AMERICA REBELS

By John Harris

Manufactured in the United States

Dust jacket photograph: Minuteman statue, Concord, Mass.
(William Ryerson, Boston Globe)

Supervising editor
David E. Young

Design/editing
Robert F. Cutting, Helen Donovan

Photography
William Ryerson, Theodore Dully

Maps
Joseph Burak, Thomas Hughes

Print directors
Bruce Howard, Douglas Dwyer

Art production
John Malionek, Gail Kaufman

Dedication

To the many considerate people who helped
in the preparation of this narrative, and especially to the most constant and cheerful helper
of them all, my wife Peg, a discerning critic.

Foreword

Roughly 200 years ago a man grown dear to his fellowmen as the sage of the common man, Benjamin Franklin, was asked by a woman what form of government the founding fathers were devising.

"A republic," replied Franklin, "if you can keep it."

At the time Franklin spoke, the people of the world were almost universally ruled by kings, most of them absolute monarchs. Launching a republic of America's 1776 size and population — with the people being their own rulers — was quite an experiment, something quite novel on this earth.

Look about us today, during our nation's Bicentennial, and ask how the experiment in democracy has prospered.

United Nations ambassador Daniel Patrick Moynihan, speaking in protest against a dictum of that assembly in 1975, made the observation that in the entire United Nations membership of 142 nations there were currently only 25 democracies. Since 1776 kingships had gone out of existence, mostly supplanted by dictatorships.

The vulnerability of mankind's experiment in self-rule has been exhibited, in this bicentennial period, by the undoing of the work of one of the greatest men of the 20th Century, Mohandas K. Gandhi, when the democracy he established was so speedily extinguished in India.

Here in the United States, on the hearth, as it were, of the doctrine given to all mankind in our Declaration of Independence, we have just been through the shame-filled experience of nearly half the electorate refraining from participation in the election of a President of the United States. And there have been reports from pollsters that all but about 15 percent of this electorate has become disillusioned with our democratic process.

How, in this bicentennial period particularly, are we to avoid the painful wonder whether the experiment of 1776 is to be carried on to a 300th anniversary? And what of a 400th?—a 500th?—a 1000th?

Winston Churchill, who rallied ideals to pit a desperately unprepared nation against the military efficiency of Adolph Hitler's tyranny, advised mankind that democracy is the worst form of goverment in this world—except for all the other forms of government. However dark and bodeful, then, may be the signs of despair—ideals are always at hand to encourage mankind to triumph, whatever the challenge. This response of steadfastness has been the same—and always successful—from the sufferings of Valley Forge to the beachheads of Great Britain that Churchill set himself to defend.

There is no better place to rediscover these ideals, and rejoice in the strength they impart, than in the tale of our nation's creation — not in the prettified and fictionalized accounts of what happened — but in the true, unadorned story, the one that takes digging and going back to the way things really happened. There may be no decorative elm tree under which Washington took command, or ringing last words from a Joseph Warren incapable of speech once struck in the head by the fatal bullet. Nor were those times, as we sense times are apt to be, filled only with heroics with an absence of doubters, trouble-makers and even traitorous men like Dr. Benjamin Church Jr.

There is, however, powerful strength in the story of a Col. Thomas Gardner, a man who gave his life at Bunker Hill, who said, "I consider the call of my country as the call of God." Or of minuteman Levi Preston, running with his musket all the way from his far-off town to the nation's first battlefield, and putting his credo in simple phrasing, "We always had been free and we meant to be free always." Or of a magnificent Maj. Timothy Bigelow, a veteran of Arnold's terrifying march through the wilderness, persisting in his patriotism despite ingratitude that brought undeserved imprisonment but later a monument in the neighborhood where he had been the leader of the Sons of Liberty.

Ideals are not all of the battlefield. Thomas Jefferson was not much as a military figure. But the words in which he immortalized ideals still, like stars, provide true guidance. How fortunate is the nation and the world to have the careers of "a brace of Adamses"—Samuel who rallied his Bostonians to action and John who devoted his wisdom to shaping a nation; or of a Mason who perpetuated a Bill of Rights; or a Washington who spurned a crown and taught his fellowmen their obligations to one another.

With such ideals there is no insistent need that this generation prepare a stone, "Democracy died here."

We should go as often as we can to the true tale—and this is the reason we have sought to present it—for if democracy were to die here, where again on this earth could it be revived? For we must bear in mind that the great experiment of American democracy was made possible, essentially, because ideals on the freedoms of mankind that grew on the soil of Great Britain, because of Great Britain's preoccupation with civil war, got a unique chance to take root in the New World. And, above all, the experiment was blessed by being made on an unspoiled continent. Where now is another such continent — and opportunity — to be found on this planet?

Two hundred years is not really a long time in the annals of the human race. But should the experiment fail, would that catastrophe not involve civilization itself? For the end of individual freedom, of free press, free assembly, free speech, already not extensively assured in this world, would mean the complete victory of the police state. What then of the dreams of those who sat in Philadelphia 200 years ago and made July 4th imperishable — and what of mankind— if despotism should inherit the earth?

—JOHN HARRIS

Table of Contents

The Boston Tea Party

Lexington-Concord Alarm

Battle of Bunker Hill

Washington's First Victory

Boston
Tea
Party

The 15 years of Revolution

"The revolution was in the minds and hearts of the people, and this was effected from 1760 to 1775, in the course of 15 years, before a drop of blood was shed at Lexington.

"The war with Britain?

"That was no part of the revolution; it was only the effect and consequence of it."

— Reflections of President John Adams, at 80 years, on events of his youth

The actions of Samuel Adams during those momentous 15 years afford the most impressive example of what John Adams meant. For Samuel Adams, John Adams's second cousin, was, above all the other patriots of that era, foremost in encouraging his fellowmen to open rebellion.

Indeed, Samuel Adams has been called the "Father of the Revolution."

Was this because he was a fire-eating, rabble-rousing rebel?

Far from that. Samuel Adams (only enemies called him a disrespectful "Sam") was generally quiet, softspoken, patient, a behind-the-scenes moulder of action. He won the minds of his fellowmen by his earnestness, his genuine democratic instincts and his unselfish dedication to preserving their liberties.

Samuel Adams did not feel that he was a rebel at all.

To him, it was the British administration that was staging a revolution. In every step he took, Samuel Adams sought to preserve the rights that the colonists had already been granted in their charters. As he saw the crisis, the British administration was conspiring to nullify the colonial charters and enslave the colonists.

In his quiet, farseeing way, Samuel Adams gathered to his cause Bostonians from all stations of life and, as his lieutenants, some younger men, Joseph Warren, his eloquent doctor; John Hancock, whose ample purse tided over many an early patriot effort; and cousin John Adams, a fledgling Braintree lawyer. Samuel Adams could tell character.

His opposition (actually directed from London) was personified in the Bay Colony by its last civil royal governor, Thomas Hutchinson. Hutchinson, descendant of the wonderful Puritan rebel Anne Hutchinson, who suffered exile and death for her beliefs, was a yes-man for his British masters. He believed in privilege, aristocracy, the rule of the few.

He, too, would eventually go into exile, but in London, where he could attend the levees of King George III. For Hutchinson lived steadfastly to "keep the past upon its throne."

In simplest terms, the 15 years can be pictured as a struggle of two men:

Samuel Adams vs. Thomas Hutchinson.

Hutchinson deeply shocked Samuel Adams. To Adams, Hutchinson was "a man that is bone of our bone and flesh of our flesh ... who has had all the honors lavished upon him ... could it be imagined that such a man should be so lost to all sense of gratitude and public love as to aid the designs of despotic power? ..."

To Hutchinson, Samuel Adams was the "grand incendiary," "the master of puppets" and "above all" the first man to speak of "independency," which to Hutchinson meant treason.

Both were men of sincere conviction.

To understand what Hutchinson risked, you can stand today on Milton Hill and look northward across what is still called Hutchinson's Field, let your view take in the coiling estuary of the Neponset River, boats glinting at its mouth, and beyond see Dorchester and all of Boston. You would be standing at the site of what was his resplendent summer retreat "Unkity," the Indian name for Milton.

And to understand what Samuel Adams challenged, you can walk the glory routes of empire, past Whitehall, Buckingham Palace, Windsor Palace, see the symbols of naval power still there in the Thames, from which the tea ships sailed to Boston; and ponder the military might enshrined in the Tower of London. Samuel Adams never saw the seat of British might, but he knew what it meant to his countrymen.

Some highlights of those 15 years will show us what aroused them to rebel, at the peril of their lives.

Britain runs short of cash

King George III, last monarch of the American colonies, acceded to the British throne in 1760. He won the hearts of Englishmen everywhere when, as the first English-bred sovereign of the Germanic House of Hanover, he slipped into his prepared address from the throne: "Born and educated in this country, I glory in the name of Britain."

Affection for the young ruler (he had just passed his 22nd birthday) was as fervent in the American colonies as in England.

Young John Hancock, expending more money than his foster father thought wise, lingered on his only trip to London to witness the showy coronation. John Adams proclaimed he was "proud of Britain," and even the patriot James Otis Jr. extolled the mother country and prayed we never put assunder what God had united.

To one and all George III was the patriot King, and it took the patriots in the American colonies until the very eve of the Revolution to learn that the detested actions of the British prime ministers and the Parliament were really the dictates of the King.

It was mighty easy at the time to swell with pride about the British empire. England, under the leadership of the Churchill-like genius of William Pitt, the elder, won in the war then just concluding with France and Spain the largest amount of territory in all England's expansionist history, vast chunks of North America, Central America, the West Indies, Africa and the huge subcontinent of India.

"Heaven be praised," exulted George III when he learned of Gen. James Wolfe's conquest of Quebec. With it, all of Canada fell to the British. This was, for the colonists, the most significant payoff to the genius of Pitt, who had fed British gold to his allies in Europe while he dispatched manpower and military might to win North America.

The colonists had contributed joyfully. So much so that Hutchinson's predecessor as colonial governor, the inept, soon to be hated Sir Francis Bernard, praised them for raising money and vying to serve the King. "Never before," said Bernard, "were the regiments so easily levied."

The colonists were canny too, for they were serving themselves as well. Now open to New England would be the undisputed fisheries of the Grand Banks, and to all the colonists the land to the west would now be rid of enemy-contrived Indian raids. The rich fur harvest was now open in the great forests. And, unrecognized then, the French and Indian War had provided military training for future minutemen.

But there remained, at the very least, two basic problems.

George III's tutoring for kingship had stressed that he should rule as well as reign. It was late in the day for this, for trying to play the role of divine right had brought King Charles I beneath the headman's axe. Yet George III wanted to maintain what the Stuarts had lost, a powerful kingship. And George III would tolerate no insubordination.

Personally a pleasant squire type, George III's idea of kingship would not let him allow his most congenial prime minister, the playmate of his childhood, Lord North, ever to be seated in the royal presence.

And, while Britain was at a new summit of power, the treasury was just about empty. Wars are costly, have to be paid in treasure or inflation, most often in both, and they produce depressions. All this hit the colonists harshly because it became British policy to secure more revenue.

The colonial trade rules, geared unabashedly for the benefit of England's own commerce, had long been outrageously restrictive, and the duties were high. They had been bearable only because enforcement in the colonies had been almost comically lax and corrupt. Revenue payments were skipped on just about every commodity and smuggling was the normal way of life.

Trying to change all this put the British administration and the colonists on a collision course.

James Otis Jr., a giant of a man in physique,

became the first rapturously admired champion of the Bay colonists when he quit his crown position as advocate general of admiralty and led the battle against the writs of assistance, warrants intended to give customsmen blanket authority to search homes and warehouses for smuggled goods.

You may still see the original setting for the trial of this issue, the council chamber in Boston's old State House overlooking the site of the Boston Massacre.

Hutchinson, in great wig and scarlet, was sitting on his first case as chief justice. (He was already the colony's lieutenant governor and held other crown posts as well — multiple officeholding that Samuel Adams made a fruitful target.) Adding greater drama, though, was the fact that many felt that this exalted judicial post rightly belonged to the father of James Otis Jr.

James Otis Sr., long a public figure and speaker of the House, had been promised this judicial vacancy, which occurred just as Bernard arrived as governor in the Bay Colony. Bernard, however, gave the post to Hutchinson, despite Hutchinson's warnings that this would offend the Otises. Hutchinson took office as the bells were still ringing for George III's becoming King.

Hutchinson later wrote: "From this time they (the Otises) were at the head of every measure in opposition. From so small a spark a great fire seems to have been kindled." This latter-day appraisal ignores the flaming dedication of young James Otis, for from a more sympathetic onlooker, enthralled young John Adams, came this imperishable judgment:

"Here this day, in the old council chamber, the child Independence was born."

Otis spoke for four hours, from early afternoon until candles were brought to illuminate the chamber. Shining on the walls were two huge paintings of the Stuart brothers, Charles II and James II, whose far from popular likenesses Gov. Bernard had found in the old State House attic, dusted off and imprudently displayed. The disputed writs of assistance harked back to the bitterly resented Stuart era.

Otis, in imagination, carried his listeners back to Runnymede and the rights bestowed by Magna Carta. He stressed the natural rights of mankind as expressed so cogently by the great British political philosopher John Locke, teacher and hero to all colonial patriots. So effective was Otis's speech, Hutchinson postponed the decision until he could hear from England.

The verdict, of course, when it came late in 1761, was against the colonists — and there was a strong feeling that Hutchinson's appointment foretold this. But Otis had exhibited to the world the principles on which the Revolutionary War would be fought. Luminous among them was the contention, mightily persuasive: "Taxation without representation is tyranny."

Otis's reaction to an offer of payment endeared him even more to his fellow colonials: "In such a case I despise all fees," he said.

Charles Paxton, native-born, crown-appoint-

Bostonian Society, Boston, Mass.

Two pence stamp — a "tuppance" (enlarged)

ed surveyor general of customs, had sought the writs under issue. He was an officious man, finally so obnoxious that the mob would be howling at his door. Paxton was determined to ferret out tax money, would go to England to help tighten revenue laws. Unconsciously, he was helping to pave the route that would lead through a succession of events to the Boston Tea Party and rebellion.

Otis had denounced the writs as "instruments of slavery . . . and villainy."

Soon something even more inflammatory came to disrupt the colonies: the stamp tax.

This revenue device had been in use in England for generations. Still, for Americans, the Stamp Act of 1765 was the first time that Parliament had attempted to impose on them a direct, internal tax. Samuel Adams had long foreseen Parliament's intentions and had been rallying Bostonians to proclaim their opposition.

Just the previous year, chairing a town meeting in old Faneuil Hall, Adams got his fellow citizens to approve his report against the trade tax that Parliament had imposed on sugar. "This, we apprehend," said Adams in the report, "annihilates our charter right to govern and tax ourselves." He had urged that this parliamentary tax be repealed as a violation of the Bay Colony charter.

King George III took no hand in the passage of the new stamp tax — he was stricken by an early attack of the royal malady, porphyria, that would one day leave him deaf, blind and demented, wandering through Windsor Castle as tragic a figure as Shakespeare's King Lear.

The Stamp Act was proposed by the King's first minister, George Grenville. Grenville was not a favorite of the King, who remarked scornfully that Grenville "had the mind of a clerk in a counting house." Grenville managed even to shock the King with his budgeting, but few in Great Britain perceived the intensity with which America would react to this latest search for revenue.

Grenville gave plenty of warning of what he was going to do before he put his plan before Parliament. He even said that he would be content if Americans preferred some other tax "provided the money be but raised." Hard money

Yale University, New Haven, Conn.
Stamp rioters stage hoisting party for a Tory

was scarce in America and a post-war slump had staggered business, all of which helped Samuel Adams's cause. He was now joined by Joseph Warren, deeply stirred by what he felt was a threat of enslavement.

Still, Parliament, indifferent or ignorant of the momentous effects of its action, passed the act by a margin that swamped the few staunch friends who spoke in behalf of the colonies.

When official word reached America (the act would take effect on Nov. 1) only Virginia's legislature was in session. Patrick Henry urged his fellow burgesses to adopt a declaration of rights called the Virginia Resolves. Two of these were so anti-parliament they were voted down amid shocked cries of "Treason! Treason!"

They were, in all, sentiments that foreshadowed the Bill of Rights, sentiments expressed against the Sugar Act the prior year by the New York Declaration and soon to be expressed by

Faneuil Hall as it looked in 1773

the Massachusetts Legislature in a set of resolves against the Stamp Act. Samuel Adams wrote them in terms so strong that Hutchinson said, "They approach very near to independence."

Massachusetts then had a novel proposal.

It was the idea of James Otis Jr., leader in the House: "A Stamp Act Congress."

The House sent letters to the other colonial legislatures suggesting a meeting in the central location of New York City to consult on the crisis created by the Stamp Act. Otis served on the Massachusetts delegation to this congress.

Hutchinson was astonished by the entire development. He wrote: "There never had been an instance of a convention of committees from the assemblies of the colonies. Nothing in their char-

ters authorized it."

The Stamp Act Congress, with nine colonies represented, conferred for 18 days and produced petitions (Otis helped to write one) to the King, Lords and Commons in England. All the petitions were spurned in Britain on the ground that the congress had not been a properly constituted ·body, as Hutchinson had noted.

It was, nevertheless, a major step for the colonies. They had experimented with the powerful technique of united action.

But events in the colonies, and especially in Boston, upstaged the congress. Boston had already erupted with rioting to an extent that had not been seen in the town since the prior century, when Bostonians tossed out the Stuart tyrant Sir Edmund Andros.

Sons of Liberty, mobs unite

Who did the rioting?

The Sons of Liberty—an exciting title given the patriots during the course of debate on the Stamp Act in Parliament.

Defending the proposed act, Charles Townshend, British fiscal authority, had rhetorically called the Americans "children planted by our care, nourished by our indulgence . . . protected by our arms. . . ."

This hyperbole brought to his feet an angered Col. Isaac Barre, friend of Americans since the days he fought side by side with them at Louisburg and Quebec.

"They planted by your care?" scoffed Barre. "No! Your oppressions planted them in America. They nourished up by your indulgence? They grew by your neglect of them," declared Barre.

"As soon as you began to care about them, that care was exercised in sending persons to rule them . . . to spy out their liberties, to misrepresent their actions, and to prey upon them, men whose behavior on many occasions has caused the blood of these Sons of Liberty to recoil within them. . . ."

The Sons of Liberty was a secret, informal organization. It was composed of activist spirits, men Gov. Bernard considered "Sam Adams's Mohawks." They were Whigs, in contrast to the crown party, the Tories. They included the whole gamut of occupations, for opposition to the Stamp Act had brought together workers and businessmen, professionals, mechanics and merchants.

Just about all these Sons of Liberty, including the waterfront musclemen, belonged to other clubs and societies, the Ancient & Honorable Artillery Company, the Masons, the Caucus.

Samuel Adams's political strength came from making the acquaintance of all these various club members in his rounds of the taverns and gathering places. Samuel Adams adored his father, a deacon and prosperous brewer who was interested in town affairs and was elected a member of the Legislature. From age 14, Samuel accompanied his father on his social-political rounds and became a steadfast, lifelong politician.

Deacon Adams founded the Caucus Club, which had groups in the North End, the center of town and the South End. Paul Revere was early among the members of the North End Caucus, where his intimate friend, Joseph Warren, was leader. Both were Masons (Otis was, too) and both became Grand Masters of the Masons. Revere was a member of the Long Club, pretty much an intellectual gathering of Harvard men—Otis, the Adamses, Warren, Josiah Quincy Jr., Hancock—which met in the upstairs office of the patriot editors of the *Boston Gazette*, Edes and Gill.

A key meeting place of the Sons of Liberty was in the small counting room, also upstairs, of the distillery of Chase & Speakman, adjoining a big elm at present Essex and Washington streets. The ground around the elm was called Liberty Hall and, after Barre made his speech, the elm was christened the Liberty Tree.

A group called the Loyal Nine acted as a steering committee of the Sons of Liberty. John Adams has described a pleasant evening he spent with them, listing them by name. John Avery, "a distiller of liberal education" (Harvard), was secretary of the Loyal Nine, writing their handbills and orders. Avery, classmate of Warren, was very close to Samuel Adams, would act in later years as his secretary and executor and became the Commonwealth's first secretary of state.

Some of these Loyal Nine would take part in the Boston Tea Party. One, Henry Bass, a young merchant and cousin of Samuel Adams, wrote a letter to his future father-in-law that is virtually the only insight that we have on how the Loyal Nine operated. They welcomed anonymity and were "not a little pleased" that others were given the credit for deeds that they set in motion.

In all of this the coaching skill and leadership of Samuel Adams is almost visible. Samuel Adams did not seek credit. Thus mystery will always surround the precise details of how things were brought about in the formative period of our revolution. John Adams has told of seeing

Samuel Adams tearing up the evidence and tossing it into the fire or to the winds so no one would come to grief because of his negligence.

Among Samuel Adams's most skillful early accomplishments was harnessing mob activity to the patriot cause.

The annual Pope's Day on Nov. 5 was a rambunctious, often bloodied holiday in Boston. Gangs from the North End and the South End, each parading behind its own Pope's cart, would clash with fists, clubs and staves. It was the local celebration of the exposure of the Gunpowder Plot (Guy Fawkes Day) back in 1605, when an attempt was made to blow up King James I and the Parliament.

A young boy was accidentally killed by a Pope's cart wheel in the 1764 brawling, with the North Enders led by Samuel Swift and the South Enders by a man who would be a Boston Tea Party stalwart, Ebenezer Mackintosh. Samuel Adams was watching, and figured a way to utilize all this energy. He would and he did get the two gangs to unite for liberty.

The year of the stamp tax marked a giant increase in his effectiveness. He was already, through years of quiet politicking, a dominant figure in the Boston town meeting, making the rounds of the clubs, writing and inspiring articles in the Whig press and preparing Boston's instructions to its legislators. Now he became one of the Boston legislators, shifting from Faneuil Hall to the old State House.

Very shortly he would be chosen clerk of the House, a key position in which, with his writing of resolves and documents and organizing propaganda, he could both shape and manage events, rallying ever greater sections of the state and colonies to oppose the despotic efforts of the King's ministers to dismantle the Bay Colony charter.

Aug. 14, 1765, would long be an occasion for a gala celebration by the Sons of Liberty.

That morning the early-rising citizens of Boston saw a straw-stuffed effigy and a big boot with a peeping devil hanging from the Liberty Tree. John Avery, working after midnight, had been among those making and putting them up. The boot, of course, was a symbol of George III's favorite Lord Bute, mistakenly blamed as an author of the Stamp Act.

The effigy was of the colony's crown-appointed secretary, Andrew Oliver, wealthy merchant, third-highest official of the Bay Colony, the man who had been designated as distributor for the stamps. Oliver was on the colony's social summit. He and Hutchinson were brothers-in-law, having married sisters, the daughters of a royal governor of Connecticut.

Shops were closed down (business was poor anyway and many people were unemployed) so everyone could come and see these summertime shenanigans. Even the crown comptroller of customs dropped by to gawk like lesser folks. He wondered aloud whose effigy this might be. Samuel Adams, looking on gave the straight-faced, tongue-in-cheek response that "he did not know, he could not tell...." He would inquire.

Gov. Bernard hurriedly assembled his councilors and sent Sheriff Stephen Greenleaf to cut down the offending symbols. The wary sheriff came, took a look, read the message of the swelling crowd and did nothing. The councilors thought this perhaps best.

Nightfall did not end the show. It enlivened it. The effigy and boot were taken down and placed on a bier, and a crowd that grew by the hundreds paraded along the main street to the old State House, paraded right through the building where Bernard, Hutchinson, Oliver and the councilors were still in perplexed session, marched down present State street toward the harbor and turned into present Liberty Square.

Nearby was a small new structure erected at the head of Oliver's Wharf. Word had spread that it was intended as headquarters for distributing the stamps. The crowd quickly leveled it, lugged the lumber, effigies and bier to nearby Fort Hill and sent them up in a merry blaze that made the summer evening even hotter.

Oliver's house, near the foot of the hill, now became a target. Oliver had just rushed home and was upstairs with his family. Roaring slogans, as they had at the old State House, the rougher members of the crowd axed open the doors, smashed windows and started breaking the furnishings and raiding the cellar.

Hutchinson, accompanied by Sheriff Green-

The Hutchinson House in the North End

leaf, had hurried to the scene and tried to stay the crowd. He was pelted with stones and debris. Oliver, now thoroughly terrified, came out on his balcony and promised that he would resign as stampmaster. He had truthfully never favored the legislation, as was the case with Hutchinson.

Early next morning Oliver obediently went to the Liberty Tree and said he would resign in a letter to London. That evening the Sons of Liberty built another bonfire on Fort Hill, much to Oliver's alarm. But this time it was in honor of his resignation.

Now the target was changed. The next night a crowd assembled in front of the residence of Hutchinson, one of the finest dwellings in the province, in Garden Court street, just off fashionable North Square. The crowd demanded that Hutchinson declare that he had not written to England in favor of the Stamp Act. He had not, but he considered it beneath his dignity to respond under this coercion. Presently a sympathetic neighbor flung open a window and gave false assurance that he had seen Hutchinson's carriage depart for his place in Milton just before nightfall. The crowd dispersed.

Hutchinson judged that the crowd "made me the principal object of popular resentment ever since Mr. Oliver had been compelled to declare his resignation." He was indeed correct.

On the very hot evening of Aug. 26, Hutchinson would be visited again, but with violence. The crowd started near the old State House with a bonfire and some firewater. The residence of reviled Charles Paxton, opposite John Gray's ropewalk in Hutchinson (now Pearl) street (on the future route of the Boston Tea Party), came next. Paxton was away and a servant averted ruin by treating the crowd to a barrel of punch.

With thirst temporarily quenched, the crowd moved back toward the old State House into present Court street to the home of William Story, register of the new Admiralty Court that arbitrarily enforced the restrictive trade laws. His windows were smashed, furniture broken and books and court papers thrown in the street. No authority existed in Boston that was capable of intervening.

Next came the newly built house of the comptroller of customs, Benjamin Hallowell, in Hanover street opposite the residence-office of Joseph Warren. The front door was broken, windows and furniture smashed, the first floor ransacked and the wines and liquors in the cellar carried out to the street to quench further the thirst arising from the hard labor of wrecking British imports.

And next it was Hutchinson's, with "Captain" Ebenezer Mackintosh in the lead. Hutchinson, a widower, had just sat down to supper with his three sons and two daughters when someone ran in and cried, "The mob is coming!" Intending to stay himself, he directed his children to flee.

Hutchinson's elder, 20-year-old daughter Sally came back and declared she would not leave without him. "I couldn't stand against this," he said, and withdrew to the other side of North Square to the house of his sister, Mrs. Samuel Mather. The patriot Josiah Quincy Jr. remarked that this move saved Hutchinson's life.

Hutchinson recalled that he had been a few minutes in the Mather house "before the hellish crew fell upon my house with the rage of devils, and in a moment with axes split down the doors and entered. My son being in the great entry heard them say, 'Damn him, he is upstairs, we'll have him!' "

Presently, one after another, messengers

came to warn Hutchinson that the mob was pursuing him. Little Hannah Mather, his niece, took him by the hand through back paths, yards and gardens to the more remote home of the baker Thomas Edes, where Hutchinson remained until 4 a.m., at which time he said, "One of the best finished houses in the province had nothing remaining but the bare walls and floors."

All his plate, family pictures and large sums of cash were gone. The furniture was cut to pieces and tossed out windows along with feathers from the slashed-open beds. Recounted Hutchinson:

"Not content with tearing off all the wainscot and hangings and splitting the doors to pieces, they beat down the partition walls, and although that alone cost them near two hours, they cut down the cupola or lanthorn, and they began to take the slate and boards from the roof, and were prevented only by the approaching daylight from a total demolition of the building.

"The gardenhouse was laid flat, and all my trees, etc., broke down to the ground. Such ruin was never seen in America."

Among Hutchinson's library books strewn in the mire was the manuscript for his history of Massachusetts. It was rescued by a neighbor, a clergyman, and can still be seen in its soiled condition in the archives of Massachusetts.

Josiah Quincy Jr., in his diary, tells how Hutchinson appeared the next morning in court so that it would have a quorum. Hutchinson was clothed, said the patriot Quincy, "in a manner which would have excited compassion from the hardest heart."

Hutchinson told the court: "Some apology is necessary for my dress. Indeed, I had no other."

Hutchinson took the occasion to say that he was sensible of his innocence but did not feel that he was obliged to answer the "questions that may be put to me by every lawless person.

"Yet," he continued, "I call God to witness — and I would not for a thousand worlds, call my Maker to witness to falsehood — I say I call my Maker to witness that I never, in New England or Old, in Great Britain or America, neither directly nor indirectly, was aiding, assisting or supporting — in the least promoting or en-

couraging — what is commonly called the Stamp Act; but, on the contrary, did all in my power, and strove as much as in me lay, to prevent it."

An overflow town meeting met that same day and, without dissent, denounced the outrages against Oliver and Hutchinson and pledged its help in preventing further disorder. Some citizens were clearly dismayed, but surely many making the vote unanimous must have taken part in the rioting.

Gov. Bernard, coming into town from Castle William, to which Hutchinson would likewise retire to protect his family, called the Council together. Hearing Mackintosh's name, Bernard issued a warrant for the cobbler's arrest.

Sheriff Greenleaf presently found Mackintosh in King street and arrested him. Immediately some men of substance warned the sheriff that if Mackintosh was jailed, it would kill plans to create a civil and military guard against new riots. Greenleaf released Mackintosh.

Eventually six or eight alleged rioters were arrested. Then, in a mass jail delivery described by Hutchinson, some men of means came into the jail in the dead of night several weeks later, made the jailer give them the keys and let the alleged rioters go free just as they were about to come to trial. Their testimony would never involve anyone else.

Nov. 1 came and left no doubt at all that the Stamp Act was a failure. There was not a single colony whose stamp distributor had not resigned, most of them under threat. In Boston the bells tolled, the minute guns fired, vessels in the harbor displayed their colors at half-mast and an effigy of Grenville (the right author this time) was hung from the Liberty Tree.

But business, for lack of legal papers, was at a standstill though no stamps were available. Boston's were still stacked unopened at Castle William. Hutchinson even gave up one of his posts, a probate judgeship, because he would not function without stamps. And Samuel Adams was trying to get things functioning without the stamps and was threatening non-importation of British goods.

Adams decided to underscore the non-functioning of any stamp agent by having Oliver re-

Library of Congress, Washington, D.C.

The Pope's cart

peat his resignation. The Loyal Nine swung into action. Rumors were spread that Oliver was reconsidering his resignation. Oliver denied this. But handbills were posted around town that Oliver was coming to Liberty Tree for a public resignation.

Oliver, foreseeing the inevitable, tried to avoid humiliation and offered to resign at the old State House. This substitute was denied. Dec. 17 was tempesty and rainy, a miserable winter day. And, irony of ironies, Mackintosh accompanied Oliver through the streets as protection.

Big men in town and 2000 citizens were on hand. The outspoken Whig justice of the peace, Richard Dana, risking reprisal from the establishment, was on hand to take Oliver's oath. Dana brought a future literary touch, for he would be grandfather to Richard Henry Dana, the seafarer and author.

Mackintosh's role was confirmation of Samuel Adams's skill.

When Nov. 5 (Pope's Day) had arrived this year, amid all these doings, there was not the slightest hint of disharmony. North Enders and South Enders marched together. Mackintosh walked arm in arm with a full-fledged colonel. Then all the Sons of Liberty attended a grand banquet at the Green Dragon Tavern. John Hancock was master of ceremonies — and Hancock also obliged by paying the bill.

The activities in Boston were a message heard in Britain.

"Americans are the sons, not the bastards, of England," declared William Pitt, now the Earl of Chatham.

Britain's greatest statesman of that age rarely appeared in Parliament because of his infirmities. Now, though his voice was feeble, he was making one of his great orations in response to George Grenville, who had said, in arguing for retention of the Stamp Act: "America is bound to yield obedience. If not, tell me when the Americans were emancipated?"

Pitt struck back:

"The gentleman asks, when were the colonies emancipated? I desire to know when they were made slaves."

Pitt said he would agree that the British kingdom was the supreme governing and legislating power for the colonies — "in everything except that of taking their money out of their pockets without their consent.

"The gentleman tells us America is obstinate; America is almost in open rebellion. I rejoice that America has resisted. Three millions of people so dead to all the feelings of liberty as voluntarily to let themselves be made slaves would have been fit instruments to make slaves of all the rest."

Something even more persuasive than rioting in America was impressing Parliament: non-importation. American merchants had agreed not to import British goods until the stamp tax was removed. John Hancock, who had a large fleet of ships, had written to his agents in London:

"In case the Stamp Act is not repealed my orders are that you will not ... ship me one article. I have wrote ... this in consideration of the united resolves of not only the principal merchants ... of this town but of those of the other trading towns of this province, and which I am determined to abide by."

Non-importation (with Americans substituting their own manufactures) badly hit the manufacturing centers of Britain. Manchester dropped three out of every 10 workmen. Thousands were thrown out of work in the midlands, in Leeds and Liverpool and in London. From Yorkshire came this irate note to the ministry:

"Our trade is hurt. What the devil have you

been doing? For our own part, we don't pretend to understand your politics and American matters, but our trade is hurt. Pray remedy it, and a plague on you if you won't."

Benjamin Franklin won international admiration when, calling himself "Franklin of Philadelphia," he appeared before the House of Commons and adroitly presented America's case for repeal. The act stipulated that the tax be paid in specie, and Franklin warned that within a year it would strip America of every farthing of cash. What business would then be possible?

The repeal was ready for the King on March 18, 1766.

George III pursed his lips as he affixed his signature and remarked: "It is a fatal compliance."

Ever after he regarded this repeal as a disaster. He was not assuaged by the companion "Declaratory Act" that affirmed the power of the King and Parliament "to make laws of sufficient force to bind the colonies and people of America in all cases whatsoever."

It was almost two months before news reached the colonies and set off such rejoicing that New York City raised two statues — one to Pitt, and an even greater one, America's first equestrian statue, to George III.

Hancock's brig *Harrison* brought the news of the repeal to Boston late on Friday night, May 16. Monday was designated for celebration. Cannon boomed, flags waved, bells rang, violins and fifes played, everyone turned out ... even Gov. Bernard joined the festivities. In anticipation of great fireworks the selectmen located two fire engines on the Common.

Paul Revere made an engraving showing the four sides of a giant obelisk of oiled paper in praise of those considered favoring colonial liberties. The night was for illumination. Pitt's likeness was lighted in windows. Extra candles illuminated houses, people carried lamps, hundreds of lanterns were hung on Liberty Tree.

There were fireworks and rockets — and these accidentally sent the obelisk, lighted inside by hundreds of lamps, up in flames. The fire engines came in handy.

Otis in his School street house and Hancock in his resplendent mansion on Beacon Hill overlooking the Common held open house. Hancock even contributed pipes (barrels of many gallons) of his Madeira wine to the celebrants and had it rolled out to the Common.

Samuel Adams should have been jubilant. Earlier in the year he had helped John Hancock win his first election to the House. John Adams recalled that he and Samuel were later walking along the mall on the Common when Samuel Adams said: "This town has done a wise thing today." "What?" said John Adams, and Samuel Adams, planning to use Hancock's purse for the patriot cause, pointed to Hancock's mansion and said, "They have made this young man's fortune their own."

Yet the celebration left Samuel Adams far from overjoyed.

He had read the wording of the "Declaratory Act." Some took it lightly as a piece of face-saving by the British ministry. But not Samuel Adams, and not farseeing men in other colonies. South Carolina's great patriot, Christopher Gadsden, who would stage a tea party in Charleston, suspected, like Adams, that they had not seen the last of the ministry's repressive schemes.

Townshend opens struggle over tea

If his words were intended as a prophecy, Charles Townshend's description of his new revenue plan of 1767 for the American colonies must certainly rank as the most inaccurate prophecy in England's political history. He was going to tax paper, painters' lead, glass and tea.

Said "Champagne Charlie," for that was his nickname:

"I know the mode by which a revenue may be drawn from America without offense."

Townshend was a big, affable, witty, ambitious fellow who had risen rapidly to be chancellor of the exchequer, for he was still quite young. He was a hard-liner, had favored the repudiated Stamp Act. Despite his personableness, he must be ranked with Grenville among the British marplots of his day.

Townshend was able to push his tax plan through Parliament because the nominal head of the administration, Pitt, friend of the colonies, was stricken by chronic illness and had virtually abdicated his premiership.

Townshend's "mode" was that he had selected what he called external (dutiable-at-the-port-of-entry) taxes instead of internal taxes. He felt that colonial spokesmen, among them Franklin, had said that these would be acceptable. But the transparent falsity of his move appeared right in the preamble of his act, in which he boldly declared that his purpose was to raise revenue.

Other provisions of his plan were also bound to outrage the colonies. He legalized the writs of assistance and declared that revenue from the taxed items could be used to pay the salaries of colonial governors, judges and customsmen, thus making them independent of colonial legislatures. To put teeth in revenue collecting, he revised the hated vice admiralty courts and established a new, enlarged customs system with continental headquarters in Boston.

Some of Townshend's ideas came directly from Gov. Bernard, to counteract a maneuver Samuel Adams had put into effect, that stripped Bernard of a Council majority. The Council would no longer be a rubber stamp for royal governors; the patriot James Bowdoin now led its majority. Bernard was thus convinced that royal sovereignty must be firmly established even if this meant doing away with the Bay Colony charter.

To get his ideas before British officialdom, Bernard had sent Charles Paxton to London to speak both for himself and Hutchinson. Paxton had long had a fixation about tightening the revenue laws against his fellow Americans.

The colonists received plenty of intimations of what was afoot long before George III on July 2, 1767, affixed his signature to the Townshend Act. But explicit news of what Parliament had done did not arrive in Boston until September, by which time Townshend, consumed by a fever, was dead, completely unaware of the irremediable damage he had devised.

Lord North succeeded Townshend as chancellor of the exchequer. North was a key figure to watch, for one day very soon he would take over the entire administration for his royal master, stage-managing one blunder after another that would inevitably force the Revolution.

Samuel Adams's first response was a Boston town meeting that voiced its opposition to the Townshend taxes and urged "non-consumption" of British products. Non-importation had helped bring down the Stamp Act. It might work a second time.

In general, however, the reaction to the Townshend Act was somewhat slow. Intercolonial rivalry and suspicions impeded workable non-importation agreements.

Tea, the most widely used of Townshend's tax targets, quickly became a symbol for all of them. Anti-tea parties were held. Substitutes for tea were publicized, Labrador Tea, Hyperion Tea, or none.

Opposition to the Townshend Act was intensified during the winter by the essays written by John Dickinson, a Pennsylvania farmer.

Then Samuel Adams tried to unite the colonies in a petition to the King. George III was still considered the benevolent father of the English world. Adams got the House to send a circular letter to the other colonies. Favorable responses came back quickly.

Hutchinson had a perspicacious reaction to Adams's scheme:

"Revolt," affirmed Hutchinson, "began here."

As the year 1768 opened, a new marplot came upon the British administrative scene, Wills Hill, Earl of Hillsborough. Benjamin Franklin, who had experienced Hillsborough's rudeness, described him as a "man of conceit, wrongheadedness, obstinacy and passion." Passion meant irascibleness. Hillsborough was named secretary of state for the American colonies.

Curiously, because they felt a tax on British export products spelled unwise economics, both Hillsborough and North at this time were in favor of outright repeal of all the Townshend taxes — but they drew back because of the growing intensity of colonial opposition. North later said he would be for repeal only when America was "prostrate" at his feet.

In March the Sons of Liberty swung into action.

With throbbing drums and wailing horns they paraded in menacing bands past the old State House and terrified Bernard with "great noise and hallooing" down the main street in front of the governor's official residence, the Province House. Bernard felt literally helpless. The Sons visited the homes of the customs commissioners and on the anniversary of the Stamp Act repeal they hung Paxton and other commissioners in effigy on Liberty Tree. The customs commissioners wanted troops sent to Boston. They, too, felt helpless. Bernard did not want the additional odium of requesting troops, so he said he could not do it without Council approval — which he knew he could not get. So the customs commissioners sent an appeal to the British naval commander in Halifax, who dispatched *HMS Romney*, 50-gun sloop-of-war.

Explosive things were sputtering now at Hancock's Wharf.

When a customsman slipped below deck to snoop in the newly arrived brigantine *Lydia*, Hancock came and ordered the man hauled on deck. Atty. Gen. Jonathan Sewall could find no

ANNO DECIMO TERTIO

Georgii III. Regis.

C A P. XLIV.

An Act to allow a Drawback of the Duties of Cuſtoms on the Exportation of Tea to any of His Majeſty's Colonies or Plantations in *America*; to increaſe the Depoſit on Bohea Tea to be ſold at the *India Company*'s Sales; and to impower the Commiſſioners of the Treaſury to grant Licences to the *Eaſt India Company* to export Tea Duty-free.

WHEREAS by an Act, made in the Preamble. Twelfth Year of this preſent Majeſty's Reign, (intituled, An Act for granting a Drawback of Part of the Cuſtoms upon the Exportation of Tea to *Ireland*, and the *Britiſh* Dominions in *America*; for altering the Drawback upon foreign Sugars exported from *Great Britain*

10 R 2 tain

British Museum, London, England

Opening words of the 1773 Tea Act

infringement of the law by Hancock since the customsman had no right to spy below deck.

A month later, on May 9, Hancock's sloop *Liberty* arrived at his wharf loaded with Madeira wine. Its skipper declared at the customshouse that he carried only a few pipes of wine. The customs officials were skeptical because this on the face of it was quite an understatement of dutiable goods. But for the present they had no contrary facts.

But they soon would.

And the muscle for them to act hove into the harbor on May 17 when the *Romney* anchored a couple of cable lengths from Hancock's Wharf.

Persistent town gossip that loads of wine had been smuggled in the *Liberty* increased the skepticism of the customsmen. Then a customs tidesman, Thomas Kirk, came forward with quite a different tale about what he claimed happened when the *Liberty* had arrived in port a month before.

One of Hancock's captains, James Marshall, came on board that night with some rugged wharfmen and tried to arrange to move some of the cargo. Kirk said he refused and was then pushed into a cabin and nailed in for three hours while he heard the banging, creaks and sounds of cargo being shifted ashore. He was then released and his life threatened if he talked.

Next day Capt. Marshall had dropped dead — some claimed from too much exertion moving cargo. Eventually Kirk got up his courage to talk to his superiors.

Customs Collector Joseph Harrison checked with the customs lawyers and was told this made the sloop *Liberty* subject to seizure. So Harrison, his son Richard, a customs clerk, and Customs Comptroller Benjamin Hallowell around sunset headed for the *Liberty*.

They were not deterred by a warning from Joseph Warren that an attempt at seizure would lead to a "great uproar" and that Warren "could not be answerable for the consequences." But there in the harbor, for the first time, was the military force of the *Romney* to back them up and they had made arrangements for its assistance.

Waterfront workers were just knocking off work, and quite a throng was on hand as the customsmen affixed to the *Liberty* the King's Broad Arrow, sign that the sloop had been seized and was now crown property. Then they signaled to the *Romney* and over came its longboat "man'd and arm'd."

This longboat, like *Romney*'s Capt. William Corner, was bitterly resented because Corner had used it in outer Boston harbor, stopping incoming vessels, and even on the Boston waterfront to impress (grab) men to fill out his depleted crew.

As the longboat took a line to tow the *Liberty*, the crowd started tossing a barrage of rocks and dirt at the longboat's crew. Corner's command "Fire!" was lost in the shouting, and presently the crowd saw the *Liberty* secured off the stern of the *Romney*.

The crowd's anger was now directed at the customsmen, who tried to flee. Josiah Quincy Jr. expressed the popular contempt for them when he likened them to locusts. Samuel Adams assailed the influx of customsmen, calling it "as dangerous to the liberties of the people as an army of soldiers."

Hallowell was bloodied and left on the ground. Harrison was beaten with clubs but managed, with his son's help, to escape. The son was knocked down and dragged by his hair. The crowd set upon a customs inspector who chanced to come by and broke his sword, tore his clothing and went off to smash windows in the homes of Harrison, Hallowell and the customs inspector general.

This was the second time a mob hit Hallowell's dwelling.

At Harrison's place the crowd found an "elegant" sailboat he was building as a gift to a member of Parliament, dragged it through the streets to the Common and set it on fire. Samuel Adams, Otis and Warren had been conferring at Hancock's house. They came to the Common and gave the Sons of Liberty the password for quitting, "To your tents!" and the rioting ceased.

Next day, Capt. Corner sent three boats, their marines with bayonets fixed, to take most of the customsmen, their families and henchmen to the safety of the *Romney*. Soon they would be shifted to Castle William, the province's fort in the harbor. Before leaving the *Romney* the commissioners sent off appeals to Gen. Thomas Gage, then Commander in Chief in New York, asking for troops, but Gage would not act without a request from Bernard.

Paxton wrote to the ministry that "unless we have immediately two or three regiments 'tis the opinion of all the friends of government that

Boston will be in open rebellion." And Hallowell set sail for London to seek help.

Meanwhile, on June 14, 1768, James Otis Jr. presided at the first of the great town meetings in Old South Meetinghouse, an overflow gathering too large for old Faneuil Hall. Otis told the throng:

"The grievances the people labor under may in time be removed: if not and we are called to defend our liberty and privileges, I hope and believe we shall one and all, resist unto blood; but, at the same time, I pray Almighty God it may never so happen."

The people were deeply troubled. They drafted a petition to Bernard. They observed that the "dutiful petition" to the gracious King — which Samuel Adams had drafted in January — was still unanswered. They noted that taxes had been imposed upon them without their consent, that they had been invaded by an armed force as though war had been declared upon them and that citizens were being illegally impressed.

They proclaimed that it would be "humiliating and base" to submit to this. They asked that the governor relieve a "justly incensed people" by halting the barbaric practice of impressment and order the *Romney* to depart.

In 11 carriages Otis, Hancock, Warren, Adams, Josiah Quincy Jr. and 17 other Bostonians rode to Bernard's summer place in Jamaica Plain to present the petition. He received them cordially and passed the wine. He did convince Capt. Corner to desist from impressment in these parts but as for getting the *Romney* out of Boston harbor, Bernard insisted that he did not have authority.

In the midst of all the town's turmoil, Bernard received peremptory orders from Hillsborough (whose timing was ridiculous) to have the Legislature rescind Samuel Adams's circular letter. Bernard, of course, did as demanded, calling home Hutchinson, then on circuit, to advise and help him. But the House stood absolutely firm.

It ordered the doors to be barricaded so that Bernard could not suddenly stop the proceedings and voted with a resounding 92 to 17 its refusal to repudiate the circular letter. Bernard, carry-

ing out Hillsborough's further orders, immediately dismissed the Legislature.

The 92 votes made the people jubilant. Fifteen Sons of Liberty joyfully commissioned Paul Revere to make a large and handsome silver bowl that would hold a gallon of punch. He created the famous Liberty Bowl. For full measure, Revere prepared a cartoon showing the 17 who voted to rescind the letter marching into hell.

Gen. Gage notified woefully worried Bernard that, pending an official request, he was having men and ships readied at Halifax. Bernard, first enjoining secrecy, confided this information to the Council in the hope of getting the Council's support. Instead, this move exposed the abhorrent fact that Bernard had been negotiating for troops.

But, unknown then to Bernard, troops had already been ordered.

On June 8, even before the *Liberty* riots, Hillsborough had sent Gage "secret and confidential" orders to send one or two regiments to Boston. And after hearing of the *Liberty* riots from Paxton and Hallowell, Hillsborough went all out. He ordered more regiments to Boston, wrote Bernard to ship troublemakers over to England for trial and told him to send the Legislature out of Boston and recognize impressment as legal in America.

On catching rumors about troops, Samuel Adams tried to mobilize public opinion. When Bernard refused to call the Legislature into session, Adams produced a substitute: The Boston selectmen would invite a convention of delegates from other towns to meet on Sept. 22.

Military might beginning to accumulate in the harbor had a chilling effect on the convention. Not all the towns sent delegates, and those who came showed their more conservative side. Massachusetts was plainly not ready yet to take up arms. Bernard denounced the gathering as illegal and ordered it to disperse. It did not, but neither did it express any new disruptive language.

Adams, skilled politician, knew when to bide his time and await the help of future events. The convention was still in session on Sept. 28, when the British warships bringing the 14th and 29th Regts. and artillery from Halifax were sighted off Nantasket. The delegates wound up their business the next day and went home.

Where to house the troops had the military command in a painful tizzy for weeks after their unwelcome arrival.

Bernard's appeal to the Boston selectmen to help him find quarters naturally got him nowhere. And his repeated efforts to get help from the Council ran into James Bowdoin's roadblock of an adamant majority. The Council slyly suggested that Bernard use Castle William, which was technically in Boston down the harbor.

Bernard assembled the Council on a warship in the harbor to see if that might help. It did not. The military commander, Lt. Col. William Dalrymple, was getting concerned that the colonials might resist the landing. So at noon Oct. 1, 1768, the full sunshine making the scarlet, gold and silver braid a dazzling show, the troops came ashore at the foot of King street.

Beneath the gloss, Dalrymple was taking no chances. The guns of the warships were loaded. Each foot soldier had been issued 16 rounds of powder and ball.

A leading Son of Liberty, William Molineux, who would be one of the foremost members of the Boston Tea Party, wanted to repulse the troops. Always a man of action, Molineux had urged fighting the redcoats at a gathering of the Sons of Liberty the prior night in his Beacon Hill mansion, just east of Hancock's. But Adams was playing for time.

Onlookers were silent as the troops with fife, drums and banners marched up King street and past the old State House. The 29th pitched tents on the Common. The 14th was housed, of all places, in Faneuil Hall, and when they overflowed this they were given all the rooms in the old State House save the council chamber. This use of public property brought vigorous protests. Hutchinson figured that 70 soldiers deserted in the first two weeks. This rate was so alarming that Gen. Gage came on from New York to try to find quarters. He knew the men could not spend the winter on the Common, and to halt desertions, he approved the execution of a young soldier who stood before the firing squad and his open grave on the Common as the regiments grimly watched.

Finally warehouses around town were rented, some right on Griffin's Wharf, future scene of the Boston Tea Party. When Gage left town on Oct. 31 quarters had also been rented for the regiments that would arrive in 10 days from Ireland. There was the brutal hint that the empire could marshal troops from all over the world to confront this town of about 16,000 souls.

Friction between the people and the troops was ceaseless. There were brawling and court actions (where the troops felt at an obvious disadvantage before patriotic justices like Richard Dana), and the poorly paid troops incensed local workmen by providing cheap labor when off-duty. The troops — "lobster-backs" to their detractors — took merciless taunting because they were forbidden to fire without orders.

Still the time came in June 1769 that Gage started removing the troops by sending the regiments from Ireland to Halifax. He asked Bernard to write him telling whether there was need for any troops remaining in Boston. Bernard hesitated to write, for his letters to his British bosses had just been exposed, shocking the colonists with his urging that the Council be appointed by the crown.

Bernard shuddered. To remove all the troops, he told Gage, "would probably have very dangerous consequences." So the fateful decision was made to keep two regiments in Boston. Hutchinson, shortly to become acting governor, had the same viewpoint, for he felt "when the troops arrived we were on the brink of ruin."

The Legislature, angry over the letters, petitioned the King to remove Bernard. But he had already been recalled by Hillsborough. When the ship taking him away, due to depart on Aug. 1, was becalmed in port, he had the miserable sport of witnessing the colonists celebrating his departure with flags waving, gunfire, bells ringing, a bonfire on Fort Hill and Sons of Liberty touching off fireworks on Hancock's Wharf.

Harvard students cut the heart out of Bernard's portrait — and later apparently did the portrait in because Harvard officials have not been able to locate it since the Revolution.

All this time Samuel Adams kept after the Townshend taxes. The merchants had voted a year's non-importation — especially of tea — that would expire Jan. 1, 1770. Business was hurting in England, and the merchants there drafted a repeal petition to Parliament but did not press it because Parliament was still in a mood to transport American troublemakers.

This did not deter an old, devoted friend of the colony, its former Gov. Thomas Pownall, a member of Parliament, from moving for repeal anyway. But the administration postponed action. A 5-to-4 majority in the cabinet, reflecting the King's firm attitude, desired to keep the tax on tea as a symbol of the right to tax the colonies. So no repeal action was taken and Hillsborough sent word to all the colonial governors saying there would be no further taxes.

The colonists suspected this was a maneuver to kill non-importation, so the Sons of Liberty intensified their campaign against merchants who were backsliders or were selling imported tea. Feelings ran so strong that some hated imports were shipped back to England. John Hancock offered his brig *Lydia* free for this purpose — even providing free crating.

In this heated atmosphere Otis got into a brawl on Sept. 5, 1769, in a King street pub frequented by Tories, the British Coffee House, just below the old State House. Otis was incensed by what he considered aspersions on his loyalty and went seeking Customs Commissioner John Robinson. Robinson was also a tall man, who, in a month, would marry the niece of Peter Faneuil, donor of Faneuil Hall.

They swung at each other with canes, then fists. More joined the fray, the lamps were smashed and in the darkness Otis was deeply wounded in the forehead. Customs Comptroller Benjamin Hallowell managed to get him away. There was a suit. Otis was awarded a big settlement but refused it, saying, "Gold will not pay for insults to honor or patriotism." His mind, already weakened, thereafter showed disturbing unbalance.

Samuel Adams, said Hutchinson, "professed principles which he owned without reserve in private discourse, to be independency." In town meeting this year of 1769 Adams did say, "Independent we are and independent we will be." And in town meeting his masterful 37-page "Appeal to the World" proclaiming the patriot cause was read.

Adams was looking though, for something more emotional than words.

It happened on Feb. 22, 1770.

In present Hanover street, North End, was the shop of Theophilus Lillie, who, said the Sons of Liberty, was breaking the non-importation agreement. A clamoring crowd, assembled by the Sons of Liberty whistling signal, gathered at a post affixed with a hand pointing at Lillie's shop. The sign said: "That is an importer of tea."

Ebenezer Richardson, a neighbor with a sour reputation as a customs informer, arrived on the scene and tried to batter down the sign. A swarm of boys arrived throwing snowballs, and when Richardson retreated into his house the crowd swelled and started tossing stones and brickbats, breaking windows. Epithets flew back and forth and then suddenly Richardson came to an upstairs window and fired swanshot into the crowd.

A 12-year-old boy, Christopher Seider, was mortally wounded and another lad, Christopher Gore, was hit in the hand and thigh. The mob grabbed Richardson and a sailor who stood by him, placed ropes around their necks and were about to hang them when William Molineux stepped in and prevented a lynching.

Samuel Adams saw to it that young Seider became the "little hero and first martyr to the noble cause." He arranged a funeral such as America had never seen. "My eyes never beheld such a funeral," said John Adams. The procession started at Liberty Tree and reached all along the main street, a poignant sight with hundreds of schoolchildren and dignitaries in chaises and chariots.

This was Feb. 26, 1770.

Just a few days later Adams would have many more martyrs.

'The horrid Boston Massacre. . . .'

A soldier seeking part-time work came around midday Friday, March 2, 1770, to John Gray's ropewalk on Hutchinson street just opposite the dwelling of Charles Paxton, the detested customs commissioner. The soldier's anger was quickly stirred when a taunting ropewalker told him to go clean the backhouse.

"Empty it yourself!" retorted the soldier and swung at his tormentor.

Beaten, the soldier returned from the nearby waterfront barracks with some of his mates of the 29th Regt. and the battling was resumed. Among the soldiers was Pvt. Mathew Kilroy, who dueled with fists and clubs with ropemaker Samuel Gray. The soldiers were drubbed by the ropemakers.

On Saturday the battling was resumed, and once again the ropemakers won. A soldier had his skull and arm broken. Lt. Col. Maurice Carr, commanding officer, got off a complaining letter to the acting governor. Maybe Hutchinson could help. After all, Hutchinson had haughtily told one crowd, "I now represent the greatest monarch on earth."

That night a sergeant was missing at roll-call, and there was a rumor that he had been killed. Next day, Sunday, Carr and some officers were illegally searching Gray's lengthy ropewalk when they got embarrassing word that the amorous soldier had returned safely. Then rumors began to spread that there would be further trouble on Monday.

Monday, March 5, Hutchinson came from his refurbished North End mansion (he had been voted compensation for the riot damages) and placed Carr's complaint before the Council. The only way genuinely to satisfy the people, he was told, would be to get the soldiers out of Boston, and get rid of the customs commissioners as well.

That evening the rumors of trouble became sensationally true. It was a brisk, winter night, a foot of snow on the ground, some ice, and in the cloudless sky a first-quarter moon. A soldier was at his sentry box outside the customshouse on King street, when a captain came past plagued by a couple of insulting apprentice wigmakers. Why didn't he pay his barber bill? The sentry swiped one of the apprentices on the side of his head. The apprentice howled and insults flowed.

It was about 8 p.m. Presently, as for a fire, church bells tolled and a crowd began to grow in addition to the groups of club-carrying townsmen who had suddenly appeared at various corners. Some now surrounded the sentry, and the apprentices dared him to come out of the sentry box. He soon did but just to retreat up the customshouse steps.

Snowballs began to fly. The sentry fixed his bayonet and lowered his musket menacingly. Henry Knox, bookseller in a nearby shop and one day to be a revolutionary general, warned the sentry that if he fired he would forfeit his life.

"If they molest me I will fire," replied the now-desperate sentry. Chunks of ice struck around him. There were cries of "Kill him!" and "Fire, damn you, fire!" until the sentry shouted across the street to military headquarters opposite the south entrance to the old State House:

"Turn out, main guard!" he pleaded. Capt. Thomas Preston, officer of the day, got the message and started striding up and down in front of the main guard, pondering what to do.

Meanwhile, violent commotion was afoot in nearby areas. In front of Murray's sugar warehouse on Brattle street and in the alley leading to it from the main street, a crush of citizens armed with clubs and sticks clashed with troops as their officers sought to get them back into the warehouse, another of the 29th's barracks.

The crowd tossed snowballs and ice and screamed, "Cowards!" and then rushed to King street, to which citizens, drawn by the bells and dread of fire, were streaming.

In Dock Square a tall man with white wig and red cloak (still one of history's mystery figures) harangued a crowd armed with cudgels, stall legs and sticks, which then pressed along the narrow lanes leading into King street and the trouble brewing there.

Further down King street more citizens

pressed in from the waterfront. Among them was Samuel Gray in search of the fire. Told by a friend that the disorder was a brawl with soldiers, Gray pledged, "I will knock some of them on the head." Remarked the friend, "Take care you don't get killed yourself." "Never fear," promised Gray.

Capt. Preston, informed several times of the sentry's peril and finally deciding to spurn restrictions, ordered a corporal and six grenadiers to fall in and headed toward the besieged sentry. It was now after 9 p.m., and even fire engines and fire buckets had been hauled mistakenly to the scene, adding to the melee.

"For God's sake, take care of your men," Knox cried, grabbing Preston's uniform. "If you fire, you die!"

"I am sensible of it," said Preston as his men, butts of their rifles set on the ground, began to load.

Preston ordered the sentry to "fall in," and now his problem was to get the soldiers back across King street, swarming with irate, shouting townspeople. He formed his men in a curving line, himself in front, and tried to persuade the townspeople to open a path.

The soldiers poked with their bayonets to get room. The crowd, pressing in, jeered, "Fire and be damned!" "Why do you not fire?"

A question was shot at Preston: "Are they going to fire?"

"They cannot fire without my orders," replied Preston.

The skirmishing and taunting grew, and suddenly a flung club struck grenadier Hugh Montgomery and he fell, dropping his musket. Rising quickly from the icy surface he fired at random. There was a drawing back, a pause, and then more firing — without any orders from Preston.

Kilroy's bullet struck Gray, who fell mortally wounded. Two bullets hit Crispus Attucks in the chest and two more struck the sailor James Caldwell. Both dropped, dying almost instantly. Attucks, born in the Bahamas, had come to market from Framingham. His name would stand high on the roll of America's black heroes.

Patrick Carr, an Irish leather worker, was heading for Quaker Lane when he was hit, and he would linger painfully until he died nine days later. Seventeen-year-old Samuel Maverick, whose half-sister was married to "Captain" Mackintosh of the Sons of Liberty, was hit fatally in the chest by a ricocheting bullet as he ran toward the old State House.

Preston was angered as his men loaded. Why had they fired? They had heard the word "Fire!" they told him. As they raised their barrels again, Preston shoved them upward, commanding, "Stop firing!" He marched them across the momentarily cleared street, into which presently even more hundreds of citizens poured as bells rang and drumsticks pounded a militia call.

Preston ordered his drummer to beat "To arms!" This would summon all the garrison. Then he sent a sergeant to notify Col. Dalrymple.

Called from the North End, Hutchinson went to the old State House, seeing the blood in the snow as he passed. Molineux was in the crowd jammed in the building and demanding that Hutchinson order the troops back into the barracks. Instead, Hutchinson went out on the balcony, promised the throng a thorough inquiry and urged all to go home in peace.

"The law shall have its course," he promised: "I will live and die by the law."

Molineux insisted that the crowd would go only if the troops did. Through a south window of the council chamber Hutchinson called over Molineux's demand to Lt. Col. Carr and Carr ordered the troops back into the barracks. The crowd left.

Justices of the peace (Dana was one of them), the military leaders Carr and Dalrymple and witnesses were called to the council chamber by Hutchinson. Sheriff Greenleaf brought Preston a warrant. By 3 a.m. Preston was put in jail midway up Queen street, and by morning the eight soldiers were imprisoned there, too, to await trial.

Later that morning, after little more than a nap, Hutchinson called a council meeting and hurried back to the old State House, where he found the Boston selectmen already on hand. They, as well as the councilors and justices, urged Hutchinson to order the troops out to

Castle William. He insisted that he had no authority to oust the King's troops.

A messenger arrived in the course of these thwarted efforts to request that the selectmen come to Faneuil Hall, where an impromptu, overflow town meeting was in progress. Citizens were telling in shocked tones about the massacre. Samuel Adams said Boston must no longer submit to military rule, and a committee of 15 was named to go to Hutchinson to get the troops sent down the harbor.

A legal town meeting was called for 3 p.m. and meantime the committee went to see Hutchinson around noon. Adams told him that only removal of the troops would prevent bloodshed, and the committee awaited Hutchinson's response. The councilors begged Hutchinson to act. Then, unexpectedly, Col. Dalrymple said that, pending Gen. Gage's approval, he was willing to move the 29th Regt. to the Castle.

Adams, hearing the offer, pounced on it and declared that, if one regiment could be removed, then both could.

Taken aback by Dalrymple's concession but still adamant, Hutchinson moved to adjourn the proceedings. Then suddenly Dalrymple asked if Hutchinson would call a council meeting for later in the day. When Hutchinson finally agreed, Dalrymple told some of the councilors that he would move the troops if they could get Hutchinson merely to "desire" him to do it.

The 1600 seats in old Faneuil Hall could not hold the crowd that came to the 3 p.m. town meeting, so everyone shifted to the Old South Meetinghouse, overflowing it so that hundreds were outside and strung all along the main street and back to the old State House to catch word of how the committee was doing with Hutchinson.

As Samuel Adams and the committee walked out of the old State House to deliver their report, there was a pathway through the throng. Adams took off his hat, bowed to townspeople on either side of his path and kept repeating, "Both regiments or none!" all the way to the Old South. Soon the report was made, and now, what was the pleasure of the meeting?

"Both regiments or none!" came in a roar.

A new committee was appointed—Hancock, Adams, Molineux, Warren, other Sons of Liberty—and at 4 p.m. it was back in the council chamber before Hutchinson. Adams restated the misery of the people and the urgency for complying with their demands. Hutchinson repeated his inability to act.

All eyes were now on Adams as he rose again, fixed Hutchinson with the awesome majesty of righteous indignation, and said in a deep, compelling voice:

"It is well known that, acting as governor of the province, you are, by its charter, the Commander in Chief of the military forces within it; and, as such, the troops now in the capital are subject to your orders.

"If you, or Col. Dalrymple under you, have the power to remove one regiment, you have the power to remove both; and nothing short of their total removal will satisfy the people or preserve the peace of the province.

"A multitude, highly incensed, now wait the result of this application.

"The voice of 10,000 freemen demands that both regiments be forthwith removed. Their voice must be respected, their demand obeyed. Fail, then, at your peril, to comply with this requisition!

"On you alone rests the responsibility of the decision; and if the just expectations of the people are disappointed, you must be answerable to God and your country for the fatal consequences that must ensue.

"The committee have discharged their duty, and it is for you to discharge yours. They await your final determination."

It was for Adams a moment of triumph, for events had given him a solution he had been seeking since the day, more than 17 months earlier, that the troops had landed in Boston. Adams later said that as he eyed Hutchinson:

"I observed his knees to tremble; I saw his face grow pale; and I enjoyed the sight."

Hutchinson had seen more than the look on Adams's face. He knew Adams had sent expresses earlier to the surrounding towns and had a signal ready for Beacon Hill. And he had seen that this was no rabble, that these were "men of the best character" as they had walked past the old State House from Faneuil Hall to the Old South. They had, as he observed, the spirit "of their ancestors when they imprisoned Andros."

Hutchinson now found all his advisers against him, and he gave in. Next day, Dalrymple's officers, feeling the evacuation would be "disgraceful" to them, sent an express to Gen. Gage, who at first approved the evacuation, then changed his mind. But the regiments were long gone before Gage's new orders arrived.

An ironic touch is recalled by John Adams. The zealous patriot William Molineux marched down King street "side by side with the commander of some of these troops to protect them from the indignation of the people." Samuel Adams must have approved this. So, who now was the "great incendiary"?

On March 8, Samuel Adams saw to it that the burial of the victims of the massacre far exceeded his earlier planning for young Seider's funeral. More than 10,000 mourners followed the four coffins around town, from Liberty Tree to Old Granary. And on March 17, three days after Carr died, his coffin and an outpouring of mourners followed the same route again. Adams, an old Puritan, knew the power of emotion.

His cousin John, looking back, put the massacre in this historic perspective:

"Not the Battle of Lexington or Bunker's Hill, not the surrender of Burgoyne or Cornwallis, were more important events than the Battle of King street, on the 5th of March, 1770. On that night, the foundation of American independence was laid."

Curiously, unknown at the time to Samuel Adams, he had scored another victory. It was on that day (March 5) that Lord North, who at the first of the year had become Britain's prime minister, started the debate in Parliament to repeal the Townshend taxes.

But North had one momentous reservation. At the wish of George III he planned to retain the tax on tea.

Public indignation against the "murderers" was so intense that Hutchinson seized every excuse available to postpone the trial of the British soldiers. Not until Oct. 28, nearly eight months after the massacre, did the trial begin before the colony's highest justices, solemnly attired in crimson robes to signify a capital offense. Chief Justice Benjamin Lynde Jr. presided.

Capt. Preston was tried first. The day after the massacre a weeping Tory friend of Preston had come into John Adams's law office and pleaded that no lawyer in town would take the case, but Josiah Quincy Jr. would if Adams would. John Adams in later life would call his acceptance "one of the best pieces of service I ever rendered my country.

"Judgment of death against those soldiers would have been as foul a stain upon this country as the executions of the Quakers or witches anciently." The Sons of Liberty had approved Quincy and John Adams defending the British soldiers. Samuel Adams was eager that Boston's reputation not be damaged, and the defense saw to it that no Bostonian served on the jury.

Six days later Preston was found not guilty. He had been unarmed and there was no proof that he had ordered his men to fire. The town was too hot for him, though, and he speedily left for Castle William.

On Nov. 27 the eight soldiers went on trial. The prosecution, as it had for Capt. Preston, included Josiah Quincy Jr.'s older brother Samuel Quincy and Robert Treat Paine, who would one day sign the Declaration of Independence. Young Josiah Quincy's father, incidentally, said he was shocked and bewildered that his son would defend "those criminals who are charged with the murder of their fellow citizens."

Eight days later six of the soldiers were found not guilty and two were declared guilty of manslaughter — Hugh Montgomery, the first to fire, and Kilroy, who shot and bayoneted Samuel Gray. Kilroy, who had fought with Gray in the earlier clash at the ropewalk, was bloodthirsty. Sheriff Greenleaf's coachman had heard Kilroy say that he had been waiting for a chance "to fire on the inhabitants" since he landed in Boston.

Hutchinson considered remitting the sentence even while Col. Dalrymple advised that it be imposed. Finally it was. The two soldiers invoked the old medieval plea of "benefit of clergy," which meant that they could read and therefore could not be executed, and Sheriff

Greenleaf came into the courtroom and branded them on the right thumbs with a hot iron.

The case was over except for the four members of the hated customs service who had been charged with shooting from the window of the customshouse. It developed that the men were nowhere near the massacre scene. The jury, without bothering to withdraw, gave a verdict of acquittal.

On April 24, 1770, Hancock's ship *Hayley* had brought news to Boston of repeal of the Townshend taxes, except the 3-penny tax on tea. In February, 300 Boston women had signed a pledge not to drink any tea until the impost was repealed. And the *Boston Gazette* in April reported that just about every merchant had likewise signed "not to dispose of any tea until the late revenue acts are repealed."

In Parliament, the great Pitt had argued that all the taxes should be repealed. Trade should be the objective with America, he said; "drawing money from the Americans by taxes was ill-judged." There was no need to keep the tax on tea as a symbol, Pownall told Parliament, for the old Declaratory Act maintained Parliament's authority.

Moreover, Hutchinson saw the wisdom of ending the tea tax. "I know not what reason may make it necessary to continue the duty on tea; but I think the repeal of it, or making the same duty payable in England, is necessary to prevent disorders in the colonies."

But Lord North did not see the wisdom. The King would not let him. So there would be plenty of agony ahead for England.

Along the way Samuel Adams would not always meet with success. He would have deep disappointments. But unswerving in his goal — which, by now, had become independency in some form for the colonies — Samuel Adams never gave up trying.

His concern that Boston might be known as a mobocracy impelled Adams, immediately after the massacre, to get a town meeting to obtain affidavits and prepare a statement on what had happened. Ninety-six depositions were quickly secured and appended to "a Short Narrative of the horrid Massacre" . . . and its causes as the patriots saw them. James Bowdoin did the writing.

It was far from objective, and its frontispiece was a print of the massacre done by the patriot Paul Revere. The propaganda was so heavy that Adams delayed circulating it in Boston where the people knew the facts — knew, for instance, that there was no "Butchers' Hall" as designated in the Revere print. The whole compilation was printed by Edes and Gill and was sent off to friends in England to furnish them with a rebuttal, if needed.

Adams kept pressure on Hutchinson. The Legislature was ordered to assemble in Cambridge. This, said Hutchinson, was on orders of the King. Adams started a two-year campaign proclaiming that the King, under the charter, had no right to issue such an order. Actually, the King had not. Hutchinson had been given discretion to return the Legislature to Boston if he wished.

Adams learned that Hutchinson had given the keys to Castle William to Col. Dalrymple. The Tories had a retreat in mind — should it become necessary.

Adams tried at once to heat this into a hot issue — but Boston was beginning to weary of turmoil.

Later in 1770, Adams had to face the fact that non-importation had become pretty much a dead letter. Intercolonial suspicions and rivalries, along with repeal of the taxes, plenty of smuggled Dutch tea, improved business and a demand for British products ended the agreement. Even Hancock freely advertised a sale of fine British imports.

"We have not been so quiet these five years," observed Hutchinson. "The people about the country have certainly altered their conduct, and in this town, if it were not for two or three Adamses, we should do well enough."

After the massacre, Hutchinson had asked to be allowed to resign. Boston, his birthplace, was more than he could handle. "If this town could be separated from the rest of the province," he daydreamed. Then, in March of 1771, he received and accepted his commission making him governor. At the same time his brother-in-law, Andrew Oliver, became lieutenant governor.

The Committees of Correspondence

The low period for Samuel Adams continued for about another year after Hutchinson got the governorship. Adams was often a man fighting single-handedly. In this difficult time he would meet his greatest personal mortification — but he would also be on his way to making his greatest contribution to uniting the colonies against Britain.

Humiliation for Adams came during the lengthy battle with Hutchinson over summoning the Legislature to Cambridge, supposedly at the King's wish. More Tory members were then in the House, and Adams was included on a committee named to acknowledge to Hutchinson that he could remove the Legislature "to Housatonic" if he desired. John Adams remarked of his cousin's chagrin that "it must have penetrated him very deeply."

Hutchinson was hopeful that the clock had been turned back a decade and that he was once again in the halcyon atmosphere of the unquestioned supremacy of Parliament.

Otis, temporarily lucid, came back to his House seat. But he was strangely jealous of the new leader, his most loyal lieutenant, Samuel Adams. Cousin John Adams had chosen not to return to the House; he wished to retire from politics altogether and had moved back to Braintree. And John Hancock was avoiding his former associates.

Samuel Adams made not a murmur against any of them. His cause was too vital to waste time on petty feelings or recrimination. He went right on politicking, moving around, handshaking, pouring out correspondence. John Adams had called this "working the political machine." Samuel Adams continued to work it. And above all, there was his writing for the press.

Hutchinson kept an eye on this writing. He observed, "In this week's paper you see the black art of Adams." Hutchinson knew the power of Adams's prose. He recognized it at once when Adams had written an analysis of the massacre under the name Vindex. And now Adams was using many pen names.

Hutchinson thought he saw a chance to win over John Hancock by offering him a seat in the Council.

As part of his courting Hancock, Hutchinson would also make him colonel in command of the Governor's Cadet Company. He even accepted him as temporary speaker of the House.

Save for Boston, Hutchinson felt he saw a "general appearance of contentment throughout the province." It was illusory.

Samuel Adams was not taking his eyes from his goal for an instant. On the first anniversary of the massacre he staged a great public memorial and oration. Revere displayed in his windows images of the martyred men and even the boy, Seider. The second anniversary was, like the first, a grand memorial. When Adams could not get his cousin, he got Joseph Warren to deliver an eloquent oration.

The Tories had picked up so much spirit they even tried to defeat Adams at the annual election to the House, May 6, 1772. His vote was less than its usual size but he was really in no danger.

On May 27, Hancock was elected to the Council. Hutchinson was overjoyed; his scheme seemed to be working. But his glee was of short duration; Hancock declined to serve and resumed active association with the patriots. To celebrate this, Hancock commissioned John Singleton Copley to paint Samuel Adams's portrait for his Beacon Hill mansion — the one with Adams pointing to the charter.

For some time Samuel Adams had been trying to establish how Hutchinson was being paid. The governor had not signed the paybill voted for him and had evaded questions about whether he was being paid by the crown. As the House was prorogued in July, Adams sent a House message to the governor asking again about his pay.

Hutchinson at last confirmed that he was being paid by the crown and, even more galling, that the money was provided by duties collected by the despised customs commissioners. To Adams this was a fundamental violation of the charter. The House angrily rejected a repair bill for Province House.

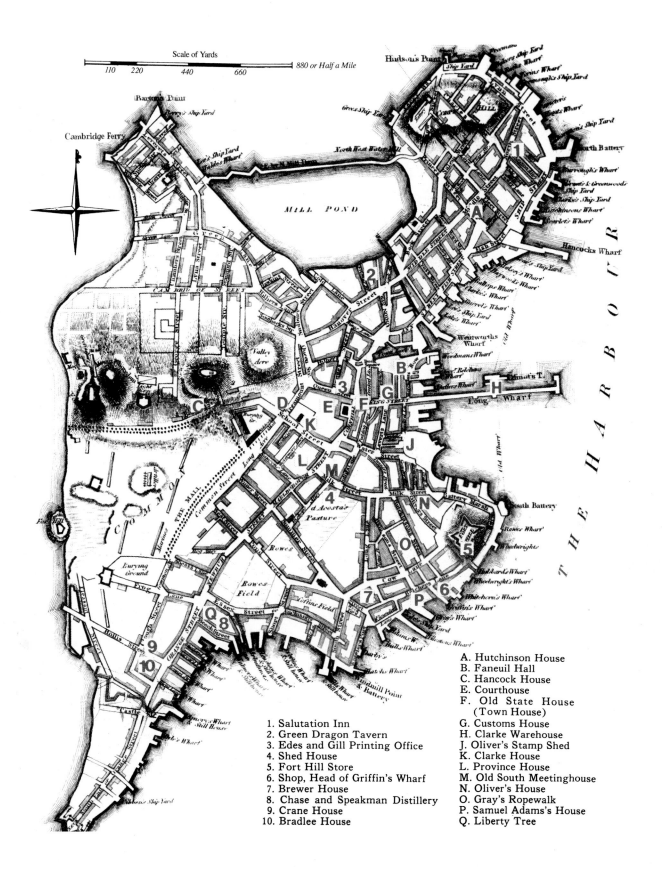

Scale of Yards

110 220 440 660 880 or Half a Mile

1. Salutation Inn
2. Green Dragon Tavern
3. Edes and Gill Printing Office
4. Shed House
5. Fort Hill Store
6. Shop, Head of Griffin's Wharf
7. Brewer House
8. Chase and Speakman Distillery
9. Crane House
10. Bradlee House

A. Hutchinson House
B. Faneuil Hall
C. Hancock House
E. Courthouse
F. Old State House
    (Town House)
G. Customs House
H. Clarke Warehouse
J. Oliver's Stamp Shed
K. Clarke House
L. Province House
M. Old South Meetinghouse
N. Oliver's House
O. Gray's Ropewalk
P. Samuel Adams's House
Q. Liberty Tree

Sons of Liberty toss tea in Boston Harbor (detail)

Ancient and Honorable Artillery Company of Massachusetts

Boston Athenaeum, Boston, Mass.

British ships and troops reach Town Wharf, Boston (detail)

State House, Boston, Mass.

James Otis Jr. denounces writs of assistance before Hutchinson

Bostonian Society, Boston, Mass.

Massachusetts Historical Society

Far left, actual tea from Tea Party, saved by participant John Crane, and his tea caddy

Left, The Edes' punchbowl

Below, The Boston Massacre

Bostonian Society, Boston, Mass.

Samuel Adams emphasizes authority of Bay State charter

Harvard University, Cambridge, Mass.

Massachusetts Historical Society

Far left, William Pitt bust, gift from Benjamin Franklin to Harvard University.

Left, John Adams

Below, "Dartmouth" under sail

Dartmouth College, Hanover, N.H.

King George III

Lord North

Gov. Thomas Hutchinson

Samuel Adams, in pulpit, John Hancock, on stairway, at the Old South before Tea Party

The burning of the Brig "Peggy Stewart"

The pay issue provoked disapproval throughout the colony. Hutchinson sadly observed, "It is not likely that the American colonies will remain part of the dominion of Great Britain another century...."

The situation became further aggravated when Adams got word that the colony's judges would get their pay by the same means as the governor. This was "despotism." Adams flailed at it in Edes and Gill's *Boston Gazette.* Then Adams put an important plan into action and in doing so, he was mightily aided by Hutchinson's stubbornness.

Adams got the town meeting formally to ask the governor whether it was true that the crown was going to pay the judges. Hutchinson spurned the question, saying that he was not required to reveal official communications. So the town asked Hutchinson to call the Legislature into session to deal with the crisis. This, ukased Hutchinson, would be treading on his prerogatives.

This high-handedness threw oil on the fires of indignation and alarm already spreading rapidly among the people.

On Nov. 2 Adams arranged another town meeting and made his momentous proposal in old Faneuil Hall that Boston name 21 members of a Committee of Correspondence to write to other Bay Colony communities to set up their own Committees of Correspondence, and hopefully extend this throughout the colonies to show the unity of the people against despotism.

The confidence of the patriots had been shaken during Hutchinson's months of contentment. Just about all of them save Adams were jittery, doubtful that his plan would meet with success. But the fervor of his conviction and persistence carried the Nov. 2 meeting, one of Faneuil Hall's most historic sessions, and his plan was approved along with drafting a declaration of the rights of the colonists.

Where had the idea of the Committees of Correspondence come from?

The title was not new. Even the East India Co. used it as one of its tools for running that General Motors-type giant of that day. The seed for its political use was in the instructions to Boston's legislators, written by Adams in 1764

against the Stamp Act. He developed it in the Circular Letter of 1768 and in his legislative committees of 1770, 1771 and 1772.

The big difference now was that the committees would be composed of local people — not high officials — and these committees would become the executive committees at local levels that would form the new, popular government of the colonies.

Characteristically, Hutchinson's immediate reaction to this idea was contempt. He thought this stance of his "vexed" the colonists. To Hutchinson, Adams's idea was, as he wrote to England, "such a foolish scheme."

But other Tories got a truer picture.

They styled it: "The source of the rebellion."

Just prior to putting the motion for the Committee of Correspondence, Samuel Adams had given a signal of what he was about to do when he concluded an article he wrote in October 1772 in the *Boston Gazette* with these words:

"Let every town assemble. Let associations and combinations everywhere set up to consult and recover our just rights."

After his plan was launched he breathed this prayer in a letter to his North Shore disciple, Elbridge Gerry:

"May God grant that the love of liberty, and a zeal to support it, may enkindle in every town!"

What Adams set in motion must have overwhelmed even him. Enthusiastic response was almost instantaneous in the colony. Hutchinson had noted sourly that, to obtain universal consent in circulating the appeal, "even a district of 200 Indians, called Mashpee, was not omitted."

With the appeal, all printed by Edes and Gill, had gone a declaration to the world of "the rights of the colonists and of this province in particular, as men, as Christians and as subjects" — pure John Locke philosophy — a document proposed and in good measure written by Adams. Benjamin Franklin, who had become the colony's agent in England late in 1770, wrote a preface and gave the declaration wide circulation in England.

To John Adams, this declaration contained the essence of what in less than four years would become the Declaration of Independence.

It was then moved by Mr Samuel Adams, That a Committee of Correspondence be appointed to consist of twenty one Persons — to state the Rights of the Colonists and of this Province in particular, as Men, as Christians, and as Subjects; to communicate and publish the same to the several Towns in this Province and to the World as the sense of this Town, with the Infringements and Violations thereof that have been, or from time to time may be made — Also requesting of each Town a free communication

Motion for a Committee of Correspondence

Boston Public Library, Boston, Mass.

Adams's motion that created the Committees of Correspondence

Franklin, in his preface for England, effectively cited the folly of the trade laws and the customs setup imposed on the colonies. The expense of keeping armed ships and soldiers to back the customs had reduced the prior year's income to "the pitiful sum of 85 pounds." Meantime, added Franklin, "tea and other Indian goods, which might have been sold in America, remain rotting in the company's warehouses. ..."

By this time Hutchinson was beginning to realize that his first estimate was wrong. He nevertheless stuck with it even when another Tory, writing in the *Massachusetts Gazette*, a Tory mouthpiece, denounced the Committee of Correspondence as "the foulest, subtlest, and most venomous serpent ever issued from the egg of sedition." Soon Hutchinson was calling the committees "very dangerous" and when he learned that they were spreading throughout the colony and into others he was genuinely alarmed.

If anyone has any doubt that there was sentiment in Samuel Adams's puritanical makeup it should be corrected by what he did as part of that famous Nov. 2 town meeting. He paid his sincere respects to James Otis Jr. by having Otis named chairman of the 21-member Committee of Correspondence, which held its first meeting the very next day in the house chamber of the old State House.

Even more, when the declaration of rights was read in Faneuil Hall on Nov. 20 for approval of the town meeting, Adams arranged that Otis act as moderator. It was a role Otis would never fill again, for he was now almost a mental wreck.

But Samuel Adams honored this great patriot, many of whose blessings to his fellowmen are now forgotten. Adams had them in mind, for he had helped, too. One of them went back to 1766, when Otis chaired the committee to construct a gallery in the House so that the people might know what was going on. It was the first true public gallery in a legislative body in the history of mankind.

Leaders of the Sons of Liberty were on that first committee besides Otis and Adams. There were Joseph Warren (who helped write the declaration), Josiah Quincy Jr., William Molineux and Dr. Thomas Young. The membership included at least three who would take part in the Boston Tea Party, and undoubtedly a greater number who would take part secretly in planning it.

Few treasures in our nation's history are

more inspiring to read than the responses the other towns, and then the other colonies, sent back to Boston. They caught the fire of liberty ignited by the declaration, repeated its words, instructed their legislators to support its ideals.

And what did they oppose? "Innovations" — that was the word they used — "innovations" being attempted by the British authorities to destroy the charter.

Hutchinson's alarm prompted him to assemble the Legislature and on Jan. 8, 1773, he lectured its members in his best judicial style, defending the supremacy of Parliament. In effect, this was his Tory manifesto.

Responses came back fast from the House led by Adams and from the Council led by Bowdoin. Their arguments were embedded in John Locke's philosophy of the natural rights of mankind and the supremacy of the people. The presentation was immensely powerful, for the fiery enthusiasm of Adams was given legal underpinning by his cousin John Adams, now back in politics and on a path that would lead him to the Presidency.

Hutchinson was chagrined to learn that his masters in England thought that he had bungled matters by reviving controversy and had merely given another inopportune opening to the patriots to stage an attack.

At this time the colonists were shocked to learn that orders had been issued to find those responsible for burning the *Gaspee* and to send them to England for trial. The *Gaspee* was a customs cutter that had been lured aground by the Rhode Island patriots and burned off Providence in June of 1772.

Of course, no "culprit" was identified and the inquiry was abandoned. But the stern orders that would destroy the jury system came just as the Virginia assembly was in session and considering Committees of Correspondence. The Virginia burgesses thereupon moved toward colonial unity by voting for a network of colonial Committees of Correspondence.

This was a tremendous stride toward the continental congress that Samuel Adams was seeking.

Meanwhile, in England, the ultimate British blunder was taking shape.

The East India Co., pushed toward bankruptcy by the millions of tons of unsold tea crammed in its warehouses near the Thames, on March 2, 1773, petitioned Parliament for a loan and a change in tea taxes that would allow it to compete, even with smuggled Dutch tea.

Hazy word of this action and debate trickled across the Atlantic by letter and ship rumor to the colonies. The Tea Act itself cleared the House of Commons and was signed on May 10. The *Boston Gazette* would mention this bare fact late in June, but it would not be until the end of the summer that the full text and facts were known in the colonies.

Hutchinson, in the interim, was to go through what he termed "detestable proceedings" at the hands of the increasingly triumphant patriots.

Hutchinson's torment this time was, like Bernard's final troubles, over letters he had sent to England four or five years previously expressing himself in favor of a number of repressive measures against the colony. Here at last was confirmation of Adams's suspicions.

"There must be some abridgment of what is called English liberty in the colonies," Hutchinson had written. This was exactly what Adams had been charging the British authorities with attempting.

The letters, in a manner never explained, had come to Benjamin Franklin, the colony's agent. There were 17 of them in all, six from Hutchinson, the rest from Lt. Gov. Oliver, Paxton and others, all addressed to a now-deceased member of Parliament, Thomas Whately, who had also been an undersecretary of the cabinet.

Franklin forwarded them to Boston to the speaker of the House with the caution that they were not to be copied or published. Adams made the most of them. He piqued curiosity by holding a locked-door, secret session of the Legislature and, as clerk, reading the letters to the House. An excuse for publishing them came with John Hancock's "disclosure" that someone had given him copies of the letters as he was walking across the Common. So the House sent the copies to the printer!

There was a big to-do in England, too.

Whately's brother issued a challenge to a duel to Sir John Temple in the belief that Temple had given Franklin the letters. Temple, son-in-law of the patriot James Bowdoin, had once been a customs commissioner in Boston but managed to retain popularity on both sides and eventually returned to Boston as England's first consul.

Temple actually had nothing to do with the letters, but accepted the challenge and wounded Whately's brother.

Franklin now disclosed that he was the one who had obtained the letters, considered them a public matter and so sent them to the colony. Franklin was hailed before the Privy Council and so unjustly assailed by the crown prosecutor that he went home, changed into homespun, and said he would use nothing else until the colonies were free. As further reprisal, Franklin was removed from his post as deputy postmaster general of the colonies.

The upshot of the to-do in the Bay Colony came late in June when the Legislature petitioned the King to remove from office both Hutchinson and Oliver.

Lord North blunders into Tea Act

Lord North was given ample, cogent warning in Parliament that he was embarking on a tax scheme impaired with a senseless provision totally unacceptable to the American colonists.

"I tell the noble lord now that if he don't take off the duty they won't take the tea," declared an incisive opponent, William Dowdeswell. Dowdeswell meant the continuing 3-penny-per-pound tax in force since Townshend's day.

The new Tea Act was far more comprehensive than continuation of the tax provision. The East India Co. was badly mismanaged, as well as facing an adverse market and smuggling. Its tea surplus was reaching a gargantuan 18,000,000 unsaleable pounds. The Tea Act contained sweeping reform of the company.

Dowdeswell, though, fired away at the 3-penny provision. To help the company's sales, the Tea Act would, while continuing this 3-penny provision in the colonies, rebate the company 12-penny-per-pound taxes that had been collected when the tea was first brought into England.

Why not, suggested Dowdeswell, cancel the 3-penny tax in the colonies and give a rebate of only 9 pennies? This would come out the same to the British treasury. The amount in revenue that the 3-penny tax produced was as puny as a "peppercorn," said Dowdeswell, compared with the loss of millions of pounds of tea sales in the American colonies.

No, North would not do it that way. He had another, sterner, purpose. He wanted to retain the 3-penny tax to signify the supremacy of Parliament and its right to tax the colonies. He brushed aside further criticism and advice, saying:

"It is to no purpose making objections. The King will have it so. The King means to try the question with America." It was North's weakness always to try to please the King, right or wrong.

Enactment of the Tea Act, regardless of its political implications, did offer a wide-open opportunity to pile up profit.

There was a scramble in England to get it.

Jockeying began in May, right after passage of the act, and continued through June and July. Letters to the East India Co. are extant showing the London agents trying to get their American customers named as consignees, or "Tea Commissioners," as they were called.

Market estimates, types of tea to include, various plans for distribution, posting of securities to assure payments to the company, division of the six percent seller's profit, prospects of beating smuggled Dutch tea (one of its greatest routes was from Amsterdam to Rhode Island)— all are mentioned recurringly in the related correspondence.

On Aug. 4 the East India directors approved their final plan and chose the consignees to whom they would send 2000 chests of tea. The company then sought ships to carry this freight, an action that soon uncovered the fact that all this bustle had gone on without considering the reaction developing in the colonies.

"The ministry," Franklin warned, "believe that three pence a pound for tea . . . is sufficient to overcome all the patriotism of an American." The East India Co.'s committee on warehouses, in charge of sales and shipping, suddenly found not every skipper in London port was eager to take tea as a cargo.

John Hancock's London colleague, George Hayley, was about to dispatch Hancock's ship *Hayley* and delayed his answer to the committee on warehouses so that he could avoid shipping any of the tea. Hayley, when he answered, cannily suggested that the *Dartmouth* was in port and would not be leaving for two weeks. Historians like to ponder the effect on the Boston Tea Party if Hancock's ship had been one of those that came into Boston harbor freighted with tea.

As word on details, still imprecise, spread in the colonies, the feelings were at first ones of amazement and despair. Had the ministry learned nothing from America's response to earlier efforts at taxation? Or from non-importation? Could the ministry be so obtuse as to believe, even for a moment, that the colonists would not see this as still another attempt at violation of their charters?

The first full text was printed in Gaine's *New York Gazette* on Sept. 6. The New York patriots issued their first warning handbill, "Alarm No. 1" on Oct. 7, and there was a meeting of merchants in honor of shipmasters who refused to transport the tea. The Committees of Correspondence got busy and America started to seethe. Soon a British officer in New York would be saying:

"All America is in a flame on account of the tea exportation."

It was in Philadelphia that the patriots took the lead in direct action. Sons of Liberty met and issued handbills: "By uniting we stand, by dividing we fall." On Oct. 16 several hundred Philadelphians assembled in their State House yard and adopted resolutions declaring anyone dealing with tea "an enemy of his country." The Philadelphia consignees were asked to resign. Some did so at once.

On Oct. 18 the *Boston Gazette* printed the names of the Boston consignees and likened them to the hated stamp commissioners of 1765. The *Gazette* assailed Lord North and "this new scheme of administration." And it suggested that the tea "be returned to England" and that the consignees be sent along, too, "to give the Premier the reasons for such conduct."

Oct. 18 was a fateful day for another reason.

The ships picked to carry the 600,000 pounds of tea for which the Lords of the Treasury had given an export license had left the port of London on various days from the end of September to the beginning of October. Strong winds as they entered the English Channel kept them sheltering at Deal. Then, on Oct. 18, the headwinds ceased and the ships started sailing down the channel toward the broad Atlantic.

What do we know about the tea ships?

On specifics, very little.

No contemporary likeness or model of any of the specific ships exist. (There are many likenesses and models of military ships of the 18th Century, but few things are rarer than 18th Century models of merchant ships.)

Likenesses do exist of merchant ships in general of that period, and there are also some modern models based on extant 18th Century building plans and designs. Conceptions of what the tea ships were like have been based on these.

All of the tea ships were known as "constant traders." These were ships carrying general cargo from London and the colonies. Usually they were built in America because construction there was less costly. They were built for profit, not showiness, and usually they traveled slowly.

The four tea ships headed for Boston were all owned in the Bay Colony. The *Dartmouth* and *Beaver* were owned by the Rotch family, Quakers of Nantucket and New Bedford. The sire, Joseph, who had three sons, was one of the greatest figures of the whaling industry, and his son William became a tycoon of this seafaring oil business.

Joseph was among the earliest settlers of New Bedford, then a part of Dartmouth, and the ship *Dartmouth* he had built on the waterfront in 1767 was the future New Bedford's first large vessel. His youngest son, Francis, then 23, was in Boston when the tea ships arrived and he was desperately anxious to get the *Dartmouth* unloaded because the Rotch sloop *Triton,* carrying whale oil, was waiting to have its cargo shifted to the much bigger *Dartmouth* for the return to London. Standby costs, called demurrage, were mounting.

The *Eleanor* was owned by John Rowe, a wealthy Boston merchant best remembered for his diary and the wharf bearing his name. He was widely liked, was a Grand Master of the Masons, leaned to the patriot side but sought in business fashion to be agreeable to both sides. This colonial Pepys left a delightful picture of Boston in those days, highlighted by his fishing trips, feasting in the taverns, partying at the great estates, giving a hand in local government.

The fourth tea ship for Boston, the one least remembered, was much smaller than the others, a brig called *William* that belonged to the Clarkes. Sire of this wealthy merchant family was Richard Clarke. He and his sons were the colony's second-largest tea importers. Top ones were the governor's sons. The Clarkes' sister Susan married the painter John Singleton Copley and they lived on Beacon Hill as neighbors of John Hancock.

The *William* would be caught in a December

gale and be wrecked on Cape Cod at Province-town, though its cargo, including Boston's first street lamps, were rescued.

The amount of tea in each whole chest was 340 pounds. The container itself weighed about 90 pounds, called the tare. So these chests of tea required heavy tackle for handling. Tea, particularly the more expensive varieties, also was shipped in half chests and quarter chests — and these lent themselves to more economical stowing of the ship's cargo.

The common, most popular variety was called Bohea. Four times as much Bohea (named for the Chinese hills where it grew) was sent in the tea ships than all of the more expensive teas put together. These more expensive ones ranged through Congo, Singlo and Souchong to the most expensive, Hyson, which cost two and a half times as much as Bohea. Bohea sold for two shillings a pound.

The Boston-bound *Dartmouth* and *Eleanor* were loaded with 114 chests each, a total combining whole and half chests; the *Beaver*, with 112 chests, and the *William*, with 58. All these vessels carried cargo other than tea.

At the same time that these ships sailed, the East India Co. dispatched tea-laden ships to the other major ports in the colonies, New York and Philadelphia in the middle colonies and Charleston in the south.

Largest tea shipment of all was on the *Nancy*, which carried a total of 698 chests of various types to New York. The *Nancy* is described in East India Co. communications as "river-built." The *Polly*, built in England in 1765, carried 600½ chests to Philadelphia. The *London*, American-owned, carried 257 chests to Charleston. Only the tea for Charleston would be landed — but not for its consignees.

In making shipments this way the company was automatically offending large numbers of dealers and merchants with whom it had previously been doing business. Normally the company sold its tea at wholesale auctions, run by "inch of candle," and the tea was then wholesaled to retailers.

Now the company, to save middleman costs, was shipping the tea to dealers of its own selection. This meant that a monopoly was being es-tablished in each of these four ports and, naturally, the company was selecting those it considered Tory sympathizers.

This cozy arrangement threw all offended groups, if they were not already there, to the side of the patriots — merchants, waterfront workers, shippers. Add to these the smugglers who did not want their way of life disturbed. And add those who feared this scheme might lead to other monopolies and to further taxes.

The East India Co. was simply flying blindly toward inevitable disaster.

The disaster was made unavoidable by Gov. Hutchinson's intransigence.

Why was Hutchinson so rigid?

He was by nature autocratic and as indifferent to people in general as Adams was considerate of them. To Hutchinson the only people who counted were the elite; all others lived to serve them and jump at their command; and, above all, to Hutchinson, the only people capable of ruling were the elite. There was not a democratic fibre in all Hutchinson's makeup.

Something else made Hutchinson doubly unbending.

It happened back in 1770, just before the Boston Massacre. On Jan. 1 of that year the non-importation agreement had formally ended. At once Hutchinson's sons, Thomas Jr. and Elisha, wanted to take their tea and British goods out of storage and sell them. Others were trying to do that, too. But the merchants' committee said that this would be in violation of the spirit of the agreement.

To be fair to all, said the committee, merchants who did not have British goods should have time to make purchases in England and bring them to the colony.

Hutchinson's sons did not agree. They had the committee's padlocks ripped from their warehouse and moved their goods "to some other place unknown to the committee." The committee demanded that the Hutchinsons bring back the goods. They refused. After protest meetings that Adams called at Faneuil Hall, boisterous William Molineux, a merchant himself, led 1000 citizens to Hutchinson's house.

What did they want, asked the acting governor from an upstairs window.

"It is not you but your sons we desire to see," replied Molineux.

As a son appeared at his side, Hutchinson proclaimed:

"I am the representative of the King of Great Britain, the greatest monarch on earth, and in his name require you to disperse."

Molineux read the town meeting's demand on his sons. The son would make no concession. Hutchinson then spoke further, saying he saw people in the crowd who had attacked his house back in 1765. The crowd dispersed.

Hutchinson still wanted to hold out when he found that his Council and the justices of the peace offered him no help. But when Tory merchants suggested that he give in to prevent violence to his sons and their property, he reversed himself and told his sons to return the British goods, mainly tea, and even to turn over the money they had collected on protested sales.

Hutchinson, reflecting later on his action, made an observation that goes a long way to explain his adamancy at the time of the Boston Tea Party. He bitterly regretted that he ordered his sons to place their goods back under the committee's padlocks. He said that he "felt more trouble and distress of mind from this error in his public trust than he had from the loss and damage to his private fortune when his house and great part of his property was destroyed" in the 1765 riot.

Further, Hutchinson did not shrink from obvious conflicts of interest. One existed in that 1770 incident and another existed at the time of the Tea Party, not just because Hutchinson was making decisions involving his sons' commitments but also because Hutchinson, though he made no public mention of this, had been involved in trying to obtain the tea for his sons in London.

He had written to an influential London merchant for his sons: "I wish you may succeed in behalf of my sons to whom I have given a hint."

Hutchinson affected all the Boston tea consignees with his stubborn attitude. In the other tea ports, even when some consignees held out a little longer than others, they all bowed to the manifest will of the people expressed at their public meetings. Even crown officials made use of available loopholes to defer to the public.

But not in Boston. The responses of the consignees to the outraged public's demand were obstinacy, deception, evasion or flight. The crown officials in Boston, customs and military, took their cue from Hutchinson.

The story of the Boston Tea Party is a story of the steadily, dramatically narrowing choices that Hutchinson's inflexible moves left to the patriots. All evidence shows that the patriots did not want to destroy the tea. They wanted to send it back in the ships it came in.

Adams knew that the eyes of the Sons of Liberty in other tea ports were on Boston. They had acted. They were watching to see what Boston would do. If the tea were to come ashore in Boston, presumably under the guns of the British ships and soldiers, Boston would have failed the other colonies. Adams's dream of assembling a congress of all the colonies would be dead.

Was Adams ready for the challenge?

At this very moment, as the tea ships were sailing, Hutchinson in a letter to his British boss, the secretary of state for the American colonies, appraised Adams as "the first person that openly and in any public assembly declared for absolute independence" and went on to say that Adams had been gradually over the years increasing his influence "until he has such an ascendency as to direct the town of Boston and the House of Representatives, and consequently the Council, just as he pleases."

Unlike Hutchinson, there was nothing autocratic about Samuel Adams. He did not move without mustering the strength that came from consulting the people. How he went about this is also a great part of the story of the Boston Tea Party, an event that would unite the colonies and lead to the outbreak of the Revolutionary War.

Assault on Clarke store

The tea consignees and the tea scheme came under constantly mounting attack throughout the colonies in October.

The Committees of Correspondence were hives of activity. On Oct. 21 the Boston committee from Faneuil Hall penned circular letters to the Bay Colony towns saying that the unity they had already established was alarming their enemies and that all conciliatory talk of the British ministry was "insidious."

At the old State House the Committee of Correspondence of the House, which was one of the six named since Virginia made its proposal in March, fired off a circular letter on the same Oct. 21 to all the colonies charging that tactics of the North ministry in America would "end in absolute despotism."

"How necessary then," pleaded the circular, "is it that each colony should take effectual methods to prevent this measure from having its designed effects."

The attack grew in meetings and in the press at the same time. The North End Caucus, composed chiefly of mechanics from the then most populous part of Boston, gathered on Saturday, Oct. 23, secretly, as was their custom, and voted that they "would oppose with their lives and fortunes the vending of any tea. . . ."

The following week, mostly rainy and cloudy, was particularly irksome to consignee Richard Clarke. He called it one of "paper skirmishes." The *Gazette* on Monday, Oct. 25, reprinted a lengthy "Scaevola" handbill from Philadelphia that was also publicized in New York. Its effect was to agitate the communities.

The handbill likened the tea consignees to the despised stamp masters of 1765 in trying to "establish parliamentary despotism.

"You are marked out as political bombardiers to demolish the fair structure of American liberty, . . ." the consignees were told, and they were asked flatly to quit this "detestable and infamous" activity.

A gathering of the Sons of Liberty the next day at New York City Hall denounced their consignees and branded their monopoly a "public robbery." "America," warned the Sons of Liberty, "is threatened with worse than Egyptian slavery. . . ."

Clarke said that in Boston there were nightly meetings of large numbers of people around town to plan ways to thwart the Tea Act. He found further attacks in the press so "inflammatory" and so designed to make the consignees "odious to the people" that he enlisted Hutchinson's help to get rebuttals printed in the Tory press.

One of those night meetings that bothered Clarke was held on Nov. 1 by the Sons of Liberty. Clarke's nerves would be really wracked that night, for the Loyal Nine, with John Avery doing the writing and Edes and Gill the printing, prepared and spread around town handbills signed by "O.C., sec'y," Avery's pen name, saying that the Boston consignees were getting a quantity of tea "destructive to the happiness of every wellwisher of his country."

At 1 a.m. on Nov. 2 there was purposeful, violent knocking at the doors of the consignees to arouse them from sleep and hand them the handbills, which went on to demand:

"It is therefore expected that you personally appear at Liberty Tree, on Wednesday next, at 12 o'clock at noon day, to make a public resignation of your commission, agreeable to a notification of this day for that purpose.

"Fail not upon your peril."

Later that morning Boston citizens found a notice, also from busy "O.C., sec'y," posted around town inviting the freemen one and all of Boston and vicinity to come to Liberty Tree and see the resignations. The Loyal Nine were obviously following the same script that they used when they brought Oliver to Liberty Tree to resign as stamp master.

On the evening prior to the big event, the Sons of Liberty met in the Green Dragon Tavern, near the Mill Pond, gathering place of the North End Caucus and the Masons, for a warm, night-before session. Among the invited guests were the Committee of Correspondence and John Hancock, which meant all the top Boston patriots were under the same roof. Their commitment was in their vote that "...the tea shipped by the East India Co. shall not be landed."

Next day a flag was hoisted atop Liberty Tree, bells in all the town's meeting places began to ring at 11 a.m. and the town crier hustled around rallying spectators. Adams, Hancock, Warren, Molineux, town officials and a crowd of hundreds were on hand at noon — but there was no sign of the consignees.

These marked men never "entertained the least thoughts," as Clarke phrased it, of being there. Instead they had gathered in the counting room above his store-warehouse at 18 Town Wharf at the harbor end of King street.

It was a close-knit group in many ways. Most of the consignees were relatives through marriage. Besides Gov. Hutchinson and Lt. Gov. Oliver marrying sisters, Oliver's brother Peter, now the chief justice, had married Richard Clarke's sister. And two of Hutchinson's children married Olivers.

The Sons of Liberty held a quick consultation at Liberty Tree and named nine, headed by Molineux and Warren, including three who would be in the Tea Party, to carry warning that the consignees by not appearing at Liberty Tree had revealed themselves "enemies of the country." Gov. Hutchinson, looking from an old State House window, saw the committee stride down King street.

It went into the Clarke building and up a flight of stairs to the counting room. Molineux was spokesman. He faced the consignees (all present except Elisha Hutchinson), a group of Clarke's brawny friends and a justice of the peace friendly to the Clarkes.

Clarke asked: "From whom are you a committee?"

"From the whole people," replied Molineux. The consignees had highly insulted the people, he added, by not appearing. He asked them to sign a paper he had, solemnly promising that they would not land or pay any duty on the tea but send it back in the same bottoms. Clarke, with what he termed "proper contempt," responded:

"I shall have nothing to do with you."

Molineux then read the resolution that the consignées would be considered "enemies of the country" and he and Warren and the others withdrew outside. A crowd had gathered. When told of the rejection and of Clarke's hauteur, the crowd uttered furious cries of "Out with them! Out with them!" Hearing this, Clarke sent a servant to bar the street door.

The crowd prevented him. The justice of the peace shouted in his majesty's name for the rioters to cease. The crowd replied with hoots and insults. Soon the hinges of the outer door were removed and the crowd swarmed in.

The narrowness of the stairway enabled the justice and about 20 of Clarke's stalwarts to stem the attack. Molineux must have passed some signal because the vigor of the assault suddenly waned and most of the crowd withdrew. A few blocked the store for about an hour and a half and then dispersed.

Clarke and the consignees were soon able to walk up the length of King street together and separate to their homes.

Hutchinson's reaction: "This seems to have been intended only as an intimation to the consignees of what they had to expect." That night a fearsome "O.C." letter to all the consignees was slipped under the door of Benjamin Faneuil, just opposite King's Chapel.

"You," affirmed the message, "boldly avow a resolution to bear a principal part in the robbery of every inhabitant of this country. ... Remember, gentlemen, this is the last warning you are ever to expect from the insulted, abused, and most indignant vindicators of violated liberty in the town of Boston."

Strong language. But the efforts of the Sons of Liberty had not succeeded. There came hints from friends of the consignees that a more legal approach might produce results. So the Boston selectmen called a town meeting to be held at 10 a.m. Friday, Nov. 5, to see what could be done about Boston consignees.

Friday, Nov. 5, was Guy Fawkes Day — old, riotous Pope's Day.

Sons of Liberty in New York would hang in effigy a tea merchant now in London, a former New Yorker, suspend the effigy on a gibbet and cart it all around the town's main streets to show their resentment.

In Boston consignee Benjamin Faneuil would conceal himself in his big house for two or three hours. But Boston's mind that day was not intent on rioting. It had the more serious business of getting the consignees to do what some in Philadelphia had already said they would do: resign.

Fully 1000 citizens were on hand in old Faneuil Hall at 10 a.m. and chose John Hancock moderator. Hancock speedily dealt with a surprise Tory handbill intended to disrupt the meeting. Would the tradesmen — the handbill was called "Tradesmen's Protest" — gather please at his right? Several hundred did. Had they sent the protest? They all cried "No!" Hancock moved to the next order of business.

In Philadelphia the patriots had drafted a set of eight resolutions that had led to some of their consignees' resignations.

Philadelphia's patriot printer William Bradford, when told that it might be difficult to arouse opposition to the tea tax, declared, "Leave that business to me." He assembled ardent colleagues at his coffeehouse, meeting place of the Sons of Liberty, and the resolutions were drafted — the first in the colonies to oppose the Tea Act.

Philadelphia adopted these resolutions at its town meeting on Oct. 16, reported in the papers of the 18th.

Now Hancock put these same resolutions before the Boston town meeting. "The sense of this town cannot be better expressed than in the words of certain judicious resolves lately entered into by our worthy brethren of Philadelphia," the Boston resolution declared. The Tea Act would render colonial legislatures "useless" and was a "violent attack upon the liberties of America" and "it was the duty of every American to oppose this attempt."

Hancock was named to head the committee of 10 to call on the consignees and ask them formally to resign. The meeting recessed to 3 p.m. At that hour the committee returned. The Clarkes and Faneuil, speaking also for Joshua Winslow, who was ailing and had gone off to his Marshfield estate, said that they could not act without the Hutchinsons and this would take until Monday.

The town meeting voted for Adams, Molineux and Warren to go back and tell these consignees that an immediate answer was expected. They could act for themselves, they were not joint consignees.

Then a committee of seven headed by Hancock, including Adams and Warren, was sent to Milton to give the Hutchinsons the same message. Within a few minutes the Clarkes and Faneuil had a letter in the hands of moderator Hancock. They could not comply, they claimed, until they learned under what terms the tea was being shipped to them. The meeting impatiently voted this response "not satisfactory," and adjourned to the next day to hear from Milton.

A big turnout of citizens was in Faneuil Hall at 11 a.m. Saturday when the committee reported that they had been able to locate only the older son, Thomas Jr. His letter for himself and brother Elisha was read. It was another version of the Clarke and Faneuil letter. Whereupon the meeting voted them both "daringly affrontive to the town," and dispersed.

"To arms! To arms!" many had cried when they had heard the Hutchinson response, and these ominous calls had drawn general applause. But moderation prevailed. Still, Boston was far from calm. On Nov. 9, Adams wrote to a friend, "One cannot foresee events; but, from all the observation I am able to make, my next letter will not be on a trifling subject."

The colonies were now carefully following one another's actions, a sign of developing unity. Pennsylvanians were saying that they hoped Boston would act with its usual spirit. A future Pennsylvania governor, Thomas Mifflin, traveling through Boston at this time, got a patriots' pledge that Boston would resist the tea cargos when he said:

"Will you engage that they shall not be landed? If so, I will answer for Philadelphia."

Would blood flow again on the streets of Boston?

Hutchinson, who seems to have had a special patent on how to get peoples' backs up, had stirred memories of bloodshed on Oct. 11, when he ordered Hancock, as commanding officer of the Governor's Cadet Company, to have the cadets in readiness with arms "whenever there may be a tumultuous assembly of people in violation of the laws. . . ." Hutchinson must certainly have expected no real help from Hancock, selectman, moderator and patriot. Certainly he got none.

Hutchinson's mood at this time — and the colony's mood — can be seen in a letter he wrote on Nov. 15 to his boss in England, Lord Dartmouth.

"At present the spirits of the people in the town of Boston are in great ferment." He bodefully wrote how his Council, while professing disapproval of tumultuous, violent proceedings of the people, would not support his efforts to help land the expected teas.

His scorn was almost visible between the lines as he said the Council felt that "the best thing that can be done to quiet the people would be the refusal of the gentlemen to whom the teas are consigned to execute their trust." Hutchinson was fast to assure his lordship that the consignees "whilst they can be protected from violence to their persons, they will not give way to unreasonable demands. . . ."

He expressed a forlorn hope:

"I wish the vessels bound to New York may arrive before those designed to this province. Gov. Tryon I know to be well disposed to do his duty, and the people there are less disposed to any violent proceedings ... than they are here; and an example of peace and good order there may have its influence here."

William Tryon was new in New York as governor. He had served many years as governor in North Carolina and had won a harsh reputation for suppressing a revolt there. He and Hutchinson were friendly correspondents. During the Revolutionary War, Tryon would lead vicious military assaults on the coastal towns of Connecticut. Hutchinson admired Tryon's backbone.

But Hutchinson's hope was not to be granted.

The tea ships would first appear in Boston ... closest of the tea ports to Europe.

Hancock's ship *Hayley,* six weeks out of London, entered Boston harbor on Nov. 17 with news that the tea ships were not far off. The *Hayley* had on board one of the consignees, Jonathan Clarke. He had been in England, had negotiated for cargo from the East India Co. and had offered the Clarke brig *William* to carry tea.

Clarke would soon be telling a different story in Boston.

Word that the tea ships were en route sparked the idea that it would be an opportune time to call a town meeting and get the issue of resignations settled. The selectmen fixed the next day, Nov. 18, for the meeting in Faneuil Hall.

Meanwhile the Clarkes prepared a jolly welcome-home party for Jonathan in their dwelling on the site next to King's Chapel, where Benjamin Franklin's statue now stands in the old City Hall yard. As the feast was being readied for the guests, Jonathan dashed off a letter to the East India Co. chairman.

He expressed his thanks for the help given to the Clarkes in becoming tea consignees and then, in quite an understatement, said that on arriving home he had found that the Tea Act was an "unpopular" measure. "I fully see that we shall meet with difficulty in executing this trust, but our utmost endeavors shall be exerted to fulfill the orders we may receive from the company."

The party had barely been seated at table when from the outside on School street came the familiar whistling of the Sons of Liberty. A crowd gathered. Horns brayed. A neighbor sought to have the crowd leave, saying that all could be settled the next day at the town meeting, when suddenly a firelog struck a spectator. Someone said it came from the Clarke house, a two-story stone, pitch-roof mansion set end-to to the street.

Pounding thudded on the front door as the women of the party were hurriedly escorted to safety on the second floor. A young man flung open an upstairs window and shouted:

"You rascals, be gone, or I'll blow your brains out!"

A pistol was fired at random. Gov. Hutchinson said this was by one of the consignees. Now the crowd attacked in earnest with big stones, bricks and clubs. The mansion was taken only recently by the Clarkes, who had lived for years in the North End as neighbors of Hutchinson. It was so splendid a residence it had once been used by a royal governor. Now the crowd smashed the windows, shutters, doors and furniture until leaders abruptly gave the signal, "To your tents."

John Hancock was moderator for the town meeting next day. It did not last long. The consignees were again asked by a committee to resign and again they wrote a letter to Hancock that this was "out of our power." They did add that they had learned that friends in England had undertaken commercial "penal engagements" on their behalf.

The meeting promptly voted the answer "unsatisfactory," and the town meeting quietly dissolved.

This placidity suggested a drastic, frightening change of pace. Hutchinson said, "This sudden dissolution struck more terror into the consignees than the most minatory resolves."

So the consignees got to thinking over their plight and hit upon a possible solution. They drafted a petition to the governor and Council telling how they had been "cruelly insulted in their persons and property," had received "insulting and incendiary letters," and that a "tumultuous and riotous assembly of people" had damaged the Clarke house for the space of two hours.

They wished "to resign themselves and the property committed to their care," the tea, to the governor and Council to land and secure "until your petitioners can be at liberty openly and safely, to dispose of the same, or until they can receive directions from their constituents," namely the East India Co.

It was a pat plan to outwit the Sons of Liberty, the selectmen and the town meeting. Hutchinson at his session the next day, Nov. 19, presented the petition to the Council. The Council, after long, probably tongue-in-cheek debate, suggested postponing action until a meeting on the 23rd.

In similar mood the Council would postpone its Nov. 23 session to Nov. 27, and that in turn to Nov. 29. Bowdoin was firmly holding the fort for the patriots.

The unifying work of the Committees of Correspondence now produced what Hutchinson called the "little senate."

The towns surrounding Boston had all signified support. On Nov. 22 Adams arranged a joint meeting of the Committees of Correspondence of Brookline, Cambridge, Dorchester and Roxbury in the selectmen's room in Faneuil Hall, where they wrote other Bay Colony towns that the choice was to surrender or resist like freemen. They were speedily joined by Charlestown.

Hutchinson said that they held almost daily consultations "like a little senate." He almost moaned in a desperate letter he wrote at Milton on Nov. 24:

"Assemblies are tolerated from night to night in the public town hall, to counsel and determine upon further unlawful measures, and dark proposals and resolutions are made and agreed to there.

"The infection is industriously spreading, and the neighboring towns not only join their committees with the committee of Boston, but are assembled in town meetings to approve of the doings of the town of Boston; and, above all, when upon repeated summoning of the Council they put off any advice to me ... under these circumstances I think it time to deliberate whether His Majesty's service does not call me to return to the Castle, where I may with safety to my person more freely give my sense of the criminality of these proceedings.

"The point to be considered is, what am I in duty bound to do?" he wailed to his brother-in-law, Lt. Gov. Oliver.

Richard Clarke, weary of trouble and with health impaired, had the day before taken himself off into the country, leaving a note to his sons. "I hereby give you full power to make whatever agreement you shall think fit respecting the tea. . . ."

His son Jonathan, clearly an enterprising fellow, judged that Hutchinson was getting nowhere with the consignees' petition, so he had started dealing with the selectmen in an effort to gain time or a solution. He dealt mainly with John Scollay, prosperous merchant who would be Boston's chairman of selectmen for 16 straight years.

It was Saturday, Nov. 27, and time had almost run out before the tea would arrive.

Jonathan called on Scollay and arranged for a 4 p.m. session with the selectmen for himself and his younger brother Isaac. Jonathan, seeking desperately to gain concessions, declared that he had been "wholly passive" and had not sought the factorship for handling tea. Shrewd Scollay noted, "Some thought this not true."

The selectmen insisted to Jonathan that the only recourse for the consignees, to satisfy the town, was to send back the tea. Jonathan demurred. He said that he would have to await the arrival of the tea to see what orders came with it, and he would then make proposals to the selectmen.

Scollay later observed that had the consignees at that moment agreed to store the tea subject to inspection, not pay the tea tax and await whatever orders would come, "I am persuaded the town would have closed with them." It was not to be. Scollay said:

"Though we labored night and day in the affair, all our efforts could not produce an agreement between them and the town."

Time for pre-planning was now gone.

In New York the consignees that day told a committee they thought "it was so much against the sense of the inhabitants that they could not execute their commission...." Nevertheless, the cautious patriots got out a broadside that anyone involved in the infamous design "... may depend upon it that we are prepared, and shall not fail to pay them an unwelcome visit, in which they shall be treated as they deserve; by THE MOHAWKS."

In Philadelphia the patriots, holding recurrent sessions at Bradford's coffeehouse, already had received the resignations of all but two of their consignees. The "Committee on Tarring and Feathering" got out warnings to the Delaware River pilots to be on the alert and to the skipper of the tea ship to "fly to the place from whence you came ... fly without hesitation ... and above all, Capt. Ayres, let us advise you to fly without the wild geese feathers."

At 10 p.m. Nov. 27, a night filled with haze and occasional rain, the first tea ship to reach the colonies, the *Dartmouth*, anchored two miles off Boston light and sent a boat ashore to pick up a pilot.

The log of the *Dartmouth* gives its movements on the next day, Sunday, Nov. 28:

British version of John Malcolm's tar and feathering

"At 4 a.m., the pilot, Mr. Minzey, came on board.

"At 6, got under way, wind WNW (west northwest), turned up ship channel and came to anchor in King's Road.

"At 11, the tide being ebb, got under way, and turned up and came to anchor under the Admiral's stern.

"At 10 at night, two customshouse officers were boarded upon us by the Castle, we being the first ship ever boarded in this manner, which happened on account of our having the East India Company's accursed tea on board."

The log showed plainly that the *Dartmouth* had already come within Boston harbor, making the tea dutiable. And, if there were any doubt about it, the tea certainly became dutiable when the customsmen came on board. Hutchinson would later try to blame Adams for ordering the *Dartmouth* to the Boston waterfront and forcing a crisis.

But when Hutchinson wrote down this contention, in his history of the colony, he was in exile in England and was trying to put the best face possible on his own behavior.

Old Puritan Boston — and on Sunday — was in an effervescence of excitement with news that the tea had arrived. Tea, under the trade laws, could not be re-entered in England. Duty would be payable the moment it was landed. If duty was not paid within 20 days after the ship's arrival, both the cargo and the ship were subject to seizure by the crown.

The deadline for paying would be midnight, Dec. 16.

There was activity on all fronts.

The Committee of Correspondence got off a circular letter by express riders to the surrounding towns informing them that part of the tea had arrived and requesting their company and advice "to prevent the impending evil" at a meeting in Faneuil Hall the next day at 9 a.m. The appeal continued:

"We request you to urge your friends in the town, to which you belong, to be in readiness to exert themselves in the most resolute manner, to assist this town in its efforts for saving this oppressed country." After all, there were British troops stationed in the Castle, and in the harbor were Adm. John Montagu's 64-gun flagship *Captain* and its two escorts.

The circular letter was written by Warren and another doctor, Benjamin Church Jr., whose philandering would lead him the following year to become a paid stooge for Gen. Gage.

Adams made other moves. He got word off to Capt. James Hall to bring the *Dartmouth* to the waterfront as soon as he could and "at his peril" land any cargo but the tea. And Molineux went to shipowner Francis Rotch, recently back from a trip to England, and asked him to agree not to enter the *Dartmouth* at customs for two days, the limit.

Scollay and the selectmen, expecting some proposal from Jonathan Clarke now that the tea had arrived, met in their Faneuil Hall chamber successively at noon and 5 p.m. and in between sent couriers looking for Jonathan. They even waited until 9 p.m., but still no Jonathan. Scollay appealed to a relative, probably brother-in-law Copley, to get Jonathan to respond for his own good.

Yeomen service was done by the Loyal Nine. They prepared the text of handbills announcing the next day's meeting to "Friends! Brethren! Countrymen!" got Edes and Gill to print them and saw to their being posted in all parts of town.

With meetinghouse bells ringing, a throng estimated at 5000 squeezed in and around old Faneuil Hall at 9 a.m. the next day, Nov. 29. A prominent merchant and patriot, Jonathan Williams, former captain and for 50 years on the rolls of the Ancient & Honorable Artillery Company, was chosen moderator and, though this was not a formal town meeting, the patriot town clerk William Cooper functioned as he always had.

The leading patriots of Boston and surrounding towns were all there. Adams had a motion:

"As the town have determined at a late meeting legally assembled that they will to the utmost of their power prevent the landing of the tea, the question be now put — whether this body are absolutely determined that the tea now arrived in Captain Hall shall be returned to the place from whence it came."

There was no dissenting voice in the roar of approval.

For more room, the meeting adjourned to the Old South, giving Hutchinson a chance to see resolute citizenry as the patriots passed by the old State House. Hutchinson was busy at the moment trying in vain to get his Council's support.

On reaching Old South, Adams immediately had another motion:

"Whether it is the firm resolution of this body that the tea shall not only be sent back, but that no duty shall be paid thereon?"

Again a roar of approval.

A Rhode Island visitor was so impressed by the high level of the discussion that he said he felt that he was "rather in the British senate than in an adventurous and promiscuous assembly of people of a remote colony." All the speeches were unrecorded.

One of the leading Sons of Liberty, and soon to be a member of the Tea Party, Dr. Thomas Young, foretold the tea's fate when he suggested to the meeting that the only way to get rid of the tea was to throw it overboard.

Hutchinson said, "Nothing can be more inflammatory than the speeches and declarations made on this occasion." They certainly got through to the consignees, who took quickly off for the Castle after the first vote to send the tea back. Hutchinson observed, "They apprehended they should be seized, and, may be, tarred and feathered and carted — an American torture — in order to compel them to a compliance."

To give time to the consignees to make the proposal for which the selectmen had been waiting, the meeting recessed to 3 p.m.

At that hour the crowd crushed back into the Old South and its vicinity and quickly adopted, without dissent, a motion that the tea should go back in the same ship it came in. Rotch was present, and so was Capt. Hall. Hall's mate had entered in the *Dartmouth* log: "The

captain went on shore, there being a great disturbance about the tea."

Rotch, just for the record, protested to the meeting, for if the tea went back as the meeting desired, the ship would be liable to seizure and Rotch would be faced with ruin. He was formally told, "at his peril," not to enter the ship at customs, and Capt. Hall was told to bring the *Dartmouth* up to a town wharf. He left to set this in motion.

To prevent any move to land the tea in a surprise action, the meeting voted to place a guard of 25 men aboard the *Dartmouth*.

The meeting was outraged when word came that the governor had that afternoon instructed the justices of the peace "to suppress any routs or riots of the people that might happen." The meeting, which had been orderly though indignant, felt the governor's order was a reflection on the gathering. A motion to that effect was passed resoundingly.

Artist Copley had come to the meeting and was talking with John Hancock, member of the board of selectmen. Presently Hancock got to his feet and told the gathering that he was informed that the consignees needed additional time to consult and make their proposal to the town. "Out of great tenderness to these persons," the meeting adjourned until the next day to get the consignees' response.

The *Dartmouth's* mate wrote in the log:

"Had a guard of 25 men come on board this night at 9 p.m."

At that time the *Dartmouth* was still anchored under the guns of the admiral's flagship. The *Dartmouth* would not be under way until the next day and then would move only to Rowe's Wharf, the wharf of the owner of the tea ship *Eleanor,* which was then not far from Boston.

The guard for that night, all volunteers, was under Capt. Edward Proctor. Among its members, mainly cadets, Ancient & Honorable artillerymen and militiamen, all accustomed to bearing arms, were 11 other men besides Capt. Proctor who would take part in the Boston Tea Party. Being aboard would be helpful training for the task ahead.

Copley seeks a compromise

John Singleton Copley was well and favorably known. His relationship by marriage to the Clarkes, who in turn were related to the colony's top officialdom, did not impair popular feeling toward the artist. His interest was strictly art, and he had with equal dedication done canvasses of patriot and Tory.

He had been talking about the plight of his relatives with his neighbor John Hancock before the meeting, and would be talking again with Hancock and Joseph Warren.

Copley, though born in the seaport of Boston, had an aversion to water. The fact that winter had arrived must have increased his uneasy feeling as he set foot in a small boat to be rowed across the harbor to the Castle. But the night was clear.

The consignees, brimming with the courage of the redcoats and weaponry that surrounded them, sent Copley off with a defiant response. The more he thought about it on his return trip the more he felt that his relatives' response would never win the town's acceptance. But his uppermost thoughts must have been on the water passage because he did not make up his mind to try to get the message tempered before he had landed.

Then he became positive and had himself rowed back to the Castle. The letter he now brought back he handed to Scollay as the meeting at Old South resumed the next day, Tuesday, Nov. 30, at 9 a.m. It was read to the meeting. It was the same old suggestion, now too late, that Scollay had had in mind.

The consignees were prepared to have the tea stored subject to inspection and until they received further instructions from London.

To the patriots any landing of the tea could mean it would eventually be taxed and sold. The consignees simply blinded themselves to the fact that this was unalterably opposed by their fellow citizens.

What action to take concerning the obstinate consignees was interrupted by the appearance of affable old Sheriff Stephen Greenleaf. He had received a letter from Gov. Hutchinson requiring him to read a proclamation to the meeting. Would the moderator allow him to go ahead? There was a surge of opposition until Adams gave his assent.

The main point of the proclamation was that the governor exhorted and required everyone assembled "forthwith to disperse and to surcease all further unlawful proceedings at your utmost peril."

"A loud and very general hiss" filled the Old South and its surroundings.

This motion was immediately put:

Would the meeting act as the governor ordered?

"No!"

Copley had seen the unfriendly reception given to the message and had a further proposal. He rose and told the gathering that he would try to prevail on the Clarkes to appear if the meeting would guarantee civility and safety for them. The meeting voted that it would. Copley was voted two hours for his attempt and there was a recess until 2 p.m.

When that hour arrived the meeting turned to other and vital agenda when Copley did not appear. In direct answer to a succession of motions, shipowners Rotch and Rowe, ship agent Timmins and Capt. Hall said that they would comply with the wishes of the meeting to take back the tea. Rotch, though, interposed the understandable objection that he had made on Monday.

The guard on the tea of the *Dartmouth* and other ships en route was put on an automatic basis. From volunteers, who were later instructed to leave their names at the printing office of Edes and Gill, there would be a new group of 25 each day "until the vessels leave the harbor." If alarmed, they could inform the inhabitants by ringing the bells in the daytime or tolling the bells at nighttime.

Six horsemen were to be appointed "to be in readiness to give notice to the country towns when they shall be required to do so. . . ."

An apologetic Copley abruptly appeared. He had exceeded his time and he hoped "they would

National Gallery of Art, Washington, D.C.

John Singleton Copley

consider the difficulty of a passage by water at this season as his apology."

He had carried the assurances of the meeting to the consignees. They felt, however, that only sending the tea back would gratify the meeting, but that this was "out of their power"; but they would do nothing to obstruct the people because "they had not been active in introducing the tea." That last thought was, of course, a direct misrepresentation of Jonathan Clarke's earlier efforts in London.

The meeting reacted as could easily have been predicted. It voted that the consignees' proposal was not in the "least degree satisfactory." Still, Copley felt he had not completely failed. He felt he had cooled resentment and any ill temper toward his relatives, as he scrawled that night in a note to them. "I think all stands well at present." He added that he thought once the *Dartmouth* was gone "you will be able to return with honour to town...."

Events would prove him quite wrong in these judgments.

The door to compromise was now closed.

Adams and the other patriots knew this as they concluded the meeting. There was a string of final resolutions ... a vote of thanks to the neighboring towns ... a vote to send copies of the whole proceedings to New York and Philadelphia ... a vote to send copies of the resolution "to prevent the landing and sale" of the tea to England and to all seaports in the province should a tea ship attempt to unload.

There would be no wavering. This was trumpeted in the resolution:

"It is the determination of this body to carry their votes and resolutions into execution at the risk of their lives and property."

Hutchinson's reaction? Writing to his friend Gov. Tryon, he pictured the meeting as a gathering of "rabble."

But next day in a letter to Lord Dartmouth he conceded that "divers gentlemen of good fortune were among them." Still, he described the gathering as "principally of the lower ranks of the people and even journeymen tradesmen were brought to increase the number, and the rabble were not excluded."

In an appraisal of the meeting he added:

"I can scarcely think they will prosecute these mad resolves; yet it is possible, and if it becomes probable I shall be under necessity of withdrawing to the Castle also, in order to defeat them as far as shall be in my power."

To Hutchinson the demands of the Old South meeting were "monstrous." And to Hutchinson, Adams was probably the man who had produced them. Speaking overall of the events at Old South, Hutchinson judged:

"All seemed to have been the plan of but few, it may be, of a single person." Former Gov. Bernard would testify to the King's Privy Council that those principally responsible were Adams, Molineux, Dr. Young and Dr. Warren — all candidates for hanging.

The fundamental significance of the meeting was completely missed by the aristocratically oriented governor. It demonstrated that organized resistance had now been achieved. The moment the meeting was concluded, Adams, as head of a committee, sent a full report to New

York and Philadelphia. There would be bell ringing and cheering when the news arrived.

The Committee of Correspondence — in effect the popular government of Boston — saw to it that accounts of the meeting were sent to all the seaports and other communities and that another watch, as voted, went on board the *Dartmouth* that night to guard the tea. In command was Capt. Ezekiel Cheever, former Charlestown selectman, now a Boston confectioner and one of the committee that had demanded the resignation of the consignees.

Among the men serving that night with him were six more future members of the Tea Party. In subsequent nights — although we do not have the entire lists — the guard would include John Hancock and George Washington's first secretary of war, Henry Knox. Quite a roll call of patriots was building in the printing office of Edes and Gill.

Early the next day, a cloudy one, the *Dartmouth* was moved by ropes from Rowe's to nearby Griffin's Wharf.

Tension in Boston, a town of less than 20,000 in 1773, was like a volcano about to erupt.

It mounted steadily.

John Andrews, Boston merchant and diarist, epitomized the town's resolution with this Dec. 1 entry:

" 'Twould puzzle any person to purchase a pair of pistols in town as they are all bought up, with a full determination to repel force with force."

Hutchinson remarked:

"Where the present discord will end, I cannot make a probable conjecture: the town is as furious as in the time of the Stamp Act."

What would he give to have Boston off his mind?

"I could be content to part with what estate I have in this town, which is not inconsiderable, if the inhabitants would be content, and it could be effected to be separated from the rest of the province. I think my government would be very easy to me."

But it is the women who expressed the mood of the moment in the most memorable words. John Adams's brilliant wife Abigail, anxious as well about her young son John Quincy Adams, who like his father would be President of the United States, wrote of her feelings to her friend, historian Mercy Warren in Plymouth, sister of the patriot James Otis Jr.

"The tea that bainfull weed is arrived.

"Great and I hope effectual opposition have been made to the landing of it. The proceedings of our citizens have been united, spirited and firm.

"The flame is kindled and like lightning it catches from soul to soul.

"Although the mind is shocked at the thought of shedding human blood, more especially the blood of our countrymen, and a civil war is of all wars the most dreadful, such is the spirit that prevails that, if once they are made desperate, many, very many of our heroes will spend their lives with the speech of Cato in their mouths.

"My heart beats at every whistle I hear, and I dare not express half my fears."

Handbills and notices in the press tell their tale of the tautness of those days. The language is all highlighted, like written screams. Word had got around that customs might pass out a permit for Capt. Hall to unload the tea. The patriots, using the signature "The people," posted in town and in press that anyone attempting to move the tea betrayed "an inhuman thirst for blood.

"This is to assure such publick enemies of this country that they will be considered and treated as wretches unworthy to live, and will be made the first victims of our resentment."

The declaration of the patriots made not a dent on Hutchinson's iron will. Indeed, he even planned orders that would make it impossible for them to send the tea back at all.

Rowe's ship *Eleanor*, Capt. James Bruce, arrived on Dec. 2 and the other Rotch vessel, *Beaver*, Capt. Hezekiah Coffin, arrived on Dec. 7. The *Beaver* had smallpox aboard and was required to tie up at Rainsford Island's quarantine. The tea was to be aired on deck while smoke fumes filled the hold.

Even in quarantine the patriots kept an eye on the tea. Quarantine officials were admonished, "by no means suffer one chest of tea to be landed or taken away by anyone. If any attempt should be made, you are immediately to dispatch messengers...." The *Eleanor* moved, on orders from the Committee of Correspondence, to join the *Dartmouth* at Griffin's Wharf.

Why there? Probably because it was more commodious than Rowe's Wharf. Rotch, after all, was eager to shift whale oil from the *Triton* to the *Dartmouth*. And all the vessels were allowed to unload cargo other than tea. Of course, it was easier for the guard to have the vessels in one place. The patriots must have had a special reason because Hutchinson noted that it was not "customary for ships from London to unlade" at Griffin's Wharf. Or maybe cautious Rowe wanted to avoid trouble.

Retreat for the tea ships was cut off on Dec. 8, when Hutchinson gave notice to Adm. Montagu not to allow any vessel to leave the harbor

Museum of Fine Arts, Boston, Mass.

Mercy Warren

without a pass. The admiral shifted his flagship and escorts *Active* and *Kingfisher* to block the channels. As Hutchinson sized up his own maneuvers he observed that "the patriots (his word) found themselves in a web of inextricable difficulties."

Boston was the only tea port now in this dilemma.

The tea ships for Philadelphia and New York had not even arrived, yet, through the activity of the Sons of Liberty, the tea consignees in both these places had publicly affirmed their resignations.

The last of the consignee holdouts in Philadelphia quit on Dec. 1 and agreed to send the tea back. That same day the New York consignees, who included some of the leading crown officials, resigned too, with the understanding that the tea would be given into the custody of Gov. Tryon until orders could come from England. This arrangement would be speedily altered when New York patriots learned that Boston had rejected such a solution.

Charleston in the Carolinas was so remote in that era that news traveled faster from Charleston to London than it did to Boston.

So Bostonians would not know for many weeks that the ship *London,* Capt. Alexander Curling, a "constant trader" to that port, had arrived on Dec. 2. The patriots there had handbills in circulation for a mass meeting the next day in the great hall over the Exchange on the waterfront, where a resolution was adopted against importing or buying any tea taxed for raising revenue in America.

The consignees evoked loud applause as they confirmed the resignations they had pledged. Christopher Gadsden, inspiring leader of South Carolina's Sons of Liberty, headed the committee to secure signatures carrying out the meeting's resolution and to enforce a boycott on nonsigners. The tea would remain in the hold of the *London* for 20 days, then be stored in the basement of the Exchange.

Contrary to reports that it rotted there, it was sold at auction two years later to help troops of the Continental Army.

Possible liabilities involved in the tea not

being landed in Boston impelled shipowner Rotch and Capt. Hall and later Capt. Bruce to go down the harbor to the Castle with a notary during the second week of December. "Out of our power" was the claim the consignees used when formally asked to receive the tea. They called attention to the guard on board and shrewdly noted that Rotch, Hall and Rowe had agreed to take the tea back in the same bottoms. The consignees declined to pay the freight or damages caused by delay until they could receive the tea.

Notarized protests were then made by Rotch and Bruce against the consignees. Later, they would be joined by the other shipmasters in protesting against those responsible for preventing the tea from being landed and for destroying the tea. Buried in all this legalism is a vivid picture of what it was like to get orders from the Committee of Correspondence in their quarters at old Faneuil Hall.

The words are those of Capt. James Bruce in a deposition he made claiming what happened to him on Dec. 2, the day he brought the *Eleanor* into Boston Harbor.

"The deponent," he testified, "was ordered to attend at 11 o'clock in the forenoon of the next day on a committee of the people of the said town, and he having attended accordingly, was then and there commanded by Mr. Samuel Adams and Jonathan Williams, Esq., in the presence of, and assembled with, John Rowe, John Hancock, William Phillips and John Pitts, Esq., and a great number of others, in Faneuil Hall, not to land any of the said tea at his peril, but to proceed to Griffin's Wharf, in said Boston, and there discharge the rest of his cargo."

"And that the said deponent was obliged to comply with said orders, and is nightly watched by 25 armed men on board the said ship, appointed, as he supposes and verily believes, to prevent the said tea from being landed."

Ironically, the John Rowe that he was facing was the owner of his ship *Eleanor*. Bruce was a Boston loyalist who would later be proscribed and banished.

On Dec. 10 it rained in Boston but there was a gale along Cape Cod that blew the fourth tea ship, Clarkes' brig *William*, on the back of the Cape near Provincetown. The *William* was a complete wreck, though its 300 street lamps for Boston and 58 chests of tea were salvageable.

Boston would not learn about this until five days later. Meanwhile, adventurous Jonathan Clarke, in his hideaway at the Castle, learned about the wreck. He promptly rowed ashore, went by horseback all the way to the tip of the Cape, got some workmen at Provincetown and put the cargo on a Salem fishing schooner he hailed and chartered to take it all to the Castle.

Tidbit of this tale is that of all the tea the East India Co. sent in the tea ships, only some tea from the *William* was ever sold in Massachusetts — though no taxes were paid. It was not a large amount. Jonathan had been helped by John Greenough, a Wellfleet justice of the peace. So Jonathan sold two chests to him on credit. Provincetown patriots burned one of these, which Greenough sold to a retailer there. The other chest, despite seizure by Wellfleet patriots, was recovered and mostly sold by Greenough.

Adams was mighty unhappy when he learned what had happened.

Patriots plan the Tea Party

"The ship must go. The people of Boston and the neighboring towns absolutely require and expect it."

Adams, as chairman of the Committee of Correspondence, was speaking to a troubled young Francis Rotch at Faneuil Hall on Dec. 11. Two days earlier the committee had called in Rotch and asked him why he had not requested customs to give him clearance on the *Dartmouth* as he had pledged he would. He replied that he was convinced he would be refused. Try anyway, he was told.

Rotch had not responded. So he had been called back on Dec. 11 and was asked again. He was advised to make application both for customs clearance and for a naval pass. He now rued his earlier pledge and went to seek legal guidance. The practical advice of John Adams, his lawyer, was not to move the ship without official clearance. It might be blown out of the water by Montagu's guns or be subject to forfeiture in every part of the King's dominions.

A meeting of the Committees of Correspondence of Boston and the surrounding towns was called for 9 a.m. Monday morning, Dec. 13, at Faneuil Hall. Only three more days remained of the 20-day period in which the patriots could act. Time was running out.

Rotch was told to appear before this little senate. Bolstered by his legal advice, Rotch was more positive of his grounds. They were the same. If he complied with his pledge he faced financial ruin. Moreover, he had given the promise originally because he felt under compulsion. He left the hall.

The little senate did not. The session ran all morning, all afternoon and well into the evening. The record, part of the official town records of Boston and beautifully extant, carries after all these lengthy hours of conferring only these few words:

"No business transacted, matter of record."

Why? Because the meeting was secret.

What, under the mounting pressure of crisis, had those men been doing all those hours?

Most details of the planning of the Boston Tea Party will never be known. They can only be surmised. The destruction of the tea would, of course, be a highly illegal act. It could involve capital punishment. It could also involve heavy lawsuits. Multiply more than 100,000 pounds of tea by our current price of tea per pound and you have a comparative estimate of the possible damages.

Secrecy — and secrecy persists in great measure right to the present — would be the patriots' best protection. The victory at Yorktown was a long way off in 1773, and meanwhile the British lion had some sharp teeth.

Tradition says that the planning was done in the gathering places of the Caucus Club, of the Long Club, of the Masons — at Salutation Inn, Green Dragon Tavern and Edes and Gill's printing office. Adams frequently visited all of them. So did the other patriot leaders and the high Sons of Liberty.

The Boston Tea Party, though, was not spontaneous. It took a lot of planning and required perfect timing. Captains and boatswains were designated for each of the ships. Men who took part did not prepare in one place, but simultaneously in a number of places all around the town. They had to know the signal. And those men had to be capable men. They must move more than 50 tons of cargo from three vessels — and move fast. The British warships were about 500 yards away and might try a repeat of the Liberty seizure.

Above all, Adams wanted the participation of the surrounding towns. Here, he had all of their leaders present at this little senate, meeting for hour after hour in urgency, in resolution, in dedication and in all-important secrecy. That laconic official record would seem to mean just the opposite: plenty of business was transacted.

To Adams, an instinctive master of public relations, one more step was vital. It must be shown to the world that there was no other choice left to men with an honorable cause than the action they were about to take.

A public meeting of all the people was called for the next day at the Old South.

The current *Boston Gazette* had just printed an item from Philadelphia that read:

"Our tea consignees have all resigned, and you need not fear: the tea will not be landed here nor at New York. All that we fear is, that you will shrink at Boston. May God give you virtue enough to save the liberties of your country!"

Would Boston fail?

The patriots already knew the answer as they left their Faneuil Hall powwow.

Handbills posted around town the next morning, Tuesday, Dec. 14, showed that others had been busy along with the Committees of Correspondence. There must have been plenty of work done by the Loyal Nine and Edes and Gill.

At the 2 p.m. hour named in the handbills a big throng assembled at the Old South.

Unity of town and country was demonstrated at once when the meeting chose as its moderator a former Boston selectman who had moved to Weston, Samuel Phillips Savage. Savage would be president of the Massachusetts Board of War during the Revolution. His son-in-law, Henry Bass, a Loyal Nine man, would be in the Tea Party.

Capt. Bruce of the *Eleanor* was asked to go to customs and get clearance for his vessel. He promptly agreed, but sized up the weaponry at Hutchinson's disposal by telling the meeting:

"If I'm refused, though, I'm loath to stand the shot of 32-pounders from the Castle."

Rotch was called.

Were the patriots picking on Rotch? Adams knew what Rotch's responses would be. Rotch had given them in Adams's presence more than once. No, the patriots were not abusing Rotch. The fact was that the seizure deadline — now only two days away — applied first to the *Dartmouth*. It had arrived at Boston five days before the *Eleanor*. How Rotch would make out would determine what ultimate action the patriots would have to take.

Above all, the world must see that the people did everything they could to save the tea and send it back — short of paying taxes on it.

Rotch was asked to go to customs and request a clearance. This time a committee of 10

headed by Adams was named to accompany him and witness the result. It was a short walk to King street and the customshouse.

Collector of Customs Richard Harrison received them. Harrison had succeeded his father as collector. As a boy, Harrison had been dragged by his hair, pelted with filth and manhandled by Boston residents when he tried to protect his father at the time that the customs seized the *Liberty*.

Harrison, unlike officials in Philadelphia, New York and Charleston, would go by the book. He would consult his superior, Robert Hallowell, comptroller of customs for North America. Rotch would have to wait until the next day to receive his answer. On hearing this report, the Old South meeting recessed to 10 o'clock Thursday, Dec. 16, only 14 hours before the *Dartmouth's* tea would become liable to seizure.

The persistence of the patriots certainly called for steady nerves.

This day, Dec. 14, the Committee of Correspondence was in session in the morning and in the evening, before and after the Old South meeting. Strategy had to be completed or kept under constant review. No record was made of what was done in those many and long, anxious hours.

Rotch, Adams and the witnessing committee members were on hand when Harrison opened his office the next morning. Hallowell was present, too, as Rotch repeated his request. Harrison gave his verdict:

"Your ship *Dartmouth* entered with me the 30th November last, with dutiable articles on board, for which the duties have not been paid. I cannot therefore give you clearance until she is discharged of those articles, consistent with my duty."

That blocked that possibility.

There was another one, hardly worth trying, but Adams wanted the record to show everything was attempted. He and the committee got Rotch to apply to the naval officer who had a bundle of passes for going by the Castle. That officer's hands were tied unless he was shown a clearance. Rotch, of course, had no clearance.

Now the only peaceful way for the *Dart-*

mouth to get out of the harbor was to get a pass from the governor.

Hutchinson, in intermittent letters, was sending Lord Dartmouth a running account of patriot activities and his comments. Hutchinson would have dearly liked to disenfranchise towns that allowed the "body of the people" to meet illegally in the guise of a town meeting.

"In the last assembly in the largest meetinghouse in town," wrote Hutchinson, referring to the Old South, "a gentleman who spoke in behalf of the consignees called upon the selectmen.

"Mr. Adams, the representative (Samuel Adams), corrected him, and remarked that they knew no selectmen at these meetings. Surely, my lord, it is time this anarchy was restrained and corrected by some authority or other."

From the patriot viewpoint, an illegally called town meeting would not be subject to suits for damages. Hutchinson missed that piece of Yankee shrewdness. He did have a reflection for Dartmouth that showed that he felt everything had started to go wrong back when the British conquered Quebec. Hutchinson's reflection, on the very eve of the Tea Party that he did so much to produce:

"Before the peace I thought nothing so much to be desired as the cession of Canada. I am now convinced, that, if it had remained to the French, none of this spirit of opposition to the mother country would have yet appeared; and I think the effects of it worse than all we had to fear from the French or Indians."

The *Beaver,* released from quarantine on Dec. 15, came directly to Griffin's Wharf on orders of the Committee of Correspondence.

And that was the day that Adams learned about the *William* being wrecked by the gale. He headed the courier who brought the news right back to the Cape with word to the patriots of Sandwich and Plymouth to help grab the tea. It was in vain.

The rain that came on the deadline day, Thursday, Dec. 16, 1773, was no damper to the excitement seething throughout the Bay area.

At least 2000 countrymen, which meant those from surrounding towns and further away, came into Boston by ferry, by boat or across narrow Boston Neck. Most came on foot. Those that came by horse and wagon added immeasurably to the traffic jam around the Old South, where 7000 citizens were expectantly gathered.

This was the greatest throng yet to come to the Old South, and it heavily overflowed the meetinghouse into the main street, the nearby lanes and over toward Province House.

A formal report was made by the committee that had accompanied Rotch to customs, and Rotch was asked to appear before the gathering. He did. As a question to him, this motion was put:

"That this body expect that he immediately protest against the customs house, and procure a pass of the governor, and that he this day proceed with the vessel to London."

Simply impractical, said Rotch, for him to do this.

So he was asked to carry his protest to the governor and try to obtain a pass to get by the guns of the Castle.

The meeting was recessed to 3 p.m., and Rotch, on horseback, started the six-mile journey to Gov. Hutchinson's beloved Unkity on Milton Hill. In the now-vanished halcyon days after the massacre trial, Hutchinson had further embellished the facade of his place with a grand portico. Those peaceful days were now a dim memory.

As Hutchinson later summarized his situation at the crucial moment, it was out of his power to have "prevented mischief" despite the presence of the military.

"The tea," he reasoned, "could have been secured in the town in no other way than by landing marines from the men-of-war, or bringing to town the regiment which was at the Castle, to remove the guards from the ships, and to take their places.

"This would have brought on a greater convulsion than there was any danger of in 1770, and it would not have been possible when two regiments were forced out of town, for so small a body of troops to have kept possession of the town."

Suspense had finally got to Hutchinson, too, and he was a troubled man. What were the patriots going to do?

Hutchinson said that Rotch made apologies about his visit and explained that he had been compelled to come to request a pass. Only if he produced a clearance could he get a pass, said the governor firmly.

The governor asked Rotch if he felt that his ship was in danger and offered him a letter to the admiral "to afford all necessary protection." But Rotch was not apprehensive about the ship. "The rage was against the tea," said Rotch. He knew he could not get hands to move the ship anyway. He declined the governor's offer.

"I asked him," Hutchinson wrote to England, "what he imagined the intentions of the people to be with respect to the tea. He said he had always supposed they had no other intention than forcing it back to England. . . ."

As Rotch left for his return horse ride to Old South, Hutchinson disclosed months later that he had a deeper worry. He had learned indirectly that a "principal leader of the people had declared . . . that if the governor should refuse a pass, he would demand it himself, at the head of 150 men . . . ." So, said Hutchinson, he was "not without apprehensions of a further application."

Meanwhile, at the Old South, the throng had reassembled at 3 p.m. It pronounced the use of tea improper and pernicious and voted, "It is the opinion of this body that every town in this province appoint a committee of inspection to prevent the accursed tea coming into any town in this province." This motion would mean a lot of tea burnings.

The throng listened to speeches by Adams, Warren, Dr. Young and Josiah Quincy Jr. The words they spoke so glowingly have all been lost save for a paragraph or two that young Quincy uttered. They exist because just a year later from England, where he went on a mission for the patriot cause, he said in a letter to his wife that his findings in England confirmed his conviction that his countrymen "must seal this cause with their blood."

He recalled similar words he had said that day in Old South, his countenance even then flushed by the illness which would cause his death when his returning vessel was in sight of his native land. There was true prophecy in the words:

"... we must be blind to that malice, inveteracy, and insatiable revenge, which actuate our enemies, public and private, abroad and in our bosom, to hope that we shall end this controversy without the sharpest, the sharpest conflicts — to flatter ourselves that popular resolves, popular harangues, popular acclamations, and popular vapor will vanquish our foes.

"Let us look to the issue. Let us look to the end. Let us weigh and consider before we advance to those measures which bring on the most trying and terrific struggle this country ever saw."

Then, just before 6 o'clock, out of the dark and the cold, for the wintry rain had ceased, Rotch came back. Huzzahs greeted him as he pressed his way into the now-candlelit meeting-house.

Rotch told the hushed multitude that he had asked for a pass and that the governor had replied that "he was willing to grant anything consistent with the laws and his duty to the King, but that he could not give a pass unless the vessel was properly qualified from the customs house . . . ."

That ended that possibility.

"A mob! A mob!" came an outcry.

Moderator Savage restored order.

Dr. Young spoke. Rotch should suffer no harm to his person or property, said Young. Rotch was a good man and had done all he could to satisfy the people.

There were two further questions for Rotch.

Under present circumstances, would he order the *Dartmouth* back with the tea?

He replied that "he apprehended it would be to his ruin."

Would he attempt to land the tea?

He replied that he had no business with it, but conceded if properly called upon to do it, he would "attempt a compliance for his own security."

Adams thereupon rose and said:

"This meeting can do nothing more to save the country."

It was a signal.

A band of men dressed Indian-style and carrying hatchets gave a war-whoop at the meetinghouse door and continued down Milk street. Their cry was answered in the meetinghouse from the gallery. A tradesman who had stood guard on the *Dartmouth* and would join the Tea Party, Adam Collson, shouted:

"Boston harbor a teapot tonight!"

There came other shouts: "Hurrah for Griffin's Wharf!" "The Mohawks have come!"

Moderator Savage rapped again for order. He had a final, prefabricated motion. The people, it proclaimed, had done everything in their power to preserve the tea without paying duty on it and had been obstructed by the consignees and their "coadjutors" in efforts to send the tea back to England. Three cheers went up as Savage adjourned the meeting.

Hundreds of spectators took off down Milk street after the Indian band.

"Adams," observed Hutchinson, "never was in greater glory."

A few paces up School street from the Old South was the dwelling of short, trim John Andrews, the merchant, who was sipping tea as Adams gave the signal. Andrews heard the whooping and shouting and rushed to the scene.

"The house was so crowded that I could get no further than the porch, when I found the moderator was just declaring the meeting to be dissolved, which caused another general shout outdoors and in, and three cheers.

"What with that and the consequent noise of breaking up the meeting you'd thought the inhabitants of the infernal regions had broke loose."

Accounts say 1000 of the Old South audience rushed down Milk street. Shipowner John Rowe said this figure was 2000, but Rowe was not present. Still, Peter Edes was there and he estimated 2000. Certainly a large number did go because the moon was up and brightly shining — and what was that whooping band of Mohawks up to?

And which way did they go? Some of the Indians were already on the tea ships as the audience broke from the Old South. They had gone down Milk street and turned right at Hutchinson street. Hutchinson was a fairly new street that ran past Gray's and other ropewalks and

was named, ironically on this occasion, after the governor. It led to Griffin's Wharf.

Were they real Indians?

Andrews wrote humorously to his brother-in-law:

"They say the actors were Indians from Narragansett."

John Adams knew they were not Indians.

"Depend upon it," he said, "they were no ordinary Mohawks."

Mackintosh, "first captain general of Liberty Tree," would say many years later, "It was my chickens that did the job."

There were some members of the Tea Party among the spectators, especially in the Old South gallery, and there were some audience participation and spur-of-the moment volunteers. No one will ever be able to identify definitely those who were just spectators, and there is uncertainty, too, about some usually included as participants.

The audience at Old South provided only a few who took part in the work to be done at Griffin's Wharf. The Old South affair was essentially an Adams performance in public relations to dramatize the fact that the patriots had come to the end of all possibilities but destroying the tea.

The actual Tea Party participants for the most part made their preparations elsewhere in Boston while the Old South meeting was in progress.

How many were there?

No one can be sure. The most likely estimate, made in the last century by Francis S. Drake, was between 110 and 130. Evidence from those who took part would indicate this range. It was adequate and practical for heavy, longshoreman's work in a restricted space. And the participants were heavily on the young side, most of them in their 20s, a dozen or so teenage, only a half dozen more than 40.

There were some individual, do-it-yourself preparations.

Two teenage apprentices, Henry Purkitt and Edward Dolbear, were at work in the cooper shop of Samuel Peck on Milk street where it reached the waterfront when they were surprised to hear whistling, probably from nearby Fort Hill. They followed it and got in the Tea Party. Peck, their master, was already in it.

Peter Slater, just turned 14, was a ropemaker's apprentice whose master, fearing trouble over the tea that deadline night, locked Peter in his chamber. Peter, hot for excitement, escaped through a window, went to a blacksmith's shop where a man already disguised told him to tie a handkerchief around his frock and put charcoal on his face and said, "Follow me!"

Twenty-year-old Amos Lincoln's master was worried, too, but had a different solution. The master obtained an Indian disguise, brought it to his North End shop, had Amos get in it, darkened Amos's face — and dropped to his knees and prayed the apprentice would be safe. Amos would serve at Bunker Hill.

Organization can be seen in Paul Revere's neighbor, John May, 25, dashing into his dwelling on North Square in the afternoon and saying to his wife, "Nabby, let me have a beefsteak as quickly as possible." As he was eating there was a rap on the window pane and he hurried out.

Or in the words of a schoolboy at the time, Benjamin Russell. He would recall "seeing through the window of the woodhouse, his father and Thomas Moore, his neighbor, besmearing each other's faces with lamp black and red ochre." Moore, now a 20-year-old wharfinger, was one of those arrested along with "Captain" Mackintosh at the time of the Stamp Act rioting.

There were much more extensive preparations. These were made in at least three places in each of the three main sections of the town. In each of them, groups anywhere from a handful to a score and more were busy improvising their Indian disguises and making ready their tools.

Elisha Story's father was a crown official, register of the court of admiralty. At the time of the Stamp Act riots, his office in King street had been invaded in the mistaken belief that stamps were stored there, and the office contents had been burned in the street. But Elisha was a patriot, a volunteer guard on the *Dartmouth*, and he told how he and other Sons of Liberty disguised themselves in an old distillery.

This, presumably, was the Chase & Speakman distillery near Liberty Tree. Chase, an owner, was a member of the Tea Party.

There were other places in the South End.

Joshua Wyeth, 16, recalled that "at the appointed time" a group of nearly 30 "met in an old building at the head of the wharf" — Griffin's Wharf. A relative of "Captain" Mackintosh, Peter Mackintosh, worked in a blacksmith shop there, and remembered seeing Thomas Spear, among others, come in to blacken their faces.

Most active spot in the South End was at the corner of present Tremont and Hollis streets. On the south corner of Hollis street was the dwelling of Nathaniel Bradlee, housewright and cistern builder. His four sons prepared there in the big front room. Their older sister Sarah got ready for the emergency a day or two earlier and helped them and her husband, John Fulton, with their disguises, then took herself off to the Tea Party.

On the north corner of Hollis street was the home of another Tea Party member, John Crane, who would be the only man injured at the Tea Party. Fifteen-year-old Joseph Lovering, who lived opposite the Bradlees and Crane on the west side of Tremont street, said he came to Crane's house and held the light while 15 Sons of Liberty put on their disguises.

In the North End some of the Sons of Liberty met at the Salutation Inn near the waterfront.

James Swan, 19, who would be wounded at Bunker Hill at the side of Joseph Warren as Warren was mortally wounded, was a clerk in a countinghouse near Faneuil Hall. Swan said that he and other young apprentices disguised themselves at the house on Hanover street where he boarded.

The venerable Green Dragon Tavern on Union street had been called the cradle of the revolution. It was a favorite meeting place of the North End Caucus mechanics and waterfront workers. Here, Joseph Warren and Paul Revere held the grand meetings of the Masons and here the Sons of Liberty and their leaders frequently met and consulted. The minutes of the Masonic meeting there that night convey eloquently by their brevity what the members were doing:

"The lodge met and closed on account of the few members in attendance. Adjourned until tomorrow evening."

Fort Hill, used long ago for harbor fill, was most accessible from the center of town. One party disguised themselves in a store on Fort Hill, said George Robert Twelves Hewes, 29-year-old shoemaker. Andrews was not on Fort Hill but he said he was told as many as 200 mustered there.

Diagonally across Milk street from the Old South was the home of Joseph Shed, 41. Adams often visited there and Shed long preserved a china punch bowl from which Adams, an abstemious man, drank. Shed and a number of other patriots donned their disguises in this house.

Best known of the gathering places in the center of town was the printing office of Edes and Gill on Queen street. In back of this was the dwelling of Benjamin Edes.

The Indians who whooped at the porch of the Old South came from this printing office, where they assembled after gathering and sharing a bit of punch in Edes's house. Edes's son Peter, who would be 17 years old the next day, told how he was not admitted to the presence of the men "for fear, I suppose, of their being known."

This is the story that Peter Edes gave his grandson:

"I recollect perfectly well that in the afternoon preceding the evening of the destruction of the tea, a number of gentlemen met in the parlor of my father's house, how many I cannot say. As I said before, I was not admitted into their presence; my station was in another room to make punch for them in the bowl which is now in your possession, and which I filled several times.

"They remained in the house 'til dark, I suppose to disguise themselves like Indians, when they left the house and proceeded to the wharves where the vessels lay. Before they reached there, they were joined by hundreds.

"After they left the room I went into it; but my father was not there. I therefore thought I would take a walk to the wharves, as a spectator, where was collected, I may say, as many as 2000 persons.

"The Indians worked smartly. Some were in the hold immediately after the hatches were broken open, fixing the ropes to the tea chests; others were hauling up the chests; and others stood ready with their hatchets to cut off the bindings of the chests and cast them overboard.

"I remained on the wharf 'til I was tired, and fearing some disturbance might occur went home, leaving the Indians working like good industrious fellows.

"This is all I know about it."

'So large a cup of tea for the fishes'

It is astonishing to find, with so many present, that only a baker's dozen of eyewitness accounts exists of the Boston Tea Party.

Six of these, including Peter Edes's, are the accounts of spectators. Among them is the brief account that the *Dartmouth's* mate, Alexander Hodgdon, put in the ship's log, and the equally brief statement Capt. Bruce of the *Eleanor* gave in his affidavit.

Strange indeed is the fact that we have nothing but silence from all the other members of the crews, who must have witnessed at least some part of the events. Were they silenced by the fear that they might be branded informers — or by the dread of tar and feathers?

Only seven participants have left eyewitness accounts of any extent. Their contradictions would puzzle a Sherlock Holmes. Their accounts conflict on the numbers involved, the numbers of witnesses, on disguises used or not used, on weapons or no weapons, even on how long they took.

Despite frequent repetitions, these accounts still make fascinating reading. They establish beyond any doubt that the party was large and hence reportable from different views. Clearly many responded spontaneously. But above all, the accounts establish that there was extensive pre-planning and that the plan was operative hours before Adams gave the signal in the Old South.

The *Dartmouth's* mate, Hodgdon, a Whig who would become the first state treasurer in Massachusetts, was among the first to see the arrival of the boarding parties on Griffin's Wharf.

Romance also came on deck. In the boarding party on the *Dartmouth* was a future general, Ebenezer Stevens, who was courting Hodgdon's sister. Stevens quickly departed to avoid compromising Hodgdon, and went to work on the tea chests of the *Eleanor.* Hodgdon wrote this in the log:

"Thursday, Dec. 16. This 24 hours rainy weather; town meeting this day.

"Between six and seven o'clock this evening came down to the wharf a body of about one thousand people. Among them were a number dressed and whooping like Indians.

"They came on board the ship, and after warning myself and the Customs House officer to get out of the way, they unlaid the hatches and went down the hold, where was 80 whole and 34 half chests of tea, which they hoisted upon deck, and cut the chests to pieces, and hove the tea off overboard, where it was damaged and lost."

Joshua Wyeth, journeyman blacksmith despite being only 16, told this graphic tale:

"Our numbers were between 28 and 30. Of my associates I only remember the names of Frothingham, Mead, Martin and Grant. Many of them were apprentices and journeymen, not a few, as was the case with myself, living with Tory masters.

"I had but a few hours warning of what was intended to be done.

"We first talked of firing the ships, but feared the fire would communicate to the town. We then proposed sinking them, but dropped that project through fear that we should alarm the town before we could get through with it. We had observed that very few persons remained on board the ships, and we finally concluded that we could take possession of them, and discharge the tea into the harbor without danger or opposition.

"One of the ships laid at the wharf, the others a little way out in the stream, with their warps made fast to the wharf.

"To prevent discovery, we agreed to wear ragged clothes and disfigure ourselves, dressing to resemble Indians as much as possible, smearing our faces with grease and lamp black or soot, and should not have known each other except by our voices. Our most intimate friends among the spectators had not the least knowledge of us. We surely resembled devils from the bottomless pit rather than men.

"At the appointed time we met in an old building at the head of the wharf, and fell in one after another, as if by accident, so as not to excite suspicion. We placed a sentry at the head of the wharf, another in the middle, and one on the bow of each ship as we took possession.

"We boarded the ship, moored by the wharf, and our leader, in a very stern and resolute manner, ordered the captain and crew to open the hatchways, and hand us the hoisting tackle and ropes, assuring them that no harm was intended them. The captain asked what we intended to do.

"Our leader told him that we were going to unload the tea, and ordered him and the crew below. They instantly obeyed.

"Some of our number then jumped into the hold, and passed the chests to the tackle. As they were hauled on deck others knocked them open with axes, and others raised them to the railing and discharged their contents overboard. All who were not needed for discharging this ship went on board the others, warped them to the wharf, when the same ceremonies were repeated.

"We were merry, in an undertone, at the idea of making so large a cup of tea for the fishes, but were as still as the nature of the case would admit, using no more words than were absolutely necessary. We stirred briskly in the business from the moment we left our dressing room. I never worked harder in my life.

"While we were unloading, the people collected in great numbers about the wharf to see what was going on. They crowded around us so as to be much in our way. Our sentries were not armed, and could not stop any who insisted on passing. They were particularly charged to give us notice in case any known Tory came down to the wharf.

"There was much talk about this business the next morning. We pretended to be as zealous to find out the perpetrators as the rest, and were all so close and loyal, the whole affair remained in Egyptian darkness."

We have romance again in the account of

A Currier & Ives depiction of the Boston Tea Party

American Antiquarian Society

athletic, tall Samuel Sprague, 20-year-old mason:

"That evening, while on my way to visit the young woman I afterwards married, I met some lads hurrying along towards Griffin's Wharf, who told me there was something going on there. I joined them, and on reaching the wharf found the Indians busy with the tea chests.

"Wishing to have my share of the fun, I looked about for the means of disguising myself. Spying a low building, with a stovepipe by way of chimney, I climbed the roof and obtained a quantity of soot, with which I blackened my face.

"Joining the party, I recognized among them Mr. Etheridge, my master. We worked together, but neither of us ever afterwards alluded to each other's share in the proceedings."

In the instance of Thompson Maxwell, a young teamster, there is direct information on how he got his orders. John Hancock gave them.

"I had loaded at John Hancock's warehouse and was about to leave town when Mr. Hancock requested me ... to be on Long Wharf at 2 o'clock p.m. and informed me what was to be done. I went accordingly and joined the band under one Capt. Hewes. We mounted the ships and made tea in a trice. This done, I took my team and went home, as an honest man should."

The Tea Party's reaction to a horse-renter named Connor comes into the recollections of three eyewitnesses. Robert Sessions, in later life a public official in western Massachusetts, recounted:

"I was living in Boston at the time, in the family of a Mr. Davis, a lumber merchant, as a common laborer. On that eventful evening, when Mr. Davis came in from the town meeting, I asked him what was to be done with the tea.

" 'They are now throwing it overboard,' he replied.

"Receiving permission, I went immediately to the spot. Everything was as light as day, by the means of lamps and torches; a pin might be seen lying on the wharf.

"I went on board where they were at work, and took hold with my own hands. I was not one of those appointed to destroy the tea, and who disguised themselves as Indians, but was a vol-

unteer; the disguised men being largely men of family and position in Boston, while I was a young man, whose home and relations were in Connecticut. The appointed and disguised party proving too small for the quick work necessary, other young men, similarly circumstanced with myself, joined them in their labors.

"The chests were drawn up by a tackle, one man bringing them forward, another putting a rope around them, and others hoisting them to the deck and carrying them to the vessel's side. The chests were then opened, the tea emptied over the side, and the chests thrown overboard. Perfect regularity prevailed during the whole transaction.

"Although there were many people on the wharf, entire silence prevailed, no clamor, no talking.

"Nothing was meddled with but the teas on board. After having emptied the whole, the deck was swept clean, and everything put in its proper place. An officer on board was requested to come up from the cabin and see that no damage was done except to the tea.

"At about the close of the scene, a man (Connor) was discovered making his way through the crowd with his pockets filled with tea. He was immediately laid hold of, and his coat skirts torn off, with their pockets, and thrown into the dock with the rest of the tea.

"I was obliged to leave the town at once, as it was of course known that I was concerned in the affair."

Curiosity again took John Andrews away from his tea, when he got wind of what was going on. He wrote:

"They mustered, I'm told, upon Fort Hill, to the number of about 200, and proceeded, two by two, to Griffin's Wharf, where Hall, Bruce and Coffin lay .... The latter arrived at the wharf only the day before, and was freighted with a large quantity of other goods, which they took the greatest care not to injure in the least, and before 9 o'clock in the evening every chest on board the three vessels was knocked to pieces and flung over the sides.

"They say the actors were Indians from Narragansett; whether they were or not, to a transient observer they appeared as such, being clothed in blankets, with their heads muffled, and copper-colored countenances, being each armed with a hatchet or axe, or pair of pistols, nor was their dialect different from what I conceive these geniuses to speak as their jargon was unintelligible to all but themselves.

"Not the least insult was offered to any person save one Capt. Connor, a letter of horses in this place, not many years since removed from dear Ireland, who had ripped up the lining of his coat and waistcoat under the arms, and watching his opportunity, had nearly filled them with tea, but being detected, was handled pretty roughly. They not only stripped him of his clothes, but gave him a coat of mud, with a severe bruising into the bargain, and nothing but their utter aversion to making any disturbance prevented his being tarred and feathered."

George Robert Twelves Hewes in 1835, when less than a dozen of the Tea Party was still living, was interviewed for "Thatcher's Traits of the Tea Party." As the meeting at the Old South ended, there was a "general huzza for Griffin's Wharf," said Hewes. He continued:

"It was now evening, and I immediately dressed myself in the costume of an Indian, equipped with a small hatchet, which I and my associates denominated the tomahawk, with which, and a club, after having painted my face and hands with coal dust in the shop of a blacksmith, I repaired to Griffin's Wharf, where the ships lay that contained the tea.

"When I first appeared in the street, after being thus disguised, I fell in with many who were dressed, equipped and painted as I was, and who fell in with me, and marched in order to the place of our destination.

"When we arrived at the wharf, there were three of our number who assumed an authority to direct our operations, to which we readily submitted. They divided us into three parties, for the purpose of boarding the three ships which contained the tea, at the same time.

"The name of him who commanded the division to which I was assigned, was Len Pitts. The names of the other commanders I never knew. We were immediately ordered by the respective commanders to board all the ships at the same time, which we promptly obeyed.

"The commander of the division to which I belonged, as soon as we were on board the ship, appointed me boatswain, and ordered me to go to the captain and demand of him the keys to the hatches and a dozen candles. I made the demand accordingly, and the captain promptly replied, and delivered the articles; but requested me at the same time to do no damage to the ship or rigging.

"We then were ordered by our commanders to open the hatches, and take out all the chests of tea and throw them overboard, and we immediately proceeded to execute his orders; first cutting and splitting the chests with our tomahawks, so as thoroughly to expose them to the effects of the water.

"In about three hours from the time we went on board, we had thus broken and thrown overboard every tea chest to be found on the ship; while those in the other ships were disposing of the tea in the same way, at the same time.

"We were surrounded by British armed ships, but no attempt was made to resist us.

"We then quietly retired to our several places of residence, without having any conversation with each other, or taking any measures to discover who were our associates; nor do I recollect of having had the knowledge of the name of a single individual concerned in the affair, except that of Lendall Pitts, the commander of my division, who I have mentioned.

"There appeared to be an understanding that each individual should volunteer his services, keep his own secret, and risk the consequences for himself.

"No disorder took place during that transaction, and it was observed at that time, that the stillest night ensued that Boston had enjoyed for many months.

"During the time we were throwing the tea overboard, there were several attempts made by some of the citizens of Boston and its vicinity, to carry off small quantities of it for their family use. To effect that object, they would watch their opportunity to snatch up a handful from the deck, where it became plentifully scattered, and put it into their pockets.

"One Capt. Conner, whom I knew well, came on board for that purpose, and when he supposed he was not noticed, filled his pockets, and also the lining of his coat. But I had detected him and gave information to the captain of what he was doing. We were ordered to take him into custody, and just as he was stepping from the vessel, I seized him by the skirt of his coat, and in attempting to pull him back, I tore it off; but springing forward, by a rapid effort, he made his escape.

"He had however to run a gauntlet through the crowd upon the wharf; each one, as he passed, giving him a kick or a stroke.

"The next day we nailed the skirt of his coat, which I had pulled off, to the whipping post in Charlestown, the place of his residence, with a label upon it, commemorative of the occasion which had thus subjected the proprietor to the popular indignation.

"Another attempt was made to save a little tea from the ruins of the cargo, by a tall, aged man, who wore a large cocked hat and white wig, which was fashionable at the time. He had slightly slipped a little into his pocket, but being detected, they seized him, and taking his hat and wig from his head, threw them together with the tea, of which they had emptied his pockets, into the water. In consideration of his advanced age, he was permitted to escape, with now and then a slight kick.

"The next morning, after we had cleared the ships of the tea, it was discovered that very considerable quantities of it was floating upon the surface of the water; and to prevent the possibility of any of it being saved for use, a number of small boats were manned by sailors and citizens, who rowed them into those parts of the harbor wherever the tea was visible, and by beating it with oars and paddles, so thoroughly drenched it, as to render its entire destruction inevitable."

William Tudor, once a young law clerk in the office of John Adams, put together a biography of James Otis from the pathetically few fragments of the papers and speeches that exist of that great patriot. Tudor did include a considerable amount of his own memoirs of the period. From acquaintanceship with some of the participants Tudor wrote:

"A band of 18 or 20 young men (no one of whom was in any disguise), who had been pre-

pared for the event, went by the Meeting House giving a shout. It was echoed by some within; others exclaimed, 'The Mohawks are come!'; the assembly broke up and part of it followed the body of young men to Griffin's Wharf. Three different parties, composed of trustworthy persons, many of whom were in after life among the most respectable citizens of the town, had been prepared, in conformity to the secret resolves of the political leaders, to act as circumstances should require.

"They were 70 or 80 in all, and when every attempt to have the tea returned had failed, it was immediately made known to them, and they proceeded at once to throw the obnoxious merchandise into the water.

"One, if not two of these parties, wore a kind of Indian disguise. Two of these persons, in passing over Fort Hill to the scene of operations, met a British officer who, on observing them, naturally enough drew his sword. As they approached, one of the Indians drew a pistol, and said to the officer:

"'The path is wide enough for us all; we have nothing to do with you, and intend you no harm; if you keep your own way peaceable, we shall keep ours.'"

Ebenezer Stevens, who would serve at both Saratoga and Yorktown, left this account, giving the incident about the mate whose sister Stevens later married:

"I went from the Old South Meeting House just after dark. The party was about 70 or 80. At the head of the wharf we met the detachment of our company (Paddock's Artillery) on guard, who joined us.

"I commenced with a party on board the vessel of which Hodgdon was mate, and as he knew me, I left that vessel with some of my comrades and went aboard another vessel, which lay at the opposite side of the wharf. Numbers of others took our places on board Hodgdon's vessel.

"We commenced handing the boxes of tea on deck, and first began breaking them with axes, but found much difficulty, owing to the boxes being covered with canvas, the mode that the article was then imported in.

"I think that all the tea was destroyed in

about two hours. We were careful to prevent any being taken away. None of the party were painted as Indians, nor, that I know of, disguised, excepting some of them stopped at a paint shop on the way, and daubed their faces with paint."

Benjamin Simpson, then a bricklayer's apprentice and later a Continental soldier, recalled:

"After the meeting in the Old South was over, there was a cry in the gallery of 'every man to his tent.'

"We repaired to the wharf. I went on board both ships, but saw no person belonging to them. In a few minutes a number of men came on the wharf, went on board the ships, then laying at the side of the wharf, the water in the dock not more than two feet deep.

"They began to throw the tea into the water, which went off with the tide 'till the tea grounded.

"We soon found there was tea on board the brig also. A demand being made of it, the captain told us the whole of his cargo was on board; that the tea was directly under the hatches, which he would open if we would not damage anything but the tea, which we agreed to.

"The hatches were then opened, a man sent down to show us the tea, which we hoisted out, stove the chests and threw the tea and all overboard. Those on board the ships did the same.

"I was on board the ships when the tea was so high by the side of them as to fall in, which was shovelled down more than once. We on board the brig were not disguised. I was then 19 years old; I am now 75."

Dr. Hugh Williamson of Philadelphia, in later years a North Carolina congressman and in 1787 one of the framers of the U.S. Constitution, was awaiting a vessel to take him to London. He was in Boston long enough to attend the great meeting at Old South at the end of November and to see some of the Tea Party. In England he was among those summoned as witnesses before the crown authorities seeking to punish the patriot leaders.

A clerk recorded Williamson's testimony before the Privy Council:

"He believes a watch was kept over the tea ships every night from their arrival, until that night on which the tea was destroyed. There was another meeting of the body of the people of Boston, and the neighboring towns, on Tuesday or Wednesday, the 14th or 15th of December, as he was informed.

"He heard the bells ringing, and saw people going to the meeting. By the report he then received, from sundry people who attended, he believes that the proceedings, which was published in the newspaper of Edes and Gill, was just. He believes there was also an adjourned meeting of the body on the 16th or 17th of December.

"In the evening of that day, about an hour after dark, he was informed that a number of people were employed in destroying the tea. He immediately went, that he might obtain full satisfaction as to this fact, and from a small eminence about 50 yards from the nearest ship, he could observe that there were people on board, who, he apprehends, were disguised. He could hear them cut open the tea chests, when they had brought them upon deck. The rioters made very little noise. On the next day the ships were said to be quite clear."

Williamson, quite evidently, was not trying to be too specific about anything that would assist the Privy Council.

Among the legal papers filed to claim damages, Capt. James Bruce of the *Eleanor* made an affidavit "against the destroyers of the tea." Bruce was joined by Capts. James Hall and Hezekiah Coffin and the mates of all three tea ships along with Francis Rotch as part owner. They testified that they were present on Dec. 16 on the ships with the tea, and went on:

"That about the hours of 6 and 7 o'clock in the same evening, about 1000 unknown people came down to said wharf, and a number of them came on board the said ship, some being dressed like Indians and they having violently broke open the hatches, hoisted up the said chests of tea upon deck, and then and there stove and threw the said chests with contents overboard into the water, where the whole was lost and destroyed."

'The tea we'll have'

Joshua Wyeth's comment, "I never worked harder in my life," was not the only one on how tiring were those three hours.

Benjamin Burton, 24, one of several men from Maine, then a part of Massachusetts, said that he had to labor with all his might. Samuel Hobbs, a 23-year-old tanner and currier from Roxbury, recalled the weight of the Bohea in a full chest as 360 pounds and emphasized they were rather heavy to lift.

The moon set a few minutes after 8 p.m. but there were lights on the ships and many of the spectators carried lanterns.

The first vessels cleared were the *Dartmouth* and *Eleanor,* which were alongside the wharf. There was only tea cargo aboard these, for they had been landing other cargo since arriving. The *Beaver* had been out of quarantine but a short time and had other cargo stowed with the tea.

As the *Beaver* was hauled closer by ropes and the patriots went aboard, the skipper, Capt. Hezekiah Coffin of Nantucket, asked for more time to shift his cargo. The patriots didn't have it. Midnight was their deadline. He was told:

"The tea we want and the tea we'll have.

"If you'll go to your cabin quietly, not one article of your goods will be hurt."

John Crane the carpenter, who was so sharp an artilleryman he was known for his perfect shots on target, was not sharp enough to duck part of a broken derrick that fell his way. He was knocked so hard that he looked lifeless. His friends carried him to a carpenter shop on the wharf and buried him under a mound of shavings. He was later found sitting up, dazed, and was taken back to Hollis street, where he soon recovered.

A young apprentice oarmaker, John Hooton, spotted a man in a small boat approaching to gather a bit of tea for himself. Hooton told how he and four other North Enders were ordered to get rid of the man, so they knocked the canoe from under him "in the twinkling of an eye."

Many of the apprentices were assigned to scattering the tea that had piled beside the ships because the tide was low and the ships sat in very little water. Purkitt and Dolbear also thoroughly smashed fragmented chests. They had found it easy to leap to and from the ship from the piles of dumped tea. After midnight, when the tide came in, it shoved the tea and debris along the shores, and later brought it out again in windrows across the harbor from the South End to Dorchester Neck.

By 9 p.m. the deed was done. Tea from 342 chests was in the salt water.

The crowds stayed to the end. Seth Ingersoll Brown, 23-year-old carpenter from Charlestown who would be wounded at Bunker Hill, told his daughters many years later of the difficulty he had getting away. He was masked, painted and had carried a club. He said that he had to fight his way through the excited crowd while avoiding discovery.

Why did he carry a club?

Those armed must have felt that they might have to use force on the ships or counteract some outside force, possibly from the military. Actually there was no chance, though none of the patriots knew this then, that the military would act. They had received no orders to do so.

Moreover, the commander down at the Castle had been importuned in messages from councilors not to send any redcoats. This might cause more bloodshed than the massacre of still-vivid memory.

Lendall Pitts, 26, an officer in Hancock's cadets, had his men line up two by two. Pitts was a son of a wealthy merchant who was a staunch supporter of Bowdoin in the Council, had a brother on the Committee of Correspondence and an older brother, Samuel, who was also in the Tea Party.

Pitts had the help of Nathaniel Barber and Capt. Edward Proctor, both members of the Committee of Correspondence and leading patriots. Proctor was commander of the first night's guard on the *Dartmouth.* Pitts had his men take off their shoes and throw any tea in them into the sea. He then had them fall back into line and headed for town with a fifer giving the cadence.

Adm. Montagu, from the house of a Tory on

Atkinson (now Congress) street, had watched the whole affair. The admiral, brother of the mighty Earl of Sandwich, commanded not only the three warships in the harbor but all the King's navy in North America.

"Well, boys, you have had a fine, pleasant evening for your Indian caper, haven't you? But mind, you have got to pay the fiddler, yet!"

Pitts shouted back to him:

"Oh, never mind! Never mind, squire! Just come out here, if you please, and we'll settle the bill in two minutes."

The admiral slammed the window. The fifer struck up again, and the men marched off, separating very shortly to their homes.

When young Joseph Lovering got home he was scolded for being out late. Sarah Fulton had hot water ready to help the men clean up. She told in later years how the four brothers and her husband were still changing their clothes when a British spy came by. They leapt into bed with the "toggery" and pretended they were sleeping. The spy seemed satisfied and left.

Joseph Pearse Palmer, hardware merchant near the town dock, gave his wife quite a fright on his return. She told the story when she was widowed:

"About 10 o'clock, hearing the gate and door open, I opened the parlor door, and there stood three stout-looking Indians. I screamed, and should have fainted, but recognized my husband's voice saying:

" 'Don't be frighted, Betty, it is I. We have been making a little salt water tea.' " He was accompanied by a King street merchant, Stephen Bruce, and a bookseller, James Foster Condy.

That night John Adams looked out from his three-story house-office on Queen street, near the old State House. He reported:

"The town of Boston was never more still and calm of a Saturday night than it was last night."

Besides the tea, only a padlock was damaged. It was quietly, anonymously replaced aboard ship the next day.

One man, Eckley the barber, was arrested a week later, imprisoned, then let go for lack of evidence.

His informer was tarred and feathered and carted through the streets. Other spies and informers turned up little evidence for Hutchinson.

The morning after the party, at breakfast, apprentices Purkitt and Dolbear noticed red paint behind the ears of their master, Peck, but made no comment.

The need for secrecy and non-recognition was ingrained in all the participants. Sprague recognized his master Etheridge as he was dumping tea into the sea and said nothing. Stevens moved fast when he realized that mate Hodgdon would recognize him. David Kinnison, another man from Maine and last survivor of the Tea Party, died in Chicago at the age of 115 still stressing how all were pledged not to reveal names of the party.

The time came in London when the solicitor general of the crown was considering that he might bring charges of treason and drew up a list of those he would have brought to England. It included Samuel Adams, Joseph Warren, William Molineux, Jonathan Williams the moderator (a cousin of Benjamin Franklin), Dr. Thomas Young and Dr. Benjamin Church Jr. The list idea was dropped for lack of evidence.

Where was Adams during the Tea Party?

He was a completely fearless man. He would hardly have gone to his home — which was very near the scene — and merely hung up his hat when the crowd left the Old South. He had to be ready for any emergency, and since he had prepared against so many contingencies, it would have been characteristic for him to be available.

This could have been at one of the club gathering places, or at old Faneuil Hall, where he functioned as chairman of Boston's Committee of Correspondence. It would have been natural to have Warren with him. After all, Molineux, who had often acted as a sort of liaison in the doings of the Sons of Liberty, and Dr. Young, were at the Tea Party and could get word to Adams.

But all went smoothly.

Yet, even that meant something for Adams to do.

The Committee of Correspondence prepared

an account of the Tea Party the next day and sent Paul Revere, who had not gone to bed until dawn after taking part in the Tea Party, riding off to bring the news to the patriots in New York and Philadelphia.

The letter Revere carried was dated Boston, Dec. 17, 1773, was unpunctuated and the "T's" were not crossed, so great was the speed of its composition:

"Gentlemen — We inform you in great haste that every chest of tea on board the three ships in this town was destroyed the last evening without the least injury to the vessels or any other property. Our enemies must acknowledge that these people have acted upon pure and upright principle."

It was Revere's first, famous ride, and he would bring back the news from New York that Charleston had spurned its tea. The colonies were learning to act together.

Tea that came from the Tea Party in small quantities may still be seen 200 years later.

It came from the shore or from the bits in the shoes and clothing of the patriots. On its accidental arrival in some of the houses of Boston that night it did not get a uniform reception.

Housewright Josiah Wheeler came home late to his house on Orange (now Washington) street in the South End, pulled off his long boots, and there was the telltale tea. A neighbor, who had been sitting up with Mrs. Wheeler, suggested:

"Save it; it will make a nice mess."

"Don't touch the cursed stuff," exclaimed Mrs. Wheeler, seizing her broom and sweeping it into the fire.

Schoolteacher William Russell found tea in his shoes when he got back to his North End dwelling and promptly shook it all into the fire.

Thomas Melvill, merchant, Princeton graduate and grandfather of the author Herman Melville, had some in his shoes when he got home. So did John May. And a future clergyman, then a child, picked some up on the shore at Dorchester Neck. These tea leaves can be seen today at the Bostonian Society in the old State House, at the Old South and at the American Antiquarian Society in Worcester. The patriots did not want any quantities to get away.

Even two weeks after the party, when they heard there was a quantity in Dorchester, "a number of Cape or Narragansett Indians" went and searched a house there. Not satisfied, they searched, as a Boston newspaper related it: ". . . at a place called Sodom, below Dorchester Meeting House, where they found a half chest, which had floated and was cast upon Dorchester Point.

"This they seized and brought to Boston Common, where they committed it to the flames."

The Boston Tea Party gave a powerful lift to the patriots in the other tea ports.

True, all the consignees in the other colonies had announced their resignations, rejecting the tea. But the tea was still en route, tempers could soften and waver and the patriots just could not be sure of success until the East India tea had arrived. Meanwhile, they kept public indignation bubbling with handbills, meetings and a drumfire of items in the press.

In New York Gov. Tryon had at first won patriot approval when his Council voted that the rejected tea would "be taken into the care of government" and stored in the fort or barracks at the foot of Broadway. But this disposition was no longer satisfactory to the New York patriots when they learned that Boston had resolved to send its tea back in the same ships.

So Tryon shifted his position. He assured the New Yorkers that he would not "use military force for the landing" of the tea. This still was not enough for the patriots. On Dec. 17, with future Gen. John Lamb presiding, 2000 New Yorkers assembled at the City Hall, then in Wall Street, and Lamb read letters from Boston and Philadelphia that both would send their tea back.

Was it satisfactory that the governor store the New York tea or, as John Lamb put it: "Shall the tea be landed?"

"No! No! No!" shouted the throng. Resolutions were immediately adopted opposing the landing of the New York tea and commending the "spirited patriotic conduct of our brethren, of the City of Philadelphia and the town of Boston, in support of the common liberties of America." The Mohawks readied themselves and pilots were cautioned to aid no tea ships into port.

Then came the electrifying news, brought by Paul Revere, that Boston had dumped its tea into the harbor! New York got this message on Dec. 21. Gov. Tryon and the consignees realized the time was ended for any trifling with the patriots. The consignees sent word to the Sandy Hook pilot boat for Capt. Benjamin Lockyer to turn back the minute he reached port and obtained provisions.

Philadelphia received Revere's message on Dec. 24, and the very next day the tea ship *Polly*, Capt. Samuel Ayres, was sighted off Chester on the Delaware River. The river pilots, honoring warnings they had received, refused any help to Capt. Ayres. He brought the *Polly* upriver on his own to Gloucester Point, within four miles of the city's center, where he was hailed by a patriot committee to anchor. He came ashore and they escorted him into Philadelphia.

For Ayres, there would be no mistaking the attitude of the Philadelphians. A public meeting was hurriedly called for Monday, Dec. 27, at 10 a.m. at the State House "to consider what is best to be done in this alarming crisis." The State House could not hold the 8000 citizens who appeared — largest gathering yet in the city's history — and they all moved into the State House yard.

Capt. Ayres listened attentively as the gathering voted that the tea must not be landed, that Capt. Ayres must not enter it at customs, that he be allowed another day to provision his ship and that he must leave immediately. A committee was named to see this was done. Finally the throng joyfully voted:

"That this assembly highly approve of the conduct and spirit of the people of New York, Charleston and Boston and return their hearty thanks to the people of Boston for their resolution in destroying the tea rather than suffer it to be landed."

Next Day Capt. Ayres went aboard a pilot boat to the *Polly*, hoisted anchor and headed downriver for London. There was no interference at any time from the governor or the customsmen. When Lord Dartmouth later protested, he was warned by a friendly correspondent in Philadelphia that opposition to duty for revenue was general in the colonies. Moreover, Joseph Reed wrote Dartmouth:

"Any further attempt to enforce this act, I am humbly of opinion, must end in blood."

There was a departure from Charleston that same day. Capt. Alexander Curling headed his tea ship *London* back across the Atlantic.

Now there was just New York.

This turned into a double climax. The denouement started on April 18, 1774, when Capt. Lockyer's *Nancy* anchored off Sandy Hook. He had had a fearful passage. A December storm had driven him from the Atlantic coast and so battered his vessel that he took it into Antigua for repairs. While there he learned of the hostility of the colonials and was fully prepared to yield as soon as he could enter a protest, just for the record.

A second storm hit him on his way from Antigua and carried away an anchor and his mizzen mast and sprung his topmast. As soon as Capt. Lockyer came to anchor, a New York patriot committee came on board. His request to come up to the city for supplies was allowed, and when he appeared the next day, there was a big crowd at the wharf "to see the man whose arrival they had long and impatiently wished."

He was accompanied to the home of one of the consignees, who told him not to go near the customshouse but to go back to England. He said he would "make all dispatch he could to leave the city," and an observation committee went with him to the *Nancy* until it should depart.

Meanwhile, a Capt. James Chambers on another vessel named *London* was headed for New York with a little deal of his own in tea. The captain had a good reputation. Only the prior October he had been among the captains of London ships honored at a Manhattan coffeehouse "for their patriotic conduct" in refusing to transport tea.

But now the patriots had received tips that Capt. Chambers might have gone back on his promise. Word from Philadelphia reached New York on Monday, the day the *Nancy* arrived, that Capt. Chambers had taken 18 boxes of fine tea on board at London port — and that the marks and numbers had been copied from the cocket (manifest) by Capt. All of Philadelphia.

Some at first suspected that Capt. Chambers might have been framed by ministerial agents.

Then on Wednesday another captain arrived from London with the same marks and numbers as Capt. All had provided.

Capt. Chambers was on a spot when he arrived Friday at Sandy Hook. He assured the pilots that he had no tea. Two members of the patriot committee examined the manifest but could find nothing. Capt. Chambers repeated his denials, so he was allowed to take his vessel to the Whitehall slip.

There, a number of intensive citizens came on board and questioned him again. No, he had no tea, he insisted. He was flatly told that this was a committee to open and examine every parcel on board and that they happened to have proof he had tea. Trapped, he confessed. He was ordered to Mr. Francis's for more questioning. Who was the shipper of the tea? Who was the owner?

Sheepishly he admitted it was all his own — all 18 quarter chests of expensive Hyson. This information was forwarded to the crowd on the wharf and the Mohawks were alerted. But the people did not wait.

At 8 p.m. they swarmed aboard and started hoisting up the tea, breaking the chests and tossing the contents into the river. By 10 p.m. the party was over and the people were "in great wrath against the captain; and it was not without some risque to his life that he escaped."

Next morning, April 23, at 8 a.m., a large flag was hoisted on Liberty Pole, ships in New York harbor displayed their colors and the bells began ringing.

"About nine," recorded Rivington's *Gazettee,* "the greatest number of people were collected at and near the coffee house that was ever known in this city. At a quarter past nine the committee came out of the coffee house with Capt. Lockyer, upon which, the band of music attending played 'God save the King.'

"Immediately there was a call for Capt. Chambers — 'Where is he? Where is he? Capt. Lockyer must not go 'til we find Capt. Chambers to send him with the tea ship.'

"This produced signs of fear in Capt. Lock-yer, who imagined some mischief was intended him; but upon assurances being given him to the contrary, he appeared composed. The committee, with music, conducted him through the multitude to the end of Murray's Wharf, where he was put on board the pilot boat, and wished a safe passage; upon which the multitude gave loud huzza's, and many guns were fired, expressive of the joy at his departure."

The committee sloop and the pilot boat bade farewell to the receding *Nancy* three leagues out from Sandy Hook at 2 p.m. Sunday afternoon.

But where was Capt. Chambers?

He had fled on the *Nancy,* leaving behind his ship and all his personal belongings. Chambers's private cache of tea was not part of the East India monopoly tea that had been shipped under Lord North's Tea Act. There never was any more shipped that way. But there were many instances of private tea deals that ran afoul of the patriots during the months that followed the Boston Tea Party.

Late in December of 1773, some Marshfield, Mass., patriots raided the cellar of a Tory and burned his tea at a spot there still called Tea Rock Hill. Thomas Newell on the last day of 1773 hied to Charlestown at noon to see the patriots there burn tea they had collected. Newell remembered that the patriots passed out "punch and wine at their own expense."

Local patriots were often active this way. Months later Newell found that the Charlestown patriots had burned another 400 or 500 pounds of tea. He did not mention punch and wine.

College boys got into the swing. Harvard barred tea. Princeton burned it and, for full measure, burned effigies of Gov. Hutchinson.

Salem schoolboys burned two chests of smuggled tea on Salem Common. Lexington assembled local tea and burned it on the green. So did Providence. Portsmouth sent off cargos of tea and assaulted the house of a persistent importer. Patriots in Weston wrecked the Jones Tavern, turning it to a shambles, for dispensing tea.

Some of the harbor dumping and tea burning were more spectacular.

One of several tea incidents in Charleston

was like the Boston Tea Party. Seven casks of tea arrived on the *Britannia*, Capt. Sam Ball. The local committee of inspection at once took charge. The *Britannia* was maneuvered out into the Cooper River and the three frightened importers were forced to stove in their own tea chests and dump the contents in the river as the crowds on the bank cheered.

Greenwich, N.J., downriver from Philadelphia, had an unexpected bonfire. Capt. Allen, on the brig *Greyhound*, was headed for Philadelphia when he was warned by the river pilots of the angry reception tea would receive. So late at night he hove into Greenwich looking for a compliant Tory who might store his tea.

He found one. But the town was watchful and plans were made for a public meeting to deal with the hidden tea. The local patriots were impatient. They gathered at night at the Fithian home near the town center and riverfront and donned Indian disguise. Soon they had carried the tea out of the Tory's cellar and, chest after chest, flung it in the flames.

Most of the names of these men have been preserved.

Several became famous — congressmen, heroes in the Revolutionary War. Richard Howell became governor of New Jersey.

The leader, Philip Vickers Fithian, in whose house the tea burners dressed, was a Princeton graduate and clergyman. He served in the Revolutionary Army and died, from exposure and camp fever, near Fort Washington on Manhattan when he was only 28. A visitor to the fort sketched Fithian's likeness just before his death.

Fithian unquestionably inspired the tea burning at Greenwich. Only a few weeks earlier, while journeying from Virginia, he had stopped at Annapolis, Md., where he learned about the most spectacular of all the tea burnings.

The 50-ton brig *Peggy Stewart*, Capt. Jackson, arrived at Annapolis, Md., on Oct. 15, 1774, from London with a large number of indentured servants and 17 full and half chests containing more than 2300 pounds of tea. The brig was owned jointly by Anthony Stewart and his father-in-law, James Dick.

Stewart was eager to dock the vessel be-

cause some of the indentured were sick and exhausted and the vessel had become leaky. He offered to pay duty on everything but the tea. The customsman was as immovable as the collector in Boston. He would not accept a partial entry, so Stewart on the spur of the moment paid duty on the entire cargo.

When the patriots of Anne Arundel County heard of this, they called a protest meeting for Oct. 19. Stewart sought to make amends with the local patriot committee. He met them on the 17th and offered to burn the tea. They thought this acceptable, and so told the public meeting when it gathered two days later.

But there were hotter heads in the gathering who did not think that burning the tea was sufficient atonement. They wanted the ship to be burned as well. They talked menacingly of tar and feathers, of destroying Stewart's house and of stringing him up on a gallows. Stewart's wife was about to give birth and her father was desperate. So much so, that when his neighbors sought to impress him that the public meeting had not voted to burn the brig, the frantic man pleaded with them "for God's sake not to meddle in the matter." Stewart yielded, too, and, accompanied by the tea consignees, he ran and set it on fire. An eyewitness reported:

"In a few hours the brig, with her sails, cordage, and every appurtenance, was effectually burnt." She was fairly new; had been built in Maryland in 1771. Maryland, it was remarked, had "out-Bostoned Boston."

Tea continued to get detestable names as colonies and mother country moved farther apart.

Substitutes for tea, however pathetically inadequate, won patriotic approval. Political cartoonists in England singled this out for special lampooning that was considered very funny in tea-drinking Britain. One of the most famous satirizes some 50 ladies of Edenton, seaport and then well-known former capital of North Carolina.

The ladies had gathered at the home of Mrs. Penelope Barker to sign an agreement that they would not import or use tea. Their substitute: dried yaupon or raspberry leaves.

Boston had more than one tea party.

Capt. Benjamin Gorham's brig *Fortune*, with 28½ chests of tea aboard, came into Boston harbor on Sunday, March 6, 1774 — more than two months after the first party.

The owner, Thomas Walley, was stunned to learn there was tea aboard. (Ship captains often acted as buyers for the owners, using their own judgment on purchases.) He frantically sought a pass to send the tea back. Collector Harrison, spouting technicalities again, refused.

The alert Committee of Correspondence sent word requesting the neighboring town committees to meet Tuesday afternoon.

But the problem was all settled the night before, when 60 Indians went aboard the *Fortune,* tied at Hubbard's Wharf, near Griffin's, and "emptied every chest of that pernicious and obnoxious herb in the ocean."

Colonies applaud Boston's deed

What did Hutchinson think of the Boston Tea Party?

"This," he wrote, "was the boldest stroke which had yet been struck in America. The people had gone too far to recede ... open general revolt must be the consequence...."

The night of the Tea Party he had been so worried and in suspense about a rumored, categorical demand for a pass to sail by the Castle's guns that he felt soothing relief "by intelligence from town of the total destruction of the tea."

Nobody had suspected, he wrote, that the tea would have been destroyed. He observed in a note to Bernard that the destruction of the tea "was what everybody supposed impossible, after so many men of property had made part of the meetings, and were in danger of being liable for the value of it."

The very next day after the party he hurried off a note to Lord Dartmouth. He had evidently got little sleep despite his feeling of relief.

"I sent expresses this morning before sunrise to summon a Council to meet me at Boston, but by reason of the indisposition of three of them I could not make a quorum." They clearly did not want to irritate the citizenry. And even valiant Hutchinson, under the guise of a visit to his sons, spent the next night at the Castle.

Hutchinson took no meaningful official action against the patriots. When his Council did meet, in the security of a Tory mansion in Cambridge, the only advice it had was that the attorney general go before the grand jury. Hutchinson knew that was pointless. No one would dare to identify anyone.

Five months, short a few days, would have to pass before Boston would learn what the official British reaction would be.

Among the patriots there was nothing but a feeling of delight that they had met the challenge and a buoyant conviction that they had acted properly. Adams was busy writing and getting others to write. The Committees of Correspondence and express riders worked tirelessly to let the world know their story.

"You cannot imagine the height of joy that sparkles in the eyes and animates the countenances as well as the hearts of all we meet on this occasion," said Adams.

To the Plymouth patriot James Warren, Adams wrote:

"The ministry could not devise a more effective measure to unite the colonies. Our committee has on this occasion opened a correspondence with the other New England colonies, beside New York and Philadelphia. Old jealousies are removed, and perfect harmony subsisted between them."

Adams, jointly with Speaker Thomas Cushing, John Hancock and William Phillips, as a committee of the House, sent a lengthy letter to the colony's deputy agent in London, Arthur Lee, for his use in promoting "the interest of this province in particular and of the colonies in general." In it they told how the patriots felt as midnight of Dec. 16 had come closer:

"Nigh 20 days were now passed since the arrival of one of the tea vessels, commanded by Capt. Hall, at which time, according to act of Parliament, it was in the power of the customs house officers to take the teas into their own possession, in order to secure the duties.

"There was just grounds to think that they intended to do it the minute the 20 days expired, and that they would attempt to land them by force, and overbear any opposition that might occur by a second effusion of blood. Under these apprehensions, the teas, on the evening of the 16th instant, were destroyed by a number of persons unknown and in disguise.

"... The destruction of the teas," they declared, after reciting the stubbornness of the cosignees, their advisers and coadjutors, "must be imputed to these obstinate enemies of our liberties. ..." We know how most of the patriot leaders felt in their own words.

John Adams, confiding detail and his usual vivid phrasing to his diary the day after the Tea Party, wrote:

"This is the most magnificent movement of all.

"There is a dignity, a majesty, a sublimity in

this last effort of the patriots that I greatly admire. The people should never rise without doing something to be remembered — something notable and striking.

"This destruction of the tea is so bold, so daring, so firm, interpid & inflexible, and it must have so important consequences, and so lasting that I cannot but consider it as an epocha in history.

"What measures will the ministry take, in consequence of this? Will they respect it? Will they dare to resent it? Will they punish us? How? By quartering troops upon us? By annulling our charter? By laying on more duties? By restraining our trade? By sacrifice of individuals? Or how?"

John Hancock wrote to his London colleague, via Capt. James Scott:

"No one circumstance could possibly have taken more effectively to unite the colonies than this maneuver of the tea. It is universally resented here."

Joseph Warren, following the party, wrote:

". . . Nothing seems able to penetrate the Egyptian darkness which is so palpable in the court atmosphere . . . .

"The unpropitious star which rules unhappy Britain has disappointed our wishes; every step taken by the administration has increased the distance between her and the colonies; and I fear, that, unless a speedy alteration is made in the system of American policy, a few years will render us as indifferent to the interests of the mother country as to that of any other state in Europe."

There was joy throughout the colonies with Boston's blow against ministerial tyranny. In his *Royal American Magazine* patriot printer Isaiah Thomas told how many "towns in this colony have met and signified their hearty approbation of the measures taken by Boston and the neighboring towns respecting the tea."

Large crowds gathered in New York in high spirits and extolled their Boston brethren when they heard the news. In Philadelphia there was "ringing of bells and every sign of joy and universal approbation." A great meeting of the people huzza'd and clapped and "rejoiced that the virtue of Boston appeared firm and triumphant." And fulsome praise came from the Carolinas.

There was no letup in patriot pressures against domestic foes or in efforts to extend control of their own government as they awaited, intrepidly, the verdict of the mother country.

Castle William was pretty cold in the winter, but it was, as Adams wrote to James Warren, "the safe asylum for our inveterate enemies. There the tea consignees, after having rendered themselves more obnoxious than even stamp masters, have immured themselves." The older men, Benjamin Faneuil and Joshua Winslow, were not there, only the Clarkes and Hutchinsons. Handbills menaced them with tar and feathers if they came to town.

Elisha Hutchinson had slipped to his relatives in Middleboro. But when he tried to visit his father-in-law in Plymouth, he soon found how bitterly matters stood.

Word of his presence headed a crowd toward Col. Watson's house and bells were tolled to bring more. Only the intercession of the local Committee of Correspondence permitted Elisha to remain that night, but he had to take off in a heavy snowstorm early the next morning. Mettlesome Jonathan Clarke did, however, manage to get aboard the *Beaver* and sail for England.

The people generally were quick to display resentment. In Boston a despised customsman, John Malcolm, managed to achieve peculiar notoriety by becoming the only man who was tarred and feathered twice. He got it first at Pownalborough (now Dresden, Maine) late in 1773. Now he ran into trouble again when Tea Party member Hewes came upon him late in January raising his cane against a boy with a sled.

The intended blow struck Hewes, who had to be taken to Dr. Warren with a severe head wound. The crowd took after Malcolm, brought him to the massacre site, flogged him, tarred and feathered him, carted him through town to the Liberty Tree and to the gallows at Boston Neck, where they gave him another beating and threatened to hang him.

This same quick-tempered reaction prevailed when the lieutenant governor, who had been the colony's original stamp master, died early in

March. Feeling ran so high against him that even his coffin, as lowered into the grave, was reviled, and his brother, Chief Justice Peter Oliver, could not attend for fear of his life.

There was no pause in the struggle against Hutchinson.

Hutchinson had decided that the best course was to leave the Tea Party alone and take a different tack. He assailed the Committee of Correspondence and said that it had the King's disapprobation. Adams retorted promptly with a stirring vindication of these committees as expressing the natural rights of the people.

The patriots moved to take over the courts. Ardent William Molineux, chosen foreman of Suffolk County's grand jury, declared that he would not serve under Chief Justice Oliver or any judge who accepted his pay from the crown. The drive of the patriots got all these judges to resign except the chief justice, a pleasant man who said, truthfully, that the provincial salary was inadequate to live on.

John Adams thought up a method of getting rid of Oliver: impeachment. This, however, technically required the cooperation of the governor. Undaunted, Samuel Adams and Bowdoin brought in the impeachment in the House and Council and went through the charade of saying the absent governor was "presumptively present," as Adams phrased it.

It worked. When the chief justice called upon jurors, grand or petit, to serve on juries, they indignantly declined to be sworn. They cited the impeachment that claimed that Oliver "had corruptly done that which hath an obvious and direct tendency to the perversion of law and justice; that he had thereby proved himself an enemy to the constitution of the province...." Royal courts were ended in the Bay Colony.

A year later the colonists would pick their own high courts and choose John Adams, then in Philadelphia, as chief justice.

Hutchinson, now completely isolated, was fed up. He prorogued the Legislature and announced that he had the permission of his royal master to take a leave of absence. The death of his brother-in-law Oliver on March 3 delayed Hutchinson's leaving. He did not want to turn over his role to the Bowdoin-dominated Council.

A vast crowd at the Old South, with tears and plaudits, listened to John Hancock deliver the annual massacre oration.

Inveterate enemies will suggest new measures against the colonies, Hancock predicted. "Therefore, let us be ready to take the field whenever danger calls; let us be united and strengthen the hands of each other, by promoting a general union among us." He lauded the work of the Committee of Correspondence. "May success ever attend their generous endeavors.

"But permit me here," he emphasized, expressing the profound hope of Adams, Warren and the other patriot leaders present, "to suggest a general congress of deputies from the several houses of assembly on the continent, as the most effectual method of establishing such a union as the present posture of our affairs requires.

"At such a congress, a firm foundation may be laid for the security of our rights and liberties."

Hancock's eloquence and spirit thrilled his listeners.

Presently dark rumors started coming across the Atlantic.

Parliament was considering punishment for Boston. Franklin sent word that violent countermeasures were under consideration. Boston's harbor might be blockaded, suggested a letter from London printed in the *Boston Gazette*. On May 2 a ship brought to Boston the King's speech to Parliament with papers on the Tea Party and Lord North's motion on a Boston Port Bill.

Boston was still unruffled.

Adams had written to John Dickinson:

"May God prepare this people for the event by inspiring them with wisdom and fortitude. They stand in need of all the countenance that their sister colonies can afford them...."

On May 10 Boston learned the worst.

It was election day. The town meeting again chose Hancock, Cushing, Phillips and Adams as representatives in the Legislature, and that same day Capt. Shayler, five weeks from London, arrived with the full text of the Boston Port Bill, which had received the King's signature on March 31.

Boston was shocked by its unanticipated severity.

As King George III was about to get into his bed on Jan. 19, 1774, he was given the news of the Boston Tea Party. He dashed off a note to Lord Dartmouth:

"I am much hurt that the instigation of bad men hath again drawn the people of Boston to take such unjustifiable steps."

First word of the Tea Party had just reached London by courier from Falmouth, where John Hancock's speedy vessel *Hayley,* Capt. James Scott, had touched land on its way to Dover and up the Thames.

The initial reaction in England, long accustomed to tales of difficulties in its colonies and with plenty of domestic troubles of its own, was as temperate as the King's. But in a few days, Gov. Hutchinson's official account reached Lord Dartmouth and the ministry started taking a sterner view.

There were a number of things to roil official tempers. The *Polly,* its tea rejected by Philadelphia, had just sailed back into the port of London. The Bay Colony's petition to remove Hutchinson and Oliver from office was at the moment being pronounced "groundless, vexatious, scandalous, and calculated only for the seditious purpose of keeping up a spirit of clamor and discontent."

And it was now that Franklin was being outrageously stigmatized before the sneering Privy Council over the Hutchinson letters. Boston, again erupting, had been an aggravation since the Stamp Act riots. The full cabinet, its anger rising, met several times. The crucial meeting came on Feb. 19.

Passengers on the *Hayley* and others from the Bay Colony newly in England were called before the Privy Council and questioned. Evidence they gave was too vague on identity to guarantee that any hangings would result from bringing charges of high treason. The cabinet proposed instead to seek a bill in Parliament that would at least padlock the port of Boston until it indemnified the East India Co.

The King was disappointed when told that there would be no treason trials. He was more convinced than ever that Britain's leniency on

taxes had contributed to this rebellious state of affairs, and he had been getting some additional bad advice from another man just back from America, Gen. Thomas Gage. Gage told him:

"They will be lions whilst we are lambs, but if we take the resolute part they will undoubtedly prove very meek. . . ."

Lord North was just as far from reality. North figured: "Four or five frigates would do the business without any military force."

The punitive legislation was prepared and the King's message to Parliament was read by North on March 7. The object was "to secure the execution of the laws and the just dependence of the colonies upon the crown and parliament of Great Britain." The issue: Were they British colonies or not?

A week later debate began on the Boston Port Bill, a measure so momentous that within a few months it would lead to the American colonies' firmly uniting and preparing to defend themselves and in a few months more would lead to open warfare. To North, Boston was the "centre of rebellious commotion in America; the ring leader in every riot."

North proposed to close Boston harbor on June 1 to any ships entering and deny any ships departure after June 15 until the tea was paid for, until injured crown officials were compensated and the King concluded that it would again be possible to carry on trade peacefully.

Public sympathy in England was with the legislation. There was a wave of feeling that Boston should be punished. America's great friend Edmund Burke described the Commons as being as "hot as Faneuil Hall or the Old South Meeting House" and called the House of Lords "a seething caldron." Even Col. Isaac Barre and former Gov. Pownall felt that Boston had earned punishment, and voted for the measure.

Burke, as Thomas Babington Macaulay once presented him, raised his voice until the old rafters of Irish oak resounded. He denounced the measure: "You will thus irrevocably alienate the hearts of the colonies from the mother country. The bill is unjust, since it bears only upon the city of Boston, while it is notorious that all America is in flames; that the cities of Philadelphia, of New York, and all the maritime towns of the continent, have exhibited the same disobedience.

"One city in proscription and the rest in rebellion, can never be a remedial measure for disturbances.

"Have you considered," he thrust, "whether you have troops and ships sufficient to reduce the people of the whole American continent to your devotion?"

Another old friend of America, Dowdeswell, also spoke against singling out Boston and convicting it without a hearing. "More mischief, more folly," he averred.

It was in vain. The King made one more of his mistaken assessments: "The feebleness and futility of the opposition shows the rectitude of the measure." The bill got his royal assent on March 31.

North was not finished. He must change things in the Bay Colony. He brought in the Regulatory Acts, which the colonies would call the Coercive Acts. They contained provisions that Bernard and Hutchinson had been long suggesting. The Bay Colony Council would be appointed by the crown, the governor would control judges, sheriffs would control juries and the town meetings would be taboo without the governor's approval, save for one annual local election.

Overbearing Lord George Germain, who would succeed Lord Dartmouth as secretary for the colonies and earn the hatred of even the British generals he controlled, gave his assessment of why town meetings should be curbed:

"The whole are the proceedings of a tumultuous and riotous rabble who ought, if they had the least prudence, to follow their mercantile employments, and not trouble themselves with politics and government which they do not understand."

North, equally blind to human values, thanked Germain for his words to Parliament. "They are worthy of a great mind," said North.

The measure passed with ease. It was May 11, and North was still not through. He brought in a Justice Bill under which trials would not have to be held in the colony but could be moved to England or elsewhere to get friendly juries.

News of Boston's second Tea Party, underlining restiveness in the colony, helped North.

He had still one more reform for Massachusetts, a Billeting Act. Troops in the Castle had not been sufficiently handy. He proposed authority to billet them anywhere in the colony, even in private houses. This brought forth another of the Earl of Chatham's great orations. He assailed North:

"Instead of making a well-concerted effort to secure the real offenders, you clap a naval and military extinguisher over their harbor, and punish the whole body of the inhabitants for the crime of a few lawless depredators and their abettors.

"I sincerely believe the destroying of the tea was the effect of despair.

"This, my lords, though no new doctrine, has always been my received and unalterable opinion, and I will carry it to my grave, that this country had no right under heaven to tax America."

In the course of North's strategy of bringing his program piecemeal before Parliament, Burke had tried to win repeal of the Tea Act and gave another of his heroic addresses aimed at conciliation. This time it was on taxation. He traced the trouble back to the 3-penny tax that still was in force from the old Townshend Act. Repeal it or there would be no peace. He lost 182 to 49, nearly four to one, a swamping.

To the King, repeal of the tea tax would be considered a sign of weakness. "I do not wish to come to severer measures," said the King, "but we must not retreat."

And the King had a view of North's entire punitive program, known to history as the Intolerable Acts:

"The die is cast, the colonies must either submit or triumph."

For the Bay Colony there would, in effect, be martial law. Gen. Gage was sent back to North America on the 20-gun frigate *Lively* as Commander in Chief and also as the next governor of Massachusetts. The same vessel carried a message to Gov. Hutchinson. Hutchinson could have the leave of absence he sought. His masters no longer considered him equal to the job.

Congress called in Philadelphia

Gen. Gage's frigate arrived at the Castle on May 13 — Friday the 13th — and he went into an immediate huddle with Hutchinson.

Boston patriots, undaunted as ever, had been busy rallying support ever since they read the oppressive terms of the Port Bill. If this could be done to Boston, it could be done to the other colonies. Adams knew the only safe course was for the colonies to unite.

Even as Gage was setting foot in the Castle, an overflow of hundreds of citizens from Boston and surrounding towns stood outside jammed Faneuil Hall, where Adams was presiding at a town meeting energetically denouncing the Port Bill that Gage had come to enforce.

Rousingly, the crowd voted against paying for the tea and approved an appeal to the other colonies to stop trading with Great Britain. Adams had written in a circular letter: "Now is the time when we should be united in opposition to this violation of the liberties of all . . . . " And now he transmitted the deep-seated belief of Boston that it would not "be left to struggle alone."

Paul Revere, carrying along some black-bordered reprints of the Port Bill, rode off with the message to New York and Philadelphia. Both would affirm support, and Philadelphia's Committee of Correspondence would send by Revere a return suggestion that a general congress be called.

Adams wrote to his Plymouth friend James Warren about the public meeting and the outrageousness of the Port Bill. Why had not the port of London been shut up when mobs surrounded the King's palace? The people must resist. Adams lauded their stamina: "The heroes who first trod on your shore fed on clams and mussels and were contented." As for Boston, said Adams:

"The people receive this cruel edict with abhorrence and indignation. They consider themselves as suffering the stroke ministerial — I may more precisely say, Hutchinsonian vengeance, in the common cause of America.

"I hope they will sustain the blow with a becoming fortitude and that the cursed design of intimidating and subduing the spirits of all America, will, by the joint efforts of all, be frustrated."

Hutchinson briefed Gage for four days at the Castle and now the day arrived for Gage to come to the town. It was May 17, windy and rainy. Boston would still show it was as urbane as the general. John Hancock and his Governor's Cadets were on the town wharf, the militia was mustered. There were salutes from the military, the ships and the batteries as Gage went up King street to the old State House.

There were three volleys and three cheers as his commission was read in the old council chamber. To the crowd, as John Andrews heard it, "he expressed himself as sensible of the unwelcome errand he came upon, but as a servant of the crown, he was obliged to see the act put in execution . . . . " An elegant banquet followed in Faneuil Hall. All was grand until, among the toasts, Gage gave one to Hutchinson.

Andrews reported, "Such is the detestation in which that tool of tyrants is held among us" that Gage's toast "was received with a general hiss."

Ironies abounded. Among the cadets and the militia Gage was unquestionably looking upon more than a quorum of the men in the Tea Party, and here they were paying respects to the man who had come as an avenger. In Gage's charge were orders to arrest — for hanging — the colonel of these cadets, Hancock. Gage, now smiling, would soon fire Hancock from that job, as Hancock quit it.

Gage would be most diplomatic about moving to arrest Adams, Warren and the other patriot leaders on Britain's wanted list. Indeed, he would even send an officer to try to win Samuel Adams with an offer of any post that he might choose. Adams's response: "Sir, I trust I have long since made my peace with the King of kings. No personal consideration shall induce me to abandon the righteous cause of my country. Tell Gov. Gage it is the advice of Samuel Adams to him no longer to insult the feelings of an exasperated people."

Gage's mission to enforce the odious act — and he must soon have sensed this — was hopeless. His power would never extend beyond Boston and Salem, where he was ordered to move the colony's seat of government. The courts could not function. Jurors would not serve. The councilors he would appoint would be forced into resignation by clamoring bands of people.

These same people who had withstood the Stamp Act and the Tea Act would not submit to what they conceived was destruction of their charter and incipient slavery. Gage's second in command, proud Lord Percy, would quickly find that the people, in defense of their cherished liberties, would "be arming and exercising all over the country."

Troops and warships investing Boston put starch in some of its citizens inclined to be Tories. They gave Adams annoyance about paying for the tea. Hutchinson from the Castle abetted the trouble. Some patriots thought this might be a way out. Even Franklin, way back in February when he felt civil war would ensue, believed paying for the tea might be a helpful way to win friends in Europe.

This had made Adams tartly declare of Franklin:

He "... may be a great philosopher, but he's a bungling politician."

As Adams saw it, "There is no crime alleged in the Act as committed by the town of Boston." He was dead set against any payment: it would admit a crime. At another in his series of "adjourned" town meetings on May 18, payment was again brought up. George Erving told the meeting he was prepared to put down 2000 pounds toward the payment and go wait on Gage to know his demands. Erving subsided when the meeting voted this down.

On June 1 the bells all over town were tolled. There was fasting and prayer led by the clergy, most all of them on the patriot side. At noon, Gage, his soldiers and ships on station, shut the port to any incoming vessels. Activity ceased along the waterfront. Stores were closed. Men were thrown out of jobs. "Violence or submission would at this time be equally fatal," Adams advised as Gage's military grip sought to enforce a tax the people had never voted.

Lord North's hope that this would isolate Boston was stillborn. Boston soon learned that the colonies had rallied without exception and embraced Boston's cause as their own.

"Don't pay for an ounce of the damned tea," Christopher Gadsden wrote to Boston, and the Carolinas sent shiploads of rice.

George Washington told the House of Burgesses:

"If need be I will raise 1000 men, subsist them at my own expense and march myself at their head to the relief of Boston."

Gifts would pour in, as would letters and resolutions pledging support and unity. Their spontaneity and ardency would bring grateful tears to the eyes of any lover of liberty. Table fish, sweet oil in carts from Marblehead ... hundreds of bushels of rye from Wethersfield and Farmington ... sheep from Windham ... Israel Putnam at the head of 130 sheep he led 100 miles from his farm ... grain from Groton, Pepperell and Wrentham ... a thousand bushels of grain from Quebec ... and on and on....

Cash, too, came from all over. It helped the poor, who went to work fixing streets and repairing empty wharves and making bricks at the town's new yard on the Neck.

June 1 was also the day that Hutchinson left for London. He had gone from Milton through Dorchester in his coach, which would soon be at the disposal of Gen. George Washington in Cambridge, and moved in a launch to the Castle. He had the paltry, departing comfort of a complimentary letter signed by 120 friends.

Hutchinson was not an evil man, he was just wrong. He truly loved this land of his ancestors and grieved that he could not live here and be buried here beside his beloved wife. His allegiance was to King and nobility, but to him the people were a mobility. In obstinacy he was a colonial edition of his royal master, George III.

Hutchinson, now nearly 63, simply did not recognize the nobility of his fellowmen, whatever their temporary lot in life, who were embarked upon the sublime enterprise of ruling themselves, thus setting out on the greatest adventure in democracy this world had yet seen, the future union of the states. Their leader, Samuel Adams, was now 52.

Hutchinson would be hurried to the King, without even a chance to change his travel clothes, the moment he reached London. He was closeted with the King for two hours and was offered a baronetcy. He told the King, "they will soon submit." And the King passed on this consistently wrong advice that same day in a note to Lord North:

"I have seen Mr. Hutchinson, late governor of Massachusetts, and am now well convinced they will soon submit. He owns the Boston Port Bill has been the only wise and effectual method."

Even as Hutchinson was leaving America, the colonies were moving irresistibly toward union. The idea of a general congress had taken firm root. Providence at a town meeting on May 17 had asked its deputies to propose one. Paul Revere had already carried to Boston the May 21 proposal from Philadelphia's Committee of Correspondence. New York proposed one to Boston on May 23 ... Virginia's House of Burgesses on May 27 ... Connecticut's Committee of Correspondence in a letter to Boston on June 3.

The movement was assisted even when Adams overreached a bit by trying, in the pattern of beating the stamp tax, to block any and all trade with Great Britain. Dr. Warren drew up what was called a "Solemn League and Covenant" for everyone to sign not only not to import any British goods but also not to sell any. People signed up, but merchants with large stocks on hand hesitated.

New York, instead, sent back word to Boston on June 7, asking that the idea be discussed at a continental congress of delegates from all the colonies. Let Boston name the time and place.

The moment for this came on June 17 at Salem.

The assembly, protesting its removal from Boston, had been meeting for some days. Gage had shifted his dwelling to Danvers to be nearby. Adams was playing for time. He wanted to allay the suspicions of Tory members, now more active with troops around, and get them to go home. He needed secrecy for what he was about to do. It had to be done fast.

Even when Warren appealed to him to be in Boston's Faneuil Hall on June 17 to beat back renewed agitation to pay for the tea, Adams had more vital business in Salem. June 17 came as the best moment to act. Only a dozen unsuspecting Tory members remained. To prevent word getting out to Gage, Adams ordered the doors locked, and then moved that the Bay Colony send delegates to a continental congress. He picked the place and the time, Philadelphia on Sept. 1.

A Tory member, pleading a call of nature, got out and hustled the news to Gage. Soon, as debate proceeded, State Secretary Thomas Flucker, who would remain staunchly a Tory though his daughter married Henry Knox, was pounding at the door and proclaiming that he had a message from Gov. Gage. When Flucker was told that the House had ordered the doors locked, he read his proclamation to the people gathered outside.

Gage had prorogued the assembly.

The session, last under royal mandate, voted a levy on each community to pay for the delegation's expenses, and then, at its own pace, ended the session.

That night, in ghost town Boston, the patriot leaders met at Warren's house, "an agreeable company," looking bravely to the future.

Aug. 10 would be the date for departure for Philadelphia.

Adams, meantime, at a great meeting in the Old South, defeated malcontents who wanted to censure the Committee of Correspondence over the Solemn League and Covenant. And he had a brush with Gage. On Aug. 9, day before the historic trip began, Adams was presiding at a town meeting in Faneuil Hall when Gage sent word that the meeting was now against the law. No, Gage was blandly told, it was not; this was not a new meeting, it was just an old adjourned one.

"Damn them," exploded once-confident Gage, "I won't do anything about it until His Majesty sends me more troops."

Early on Aug. 10 the Bay Colony delegates — Samuel Adams, John Adams, Thomas Cushing and Robert Treat Paine — gathered in the parlor of Speaker Cushing's house and then climbed into the coach. Warren, who would be the commanding figure in the colony in Samuel Adams's absence, and Molineux on horseback followed the coach as it passed daringly beside the Common where British soldiers were encamped.

It would be a festive journey — with warm welcomes all along the route, the first a banquet at Widow Coolidge's Tavern in Watertown. Two of the toasts were: "Our worthy friend and patriot, Mr. Samuel Adams"; and "In memory of the first Committee of Correspondence in America, and all those who dared to support our glorious cause in times of danger."

In England, George III sized up the situation:

"The New England governments are in a state of rebellion. Blows must decide."

Minutemen were already stirring.

Lexington-Concord Alarm

Why America was ready to fight

A man has to feel conviction most profoundly, from hair-tip to toes, in the clench of his teeth, in his stomach, head and heart, to face, musket in hand, the troops of his own land.

These troops suddenly must look like deadly enemies — these same soldiers who for so long have been the living symbols of glory and of admired traditions, won on worldwide battlefields.

Americans of 1775 had this intense conviction.

Lord Percy, a nobleman from Northumberland and one of Gen. Gage's more skilled subordinates, on April 19, 1775, saw how these Americans "advanced within 10 yards to fire at me and other officers though they were morally certain of being put to death themselves in an instant." Percy had this telltale comment: "I never believed, I confess, that they would have attacked the King's troops. . . ."

The mounting dictates of a faraway ministry had convinced Americans that the only alternative to risking death was to live under a form of despotism alien to Americans since they first arrived on this continent.

The Boston Port Bill of 1774, initial punishment for the Boston Tea Party, had turned out to be only a starter.

It was unfair, for it struck alike at the guilty and the guiltless. It was unfair because the men who took part sincerely believed that the distant ministry had left freemen no other choice. It was unfair most of all because the reaction of Lord North's ministry was to retaliate, rather than to strive to understand the reasons for the protest in Boston.

It was the flood of punitive parliamentary acts that came swiftly after the Boston Port Bill that tipped the scales for war — acts that sought to stamp out hard-won charter rights. These the British administration even called "Coercive Acts." Typically, 36 members of the Governor's Council would be picked in London and appointed by writs of mandamus — no longer would they be elected by the people's House of Representatives. Judges and juries would be strictly London-directed.

Most detested of all was the act euphemistically called "An Act for better regulating the government of the Province of the Massachusetts Bay."

Among its provisions was the virtual death of the town meeting. Americans amply understood what this meant. Their town meetings — and every community then had one — had grown to be little democracies. Every voter could have his say on just about everything touching his daily life. Moreover, from these town meetings the voters in effect ran the province, for after they sent their delegates to the House of Representatives, they drafted instructions on how the representatives should vote. It was home rule all the way, and Lord North's ministry would destroy it. This, as the provincials saw it, would constitute political slavery.

For long, mistaken months the Americans would feel it was only Lord North's ministry that was the enemy, and not the King. The troops would come to be scorned as "the ministerial army." On the extant, original mustering of the minutemen of Concord appears this pledge:

"1. That we whose names that are hereunto subscribed will defend Majesty King George the Third, his person, crown and dignity.

"2. That we will at the same time to the utmost of our power and ability defend all and every of our charter rights, liberties and privileges and will stand at a minute's warning with arms and ammunition to do so."

Lord Dartmouth, transmitting the Coercive Acts act by act from London to Gen. Gage, knew what was at stake:

"The authority of this kingdom over its colonies must be vindicated. . . . It is not only its dignity and reputation, but its power, nay its very existence depends upon the present moment. . . ."

Danvers minuteman Levi Preston, then young, now vivid to us only in a likeness made in his far-advanced years, knew what was at stake, too, when he shouldered his musket and practically ran much of the way to the battlefield on hearing the Lexington Alarm.

"We always had been free," said Preston, "and we meant to be free always."

Gage's harsh duty

Gen. Thomas Gage was feeling mighty ebullient while conversing with King George III, at the very summit of British power ... power that had brought Great Britain to world supremacy in the year 1774.

His Majesty was still disturbed by the unmitigated defiance the Boston Tea Party had exhibited to the authority of Parliament, and, implicitly, to his own autocratic views of kingship. Boston was about to be punished by clamping shut its port and with other severe parliamentary measures yet to be drafted, and the King was seeking a man to make Boston submit.

How much manpower would it require, asked the King.

Four regiments should do, Gage told his royal master — an amazing miscalculation possibly induced by the bliss Gage felt while in the royal presence. The King gratefully accepted this misadvice, for he considered that Gage was in a position to know. Gage, in England on leave, had spent two decades in America, had married an American and for years had been in command of all the military forces in North America.

This conference was in impregnable London — right in the King's palace. Four regiments indeed! A handful, really, not even a couple of thousand men.

Early in April 1774, Gage's superior, Lord Dartmouth, secretary of state for the colonies, directed Gage to board His Majesty's ship *Lively* and sail with the first fair wind to Boston, commissioning him under the Great Seal as the captain general and governor in chief of His Majesty's Province of Massachusetts Bay. Dartmouth wrote minute orders for Gage to put into effect the punishment decreed by Parliament "for enforcing a due obedience."

In later life Gage, a generally reserved, taciturn man of noble descent, would confide that he had always been ready to return to his military duty "but was adverse to taking the government of Massachusetts Bay." Gage would find that the orders that Dartmouth prepared for him would virtually tie his hands.

Dartmouth instructed Gage that "your authority as the first magistrate, combined with your command over the King's troops, will, it is hoped, enable you to meet every opposition and fully to preserve the public peace by employing those troops with effect."

But Dartmouth had added:

"The King trusts however that such necessity will not occur, and commands me to say that it will be your duty to use every endeavor to avoid it...." Further, said Dartmouth, "At the same time the sovereignty of the King and His Parliament over the colonies requires a full and absolute submission."

Even clear-cut, nonconflicting provisions of Gage's orders proved unsuccessful, though Gage did try to put them into effect.

Gage dutifully plunged the bustling port of Boston into economic doldrums and unemployment on June 1 by preventing the entry of merchant ships. Samuel Adams promptly headed a Donations Committee, and money and food flowed from all the colonies to help Bostonians suffering in the common cause. When South Carolina sent rice and other colonies sent sheep, Gage felt that Bostonians must soon realize this supply was "too precarious ... and must fail them."

Gage did not immediately detect the awesome, gathering might of colonial unity. He fancied that Bostonians would receive from the newly assembled Continental Congress "little more than fair words." Gage even had the misty self-deception that most of the other colonies felt that Boston should begin by indemnifying the East India Co. for the tea that had been tipped into the harbor.

Gage faithfully studied Dartmouth's orders that told him to use his "utmost endeavors to obtain sufficient evidence against the principal actors" in the Boston Tea Party, for the "King considers the punishment of these offenders as a very necessary and essential example to others...." But Gage was also told to forgo arrests if he could not get convictions, for, said Dartmouth, failure to convict would be "disgraceful to government."

Gage did soon come to realize, and so informed Dartmouth, that arresting any leaders "would be the signal for hostilities."

Even Gage's moving the provincial government to Salem, part of the punishment plan for Boston, failed. Salem would take no advantage of Boston's economic distress. To be near there, Gage moved into the Danvers summer home of Tory "King" Hooper of Marblehead and tried to run the province — and all North American military affairs, too — from an office a stone's throw from present Danvers center.

Through June, July and August Gage's hopes for a peaceful solution were repeatedly dashed. Samuel Adams outwitted him by dispatching and financing a delegation to the First Continental Congress. Tories picked in London to serve as Gage's councilors — the so-called Mandamus Councilors — wilted from office when their outraged neighbors, often in throngs, demanded that these traitors to the people resign. The crown-chosen, crown-paid judges could get no jurors to serve.

What had happened?

The patriots — "the faction," Gage called them — had learned details of further punitive measures being devised by Parliament, the repressive acts that the patriots had quickly, angrily characterized as the "Intolerable Acts." They were preparing to resist them.

By the end of August, Gage abandoned the shift to Salem and hastened back to Boston.

Gage's impression of the collapse of imperial authority in Massachusetts, and beyond its borders, is recorded step by step in his official reports to Dartmouth, a litany of deterioration. "Tho I saw things were bad when I wrote from Salem, I found them much worse than I expected when I arrived here," Gage informed Dartmouth.

Mandamus Councilors were fleeing their homes to shelter behind the British troops in Boston. Gage explained that he had come to Boston because the councilors did not dare to meet him in Salem. "I hope His Majesty will approve of my consenting to their request."

He also shifted to Boston to attend the Superior Court and to decide on sending troops to protect the courts in Worcester. "Civil government," wrote Gage, "is near its end, the courts of justice expiring one after another." He expressed the hope that Dartmouth would submit what should be the next move to "His Majesty's superior wisdom."

There was no blithe talk now about a mere four regiments.

To stem the torrent, Gage judged, would require "that a very respectable force should take the field." This was no rabble confronting him, said Gage, "but the freeholders and farmers of the country.

"A check anywhere," he concluded, "would be fatal, and the first stroke will decide a great deal."

Gage's confidential letters to his longtime acquaintance, Lord Barrington, secretary of war, were even more expressive. To Barrington, Gage was shortly writing:

"Affairs here are worse than even in the time of the Stamp Act. I don't mean in Boston, but throughout the country. The New England provinces, except part of New Hampshire, are I may say in arms, and the question is not whether you shall quell disturbances in Boston, but whether those provinces shall be conquered. . . .

"From appearances, no people are more determined for a civil war, the whole country from hence to New York armed, training and providing military stores. . . ."

Bulky Col. William Brattle, commander of the 1st Regt. of Middlesex and major general of the province's militia, sat down on Aug. 29, 1774, at his desk in his mansion (still standing) near Harvard Square, Cambridge, at the head of Tory Row, and wrote a letter to Gen. Gage that nearly got the Revolutionary War off to an early start.

At the very least it provided a rehearsal for the following April 19, the day the war would begin.

The times had become far from easy for the Tories, and the hearty colonel, who had once marched with Sons of Liberty in days before the Boston Tea Party, was now definitely Tory. He must have thought himself pretty slick in the veiled way in which he worded his letter, which Gage, on his way to a dinner, accidentally dropped on a Boston street. Patriots took one glance at the missive and read it for what it was: a tip-off to the general.

Brattle's letter told Gage that the Medford selectmen had just taken their town's stock of powder from the powder house (still standing), on Charlestown's (now Somerville's) Quarry Hill, leaving only the King's powder isolated there. Selectmen of all the other Middlesex towns had been quietly withdrawing their town stocks from Quarry Hill since Charlestown's selectmen started the run back in July.

Gage's first reaction was to order Brattle to deliver to High Sheriff David Phipps some powder and two fieldpieces only recently obtained by Brattle for his regiment.

Gage had just written to Dartmouth, "It is agreed that popular fury was never greater in this province than at present, and it has taken its rise from the old source at Boston, tho it has appeared first at a distance .., .

"In Worcester they . . . openly threaten resistance by arms, have been purchasing arms, preparing them, casting ball, and providing powder, and they threaten to attack any troops who dare to oppose them."

Gage, as Brattle's letter implied he should, had been gathering in any weaponry he could keep from the faction. He had suddenly seized what Boston had in its magazine on the Common. The patriots, of course, were as eager to keep war supplies from the King's troops. Only weapons and gunpowder stood between them and political slavery, as they saw it, and gunpowder, almost exclusively of British and foreign manufacture, was bound to be in short supply.

Patriots were preparing against the hostile way events were shaping. At the very moment the Medford selectmen acted, John Hancock's chief skipper, Capt. James Scott, was on the high seas headed for Salem with a secret cargo of gunpowder. Far and wide the towns were making ready, just as Gage warned Dartmouth.

Times were mighty bad in Boston. The Donations Committee thought up street repairing and brick making, and improvised public-service jobs for the unemployed. Bostonians who could go into the countryside to live with relatives made a touching counterstream to the Tories fleeing to Boston to escape their irate, threatening neighbors.

Things were bad for the British troops, too. The desertion rate was so worrisome to the general that he ordered deserters executed on the camp parade on the Common. The patriots added to the natural friction sparked by an occupying force by burning hay, sinking barges of brick or refusing to work on barracks in which Gage wanted to winter over his troops. Everywhere there was emotional signing of covenants not to buy British goods, a tactic that had helped gigantically to repeal the old Stamp Act.

Gage's greatest trial, and most menacing, was the rash of fiery county meetings.

The detested act that restricted town meetings had made no mention of county meetings. The canny Yankees promptly, wryly noted this oversight, exhibiting a hairsplitting trait that drove Gage to distraction. So patriots flocked to county meetings to denounce the parliamentary measures and brand anyone acting under them as traitors.

"It is needless to trouble your Lordship with daily publications of determined resolutions not to obey the late acts of Parliament," Gage wrote Dartmouth. "They talk of fixing a plan of government of their own, and as far as it can be seen, nothing less than the conquest of almost all the New England provinces will procure obedience to the late acts of Parliament for regulating the government of the Massachusetts Bay."

Two days after Brattle wrote his missive, Gage, almost in a seeming afterthought, ordered that the powder at the powder house on Quarry Hill be seized and taken to Castle William, the King's secure fort in Boston harbor.

This order put the fat in the fire, and would shortly force Brattle to flee for his life.

The Cambridge powder alarm

Gage's orders for the seizure were carried out swiftly.

Two hundred and sixty redcoats, under command of Lt. Col. George Maddison, marched from the Common down to the end of King street to Long Wharf and entered 13 barges. It was sunrise, Sept. 1. They moved up the Mystic River, past Bunker Hill, disembarked at Ten Hills, Gov. John Winthrop's old farm, then marched across Winter Hill to Quarry Hill and the powder house.

This was an old windmill built in the early 1700s from slate in the nearby quarry. It stood 40 feet high with three heavy floors sturdily supported by great oak beams and housed but 250 half barrels of the King's powder. Maddison's men removed these while a detachment hied off to Cambridge to pick up the powder and fieldpieces Brattle had given to Phipps.

Soon all these supplies were stowed in Castle William. Maddison's mission had worked as smooth as magic.

Trouble started when news of what Maddison had done moved through the countryside like prairie fire, inspiring wild, doom-sounding rumors. Expresses sprang on horseback. Beacon fires were lighted on hills. The rumors swelled as they traveled farther and farther. Men seized their arms: muskets, clubs, pitchforks.

Cambridge, Brattle's bailiwick, was the storm center, though little happened there that night save at the mansion of Atty. Gen. Jonathan Sewall near the middle of Tory Row.

A moderate crowd gathered, "mostly boys and Negroes," but when someone in the Sewall household opened a window and fired a gun, the crowd — like the angered crowd in Boston's School street in Tea Party days — was "provoked to break the windows, but very soon left the house without doing further damage."

The stage was being set for far greater excitement. Near Sewall's house was (and still stands) the 17th Century mansion of elderly Judge Joseph Lee, a Mandamus Councilor. While the crowd was at Sewall's house, a horseman from Concord sped to Lee's and told him of the throngs gathering in the distant countryside. Lee needed to hear no more. He sat down and wrote his resignation to Gage.

On the other side of Harvard Square from Brattle's mansion was the home of another Mandamus Councilor, Samuel Danforth, a man rapidly approaching his 78th birthday. Danforth, who fancied himself as a scientist and wrote letters to Benjamin Franklin, had spent all his life in local, provincial and judicial offices.

Danforth could sense danger and had gone to Boston, resignation in hand, to give it to Gage. Gage had refused to accept it because Danforth, like some of the other timorous councilors, had been sworn in secretly and Gage felt that there matters should stand.

The crisis came in a rush the next day, Sept. 2, a scorching hot day.

Thousands of citizens armed with sticks gathered on Cambridge Common while at the far end of Tory Row a large body of people from several outlying towns surged along the Watertown road past the great mansion (now called Elmwood) of Lt. Gov. Thomas Oliver. Oliver had not sought his office. Like other Mandamus Councilors, Oliver's name had been picked in London by Lord Dartmouth from a list drafted by former royal Gov. Thomas Hutchinson.

An immensely rich, pleasant man, a lieutenant colonel in Brattle's regiment, Oliver, now 40, had purchased 100 acres on Tory Row and built his mansion to be the neighbor of his brother-in-law, Col. John Vassall. They had married each other's sisters.

Oliver was begged by worried friends to speak to the passing throng. He went out and asked why they had come. They told him they "came peaceably to inquire into their grievances, not with design to hurt any man." Oliver recounted, "I perceived they were landholders of the neighboring towns, and was thoroughly persuaded they would do no harm." The throng continued toward Cambridge Common, where they encountered an electrifying rumor that "troops were on the march from Boston."

Oliver, too, went to the Common, where, he

said, "I was desired to go and intercede with His Excellency to prevent their (the troops') coming." He first wrote this note to Gage:

"The town is full of people from all quarters. I have given them assurances of no troops coming out, and I hope no consideration will induce you to send any such, as it will be attended with the most fatal consequences, and particularly to Your Excellency's most obedient servant, Thomas Oliver."

Meanwhile, messages had been arriving since 6 a.m. at the Hanover street home of Dr. Joseph Warren, Samuel Adams's chief lieutenant and key leader of the Sons of Liberty in Boston now that Adams had left for the First Continental Congress in Philadelphia. One messenger, as Warren wrote to Adams, told how the Middlesex people were "highly incensed against Mr. Brattle and some others, and advised that some people from Boston should go up to Cambridge."

On the heels of this messenger came a billet. Warren was "requested to take some step in order to prevent the people from coming to immediate acts of violence, as incredible numbers were in arms, and lined the roads from Sudbury to Cambridge."

Warren gathered some members of the Boston Committee of Correspondence, went over the ferry to Charlestown and met Charlestown patriot Richard Devens and members of the Charlestown committee and members of the Cambridge committee who had come to urge that all hasten to Cambridge to meet the emergency.

"On our way," said Warren, "we met the Lt. Gov. Oliver." Oliver told them his errand. "We thought his precaution good, and proceeded to Cambridge."

Oliver arrived at Province House, Gage's official residence on Boston's main street, as Gage was writing to Dartmouth, so Gage inserted:

"A vast concourse of people assembled this day from various parts about eight miles hence; they have frightened and pursued many obnoxious people as they term them. Nobody has asked assistance, and I have just received a letter from Mr. Oliver the Lieutenant Governor to beg I would on no account send any troops there,

Brattleboro, Vt. Library

Col. William Brattle

or it would prove fatal to him." Now Gage gave Oliver assurances in person, and Oliver headed back.

On the way, he met the much-troubled high sheriff hurrying to Boston. Self-confident Oliver persuaded Phipps to turn back. "They thus both fell into the snare," Gage told Dartmouth.

Harvard Square was jammed with upwards of 4000 aroused citizens as Warren arrived.

Old Danforth was on the steps of the courthouse seeking, in a very feeble voice, to placate the throng. He assured one and all that he had resigned his office, since he found there was "a general sense against his holding a seat at the Council." And, taking no more chances, he left forthwith for his son's house in Boston.

Lee read to the throng the resignation he had written to Gage and promised that he would not act under the hated law.

Sheriff Phipps next joined the line of political sinners with a pledge, read from the same courthouse steps, that he would carry out no more orders under the heinous act of Parliament.

Oliver, on getting back to Cambridge, conferred with the patriot committee, assured members that no troops were coming, was thanked and was about to leave when a member abruptly suggested that Oliver resign his seat. Oliver later:

"As Lieutenant Governor, I stood in a particular relation to the province in general, and therefore could not hear anything upon that matter from a particular county. I was then pushed to know if I would resign when it appeared to be the sense of the province in general; I answered that when all the other Councilors had resigned, if it appeared to be the sense of the province I should resign, I would submit." Oliver's response was voted acceptable. Oliver left.

When this was reported to the throng all was well received and the lopping of political heads seemed, for the present, to be over — but events took a sudden turn.

Into the square in his post chaise, accompanied by a mounted servant, rode one of the most disliked men of the colony, Benjamin Hallowell, a customs official since stamp-tax days. Hallowell, who had married a woman of fortune, was en route from Salem to his palatial residence near Jamaica Pond. An outspoken individual, short-tempered, too, he was noted for his arrogance. Epithets passed between Hallowell and the throng.

Nearly 100 men on horseback took after him. Patriot leaders — Warren, Dr. Thomas Young of Boston, Richard Devens, Capt. Thomas Gardner of Cambridge, who would soon succeed to the command of Brattle's regiment — galloped after the horsemen and called on them to desist. There was more urgent business: getting Mandamus Councilors out of office.

One small horseman still pressed after Hallowell. Hallowell fired his pistol at him, leaped from his chaise, mounted his servant's horse and fled toward Boston, crossing Boston Neck, where his horse collapsed, then running all the way into the camp on the Common. He blurted his fears that the mob was coming. Soldiers were sent out to reconnoiter. They reported "all was quiet near the town," but their going out sped another false rumor to Cambridge:

The troops were coming out after all!

The crowd, 4000 strong, headed at once for Oliver's mansion at the end of Tory Row.

Oliver had noticed the large companies still pouring past into Cambridge, felt apprehensive and was getting into his carriage when the throng from Harvard Square, every fourth man armed, surrounded the mansion. A committee of five leaders entered and asked him to sign a resignation. He protested about false dealings. The committee excused themselves, explaining that the people were dissatisfied.

"... They pressed up to my windows, which then were opened; I could from thence hear them at a distance calling out for a determination, and, with their arms in their hands, swearing they would have my blood if I refused," recalled Oliver. He became worried about the calamities he might occasion his wife and six children, agonizing in the next room.

"With a hurry of mind and conflict of passion," said Oliver, he then signed his resignation, but first adding a sentence that his house was surrounded and he was doing so under duress. He, too, fled to Boston, reported "in the greatest distress" to Gage and soon resumed his titles.

It was sunset. The people left Tory Row. The powder alarm, though, was not over, not while the distress call kept spreading through the land.

Old hero Israel Putnam, on his Connecticut farm, got the word next morning, Sept. 3. Only two weeks earlier, Old Put had brought a flock of sheep to help Boston's distressed and had put up at Warren's house. Putnam spread the alarm farther, for he was told that Boston had been bombarded and six patriots had been killed as they were robbed of their gunpowder. He headed for Cambridge.

Putnam's letter beseeching help was printed and the next day, Sunday, was read in most Connecticut churches, and an estimated 20,000 men with arms started marching for Cambridge from town after town.

An express sent by Putnam reached New York on Sept. 5. The report was, "We were shocked with an alarm that Gen. Gage had robbed the magazine of the powder ... and six men killed. ... It is said above ... 50,000 men were in motion for the relief of Boston. ..."

Putnam's express reached Philadelphia on Sept. 6.

The Continental Congress, originally called for Sept. 1, had not got going until Sept. 5. It was 2 p.m. the next day, wrote Robert Treat Paine, that Putnam's express arrived and "we were informed that the soldiers had fired on the people and town at Boston. This news occasioned the Congress to adjourn to 8 p.m. The city of Philadelphia in great concern; bells muffled rang all p.m.

"Shocked John Adams wrote to Abigail:

"Every gentleman seems to consider the bombardment of Boston as the bombardment of the capitol of his own province. Our deliberations are grave and serious indeed."

Contradiction of the rumor reached Philadelphia two days later. The horrid news, as John Adams called it, "made us miserable for two days, 'War! War! War!' was the cry." A relieved Adams could now write in his diary:

"The happy news was brought us, from Boston, that no blood had been spilled, but that Gen. Gage had taken away the provincial powder from the magazine.... This last was a disagreeable circumstance."

As the commotion subsided, Paul Revere wrote to his friend, John Lamb, leader in New York:

"The spirit of liberty was never higher than at present; the troops have the horrors amazingly. ..."

The powder alarm had shown Bostonians they would have help.

Warren judged that the province now felt that "the cord by which they were bound to the King of Britain has been by his act, cut in sunder." Of Gage's troops, Warren said exultantly:

"Had the troops marched only five miles out of Boston, I doubt whether a man would have been saved of their whole number."

Colonies acclaim Suffolk Resolves

Before he took off for the First Continental Congress, Samuel Adams discussed county meetings with Joseph Warren. Adams's purpose, just as when he staged the grand public meeting in the Old South Meetinghouse prior to the Boston Tea Party, was to make clear to all the world why the patriots were opposed to the Intolerable Acts.

Warren, a tireless letter writer, would keep Adams steadily informed on how the patriot cause was faring in Boston.

Disturbing word about Parliament's intention had been trickling across the Atlantic to Boston even before the King signed the crucial act for "better regulating" Massachusetts on May 20. (The patriots called it the "Regulatory Acts.") In the slow fashion that news traveled in those days, Gage did not receive official notice until Aug. 6. By then the patriots regarded the act as a move to destroy their charter.

A pioneer county convention was called by patriots in Berkshire County, at Stockbridge, on July 6, before the terms of the Regulatory Act were precisely known, and the 60 delegates denounced Parliament's drive to take away liberties granted by the old William and Mary charter.

It was not until August, though, that the succession of county meetings from Berkshire to Plymouth, and Bristol to Cumberland in present Maine, got under way, reaching a peak of international significance in the Suffolk Resolves.

Worcester led the way. Delegates from 20 Worcester County towns met on Aug. 9 in the home of an innkeeper, Mary Sternes, and drafted a set of resolutions "to oppose the torrent of tyranny rushing upon us." The delegates declared that Parliament's attempt to kill their charter dissolved the union with Great Britain. To save themselves and their posterity from "inevitable ruin," they urged all towns to "prevent the execution of these most alarming acts of Parliament."

Worcester, promoting unity, suggested to the Boston Committee of Correspondence (and these were the days when these local committees were,

in effect, running the province's towns) that it determine a plan of action for the entire colony.

The patriots had already been conferring. Five days after Adams's departure, the Boston Committee of Correspondence named Warren to head a delegation to a convention of Suffolk County, which then included a far greater part of eastern Massachusetts. This gathering assembled on Aug. 16 at Col. Tom Doty's tavern in Stoughton, but because some towns had not received timely notice to elect delegates, a later meeting was set for Sept. 6 at Richard Woodward's inn at Dedham.

Meantime Warren wrote to Adams, "I shall take care to follow your advice respecting the county meetings, which, depend upon it. will have very important consequences.

"The spirits of our friends rise every day; and we seem animated by the proofs, which every day appear, of the villainous designs of our enemies, which justify us in all we have done to oppose them hitherto, and in all that we can do in the future."

Faneuil Hall was the setting on Aug. 26 for the coordinating session that had been urged by Worcester. Delegates from Worcester, Middlesex, Essex and Suffolk took part, and here, in private, the patriots devised what all the counties should do. Next day the wisdom of their fateful gathering was expressed in resolutions. The preamble language was strong.

Parliament had acted "without the least color of right or justice...." This action constituted "a complete system of tyranny.

"Persons are appointed to fill certain offices of government in ways and under influences wholly unknown before in this province....

"No power on earth has a right without the consent of this province, to alter the minutest tittle of its charter...."

So the patriots advised all counties that:

—A provincial congress was necessary to counteract despotism, and counties would act "wisely by choosing members as soon as may be...."

—Every illegally named officer be opposed "as a traitor cloaked with a pretext of law."

—"The military art ... ought attentively to be practised by the people of this province as a necessary means to secure their liberties...."

This program of action would be ratified in open county meetings that followed — Middlesex at Concord on Aug. 30, Worcester at Worcester on Aug. 30, Essex at Ipswich on Sept. 6, Suffolk at Milton on Sept. 9 and, still later in the month, the county conventions in Cumberland, Hampshire, Plymouth and Bristol

A provincial congress was to be the patriots' principal response to Parliament.

They seem to have agreed well in advance upon a date for creating their congress. For on Aug. 30, when the 130 delegates gathered in the Worcester County courthouse and the 150 Middlesex County delegates gathered at Concord, they both picked Oct. 11 — the actual date that the congress would eventually meet for the first time at Concord.

The spirit of the resolutions adopted in county conventions breathes indignation and defiance.

Little wonder! The men participating — in many cases the leaders of the conventions — included individuals who had already shared the risks of the Boston Tea Party. They were men who would respond to the Lexington Alarm, some would suffer wounds, some would die that day and some would face the redcoats at Bunker Hill and give their lives. Their conviction of purpose was boundless.

Most flaming of the language was in the Suffolk Resolves.

These were in the words of Warren, a shining figure in our galaxy of early patriots. He was closest of all to the father of our Revolution, would be in effect the patriot governor of the province and would die a hero on the battlefield of Bunker Hill.

We know Warren's mood as he approached writing the resolves. In one of his letters to Samuel Adams, Warren pictured the colony's plight:

"You will, I am sure, consider the great difference that there is between this and the other colonies.

"Their commerce glides in its usual channels.

"Their charters have not yet been torn to pieces by the harpies of power.

"They retain their usual forms of trials by juries, in courts duly constituted.

"What is left for us? If we acquiesce but for an hour, the shackles will be fixed forever.

"Our all is at stake. We must give up our rights, and boast no more of freedom, or we must oppose immediately."

Gage felt the drift of events. The powder alarm and now the county conventions alarmed him. The worried general, who had lightly brought a military force to punish Boston, now sat in Boston, to which he had withdrawn that force, ironically busying himself on finding ways to protect those very soldiers. He decided to strengthen the fortifications on Boston Neck, then a narrow isthmus and the only land approach to Boston.

The Boston selectmen went to Gage to protest. He assured them that he had no hostile intentions against the people, and went right on with the fortification. This was on Sept. 5, 1774. Next day, the Suffolk convention reconvened in Dedham. Warren and a committee were chosen to prepare resolutions, and the convention adjourned to meet on Sept. 9 at the house (still standing) of Daniel Vose in Milton.

The final stage for the Suffolk Resolves was now set. A patriot from Braintree, Joseph Palmer, would preside. Palmer was a provincial leader, businessman and philanthropist. His son took part in the Boston Tea Party. Palmer would play a key role in bringing the Provincial Congress into life and would serve on the all-important Committee of Safety in the Lexington Alarm and in the patriots' fortifying of Bunker Hill.

Warren's inspired, exciting prose shines in memorable phrases in the preamble. Among them:

"On the fortitude, on the wisdom, and on the exertions of this important day, is suspended the fate of this new world, and of unborn millions."

The phrasing of the resolutions was so hard-hitting it made ultraconservatives consider it a manifesto of rebellion.

Boston Athenaeum, Boston, Mass.

Joseph Palmer

Like the county gatherings of Worcester and Middlesex, Suffolk, too, called for a provincial congress to meet on Oct. 11. Four of the resolutions were mortal blows to Gage's government.

Local tax collectors were told to withhold public monies from the royal provincial treasurer until there was a legal civil government. Gage was warned that his plans to arrest patriot leaders would result in the patriots' taking hostage "every servant of the present tyrannical and unconstitutional government...."

A patriot militia was to be established, by each town electing new militia officers, thus tossing out any Tories still holding military commissions. Immediate training in the art of war was urged to confound enemies who "have flattered themselves that they shall make an easy prey of this numerous, brave and hardy people."

The final resolution, one based on the experience gained in the powder alarm and looking prophetically forward to the Lexington Alarm, instructed members of the Committee of Correspondence or selectmen to dispatch couriers to neighboring towns for aid "should our enemies, by any sudden maneuvers, render it necessary to ask aid and assistance of our brethren in the country...."

Further, towns receiving these appeals "shall dispatch others to committees more remote, until proper and sufficient assistance be obtained...."

This in total was the prescription of the Suffolk Resolves for combatting "attempts of a wicked administration to enslave America."

Warren was named head of a committee of 15 to go directly to Gage with an address protesting the fortification on Boston Neck and its arming with cannon he had removed from the Common. The heart of the address to Gage was:

"The people of this county are by no means disposed to injure His Majesty's troops; they think themselves aggrieved and oppressed by the late acts of Parliament, and are resolved, by Divine assistance, never to submit to them, but have no inclination to commence a war with His Majesty's troops...."

Gage hedged about receiving the address. He proposed he be shown a copy of it "in a private way." This was on Friday. When the patriots assented and gave him a copy, Gage set the following Monday at noon to receive Warren and the committee.

Meantime, on Sunday, Warren sent for his North End neighbor and friend Paul Revere, and sent him galloping to Philadelphia with the Suffolk Resolves, another Revere mission associated with momentous events.

On Monday, Warren and the patriots appeared at Province House. Gage was at first at his diplomatic best.

"Good God, gentlemen," said Gage, "make yourselves easy, and I will do so. You have done all in your power to convince the world and me that you will not submit to the Acts, and I'll make representation home accordingly, for which I will embrace the earliest opportunity."

Beneath smiles both sides were engaged in grave maneuvering. Gage had some questions.

"I would ask, what occasion there is for such numbers going armed in and out of town, and through the country, in a hostile manner? Or, why were the guns removed, privately, in the night, from the battery at Charlestown?"

Warren declared:

"That no person had, so far as he had been informed, taken any steps which indicate any hostile intention, until the seizing and carrying off the powder from the magazine in the county of Middlesex. . . ."

After Warren and the committee left, they decided that Gage's written reply was not satisfactory. Twice Warren went back to Province House and handed the colonial secretary, Thomas Flucker, a further address expressing their concern. Gage twice declined to meet again with Warren, saying that he had "given all satisfaction in his power."

In a move of high statesmanship, Gage did write to London and suggest that the Coercive Acts be suspended. His suggestion was something of a shocker, for the obtuse ministers of George III had no conception of the way the crisis was spreading and intensifying. Instead, Gage's sage proposal was the beginning of his downfall at Whitehall.

Revere, in the spectacular speed of only five days, delivered the Suffolk Resolves to the Continental Congress on Sept. 16.

The distress and the courage of the Bay Colony people portrayed in Warren's eloquence deeply moved the members of the Congress, which was still in its early cautious, conservative, conciliatory period so distressful to the more ardent members such as the Adamses. John Adams looked around the chamber:

"I saw the tears gush into the eyes of the old, grave, pacific Quakers of Pennsylvania.

"The esteem, affection, the admiration for the people of Boston and Massachusetts which were expressed, and the fixed determination that they should be supported, were enough to melt a heart of stone."

Samuel Adams, whose master hand almost visibly produced the outpouring of the county resolutions, spotted immediately the far-reaching import of the action of the Continental Congress when it voted approval of the Suffolk Resolves on Sept. 17.

"I think I may assure you," he wrote, "that America will make a point of supporting Boston to the utmost."

All the colonies would hang together. Massachusetts would have national support in its ordeal.

Revere sped back to Boston with this news to Warren and to the anxious Bay Province.

Patriots create own government

Gage, back on Sept. 1, had routinely issued precepts for the Great and General Court to assemble at Salem on Oct. 5.

As the days passed he became aware from the resolutions of the county conventions that there would be nothing ahead for him in such a meeting but trouble. About him in Boston his imperial government seemed to be toppling. His fortification of Boston Neck had further aggravated his difficulties with the people.

The disease, as Gage called the patriots' resistance, might some time ago have been confined to Boston and been eradicated there with ease. "But now," he imparted plaintively to Dartmouth, "it is so universal ... there is no knowing where to apply a remedy."

Warren gleefully wrote to Adams of the people's retaliating against the soldiers for treating them "as enemies rather than as fellow subjects." A load of straw was headed into Boston for the troops. "The high sons of Roxbury gave it to the flames," wrote Warren.

Citing something far more irritating to Gage, Warren said that late in September "about 200 carpenters were employed the last week in providing barracks for the troops. This week the works are entirely forsaken." Gage tried to make a deal with John Hancock to get the barracks built. Hancock refused, so Gage sent off to the British base in Halifax for workmen.

On Sept. 28, Gage made a vital play for time. Beneath the awesome embellishment of the royal arms he issued a proclamation canceling his call for the Great and General Court to meet him in Salem. It was highly inexpedient, he explained, in the "present disordered and unhappy state of the province." He would not be in Salem on Oct. 5 and, in effect, told all newly elected representatives to stay away.

The patriots were not to be deterred. Boston and town after town, carrying out the goal of the Faneuil Hall meeting, had handed their newly chosen representatives instructions to vote to create a provincial congress. This was far indeed from what Gage had in mind when he had initiated the precepts for the elections.

Thus on Oct. 5, 90 representatives resolutely gathered in the large first-floor courtroom of Salem's Town House, a dignified chamber with the royal arms of George III high on the wall. Other customary regal refinements were missing, no one to swear them in, no royal governor. The delegates went through the appearance of awaiting Gage.

There was unexpected excitement.

At 3 a.m. the next day a fire erupted in a warehouse and consumed two dozen buildings in the center of Salem, scorching and blistering the paint of the town house.

The representatives, though, had greater things to talk about. Warren, in the days before the meeting, had been seeking advice from Adams on a weighty question. Some counties felt that the killing of the charter by Parliament had broken the bond with the King and that the delegates should create an entirely new form of government. Other counties felt it would be best to resume the old charter. What to do?

Adams wrote back to Warren that unity was fundamental. Adams feared that any new form of government would not sit well with the middle and southern colonies. So Warren could use this free time in Salem politicking on behalf of the revered old charter of William and Mary.

On Thursday the delegates, gladly giving up on Gage, elected John Hancock their presiding officer and appointed Benjamin Lincoln clerk.

By Friday, Oct. 7, the delegates were ready to carry out their foremost instruction.

Gage's proclamation, they declared, was "unconstitutional, unjust and disrespectful to the province." The people were under "just apprehensions of slavery" with Gage's military superceding constitutional government and they must act to preserve their freedom. They thereupon voted to "resolve themselves into a Provincial Congress" and adjourned to meet in the courthouse at Concord on Oct. 11.

The old courthouse in Concord's main square was too small when the delegates assembled that morning. Instead of 90 representatives, there were now 288. Over the weekend, delegates

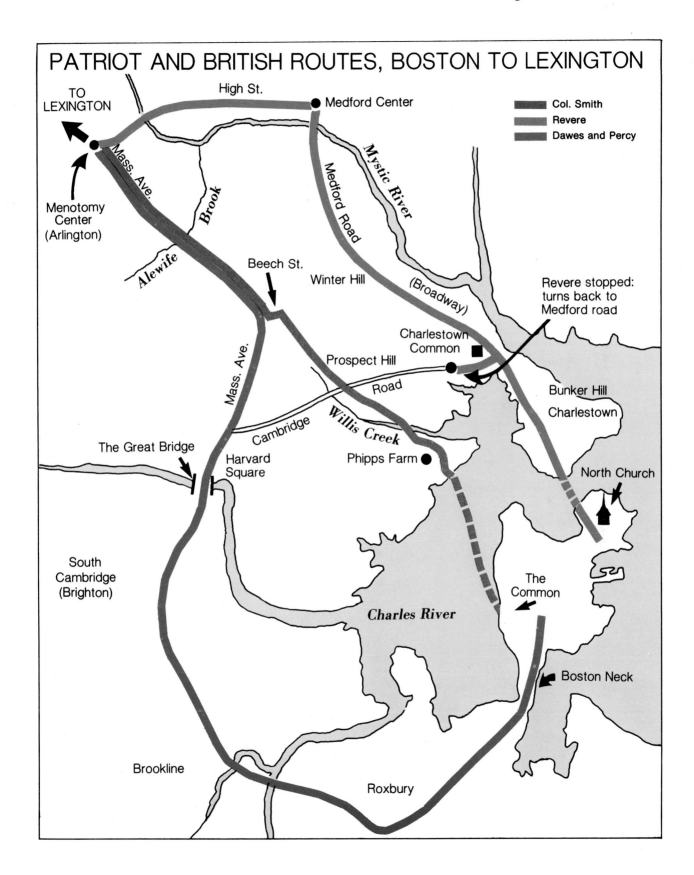

PATRIOT AND BRITISH ROUTES, BOSTON TO LEXINGTON

TO LEXINGTON

High St.

Medford Center

Col. Smith
Revere
Dawes and Percy

Mystic River

Mass. Ave.

Brook

Medford Road

Menotomy Center (Arlington)

Alewife

Beech St.

Winter Hill

(Broadway)

Revere stopped: turns back to Medford road

Charlestown Common

Mass. Ave.

Prospect Hill

Road

Bunker Hill

Charlestown

Cambridge

Willis Creek

The Great Bridge

Harvard Square

Phipps Farm

North Church

South Cambridge (Brighton)

Charles River

The Common

Boston Neck

Brookline

Roxbury

Foot of the Common and Back Bay where Smith's expedition entered boats to cross to Cambridge

Col. Leslie agrees to token march at North Bridge, Salem

John Hancock

Independence National Historic Park, Philadelphia, Pa.

Cary Memorial Library,
Lexington, Mass.

Brig. Gen. Hugh Percy

Cary Memorial Library,
Lexington, Mass.

William Dawes Jr.

The Hancock-Clarke house in Lexington

William Ryerson, Boston Globe

Adams National Historic Site,
Quincy, Mass.

Dr. Joseph Warren

The battle scene at North Bridge in Doolittle 1775 print

Capt. Isaac Davis, with his minuteman company, leaves from Acton

John Singleton Copley
(Collection of Mr. and Mrs. Paul Mellon)

Gen. Thomas Gage

National Army Museum,
London, England

Lt. Col. Francis Smith

Lexington Historical Society,
Lexington, Mass.

Maj. John Pitcairn

William Ryerson, Boston Globe

*Powder House on Quarry Hill,
Somerville, Mass.*

Museum of Fine Arts, Boston, Mass.

Paul Revere

William Ryerson, Boston Globe

Minuteman statue faces British approach route outside Buckman Tavern in Lexington

"The Dawn of Liberty" on Lexington Green, painting by Henry Sandham

Redcoats on retreat from Concord

had been arriving from all the towns to attend this historic first session of the people's own government. They shifted the few paces to the much bigger meetinghouse.

There, with speed equal to the emergency distressing them, they put self-government back in action.

We do not have the words they spoke; only a few of their faces are known. But we do know that here were men of heroic stature: John Hancock, who would be the first to sign the Declaration of Independence; Artemas Ward, who would command our first army; Benjamin Lincoln, who would at Yorktown receive the sword of defeated Lord Cornwallis; men who would serve in highest state and national offices, men who would be leaders in the arts of peace, men who would fight, bleed and die in our nation's earliest battles.

Boston Public Library,
Boston, Mass.

British political cartoon "Gage Unhorsed"

The patriotic Concord minister, Rev. William Emerson, who would give his life in the coming struggle, was chosen as chaplain and led the prayer.

The delegates formally implored Gage to remove the fortress at the entrance of Boston. "It is with the utmost concern," they told him, that "we see your hostile preparations, which have spread such alarm throughout this province and the whole continent, as threatens to involve us in all the confusion and horrors of a civil war. . . .

"The rigorous execution of the Port Bill, with increased severity, must eventually reduce the capital and its numerous dependencies to a state of poverty and ruin.

"The acts for altering the charter and the administration of justice in the colony, are manifestly designed to abridge this people of their rights, and to license murders; and, if carried into execution, will reduce them to a state of slavery. . . ."

After four days in Concord, the delegates adjourned to the courthouse in Cambridge on Monday, Oct. 17. They promptly shifted to the larger meetinghouse. It was in this building, during the ensuing 12 days, that the delegates, working day and night except Sunday, put together the framework of civil government and of a military body for its defense.

Henry Gardner of Stow, a delegate, was named receiver general, and all taxgatherers were told to send public monies to him instead of the royal treasurer, Harrison Gray, a Tory who had declared that the Tea Party perpetrators should burn in hell.

All remaining Mandamus Councilors (the count was now down from 36 to 15, confined to Boston) were given 10 days to quit.

The delegates received word from Gage that what they were calling a fortress "unless annoyed, will annoy nobody." They responded by telling off Gage. The honor of British troops, they said, "is sullied by the infamous errand on which they were sent to America." They pointedly reminded Gage, who had kept calling the law on them:

"You must know that barely keeping a

standing army in the province, in time of peace, without the consent of the representatives, is against the law . . . a grievance which this people could not, with due regard to their freedom, endure, was there not reason to hope that His Majesty, upon being undeceived, would order redress."

Gage had been perfectly right when he had sent word to Dartmouth, by his packet ship *Scarborough,* that "civil government is near its end."

Former Royal Gov. Thomas Hutchinson, in exile in England and writing his history of the colony, pinpointed the reason for the collapse:

"The people, by their own authority, formed a legislative body and from that time all pacific measures for restoring their former dependence upon the supreme authority of the British dominions, were in vain and to no purpose."

The Continental Congress on Oct. 8 voted its support:

"This Congress approve the opposition of the inhabitants of the Massachusetts Bay to the execution of the late acts of Parliament; and if the same shall be attempted to be carried into execution by force, in such case all America ought to support them in their opposition."

Gage's suggestion of suspending the acts would reach King George III, and His Majesty would pronounce the advice "the most absurd that can be suggested. . . ."

Concord Free Library,
Concord, Mass.

Rev. William Emerson

As for the colonies, George III felt:

"We must either master them or totally leave them to themselves and treat them as aliens. . . ."

The patriots did not yet know that there was no hope of any royal redress.

Minutemen enlisted to defend people's rights

Minutemen!

In the annals of American gallantry no title stands higher.

Yet minutemen, though covered with military glamour, had but a brief role in our history. They were a people's army, an impromptu force, the spearhead of our Revolutionary War.

They came together for just one campaign, the opening one. Though they would continue to furnish leaders throughout the war, they soon would be blended into a more regular military force that was formed during the siege of Boston.

Minutemen had their birth — but not yet their name — during the same, first, 12-day session of our first Provincial Congress at Cambridge that recreated civil government. Once again we do not have the speeches or debate, but the minutes underscore the anxiety that underlay the long hours of seeking a secure defense.

All was caution. Still, right in the innermost counsel of the Congress there was a man, a respected doctor, who would be revealed months later as an informer passing on inside information to Gage.

Before there was any debate at all, the order was given that the "galleries be now cleared and the doors of the house be kept shut during the debates. . . ." Intermittently, in the coming days, the minutes would record precautionary resolves: "Keep all debate secret" or "enjoining secrecy" or that any talk about military supplies be done "with the greatest secrecy."

The profound fear of the delegates was that Gage, by his powder and cannon seizures, was making extreme efforts "to place the province entirely in a defenseless state."

Col. William Heath of Roxbury, who would become the only general officer on the battlefield at the Lexington Alarm, was named head of a committee of five military men to report on the state of the province's armed forces. This was on Wednesday, Oct. 19. Next day, a committee of 13, chosen by county, dug into the problem of the province's safety.

This earnest defense study and debate continued day and night Friday and Saturday. Late on Saturday they seemed to think they had a plan, then it was recommitted; and all day the next Monday the debate continued. That day the Congress named Col. Jeremiah Lee of Marblehead and a committee to advise on when to procure powder, ordnance and ordnance stores. The committee sat forthwith and reported right back: "Now!" Warren and more military men were quickly added to this committee to report directly on quantities and costs. Other defense committees were expanded, too.

By Wednesday, Oct. 26, a plan was ready. It was delegated, it was amended and it was read and voted on, paragraph by paragraph.

It was in these paragraphs on the militia that the minutemen were born. One paragraph instructed militia companies that had not already done so to meet and elect their officers to take command of companies; then these officers were to meet and elect field officers. Next came these words:

"Field officers so elected, forthwith endeavor to enlist one quarter at least of the number of the respective companies and form them into companies of 50 privates at the least, who shall equip and hold themselves in readiness to march at the shortest notice. . . ."

Selectmen of the towns were to provide a full stock of arms and ammunition "without delay" where needed, and the men were to train and perfect themselves in military skill because "the security of the lives, liberties, and properties of the inhabitants of this province, depends, under Providence, in their knowledge and skills in the art military. . . ."

Oct. 27 was a day of notable decisions. The Congress named Hancock and Warren to head a committee of nine, later increased to 11, as a quick-action, executive committee for the province. It was called the Committee of Safety, and was to be in charge of about everything — organizing and ordering the militia, meeting emergencies, supervising supplies, making recommendations to Congress.

Safety's Siamese twin committee was to be the Committee of Supplies.

Senior military officers, all veterans of the French and Indian Wars, were chosen. Chief command went to Jedediah Preble of Maine; second in command, Artemas Ward of Shrewsbury; third in command, Seth Pomeroy of Northampton. Later the Congress would add Col. John Thomas, a doctor of Kingston, and Col. William Heath. Ward would take top command when brave old Preble, close to 70 and ailing from gout, had to decline.

How did the minutemen get their name?

A sturdy patriot of Worcester County, Col. William Henshaw of Leicester, on Nov. 24 petitioned a late session of this Congress for permission to have his minutemen use the improved Norfolk exercises instead of the old 1764 discipline established for His Majesty's troops. Here was the first use of "minutemen," doubtlessly confirming usage already in effect among the men.

First official use by the Provincial Congress came in a Dec. 10 address to the people:

"We now think that particular care should be taken by towns and districts in this colony, that each of the minutemen, not already provided therewith, should be immediately equipped with an effective firearm, bayonet, pouch, knapsack, 30 rounds of cartridges and balls, and that they be disciplined three times a week, and oftener, as opportunity may offer...."

Gen. Gage was asked officially by the Continental Congress about his fortifying Boston Neck. He wrote to Philadelphia that he was merely doing his duty in view of hostile preparations by the people and that he hoped the dispute would end like "the quarrel of lovers" with an increased affection "they ought to bear each other."

Things just were not that way. There was now a desperate race, with each side striving to gather strength.

Gage had not been able to augment by much his original four regiments. After the powder alarm and the surprising outpouring of patriots, Gage did bring Gen. Frederick Haldimand, his second in command, and some troops from New York and Halifax, but Gage's Oct. 30 suggestion to Dartmouth that he could use 20,000 men had

already been vetoed by Dartmouth, who had written Gage that the approach of winter meant transports "must be postponed until spring."

British officers spiked cannon to keep them from the patriots. The patriots, among them William Dawes Jr. and some Tea Party men, snatched two cannon right from the Common, carted them, beneath manure, over Boston Neck and christened them the "Hancock" and "Adams." Men drilled on the town greens. Women made cartridges. Village anvils turned out swords.

The Committee of Safety set to work building caches of arms and stores in Worcester and Concord.

King George III's ministers well knew the drastic intent of their action when His Majesty on Oct. 19 signed an Order in Council banning the export of arms and ammunition from Great Britain.

Britain had long been the supplier of these necessities to the colonies — indeed, had used restrictive mercantile laws to protect the British monopoly.

Word of the King's deed was sped to Gage and all the royal governors on *HMS Scarborough,* which arrived in Boston harbor on Dec. 3. The news reached the Bay Province's patriots, however, by way of Rhode Island, where the patriot-dominated General Assembly on Dec. 5 sent the Provincial Congress a copy of Dartmouth's letters and of the Order in Council.

That same day the Rhode Island Assembly, to outwit its Tory-minded Gov. Joseph Wanton and the Tories of Newport, directed Col. Joseph Nightingale to remove from Newport to Providence all but a token amount of cannon, powder, shot and stores at Fort George overlooking Newport harbor.

To the dismay of Newport Tories, or their "exceeding wroth," as patriot diarist Rev. Ezra Stiles phrased it, Col. Nightingale accomplished his mission over a three-day period, Dec. 8-10, with a small fleet of Providence packets. Stiles noted with joy that Gage's man-o'-war *HMS Rose* arrived on Dec. 11, Sunday morning, "just after the vessel with the last guns sailed for Providence."

In Boston, Warren's Committee of Correspondence got word of Rhode Island's success and had been alerted that troops in Boston were being put aboard Gage's transports. Outside of Boston, already in Gage's hands, and the powder at Newport, the only other royal magazine on the New England coast was Fort William and Mary in the harbor of Portsmouth, N.H.

Paul Revere was dispatched there, maneuvering a pass to get out of Boston, then speeding as best he could along the ice- and snow-covered highway so that he reached Portsmouth on the afternoon of Dec. 13. He went to the residence of prosperous patriot merchant Samuel Cutts, head of the Portsmouth Committee of Correspondence. Revere brought word that Gage was sending a force to strengthen the garrison at Fort William and Mary and news of the King's ban on arms and of Rhode Island's coup.

Cutts quickly gathered other members of the local committee and, after conferring, they resolved to raid the fort the next day. New Hampshire's Royal Gov. John Wentworth, sensing trouble, sent word to the fort's commander, Capt. John Cochran, to be on his guard.

At noon next day, Dec. 14, the Sons of Liberty marched through Portsmouth with fife and drum, and 200 eager volunteers joined them. Gov. Wentworth sent his august chief justice to the town square to warn them against rebellion and to tell them to disperse. There was no stopping them. They boarded boats and scows at the waterfront, went the two miles across the harbor to the fort and were joined there by 200 more New Castle patriots.

Cochran said they all reached the fort at 3 p.m. He warned them not to enter at their peril. Cochran recalled to Wentworth:

"They replied they would. I immediately ordered three four-pounders to be fired on them, and then small arms; and before we could be ready to fire again, we were stopped on all quarters."

Cochran and his ineffectual corporal's guard of five men were secured and bound, with the patriots giving three huzzas and hauling down the King's colors. Cochran bravely refused to turn over any keys, so the patriots, with axes and crowbars, opened the magazine and removed roughly 100 barrels of gunpowder, leaving a single barrel. In an hour and a half, they had these on gondolas — local shallow draft sloops — and on their way inland to Durham for concealment and dispersion.

A Portsmouth leader in the raid, wealthy merchant Capt. John Langdon, sent word to the Durham leader, Maj. John Sullivan (both future governors), that there was a rumor that Gage was sending warships. Sullivan decided he better get more munitions from the fort. He gathered patriots of his area and headed for Portsmouth as Wentworth was writing to Gage about Revere's doings and the threat of more "outrage" unless Gage sent aid.

Next night, Sullivan and his 70 followers went to the fort and removed 16 cannon, a variety of cannon shot and 60 muskets. The weather had turned bitter cold and ice formed on the Oyster River leading to Durham, so the haul was delayed. To protect it, Col. Nathan Folsom and the men of Exeter came the next day, Dec. 16, to Portsmouth and left peacefully when the munitions were en route.

In later life Sullivan, then a general, recounted how the river "was froze far down and we were about two days in sawing the ice and getting up the boats." Legend tells us that some of the gunpowder was hidden beneath the pulpit in the meetinghouse next to Sullivan's house, still standing by the river, and that the gunpowder filled patriot muskets during the siege of Boston. Wentworth wrote a chagrined letter to Gage to describe how he had drums beat to summon militia to help Cochran hold the fort. None would serve. He confessed he could not raise a dozen men including all around him:

"It was impossible for me, with four Councilors, two justices, one sheriff, Mr. Macdonough and Benning Wentworth, to subdue such multitudes, for not one other man would come forth." Quite an eloquent sidelight of Tory support!

British orators plead to prevent war

The new Parliament, George III's 15th, the one that would split the American colonies from the British empire, assembled at Westminster to hear the King's speech from the throne.

The Tory majority in the Parliament had been sharply increased by a political maneuver. The Boston Tea Party had even convinced some staunch friends of the colonies that some punishment should be imposed. On what seemed this wave of approval, Lord North had abruptly called a general election. The gain in Tory seats delighted both him and his master, the King.

North felt he could now pursue his policy of "unconditional submission."

The King's speech put it into words:

"You may depend on my firm and steadfast resolution to withstand every attempt to weaken or impair the supreme authority of this legislature over all the dominions of my crown. . . ."

Lord Camden, in a rare protest against a royal address, got nine of the Lords to join in a signed request for information on the damage of the Coercive Acts before plunging the empire "into all the calamities of a civil war."

The greatest British statesman of that era, William Pitt, the Earl of Chatham, told the House of Lords that North's election maneuver had won by misrepresentation. British voters had been told it was merely a faction in Boston which was opposed to lawful government.

"But now, my lords," Chatham warned, "we find that instead of suppressing the opposition of the faction at Boston, these measures have spread it over the whole continent. They have united the whole people, by the most indissoluble of all bonds—intolerable wrongs."

Just before Christmas, the King was offered the conciliatory address that the First Continental Congress had voted and sent across the Atlantic. The King declined to look at it. He busied himself thinking up ways to get action from Gage and was calling Gage his "mild general."

The King fancied that he had a splendid solution. He would send Lord Jeffrey Amherst, victor in the last French and Indian War, to re-place Gage. Amherst refused. Amherst would not fight against the men who had helped him win his victories. The King, in his own handwriting, has left lists of other generals he considered, among them three major generals he would eventually send to bolster Gage.

North meanwhile perfected his plans to have the new Parliament confirm the Coercive Acts by declaring Massachusetts in rebellion and by shutting the North Atlantic fisheries, their major source of livelihood, to Yankee fishermen. North also planned to assemble manpower he considered adequate to enforce his program.

North had a quite formidable obstacle to the parliamentary moves he now set in motion. The obstacle was the Earl of Chatham.

Chatham had invited Benjamin Franklin as a guest in the visitors' gallery. In it, too, was the brilliant young patriot Josiah Quincy Jr., already mortally ill, who had been sent to England by Samuel Adams to help Bostonians understand the severe, inexplicable reactions of the North ministry. Quincy, for his journal, took hasty notes of Chatham's words, for Chatham spoke extemporaneously, after the fashion of those times.

Franklin would say later that in Chatham's oratory he gratefully heard for once both "wisdom and eloquence" united.

It was Jan. 20, 1775.

Petition in hand, Chatham, who suffered tortures from gout, rose to speak. He had risen on a similar occasion 20 years back when the empire was faced with destruction in the era of Gen. Edward Braddock's defeat and reverses all around the globe during the French and Indian War. He had taken over then as prime minister, fought back at Minden, Quebec and in India, and won the French and Indian War.

But the King did not like Chatham's wisdom or greatness and wished "to be relieved of his superiority."

"A trumpet of sedition" was the King's phrase for Chatham.

Quincy wrote that Chatham "seemed like an old Roman senator, rising with the dignity of age, yet speaking with the fire of youth." Chatham's petition beseeched the King to order immediate withdrawal of Gage and the troops from Boston to open the way for a plan of concord, the only prescription to keep the empire intact.

"My lords," said Chatham, "I am happy that a relaxation of my infirmities permits me to seize this earliest opportunity of offering my poor advice to save this unhappy country, at this moment tottering to its ruin. But as I have not the honor of access to His Majesty, I will endeavor to transmit to him, through the constitutional channel of this House, my ideas on American business, to rescue him from the misadvice of his present ministers. . . .

"I wish, my lords, not to lose a day in this urgent, pressing crisis. An hour now lost in allaying the ferment in America, may produce years of calamity.

"The fate of this kingdom hangs upon the event of this controversy. . . .

"We ought to seize the first moment to open the door of reconciliation. It will soon be too late. . . .

"I know not who advised the present measures; I know not who advises to a perseverance and enforcement of them; but this I will say, that whoever advises them, ought to answer for it at his utmost peril. . . .

"But somebody had advised His Majesty to these measures, and if His Majesty continues to hear such evil counsellors, His Majesty will be undone. His Majesty may indeed wear his crown, but, the American jewel out of it, it will not be worth the wearing.

"What more shall I say? I must not say the King is betrayed; but this I will say, the nation is ruined. . . .

"In the last Parliament, all was anger—all was rage. Administration did not consider what was practicable, but what was revenge. . . . The ruin of the nation was a matter of no concern, if administration might be revenged.

"The Americans were abused, misrepresented, and traduced, in the most atrocious manner, in order to give a color, and urge on the most precipitate, unjust, cruel, and vindictive measures that ever disgraced a nation. . . ."

Like a great mosaic, Chatham's speech must be assembled piece by piece. There are many passages of it available from those who were present. They do not agree on the exact wording or the order. We do, though, have highlights, these among them:

"I contend not for indulgence, but for justice for America. . . .

"Let the sacredness of their property remain inviolate; let it be taxable only by their consent, given in their provincial assemblies, else it will cease to be property. . . ." Americans, said Chatham, were heirs, too, to British resistance to "arbitrary taxation" back to the days that cost King Charles I his head.

Gage, he said, was not to be blamed for leading an "army of impotence. . . . His tameness, however disgraceful, cannot be censured. . . . Woe to him who sheds the first, the unexpiable drop of blood in an impious war with a people contending in the great cause of public liberty.

"I tell you plainly, my lords, no son of mine, nor any one over whom I have influence, shall ever draw his sword upon his fellow subjects."

Chatham praised American behavior and the American Continental Congress. "They chose delegates by their free suffrages; no bribery, no corruption, no influence there, my lords. . . . They do not ask you to repeal your laws as a favor; they claim it as a right . . . they demand it. . . . I tell you, the acts must be repealed; they will be repealed; you cannot enforce them.

"The ministry are checkmated. . . . Repeal, therefore, my lords, I say. . . . We shall be forced ultimately to retract; let us retract whilst we can, not when we must. . . . I stake my reputation on it; I will consent to be taken for an idiot if they are not finally repealed."

Giving America's population, Chatham said, "My lords, there are three millions of Whigs; . . . three millions of Whigs, my lords, with arms in their hands, are a very formidable body. It was the Whigs, my lords, that set His Majesty's royal ancestors on the throne of England. . . .

"My lords, there is no time to be lost; every moment is big with dangers.

"Nay, while I am now speaking, the decisive blow may be struck, and millions involved in its consequences. The very first blood will be a wound that will not easily be skinned over. Years, perhaps ages, will not heal it."

How Chatham's words must have glittered to Quincy and to Franklin — and the common sense ring in their ears. Quincy wrote that the tales of ancient Greek and Roman orators working wonders in the Senate and in the field "no longer appear fabulous."

Yet it was of no avail. North's machine demolished Chatham's petition, 18 to 68. Twelve days later, on Feb. 1, when Chatham, with Franklin assisting him in the drafting, brought in a proposed act to settle the troubles with America, it was immediately beaten, 32 to 61.

Very next day North's motion for an address to the King declaring Massachusetts in rebellion was carried 2 to 1. The King and North saw to it that there was a "large attendance" of members when the speaker of the House of Commons came, with great pomp, to St. James's Palace on Feb. 9 to present the address on rebellion.

North speedily pushed through the rest of his program. On Feb. 10 he moved to close the fisheries to Americans. After July 20, offending vessels would be liable to search and seizure. Edmund Burke, once secretary of the ministry that repealed the odious Stamp Act, assailed the measure, saying this "scheme of Parliament was new and unheard of in any civilized nation, to preserve your authority by destroying your dominions."

Charles Fox, House leader of the Whigs, said the measure was meant for nothing but to exasperate the colonies into open and direct rebellion and "to give an opportunity for drawing the sword and throwing away the scabbard."

Widely remembered from this historic debate was what Lord Sandwich, lord of the Admiralty, had to say in belittling the Americans:

"Suppose the colonies do abound in men," sneered Sandwich, "what does that signify? They are raw, undisciplined, cowardly men.... Believe me, my lords, the very sound of a cannon would carry them off ... as fast as their feet would carry them."

Over in the House of Commons, Col. Isaac Barre, who had fought under Wolfe at Quebec, replied to the "Noble Lord at the head of the Admiralty. As to cowards — the very corps that broke the whole French column and threw them into such disorder at the siege of Quebec, were three parts composed of these cowards."

North's machine, well lubricated with patronage, power and cash, as Chatham had intimated, performed again, and the fisheries ban was voted. The machine performed still again when Edmund Burke, on March 22, made his great oration in the House of Commons in a desperate effort to bring conciliation. His words, like Chatham's, still ring gloriously in the cause of liberty:

"An Englishman is the unfittest person on earth to argue another Englishman into slavery.

"I do not know the method of drawing up an indictment against a whole people."

It was then already, as Chatham feared, too late.

By the timg Burke's speech was going westward across the Atlantic it would pass the news of the battles of Lexington and Concord en route to England.

Salem turns back redcoats

Gage, in his conflicting roles as enforcer and pacifier, was trying through the winter to use extreme caution. Yet it did not spare him from being led, as he confided to Dartmouth, "into a mistake."

To offer some show of authority despite government's being "so totally unhinged," Gage established the practice of sending detachments of his troops out of Boston for short marches into the neighboring communities.

Once Gage sent troops to the South Shore. The Tories of Marshfield in January requested troops. Gage embraced the appeal under the illusion that he was gaining inland support. He sent Capt. Nigel Balfour and 100 soldiers. Their presence further outraged the patriots, and Balfour and his men would flee the moment they got wind of the Lexington Alarm.

In February, Gage got information that impelled him to send a force — this time 200 men — to the North Shore.

An informer's secret letter to Gage gave details of the chain of command of the province's 15,000 minutemen — "the picked men," said the informer, "of the whole body of militia." It told how they were to be summoned by express riders, the number of their fieldpieces and how they were collecting military stores at Concord and Worcester. It also contained these words:

"There are eight fieldpieces in an old store, or barn, near the landing place at Salem; they are to be removed in a few days, the seizure of them would greatly disconcert their schemes."

Gage thought that these must be eight fine brass fieldpieces obtained from Holland or some other foreign place. So he made plans for a secret expedition. He would use 200 men of the 64th Regt. in barracks at Castle William — out of sight of Bostonians — and he picked Sunday, Feb. 26, for them to embark on their mission.

Boston patriots, warned that something was afoot, were on the alert. Paul Revere and friends rowed out to the Castle Saturday afternoon to watch. Under orders to the Castle to hold all visitors, Revere and friends were detained — as was the Castle's milkman, who happened to arrive that day. Revere would be making no repeat this time of his ride to Portsmouth.

Revere was forced instead to watch Col. Alexander Leslie as he shipped off with the 200 soldiers, for no visitors would be released until Leslie returned.

It was Sunday noontime when the transport arrived at Marblehead. The soldiers were kept below deck until after 2 p.m., when the townspeople would be gathered in their meetinghouse. Now the troops emerged, landed at Homan's Cove, loaded, affixed their bayonets and stepped off on the five-mile march to Salem.

The Marbleheaders moved, too, sending expresses to spread the alarm. Maj. John Pedrick, merchant and militiaman, mounted his horse and headed for Salem. Presently he came abreast the British soldiers and Col. Leslie. They were acquainted. Leslie, son of a Scottish Earl and an adviser to Gage, had spent some time in the area, for it was his men who had camped near Gage's Danvers residence while providing his bodyguard.

Leslie had his troops shift so Pedrick could pass. When out of sight, Pedrick resumed his gallop, sped into Salem's Town House Square and alarmed the Salem congregation listening to their young minister, Rev. Thomas Barnard Jr. The people poured into the street as bells began to ring and drumsticks to beat.

Most concerned was Col. David Mason, engineer, commissioned by the provincial leaders to assemble cannon. At the moment he was secretly mounting eight old cannon removed from a ship — not fine new brass cannon as Gage had been told. But all cannon were precious to the patriots. Mason and his young helpers hurried to cart the cannon across the North Bridge to a blacksmith shop on the road to Danvers.

A stablekeeper, Benjamin Daland, galloped express to Danvers to alarm the patriots there.

Leslie, on reaching Town House Square, ordered his men to halt outside Rev. Barnard's meetinghouse. Presently John Sargent, half-brother to the obnoxious Mandamus Councilor William Browne, made his way to Leslie and whispered in his ear. Leslie at once ordered his men forward in the direction Mason had taken with the cannon. But Leslie had to come quickly to a halt, for Mason had taken the precaution of raising the draw.

Leslie's temper turned taut. The draw must be lowered at once! No one obeyed. The townsmen's eyes were intent on Leslie's face. Why did he have to cross the bridge? Because, he fumed, he had orders and he would obey the orders if it cost him his life and the lives of others. He talked to one of his officers. It was talk of firing.

"Fire?" said John Felt to Leslie, "you'd better be damned than fire!" Felt, 50-year-old shipmaster and one of the proprietors of the drawbridge, had strode near Leslie from the meetinghouse to the bridge. Felt quickly added:

"You can have no right to fire without further orders. If you fire, you will all be dead men!"

Leslie knew Felt was telling the truth on the way the law stood. Leslie nodded to his officers, huddled and consulted while the townspeople cried out increasingly vehement taunts.

Leslie's eyes caught sight of two gondolas stranded by the ebb tide. He could ferry soldiers over! Felt watched Leslie's eyes and got the same message. Felt, owner of one of the gondolas, nudged some of his companions and they set to crashing the bottoms of the gondolas with axes. Leslie irately sent soldiers to stop the scuttling.

The redcoats ran to the gondolas, pushed the scuttlers with bayonets. Some, including Joseph Wicher, were pricked and shed blood. The effort of the redcoats was in vain anyway because the axed craft would no longer float.

At this juncture, Rev. Barnard, concerned for his flock, appealed to Leslie to restrain his men "from pushing their bayonets.

"He told me," recounted Barnard, "they were much insulted, and intimated his determination to pass over the bridge. . . ."

Leslie told one and all: "I'm on the King's highway and I won't be stopped."

Someone in the crowd called back:

"It is not the King's highway. It is a road built by the owners of the lots either side, and no King, country or town has anything to do with it."

The impasse had persisted for more than an hour. The February day grew colder; the sun dropped toward setting. Leslie asked Felt if he had authority to lower the draw. "No authority," responded Felt, "but there might be some influence."

Leslie, a brave, levelheaded man, appraised the situation. Col. Mason prodded with words from the top of a ladder slanted up the raised draw. Mason called down to Leslie that expresses had been sent into the country and soon there would be thousands of minutemen. Col. Timothy Pickering, who less than two weeks earlier had been voted command of Mandamus Councilor Browne's former regiment, had armed men on the way, too.

Rev. Barnard gathered Felt, Pickering and other patriots beside him as he got Leslie's pledge that if the draw were lowered the redcoats would not march above 30 rods.

Why 30 rods? Just another 15 rods farther would have brought Leslie's troops to the blacksmith shop where Mason had concealed the cannon.

The argument set, the draw was lowered. Leslie's troops, Pickering related, "passed over, marched a few rods, returned, and with great expedition went back again to Marblehead, where they embarked on board the transport without delay."

Leslie's withdrawal averted the eruption of war for nearly two more months. Just after Leslie had his column do an about-face, the minutemen of Danvers hove into sight. Other minutemen from other towns were moving along the highways, until released by messengers sent by Salem patriots.

A parting taunt was shouted from a window by Sarah Tarrant:

"Go home and tell your master he sent you on a fool's errand, and has broken the peace of our Sabbath. What! Do you think we were born in the woods to be frightened by owls?"

Warren risks life honoring massacre victims

Samuel Adams and Gen. Gage would have agreed on one thing as they approached the fifth anniversary date of the Boston Massacre on March 5, 1775.

Boston was a tinderbox.

Gen. Gage "was apprehensive of a riot" when he learned that the selectmen were planning a procession through the streets on the night of the traditional public oration. Gage sent for them and warned them to cancel the procession as it would most likely produce a disturbance. For double safety, Gage ordered all regiments to be ready to turn out at a moment's notice, and he strengthened the guards.

Angry reaction was fomented among the soldiery by the way in which the announcement of the oration was billed "to perpetuate the memory of the horrid massacre perpetrated on the evening of the Fifth of March, 1770, by a party of soldiers under the order and eye of Capt. Thomas Preston of the 29th Regiment. . . ." Rumor spread in the barracks that the orator would be killed. The troops took the very idea of the oration as a great insult.

British officers let it be known that they would be on hand to resent any slights or aspersions on the military. As for the people, one of the British officers who attended, Lt. Frederick Mackenzie, a meticulous fusilier, wrote in his diary:

"The townspeople certainly expected a riot, as almost every man had a short stick, or bludgeon, in his hand; and it was confidently asserted that many of them were privately armed." A violent oration, he wrote, could have induced the officers to give "the signal for battle. It is certain both sides were ripe for it, and a single blow would have occasioned the commencement of hostilities. Samuel Adams had identical feelings. In selecting Joseph Warren to deliver the oration, Adams observed that it was best to have someone experienced (Warren had previously delivered the Massacre oration in 1772) "as we may possibly be attacked in our trenches."

Tension was heightened by the event being put over to Monday, March 6, because the actual anniversary fell on a Sunday. No Samuel Adams touch was omitted. There would be a public collection for unlucky Christopher Monk, "a young man now languishing under a wound he received in his lungs, by a shot from Preston's butchering party of soldiers on the 5th of March, 1770."

The meeting — the now-customary "adjourned" town meeting — would start at Faneuil Hall and the gathering would move, Samuel Adams style, along the main Boston street to resume at 11:30 a.m. in the Old South Meetinghouse. The marchers would be quite visible to the colony's royal governor, Gage, whose residence, Province House, was diagonally across the street from the Old South.

Warren had sought the post of danger. He wanted one and all to know that the Yankees had "no want of courage." Like a Daniel in the lions' den, he would be in the very heart of a town garrisoned by his foes. The doors were opened early, and spectators filled the edifice to overflowing. Warren had to raise a ladder outside the window above the pulpit to make his entry.

Warren wore a toga, and Adams saw to it that the pulpit was draped appropriately in black.

Near Warren in the pulpit were other patriot leaders: moderator Samual Adams, John Hancock and the other selectmen, patriot clerk William Cooper. What a haul these men would have made for shipment to London and administration vengeance. The impatient King had already dispatched orders for their arrest, back in January during Parliament's debate on declaring Massachusetts in rebellion, but the orders would not arrive until April 16 — and then the leaders would be beyond the King's grasp.

Caustic Lt. John Barker of the King's Own Regiment, the 4th, imagined there would be a riot in the Old South that would be "fatal to Hancock, Adams, Warren, and the rest of those villains as they were all up in the pulpit together. . . ." He did not approve of such an exit from life for them; instead, he said, "I hope we shall have the pleasure before long of seeing them do it by the hands of the hangman."

As Warren was about to speak, Adams noticed about 40 British officers, all in their dazzling scarlet and gold, standing in the aisles. He asked some early-comers in the front pews to give the seats to the officers, and Gage's elite took the pews or sat on the stairs leading to the pulpit.

Warren's words were followed attentively. Some ill-suppressed groans from the military sprinkled occasional applause. Capt. Benjamin Chapman of the Royal Irish, the 18th Regt., did thrust out a handful of pistol bullets, but Warren, without pausing, neatly dropped a handkerchief so it covered the captain's hand.

Warren's flaming eloquence was far above mere pinprick jabs at the military. He spoke of how the nation grew, of the natural rights of mankind, of the rise of administration aggression against those rights, and of a result of this, the Boston Massacre and its horrors.

"Who spread this ruin 'round us? Was it the usual enemies?" he asked rhetorically.

"No: none of these. But how astonishing! It is the hand of Britain that inflicted the wound. The arms of George, our rightful King, have been employed to shed that blood which freely would have flown at his command when justice, or the honor of his crown, had called his subjects to the field."

Warren assailed the evil acts of Parliament with their intended destruction of ancient liberties.

"Our country is in danger, but not to be despaired of. Our enemies are numerous and powerful; but we have many friends, determined to be free, and heaven and earth will aid the resolution.

"On you depend the fortunes of America.

"You are to decide the important question on which rests the happiness and liberty of millions yet unborn. Act worthy of yourselves. . . .

"But, pardon me, my fellow citizens, I know you want not zeal or fortitude. You will maintain your rights, or perish in the generous struggle. However difficult the combat, you will never decline it when freedom is the prize.

"An independence of Great Britain is not our aim. No; our wish is, that Britain and the colonies may, like the oak and the ivy, grow and increase in strength together. But whilst the infatuated plan of making one part of the empire slaves to the other is persisted in, the interest and safety of Britain as well as the colonies require that the wise measures recommended by the honorable, the Continental Congress be steadily pursued. . . .

"But if these pacific measures are ineffectual, and it appears that the only way to safety is through fields of blood, I know you will not turn your faces from our foes, but will undauntedly press forward until tyranny is trodden under foot. . . ."

Commotion threatened when Adams moved to thank Warren for his "elegant and spirited oration." Some officers pounded their canes, some hissed, some stood and cried out "Fie! Fie!" A few spectators mistook this for a cry of "Fire!" and began jumping from the lower windows.

Just at that moment the troops of the 43rd Regt., with drums and fifes playing, returned from a short march into the countryside and halted for a few minutes opposite the meetinghouse. To show how notions spread, we have the word of Ens. Jeremy Lister of the 10th Regt., who was outside. When Lister saw people jumping from the windows, he fancied that the escapees feared that the troops of the 43rd Regt. were "going to fire into the church or at least take them all prisoners."

Emotions were soon brought under control, including those of a woman among the spectators, who was so upset by the behavior of an officer that she threatened to wring his nose. The assemblage had certainly attained its announced purpose of showing "the ruinous tendency of standing armies being placed in free and populous cities. . . ."

Gage plans to destroy arms

Those reports that Gen. Gage had been getting of patriot supplies and munitions accumulating at Worcester and Concord had increasingly occupied his mind. He felt he must do something about them.

He had written to Lord Barrington that matters must be brought to a conclusion "to determine on which side of the Atlantic the supremacy is to be fixed." He knew his promised reinforcements would arrive in the spring. Meanwhile, "to command the country," he had his troop detachments, with colors flying, increase their marching into the countryside.

He needed to do more. He must have exact information about the political thinking, especially the intentions, of the patriots. To accomplish this he used the King's gold and managed to get right inside the patriot council. He got his information secretly from the venal doctor, Benjamin Church Jr., unsuspected intimate of Samuel Adams, Hancock and Warren.

Church, son of a deacon, seemed to be living high, possibly beyond his means. Worse, from puritanical Samuel Adams's viewpoint, Church was an unfaithful husband with many mistresses. Just when Church found the King's gold irresistible remains a mystery, but by March Gage was writing to Dartmouth that he had obtained a very special source of intelligence, too important to identify in writing.

Church must have begun his two-faced role by then, for Paul Revere learned that all at once Church "had several hundred new British guineas." Revere added that he had never felt that Church was a man of principle, and Joseph Warren, too, "had not the greatest affection for him." Still, Church, tireless and able patriot writer, seemed a genuine Son of Liberty.

To obtain information on the terrain — roads, rivers, possible fords, heights, passes, open or wooded countryside — Gage could send out military spies. He issued a general order asking for officers "capable of taking sketches" of the country, made his choices and on Feb. 22 prepared detailed spying instructions for Capt. William Brown, 52nd Regt., and Ens. Henry deBerniere, 10th Regt.

They started out the very next day on an eight-day mission sketching as far inland as Worcester, catching exciting glimpses of the resolution of the patriots and experiencing hairbreadth escapes from citizens angered by their presence. They did try to disguise themselves as countrymen "in brown cloaths and reddish handkerchiefs round our necks," but it was all in vain.

A black woman in Brewer's Tavern, a patriot gathering place in Watertown, had seen Capt. Brown five years earlier in Boston and knew he was an officer. She brought them dinner, but eyed them attentively, and when they disarmingly remarked that it was a very fine country, she meaningfully replied:

"So it is, and we have got brave fellows to defend it." This so disconcerted the spies that they settled their bill quickly and hastened on to the Sign of the Golden Ball, a tavern in Weston run by Isaac Jones, "a friend to the government." The woman's alert spread fast that there were spies around.

Brown and deBerniere, helped by another Tory tavernkeeper also named Jones, sketched Worcester from its hills and headed back. Pausing Monday night at Buckminster's, a patriot tavern in Framingham, they looked out and saw minutemen assembled for training. It was 6 p.m.

DeBerniere wrote: ". . . The company of militia were exercising near the house, and an hour after, they came and performed their feats before the windows of the room we were in. We did not feel very easy at seeing such a number so very near us; however they did not know who we were, and took little or no notice of us.

"After they had done their exercise, one of the commanders spoke a very eloquent speech, recommending patience, coolness and bravery (which indeed they very much wanted), particularly told them they would always conquer if they did not break, and recommended them to charge us cooly, and wait for our fire, and everything would succeed with them. . . .

"After so learned and spirited an harangue, he dismissed the parade, and the whole company came into the house and drank until 9 o'clock, and they returned to their respective homes full of pot-valour."

Sneers at patriot valor were common in the British camp. They ill became the two spies. Next night, in the hospitable Weston tavern of Jones they were fearful enough to send Capt. Brown's sergeant back to Boston with their sketches, before backtracking next day to Marlboro. It was March 1, and snow poured down, a scene bitter and cold.

Marlboro's Tory squire, Henry Barnes, made them welcome in his mansion, spreading a fine meal. They were about to eat when a party of Marlboro liberty people, despite the wretched weather, gathered outside, and the spies fled back to the warm nest of "our friend Jones" in Weston, and then back to Boston, carefully avoiding the center of Watertown.

Three Mondays later, March 20, Brown and deBerniere went overnight to Concord by way of Weston to see "what quantity of artillery and provisions" were stored there. A Concord woman showed them the way to the house of Daniel Bliss, Tory brother-in-law of the patriot clergyman, Rev. William Emerson.

Bliss set a splendid table to entertain them. Presently the woman who had given them directions dashed in in tears. She was told, she sobbed, that "if she did not leave town, they would tar and feather her for directing Tories in their road."

Bliss gave the men details on the patriot supplies. There were 14 pieces of cannon — 10 iron, 4 brass — poorly mounted so that their elevation was fixed. He also told them that he had been sent a threat that "they would not let me out of town alive." So the spies took Bliss to Boston with them, along what would shortly be "Battle Road," and he never returned to Concord.

Incredibly, the spies, going over this road less than a month before warfare would flame along every mile from Concord to Charlestown, gave this verdict to Gage: "The road is very good almost all the way."

They did spot "one very bad place" between Lexington and Menotomy (now Arlington) that

William Ryerson, Boston Globe
Maj. John Buttrick monument in Concord

they did not name. Possibly it was the "Foot of the Rocks," not far from where Warren would nearly lose his life.

Gage sent out a third spy, John Howe, on April 5 to find "the best route to Worcester to take an army to destroy the military stores deposited there." He covered about the same roads and took letters from Gage to the Tory friends, Squire Barnes and the two tavernkeepers named Jones.

Lt. Col. Francis Smith, shortly to be sent in command of the April 19 mission to Lexington and Concord, set out with Howe. They, too, effected countrymen's attire, leather breeches and blue mixed stockings. It worked fairly well for Howe but was near disaster for Smith when they came to the first tavern in Watertown.

The black woman — whose name has not come down to us — waited on them. When Smith, pretending they were workmen, asked her where they might get employment, she looked him in the face and said:

"Smith, you will find employment enough for you and all Gen. Gage's men in a few months." Smith was thunderstruck. They paid quickly and had gone a short way when Smith decided it was best that he return to Boston. He handed Gage's letters to Howe, who last saw Smith "running through the barberry bushes to keep out of sight of the road."

Howe's mission took him a week. He had to flee into a swamp, after leaping from a back window at Squire Barnes's, when the Marlboro patriots came again to the place, this time with tar and feathers. Posing as a gunsmith, Howe did manage to meet Maj. John Buttrick, dine with patriots and see the cannon at Concord. Everywhere he found that the people were expecting the regulars.

On the Lexington road he met a 77-year-old man cleaning his musket and asked him what he was going to kill. The old man replied that there was a flock of redcoats of Boston who would soon be out and he "meant to try and hit some of them, as he expected they would be very good marks."

Exactly a week before the Lexington Alarm, Howe got back to Boston and gave Gage his report:

"If they should march 10,000 regulars and a train of artillery to Worcester, which is 48 miles from this place, the roads very crooked, stony and hilly, the inhabitants generally determined to be free or die, that not one of them would get back alive."

Howe was asked: What about destroying the stores at Concord, only 18 miles inland? Howe said he told Gage:

"I thought 500 mounted men might go to Concord in the night and destroy the stores and return safe, but to go with 1000 foot (soldiers) to destroy the stores the country would be alarmed;

that the greater part of them would get killed or be taken." Gage thanked the 22-year-old soldier.

But Gage, who had mounted dragoons coming as part of his promised reinforcements, either missed or ignored Howe's advice to send mounted men. Gage did, though, rule out a foray to Worcester. He would instead try one to Concord.

The latest London news arriving by vessel at Salem on April 2, 1775, told the patriots there was no longer any uncertainty: A crisis was starkly at hand.

The newspapers carried the wording of the parliamentary address to George III that in Massachusetts "a rebellion at this time actually exists." And there, too, was the aggressive response of the King at St. James's: "You may depend on my taking the most speedy and effectual measures for enforcing due obedience to the laws. . . ."

Further, the King, to support his crown and Parliament, would increase his forces by sea and land.

There would be still another Coercive Act. But the newspapers, for it was early February when the vessel left England, told only of Lord North proposing the restraining bill that would keep Yankee fishermen from their livelihoods in Newfoundland waters.

And there was still further startling news. The patriots managed to secure a private letter addressed to one of the hated Boston customs commissioners and read in it that firm orders were coming to arrest the leading patriots of the province and send them to England for trial.

Lord Percy, a top officer under Gage, wrote relatives about the effects of the news:

"This has convinced the rebels (for we may now legally call them so) that there is no hope for them but by submitting to Parliament; they have therefore begun seriously to form their army. . . . They are every day in greater numbers evacuating this town and have proposed in (Provincial) Congress, either to set it on fire and attack the troops before a reinforcement comes, or to endeavor to starve us. . . ."

Relations between the troops and Bostonians had grown increasingly malicious since Warren's massacre oration. Two days later, a minuteman from Billerica, Thomas Ditson Jr., seeking to purchase a musket, was decoyed into a barrack on the Boston waterfront, tarred and feathered head to foot and carted around town by officers and men of the 47th Regt. until Gage, hearing of it, sent orders it be stopped.

The president of the Provincial Congress, John Hancock, was a target for the redcoats' rancor. A gang of soldiers came up Beacon Hill and hacked his fences. Two days later some sergeants and soldiers, pretending to examine the Hancock stables as a possible barrack, when ordered away, declared insultingly that it would "soon be theirs." Gage put a stop to that, too.

But terrorizing marches into the countryside were continued. Lord Percy took off at 6 a.m. on March 30 from the grand parade on the Common at the head of five regiments. Marching in column was Lt. John Barker of the King's Own, who wrote:

GENERAL GAGE's
INSTRUCTIONS,
Of 22d *February* 1775,

To Captain *Brown* and Ensign *D'Bernicre*, (of the army under his command) whom he ordered to take a sketch of the roads, passes, heights, &c. from *Boston* to *Worcester*, and to make other observations :

With a *curious*

NARRATIVE

Of OCCURRENCES during their mission; Wrote by the *Ensign*.

Together with an ACCOUNT of their doings, in consequence of further Orders and Instructions from General *Gage*, of the 20th *March* following, to proceed to *Concord*, to reconnoitre and find out the state of the provincial magazines ; what number of cannon, &c. they have, and in what condition.

ALSO,

An ACCOUNT of the Transactions of the *British* troops, from the time they marched out of *Boston*, on the evening of the 18th. 'till their *confused*

Lexington Historical Society,
Lexington, Mass.

Gage's Feb. 22 instructions to spies

"It alarmed the people a good deal. Expresses were sent to every town near; at Watertown about nine miles off, they got two pieces of cannon to the bridge and loaded 'em but nobody would stay to fire them. At Cambridge they were so alarmed that they pulled up the bridge. However they were quit of their fears, for after marching about the country for five hours we returned peaceably home."

In neighboring towns, patriots mustered and equipped themselves to march. Such a confusing situation was actually being pondered that very moment by the Provincial Congress at Concord. The resulting guideline, stated in unanimous resolution, was to have a far-reaching, ruinous effect on Gage's April 19 plans when informers would secretly pass it along to him. It read:

"Whenever the army under command of Gen. Gage, or any part thereof to the number of 500, shall march out of town of Boston, with artillery and baggage, it ought to be deemed a design to carry into execution by force the late acts of Parliament ... and therefore the military force of the province ought to be assembled ... to act solely on the defensive so long as it can be justified on the principles of reason and self-preservation and no longer."

This was Samuel Adams's thinking: Let the British be the aggressor, let them fire the first shot.

Only a few weeks earlier, Warren expressed the opinion that if Gen. Gage actually led out his troops to enforce the acts, "Great Britain may take her leave, at least of the New England colonies, and, if I mistake not, of all America."

The thought of all patriots was now on the leaders gathered in anxious, secret session at Concord. They would call the signals. True, the London news did throw the Provincial Congress "into great consternation" — but not into fear or inaction. The increased tempo as the clash came closer can be felt intensely even in the lean minutes of the proceedings.

The towns had already been warned that any relaxation would bring the "utmost danger" to their liberties; they must gather arms, and their men must drill. Now in rapid succession the delegates produced "rules and regulations for the Massachusetts Army," repeated cautions to the Committees of Correspondence to have their militia and minutemen ready, sought to organize companies of artillery, advised Bostonians to move out into the country.

On April 8 the delegates took a giant step. They not only voted that "the present dangerous and alarming situation" required that they form their army, but also that they send delegates to New Hampshire, Rhode Island and Connecticut to build a New England army to combat "ministerial vengeance." In a message two days later to their sister colonies, the delegates said that in view of their being declared in rebellion and Gage's "daily and hourly preparations:

"This Congress have come to a full conclusion, that very little, if any expectation of the redress of our common and intolerable grievances is to be had from the humble and dutiful petition and other wise measures of the late honorable Continental Congress...."

Hancock, busy as he was presiding, missed but few of the meetings of the all-important Committee of Safety, of which he was also chairman. This committee, often with the Supplies Committee, had been assembling intermittently at taverns around Boston to prepare an army of 15,000 men and to arm, provision, direct and protect them.

It was this committee that ordered tons of brimstone and guns and powder, shifted around the cannon, organized couriers, sent orders to towns to make cartridges and sent warnings to Concord's Col. James Barrett to have sufficient and faithful men to guard the colony's magazine and "have a suitable number of teams in constant readiness, by day and night, to remove the stores" if in peril.

On Saturday, April 15, the Provincial Congress adjourned after taking another look at the London news, concluding it showed only "hostile intentions of the British Parliament toward this colony." Hancock and Adams retraced the seven miles to Lexington, to the Hancock-Clarke House, once the home of Hancock's grandfather, where these provincial leaders had been staying while preparing to leave shortly as delegates to the Second Continental Congress.

Meanwhile, Warren, who risked continuing to dwell in Boston as head of the Boston patriots, where he could keep abreast of any emergency, was brought some information that aroused suspicion.

HMS Somerset, 68-gun man-o'-war, fresh out of drydock for repairs, had been moved. Adm. Samuel Graves had had soundings made and determined that the big vessel could be safely placed between Boston and Charlestown. So, on April 11, he had ordered Capt. Edward LeCras to place it "exactly in the ferryway."

Then, on April 15, Warren learned that Gen. Gage had ordered that his shock troops — the big grenadiers and the light-infantry companies — be relieved of their regular duties. About midnight that night, the boats of the squadron were put over the side and nested at the sterns of the men-o'-war. Clearly, Gage was planning some action.

Warren sent for Paul Revere. On Sunday, Revere galloped to Lexington to carry Warren's urgent warnings to Hancock and Adams. Something grave was afoot.

Governor orders mission to Concord

"What they intend to do I can't pretend to say, . . ." Gage wrote on April 12 to the governor of North Carolina, referring to what Gage called a "newfangled legislature termed a Provincial Congress" sitting at Concord.

Fact was, however, that Gage, through his informers, knew very well what the Provincial Congress was doing. This pleased him immensely. His difficulty was not inability to get information. It was his interpretation of it and his timing that led him to blunder.

He studied the informer's April 3 report that the Provincial Congress had decided that there should be an alert of its military forces only if 500 or more of Gage's troops marched out "with artillery and baggage." So, he concluded he would send his initial force to Concord without artillery and baggage.

On April 9, midway in the debate of the Provincial Congress on trying to raise a New England army, Gage received an informer's letter giving him all the developments, even to the discussion getting under way about sending delegates to the other New England colonies. This, in Gage's mind, had to raise the prospect that his forces, currently numbering about 4000, might have to face still greater odds.

On April 11, Gage received a crucial, secret letter. His informer told him that the patriots had been talking about seizing Fort Pownall on the Kennebec River (to which Gage already had ships headed to grab its cannon and supplies) and had further talked about raising a New England army; but, most important of all, the informer had some advice:

"A sudden blow struck now or immediately on the arrival of the reinforcements from England, should they come within a fortnight, would overset all their plans."

Long ago Gage had written to Lord Dartmouth what seemed his scheme for meeting the crisis: "A check anywhere would be fatal, and the first stroke will decide a great deal. We should therefore be strong and proceed on a good foundation before anything decisive is tried." Gage seemed to have forgotten complete-ly his own cautious plan, now that he had in hand this April 11 recommendation. He decided that he would not wait for more reinforcements, or for the mounted dragoons. He would change his timing. He would do what his paid informer proposed.

He would send another secret expedition, this time to Concord.

So he issued orders for the boats and the men to do the deed. The men would be his very best troops. He had 10 full regiments and part of another. Each regiment was composed of 10 companies. Two companies out of the 10 in each regiment were superior troops, one, a company of grenadiers, the biggest, strongest, most impressive men, used as shock troops; the other, a company of light infantry, spry, vigorous, fast men, used for flanking purposes or speed.

It was not difficult for Gage's troops, or the patriots, to guess that some action was in the making, an amphibious action. The patriots had countless volunteers as observers. Paul Revere and many of his mechanic friends (as they had done on the Portsmouth alert) kept a watch on the British. And patriots had been designated to watch all around Boston — in Roxbury, Cambridge, Charlestown — to report any suspicious moves by the British. Couriers were always in readiness.

When Lt. Barker read the general order on the superior troops he wrote in his journal:

"I dare say they have something for them to do." Barker was not bluffed, anymore than the patriots were, by Gage inserting in the general order that the troops were going to be trained in new exercises.

That weekend two of His Majesty's vessels, the *Nautilus* and the *Falcon,* both very leaky from "blowing weather in their passage," arrived with messages from Whitehall. The *Nautilus* came on Friday, and the sloop-of-war *Falcon* came Sunday, April 16. The latter brought secret orders to Gage that Lord Dartmouth had written on Jan. 27, during the height of the punitive debate in Parliament.

Dartmouth, of course, was sending the royal

and official reaction to what had been going on in Massachusetts four long months earlier. Dartmouth told Gage that he could not have 20,000 troops, which would amount to a war establishment, and, Dartmouth wrote, "I am unwilling to believe that matters are as yet come to that issue." This was the erroneous official British position with the outbreak of war only three days away.

Now came the direct orders, wind of which had already kept Hancock and Adams out of town and beyond Gage's power:

"It is the opinion of the King's servants, in which His Majesty concurs, that the first and essential step to be taken towards re-establishing government, would be to arrest and imprison the principal actors and abettors in the Provincial Congress (whose proceedings appear in every light to be acts of treason and rebellion)...."

Then came instructions that must have buttressed the decision that Gage had already made to go ahead with his expedition to Concord. Dartmouth told him that if, using every precaution and secrecy, he made a move to arrest the patriot leaders, and if this became the "signal for hostilities" that Gage had expected, then, said Dartmouth:

"It will surely be better the conflict should be brought on, upon such ground, than in a riper state of rebellion."

Gage was studying Dartmouth's letter (which was quite lengthy) just about the time that Revere, dispatched by Warren, was on his Lexington mission to acquaint Hancock and Adams with warnings of an impending expedition, possibly aimed at them, too.

On his way back Revere, knowing he would have to go out of Boston again if the British actually moved, visited with patriot leaders in Charlestown to arrange signals. Should the British, who already had Revere well identified as a patriot express, prevent his next departure, Revere said, he would arrange for some lanterns in the steeple of the Old North Church: "One, if by land, and two, if by sea...."

Sunday gave Gage time to think out the secret orders he would be giving to Lt. Col. Smith of the 10th Regt., the garrison's senior lieutenant colonel, a man who had been in army service in the colonies for a dozen years. These would be mighty important orders — the first major move against the patriots.

Monday, April 17, was a bustling day for the patriot inner circle. The committees of Safety and Supplies met at Concord. Hancock was mindful of Revere's Sunday ride to Lexington, and the other members had a sense of increasing urgency. They discussed forming artillery companies, chose possible captains, arranged artillery pay, but wound up their meeting by protectively ordering some cannon removed from imperiled Concord — two mortars to Acton and four 6-pounders to Groton in care of Col. William Prescott.

The committees voted to meet quickly again the next morning at Mr. Wetherby's Black Horse Tavern on the Cambridge-Concord highway near the center of the village of Menotomy.

By Tuesday, Gage made changes in Smith's orders. At first, as still appears in the preliminary draft, Gage employed words, supplied by informers, to specify locations and quantities of the war supplies at Concord. But Gage had received secret word just that day that some of the provisions and stores had been removed hastily. Gage consequently shortened the orders and contented himself with giving Smith a map that merely indicated locations.

Smith was ordered to go "with the utmost expedition and secrecy." He was to send his "best marchers (light infantry) on with expedition" to secure the two bridges at Concord. There would be (thanks to Gage's informers) no artillery and baggage, but some artillerymen in chaises would be sent ahead with hammers and spikes to destroy cannon. And stressing secrecy again, Gage wrote in the final orders:

"A small party on horseback is ordered out to stop all advices of your march getting to Concord before you." Gage, as events turned out, would have neither secrecy nor speed.

Patrols, the small party on horseback, left Boston disarmingly in time for casual midday meals. One patrol in particular went to Cambridge to dine. Just about that time the seamen were coming off watch from the warships that were stationed in a ring around the Boston peninsula. From that moment on, an observer in Boston would have to have been sightless not to detect an expedition was afoot.

The adjutant of the Royal Welsh Fusiliers, Lt. Mackenzie, wrote in his diary: "It was pretty generally known, by means of the seamen who came shore from the ships, about 2 o'clock, that the boats were ordered to be in readiness."

The patrol that went to Cambridge was not the only concerned group dining there that afternoon. The members of Safety and Supplies dined at the Black Horse Tavern after a mighty diligent session, which involved countermanding prior orders that would have moved gunpowder to Concord, splitting and shifting supplies among nine towns, ordering Col. Barrett in Concord to bury munitions and entrusting the papers of both committees to one of the members, Abraham Watson.

Redcoats and patriots seem to have finished their meals at the same time. The patrol started moving along the highway toward Menotomy while Safety Committeeman Richard Devens bade good-bye to three members staying the night at the tavern and rode off in his chaise for his home in Charlestown. En route he was going to drop Watson and the committee papers at Watson's house in Cambridge. Soon they caught sight of the patrol. Devens recalled:

"We rode some way after we met them, and then turned back and rode through them, went and informed our friends..." staying at the Black Horse Tavern. One of this trio, Elbridge Gerry, who would be a signer of the Declaration of Independence, a governor and Vice President of the United States, sent off an express to warn Hancock and Adams of "some evil design." Devens resumed his trip to Charlestown.

Hanock and Adams got further warning.

Eighteen-year-old Solomon Brown, returning to Lexington from the Boston market, passed through the British patrol, glimpsed arms beneath the officers' cloaks and hastened to report what he had seen to William Munroe, orderly sergeant of Capt. John Parker's Lexington minutemen. Munroe hurriedly turned over his tavern to his neighbor John Raymond, who would be killed in a few hours, collected eight minute-

men and posted a guard outside the Hancock-Clarke House.

The British patrol, of nine or 10 officers and men, inquired about the location of a "Clarke Tavern" but went through Lexington about 8 p.m. toward Concord without attempting to approach the Hancock-Clarke House. The patrol's passage induced about 40 anxious Lexington minutemen to assemble at the Buckman Tavern on the highway beside the Lexington Green.

Gage had set 8 p.m. for action and briefing in Boston.

By "desire of the general," Adm. Graves had ordered all boats of the squadron to be assembled along the side of *HMS Boyne,* a 70-boat man-o'-war, at 8 p.m., and all the boat officers to follow directions that would take them around the North End and up the Charles River to the foot of the Common.

At 8 p.m. the commanding officers of Gage's 11 regiments met with Gage at his headquarters. Lt. Mackenzie said that they were then "ordered to have their respective Grenadier and Light Infantry companies on the beach near the Magazine guard exactly at 10 o'clock . . . with one day's provisions in their haversacks, and without knapsacks." They were directed to order their companies to parade quietly at their respective barracks, to march to the places of rendezvous in small parties and, if challenged, to answer "Patrole!"

Talking about the troops, Rev. Jeremy Belknap said: "Just as it was time to march, they were waked up by the sergeants putting their hands on them, and whispering gently to them; and were even conducted by a back way out of the barracks, without the knowledge of their comrades, and without the observation of the sentries. They walked through the streets with the utmost silence. It being about 10 o'clock, no sound was heard but of their feet; a dog, happening to bark, instantly was killed by a bayonet.

"They proceeded to the beach under the new powder house, the most unfrequented part of the town; and there embarked on the boats which had their oars muffled to prevent a noise."

Some officers volunteered to go. Ens. Lister of the 10th Regt., billeted in the same lodgings with the grenadiers, went off to the Common out of curiosity. Here he learned of a malingering lieutenant and volunteered to replace him despite Lt. Col. Smith's humane persuasion not "go into danger" for such a man. Lister insisted on going along. Lister said he felt that "it would be rather a disgrace for the company to march on an expedition, more especially it being the first, without its complement of officers."

Lt. William Sutherland of the 38th Foot, an enthusiastic soldier who had been in the army for a decade and a half, could not resist joining. "About 9 o'clock I learned there was a large detachment going from this garrison, on which I immediately resolved to go with them, and meeting a few men in the street accounted, I followed them and embarked on the Magazine guard."

Lt. Mackenzie, on hand as adjutant of his regiment to see his two companies safely under way, had got his grenadiers and light infantrymen to the beach, the first complete units to arrive.

"Here we found a number of men-o'-war and transport boats in waiting. As there was no public officer attending to superintend the embarkation, which it was evident would take up a good deal of time, our two companies, with the approbation of the officers of the navy, embarked in the nearest boats, and pushed off a little way from shore.

"As the other companies arrived soon after, as many men embarked as the boats would contain. By this time Lt. Col. Smith of the 10th, who was to have the command, arrived, and with him Maj. Pitcairn of the marines. The boats then put off, and rowed toward Phipps's farm, where having landed the troops they returned for the remainder and landed them at the same place. This was not completed until 12 o'clock."

In all about 700 redcoats were embarked near Fox Hill (now vanished), were rowed past the guns of the *Nautilus* stationed off Magazine Point and were carried across the mile and a quarter of tidal water from Boston Common to Phipps's isolated farm on a hill above the salt marshes on the Cambridge shore.

Warren sends out Dawes, Revere

Warnings that the British troops were on the march got to Lexington so far ahead of the redcoats that the patriots would begin to wonder if the alarm were genuine.

Gage, to his utter dismay, would learn quite early that secrecy was breached and that his expedition would have no advantage of surprise. After Gage told Lord Percy the objectives of the troops, then embarking, and had cautioned Percy about absolute secrecy, Percy discovered almost at once that there was none. On his way to his quarters Percy saw a group of men on the Common and heard one say:

"The British troops have marched, but they will miss their aim."

"What aim?" inquired the astonished Percy.

"The cannon at Concord," came the response.

Percy dashed back to Province House and told Gage, and Gage gave peremptory orders that no one was to be allowed to leave Boston.

There had been hints aplenty long before Warren acted. There was the seamen's tale. Then a groom at Province House told the patriots of hearing officers say that there would be "hell to pay tomorrow." Warren just wanted to be sure that the troops were actually under way.

Then he sent for a near neighbor, William Dawes Jr., and dispatched him to Lexington by the land route over Boston Neck. Dawes, a resourceful young man, would have to get past the guards. Warren sent next for Paul Revere, another neighbor, to take his message by the shorter route across the water and along the Charlestown road should Dawes fail to get through.

Revere hurried to Warren's house. Warren's message: The regulars were really "marching to the bottom of the Common," where boats were ready to take them, "it was supposed," either to Lexington to seize Hancock and Adams, or to Concord.

"I left Dr. Warren's," said Revere, "called upon a friend, and desired him to make the signals." Robert Newman, the friend, was the 23-year-old sexton of the Old North Church. Capt. John Pulling, another friend, stood guard as Newman climbed the steeple to display two lanterns to Charles Devens, Col. William Conant and several other patriots watching on the Charlestown shore. The lanterns would also be seen in Boston, and Newman would be arrested by British soldiers. Capt. Pulling, disguised as a sailor, would flee in a fishing vessel.

Revere meantime went home, put on his boots and surtout and had two friends—Joshua Bentley and Thomas Richardson — row him across the Charles River "a little to the eastward where the *Somerset* man-o'-war lay. It was then young flood, the ship was winding, and the moon was rising."

Watch on the *Somerset* must have been looking at the moon, for Revere crossed the river undetected.

The instant Charles Devens had seen the lanterns, he had hurried off an express, who never arrived, to tell Gerry, Hancock and Adams that "the enemy were certainly coming out." Devens had just come from an emergency meeting at which it was decided to call the Provincial Congress back into immediate session at Concord because of the "alarming crisis." Devens had also sent expresses at "utmost speed" to inform each member.

Revere landed and told Devens that the "troops were actually in their boats." Devens got a horse from Deacon Larkin's nearby barn and, while it was being prepared, told Revere how he had come down the road from Lexington after sundown that evening and that he had met 10 British officers, all well mounted and armed, going up the road. Ahead for Revere would be troublesome encounters with Gage's patrols.

"I set off upon a very good horse," related Revere. "It was then about 11 o'clock, and very pleasant. After I got past Charlestown Neck, and got fairly opposite where Mark (a murderer executed 10 years earlier) was hung in chains, I saw two men on horseback, under a tree. When I got near them, I discovered they were British officers. One tried to git ahead of me, and the other to take me.

"I turned my horse very quick, and galloped towards Charlestown Neck, and then pushed for the Medford road. The one who chased me, endeavoring to cut me off, got into a clay pond ... I got clear of him. . . .

"In Medford, I awakened the captain of the minutemen; and after that, I alarmed almost every house, 'till I got to Lexington."

It was about midnight. Sgt. Munroe and his men were still on guard at the Hancock-Clarke House, and inside, in the room to the left of the front doorway, Hancock and Adams had just retired. In the upstairs bedroom, Hancock's young fiancee, beautiful Dorothy Quincy, and her chaperone, Hancock's aunt Lydia, had also gone to bed. The dwelling (still standing and with furnishings the patriots used) was now the home of the Lexington patriot minister, Rev. Jonas Clarke, who had married Hancock's first cousin. Hancock knew the place well from boyhood when it was the manse of his grandfather.

It would not be long before some wounded minutemen would be brought into the house and a stray British musket ball would whizz by Aunt Lydia's head as she would lean out a window to see what was happening on the Green.

Revere asked admittance. Munroe told him that the family had just retired and requested that "they might not be disturbed by any noise about the house."

"Noise!" exclaimed Revere, "you'll have noise enough before long. The regulars are coming out!"

Rev. Clarke raised his bedroom window, on the upper floor. Who was there? Revere replied he wanted to see Hancock and Adams.

Hancock heard the exchange. He called out: "Come in, Revere. We are not afraid of you." Revere delivered Warren's message. A half hour later, Dawes, who had been slipped past a friendly guard at Boston Neck, arrived. The two expresses refreshed themselves, mounted and headed for Concord.

The old belfry, which then stood back of the meetinghouse on Lexington Green, had rung out the alarm brought by Revere, and most of Capt. John Parker's 144 minutemen were assembling. Parker, descendant of earliest Bay settlers, was

45 years old, a large-framed man, with muscles toughened by toil on his farm to support his wife and seven children. An ardent churchman, Parker was a keen follower of his eloquent friend, Rev. Clarke, leader of Lexington's Sons of Liberty.

Parker sent a scout down the road toward Boston to check on the British. Within the hour the scout came back. He had seen no British troops. Capt. Parker released his company with instructions to reassemble at the beat of the drum. Those who lived at a distance went into the Buckman Tavern, where jovial John Buckman, fellow minuteman, could help lighten their wait for further orders. The night had been getting chilly.

As Revere and Dawes rode out of Lexington, they were joined by a high Son of Liberty from Concord, Dr. Samuel Prescott, who had been in Lexington visiting his fiancee, Miss Lydia Mulliken.

Revere mentioned that they had better alarm all the inhabitants 'til they got to Concord. "The young doctor much approved of it," Revere said. Presently Dawes and Revere stopped to alarm some people at a house where Lincoln minuteman Nathaniel Baker was courting his future wife. Baker hurried off to Lincoln spreading the alarm, and later that morning would be at Concord's North Bridge. As Revere's companions had been talking with Baker, Revere recalled, "I was about 100 rods ahead, when I saw two men, in nearly the same situation those officers were near Charlestown." Revere had met with another patrol, the one that had passed through Cambridge and Lexington.

Revere yelled to Dawes and Prescott to come up. In an instant there appeared four British officers, armed with pistols and swords. Dawes tugged his reins, his horse turned and he escaped. Prescott, who had been closer, and Revere were forced into a pasture. Prescott got free by jumping his horse over a low stone wall as Revere attempted to flee into the Lincoln woods.

"When I got there," said Revere, "out started six officers, on horseback, and ordered me to dismount." Revere found he was not alone. There were four other prisoners, a one-armed peddler, and three Lexington minutemen — young Solomon Brown, who had first encountered this patrol back in Cambridge, Elijah Sanderson and Jonathan Loring, three men Capt. Parker had sent out as scouts to report what the patrol was doing.

Revere was questioned by one of the officers:

"Where I came from, and what my name was? I told him. He asked me if I was an express? I answered in the affirmative. He demanded what time I left Boston? I told him; and added, that their troops had catched aground in passing the river, and that there would be 500 Americans there in a short time, for I had alarmed the country all the way up."

Other officers came at Revere at a gallop. Revere said that the commander of the patrol, Maj. Edward Mitchell, 5th Regt., now "clapped his pistol to my head, called me by name, and told me he was going to ask some questions, and if I did not give him true answers, he would blow my brains out." There was nothing new asked by Mitchell, who thereupon told Revere to mount and searched him for arms and all headed for Lexington.

"We rode until we got near Lexington Meetinghouse, when the militia fired a volley of guns, which appeared to alarm them very much. The major inquired of me how far it was to Cambridge, and if there was any other road?"

Maj. Mitchell, deep in hostile country, was clearly alarmed. He noticed that the big grenadier sergeant leading Revere had tired his horse, so he ordered Revere to dismount and gave Deacon Larkin's horse to the sergeant. Bridles and girths were sliced and the prisoners were set free as the patrol, virtually in flight, headed toward Cambridge.

Prescott meantime had emerged from the woods at the dwelling of Sgt. Samuel Hartwell of the Lincoln minutemen. His wife Mary, at Prescott's request, hurried back to the house of her neighbor, Capt. William Smith, who raced to Lincoln center, gathered his Lincoln minutemen, and started off for Concord. They would be the first outside minuteman companies to arrive there. Prescott had galloped on to alarm Concord.

Revere made his way through the Lexington burying ground and pastures back to the Hancock-Clarke House. "I told them my treatment, and they concluded to go from that house toward Woburn." Hancock had been proclaiming that he would join the minutemen in any skirmish, while Adams had been trying to dissuade him. They were of the "cabinet," said Adams, and must leave soon for the Continental Congress.

They did take off in a chaise. Revere and Hancock's clerk, his nephew John Lowell, went along with them two miles to the dwelling of James Reed, captain of the Woburn Precinct (now Burlington) minutemen. Hancock remembered something important when he got to Capt. Reed's — his trunk, left in Buckman Tavern.

Hancock sent Revere and Lowell back to get it and to "find what was going on."

It was 2 a.m. by the time Smith gave orders for his force to start marching.

Besides trips for the troops, the boats had to transport supplies, food, munitions, horses for the officers. The boats could not come all the way in the marsh, so the men had to wade in water up to their knees to get ashore. There they waited two precious hours, the moon-lit wetland a contrast to scattered lights on the Boston shore.

Food, a day's rations, was distributed to the soldiers and each was given 36 rounds of ammunition.

The march, wrote Ens. Lister, "was at first through some swamps and slips of the sea." Smith went along a cart road of Lechmere Point that circled 'round Phipps's lonely farmhouse and led to Willis Creek. There was a small bridge over the creek but Smith, striving to preserve secrecy, ordered his men to wade quietly rather than tramp over the creeking planks.

"The tide being in we were up to our middles before we got into the road," said Lt. Sutherland, recalling a wet, far from appealing way to begin a 40-mile march on a chilly night.

They moved toward the old Cambridge Path (through what is now Union Square, Somerville), passed by the few houses along Charlestown lane that would be called "Milk Row" by dairy farmers going to market (now Somerville avenue and Elm street), and then went left the short distance of Beech street, then right into the Lexington road (now Massachusetts avenue).

They did not go by unseen. A widow ran in her night clothes to her neighbor, Samuel Tufts, who dashed off on his horse to alarm Cambridge.

As the troops came to the Black Horse Tavern, their tread awakened the three Marblehead committeemen, Gerry, Col. Azor Orne and Col. Jeremiah Lee. Partly dressed, they gazed from their upstairs windows at the passing column. Suddenly an officer and file of soldiers peeled off and headed for the tavern. The patriots scampered downstairs. Gerry grabbed a doorknob to get out. The tavernkeeper screamed:

"For God's sake, don't open that door!"

It led into the highway! Instead, he guided them to the back door and into the short stubble of a cornfield.

They kept close to the cold, damp earth to conceal themselves as the soldiers searched the tavern. Gage had made no mention in his written orders to Smith to arrest leaders of the Provincial Congress. Such arrests, which the King and Dartmouth ordered in instructions Gage had received only three days earlier, may have been given orally. If so, did they include Hancock and Adams?

The search, seemingly fruitless, did have fatal consequences. Col. Lee died within a month from the exposure.

Smith, coming toward Menotomy center, decided it was time to send a fast-moving detachment on ahead to secure the two bridges in Concord, as Gage had ordered. He dispatched Maj. John Pitcairn, his second in command, with six of his 10 companies of light infantry. Hardly had he done this than Smith heard the alarm bells of Menotomy start to clang and heard the fire of signal guns.

Smith thereupon sent a messenger galloping back to Gage to request reinforcements.

Gage, worried about Percy's discovery on the Common, had been considering reinforcements even before Smith asked for them. At 4 a.m. he issued orders for Percy to take his First Brigade, approximately 1000 troops, this time with artillery and baggage, to help Smith.

Altogether the troops under Smith and Percy would comprise nearly half of all Gage's force. This, too, disturbed Gage because he suspected (and later events would disclose) that the citizens of Boston had ample weapons — flintlocks, bayonets, blunderbusses — to mount a rising. As a safeguard, Gage ordered all his remaining troops in barracks to be under arms and prepared to move instantly.

Pitcairn, on getting Smith's command, sent a small advance patrol of a sergeant and six or eight men in front of his column. Lts. Sutherland and Jesse Adair went with it. As it moved through the center of Menotomy, Adair called back to Sutherland, "Here are two fellows galloping express to alarm the country." Sutherland and a Tory volunteer, one of several who went with Smith, seized the two men. Pitcairn ordered them kept as prisoners.

Lexington Historical Society,
Lexington, Mass.

William Diamond's drum

But they were not expresses. They were two young Woburn men, their produce in their panniers, who had been headed for the early Boston market. One of them would be killed within two hours. They were forced to go with the column along with two Lexington farmers, also bound for market, who had been captured previously.

Despite the early hour there was quite a number of travelers on the highway.

Lt. William Grant of the Royal Artillery, in command of the engineers sent ahead in a chaise to wreck cannon, was overtaken by Sutherland. Grant "told us," said Sutherland, "the country, he was afraid was alarmed, of which we had little reason to doubt as we heard several shots, being then between 3 and 4 in the morning, a very unusual time for firing. . . ."

Moments later, along came Maj. Mitchell and the fleeing patrol. Mitchell told Sutherland that they had found "the whole country was alarmed and had galloped for their lives . . . they had taken Paul Revere but was obliged to let him go after having cut his girths and stirrups."

Into the Pitcairn net, at a gallop, came another of Capt. Parker's scouts, near the Foot of the Rocks. The column passed the (still-standing) dwelling of Capt. Benjamin Locke of the Menotomy minutemen and came upon a man in a sulky who told them there were 600 minutemen "assembled at Lexington with a view to opposing us." Sutherland had him repeat this for Pitcairn.

His curiosity keenly piqued, Sutherland rode off the highway to the left and said he "saw a vast number of the country militia going over the hill with their arms to Lexington." On the way back he captured one of them, Lexington minuteman Benjamin Wellington, taking his firelock and bayonet. Wellington, far from daunted, circled through the woods and swamp and would be in line with Capt. Parker's minutemen on the green.

Pitcairn, to prevent surprise, put out flankers and moved on toward Lexington center. "We saw shots fired to the right and left of us," said Sutherland, "but as we heard no whizzing of balls, I concluded they were to alarm the body that was there of our approach."

The situation grew more serious as the column approached the center.

"On coming within gunshot of the village of Lexington a fellow from the corner of the road on the right hand cocked his piece at me, burnt priming (flashed in the pan)," related Sutherland. "I immediately called to Mr. Adair and the party to observe this circumstance, which they did, and I acquainted Maj. Pitcairn of it immediately."

In their consternation, neither Pitcairn nor Sutherland noticed that Capt. Parker's final scout, Thaddeus Bowman, had caught sight of the column, had wheeled his horse about and sped back to the Buckman Tavern yelling, "Captain Parker! Captain Parker!" Captain Parker heard him and ordered his drummer boy, William Diamond, to beat the call to arms.

On the other side of the center, Maj. Pitcairn heard the drumbeat and alarm guns, ordered his column to halt, prime and load, then move at double time toward Lexington Green.

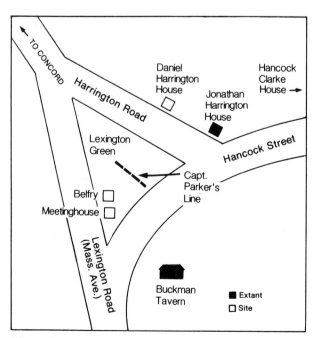

Map shows points of conflict in Lexington

'If they want to have a war . . . .'

Capt. Parker's men came hurriedly out of the Buckman Tavern as they heard Parker's command to the drummer.

A few moments before Bowman had given his frantic message that the redcoats were at his heels, two young men from Woburn had joined the small band of Lexington minutemen.

The bell tolling in the old belfry had awakened Sylvanus Wood of Woburn, who soon would take some of the first British prisoners. His companion, Robert Douglass, a Maine man who had come to visit his father, was awakened by an express carrying the alarm to Woburn. Wood and Douglass had come running with their muskets.

Wood recalled that as the minutemen came out of the tavern and reached the roadway, Capt. Parker shouted: "Every man of you who is equipped, follow me, and those of you who are not equipped, go into the meetinghouse and furnish yourselves from the magazine, and immediately join the company."

Three minutemen—Joseph Comee, Caleb Harrington and Joshua Simonds—dashed to the meetinghouse, a few yards farther on the green and just short of the old belfry.

Capt. Parker, a "great, tall man with a large head and a high, wide brow," as his grandson described him, strode deeper upon the green so that his men could form a line. Drumbeat, bell toll and alarm guns would bring more minutemen, but at this moment Wood made a count of those forming in the line, and the count was only 38.

More minutemen were coming, though, by the roadways bordering the green, from the woods beside and back of the few houses, only eight or 10 in this part of the town.

Sgt. Munroe, Capt. Parker's orderly, told those arriving to form a second line. Now there were 77 men.

It was daylight, the young leaves on the trees wore the fresh green of springtime, a setting of rustic beauty as the sun was about to sparkle through the branches. But there was no time for enjoyment. The business of these men

was grim. And its danger could be read on the tense faces of mothers, wives, sisters and children, the 40 or more spectators watching from dwellings or around the green.

Capt. Parker presently heard the crunch of the redcoats' boots on the roadway.

"Stand your ground," he called to his men. "Don't fire unless fired upon. But if they want to have a war let it begin here!"

Maj. Pitcairn must have had several things on his mind as he swung his horse toward the green. Two miles back he had received intelligence that "about 500 men in arms were assembled, determined to oppose the King's troops." This rumor had brought him dashing to the head of his six companies, where he was then told of the attempted shooting of his officers — or was it an alarm gun firing, that musket Sutherland said had "flashed in the pan"?

Pitcairn recognized instantly that the minutemen, far fewer in numbers than he had been told, were not obstructing his roadway to Concord. They were, indeed, some 100 yards or more away from that road, and deep on the green. But Pitcairn could not, with security, leave an armed body of men on the flank of the troops, now, or later, when those troops would return this way.

Pitcairn's light infantry caught sight of the minutemen, too, and realized instantly how few they were.

Capt. Parker eyed the approach of the redcoats. Like Pitcairn, Parker had had advance information. He knew of the "officers riding up and down the road, stopping and insulting people." He had been told that "a number of the regular troops were on their march to take the province stores at Concord." He had then consulted with his men and they had concluded:

"Not to be discovered, nor meddle, or make with said regular troops, if they should approach, unless they should insult or molest us."

Capt. Parker, as the redcoats came on, could see at first glance that his small band was far outnumbered. He realized that these troops coming in column, rank on rank, might be followed by even greater numbers. Parker was a veteran

Joshua Simonds

of the French and Indian Wars. He knew what he must do as the regulars wheeled from the roadway toward the green.

"Upon their sudden approach," said Parker, "I immediately ordered our militia to disperse and not to fire."

But the redcoats did not maintain their rigid order. Parker said that they came "rushing furiously on."

Long pent-up bitterness propelled the redcoats, both officers and men. Theirs was the vindictive spirit that had made them bully and later burlesque Joseph Warren's massacre oration. Theirs was the animosity that had turned officers and men into a military gang that little more than a month ago had carted minuteman Thomas Ditson Jr. in tar and feathers. Hate flared, blind hate, against these countrymen standing on the green, these men who could now legally be called rebels.

Officers, mounted, spurred forward, among them Sutherland. To him the patriots were an "armed mob." As the minutemen — most, but

not all of them — began to disperse, they looked an even more meager band, and the redcoats reacted with huzzas and shouting as they ran forward. "The light infantry," said Pitcairn, observing some minutemen withdrawing, "ran after them."

"I instantly called to the soldiers not to fire, but to surround and disarm them," said Pitcairn. Several times he repeated his order.

But disorder had taken over.

Officers, from their saddles, yelled to the huzzaing, running regulars. Sutherland said that he heard several officers call out to the minutemen:

"Throw down your arms and you shall come to no harm." Sutherland said he could hear Pitcairn's voice calling out: "Soldiers, don't fire, keep your ranks, form and surround them."

Ens. Lister, in the very van of the light infantry, could hear Pitcairn call to the minutemen "to disperse."

There were several British officers on the green, among them Maj. Mitchell and the officers of the patrol that had captured Revere earlier in the morning and threatened to blow his brains out. Elijah Sanderson, a minuteman, but without weapon and forced to be a spectator, heard one British officer declare as he advanced toward the minutemen: "Damn them....We will have them."

No doubt the confusion was prodigious — a genuine military melee.

Amid the shouting and the rushing there came, suddenly, a shot. Paul Revere heard it. He had just come from the Buckman Tavern, where he and Hancock's clerk had gone to fetch Hancock's trunk. From a tavern window Revere had seen the redcoats approach the green, and now, passing among the minutemen and carrying the trunk, he heard the shot and saw smoke in front of the redcoats.

The shot appeared, said Revere, "to be a pistol."

Pistol? The British officers were the only ones there who had pistols.

Others on the scene also thought it was a pistol. Minuteman Benjamin Tidd, back from carrying the alarm to Bedford, said it was a pistol. So did three more spectators, Joseph Abbott, Levi Mead and Levi Harrington. Abbott and Harrington saw British officers fire "a pistol or two on the Lexington company."

Minuteman Thomas Fessenden, also forced to be a spectator — cut off, like the others, from access to the meetinghouse magazine — said he saw a British officer brandish his sword and yell, "Disperse, you rebels," while another officer, about 30 feet behind the first one, fired a pistol at the minutemen.

Simon Winship of Lexington saw much the same thing. Winship, who was among those taken captive by Pitcairn's advance patrol, had seen the redcoats prime and load at Pitcairn's command and now saw, on the green, an officer "flourishing his sword, and with a loud voice giving the word 'Fire!'"

Another spectator, William Draper of Colrain, heard the huzzas and then the command:

"Fire! Fire! Damn you, fire!"

Fessenden added that the officer who flourished his sword and yelled "Fire!" had shifted his sword and "pointed it down towards the militia and immediately . . . the regulars fired a volley."

Confused as the scene was with shouts, cries of "Fire!" and "Don't fire!" curses, the regulars with primed and loaded weapons and trigger-eager fingers and emotions laden with malice and profound resentment, there is certainty that the first shot, followed by a few nervous, scattered ones, led to the redcoats' firing a volley. Each side would claim that the other fired the first, the fateful, the momentous shot. But there was no question which side fired the volley.

Thomas Rice Willard looked from the window of the Daniel Harrington house, which once stood on the edge of the green, and faced the approaching redcoats. Willard saw an officer at the side of the regulars and heard him shout to the minutemen, "Lay down your arms — damn you — why don't you lay down your arms."

Lay down arms! This was the very heart of the conflict. No minuteman would willingly lay down his arms. His arms — and the colony's military supplies the redcoats were seeking to destroy — were all that stood between the minute-

men and outright submission to what they ardently, profoundly believed was ministerial tyranny.

Lt. William Tidd, Parker's second in command, and 33 minutemen with him would declare that they began to disperse at Parker's command and that "whilst our backs were turned on the troops, we were fired upon by them. . . ."

Cpl. Samuel Sanderson, with 13 other minutemen, would declare the same thing:

"Some of our company were coming to the parade, with their backs toward the troops, and others on the parade began to disperse, when the regulars fired on the company. . . ."

Minuteman John Robbins, who would be wounded, was one of those who did not leave on Parker's command. Robbins was in the front line. As he stood his ground, the oncoming redcoats seemed to him to be "a thousand . . . 60 or 70 yards from us, huzzaing, and on a quick pace toward us, with three officers in their front on horseback, and on full gallop towards us; the foremost of which cried, 'Throw down your arms! — ye villains! — ye rebels!'"

Then, said Robbins, the same officer ordered his men:

"'Fire! — by God! — Fire!' at which moment we received a heavy and close fire from them; at which instant, being wounded, I fell and several other men were shot dead by me."

Robbins was referring to two volleys fired by the redcoats in rapid succession. After the first volley "all was smoke," said Elijah Sanderson. He was forced to be an onlooker, for he found, after the British patrol released him, that his brother had borrowed his gun. "Seeing nobody fall," said Sanderson, he was sure that the redcoats had used no musket balls in the first volley.

On the right side of Capt. Parker's front line stood two brothers, Cpl. John Munroe and, to his left, Ebenezer Munroe. After the first volley John turned to Ebenezer and remarked that the redcoats seemed to have "fired nothing but powder."

But the second volley, maybe fired lower than the first, was lethal.

Some minutemen had remained in position because they may have failed to hear Capt. Parker's command. But not Jonas Parker, the captain's first cousin. Jonas Parker stood his ground as on a bedrock of individual conviction. Only a few days earlier he had told Elijah Sanderson of his determination "never to run from before the British troops." Now, as those troops approached, Sgt. William Munroe had seen Jonas Parker standing in the front line, his hat flung on the sod between his legs, and in the hat his musket balls and flints. Sgt. Munroe heard Jonas repeat that "he would never run."

Jonas Parker died where he had taken his stand.

Sgt. Munroe said:

"He was shot down at the second fire of the British, and, when I left, I saw him struggling on the ground, attempting to load his gun, which I have no doubt he had discharged at the British. As he lay on the ground, they ran him through with the bayonet."

That second volley leveled minutemen either side of Jonas Parker. Young Isaac Muzzey was killed instantly. Jonathan Harrington Jr., mortally wounded in the chest, stumbled and crawled toward his house, still standing beside the green. From a window, his young wife witnessed his agony, the blood gushing as he stretched his arm toward her. She rushed to the door as he approached, and he died at her feet.

Ens. Robert Monroe was third in command of the minutemen. He was the father of minutemen John and Ebenezer Munroe and would be 63 years old in two more weeks. His daughter Anna, married to minuteman Daniel Harrington, was watching them all from her window as Ens. Munroe was struck and killed as he turned from the line toward a stone wall bordering the Buckman Tavern land.

Minutemen John Brown and Samuel Hadley were blasted down and killed as they sought the shelter of a swamp behind the Harrington houses.

Maj. Pitcairn said that "several shots were fired from a meetinghouse on our left." The three minutemen who had entered the meetinghouse had found themselves cut off by the advance of the British column on the green. They had fetched two small casks of powder down to the gallery when they heard the first British volley.

Caleb Harrington and Comee fled from the doorway that faced the green. Redcoats saw them and fired. Harrington was killed instantly. Comee, hit in the arm, managed to race to a nearby house, flee through it and escape into the woods. Joshua Simonds aimed his musket at one of the powder casks he had opened and was prepared to blow up the building and himself if the redcoats entered.

Pitcairn said that after the first shots, "without any order or regularity, the light infantry began a scattering fire, and continued in that situation for some little time, contrary to repeated orders both of me and the officers that were present." Lt. Barker, 4th Regt., also said that the troops, after the first shots, acted "without any orders."

Ebenezer Munroe was wounded in the arm by the second volley. "I'll give them the guts of my gun," he said to his brother John and fired at the redcoats.

"As I fired," said Ebenezer, "my face being toward them, one ball cut off a part of one of my earlocks, which was then pinned up. Another ball passed between my arm and my body, and just marked my clothes.

"As we were retreating, one of our company, Benjamin Sampson, I believe, who was running with me, turned his piece and fired. When I fired, I perfectly well recollect of taking aim at the regulars. The smoke, however, prevented my being able to see many of them. The balls flew so thick, I thought there was no chance for escape, and that I might as well fire my gun as stand still and do nothing."

Cpl. John, Ebenezer's brother, after seeing the bayoneting of Jonas Parker beside him, said, "I retreated about 10 rods, and then reloaded my gun a second time, with two balls, and, on firing at the British, the strength of the charge took off about a foot of my gun barrel." What that overcharge did to John Munroe's musket may still be seen at the Munroe Tavern.

Nathan Munroe and Solomon Brown managed to reach Buckman's stone wall. There, Nathan, with the British less than 100 feet away, "turned and fired at them." Brown, too, fired from behind the stone wall, ran to the back steps of the tavern and fired again, ran through the tavern to the front door and continued his firing.

Lt. William Tidd, fleeing up the North road that led past the green to Bedford, was pursued for 500 feet by an officer on horseback who yelled at him, "Damn you, stop, or you are a dead man!"

Tidd said that he found he could not escape unless he left the road. "Therefore I sprang over a pair of bars," he said, "made a stand, and discharged my gun at him; upon which he immediately returned to the main body...." Tidd thought his pursuer might have been Maj. Pitcairn.

More likely, the pursuer was Lt. Sutherland, whose horse bolted at the early gunfire and "galloped with me down a road above 600 yards" before he was able to turn.

The regulars, said Cpl. Munroe, "kept up the fire, in all directions, as long as they could see a man of our company in arms."

On the opposite side of the green two minutemen, Amos and Ebenezer Lock, who had started back to their homes after the earlier alarm, heard the firing and hurried back. As they came over the stone wall of the Buckman Tavern, they found Asahel Porter of Woburn shot through the body. Porter, captured early in the morning on his way to market, had been released with a fellow prisoner and had been cautioned not to run.

He did run, however, when he must have felt he was a safe distance, but a different redcoat, believing Porter was fleeing, shot him. On seeing the dead body, Ebenezer Lock was so revolted he took aim, Amos said, "and discharged his gun at the Britons."

Besides the dead there were nine wounded. Among them was a black man, Prince Estabrook, and Jedediah Munroe, who would be killed later in the day. There was also John Tidd, struck by a saber on the head; John Robbins, crippled for life; Nathaniel Farmer, Solomon Pierce and Thomas Winship.

Lt. Barker put the British losses succinctly. "We had a man of the 10th light infantry wounded, nobody else hurt. The man was Pvt. Johnson, hit in the thigh. At the same time Maj. Pitcairn's horse was hit twice, but the major could be no more specific than to say that the horse was hit "from some quarter or other."

Losses among minutemen in the buildings and the spectators in the houses could have meant further tragedy, save for an order issued by Lt. Col. Smith when he arrived at the green, Lt. Sutherland said:

"Col. Smith turned to me, asked me, 'Do you know where a drum is?'" Sutherland found a drummer and Smith ordered the drummer to beat, "To Arms!" At this, said Sutherland, "the men ceased firing."

Col. Smith later wrote to a friend that the troops had "been fired on from the houses repeatedly, were going to break them open to come to those within." Smith said he feared that if the enraged troops did this "none within could well be saved" and that he requested the drummer

Lexington Historical Society, Lexington, Mass.

Cpl. John Munroe's musket

because "I was desirous of putting a stop to all further slaughter of those deluded people."

The shooting overall had been over quickly and during it the sun came up. The expedition now began to reform its ranks. Lt. Barker said that the regulars "formed on the Common with some difficulty, the men were so wild they could hear no orders." And Lt. Sutherland, who told of three shots being fired at Smith from Buckman Tavern, said that he overheard Smith and Pitcairn regretting "the great warmth of the soldiers in not attending to their officers and keeping their ranks."

Rev. Jonas Clarke, incensed by the carnage and the troops' behavior, watched as they "drew up and formed in a body on the common, fired a volley and gave three huzzahs, by way of triumph...." Then to the music of fife and drum the redcoats resumed their march to Concord, and Rev. Clarke turned his attention to the bodies of the dead minutemen being carried into the meetinghouse.

Those dead and the wounded were a tragic loss to so small a settlement. So many were related. More than half of all the town's 144 minutemen came from only 14 families. Four families alone represented fully a third of the company: Munroes, Harringtons, Smiths, Reeds. In it were at least 10 pairs of fathers and sons. A father killed and a brother wounded, Anna Harrington, looking out on the green, also could see husband, brother-in-law, cousins and her 14-year-old son. And hers was only one bereaved household.

Nevertheless, resolutely, the men of Lexington, in greater numbers, would come together again this day at Capt. Parker's call — and more would be wounded, more would die.

After the regulars marched away, six stragglers (the first one seized by Joshua Simonds on emerging unharmed from the meetinghouse) were taken as the first British prisoners of the Revolutionary War. Ebenezer Munroe took their muskets into the Buckman Tavern and distributed them to minutemen who had none of their own. These muskets would be handy when the redcoats came back in the afternoon.

The prisoners were taken by Capt. James Reed to his dwelling in Woburn Precinct, where John Hancock and Samuel Adams had fled.

A short time after the first shots on the green, Hancock and Adams left Capt. Reed's house to flee deeper into Woburn. They passed minutemen marching along the highways, and one of the minutemen near the Reed house said that he heard the Lexington musketry. So could Adams, and he remarked to Hancock:

"Oh, what a glorious morning it is!"

Hancock thought that Adams referred to the bright spring day. More likely, Adams, who could see all around him the eager patriot response, would feel as he did when thousands rallied to the powder alarm. At that time the patriot Thomas Young, who was there, wrote to Adams that Adams could have seen "the temper of your countrymen in the condition your every wish, your every sigh for years past, panted to find it, thoroughly aroused and unanimously in earnest; something very important must inevitably come of it."

If Smith had any secret orders for the arrest of Hancock and Adams, events on the green canceled them.

'The war has begun!'

Lexington, a town of roughly 1000 souls, much fewer than the shire town of Concord, and strictly a farming community of little more than 120 families, might seem an unlikely place in which to change the destiny of two tremendous nations.

Far from being unique, Lexington was typical of countless New England communities. So the accident of Lexington's historic choice seems to emphasize the way that the overwhelming number of Americans of that day felt. Their men would respond because they believed passionately in their cause. In town after town there was many a preacher who, like Rev. Jonas Clarke, had been repeatedly preaching:

"The voice of liberty is the voice of God."

After Lord North, stubbornly ignoring the warning of the Earl of Chatham that "it would soon be too late" for reconciliation, had piled one Intolerable Act upon another, the issue in America was no longer merely taxation without representation. The colonists now believed that every one of their ancient liberties was at stake.

The sturdiness with which minutemen stood up to the crisis could be seen on April 19 on the countenance of Capt. Parker. He was a man inspired, a man sure of himself. That day, said the last survivor of the battle, Capt. Parker "looked as though he could face anything."

It just had to take unbounded courage to confront the trained, finely equipped, fully supplied regulars of the world's foremost power, backed with the world's greatest command of wealth, battalions and fleets.

Yet thousands of minutemen and militiamen were ready, even zealous, to take the awesome risk.

They responded throughout New England with exactly the enthusiasm and numbers that had troubled Gen. Gage's thoughts—thoughts that had impelled him to ask for what seemed to Great Britain to be a staggering total of reinforcements—and had made Gage wonder, with dread, where he should send his redcoats to stem the mounting rebellion.

The shouts of Dawes and Revere in the night brought into action first the men of the towns through which they sped, and companies formed in haste at the meetinghouses and on the greens.

Men of Charlestown, directly under the cannon of British men-o'-war, would be in arms despite Gage's threats. Men of the Boston Tea Party would serve again from Roxbury and Cambridge, and from Cambridge, one of them, John Hicks, would this time give his life. Minutemen gathered in Brookline, Medford and Menotomy—many would die, many would be wounded.

Dawes and Revere we know well. But countless expresses, picking up the first alarm, would fan out across the countryside—their names mostly unknown, as are most often their routes, long lost in the endless shiftings of highways.

An express on a white horse dashed into the center of Worcester. "To arms! To arms! The war has begun!" cried this messenger. Foaming and bleeding from desperate spurring, the horse collapsed, but was replaced with another mount and the express galloped on.

The fearsome message was rushed to other colonies.

Time and again in that rural, provincial world it would come to men at work in their fields. Beloved Israel Putnam, hearing the alarm as "on the wings of the wind," would leave his plow in the furrow and rush to arms.

The Connecticut governor's son, John Trumbull, would march at once, describing the occasion, for wild rumor would accompany the alarm:

"The blood of our brethren cried from the earth, and the cry was heard throughout New England."

New Hampshire's popular hero John Stark would get the word of Lexington while he was in his sawmill in Amoskeag at the falls of the Merrimack River. He would rush to his dwelling, get his gun and ammunition and gallop away, urging volunteers as he passed to rendezvous with him at Medford. Over on New Hampshire's western side, in Keene, Capt. Isaac Wyman would gather his minutemen at his tavern and all would take off for the battlefield.

When the alarm would reach Providence, 1000 Rhode Island men would march northward.

Though word of the British march and the battle was carried as fast as fleet horses could bear, it did not reach these remote areas until a day or two after April 19. But the men came on, merely changing direction toward Cambridge as news was encountered of developments and death on the battlefield. It would be from these assembling forces that the patriots would begin organizing the later siege of Gage and his redcoats in Boston.

The minutemen and militiamen who did reach the battlefield on April 19—a battlefield that would stretch from Concord to Charlestown—came that day from four Bay Province counties, Suffolk, Norfolk, Essex and Middlesex. From these counties only the minutemen and militiamen of some 30 towns could get to the battlefield in time to meet the redcoats.

More than 30 modern communities are involved historically, because many 18th Century towns were later subdivided, among them Somerville from Charlestown, Menotomy from Cambridge, Carlisle from Concord, Wayland from Sudbury and Natick and Wellesley from Needham.

The scene in all 30 towns during the night and the morning hours was one perfervidly repeated: the shout of the express rider; the ringing of the bell in the meetinghouse; the beat of the drum; the firing of alarm guns; in some places bonfires ignited or triple firing of muskets to project the message onward; sergeants forming up their men; women preparing food or flight with the children; the men hastening to battle.

Many of these marching patriots passed through Bedford and Watertown, each at a crossroads to the battlefield. The old Mill Bridge at Watertown provided a crossing of the Charles River. Beyond the bridge, the lower road from Watertown led to Menotomy, the upper one to Lexington and Concord. Companies, like the many passing through from Needham, were given impromptu refreshments by the Watertown women.

A Bedford woman told her impressions in her town:

"All day long the bells were ringing, the guns were firing, people were dashing back and forth on horseback, and all I could learn was that there had been an awful fight, ever so many killed, and I thought certain my husband must be one of them."

The variety of weapons carried by the men bespoke the volunteer nature of their enterprise. Uniformity was nonexistent. There were old family flintlocks used in picking off a woodchuck or raccoon, old French weapons captured mayhap at Louisburg or in the back-and-forth warfare around Lake George, an occasional bayonet, muskets of infinite-sized smooth bore, homemade weapons of countless character.

The men of those 30 towns came from all directions:

They marched from towns in and near the Merrimack Valley.

Tewksbury's captain of minutemen, John Trull, lived near the Merrimack River. At 2 a.m. an express galloped from the town's center and shouted, "Captain Trull! The British are on their way to Concord. I have alarmed all the towns from Charlestown to here." Capt. Trull grabbed his gun and discharged it three times from his bedroom window. Across the river, the captain in Dracut acknowledged the signal by firing three musket shots.

The Andover men were already marching when they learned of the killing on Lexington Green. In Billerica, Thomas Ditson Jr., and other Ditsons, lived on the Woburn road and were first to get the alarm coming from Woburn. They were off fast to muster on Billerica Common — ready to repay the redcoats for Ditson's tar and feathers. One of the captains at Chelmsford was in such a rush he marched off saying he could not wait even for the customary prayer!

Minutemen came from towns on the North Shore.

Two Lynn minutemen — one of them young, newly married Abednego Russell, who would be killed this day — were on the seashore hunting ducks. When they got word there was trouble "up country," they threw down their ducks and ran by Lynn Common to catch up with their company.

Beverly's minutemen would travel the farthest of any to join this day's struggle. Beverly's young Reuben Kennison was at work in his hillside field when he heard the bell ringing its alarm in the meetinghouse at Salem Village (now Danvers). He grabbed his flintlock and joined the minutemen of nearby Danvers.

Only the men of Lexington would suffer more killed than would the men of Danvers, and Kennison would be among those killed. The men of Danvers, tanners, potters and millers, rushed to get their arms, formed at the sound of the bell and the drum, shared in the preacher's prayer. They moved fast, covering in four hours the 16 miles to the battlefield. They went "full half the way upon the run," said Capt. Gideon Foster, their commander. Many of them were named Putnam, for Danvers was the birthplace of the hero Israel Putnam. And, en route, they would meet and be joined by more Putnams among the Medford minutemen.

And on came the minutemen from towns to the south and to the west.

Needham's losses would be exceeded only by those of Lexington and Danvers. Ens. Ephraim Bullard, whose son was a drummer in his company, gave the alarm by running up a hill back of his tavern and firing his gun three times. Men from West Needham (now Wellesley) gathered at the tavern.

In East Needham (now Needham) the alarm came from Dedham, and the militia formed near the minister's house, where the ammunition was kept. From Needham Leg (now Natick) Lt. John Bacon, who would be killed, came at a gallop. The march led across the Charles River into Newton, and then again across the Charles, over old Mill Bridge, into Watertown.

The alarm from Dedham reached Dover, and Elias Howe, who would give his life, left his harrow in the field and rushed off to join the minutemen.

On the field outside the Buckminster Tavern in Framingham, where Gage's spies had contemptuously watched them train, the minutemen of Framingham formed and marched off by the Old Connecticut Path to Concord. With them

was a black man, Peter Salem, who would win further renown at Bunker Hill. Since no slave could be mustered, Maj. Lawson Buckminster assented to his liberation and Salem went as did other freemen to defend their rights.

Many are the tales of individual fortitude among the minutemen hurrying to the battlefield.

Newton's oldest participant, 76-year-old Noah Wiswall, went with a company commanded by one of his sons. In it were two other sons and some sons-in-law. Wiswall went along, he said, because "he wanted to see what the boys were doing." He was injured in the hand by a British musket ball, kept right on fighting and got a redcoat's musket as a trophy.

In the oldest part of Watertown, Joseph Coolidge, father of seven young children, caught the sound of the alarm bell and heard the alarm guns. He unhitched his team from his plow, told his wife where he had buried the tax money (he was collector in his section of town) and hurried to Watertown center. There, not waiting for his company, he took off for the battlefield, acting also as a guide to some of the Needham minutemen. He would lose his life this day.

In the rally of the minutemen there is a tale that epitomizes the spirit of these patriots as they sped to answer the alarm.

Jonathan Harrington, 16, a fifer in the minuteman company, was asleep when the early alarm came to Lexington. His mother ran to his bedroom and awakened him:

"Jonathan, Jonathan," she gasped, "get up! The British are coming and something must be done."

All these minutemen from the 30 towns would fight the redcoats at various places along the eventual British retreat out of Concord to Charlestown.

There were, in addition, minutemen who would fight the redcoats in Concord itself, at the old North Bridge. These men were moving toward this battlefield even as the redcoats were marching the seven miles from Lexington to Concord, as Col. Smith expressed it, "without anything further happening." Smith would find happenings aplenty when he reached Concord.

Redcoats approach Concord

After Paul Revere's capture, Dr. Samuel Prescott had galloped by Meriam's Corner and along the highway past his own house and the meeting place of the Provincial Congress to warn Concord. Patriots heard his shouts, and presently the bell atop the Concord Town House was clanging.

Rev. William Emerson, young chaplain of the Provincial Congress and the community's patriot preacher, wrote in his diary:

"This morning between 1 and 2 o'clock we were alarmed by the ringing of ye bell. . . ."

When Rev. Emerson, who lived in the manse still standing by the North Bridge, heard the bell, he grabbed his musket and was the first to come running to the town square. At the far end stands the Wright Tavern, which had been used as a workshop and inn by the members of the Provincial Congress. Now it was pressed into use as headquarters for the assembling minutemen and militia.

Col. James Barrett dashed up on his horse. Ever since he had received urgent word to move or secure the military stores, he had given all his energy to the task. He got Prescott's message and hurried away to intensify his efforts, while in town, all available teams were pressed into action to help get the precious supplies secreted or carted away.

The Concord men were anxious both for further news and to send on the alarm. Dr. Prescott sped out of Concord to other towns. Concord minuteman Reuben Brown, a saddler, was sent down the Lexington road in the hope of getting information about what was really afoot at Lexington.

Meanwhile, the Concord men, those no longer needed for shifting supplies, were joined at the tavern by two companies of Lincoln men, Capt. William Smith with the minutemen and Capt. Samuel Farrar with the militia. They brought with them shocking rumors that there had been shooting on Lexington Green. More than ever, the Concord men were desperate for news.

Reuben Brown got to Lexington and was riding down Concord Hill, which approaches the green, when he saw the British fire and the obscuring belch of gunsmoke. He did not tarry an instant, swung his horse about and galloped for Concord.

Maj. John Buttrick asked him pointedly whether the British he had seen had fired actual bullets.

"I do not know," said Brown, "but I think it probable."

The Concord drummer beat the call.

Cpl. Amos Barrett of Concord estimated that even before sunrise there were about 150 men assembled. Then, said he, "we thought we would go and meet the British." Concord Capt. George Minot thought it vital that the patriots also occupy the nearby ridge, with the liberty pole, overlooking the town. Minot took his men there while the others marched along the Lexington road toward the oncoming redcoats and in about a mile and a half, said Cpl. Barrett:

"We see them acoming, we halted and stayed 'til they got within 100 rods, then we were ordered to the about-face and marched before them with our drums and fifes agoing and also the British. We had grand music."

Lincoln minuteman Amos Baker was in the patriot force.

"I saw the British troops coming up the road that leads on to the common at Concord," said Baker. "The sun shone very bright on their bayonets and guns." Those bayonets, 21 inches long and affixed at the end of the regular British musket, the 4½-foot Brown Bess, was about the most dreaded weapon the patriots had to face.

The mile-or-so-long road into Concord from Meriam's Corner is commanded on its right by the ridge. Lt. Barker wrote that when Smith's redcoats arrived at Meriam's Corner they saw that "country people had occupied a hill" overlooking the road. Smith ordered his light infantry to ascend the hill and march along the ridge while the grenadiers kept to the highway. This promptly cleared the ridge. "The Yankees," said Lt. Barker, "quitted it without firing."

The far-outnumbered patriots drew back

along the ridge to where Capt. Minot and his men had originally gone, and where Minot was joined by the Concord and Lincoln men who had marched back in front of the redcoats. There was no doubt now that there were far more redcoats than patriots, so the patriots shrewdly withdrew to a hill farther from the village, a hill overlooking the North Bridge.

"We marched into town," said Barker, "after taking possession of a hill with a liberty pole on it and a flag flying which we cut down."

The patriots, from their adjoining hill, could see clearly this hateful destruction. They could also see Col. Smith and Maj. Pitcairn ascend to the ancient, hilltop cemetery near the hacked liberty pole and study the countryside through a spyglass. Smith promptly went ahead with the orders Gage had given him, dispatching troops to seize the two bridges that led over the rivers into Concord.

One company under Capt. Munday Pole was sent to the South Bridge over the Sudbury River, which flows into the Concord River. A much larger detachment of six companies under Lt. Lawrence Parsons was sent to the North Bridge over the Concord River, both to secure the bridge and to search Col. Barrett's dwelling for military supplies.

Parsons's men stepped out "glittering in arms," as Rev Emerson observed them, "advancing toward us with the greatest celerity." The patriots took hurried counsel. Some were for making a stand. Rev. Emerson could see his own threatened manse across the road, just to his right. "Let us stand our ground," advised the courageous preacher, "if we die, let us die here!"

Others were for withdrawing. Rev. Emerson did concede that "others more prudent thought best to retreat 'til our strength should be equal to the enemy's by recruits from neighboring towns." This was the view of Col. Barrett, who had just arrived at the hill after concealing the supplies.

Barrett, in top command though handicapped in getting around on foot, ordered all the patriots to withdraw across the North Bridge and to go up the sloping elevation of Punkatasset Hill, overlooking the bridge, a maneuver they quickly began before Parsons and his six companies reached the bridge.

On arriving, Parsons posted one company at the bridge, marched across, posted two more companies on small hilltops across the river that commanded his route, then started off on the two-mile stretch to Barrett's. Parsons had three companies with him, would soon be joined by a fourth company sent by Smith and had as a guide Ens. deBerniere, the spy who had obtained the secret location of patriot supplies on his recent visit with the Tory Daniel Bliss.

At this menacing move by Parsons, Barrett galloped ahead to his farm to give his family and men there warning and last-minute instructions.

Barrett's order to the patriots had been prudent indeed. They reassembled on top of Punkatasset Hill. During the hour or more they waited, they could see the emergency plans made by the Provincial Congress come magnificently into effect as their numbers swelled.

Bedford had been alerted, doubly so. Josiah Nelson of Lincoln had been assigned to carry the alert to Bedford if the British came out. When Nelson heard Maj. Mitchell's midnight patrol (with Revere a captive), he had plunged out into the dark to inquire if these strangers knew anything about the British coming. "We will let you know when they are coming," replied one of the officers, and gashed Nelson's head with his sword.

Despite the injury, the first inflicted on April 19, Nelson made his way to Bedford after the patrol released him and his wife had dressed his wound. He alerted the part of Bedford near Lincoln. Two Lexington minutemen sent earlier by Capt. Parker had gone to Bedford center. Bedford Capt. Jonathan Willson, who later this day would lose his life, rallied his minutemen at Sgt. Jeremiah Fitch's tavern near Bedford center. The men ate hurriedly. Capt. Willson had a word of cheer:

"It is a cold breakfast, boys, but we will give the British a hot dinner. We'll have every dog of them before night." Capt. John Moore gathered the Bedford militia, and presently both companies were on the highway to Concord.

The men of Carlisle, then part of Concord,

had mustered to the sound of drum and horn, and headed for Concord.

When the alarm reached Westford, Lt. Col. John Robinson was unwilling to lose the time it would have taken him to go to the center of Westford and headed instead on a much more direct route to Concord. He gave orders for his men to muster at the church in the center and follow him, and he left word about sending food by horseback. As Robinson sped to Concord he was joined by an ardent patriot minister, Rev. John Thaxter, a friend of Rev. Emerson, who had come galloping with his brace of pistols.

Robinson would be one of the highest-ranking officers in the encounter now shaping at the North Bridge.

Other volunteers had started for Concord as individuals, not in company formations, from neighboring Littleton, Chelmsford, Stow and Groton. Nathan Corey and eight other Groton minutemen, curious about the brass cannon transported Tuesday to their town from Concord, had decided to go immediately to see what was doing.

"We travelled all night, carrying lighted pine torches a part of the way, and we reached Concord at an early hour of the morning. We all went and got some breakfast at Col. Barrett's house." They went to the center of Concord and then, with the Concord and Lincoln men, withdrew to Punkatasset Hill.

Next to Concord, Acton would have the most companies at the old North Bridge, two of militiamen and one of minutemen led by young Capt. Isaac Davis, who would be the first patriot to be killed at the bridge.

Just before dawn a horseman had galloped into Acton and pounded at the door of militia Capt. Joseph Robbins. "Captain Robbins! Captain Robbins! Up! Up! The regulars are coming to Concord. Quick as possible alarm Acton." Robbins's son jumped on a horse and sped the mile or so to Capt. Isaac Davis and, within an hour, Davis had his men ready to march. All four Davis youngsters were sick as Davis left with this poignant farewell to his wife, "Take good care of the children."

This imperative scene was repeated in South Acton. A swift horseman shouted the alarm at the dwelling of Col. Francis Faulkner of the Middlesex militia. Faulkner, partly dressed, fired his musket three times, and almost instantly came a responding three shots as the signal spread and a third Acton company assembled and headed for Concord.

As the critical wait on Punkatasset Hill passed, the number of patriots mounted toward 400. Beneath them on the slope, the three companies of redcoats near the North Bridge numbered about 100, and the redcoats out of sight at Barrett's numbered about 130.

The patriots appraised the situation and moved down from Punkatasset Hill to the lower height of the Buttrick field, much closer to the redcoats at the bridge.

The redcoats appraised the situation, too. They could see the patriot numbers growing though, as Lt. Barker observed, the patriots were covered by a wall. To him the number of the patriots on the hill already seemed 1000.

Capt. Walter S. Laurie, 43rd Regt., was in command of the three companies of light infantry that Parsons left to guard the bridge and the river road. As the patriots moved down to the Buttrick field, the two companies, of the 4th and 10th Regts., posted on the far side of the bridge prepared to move from their hillocks back toward the bridge. Laurie noticed their motion.

"Upon this," he said, "I sent Lt. Robertson of my own company to acquaint Col. Smith of my situation, desiring he would send some of the grenadiers to support me in case of their attacking. Mr. Robertson brought for the answer that two companies would be sent to me."

There was no question that the redcoats of the 4th and 10th companies, as Barker said, "were expecting to be attacked." Lt. Sutherland, always eager to be at the height of the action, was vexed when he learned more officers and men had gone ahead to join Parsons. Sutherland begged a couple of men from the 10th and took off for Barrett's farm. Suddenly one of his two men, the sergeant, called to him: "Sir, the company of the 4th are retiring."

Sutherland caught the reason for the withdrawal.

"I looked to my right and saw a large body of men marching almost within pistol shot of me. It struck me it would be disgraceful to be taken by such rascals and I made the best of my way for the bridge . . . 'til I joined Capt. Laurie."

As the 4th drew back, so did the 10th.

Ens. Lister said that Lt. Waldo Kelly, in command of the 10th in the absence of Parsons, consulted with the officers and all but Lister favored drawing back. Lister's objection was that their position was on a steepish hill and that they would be "under the muzzles of the rebels' pieces." Lister was overruled. "Luckily for us," he admitted, there was "not a shot fired."

The position of the three companies, two of them with the Concord River at their back, would grow even more precarious. For this, they could thank their grenadier comrades who were busy back in Concord Village seeking out military stores marked on the spy-inspired map that Gen. Gage had furnished Smith.

Several fires were set by the grenadiers. Right in the town square in front of the town house, a blaze was made of gun carriages. Cpl. Amos Barrett said that there were a number of entrenching tools found in the town house and these were carried out and burned, too. "At last," recounted Barrett, "they said it was better to burn them in the house and (did) set fire to them in the house."

A few houses along the Lexington road, the grenadiers set a fire in Reuben Brown's harness shop, where he had been making mounts for cannon. And, on the far side of the village near the South Bridge, Capt. Pole added to the startling scene by locating and burning wooden barrels packed with wooden plates and spoons.

The smoke rising from the fires was in clear view of the patriots in Buttrick's field, where Joseph Hosmer, acting as adjutant to Col. Barrett, was directing the formation of the companies already there and those arriving. Hosmer, a farmer, only recently had won great admiration when, with eloquence inspired by fervor, he had publicly replied to a polished speech by "Tory" Bliss ridiculing the Sons of Liberty.

What, with these fires, were the redcoats up to?

Concord Free Library, Concord, Mass.

Joseph Hosmer

The patriots could not be sure. They did not know that the grenadiers would extinguish the blazes when besought by the few townspeople who did not flee. The fire in the town house (which was also the county courthouse) would be doused with pails of water after an appeal from a 71-year-old widow, Martha Moulton, whose little house was right next door to the endangered square.

Barrett held a council on the hillside. Officers and patriot leaders of Concord joined in it, and as they were discussing their course of action, Adj. Hosmer uttered the question on most of their minds:

"Will you let them burn the town down?"

None dissented as they immediately resolved "to march into the middle of the town for its defense, or die in the attempt."

Capt. William Smith of Lincoln, younger and only brother of Abigail Adams, offered to take his minuteman company down to the river and clear the redcoats from the bridge. Barrett, veteran of the French and Indian Wars, had something more to employ than this raw courage, and decided to assign the head of the column to Capt. Isaac Davis.

Why? Davis was a gunsmith and he had equipped all the young men of his company with bayonets. Amos Baker, only Lincoln patriot present with a bayonet, said he heard Barrett and Davis mention this. Bayonets were a pretty scarce item in the patriot arsenal and, said Baker: "It was not certain whether the British would fire, or whether they would charge bayonets without firing."

Davis assured Barrett: "I haven't a man that's afraid to go."

Barrett thereupon gave his order to the men to march to the North Bridge, "pass the same, but not to fire on the King's troops unless they were first fired upon." Barrett was heard to repeat his caution several times. This was the order of the Provincial Congress. It was also the dictate of Barrett's judgment. Rev. Emerson has told us:

"We were the more careful to prevent beginning a rupture with the King's troops, we were then uncertain what had happened at Lexington, and knew not they had begun the quarrel there by first firing upon our people and killing eight men upon the spot." Concord had heard many rumors, but confirmation was yet to reach there.

The men, two by two, started to file down the hill with Maj. John Buttrick, Lt. Col. John Robinson and Capt. Isaac Davis in the lead.

Luther Blanchard, fifer, and Francis Barker, drummer, played the same martial air they had when their company left Capt. Davis's house in Acton, "The White Cockade."

As these brave, determined men marched along, another young fifer, John Buttrick Jr., son of the major, overheard a touch of 18th Century military courtesy. He recalled that Maj. Buttrick offered to give his superior in rank, Lt. Col. Robinson, the command, but Robinson, while asking to share the danger, declined to take the honor from the local commander.

Sight of the oncoming patriots stirred near-panic among the redcoats at the bridge.

Sutherland said that "Capt. Lumm galloped back as hard as he could to hasten the reinforce-

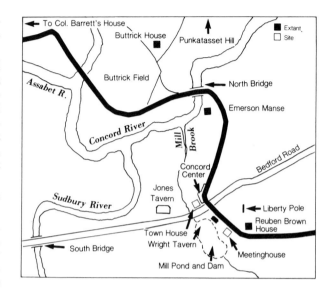

ment." Lister, totally forgetting that Parsons and his men would have to return this way, proposed destroying the bridge. The officers hastily agreed with Laurie that they should all withdraw across the bridge, and did so, giving orders to raise a few planks. Sutherland remembered:

"I being last that came over and raised the first plank myself."

Buttrick shouted to the redcoats to stop lifting the planks, and called to his column to step faster.

Laurie then attempted to execute a maneuver that Lt. Barker complained Laurie should have "done at first and then he would have had time to make a good disposition, but at this time he had not, for the rebels were got so near him that his people were obliged to form the best way they could as soon as they were over the bridge."

What Laurie tried to get his men to do was form for street fighting. He wanted the 4th company in front and the 10th behind it to shift into a column of squads to provide a succession of volleys, and he ordered his own 43rd company to deploy along the riverbank on either side to act as flankers and prevent the patriots from crossing. The maneuver would fail.

Suddenly there were shots.

No argument as at Lexington — Laurie conceded that the shots came from his side. The rebels, he said, "were close upon us, and I imagine myself, that a man of my company (afterwards killed) did first fire his piece...."

Barker, whose 4th company was in front, said, "The fire soon began from a dropping shot on our side."

Cpl. Amos Barrett of Concord, marching in double file in the third company in the patriot column, saw the British start the shooting "when they fired three guns one after another. I see the balls strike in the river on the right of me. As soon as they fired them they fired on us. Their balls whistled well." Acton patriots, too, saw and recalled all this.

One of these musket balls passed under the arm of Col. Robinson, struck the side of Luther Blanchard, and, still not spent, struck Jonas Brown of Concord. Blanchard, the 19-year-old fifer, would die a few months later from the effects of his wound.

The patriots kept pressing forward.

The front British squad fired a volley. In Laurie's words: "The company of the 4th Regt. gave a fire, as did a few of my own (company) from the flanks...."

It was a deadly volley.

Capt. Davis was taking aim when struck in the heart by a musket ball. He was flung into the air, was dead when he fell back on the river-bank. His brother Ezekiel Davis was wounded when a shot grazed his head. The same volley killed young Abner Hosmer, a private in Davis's company. Another member of the company, Thomas Thorp, was near Davis and some blood landed on his clothing. Thorp, who would serve throughout the war, often said that he could see that blood and he "never could and never would give up the cause."

Maj. Buttrick, leaping in outrage into the air, shouted to his men:

"Fire, fellow soldiers, for God's sake, fire!"

All the patriots fired, said Cpl. Barrett, "that could fire and not kill our own men."

The redcoats, among them the men of the 10th Regt. who had fired upon the small band of patriots who had stood earlier in the day on Lexington's green, took to their heels.

Sutherland had led some of Laurie's flankers, three or four, over the stone wall by the roadside near the Emerson manse. It was probably the fire of these men into the river that had first caught the eye of Cpl. Barrett. They brought down upon themselves the musketry of the minutemen. Sutherland said:

"When I was loading again and in the act of firing I received a shot a little above my right breast which turned me half 'round, when I heard Capt. Laurie exhorting his men to rally and fire. I called to Capt. Laurie I was wounded and made the best of my way, leaving two of the men that turned out with me dead on the spot and myself retiring under a fire from the enemy...."

Laurie's maneuver had collapsed. Laurie himself described his men fleeing. He said that after the 4th company fired its volley, and after some more shots from the flankers, "the whole went to the right about, in spite of all that could be done to prevent them."

They took off, said Barker, after the front company fired, "there being nobody to support the front company. The others not firing, the whole were forced to quit the bridge and return toward Concord...."

Lister wrote:

"We was obliged to give way, then run with the greatest precipitance...."

Cpl. Baker and the minutemen came to the bridge. Baker said:

"When I got over, there was two (regulars) lay dead and another almost dead. We did not follow them. There was eight or ten that was wounded and arunning and hobbling about looking back to see if we was after them."

A short way along the road back to Concord, the fleeing redcoats met ponderous Col. Smith marching at the head of a relief of grenadiers. Smith's size probably slowed their march, but Lister called the arrival of the grenadiers fortunate. While they were too late to help at the bridge, "yet they served as a cover for us to draw up our scattered company...."

About half the patriots ascended a hill and soon moved closer behind the ridge where they could observe the town center and what the redcoats were doing. The fires were extinguished now, and seeing the hundreds of troops at Smith's command must have reassured the patriots of the wisdom of awaiting more minutemen before rejoining the battle.

The other half of the patriots went back across the bridge, picked up the bodies of Capt. Davis and Hosmer and bore them to Maj. Buttrick's house on the hill.

Besides the two patriots killed, there were four wounded. Of the redcoats at the bridge, four of their eight officers were wounded. One would die, a prisoner, in a few days. Three redcoats were killed while a sergeant and four privates were wounded.

The patriots watching Smith's movements could get no clear idea of what he was doing. Smith seemed to have none either, with his troops tired, the wounded to be attended to, his concern about what was happening to Parsons. Rev. Emerson said that "the enemy by their marches and counter marches discovered great fickleness and inconstancy of mind, sometimes advancing, sometimes returning to their former posts."

Lister, on his side, told how he was assigned "to watch the motions of the rebels." He was as puzzled as they were. "We was kept continually running from hill to hill as they changed their positions," said Lister.

Unseen by both forces at Concord center, Parsons went about his task at the Barrett farm in complete ignorance of what was happening at the bridge. The last of the patriots' light cannon and muskets just had been plowed over in furrows and the plowman barely had withdrawn as the redcoats came past the Barrett sawmill to the farm. Other supplies, on Barrett's last-minute orders, had been hidden in the nearby woods.

Musket balls, flints and cartridges secreted beneath feathers in barrels in the attic were missed. A search of Col. Barrett's "muster room," as he called it, the room from which he ran the militia and minutemen, gave them nothing. They merely found the obvious, some cannon carriages, and prepared to burn these so

near the barn that Barrett's plucky wife protested. The fire was made instead in the roadway in front of the farmhouse.

Barrett's 25-year-old son Stephen, back from directing the Sudbury minutemen to avoid the South Bridge, entered the farmhouse. A British officer clamped his hand on Stephen's shoulder and placed him under arrest. Mrs. Barrett spoke up again. This man was her son, not Col. Barrett. Stephen was released.

Spy deBerniere plainly was no help. Without his Tory friends he could not identify one of the best-known men in Middlesex County, for Col. Barrett not only was a most trusted custodian of the provincial supplies and commanding officer of the militia and minutemen, but also was a Concord delegate to the Provincial Congress and one of those who had voted the Congress into existence.

Arrest? This sounded like Col. Smith when he had stopped at the Black Horse Tavern in Menotomy. Had Smith, after all, been given oral orders for arrests and never had his chance to impose them on Hancock and Adams?

Soon the Parsons detachment, returning, approached the North Bridge. On the hill were the patriots who had brought back the bodies. "They never attacked us," said deBerniere, and added: "They had taken up some of the planks of the bridge, but we got over. Had they destroyed it, we were most certainly lost."

Parsons's detachment saw bodies of redcoats near the bridge. One of the bodies seemed mutilated. It had been struck by a hatchet moments after the patriots had first driven the redcoats from the bridge. A youth, intending to join the fast-moving patriots, had seen the fatally wounded redcoat move and, in battlefield fright, had hit the unfortunate man with a hatchet.

Parsons's men, shocked by the sight, spread a tale of atrocity to their comrades on reaching Concord center. It was, like all atrocity tales, promptly magnified. Lister, who had been in the engagement at the bridge but had not seen the wretched victim of warfare, gave this exaggerated account:

"Four men of the 4th company killed, who was afterwards scalped, their eyes gouged, their

Bedford Library, Bedford, Mass.

Flag of the Bedford men

noses and ears cut off, such barbarity exercised upon the corpses could scarcely be paralleled by the most uncivilized savages. . . ." The horror tale grew worse on repetition despite two denying affidavits from the men who buried the two redcoats found near the bridge.

Smith's search for patriot war supplies had proved no more productive than Parsons's had at Barrett's farm. There, as deBerniere put it, "we did not find so much as we expected, but what was there we destroyed." Besides the items burned, there were some barrels of flour and kegs of musket balls located and dumped in the now-vanished millpond. Most were salvaged.

Of cannon, the most important weaponry marked on Smith's spy map, little was found. Barker recorded in sour comment on the patriots' last-minute dispersion that cannon "had

been there but had been taken away that morning."

Thorough Maj. Pitcairn, however, did uncover two iron 24-pounders in the tavern of Ephraim Jones, keeper of the nearby jail on the main square.

Jones had his door locked. On Pitcairn's orders the grenadiers pounded on the door. Jones refused them entry. Pitcairn ordered the door smashed, and when it was bashed open, he rushed in and collided with Jones. The major forced Jones to uncover the cannon in the jail yard, and trunnions were knocked off. Pitcairn then strode diagonally across the street into Amos Wright's tavern, now headquarters for the redcoats, and ordered himself a brandy and water.

Gen Gage, taking the language of Smith's report, would say that during the many searches the grenadiers made in Concord, they found the people "sulky; and one of them even struck Maj. Pitcairn."

Pitcairn, when the brandy and water was placed before him, may have been confirming the tale of being struck, for he plunged his finger into it and told his companions that he hoped he should "stir the Yankee blood so before night."

By noon Smith had given all the precious time he could to allowing Parsons's men to be rested, and to treating the wounded soldiers. Two of the wounded officers were sent ahead on chaises purloined by the redcoats. Then Smith gave the command to march, and the column started back for Boston with the grenadiers on the Lexington road and some light-infantry flankers on the ridge.

On the other side of the ridge, across the section that Rev. Emerson called "ye back way through ye great fields," the minutemen and militia came from the hills and the ridge and started marching and running in pursuit, toward Meriam's Corner.

Volley opens 16-mile battle

How the patriots reacted lives in the words of Cpl. Amos Barrett:

"We was soon after them. When they got a mile and a half to a road that comes from Bedford and Billerica they was waylaid and a great many killed."

This road enters the Lexington road beyond the end of the Concord ridge near the still-standing Meriam farmhouse, Concord's oldest dwelling and even then a good century old. Along this road the men of Billerica and Reading, who had come by the Bedford crossroads, approached the corner.

From across the great fields — along with the men who had fought at the North Bridge — came men from Sudbury and Framingham. The number of patriots pursuing the British column at Meriam's Corner now exceeded Col. Smith's force.

A young Reading doctor, John Brooks, who would become governor of his state, had a young minister in his minuteman company, Rev. Edmund Foster, who was so enthusiastic a patriot that when he heard the alarm guns fired he had gone running to Maj. Brooks to ask when they were going to Concord. Brooks had responded: "Immediately."

The Reading men had left their horses at Bedford and marched toward Meriam's Corner. Rev. Foster said:

"A little before we came to Meriam's Hill (the ridge), we discovered the enemy's flank guard, of about 80 or 100 men, who, on their retreat from Concord, kept that height of land, the main body in the road. The British troops and the Americans, at that time, were equally distant from Meriam's Corner.

"About 20 rods short of that place, the Americans made a halt.

"The British marched down the hill with very slow, but steady step, without music, or a word being spoken that could be heard. Silence reigned on both sides.

"As soon as the British had gained the main road, and passed a small bridge near that corner, they faced about suddenly, and fired a volley of musketry upon us. They overshot; and no one, to my knowledge, was injured by the fire. The fire was immediately returned by the Americans, and two British soldiers fell dead at a little distance from each other, in the road near the brook.

"The battle now began, and was carried on with little or no military discipline and order, on the part of the Americans, during the remainder of that day. Each one sought his own place and opportunity to attack and annoy the enemy from behind trees, rocks, fences, and buildings, as seemed most convenient."

Maj. Brooks cannily had some of his minutemen shield themselves behind the Meriam farmhouse and barns.

Ens. Lister, the 22-year-old Yorkshireman, about to be wounded, was among the light-infantry flankers who had come down from the ridge to Meriam's Corner. He recounted:

"As we descended the hill into the road the rebels begun a brisk fire but at so great a distance it was without effect, but as they kept marching nearer when the grenadiers found them within shot, they returned their fire. Just about that time I received a shot through my right elbow joint which effectually disabled the arm. It then became a general firing upon us from all quarters. . . ."

In a few moments Cpl. Barrett came to the bridge near Meriam's Corner. He said:

"When I got there a great many lay dead and the road was bloody."

The patriot force was now formidable. Col. Smith could well be hungering for sight of the reinforcements he had requested long before daybreak, and for which he may have forlornly lingered longer in Concord center.

Sudbury, then the largest town in Middlesex County, had sent a large force, six companies. Already present from West Sudbury (now Sudbury) was the minuteman company under Capt. John Nixon, who would become a general in the war, and the militia under Capt. Aaron Haynes.

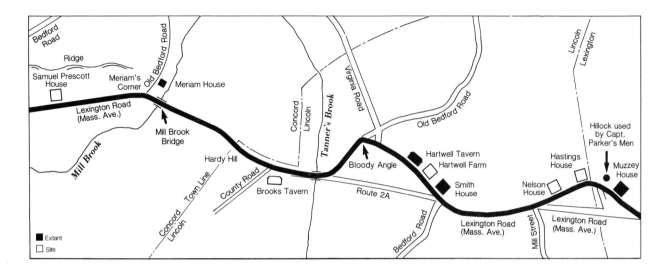

The spirit of these men was that of Deacon Josiah Haynes, the captain's cousin.

The deacon, aged 79 years, was offended by being put in the over-age, alarm company, so he had grabbed his powder horn and musket and marched along with the minutemen. Shortly, the deacon would be killed. With him were many Haynes cousins equally spirited, among them the company drummer, the captain's son, Aaron Haynes Jr., just turned 16 years old on this day.

With the Framingham men was Daniel Hemenway, in the same company as Peter Salem. Hemenway would be badly wounded.

Capt. Ebenezer Bridge, commanding the minutemen from Billerica, would, like Salem, be among the heroes at Bunker Hill.

The men of Stow were here, aroused by Dr. Samuel Prescott on his gallop beyond Concord. Two companies from Chelmsford were on hand, one led by Capt. Oliver Barron, who would be wounded, and the other by Capt. Moses Parker, who would die a hero at Bunker Hill. Here, too, were three companies of militia from Woburn and the men of Westford under Capt. Oliver Bates, who would be so grievously wounded that he would die the coming July 4.

The bridge near Meriam's Corner was over a small, winding brook that flowed toward Concord center and formed the millpond into which

the British had dumped their skimpy spoils of flour and musket shot. The brook, in its earlier meanderings through Lincoln, was also known as Tanner's Brook and would come again into the battle.

Once the redcoats crossed the small bridge and the brook, the battle was not only intensified but was of a nature distinctly different. On Lexington Green and at Concord's North Bridge, the patriots had sought to form a line or column, and, if called upon, to stand and fire at their foe. Now, and all the way to Charlestown, there would be no more of this European-type exchange.

The patriots would take instead to a style better adapted to their countryside. It would confound and outrage the redcoats.

Lt. Sutherland called these tactics a "cowardly disposition." To him the patriots were "concealed villains." Ens. Lister reviled the patriots' "skulking way behind hedges and wall."

A British soldier wrote: "We did not see above 10 in a body, for they were behind trees and walls, and fired at us, and then loaded on their bellies." Another complained: "They never would engage us properly." And Col. Smith, in his official report, criticized the patriots because, he said, they "did not make one gallant attempt ... but kept under cover."

Furthermore, Lexington and Concord gunfire had been basically skirmishes. Beyond the Mill Brook the battleground would be a continuous stretch. There would be bloodshed all the way to Charlestown, and deaths would mount sharply on both sides.

Beyond the brook the land sloped upward to Hardy's Hill in Lincoln. Disaster would increasingly confront Smith as his regulars marched on.

There was no reason in the world why the patriots should have further tried the European manner of warfare. It would merely have made them targets for the grenadiers' bayonets. They had no top commander present to coordinate their efforts. And these tactics they were adopting from necessity — and some war experience in the American forests — would prove highly successful.

Within four more miles these patriot tactics would have Smith's force completely demoralized and near collapse.

On Hardy's Hill a country road came into the Lexington road at an angle near the old Brooks Tavern, and along this road came the companies from East Sudbury (now Wayland) with the minutemen under Capt. Nathan Cudworth. They immediately scattered into positions in the woods on either side and blasted at the retreating redcoats with a constant fire.

On the other side of the Lexington road the West Sudbury men, under Lt. Col. Ezekiel Howe, who had come across the field from Meriam's Corner, now poured on their fire as the British went down the hill to the little bridge over Tanner's Brook.

A redcoat's musket ball struck and killed Sudbury's Asahel Reed. In the furious musketry still other Sudbury heroes were wounded, old and young, 69-year-old Thomas Bent and 24-year-old Joshua Haynes Jr., whose 19-year-old cousin of the same name would soon give his life to his country at Bunker Hill.

Beyond Tanner's Brook the Lexington road, once again climbing a hill, made a turn to the left and, very shortly, made a right-angle turn to the right and continued on past the still-standing dwellings of Sgt. John Hartwell and Capt. William Smith. This would be the scene, especially this right-angle turn with dense woods and thickets on either side, of some of the day's goriest fighting.

It would be called "the Bloody Angle."

The possibility of ambushing the redcoats at this spot occurred to many of the patriots. Bedford's Capt. Jonathan Willson hurried his minutemen by Tanner's Brook to take a commanding position in the woods in the angle. Capt. Willson, who would within minutes lose his life, was accompanied by his brother-in-law Thompson Maxwell. They were married to half-sisters.

Maxwell, a teamster, hailed from Bedford but was living at Amherst, N.H. He was stopping at Bedford to break his trip to the Boston market. On a similar trip in 1773, Maxwell had met John Hancock and become a member of the Boston Tea Party.

This trip Maxwell had been in Boston on the eve of the battle and had seen movements in the British camp that intimated impending action. He had sat up until early morning discussing them with Capt. Willson. Maxwell would recall:

"Next morning early he (Willson) had orders to march with his company to Concord; he requested me to go with him. I went well armed and joined in the fight. My brother (Willson) was killed; next day I hired a man to drive my team home, and never went home 'til after the battle of Bunker Hill."

Men from Woburn took positions in the wooded ambush. They had come by way of Lincoln Meetinghouse. Future Gov. Loammi Baldwin told how they had come to the bridge at Tanner's Brook "and then concluded to scatter and make use of the trees and walls for to defend us, and to attack them. I had several good shots."

Minuteman Daniel Thompson was one of three brothers from Woburn. When he had first heard the alarm he had sped on his horse to arouse others. One man asked him if he wasn't too hasty. Thompson told him:

"I tell you that our tyrants are on their march to destroy our stores, and if no one else opposes them, I will!"

Minuteman Nathaniel Wyman, a member of Capt. John Parker's Lexington company, had moved farther along the road to get in his repayment for what the redcoats had done that morning on Lexington Green. He was among the patriots waiting in the woods.

Rev. Edmund Foster had come across the fields from Meriam's Corner with the Reading men. He said:

"The enemy retreated and were followed. We saw a wood at a distance, which appeared to lie on or near the road the enemy must pass. Many leaped over the wall and made for that wood. We arrived just in time to meet the enemy.

"There was then, on the opposite side of the road, a young growth of wood well filled with Americans. The enemy was now completely between two fires, renewed and briskly kept up. They ordered out a flank guard on the left to dislodge the Americans from their posts behind large trees; but they only became a better mark to be shot at."

Bodies of eight redcoats were found at the angle in the road, and a large number were wounded.

The patriots' cost was high, too, because of the flankers. This was the part of the highway where deBerniere had completely missed the

hazards on his spy trip. Now, on the march back, he said, Col. Smith "put out flankers more numerous and further from the main body." It was these flankers closing in on the minutemen in the woods who killed and wounded so many patriots.

Capt. Willson, Nathaniel Wyman and Daniel Thompson all died at the Bloody Angle. There were wounded, too. Job Lane of Bedford had his leg so shattered it had to be amputated.

Daniel Thompson's oldest brother, Samuel, had told his 15-year-old son Jonathan to take care of his mother. Instead, Jonathan, borne on the excitement of a people's mobilization, had found an old musket and had tagged along.

Moving away from the Bloody Angle, Samuel unexpectedly caught sight of Jonathan. "Why, Jonathan, you are here!" said the father, then, accepting it, added, "Well, take care of yourself. Your uncle Daniel has been killed. Be prudent, my son, and take care of yourself."

Loammi Baldwin watched the redcoats as they moved beyond the Bloody Angle. He said: "The enemy marched very fast, and left many dead and wounded and a few tired."

The redcoats came now to the two Hartwell

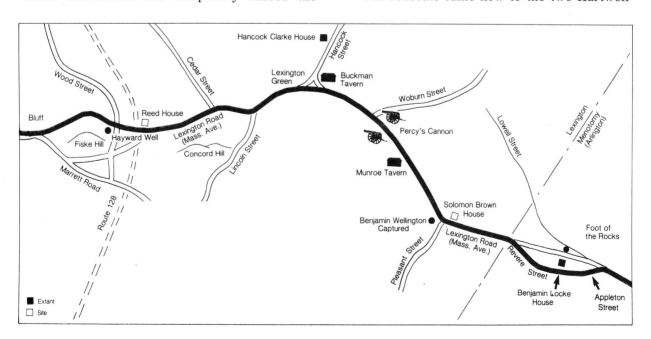

dwellings, Ephraim Hartwell's tavern; in which Sgt. John Hartwell of the Lincoln minutemen lived; and the Sgt. Samuel Hartwell farmhouse, where his brave wife Mary, who had carried the Lincoln alarm for Dr. Samuel Prescott, was caring for her children in the absence of her husband on the battlefield.

During the day she had seen "an occasional horseman dashing by, going up and down, but heard nothing more until I saw them coming back in the afternoon, all in confusion, wild with rage, and loud with threats.

"I knew that there had been trouble, and that it had not resulted favorably for the retreating army.

"I heard the musket shots just below, by the old Brooks Tavern, and trembled, believing that our folks were killed.

"Some of the rough, angry soldiers rushed up to this house and fired in; but fortunately for me and the children, the shots went into the garret, and we were safe. How glad I was when they all got by the house...."

That night Mrs. Hartwell could not sleep because she knew that "there were British soldiers lying dead by the roadside." Next morning when Ephraim Hartwell hitched up his oxcart and brought five of the British dead to the old Lincoln cemetery, she got to thinking compassionately of their loved ones across the Atlantic, took her children and followed the rude hearse.

"I remember how cruel it seemed to put them into one large trench without any coffins. There was one in a brilliant uniform, whom I supposed to have been an officer. His hair was tied up in a cue (queue)."

A number of other British dead along the main road in Lincoln were buried in unmarked graves near where they fell. One grenadier was shot between the Hartwell houses. Next beyond these houses was the farmhouse of the commanding officer of both Hartwell sergeants, Capt. William Smith. A grenadier left wounded was carried into the Smith house and died there three days later. His wounds were so painful he begged to be killed.

The patriots suffered, too. Three of the four Concord captains were wounded in the pursuit. But the British losses much exceeded those of the patriots. A Lincoln minuteman, William Thorning, had a miraculous escape when caught between the fire of the main British column and the flankers. He managed to hide behind one of a number of huge boulders on the roadside farm of Josiah Nelson and quickly picked off two redcoats.

Still another redcoat was shot in the doorway of the last house in Lincoln, the Samuel Hastings house. Here again the wounded man was given shelter, but died of wounds.

Col. Smith, in his report to Gage, would say that once he left Concord, the enemy "began to fire on us from behind walls, ditches, trees, etc., which, as we marched, increased to a very great degree, and continued without the intermission of five minutes altogether...."

For Smith, the worst was awaiting him in Lexington, which he now approached.

Redcoats flee from Lexington

Lexington's minutemen led by Capt. Parker were waiting for the returning redcoats on a hillock just across the Lincoln-Lexington line. With them were men from Cambridge in Capt. Samuel Thatcher's command.

The hillock was at a curve in the road between the Hastings house and that of John Muzzey. While Samuel Hasting's house was in Lincoln, he, like John Muzzey, was a member of Capt. Parker's company. So was Hasting's son and so were three of Muzzey's sons. One of them, Isaac, the oldest, had been killed earlier on Lexington Green.

These men gathered on the hillock, some overlooking their homes, and with deep-rooted determination leveled their muskets at the disspirited, desperate redcoats practically fleeing from Lincoln.

The British column was so shattered that Col. Smith, seeing it virtually disintegrating, sought frantically to restore some military cohesion. Just beyond the Muzzey house, the road curved around a high bluff and started to ascend the slope of Fiske Hill. Smith posted a rear guard on the bluff and ordered his officers to force the men into a column on the road.

The effort failed as the patriots, moving fast from the hillock, sent Smith's rear guard pellmell down the bluff, adding to the military disarray on the road.

The redcoats developed still another problem, ammunition. Lt. Barker told how both sides had been keeping up an "incessant fire" though the rebel fire was more effective because "they were so concealed there was hardly any seeing them." The rebels' numbers were always increasing, said Barker, "while ours was reducing by deaths, wounds and fatigue, and we were totally surrounded with such incessant fire as it's impossible to conceive. Our ammunition was likewise near expended."

DeBerniere had the same dejected report: "When we arrived within a mile of Lexington our ammunition began to fail, and the light companies were so fatigued with flanking they were scarce able to act, and a great number of wounded scarce able to get forward, made a great confusion. Col. Smith had received a wound through his leg, a number of officers were also wounded, so that we began to run rather than retreat in order — the whole behaved with amazing bravery, but little order; we attempted to stop the men and form them two deep, but to no purpose, the confusion increased rather than lessened."

Rev. Foster pictured the military shambles and what happened to Maj. Pitcairn, who had been trying with Smith to re-establish order in the collapsing column: "An officer, mounted on an elegant horse, and with a drawn sword in his hand, was riding backwards and forwards, commanding and urging on the British troops. A number of Americans behind a pile of rails, raised their guns and fired with deadly effect.

"The officer fell, and the horse took fright, leaped the wall, and ran directly towards those who had killed his rider." Pitcairn was unhorsed, but he was not killed. However, along with his horse, Pitcairn's superb brace of pistols was captured and soon presented to the popular hero Israel Putnam. Putnam used them throughout the war.

There was no letup in the patriot attack on Fiske Hill. "We fired on them, and continued so to do, . . ." said Lexington minuteman Nathan Munroe. Jedidiah Munroe, wounded on Lexington Green in the morning encounter, was now mortally wounded in the struggle on Fiske Hill. Sudbury's valiant old deacon Josiah Haynes, who had pursued the redcoats from Meriam's Corner, now lost his life in the furious musket fire.

At the foot of Fiske Hill young James Hayward of Acton paused at the well of the Fiske farmhouse. A redcoat emerging from the house raised his musket to Hayward, exclaiming, "You are a dead man!"

"And so are you!" replied Hayward, bringing up his weapon. Each fired. The regular dropped dead and Hayward, mortally wounded, would die in a few hours.

Only one more hill remained before Lexington center, Concord Hill, higher than Fiske Hill. Over this, under continual fire, the redcoats literally ran. Behind them on Fiske Hill would later be the graves of many regulars, marked and unmarked. And now the fleeing British even abandoned their wounded.

Between the two hills was the homestead of a Lexington minuteman, Thaddeus Reed. Three wounded redcoats were borne into it, died and were buried nearby. Three more wounded redcoats were abandoned in the flight over Concord Hill and these, with the help of Rev. Foster, would be carried into Buckman Tavern, and one would die there. Panic had seized the fleeing regulars. They rushed right past Lexington Green.

These were the troops who only this morning, in their illusion of invincibility, had fired so eagerly, so contemptuously at the farmers who had gathered solely to defend their ancient, hard-won rights. None, at sunrise, would have imagined that roughly nine hours later there would be this swift, this ignominious retribution.

For the redcoats now, here where their volley had signaled the beginning of the Revolutionary War, there was only the hot urgency of flight. DeBerniere said: "At last, after we got through Lexington, the officers got to the front and presented their bayonets, and told the men if they advanced they should die; upon this they began to form under a very heavy fire."

They were slightly beyond Lexington Green and in the center of the town. And now, suddenly, rescue was at hand: the first brigade, one of three brigades under Gen. Gage. One thousand men strong, the brigade had arrived under the command of one of Great Britain's highest noblemen, Lord Percy of Northumberland, on a traditional white horse of the Percys.

Ens. Lister has helped to preserve the emotions of the regulars at this moment. They were met by Percy, said Lister, "to our great joy, our ammunition being then nearly expended."

The struggle on Fiske Hill

Lt. Barker has helped recall events, too. He said:

"We had been flattered ever since the morning with expectations of the brigade coming out, but at this time had given up all hopes of it, as it was so late.

"As soon as the rebels saw this reinforcement, and tasted the field pieces, they retired, and we formed on a rising ground and rested ourselves a little while, which was extremely necessary for our men who were almost exhausted with fatigue."

If Percy's brigade had not arrived, said Barker, with so few of Smith's men having ammunition left and the men too fatigued to put out flankers, "we must soon have laid down our arms, or been picked off by the rebels at their pleasure...."

One British soldier present, a future historian, said some of the regulars "were obliged to lie down for rest on the ground, their tongues hanging out of their mouths, like those of dogs after a chase."

Percy has left a commander's view of the military extremity Smith had reached. Percy wrote to his father, the Duke, and told how he had met Smith's regulars "surrounded by rebels, having fired almost all their ammunition.

"I had," he added, "the happiness ... of saving them from inevitable destruction."

The fieldpieces mentioned by Barker were two 6-pounders placed on two hillocks commanding the village. Percy ordered them fired at the rebels and said, "The shot from the cannon had the desired effect, and stopped the rebels for a little time, who immediately dispersed and endeavored to surround us, being very numerous."

One cannonball pierced the meetinghouse on the green, another hit minuteman Daniel Harrington's house on the edge of the green. Loammi Baldwin of Woburn was approaching Buckman Tavern "with a prisoner before me when the cannon began to play. I retreated back toward the meadow, north of the meetinghouse, and lay and heard the balls in the air and saw them strike the ground."

Cannon fire was terrifyingly novel to most of the minutemen and they scurried to take cover. But they did not depart. Their numbers, as Percy noted, continued to grow. Three companies of men arrived from Newton, and along the road from Watertown came the patriots' first general officer, Maj. Gen. William Heath, and with him Dr. Joseph Warren, soon to be named the patriots' de facto governor of the province.

Heath, longtime military and civic leader in Roxbury and a member of the Provincial Congress, and Warren had come by way of Watertown to get to the rear of the British. They had just attended a morning session of the Committee of Safety at the Black Horse Tavern.

Heath and Warren now rallied the patriot forces after the cannonade, and soon the minutemen started moving in on Percy's position.

It was well after 2 p.m.

Percy had been much longer marching to Lexington than had Smith, who came via the marshes of Cambridge. Percy's route of course was a few miles longer, the land route via Boston Neck, Roxbury, Brookline and South Cambridge (now Brighton) to the Great Bridge (site of the present Larz Anderson bridge).

It was not the route that was the problem. Percy's departure had been hexed by a pair of military blunders.

Worried Gen. Gage had planned the brigade departure for 4 a.m. But it was nearly 9 a.m.—five hours later—before Percy had given the command to march out of Boston.

Gage's original orders for the reinforcements had been left for a brigade major who was away from his quarters. This error was not discovered until after Smith's express arrived with his appeal for reinforcements. New orders were issued at 6 a.m., which is the time Lt. Mackenzie, Royal Welsh Fusilier who marched with Percy, said he got orders to be on the grand parade on the Common.

By the "utmost expedition," said Mackenzie, who was adjutant of the regiment, he got his men to the Common at 7:30.

The second blunder cost another hour. Orders for the marine detachment had been sent to the quarters of Maj. Pitcairn through staff failure to recall that the major had left earlier with Smith. This was not discovered until 7:30, and it took an hour for the marines to get their equipment and reach the parade and form up.

To save time, Percy refused to take along more than 24 rounds for each of his cannon. He decided that the 140 rounds available for him in a wagon near the Common would retard his march and he "did not imagine there would be any occasion for more than there was in the side-boxes." The cannon, anyway, would slow his march.

While en route, Percy had no knowledge of what had been happening to Smith's expedition. Capt. William Glanville Evelyn, a clergyman's son in the King's Own, 4th Regt., wrote to his father overseas that the three regiments and the marines with Percy marched out from Boston "little suspecting what was going on.

"We observed on our march as we went that the houses along the road were all shut up as if deserted, though we afterwards found these houses were full of men, and only forsaken by the women and children."

Lt. Mackenzie got the same bodeful impression so in contrast with the spring morning. "Few or no people were to be seen; and the houses were in general shut up. . . ."

There were clearer signs of hostility. On arrival at the Great Bridge, a name that went back to its being the first bridge across the Charles River, Percy found that the planks had been taken up—but, curiously, had been left conveniently on the opposite shore. Capt. John Montresor, well-known mapmaker and royal engineer, was busy having the planks put back.

Percy's delay was brief, but his baggage train had greater delay, was left behind and very shortly would be captured by the old men of Menotomy.

Percy got his first intimation of trouble ahead when he heard shots and met, riding along propped in bedding in a stolen chaise, a British officer who had been wounded at Concord's North Bridge, little Lt. Edward Thornton Gould, who, a bit farther on, would be captured by the same old men of Menotomy.

Gould's breathless tale of what the rebels had done astounded Percy.

"I never believed, I confess," Percy would confide, "that they would have attacked the King's troops. . . ."

Percy pressed on. Mackenzie said that at first they "heard some straggling shots." Then: "As we advanced we heard the firing plainer and more frequent, and at half past two, being near the church (meetinghouse) at Lexington, and the fire increasing, we were ordered to form the line . . . but by reason of the stone walls and other obstructions it was not formed in so regular a manner as it should have been. . . ."

"The village of Lexington lay between both parties.

"We could observe a considerable number of rebels, but they were much scattered, and not above 50 of them to be seen in a body in any place. Many lay concealed behind the stone walls and fences. They appeared most numerous in the road near the church, and in a wood in the front, and on the left flank of the line where our regiment was posted. A few cannon shots were fired at those on, and near the road, which dispersed them. . . ."

The cannon fire of Percy's was the first of the Revolutionary War.

Presently, the rebels, said Mackenzie, "endeavored to gain our flanks, and crept into the covered ground on either side, and as close as they could in front, firing now and then in perfect security. We also advanced a few of our best marksmen who fired at those who showed themselves."

The musketry of the patriots was effective despite all Percy's precautions. Seven officers were wounded and a large number of redcoats were killed or wounded.

Percy used his 30- or 45-minute halt to allow Smith's men to rest and the wounded to be treated at the Munroe Tavern, where John Raymond, Munroe's crippled neighbor, was forced to serve the redcoats drinks.

Several roadside buildings, barns and shops, which Percy felt the rebels were using as shelters or for gunfire, were ransacked and burned, stone walls were pushed over and other buildings were pillaged. Now that some redcoats were getting into abandoned houses, the looting, which started back in Lincoln, grew steadily

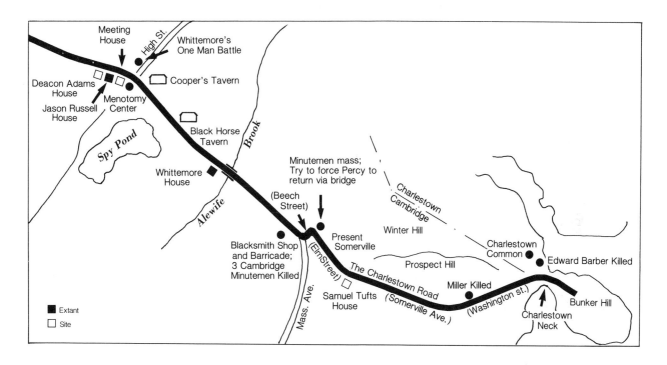

worse, but would cost some trapped redcoats their lives.

Percy, with miles ahead to Boston and the patriot assault continuing, decided shortly after 3 p.m. that he should start back. He assigned the most dangerous post, the rear guard, to Mackenzie's Royal Welsh Fusiliers.

A few redcoats in the taproom of the Munroe Tavern, as a parting gesture, committed an outrage that was a foretaste of barbarities ahead against unarmed civilians. They took shots at the old crippled John Raymond and mortally wounded him as he tried to flee through a back door into the garden.

Percy, as acting brigadier general, was now in command of the expedition and had superceded wounded Lt. Col. Smith. Smith's tired,

wounded and battered men were placed in front of the formation and were covered by Percy's brigade. This was Percy's plan, with strong flanking parties and with the marines and his other two regiments to alternate in the rear to relieve the Royal Welsh Fusiliers.

Fighting, with minutemen from the four counties taking positions along the route ahead, was far from over.

Indeed, the hardest and bloodiest fighting of the entire day was still to come.

Percy's white horse would be shot—not a slight feat in view of the flankers and the musket of that day, a smooth-bore weapon without modern sights and effective at up to less than 200 feet.

Menotomy: The bloodiest fighting

Percy, picturing the harassment of his force by the minutemen, said that they kept about his men with incessant fire wherever they went "like a moving circle."

Mackenzie said it began before they had been a mile on the road from Munroe Tavern. This was in East Lexington.

"Numbers of armed men on foot and on horseback were continually coming from all parts guided by the fire...." The regulars were hit "from all quarters, but particularly from the houses on the roadside and the adjacent stone walls.

"Several of the troops were killed and wounded in this way, and the soldiers were so enraged at suffering from an unseen enemy, that they forced open many of the houses from which the fire proceeded, and put to death all those found in them."

Barker put it stronger:

"We were now obliged to force almost every house in the road, for the rebels had taken possession of them and galled us exceedingly." He recalled: "When we got to Menotomy there was a very heavy fire...."

Wounded Ens. Lister, who had a musket ball removed from his arm while he was at Munroe Tavern, has left a graphic picture of what the patriot assault was like:

"I found the balls whistled so smartly about my ears I thought it more prudent to dismount and as the balls came thicker from one side or the other so I went from one side of the horse to the other for some time, when a horse was shot dead close by me, that had a wounded man on his back and three hanging by his sides. They immediately begged the assistance of my horse which I readily granted, and soon after left him wholly to their care."

The column was now moving across the base of present Arlington Heights, then a rocky, wooded section called the Foot of the Rocks. It gave cover to many of the pursuing minutemen and a vantage from which to fire upon the retreating column as it passed near the still-standing dwelling of Menotomy Capt. Benjamin Locke. Farther on, the road descended to the Arlington plain.

Along this flaming stretch, from the Foot of the Rocks through the center, would now occur more than half of all the patriot and redcoat casualties of the day. Percy's men were lively and angered. There would be barbarity, looting and slaughter. The minutemen, incensed by the outrages, would strike back with power augmented by fully three dozen companies from half as many towns now reaching the battlefield.

Below the Foot of the Rocks, Percy swung around his cannon and fired to scatter his attackers.

Gen. Heath told how he was several times greatly exposed to danger and how on this plain Dr. Joseph Warren, "who kept constantly near me, and was then but a few feet distant, a musket ball from the enemy came so near his head as to strike the pin out of the hair of his earlock."

Heath told of a fearless doctor who, finding he could not equal a flanker's skill with the bayonet, reversed his musket and used it to club his opponent to the ground. He thus recounted what his squat, muscular Roxbury neighbor did then:

"On this plain, Dr. Eliphalet Downer, in single combat with a British soldier, killed him on the spot by thrusting nearly through his body with his bayonet."

DeBerniere described the center of Menotomy as "a village with a number of houses in little groups extending about half a mile."

Unobstructed now by the rocky ground of the heights, Percy put his flankers far out on either side of this stretch, as he moved his column toward the center with its dominant meeting-house steeple.

The patriots from the roadside houses, said deBerniere, "kept a very heavy fire, but our troops broke into them and killed vast numbers; the soldiers showed great bravery in this place, forcing homes from whence came a heavy fire, and killing great numbers of rebels."

But all was not bravery.

On the right, on approaching the center, was the home of Deacon Joseph Adams, who had fled to the nearby hay barn of the local minister. There, redcoats prodded after him with bayonets. Back in the Adams house, still ill in her bed, was the deacon's wife, Hannah, and her new baby. Her life was menaced with a bayonet. She was forced to flee to the corn house while some soldiers looted and set the dwelling on fire. Five other Adams children, who had been hiding under the bed, put the fire out.

A short distance away was the farmhouse of neighbor Jason Russell, which was now to become the bloodiest scene of the day.

Russell, 58 years old and lame, had taken his wife and youngest son to a dwelling high on the slope back of his house, then returned to defend his home. He used some bundles of shingles to block the gateway in his long stone wall. Here he was joined by minutemen from Danvers under Capt. Israel Hutchinson, Capt. Gideon Foster, a strapping 26-year-old, and by other minutemen and militiamen from Needham and Lynn.

The Danvers minutemen had made such haste to reach the battlefield that 16-year-old Amos Putnam, relative of hero Israel Putnam and one of the numerous Putnams present in the patriot forces, had collapsed en route and died.

As the British column came along the main road, the men at the stone wall and around the Russell yard opened fire. The British force seemed bigger to Capt. Foster than his men had expected. Capt. Foster recounted:

"I discharged my musket at the enemy a number of times (I think 11) with two balls each time, and with well directed aim. My comrade, Mr. Cleaves of Beverly, who was standing by my side, had his finger and ramrod cut away with a shot from the enemy."

Young Reuben Kennison of Beverly, whose wife had run after him to bid an endearing farewell as he left Ryal Side (part of Beverly) to join the Danvers minutemen, was struck by British musket balls and killed in the Russell yard. Some of his young Danvers comrades died here, too, among them 22-year-old Jotham Webb attired in his wedding suit. On leaving his bride Webb had said: "If I die, I will die in my best clothes."

The youngest of the Danvers men who lost their lives in battle, Perley Putnam, 21 years old, was killed in the Russell yard. Samuel Page, the son of a Danvers militia captain, was trying to reload his musket and broke his ramrod. He turned to borrow Putnam's and as he did there were shots from behind them. Young Putnam dropped dead at Page's feet.

The patriots looked behind them.

"They are our own men!" exclaimed Capt. Hutchinson.

"No!" cried Aaron Cheever, "they are regulars, don't you see their red coats?"

Some of the minutemen fled to a nearby apple orchard.

Page escaped in a hail of musket balls. Others headed for the shelter of the Russell farmhouse. Russell himself, handicapped by his limp, was pierced by musket balls as he reached the door and was bayoneted mercilessly by the infuriated flankers rushing into the dwelling.

Two minutemen from Lynn, Timothy Munroe and Daniel Townsend, had been firing from behind the house. "There is another redcoat down," said Townsend, who had just fired, when Munroe looked around and saw the flankers. Both dashed for the Russell house and were seeking a door to the cellar when the flankers burst in.

"Townsend," said Munroe, "leaped through the end window, carrying sash and all with him, and instantly fell dead."

Munroe ran as had young Samuel Page, but Monroe was hit by a musket ball in the leg. He still managed to escape — an extraordinary escape, for in the musketry aimed at him from both the column and the flankers he could count 32 holes in his hat and clothes.

The patriots within the Russell dwelling were butchered by the bayonets of the revengeful flankers. Some patriots managed to find the stairway to the cellar and threatened to kill any redcoat who came down. A redcoat tried and was shot. Most of the seven Danvers men killed — all but one of them in their early 20s — were in the slaughter of the Russell House.

Lt. John Bacon of what is now Natick was with a Needham comrade on a ledge of rocks behind a stone wall. Bacon, veteran of the French and Indian Wars, was trying to take careful aim at the passing redcoats. His companion, old Joseph Hawes, was worried about flankers. Presently Hawes cried: "Run or you are dead, here's the guard!" Bacon was killed trying to climb over the stone wall.

The dead patriots within and near the Russell farmhouse were later carried into a first-floor room and placed side by side. There were a dozen, among them Jason Russell. Mrs. Russell, seeking her husband, came back to the (still-existing) bullet-scarred dwelling. "The blood in that room," she said, "was almost ankle deep."

The battle now raged closer to the center and the meetinghouse.

Death struck all over the area. A Salem baker, Benjamin Peirce, was killed moving across a field. Jonathan Parker and Aaron Fisher, Needham militiamen, were behind a barn trying to pick off redcoats on the main road. Flankers took them by surprise. Fisher escaped, Parker was killed as he ran toward the woods.

Sgt. Elisha Mills, another Needham militiaman, was firing from the same barn. As he stepped out and raised his musket to fire, flankers hit and killed him with a half-dozen musket balls. The sergeant left a wife and six children as did his cousin, Amos Mills, a Needham minuteman who also lost his life.

At the corner of the meetinghouse, Elias Howe of what is now Dover, son of a deacon, was taking aim with his brother-in-law Aaron Whiting. Howe edged forward, was caught by a British musket ball and was killed. Sixty-three-year-old Henry Putnam of Medford, cousin of the Danvers' Putnams, was killed near here, too, and his son Henry Jr. was badly wounded.

The roadway in front of the meetinghouse, which the British had now reached, was disarmingly tidy. The old men of Menotomy had seen to that, to conceal what had happened there earlier in the day to Percy's belated baggage train loaded with military supplies.

Word that the baggage train had been delayed at the Great Bridge had been carried quickly to Menotomy. The old men, exempt from service, had gathered at the Cooper Tavern in Menotomy center, where the Medford road enters the main road, to figure what they could do. They picked as their leader David Lamson, a half-Indian and veteran of the French and Indian Wars.

The small band of about a dozen was joined by Rev. Phillips Payson of Chelsea as they waited.

When the wagons had approached, Lamson called to the sergeant to surrender. In response, the sergeant lashed the horses to pick up speed and, as he did so, the old men opened fire from behind a stone wall about opposite the meetinghouse. Two regulars were killed, others wounded and the rest took off for nearby Spy Pond, where elderly Mother Bathericke was cutting dandelions. They threw their arms into the pond and surrendered to the astonished old woman. She took them to the home of Capt. Ephraim Frost and told them: "If you ever live to get back, you tell King George that an old woman took six of his grenadiers prisoners."

Close to this spot some of Percy's men got an amazing, fiery reception from another old man, Samuel Whittemore, who was 78 years old. His house, still standing, was near Menotomy (now Alewife) Brook. Awakened by Percy's march outward, Whittemore declined to flee with his wife and said that he was going up town.

The old French and Indian War officer oiled his musket and pistols, sharpened his sword and took up a position by a stone wall near the Cooper Tavern. As Percy's men passed the meetinghouse, Whittemore picked off a redcoat. Flankers approached him. He killed one with one pistol, and, with the other, wounded a flanker mortally in the chest. Then the flankers clubbed and bayoneted him, leaving him for dead.

When Whittemore later was taken into Cooper Tavern, bleeding "like an ox," the doctor said that there was no hope. Too many others needed attention. But the doctor eventually treated him. Whittemore responded — and lived 18 more years despite having been left twice for dead.

A final outrage against unarmed civilians was committed before the redcoats left the village.

It happened in the same Cooper Tavern.

A member of one of the oldest families in the town, Jason Winship, 45, a cousin of Mrs. Jason Russell, was spreading the glad tidings of a very special family event. Winship's first wife had died in child-bed, four more of his children had died at birth and now, at last, the family had its first son, and he was to be baptized this coming Sabbath. Jason had met with his brother-in-law, Jabez Wyman of Woburn, to toast the coming event.

Tavenkeeper Benjamin Cooper had prepared a festive drink, flip, made with egg, sugar and spices.

Wyman, though he had a long ride home with the news of the christening, told Winship: "Let us finish the mug, they won't come yet."

But the redcoats were hurrying, and they did come. The tavernkeeper and his wife, who managed to escape to the cellar, told how a hundred bullets suddenly tore through the tavern and enraged troops rushed in. The Coopers said:

"The two aged gentlemen were immediately most barbarously and inhumanly murdered by them, being stabbed through in many places, their heads mangled, skulls broke, and their brains out on the floor and walls of the house."

The following Sabbath the christening of the infant Jason Winship was held, and that same day in the same meetinghouse the bereaved families gathered for a memorial service to all the men who had died as the retreating redcoats swept through Menotomy.

Percy, when he crossed the brook into Cambridge, made a choice that was vital to his expedition.

Sir Henry Clinton, who would be one of the successors to Gen. Gage as Commander in Chief in the colonies, attributed even more significance to it when he later observed to Percy:

"I have always thought and said that had not Your Grace decided at Cambridge to move by Charlestown instead of Roxbury, there would have been that day an end of British government in America."

About a mile ahead of Percy, on the left, was the Charlestown road, the one Col. Smith had used coming out. It runs along Beech street, near Porter Square. Percy had several compelling reasons to take this road instead of returning the way he had come, which was straight ahead through Harvard Square to the Great Bridge. Percy has stated the reasons why he chose the Charlestown road:

"Lest the rebels should have taken up the bridge at Cambridge (which I find was actually the case), and also as the country was more open and the road shorter."

The Charlestown road was five miles shorter than returning by Boston Neck, and it would bring Percy's column much more quickly within the support of the British warships.

Percy could have been more explicit about one of his reasons. The redcoats had been accompanied by several Tories. The leading one was wealthy Abijiah Willard of Lancaster, a Mandamus Councilor. Willard would tell in England how he had forewarned Percy that the rebels had again lifted the planks of the Great Bridge.

This bridge operation was part of Gen. Heath's hopeful strategy to crush the entire expedition.

Gen. Heath may have discussed it at the meeting of the Committee of Safety in the morning. He did start staging it when he and Dr. Joseph Warren went through Watertown on their way to Lexington. Heath had told the Watertown militia to go downriver, take up the planks replaced for Percy and form a barricade on the far side. Then the patriots would have themselves and the unfordable river to defeat the returning redcoats.

Percy's choice nullified these preparations. But he would shortly encounter a residual part of Heath's strategy when he would start moving along the Charlestown road.

En route to it, Percy brought more killing and terrorizing to Cambridge. He had kept out his strong flankers as he moved along the plain and, now that he was through the heavier gunfire in Menotomy, he shifted the marines to his rear guard and relieved the Welsh Fusiliers who, said Mackenzie, "had expended a great part" of their ammunition.

On Percy's right, and not far from the Charlestown road, was a blacksmithy. In the yard some patriots of Brookline and Cambridge had made a barricade of empty casks, had their muskets ready, awaiting the column of redcoats.

They did not see the flankers until it was too late. Here, the highest-ranking patriot to lose his life this day, Maj. Isaac Gardner of Brookline, a leading official of his town, was killed as he stepped back to get a drink.

Here died two Cambridge patriots, John Hicks, 50, who had been among the Sons of Liberty emptying the huge chests at the Boston Tea Party, and Moses Richardson, 53. Richardson was the campus carpenter at nearby Harvard University and lived just off Cambridge Common.

The wife of a noted Harvard professor, Mrs. John Winthrop, has left a touching description of how women and children fared when they left those empty dwellings in Cambridge and Menotomy and, indeed, any dwelling along the route of warfare. She wrote to Mercy Warren of being awakened by drumbeats and bells and learning that Smith's troops had gone "to murder the peaceful inhabitants.

"Not knowing what the event would be at Cambridge at the return of these bloody ruffians, and seeing another brigade (Percy's) dispatched to the assistance of the former, looking with the ferocity of barbarians, it seemed necessary to retire to some place of safety 'til the calamity was passed....

"We were directed to a place called Fresh Pond, about a mile from the town; but what a distressed house did we find there, filled with women whose husbands were gone forth to meet the assailants; 70 or 80 of these, with numbers of infant children, crying and agonizing for the fate of their husbands!

"In addition to this scene of distress, we were for some time in sight of the battle, the glistening instruments of death...."

Then she learned that it was "useless to return to Cambridge, as the enemy were advancing up the river and firing on the town. To stay in this place was impracticable....Thus with precipitancy were we driven to the town of Andover, following some of our acquaintance, five of us to be conveyed by one poor, tired horsechaise. Thus we began our pilgrimage alternately walking and riding, the roads filled with frighted women and children, some in carts with their tattered furniture, others on foot fleeing into the woods.

"But what added greatly to our horror of the scene was our passing through the bloody field at Menotomy, which was strewed with mangled bodies. We met one affectionate father with a cart, looking for his murdered son, and picking up his neighbors who had fallen in battle, in order for their burial...."

The Charlestown road into which Percy marched his column went only a few hundred feet before making a sharp right turn and looping around Prospect Hill into what is now Union

Massachusetts Historical Society

Maj. Gen. William Heath

Square in Somerville. It was at this sharp turn that Gen. Heath had posted a patriot force in the hope that it could force the British to shun the Charlestown road and return by way of the torn-up bridge and barricade. Percy promptly noticed the patriots "drawn up together."

Heath had not weighed the terrifying effect of the cannon. The patriots made a brave attempt (there are nameless British dead buried here) but withdrew when Percy's cannon, unburdened of wounded that they were carrying, were wheeled up and opened fire.

The sun was setting as Percy's column, still under patriot fire, passed through Union Square and headed to Charlestown Neck, about a mile away. Percy had to use his cannon again against patriots on Prospect Hill on his left. It was along here that 66-year-old James Miller made a one-man stand like Samuel Whittemore in Menotomy. But Miller was killed.

Miller's house was on the hillside near Percy's route. He and a companion sent several shots at the redcoats and then were spotted. "Come, Miller, we've got to go!" yelled the companion.

"I'm too old to run," replied Miller, who kept firing and was presently brought down by a hail of musket shot.

In the twilight the flashes of the muskets and the belch of the cannon could be seen across the harbor by spectators in anxious watch on the hills of Boston. They also were seen by Col. Timothy Pickering as he arrived atop Winter Hill with 300 minutemen from Salem. The colonel, who never had felt certain that he could be in time to reach the battlefield, had made halts, but now had his men prime and load and hasten ahead.

He sent off an aide to get orders from Heath.

Percy's column, also hurrying, moved across Charlestown Common and Charlestown Neck at dusk.

Heath ordered Pickering to make no attempt to follow or attack the column. Heath knew it was supported by the cannon of the British warships. Musketry alone would be futile.

One final outrage preceded the redcoats' pausing, tired but safe at last, on Bunker Hill.

At Charlestown Neck, on the way to the ferry, was the dwelling of a sea captain, his wife and their 13 children. A son, 14-year-old Edward Barber, was peering into the dusk from a window, as any boy might, to watch what was going on. A redcoat saw him, fired, and young Barber instantly was killed.

As in Cambridge, there also had been panic in Charlestown. Dr. Joseph Warren received early word by express of what had happened in Lexington, left Boston by ferry, and hurried on horseback through Charlestown. He confirmed, as he galloped, that there had been shooting. Charlestown men started for the battlefield. School was called off. Many people scurried to leave town.

To go? To stay? People were in agitation for hours. Gage, with Charlestown under the 68 cannon of *HMS Somerset,* menaced the selectmen with "disagreeable consequences" if a single man more — like patriot James Miller — was to take up arms. Word came that the Great Bridge was blocked. Charlestown was now positive that the redcoats would come back this way. And soon came the confirmation of distant gunfire. The shooting of young Barber prompted rumors of massacre.

In this wild confusion a truce was reached. The selectmen would see that nothing was done against the regulars if they would not harm the people or destroy dwellings.

One in every six redcoats in the expedition was a casualty. There were 65 killed and many of the wounded would die. Boats of the *Somerset,* the same boats that had helped to ferry Smith's expedition from the foot of the Common, now carried 180 wounded back to Boston, where this number would overtax the regimental hospitals.

Pickets came back in the boats and Capt. Montresor started building a redoubt on top of Bunker Hill to command Charlestown Neck. It would be after midnight before all the men of Percy's force were back in their barracks in Boston.

The patriot casualties were 97 in all, 49 of them killed. Many would die from wounds. The church on Cambridge Common was swiftly converted into a hospital and doughty Dr. Eliphalet Downer, winner of his duel in Menotomy, and Dr. John Brooks, the major who had led his Reading minutemen at Meriam's Corner, both straight from the pursuit of Percy, started at once to treat the wounded.

Wounds with the weaponry of those days were frightful, most often leading to amputations, with no anesthetic but rum. Musket balls, usually home-moulded, were three-quarters of an inch thick, not the thinner bullets of modern times.

Muskets were more a weapon of terror than precision. Dr. William Aspinwall of Brookline, despite a blind eye, went along with Maj. Isaac Gardner to fight in Cambridge, where Gardner was killed. Aspinwall said he preferred, when reloading his musket, to stand in front of a tree facing the enemy rather than chance the marksmanship behind him of men of his own side.

Some patriots were killed by patriot fire while, as prisoners, they were forced to march with the British column.

The outcome of this long day of fighting, though, was an unmistakable victory for the embattled farmers.

Percy, filled with new-found respect, said: "Whoever looks upon them as an irregular mob will find himself much mistaken. They have men among them who know very well what they are about, having been employed as rangers against the Indians and Canadians; and this country, being much covered with wood, and hilly, is very advantageous for their method of fighting.

"You may depend upon it that the rebels have now had time to prepare, they are determined to go through with it, nor will the insurrection turn out so despicable as it is perhaps imagined at home."

George Washington, soon to come to Cambridge as Commander in Chief, saw in the head-long British retreat a response to Lord Sandwich's slur, during the parliamentary debate with the Earl of Chatham, that the provincials were little more than cowards. What had happened, Washington said, "may serve to convince Lord Sandwich, and others of the same sentiment, that the Americans will fight for their liberties and property, however pusillanimous in his Lordship's eye they may appear in other respects." Fact was, said Washington:

"If the retreat had not been as precipitate as it was, and God knows it could not well have been more so, the ministerial troops must have surrendered, or been totally cut off."

After the fighting had subsided, Heath called all his officers to meet with him at the foot of Prospect Hill and there held the Revolutionary War's first Council of War. A guard was ordered posted at Charlestown Neck. Cambridge would be the main patriot camp — within two days there would be assembled some 20,000 minutemen and militia, while others still came spontaneously from all over New England in response to the Lexington Alarm.

Heath's Council of War marked the beginning of the patriot siege of Boston.

What was yet to come, neither side knew, for the Declaration of Independence was still 15 months in the future. But those who had come from England to punish Boston would come to understand, now that King George and Lord North had provoked a revolution and eight long years of battle, that soon the only power that would remain to them in Boston would be to leave it.

Washington put the heart of the conflict in his comment on Lexington and Concord:

"Unhappy it is . . . to reflect, that a brother's sword had been sheathed in a brother's breast, and that the once happy and peaceful plains of America are either to be drenched with blood, or inhabited by slaves. Sad alternative! But can a virtuous man hesitate in his choice?"

The April 19 heroes

George Washington was among the earliest pilgrims to these scenes where our War of Independence began. He visited Buckman Tavern, where Capt. Parker's minutemen had gathered, and he dined at Sgt. Munroe's Tavern, where Lord Percy paused and had his wounded treated during the British retreat.

Washington wrote that he had come to see "the spot on which the first blood was spilt on the 19th April, 1775."

There are, besides these scenes and the entire length of the battlefield, many reminders: some dwellings, muskets, powder horns and swords, some clothing, a few other objects, some affidavits.

But what was the appearance of the embattled farmers?

We do not have the likeness of any of the leaders at Lexington and Concord — Capt. Parker, Col. Barrett, Lt. Col. Robinson, Maj. Buttrick. Nor do we have a likeness of any minuteman killed that day. Even likenesses of participants, as they looked then, are as scarce as are those of participants in the Boston Tea Party. The luck, then, that gave us a picture of a youthful Paul Revere — because artist Copley paid a debt with a portrait — was not repeated. Most often the likenesses we have are the wizened ones of age — Levi Preston, Amos Baker and the once-young fifer Jonathan Harrington.

For most of the day's heroes who died we have only their graves — and for some, even these are unknown.

When John Hicks did not come home as he had from the Tea Party, his wife sent their 14-year-old son to seek him. The boy found his father's body by the Cambridge roadside.

The young son of Moses Richardson found and helped to carry his father's body, with the other dead, to a common grave in the old cemetery off Cambridge Common. Richardson had fought at Quebec and made the casket for the victor, General Wolfe. For Richardson there was no time for a casket. His son jumped into the grave and covered his father's face with his cloak.

The son of Lt. John Bacon of Natick came to Menotomy seeking news of his father. The dead there, nine of them from the Jason Russell House, had already been buried in a common grave. Some of their clothing had been left in a schoolhouse. Bacon's son said that the instant he entered the schoolhouse he knew that his father was dead, for his eyes caught sight of his father's old striped hat.

Gen. Heath, the day after the battle, detailed Capt. Ebenezer Battle's Dedham company to go over the route and bury the remaining dead. Some of the haste of burial had been to conceal from an adversary what had happened.

There were common burials in Lexington, in Acton, in the old cemetery at Arlington, where lie dead heroes of Menotomy, Needham and Lynn, in Cambridge and in the old burying place at the Peabody-Salem boundary.

There were individual burials — among the loneliest seems that of young Reuben Kennison of Beverly in a family plot on the hillside where he and his bride built their now-vanished house and began their all so short wedded life.

Most often in communities away from the battlefield the scene was like that in the old South Meetinghouse in Danvers. The men of Danvers had obtained a carriage in Menotomy to bring home their many dead. They paused the first night at Medford. Next day they reached their town and the people came.

On Friday two companies from Salem arrived with military honors. The church was filled for the service. The companies, on the way to the cemetery, marched with reversed arms and muffled drums. As the procession reached the old burying ground, some bands of soldiers coming toward them moved to either side of the road to let the mourners pass.

Then the bands of soldiers, from Newburyport, Salisbury and Amesbury, continued on their way to Cambridge as volunteers in the gathering siege of Boston.

Battle of
Bunker Hill

Word of Lexington shooting spreads

The dreaded message, carried frantically by word of mouth and galloping express, moved across the land in shock waves from the Lexington and Concord Battle Road:

"War has begun!"

Newspapers and pamphleteers spread far and wide the poignant list of the dead and the wounded.

Writing exists that shows at least one way in which the news was rushed from Watertown across colony after colony until it reached the Carolinas.

It was near 10 o'clock on the morning of April 19 that patriot leader Joseph Palmer of Germantown (now Braintree) grabbed a piece of paper, quickly wrote a message "to all friends of American liberty" and sent Israel Bissell galloping from Watertown southward "charged to alarm the country quite to Connecticut. . . ."

Palmer had presided at the voting of the Suffolk Resolves, was a key figure in creating and running the Provincial Congress and would have a vital role in the patriot seizure of Bunker Hill. Bissell, a patriot express rider, knew every turn on the postroad to New York.

Palmer's message was sped from town to town in Connecticut, was copied, endorsed and forwarded by members of local Committees of Correspondence or Safety or both. It reached New York City at noon on April 23. An overnight gallop brought it next afternoon to Philadelphia, where it was hastily copied on a handbill at the printshop of the patriot printer William Bradford and was spread even farther by three Philadelphia newspapers.

New horses, new riders, rushed the message to Baltimore and to the Virginia capital of Williamsburg by the night of April 28. Many additional messages had been added along the way, and here the Williamsburg printer the next day appended these words:

"This morning the Committee of Correspondence met, and have determined to send expresses to the southward. It is now full time for us all to be on our guard, and to prepare ourselves against every contingency. The sword is now drawn, and God knows when it will be sheathed."

The message went on and on, to the Carolinas and to Georgia, to all the colonies. The minutemen who had fought at Lexington and Concord and all along the retreat of the redcoats back to Boston would not be alone in their struggle. In South Carolina the patriots of Charleston, on hearing the news, swarmed into the royal arsenal and distributed arms to the people much as did the patriots of Georgia at Savannah, where they promptly took over the royal magazine.

This united backing of the colonies was essential to preserve the liberties for which the patriots had responded to the Lexington and Concord Alarm. Dr. Joseph Warren, foremost of the Bay Colony patriots now, with John Hancock and Samuel Adams on their way to Philadelphia to the Second Continental Congress, had learned as an eager disciple of Adams how important it also was to win worldwide approval.

In Great Britain the patriots had many ardent friends, especially the greatest British statesman of the century, William Pitt, the Earl of Chatham. Warren and the Bay Colony patriots, in true Samuel Adams style, lost no time in making an effort to strengthen friendly sympathies and win still wider popular understanding and support.

Warren was certain that Gen. Gage would be dispatching his official version of the battle to Great Britain. The patriots appreciated the immense advantage to their cause of reaching Great Britain ahead of Gage with the news and with their own account of what had happened on the battlefield.

Warren became the key figure in this hurried endeavor.

The Provincial Congress, which had adjourned, was speedily called back into session after the outbreak of fighting on April 19. It reconvened at Concord on April 22 and shifted in the afternoon to the Watertown Meetinghouse, now vanished, to be nearer the impromptu patriot army that had assembled in an arc around Boston with its headquarters in Cambridge.

A top order of business that troubled day was to designate Elbridge Gerry as head of a committee of nine to obtain depositions from those who had fought at Lexington and Concord.

So anxious were the members of the Congress about meeting the responsibilities suddenly confronting them that they even sat next day, April 23, a Sunday, a day then when all business but churchgoing was reverently suspended. It was on this day that they elected Warren their presiding officer, in effect patriot governor of the province, and named a fellow hero of the Suffolk Resolves, Joseph Palmer, secretary.

Twenty-four hours later, Gen. Gage, who had collected reports from his major officers engaged in the Lexington-Concord expedition, sent off his dispatch to Lord Dartmouth by Lt. Joseph Nunn, Royal Navy, on board the express packet *HMS Sukey.*

The patriots fully realized that they were now under a handicap in their oceanwide race with Gage. But the situation did not dismay them. New Englanders, who had for generations been winning a living from the sea, long had provided some of the best sailors in the world. Their bid for success this time:

The sensational voyage of a small Salem vessel named the *Quero.*

The Watertown setting of the Provincial Congress was bustling with activity as the patriots perfected their plans from Sunday, April 23, through Wednesday, April 26.

Secrecy still shrouds the debate in the old meetinghouse, but it was long and persistent. There were urgent sessions as well in the nearby houses, where the delegates held committee meetings, dwelt or did their assigned chores. Members taking depositions met minutemen, and some British prisoners, too, from Sunday to Tuesday at Lexington, Lincoln and Concord.

John Hancock, pausing at Worcester on his trip with Samuel Adams to the Continental Congress, stressed in a letter back to Warren on Monday the importance of depositions showing "the certainty" of the British troops' "firing first." The depositions made this point so well there would be uncertainty for many years whether the minutemen on Lexington Green had fired back at all!

Wednesday was crowded with action.

Richard Derby, prominent Salem merchant who had helped to thwart Col. Leslie at Salem's old North Bridge back in February when Gen. Gage had sought to destroy the military supplies there, was a member of the Provincial Congress. Derby offered to make available one of his vessels, the schooner *Quero,* to outrun Gen. Gage's packet *Sukey.*

The 62-ton *Quero* was small, could be prepared quickly for sea and, above all, was a fast sailer. Derby's son, Richard Jr., was prepared to make the *Quero* ready to put out from Salem, and another son, John, was willing to be its skipper. The Provincial Congress accepted, and Warren signed the formal orders to Richard Derby to proceed with making the *Quero* shipshape for departure.

This same day, Warren signed an address he had been working on to the people of Great Britain and also signed a letter to Benjamin Franklin, agent in London for the province of Massachusetts.

The patriots did not know that Franklin, who had seen King George III's subservient Parliament vote down the Earl of Chatham's proposal to order the recall of Gage's troops from Boston, was already on the high seas, homeward bound, finally convinced that war was inevitable. Still in London, ready to carry on for Franklin, was an associate, Arthur Lee of Virginia.

Warren's message to Franklin was to ask his help for Capt. John Derby and request Franklin to print and "disperse through every town in England" the papers that Capt. Derby would bring — the depositions, the news account, the address to the people of Great Britain. All of these, Warren declared, would show "we are at last plunged into the horrors of a most unnatural war."

Referring to Gage, Warren wrote: "Our enemies, we are told, have despatched to Great Britain a fallacious account of the tragedy they have begun. ..." In his letter to Dartmouth, a letter then traveling toward London on the *Sukey,* Gage gave a bare-bones, temperate account, but claimed that it was the men at Lexington (Gage called them "a body of men within six miles of

Concord") who "first began to fire" upon the King's troops.

Warren, in his address to the people of Great Britain, told how the minutemen had assembled at Lexington Green because they had been alarmed by Gage's secret expedition and had learned of the troops' arresting and abusing innocent people along their march. These troops committed ravages that, said Warren, "would disgrace the annals of the most uncivilized nation."

The Lexington minutemen had begun to disperse, Warren asserted, but despite this, "the regulars rushed on with great violence; and first began hostilities by firing on said Lexington company."

All these happenings, said Warren, sprang from "ministerial vengeance against this colony, for refusing, with her sister colonies, submission to slavery. . . ." Warren added that even this has not "detached us from our royal sovereign," but "to the persecution and tyranny of his cruel ministry we will not tamely submit." He concluded with these ringing words:

"Appealing to heaven for the justice of our cause, we determine to die or be free."

Warren's address, for most Britons, would be their first knowledge war had begun and reasons for it.

On Thursday, April 27, Warren also wrote a letter to Arthur Lee, the agent who would carry out the requests made to Franklin. Warren gave a striking capsule picture of the way things stood at that moment. He said that he was surrounded by 15,000 or 20,000 men (minutemen and militia) and that the rage of the people was so inflamed by the barbarous effusion of blood they might "attack Gen. Gage and burn the ships in the harbor."

Warren warned prophetically: "Lord Chatham and our friends must make up the breach immediately or never. The next news from England must be conciliatory, or the connection between us ends, however fatal the consequences may be."

This same day, April 27, Warren signed and gave Capt. Derby his orders "to make for Dublin, or any other good port of Ireland, and from thence to cross to Scotland or England, and hasten to London." This direction was given to escape any British cruisers in the English Channel. Derby was to "forthwith deliver his papers to the agent on reaching London." Warren appended:

"P.S. You are to keep this order a profound secret from every person on earth."

Capt. Derby slipped out of Salem on the night of April 28, evading *HMS Lively,* a 20-gun sloop, which had been lying off Salem, Marblehead and Beverly for days to keep an eye on patriot maritime activities. It was *HMS Lively* that shortly, lying off Charlestown, would fire the first cannon shot — indeed, the first shot of all — in the battle of Bunker Hill.

The *Sukey's* four-day lead was swiftly overcome by the *Quero.* The *Sukey* was a 200-ton vessel and heavily loaded, while the much lighter *Quero,* without passengers or cargo, carried only ballast to stabilize her yacht-like hull in the rough swells of the Atlantic. She made the passage in a spanking 29 days.

Plenty of intentional mystery concealed Capt. Derby's movements in his two or three days on English soil. Our best source for what he did there is the penny-pinching expense bill, with no charge for his services or vessel, that he later submitted to the province of Massachusetts Bay.

Differing from the orders Warren had given him, Derby headed, despite its risks, straight for the British Channel so familiar to American seamen. He brought the *Quero* into one of the many coves on the Isle of Wight, took off by boat for Southampton, taking the wise precaution of heading the *Quero* back westward along the channel to meet him later at Falmouth. He took post chaise to London and was in his lodgings there on Sunday, May 28.

Lee was given all the documents and also the news accounts of Lexington and Concord fighting that appeared in the April 21 and April 25 issues of the "Salem Gazette." All of it then was handed to the patriots' friend — and foe of King George III's yes-man Parliament — Lord Mayor John Wilkes, at Mansion House, his official residence in the heart of old London.

John Derby

Custom House, Salem, Mass.

Next day the news was out. A man landing from outer space would barely have topped the sensation spread by Capt. Derby. King George III, who got the news at his Kew Palace, claimed the account had been made "favorable as possible for the insurgents." There was widespread consternation. London merchants feared for their trade. The market was shaken.

The Bay Colony's former royal governor, Thomas Hutchinson, currently a court favorite, hustled off with the news to Lord Dartmouth, who, said Hutchinson, "was much struck with it." Lord Dartmouth, and all Whitehall, was deeply embarrassed, for they had yet to hear from Gen. Gage. Next day, in the official gazette, Dartmouth cautioned the public that "no advices have as yet been received in the American department of any such event."

Lee's reponse was to emphasize that the accounts and depositions were available to the public at Mansion House. "Read them and judge if they be true or false!"

Dartmouth got off a message to Gage: "It is very much to be lamented that we have not some account from you of the transaction."

"Bella, horrida bella!" exclaimed Hutchinson in Latin. "War, horrid war! I hear one and another of the King's ministers say there is no receding. And yet to think of going on makes me shudder."

British authorities thought of arresting Capt. Derby, reconsidered and felt it would be impolitic. They did send customsmen searching for his vessel in the inlets of the Isle of Wight — and, thanks to his foresight, found nothing. Meantime, on June 1, he slipped out of London by stage, then by post chaise all the lengthy journey to Falmouth, not far from England's most southwestern cape, Land's End.

Still no word from Gage. A curate from Kent, John Horne Tooke, an intimate of Lord Mayor Wilkes, claimed that what the regulars did at Lexington and Concord was murder and sought to raise a fund to give Benjamin Franklin for the American widows and orphans of the victims. Tooke was charged with libel, tried at Guild Hall, fined and imprisoned for a year.

Belated *HMS Sukey* reached England on June 9. Its arrival underscored the success of Capt. Derby's mission, for the British public found its report was virtual confirmation of the American account save for one, though a crucial, detail. Gage claimed, of course, that the Americans had fired first.

But the American claim that it was British regulars who began the shooting had already won such acceptance that some Britons wore mourning bands to sympathize with the Americans who, as John Horne Tooke put it, "faithful to the character of Englishmen, preferring death to slavery, were, for that reason, inhumanely murdered by the King's troops."

On July 18, returning as he had gone, in ballast, Capt. Derby would appear at Cambridge headquarters to report on his mission to Gen. George Washington, who by this date had been named Commander in Chief of the American army and had arrived in Cambridge about two weeks after the battle of Bunker Hill.

Gage double cross disarms Bostonians

Letters and diaries aplenty tell of the extreme way life was altered in and around Boston by the events of April 19.

Artist Henry Pelham early that very day decided to take his chaise and go to Cambridge to bring relatives back to Boston. Pelham, writing to London, told his half-brother John Singleton Copley, the eminent painter, how he had scolded the ferryman for refusing him passage to Charlestown because the wind was high, how he was forced to take the long way by Boston Neck and, returning, had to go 13 miles still farther through Watertown because the patriots had taken up the planks of the Great Bridge at Cambridge.

Pelham later was grateful that he had been compelled to make the 30-mile trip:

"Had we returned through Charlestown we should have been in the midst of the battle." He found that the country was in "utmost confusion" and, as for conditions in Boston, he wrote to an uncle:

"Words are wanting to describe the misery this affair has produced among the inhabitants of this town. Thousands are reduced to absolute poverty who before lived in credit. Business of any kind is entirely stopped."

Boston merchant John Rowe, owner of one of the Tea Party ships, wrote in his diary: "All business at an end and all communications stopped between town and country. No fresh provisions of any kind brought to this market so that Boston is in a most distressed condition."

British soldiers just from the battle wrote about it. Ens. Henry deBerniere observed: "In the course of two days from a plentiful town, we were reduced to the disagreeable necessity of living on salt provisions, and fairly blocked up in Boston." George Harris, a future lord, who would be desperately wounded at Bunker Hill, wrote:

"However we block up their port, the rebels certainly block up our town, and have cut off our good beef and mutton, much to the discomfiture of our mess."

Gen. Gage had far greater concerns than the regimental mess or the regimental hospitals with their many battle wounded. He could walk up any hill in Boston and see thousands of patriot soldiers, from all over New England, encircling and blocking Boston on the south, west and north of him. Should they attack, he was profoundly worried that the rebels living within Boston might stage an uprising or burn the place.

Joseph Warren had many worries, too, working long hours daily on the military, civilian, diplomatic problems besetting the patriots. None was more pressing to him, though, than the plight of the people now suddenly cut off in Boston, a virtual British garrison, with Gage preventing all exit and vigorously increasing its fortifications.

Gage summoned chairman John Scollay and the other Boston selectmen to his headquarters, Province House, to try for an accord. He wanted Bostonians to agree not to attack his troops if the patriot army should attack Boston. The selectmen called a town meeting at Faneuil Hall, and it continued its deliberations that weekend, all Saturday and Sunday. When Scollay and his group reported assent on Gage's first request, he came up with still another.

Gage would open the exits from Boston, even have his admiral provide small craft for water departure, if the Bostonians would surrender their weapons to the selectmen.

Gage quickly found that the Bostonians would take no action without consulting the patriot leadership in Cambridge. This meant dealing with Joseph Warren, who was officially chosen president of the Provincial Congress that weekend.

Warren, the day after the battle, April 20, had already written to Gage about "the unhappy situation into which this colony is thrown." Warren said much still could be done to alleviate misfortunes if "the contending parties may rely upon the honor and integrity of each other for the punctual performance of any agreement...."

For his part, Warren wrote that "everything promised shall be religiously performed." Then he offered: "I should now be very glad to know from you, sir, how many days you desire may be allowed for such as desire to remove from Boston, with their effects; and what time you will allow the people in Boston for their removal."

Gage did not feel he could carry on direct communication with a rebel leader, but was willing to communicate with Warren through the Boston selectmen. In this way there were, in effect, negotiations on Bostonians' leaving without arms or ammunitions. On Saturday, April 22, after talking over Gage's proposals with Safety committeemen, Warren penned his approval to the Boston selectmen.

On Monday, April 24, as Rowe and other Boston diarists and writers noted, "This day the inhabitants carried in their arms." As the week progressed the arms stacked at Faneuil Hall, eventually under British sentries, included 1778 muskets, 634 pistols, 973 bayonets and 38 blunderbusses, though only the Lord knows of what vintage or utility.

We can appreciate Gage's relief by the remarks of Lt. John Barker of the King's Own Regiment. Of the turn-in of weapons Barker wrote in his diary:

"I fancy this will quiet him (Gage) a little for he seemed apprehensive that if the lines should be attacked the townspeople would raise and assist; they would not give up their arms without the General promising that they should have leave to quit the town, as many as pleased."

There were further negotiations during this week. Gage wanted loyalists from the countryside admitted to Boston on the same terms of no arms, no ammunition. Warren and Safety committeemen at Cambridge went over proposed agreements. Sunday, April 30, day of further accord, the Provincial Congress, too, was in session all day from 7 a.m. Warren, before going to seek approval of the Congress, wrote to the selectmen of "My ever-dear town of Boston."

"No person now in Boston," said Warren, "is more deeply sensible of the distress, nor more desirous of relieving our brethren there, than the members of this committee. Encouragement will be given tomorrow to the wagoners in the country to repair to Boston, to give all possible assis-

tance to our friends in the removal of their effects." Warren asked Gage, for a second time, about increasing the limit Gage had imposed of only 30 wagons to enter Boston at one time.

The permitted number of wagons continued unsettled, but by late April 30 a system of passes was arranged, and the Provincial Congress approved and ordered the agreement printed. Warren and the Provincial Congress started forming plans, based on town quotas, of moving out and rehousing in the countryside 5000 Bostonians who were without funds.

Suddenly the accord began collapsing. Gage, in a letter to Lord Dartmouth, blamed it on a "great clamour" made to him by the loyalists in Boston. They impressed upon Gage their dread that once the patriot faction was out of Boston, the place would be set in flames. Better, they argued, to retain these people as sort of hostages for the security of the town.

Gage used many pretexts to impose a brake on the outflow. There was disagreement on whether "merchandise" was to be included in a person's "effects." Passes became more difficult to obtain from the British officer in charge.

Patriot confidence in Gage's word vanished fast. On May 2, Warren, concerned (groundlessly, as it later developed) by Connecticut Gov. Jonathan Trumbull's sending agents to quiz Gage and suggest a cessation of hostilities, wrote to Trumbull that he must not be sensible of the "miseries to which Gen. Gage's army have reduced this wretched colony.

"We have lost the town, and we greatly fear for the inhabitants of Boston," wrote Warren, "as we find the general is perpetually making new conditions, and forming the most unreasonable pretenses for retarding their removal from that garrison.

"No agreement or compact with Gen. Gage will in the least alleviate our distress, as no confidence can possibly be placed in any assurances he can give. . . .

"Our relief now must arise from driving Gen. Gage, with his troops, out of the country, which, by the blessing of God, we are determined to accomplish, or perish in the attempt."

Gov. Trumbull quickly sent a reassuring response. Connecticut would support the Bay patriots in the struggle for American liberty.

Lt. Barker compassionately noted on May 4: "Numbers of people are quitting the town every day with their families and effects; its a distressing thing to see them for half of them don't know where to go to, and in all probability must starve."

But soon the outflow became a painful trickle. Rev. William Emerson of Concord had an errand in Boston at this time, went in and out by the Charlestown ferry. Emerson said:

"The people in great distress in Boston, great difficulty in getting a permit to come out of the town. The guard very strict in searching all that come out of town to see that they carry no merchandise out."

By May 6, merchant John Andrews wrote: "This morning an order from the governor has put a stop to any more papers (passes) ... not even to admit those to go who have procured them already."

By May 10 Gage's double cross was unmistakable. The Provincial Congress, which a few days earlier had called him "an unnatural and inveterate enemy of the country," sent him a public letter asking him to halt flouting an agreement made with the selectmen to help a distressed people.

Warren, in a final effort, also sent along a letter he wrote privately to Gage to appeal to his conscience not to "sacrifice the interest of Great Britain and the peace of the colonies" and re-

quested "for the last time" that Gage stop "hearkening to the mad advice of men who I know have deceived you." This, too, failed.

Warren soon was writing to Samuel Adams in Philadelphia: "Gen. Gage, I fear, has trepanned the inhabitants of Boston."

There remained only the alternative that Warren had cited to Gov. Trumbull. The patriots must drive "Gen. Gage, with his troops, out of the country. . . ."

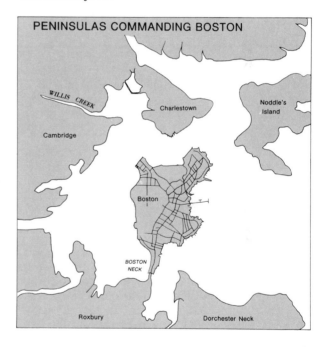

PENINSULAS COMMANDING BOSTON

Boston becomes a bleak citadel

A curiosity of the British retreat on April 19 back through Charlestown was that Gen. Gage, in protecting Lord Percy's force after it had crossed Charlestown Neck, ordered a redoubt both raised and dismantled on Bunker Hill.

In less than two months, Gage would be risking his entire army to control Bunker Hill, and yet on the day after Percy's retreat Gage simply gave it up. An officer who fought along with Percy on the British march, Lt. Frederick Mackenzie, wrote on April 20 in his diary about Gage's temporary redoubt on Bunker Hill:

"It was in a good state of forewardness this morning when Gen. Gage, having determined to abandon Charlestown, gave orders for its being demolished, and the troops to be withdrawn into Boston; which was done by 4 o'clock in the afternoon."

Just a brief look at Boston's geographical situation on a map of the 1770s quickly demonstrates the strategic situation that produced all the decisive military developments in the area, from the battle of Bunker Hill to George Washington's occupying Dorchester Heights and driving the British army out of Boston.

Boston, a peninsula connected to the mainland on the south by a narrow isthmus, Boston Neck, was about a third its present size, its coves and flats, especially the great Back Bay area, still covered by tide instead of landfill. Today's surviving hills, used in part for that landfill, were then higher.

Boston, into which Gage withdrew his troops, could be made defensible by fortifications. The town was, however, dominated by the heights of two other peninsulas from which siege-size cannon, then not yet a part of the patriot weaponry, could control Boston and make it untenable.

On the north of Boston was the Charlestown peninsula, the great, then-unfilled cove on its west side still a millpond, marsh and tideland. Bunker Hill near the Charlestown Neck, and lower Breed's Hill, just across the river and harbor from Boston's North End, controlled the Charlestown peninsula, and could make things hot for Boston's North End or shipping.

To the southeast of Boston was the Dorchester peninsula with its hills, Dorchester Heights, and particularly a hill, now vanished, which was closest to Boston's South End, Nook's Hill. It was Washington's fortifying Nook's Hill that ultimately would cause the British forces to take to their ships and go.

Why did Gage refrain from taking the heights in Dorchester and withdraw from Bunker Hill? He knew their military value. Vice Adm. Samuel Graves, in command of the British squadron at Boston, urged Gage to burn the towns of Charlestown and Roxbury and seize the heights.

Gage, who had besought Lord Dartmouth to send him reinforcements, was worried that his roughly 4000 troops were not sufficient to hold territory beyond Boston itself or to face a possible patriot assault and a simultaneous uprising of the patriots still in Boston, those he had wanted so eagerly to disarm.

Lt. Barker, encamped on a western slope of Beacon Hill, has given a lively, day-to-day account of the agitation and bustle in the British forces in their efforts to make Boston more secure in the days that followed the retreat from Concord and Lexington. Barker noted:

"Ever since the 19th we have been kept in constant alarm; all officers ordered to lay at their barracks."

Barker seems to have Vice Adm. Graves criticizing Gage's abandonment of Charlestown, for Graves ordered a battery built on top of Copp's Hill in the North End, to protect his biggest warship HMS Somerset, which he had stationed near the Charlestown ferryway. Barker said Graves wanted to defend the warship "from any battery which might be raised against her on a hill on the Charlestown side."

All over Boston, said Barker, Gage had his troops strengthen fortifications — on Fort Hill and on Beacon Hill, where he threw up "a small works ... which can command the town." Most extensive fortifying was at Boston Neck, where, Barker wrote:

"We have now almost finished a battery of

ten 24-pounders at the blockhouse; it is fronting Dorchester Hill where the general is afraid the rebels will erect batteries against us." Lt. Barker made this diary entry on May 4, confirming this early that fears of the heights around Boston had been plaguing Gage.

Barker added this curious sidelight on the rebels, who, as he phrased it, had erected their standard at Cambridge:

"They call themselves the King's Troops and us the Parliament's. Pretty burlesque!"

The patriot force, though each side was nervous about what the other might do, clearly was no laughing matter to Gage. The patriots made prompt use of the Lexington-Concord Alarm to start building a force to expel Gage from their Bay capital. John Hancock, en route to Philadelphia, sent word: "Boston must be entered; the (British) troops must be sent away."

Joseph Warren already was busy organizing this very effort when Hancock's message arrived. Warren and the Committee of Safety that Warren headed sat day and night in one side of the Hastings house — a dwelling, now gone, which belonged to the steward of Harvard College, Jonathan Hastings — while on the other side of the house, Gen. Artemas Ward, our first Commander in Chief, was trying to operate the patriot army.

From the windows of the Hastings house, just off Cambridge Common, Warren could see the patriots gathering on the morning of April 20 as he wrote a circular letter to all the towns, a letter seething with indignation and urgency:

"The barbarous murders committed on our innocent brethren, on Wednesday the 19th instant, have made it absolutely necessary that we immediately raise an army to defend our wives and our children from the butchering hands of an inhuman soldiery ... who will take the first opportunity in their power to ravage this devoted country with fire and sword....

"Our all is at stake....

"Every moment is infinitely precious....

"We beg and entreat, as you will answer to God himself, that you will hasten and encourage by all possible means the enlistment of men to form the army, and send them forward to headquarters at Cambridge...."

This was the customary way of doing things, to ask the towns to raise troops.

But the times were extraordinary and demanded extraordinary solutions.

There on Cambridge Common and its vicinity were assembling thousands of minutemen and militiamen, most of them too late to get into the action of April 19. Could they possibly become an immediate army?

They offered, though, only a brief opportunity. These men shortly would melt away, for they had come freely, could go freely, were under no orders to remain. Their unselfish, volunteer arrival has best been described by Warren in a letter he would send, with deep admiration, to Samuel Adams:

"A sudden alarm brought them together, animated with the noblest spirit. They left their houses, their families, with nothing but the clothes on their backs, without a day's provision, and many without a farthing in their pockets. Their country was in danger; their brethren were slaughtered; their arms alone engrossed their attention."

Warren and his committee made an impromptu, extraordinary decision to try to form an army directly out of these men. The patriot leaders had known right along that so loosely knit an organization as the minutemen would have to be replaced, and had even started to do so before April 19. Officers would be commissioned instead of being elected. This would bring more discipline. On April 21 Warren and his committee voted to raise an 8000-man army and to prepare enlisting forms.

Two days later, the Provincial Congress, urged by Gen. Ward, voted instead to field a 30,000-man army and called upon the other New England colonies for proportional help in sending men. Massachusetts would try to raise a quota of 13,600. Enlistment would be for the rest of the year — more than eight months of service.

These endeavors came none too soon.

The spontaneous army, almost as spontaneously, had begun to vanish.

Gen. Ward, 47, judge, legislator, veteran of the French and Indian Wars, was ill in bed at his Shrewsbury farmhouse when he got word of the Lexington-Concord Alarm. At daybreak on April 20, he mounted his horse, hastened past marching minutemen and arrived in the afternoon at Hastings House. There, he held his first Council of War.

He called for gunpowder and other military supplies and sent Maj. Gen. William Heath, whom he had just supplanted as top commander, to reinforce Brig. Gen. John Thomas of Kingston, doctor and French and Indian War veteran, who was commanding the patriot forces gathered at Roxbury to block the British on the land exit from Boston Neck.

Through the minutes in Ward's orderly book glow his massive problems of trying to furnish food and shelter to the multitude of men comprising his transitory army. Harvard steward Hastings was made temporary army steward. Harvard and nearby buildings were made barracks, Harvard kitchens and campfires helped provide the army mess. Still, spring planting and personal needs drew the men steadily homeward.

The drain was so strong that by April 23 Ward wrote plaintively to the Provincial Congress:

"My situation is such that, if I have not enlisting orders immediately, I shall be left all alone."

The impromptu plan to enlist minutemen right on the scene succeeded. Twenty regiments were sought, their colonels already designated once they enlisted all their men. Fully half of these complements were filled within a week from the men who had marched to Cambridge.

But recruiting officers, with their "beating orders" (enlistment papers), had to return to the towns to enlist still more men — many of whom had departed without joining up. So there were nervous moments such as Ward had felt, moments when Gen. Thomas marched his depleted force repeatedly around the hill in Roxbury to conceal his weakness from the British.

There were sudden alarms. On May 6, Gage received some reinforcements he had ordered from Halifax, and their arrival spread rumors in the patriot camp that the British were about to launch an attack. The meager patriot army was ordered to lie all night with its arms ready. The Provincial Congress, imposing utmost secrecy, anxiously ordered the Committee of Supplies to obtain military stores from "any place whatever."

Next day, rumors persisting, the Provincial Congress met thrice in session, despite its being Sunday, to appeal for arms and bayonets from any colony. Ward was worried the British assault would come on Roxbury and wanted the patriots to seize Dorchester Heights. The towns were asked to send the militia. But Gen. Thomas "much despaired" of taking Dorchester Heights immediately, for lack of men, lack of cannon, lack of artillerymen able to fire cannon and the menacing British batteries at Boston Neck.

Warren put in words the mood in Massachusetts:

"No business but that of war is either done or thought of in this colony."

In mid-May, Gage wrote to Lord Dartmouth and reported all the enlisting that was going on in Massachusetts and "in most of the provinces," and then he added:

"It seems impossible to be long before we come again to blows."

Plans to seize cannon formulated

Bunker Hill and Dorchester Heights were manifestly on Joseph Warren's mind when he wrote on May 14 to Samuel Adams:

"If a number of large battery cannon, with proper ammunition, could be procured, I believe we should soon settle the business with Mr. Gage."

Only two days earlier, concerned about assaults Gage might make, the patriot military and civil leaders had held a joint Council of War to discuss fortifying some highlands around Boston. Fortifications were proposed on Winter and Prospect hills and "also a strong redoubt to be raised on Bunker's Hill, with cannon planted there."

Two men who would win eternal honor in the battle of Bunker Hill, Connecticut's Israel Putnam and Pepperell's William Prescott, ardently favored fortifying Bunker Hill. However, the civil and military chiefs, Warren and Gen. Ward, were opposed because of the lack of cannon and powder. They knew a redoubt would mean a challenge to Gage and they felt that the patriots were not yet equipped for a general engagement.

Warren had something further in mind when he wrote his May 14 letter to Adams. A few days earlier he had helped to provide orders to a newly arrived, enthusiastic volunteer from Connecticut, Benedict Arnold, to capture the fortress of Ticonderoga and fetch its big battery cannon to drive the British out of Boston.

Ticonderoga had long fascinated Americans. The fortress, built and rebuilt, taken and retaken many times during the French and Indian Wars, was located strategically on the great wilderness water highway of the Richelieu River, Lake Champlain, Lake George and the Hudson River that flowed between Canada and New York. A hostile force could use it for invasion or to cut off New England.

A year earlier, in 1774, when war with Great Britain seemed approaching, Samuel Adams wondered what the Canadians and the Indians along the New England frontier (Massachusetts then included Maine) might do if war came. The Provincial Congress wrote to these people, and early in 1775 sent John Brown, Pittsfield lawyer and member of the Congress, to Canada to learn their intentions. Brown, during his travels through the New Hampshire Grants (now Vermont), obviously conferred with the fiery leader of its Green Mountain Boys, Ethan Allen. In a letter March 29 from Montreal to Samuel Adams and Joseph Warren, Brown wrote:

"One thing I must mention as a profound secret. The fort at Ticonderoga must be seized as soon as possible should hostilities be commenced by the King's troops.

"The people of the New Hampshire Grants have engaged to do this business and, in my opinion, are the most proper persons for the job."

This was the first recorded suggestion about seizing Ticonderoga on the outbreak of the revolution. Its purpose was strategic. Others, with a different aim, also thought of its capture. But their immediate purpose was to acquire Ticonderoga's cannon to expel the British from Boston. Among these enthusiasts was Arnold.

When news of the shooting on Lexington Green reached New Haven, Arnold assembled his "Governor's Guards" militia company. Capt. Arnold, 34, a man of medium height, muscular, athletic, merchant and sea trader, was instinctively aggressive. He was delayed temporarily by the conservative local officials' denying him gunpowder. Finally he gave them five minutes to hand him the keys or he and his men — and some Yale students who had joined — would break open the stores. He got the powder.

On his march to Cambridge, he encountered a Hartford patriot, Samuel Holden Parsons, lawyer, legislator, future general, who was on his way back from Cambridge to recruit soldiers. They discussed the patriots' need for cannon. Arnold's horse trading in Quebec and Montreal had brought him acquaintances there, and information.

Parsons said that Arnold "gave him an account of the state of Ticonderoga, and that a great number of brass cannon were there."

Brass cannon, of course, were the best.

Sunday, April 30, the day after Arnold reached Cambridge, he appeared before Warren's Committee of Safety with a proposal: The fort at Ticonderoga was in ruinous condition, manned by only 40 or 45 men, had considerable stores, had lots of cannon — Arnold mentioned 80 pieces of cannon, 20 pieces of brass cannon, mortars and still more in the satellite forts — and he wanted to lead an expedition to get them.

Warren, other Safety members and Gen. Ward eagerly conferred. On Tuesday they urged the Provincial Congress to give Arnold cash, gunpowder, lead balls, flints and horses. On Wednesday, May 3, Arnold was made a colonel and was authorized to enlist up to 400 soldiers in the western part of Massachusetts and the neighboring colonies.

A sentence in Arnold's orders, which, curiously, were prepared by the still-unsuspected traitor, Dr. Benjamin Church Jr., emphasized the desperate need of the army at Cambridge for cannon. Arnold was precisely instructed: "You are to bring back with you such of the cannon, mortars, stores, & etc., as you shall judge may be serviceable to the army here."

Arnold was never slow to action. He headed via Deerfield to the Berkshires, arranging for recruits as he advanced, filled with ambition and confidence, on his first mission as a top commanding officer. What he did not know at the start was that there were others heading for Ticonderoga on the same mission — and they, too, considered themselves in top command.

Parsons, after his chance encounter with Arnold, had sped to Hartford, consulted with some Sons of Liberty, who borrowed money from the Connecticut treasury and on April 28 sent two agents to arrange for an assault on Fort Ticonderoga. The patriots then located Heman Allen, who was visiting in Hartford, and sent him riding posthaste to Bennington to alert his brother Ethan Allen and the Green Mountain Boys. On April 29, also sent by the Hartford patriots, Capt. Edward Mott headed northwest with six recruits to take command of all the Connecticut men.

By the time they crossed into Massachusetts, Mott's party had increased to 16 recruits. "We meant to keep our business a secret and ride through the country unarmed," recalled Mott, "until we came to the new settlements on the Grants."

On May 1, Mott and the Connecticut men paused in the heart of Pittsfield at the tavern of James Easton, patriot, deacon, colonel of the Berkshire militia. In the Easton tavern, by happy coincidence, was John Brown, who only a few weeks earlier had been in the Grants and talking with Ethan Allen about taking Ticonderoga.

Mott promptly shared his secret with Brown and Easton, and presently they were ready to join Mott and enlist some men from Massachusetts to join the expedition. Forty-seven Berkshire men, from Pittsfield, Jericho (now Hancock) and Williamstown were mustered from Easton's regiment, and all headed north to Bennington.

Catamount Tavern, a frontier hostelry, was the Bennington headquarters of Ethan Allen and his Green Mountain Boys. From its shelter, and especially from its taproom, where they hoisted mighty "stonewalls," a concoction of rum and hard cider, they maintained what law there was in the mountains and forests and scattered farmlands of the unorganized Grants.

Ethan Allen, a giant in buckskin, powerful, magnetic, inspiring, was the fearless embodiment of the spirit of independence that would create Vermont. Since the end of the French and Indian Wars, pioneers had trekked to the Grants and purchased land based on New Hampshire deeds. But wealthy, vast landholders in New York claimed that they owned the land and their agents tried to make the Green Mountain pioneers pay again or get out. Ethan Allen for years had been the Green Mountain champion against the hated Yorkers. New York had outlawed Ethan and put a price on his head.

Allen and leaders in the Grants gathered quickly in Bennington when they got news of the Lexington Alarm and, as Allen expressed it, "attempted to explore futurity, but it was found to be unfathomable." How would the outbreak of war effect their struggle with the Yorkers? What of the Grants' petition for resolution of the dispute pending in London?

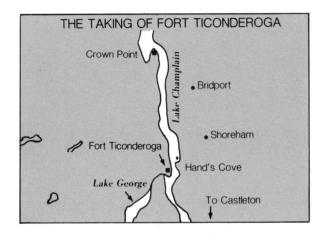

THE TAKING OF FORT TICONDEROGA

Crown Point

Lake Champlain

Bridport

Shoreham

Fort Ticonderoga

Hand's Cove

Lake George

To Castleton

The debate was still on when Heman Allen burst in with Connecticut's request to Allen. Then Capt. Mott arrived on May 7 with the official appeal for Allen to surprise and take the fortress at Ticonderoga. Their arrival decided the debate.

"This enterprise," recounted Allen, "I cheerfully undertook; and, after first guarding all the passes that led thither, to cut off all intelligence between the garrison and the country, made a forced march from Bennington." Allen had sent out scouts to watch the wilderness paths and spread his wolfhunt call for his Green Mountain Boys.

Leaders of the expedition gathered Monday, May 8, at Castleton "to conclude," said Mott, "in what method we would proceed in order to accomplish our design." Mott was chosen chairman of the gathering.

They decided to make two attempts to provide boats for taking their force across Lake Champlain. Thirty men would be sent to Skenesborough (now Whitehall, N.Y.) to seize the baronial estate of Maj. Philip Skene, a loyalist, and especially to appropriate his schooner and boats. A volunteer would be sent to Crown Point to see if a relative stationed there could, by "some strategem," hire the King's boats.

Most important of all, Mott recorded:

"It was further agreed that Col. Ethan Allen should have the command of the party that should go against Ticonderoga, agreeable to my promise made to the men when I engaged them to go, that they should be commanded by their own officers."

Allen set out on the roughly 20-mile trip farther north to Shoreham, where the expedition would rendezvous. Shoreham is on the east bank of Lake Champlain and across from Fort Ticonderoga. Other leaders still at Castleton busied themselves about packhorses, provisions and picking the men to go to Skenesborough when suddenly they were, as Mott phrased it, "shockingly suprised" by the arrival of Arnold.

Arnold had been hurriedly organizing his expedition from the Berkshires through the Grants and earlier in the day, from Rupert, midway between Bennington and Castleton, had sent a further appeal to the Berkshire towns "to send forward as many men to join the army here as you can possibly spare." He signed his message: "Commander of the Forces." Either at Bennington or Rupert he must have discovered, to his unbounded chagrin, that a prior expedition was shaping, and accompanied by only a servant, had come at a gallop to Castleton.

Mott has left a description of that late-evening arrival:

"Col. Arnold came to us, with his orders, and demanded the command of our people, as he said we had no proper orders.

"We told him we could not surrender the command to him, as our people were raised on condition that they should be commanded by their own officers.

"He persisted in his demand, and the next morning he proceeded forward to overtake Col. Allen."

It was now rendezvous day, May 9, and the place was at Hand's Cove, an inlet shielded by trees from Fort Ticonderoga, more than a mile across the water.

A determined, thwarted Arnold spurred his mount toward the cove to confront Ethan Allen.

Ethan Allen captures Ticonderoga

Mott wrote in his journal:

"When Col. Arnold went after Col. Allen, the whole party followed him, for fear he should prevail on Col. Allen to resign."

Nothing would have been more unlikely, as the men from Connecticut discovered when the two colonels met at the head of Hand's Cove. The giant Allen was not a man to be domineered, or, for that matter, to be impressed by a legal paper from Massachusetts any more than he was by the decrees of New York that had outlawed him.

The decision at the cove was really made, though, by the Green Mountain Boys.

Arnold's claim to the top command, Mott wrote to the Massachusetts Provincial Congress, "bred such a mutiny amongst the soldiers which had almost frustrated our design." Not one of the soldiers there at the cove (Allen estimated 230, Easton estimated 240) had come at Arnold's call.

"Our men," Mott wrote, "were for clubbing their firelocks and marching home, but were prevented by Col. Allen and Col. Easton, who told them that he (Arnold) should not have the command of them, and if he had, their pay would be the same as though they were under their command; but they would damn the pay, and say they would not be commanded by any other but those they engaged with."

Arnold asserted that Allen agreed to give him a joint command. Allen has left nothing specific, though the two colonels would be close together during the immediate capture of the fort. At the moment, Allen was full of anxiety about how he would get his men across the lake. He had stationed lookouts by the shore. The boats he expected from Skenesborough or Crown Point did not appear.

"It was with the utmost difficulty," Allen wrote in later years, "that I procured boats to cross the lake."

The moon set, the wind from the north grew stronger and ruffled the lake, and the night was passing. Still no sign of the boats. And this, May 10, was to be a momentous day, at the fort across the lake, and at faraway Philadelphia, where the Second Continental Congress was to begin its deliberations. Suddenly the sentinels caught sight of something moving on the dark water.

There were two flat-bottom scows, brought by volunteers from Bridport some 10 miles to the north. Ferrying by these would be frustratingly slow. Allen and Arnold, Easton and Brown, too, got across, and 83 men were landed north of Willow Point, but there were far more of the men, under Allen's top lieutenant, Col. Seth Warner, still awaiting passage when, Allen observed:

"The day began to dawn, and I found myself under a necessity to attack the fort, before the rear guard could cross the lake."

No lights had yet appeared at the fort. Surprise of the sleeping garrison still would be possible. The task ahead, said Allen, was "viewed hazardous," so he assembled the band of 83 on the beach and, in a low tone to avoid alerting the garrison, Allen said:

"Friends and fellow soldiers:

"You have, for a number of years past been a scourge and terror to arbitrary power. Your valor has been famed abroad, and acknowledged, as appears by the advice and orders to me, from the General Assembly of Connecticut, to surprise and take the garrison now before us.

"I now propose to advance before you, and in person, conduct you through the wicket gate; for we must this morning either quit our pretensions of valor, or possess ourselves of this fortress in a few minutes; and, inasmuch as it is a desperate attempt, which none but the bravest of men dare undertake, I do not urge it on any contrary to his will.

"You that will undertake voluntarily, pose your firelocks."

The men, drawn in three ranks, assented with their weapons silently raised.

A road led from the beach and up through woods toward the fort, curved around a wall and past a ruined curtain barrier with a breach in it. Allen, with Arnold beside him, led the men through this breach. In front of them was the wicket gate that opened into a long, arched, covered passageway to the parade of the fort, a quadrangle bordered with limestone barracks.

It was now, as Allen described it, "the gray of the morning."

The wicket gate was open.

"Col. Arnold entered the fortress with me side by side," Allen wrote, within a few hours, to of all places, Albany.

Allen came at once upon a foe:

"I found a sentry posted," he recalled, "who instantly snapped his fusee at me; and I immediately ran towards him, and he retreated through the covered way into the parade within the garrison, gave a halloo, and ran under a bomb-proof."

This sentry, said Col. Easton, was thereupon "seized and confined."

Allen had his men form quickly on the parade. "The garrison being asleep, except the sentries," said Allen, "we gave three huzzas which greatly surprised them." Whereupon the Green Mountain Boys and their allies, with cries of "No quarter!" surged pell-mell at the barracks and the startled regulars.

The victory cry had penetrated the drowsy guardroom, and out dashed a redcoat. Allen said that this sentry, with his bayonet fixed, charged at one of the Green Mountain band, Col. Easton, and slightly wounded him.

"My first thought," said Allen, "was to kill him with my sword; but in an instant, I altered the design and fury of the blow to a slight cut on the side of the head; upon which he dropped his gun, and asked for quarter, which I readily granted him, and demanded of him the place where the commanding officer kept. He showed me a pair of stairs in front of a barrack, on the west part of the garrison, which led up a second story in said barrack, to which I immediately repaired."

Even a slight slash from Allen's potent sword could be ghastly. The sentry was lucky. A comb in his hair deflected the full force of Allen's blow.

At the head of the outside wooden stairway that the sentry showed Allen were the quarters of the commanding officer of the fort, Capt. William Delaplace, 26th Regt., and adjoining were those of his first subaltern, Lt. Jocelyn Feltham. Feltham, who had been unwell for two or three nights, was easily awakened by "numbers of shrieks and words, 'No quarter! No quarter!' from a number of armed rabble.

"I jumped up, about which time I heard the noise continue in the area of the fort. I ran undressed to knock at Capt. Delaplace's door and to receive his orders or wake him. The door was fast, the room I lay in being close to Capt. Delaplace's. I stepped back, put on my coat and waistcoat and returned to his room, there being no possibility of getting to the men, as there were numbers of the rioters on the bastions of the wing of the fort on which the door of my room and the backdoor of Capt. Delaplace's room led.

"With great difficulty I got into his room ... and asked Capt. Delaplace, who was now just up, what I should do, and offered to force my way if possible to our men." Presently, partly dressed, Feltham opened the door to the parade and saw:

"The bottom of the stairs was filled with rioters and many were forcing their way up, knowing the commanding officer lived there, as they had broke open the lower rooms where the officers live in the winter, and could not find them there.

"From the top of the stairs I endeavored to make them hear me, but it was impossible. On making a signal not to come up the stairs, they stopped and proclaimed silence among themselves. I asked them a number of questions, expecting to amuse them 'til our people fired, which I must certainly own I thought would have been the case."

Allen, said Feltham, declared he "must have immediate possession of the fort and all the effects of George III, those were his words, Mr. Allen insisting on this with a drawn sword over my head and numbers of his followers' firelocks presented at me, alleging I was commanding officer and to give up the fort, and if not complied with, or that there was a single gun fired in the fort neither man, woman or child should be left alive in the fort."

Amid the hubbub Allen suddenly learned that Feltham was not his man. Vermont tradition tells us that Allen, in a voice like thunder, roared at the sulking captain something—minus frontier profanity—like:

"Come out of there, you damned old rat!"

In his latter account Allen phrased it:

"I ordered the commander, Capt. Delaplace, to come forth instantly, or I would sacrifice the whole garrison." The captain stepped out.

"I ordered him to deliver me the fort instantly," recalled Allen. "He asked me by what authority I demanded it. I answered him: 'In the name of the great Jehovah, and the Continental Congress!'

"The authority of the Congress being very little known at that time, he began to speak again; but I interrupted him, and with my drawn sword over his head, again demanded an immediate surrender of the garrison; with which he then complied, and ordered his men to be forthwith paraded without arms, as he had given up the garrison.

"In the meantime some of my officers had given orders, and in consequence thereof, sundry of the barrack doors were beaten down, and about one-third of the garrison imprisoned, which consisted of the said commander, a Lt. Feltham, conducter of artillery, a gunner, two sergeants, and 44 rank and file; about 100 pieces of cannon, one 13-inch mortar and a number of swivels."

Allen had undeniable cause to rejoice.

"The sun seemed to rise that morning," he said, "with a superior luster; and Ticonderoga and its dependencies smiled on its conquerers, who tossed about the flowing bowl, and wished success to Congress, and the liberty and freedom of America." Allen then sent Col. Warner and the rear guard to take the fort at Crown Point, which they speedily did, along with more prisoners and "upwards of 100 pieces of cannon."

Now the entire prize, the gateway to Canada, was in the patriots' hands.

True, the main fort was in such ruinous shape that the top British engineer in the colonies made a survey that showed "it would require more to repair it than constructing a new fort." Ticonderoga had been militarily neglected since the end of the French and Indian Wars. Roughly half its meager garrison comprised worn-out soldiers, some lame or unable to stand fatigue duty. With them were their families, many women and children. All the men nevertheless were experienced, trained regulars.

Gage, and his top officer in Canada, Gen. Guy Carleton, had made belated efforts to strengthen the garrison. A lieutenant and some reinforcements arrived just after the fort was surprised, and were captured. But security had been lax. Noah Phelps of the Connecticut men was able, the day before the capture, to enter the fort, pretending need of its barber, and reconnoiter.

Ethan Allen's blunderbuss

Ft. Ticonderoga, N.Y.

Still, here were the cannon so anxiously awaited in Boston; and it eventually would be these very cannon that would drive the British out of Boston. And here was one of the most strategic spots in all the colonies. Within the next few days Arnold, by commencing naval exploits in a captured schooner, would win command of Lake Champlain. His enterprise would forestall a British invasion from Canada for two years, helping to seal the invasion's eventual doom.

After the capture of Fort Ticonderoga, developments connected with it—all of them affecting the siege of Boston—took some strange twists.

There was another leadership clash.

"Col. Arnold challenged the command again," said Mott, "and insisted that he had a right to have it; on which our soldiers again paraded and declared they would go right home, for they would not be commanded by Arnold.

"We told them they should not, and at length pacified them; and then reasoned with Arnold, and told him as he had not raised any men, he could not expect to have the command of ours. He still insisted that as we had no legal orders to show, he had a right to take the command. On which I wrote Col. Allen his orders."

These orders, though, said nothing specific about cannon being taken to Boston. Arnold's did. Still, Arnold had no men, and when the recruits he had sought in the Berkshires did begin to appear in a few days, Arnold took off on his naval campaign. Meantime, Arnold said, he was not consulted, was "often insulted ... often threatened with my life and twice shot at."

Word of the clash got back to Cambridge and Hartford and Albany. These colonies' leaders were sending letters by express back and forth to avoid any hurt feelings, for Cambridge and Hartford patriots, after all, had commissioned Allen and Arnold to seize a fort that was within New York's territory.

Boston's anxiety for cannon prompted Warren, in one of these letters to Hartford, to urge patriots there to solve the disputes at Ticonderoga by their putting Arnold in charge of the cannon to "bring them down in all possible haste." Gage's army in Boston, said Warren, had the advantage of "as fine a train of artillery as ever was seen in America."

The unexpected, unbelievable reaction of the Second Continental Congress to news of the capture of Ticonderoga shocked all patriots in New England and New York, too. Allen had given Pittsfield's John Brown the honor of going express to Philadelphia with the news of the victory.

The Continental Congress, which assembled May 10 within a few hours of Allen's taking the fort, was nonplussed by Brown's message. Lexington and Concord was a defensive action. Ticonderoga was aggression. And the Congress at the moment was in the mood to seek conciliation with Great Britain.

It ordered that the captured ordnance be taken south on Lake George with a view to returning everything to His Majesty when "former harmony" was restored. Ticonderoga and Crown Point were ordered abandoned! At once, Massachusetts, Connecticut, New Hampshire and New York appealed to the Continental Congress to retain the forts against the prospect of Gen. Carleton in retaliation invading from Canada.

Even Allen and Arnold saw eye to eye on this, and wrote similar appealing letters to Philadelphia. Congress soon reconsidered and agreed to keep the forts, but there would be none of the Ticonderoga cannon available when a crisis would come shortly at Bunker Hill.

One of the strangest twists of all was the manner in which Gage learned that Fort Ticonderoga had been captured.

Gage's agents intercepted and copied a letter Warren wrote, giving the joyful news to his prospective father-in-law, John Scollay. Gage read the copy, and got off a letter at once to his chief, Lord Dartmouth, telling of the capture and saying "the fort was not to be taken, unless by surprise." Which, of course, was exactly the way it was done.

Fight for Boston Harbor islands

Lt. Barker of the King's Own caught quite a sight on the afternoon of May 13, as he looked from his regiment's encampment on top of West Hill, the third, westernmost peak of Beacon Hill.

Across the water and along the Cambridge marshes, where the patriots had been building a square redoubt, Barker could see 300 Yankee soldiers parading. Moreover, at the same time, as he looked northward to Charlestown, there was an even bigger Yankee parade. Barker estimated that "between 2000 and 3000 of the rebels came from Cambridge, marched over the Neck at Charlestown and up the height above the town...."

This was all an enterprise of the restless old warrior Brig. Gen. Israel Putnam to inspire his men with confidence and shake his fist at Gage's garrison in Boston. Putnam, at the May 12 powwow of the patriot chiefs, had favored immediately fortifying Bunker Hill. The chiefs' decision was to postpone this action, so Putnam next day went ahead with the march of his men and his show of defiance to the redcoats.

Actually, Putnam had only 2200 men on his march. These were all the men he had in Cambridge except the guards. He marched them over Bunker Hill, Breed's Hill and along the main street to the marketplace near the ferryway to Boston. *HMS Somerset* was on station nearby, so Putnam's men gave a war whoop before marching away.

If Putnam's men had fired on the warship, Barker declared, its gunners "had everything ready for action, and must have destroyed great numbers of them, besides putting the town in ashes."

However, action between the two forces in May — in the weeks leading to the battle of Bunker Hill — was confined pretty much to the ocean side of Boston. The patriot army, despite blocking any supplies entering Boston from Roxbury or Charlestown, had inadvertently left the cattle, sheep, produce and hay on the islands of Boston harbor still within grasp of the British squadron. Gage's garrison could use it all. "Our supplies from the country," Gage wrote to England, "are cut off...."

British foraging parties were sent around the harbor. These put the farmers in a dilemma: whether they sold or refused to sell would make them offend one side or the other. British troops went to Lovell's Island in April, seized cattle from two protesting farmers' wives and left behind chits for payment. Foraging parties were a threat to the coastal communities, too.

Warren and the Committee of Safety on May 14 resolved that local officials should remove all livestock from Boston's two biggest harbor islands, Noddle's (now East Boston) and Hog (now Orient Heights), and also from Snake Island (off Winthrop) and the seacoast of Chelsea, which then included Winthrop and all of what is now Revere. If necessary, the officials could use some of Col. John Stark's regiment posted at Medford.

Little action followed, but on May 21 it was speeded by a skirmish in the southern part of the harbor at Grape Island, just off Weymouth.

Gage desperately needed hay. On the eve of Sunday, May 21, three sloops, an armed cutter and 30 soldiers were sent for the Grape Island hay, creating an alarm that there would be a landing at Weymouth. Gen. Thomas rushed off three companies from the Roxbury encampment to help. The British detachment appeared Sunday morning off Weymouth's Fore River. On the shore drums beat, bells rang, alarm guns were fired. Minutemen gathered, residents fled. Soon, amid the panic, it became clear that the redcoats were interested only in the island, which was far enough offshore so that the patriot fire was ineffective.

Still, there was an exchange of gunfire as the soldiers carried hay and piled it on the shore. When the tide came in, the patriots were able to float some lighters and headed for the island. They landed on one end and the British fled from the other, occasionally firing their swivel guns. The patriots burned a barn and 70 or 80 tons of hay and removed the cattle. The British got only seven or eight tons of hay.

Warren had rushed to the scene, joining the patriots and helping to inspire their success. Abigail Adams missed none of the excitement.

She wrote to her husband how men of Weymouth and neighboring towns rushed to arms, how both of Adams's brothers took part and how the younger one was one of the first to reach Grape Island.

Warren and the Provincial Congress, urged by the Committee of Safety, debated removing "immediately" the livestock and hay from Noddle's and adjacent islands. Gage, through his informers, got wind of this. On May 25, the very day he had sent a captain and 50 men to snatch hay on Long Island, Gage scrawled an agitated note to his naval commander, Adm. Graves, warning that he had just learned that "the rebels intend this night to destroy and carry off all the stock on Noddle's Island."

Gage's warning was a day early. It was not until the night of May 26 that the patriots acted. On orders from Gen. Ward, Col. Stark and upwards of 200 men marched from Medford, along the Malden marshes, around Chelsea Creek by Rumney Marsh (now Revere) and the meetinghouse, where he was joined by Chelsea men, and down toward Pullen Point (now Winthrop), to where his men could ford the narrow creek to the road on the east end of Hog Island.

Stark knew the area well. He and his men had been here in April to help defend it from foraging parties. He had come another time, for Ward, to study the possibility of placing a battery on Noddle's Island. This time there were with him as well 200 to 300 men under Col. John Nixon. Next morning, May 27, the patriots removed a few horses and cattle and more than 400 sheep from Hog Island to the mainland.

In the afternoon they waded, knee-deep, across the creek to Noddle's Island and started moving cattle and destroying things useful to the British. The entire island was rented to Henry Howell Williams, who had a residence, many buildings, barns, horses, cows and lots of sheep and hay. Williams had been supplying the British and passing merchant ships. Though Adm. Graves scorned Williams, who was a quartermaster sergeant for the patriots, Graves nevertheless rented a storehouse to hold naval stores he felt an "impossibility of replacing." Williams was one of those harbor dwellers with a dilemma.

Presently, between 2 and 3 p.m., the British caught sight of what the patriots were doing. Graves, from his 50-gun flagship *HMS Preston*, ran up his signal, a red flag, for the marines to land and sent off the schooner *HMS Diana*, skippered by his nephew Lt. Thomas Graves, to move up Chelsea Creek and cut off the patriot retreat. The *Diana* carried four 4-pounders, 12 swivel guns and 30 men. The patriots, pursued by the marines, retreated toward Hog Island. After wading across the intervening creek they found a ditch and staved off the marines.

"The bullets flew very thick," recalled minuteman Asa Farnsworth of Groton, a member of Col. Nixon's regiment.

The patriots also endured shot from the *Diana* as it moved up the main part of the creek. Most withdrew across Hog Island the way they had come, and on reaching the mainland sent an appeal for reinforcements. They also maintained fire on the *Diana*, which kept moving up the creek despite low tide. Graves had ordered his nephew "to get up as high as possible to prevent their (the patriots') escape."

There was no slack in the patriot fire, mainly from ditches in the Chelsea-side marshes. Soon, though, around 6 p.m., the *Diana* was in difficulty. The wind fell, the tide turned against her. The admiral sent the tender of *HMS Somer-*

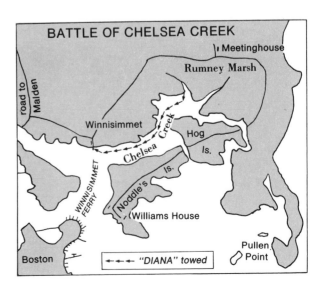

set (the *Britannia*) and 11 barges, with swivels mounted, from ships of the squadron, to assist the *Diana*. The barges, their men at the oars, took *Diana* in tow, and she began to move, still under fire, back along the creek. Progress was desperately slow.

While the shore of the creek was mostly marsh, there was sound ground ahead in the area where the ferry from Boston docked at Winnisimmet (now Chelsea), and in this area Israel Putnam placed some men after he arrived about 9 p.m. Warren was with him, boosting morale, and, for the first time in the Revolutionary War, a pair of patriot cannon, which they had brought, was ready for action. Putnam now had command of about 1000 men along the creek.

On arrival, Putnam had waded in the marsh and water and called to the *Diana* to surrender and had promised that its men would be given quarter. Lt. Graves's response was some cannon shot. The patriots returned the shots. Firing continued intensely despite the darkness, and was joined by extra British cannon sent to Noddle's Island. Patriot fire finally forced withdrawal of the men in the barges, who cast off and left the *Diana*.

A sudden breeze drove the *Diana* hard aground shortly before midnight. Her crew kept fighting, even propped her from the side as the tide receded, but had to flee with their wounded to the *Britannia* when the *Diana* fell on her beamends. Soon the *Britannia*, too, was forced to withdraw with at least one seaman dead, one dying and many wounded on her deck.

The patriots, knowing they could not keep the *Diana* in view of the British control of harbor waters, stacked hay and set her afire about 3 a.m. after removing anything useful, especially the cannon. Because of darkness, distances and ditches, the casualties were not many — only four wounded among the patriots.

The patriots were certain (as the British were on their side) that they killed a great many of the enemy. Gage, in his report to Whitehall, said only two were killed and a few wounded. Gage's brother-in-law, Dep. Adj. Gen. Stephen Kemble, said "two or three killed." Adm. Graves said that besides the dead and wounded on the

Boston Athenaeum, Boston, Mass.

Lt. Thomas Graves

Britannia "several were wounded in the schooner and other boats."

This encounter was by no means the end of skirmishes and raids on the islands. In succeeding days, the patriots returned until they had burned all the structures on Noddle's Island and removed all livestock, and they made similar visits that removed 500-odd sheep and cattle from Peddock's Island and 800-odd from Deer Island. There would be many forays to harbor islands for hay.

When Putnam, his clothing up to his waist telltale of soaking and mud, got back to Cambridge, he remarked to Warren and Ward:

"I wish we could have something of this kind to do every day. It would teach our men how little danger there is from cannonballs."

One of the most important effects of the action in Chelsea Creek came in Philadelphia. Warren had been writing to Samuel Adams about the wisdom of the Continental Congress's assuming control of the New England army now besieging Boston. Twice the Provincial Congress supported him with urgent appeals. The thrilling news of the Chelsea battle arrived as the Continental Congress was picking general officers, and brought a major generalship to daring and energetic "Old Put."

There was a curious aftermath of the battle, too.

The four cannon captured from the *Diana* were carefully carted, on orders of Warren's Committee of Safety, to Cambridge and added to the skimpy patriot magazine. Tradition tells us that these four would be moved into battle again at Bunker Hill and the patriots would save only one of them.

Gage's superspy, Dr. Church, gave the besieged general ample, specific warning that the patriots were contemplating decisive moves with regard to the strategic heights that dominated Boston. Within 24 hours of the patriot leaders' secret discussion, Church on May 13 informed Gage:

"They intend shortly to fortify Bunker's and Dorchester Hills."

Both sides, however, still hesitated to act from concern that they were inadequately prepared. Battery cannon for the patriots still were not at hand. And George III's "mild general" did not wish to repeat the bad timing that had impelled him to send his troops on the April 19 mission before his mounted dragoons had arrived. Gage would await reinforcements.

Transports were bringing them fairly steadily as Lord Dartmouth had promised, though not in the numbers Gage felt he should have. Light dragoons did arrive, imposing on Gage additional supply problems of horses and hay, and there came more men to fill out the regiments already in Boston, and more regiments as well. On May 25 there was a sensational arrival. *HMS Cerberus* entered Boston harbor with three well-known major generals.

John Burgoyne, "Gentleman Johnny," man of fashion, playwright, member of Parliament, son-in-law of Lord Derby, had been told by the captain of a passing packet that there were thousands of country people confining Gage's troops in Boston. Burgoyne asked the captain how many regulars were in Boston, and the captain replied there were 5000.

"What!" exclaimed Gentleman Johnny. "Ten thousand peasants keep 5000 of the King's troops shut up! Well, let us get in and we'll soon find some elbow room!"

This was why George III had sent the major generals, to put some military thrust into his "mild general." The two other major generals were younger than Burgoyne but his military seniors — William Howe, courageous, self-indulgent, distant relative of the King, leader of the British soldiers in scaling Wolfe's Cove to take Quebec in '59, and Henry Clinton, competent, difficult, American-born aristocrat.

"As our generals have now arrived," Lord

Dr. Benjamin Church Jr., superspy, tips Gage that patriots plan to fortify Bunker Hill

Percy wrote to England, "I take it for granted that something will be undertaken." The newly arrived generals took a look around and saw immediately that the security of Boston depended on taking the neighboring heights. Clinton was surprised that this had not already been done. Gage, at any rate, was in a better position now to perfect his planning.

May 25 was a pleasing day, too, for the patriot leader. On arriving at his office in Watertown, Warren got the news of Arnold's successful Canadian raid at St. John's, of New Hampshire's voting to raise 2000 or more men, and of a company of troops arriving from Rhode Island with a train of artillery. Warren, thinking of Ward, sent off the encouraging news to Hastings House "to the general's room," he said, "as I love to give pleasure to good men."

The patriots were striving to augment their new army of eight-month recruits. Only a few days earlier, Ward had written to Warren that the regiments must be settled immediately, their officers commissioned and the soldiers mustered, "if we would save our country." Ward himself was formally commissioned at once, and beating papers were put in circulation to enlist men for the regiments.

So that there should be no question about the civilian control of the military, Warren and the provincial leaders were also urging the Continental Congress to give its legal blessing to the Provincial Congress. Meantime, to keep close to the people, a new Congress was elected and the Third Provincial Congress (practically the same members) assembled in Watertown.

The political gulf that now divided motherland and colony was apparent in the inaugural sermon preached, on this occasion, by the chaplain of the besieging army, President Samuel Langdon of Harvard College. In the future, he told his audience, he clearly could see "a final separation of the colonies from Great Britain . . . ."

Reinforcements for Gage continued to reach Boston. He even had Adm. Graves send a ship to cruise off New York to watch for four regiments destined for that province and "to order them to join the troops here, where the rebels have collected their main force." It was now June 12 and

Gage had made up his mind. His thinking at this moment is in a letter he sent to Dartmouth, a letter considered so significant in London that a copy of it exists among the papers of George III — in the handwriting of the King himself.

Gage estimated to Dartmouth that it would take at least 32,000 soldiers — 15,000 of them to be stationed in Boston — to quell the rebellion. This was a staggering figure, for it represented far more than half of all the soldiers Great Britain then had under arms on the entire earth.

Gage had analyzed the situation that confronted him in Massachusetts. He wrote:

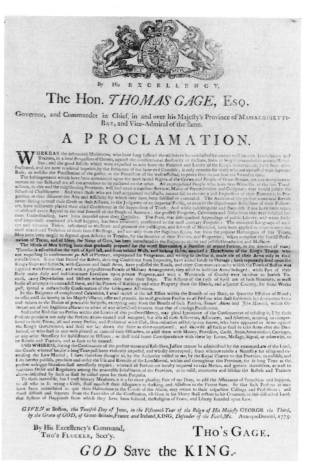

Gage's June 12 proclamation

W. L. Clements Library,
Ann Arbor, Mich.

"I see no prospect of any offers of accommodation and have therefore issued a proclamation for the exercise of the law martial." Some marines, royal artillery and more light dragoons had just arrived. A few more reinforcements were soon expected, he said, and then added:

"I do not however design to wait long for them before I make an attempt upon some of the rebels' posts, which becomes every day more necessary."

He was planning, at that very moment, to act within a week.

The proclamation he mentioned was issued June 12.

Like the augmentation of Gage's army, the proclamation was a signal that action was impending. It proclaimed much more than martial law. In the orotund phrasing of playwright Burgoyne, it granted the King's pardon to all rebels who "shall forthwith lay down their arms and return to the duties of peaceable subjects" — all but Samuel Adams and John Hancock.

Those traitors, proclaimed Gage, must face "condign punishment," veiled language for hanging.

The patriots prepared a counter proclamation. It would offer peace to all but Gage, Adm. Graves and the three hold-out Mandamus Councilors, the hated Jonathan Sewall, Charles Paxton and Benjamin Hallowell, all sheltered behind Gage's lines. But the patriots did not issue their response. They had more urgent business.

Gage's three major generals, in letters and comments, have preserved in essence the plan Gage drafted in his sessions with them at Province House, and said all had assented. He would launch an attack to take Dorchester Heights, swing in an arc through Roxbury, Brookline, Cambridge and Charlestown, crushing the rebel force, and reoccupy Bunker Hill.

Dorchester peninsula, from the neck to the point opposite Castle Island, would be the first objective. Burgoyne has put the first maneuver most succinctly:

"Howe was to land the transports on the point; Clinton in the Center; and I was to cannonade from the causeway or the neck (Boston Neck); each to take advantage of circumstances. The operation must have been very easy."

The time Gage picked to start the operation: Sunday, June 18, at daybreak.

But the patriots also would have a plan — for the day before June 18.

Patriots plan a surprise

The patriot plan was an improvisation, something with which they hoped to upset Gage's project of breaking out of Boston southward across the neck.

They would fortify the heights of Charlestown on Gage's north, the opposite side of the Boston peninsula, "to defeat," as the Committee of Safety later wrote, "this design of our enemies." Patriot intelligence had been as thorough as that of the British. The information on which the patriots were now to act suddenly came to them, Joseph Palmer wrote afterwards for the Committee of Safety, "about the 14th ult.," which was June 14, three days before the battle. It came inopportunely, though, for the patriots were still in the midst of striving to organize and supply their army.

Roughly a week earlier, on June 6, the general officers had made another survey of Dorchester Heights. Their decision was the same as they had made a month earlier at their May 12 powwow. As yet, they did not have cannon or powder sufficient for so hazardous an enterprise.

Brig. Gen. Thomas, in command of the patriots' right wing, had been under alarm many times that the British would try to take Dorchester Heights.

Indeed, Gen. Ward and Thomas had frequent communication on this danger. Thomas kept men posted at Dorchester Neck in the daytime, pickets there at night and still more at Dorchester Point opposite powerfully armed Castle Island. The British watched, too. Even during the June 6 survey they fired three cannon balls at the patriot generals but, as a Yankee soldier there reported, "did no harm."

The confused state of the growing army was bedeviling the patriots. Too many enlisting orders had been issued. There were rivalries over commissions among the officers, and among the men there was too often intense feeling as to the regiments in which they were willing to serve. The Provincial Congress gave stringent directions to the Committee of Safety to try "reducing the army to order." To help, the Congress was preparing to name more generals, major, brigadier and adjutant.

It was amid this anxiety that Gage's June 12 proclamation reached the patriot camp. The people of Massachusetts, as the patriots were quick to notice, had been "in the most explicit manner declared rebels." No question, Gage was about to spring. That very day Ward directed the New Hampshire regiment of Col. James Reed to move deeper into Charlestown. Reed posted his men at Charlestown Neck and sent sentinels to Bunker Hill.

Like a bolt of lightning, specific intelligence of Gage's plan came next to the patriot leaders. Joseph Palmer said "about the 14th." Likely, it came the 13th. On that day the Committee of Safety resolved that "the debates and determinations of this committee be kept in profound secrecy." Determinations poured from the committee, prefaced with the urgency:

"It is daily expected that Gen. Gage will attack our army now in the vicinity of Boston."

Each colonel must make immediate returns on his unit's condition and equipment. Colonels must report immediately "the number of men destitute of arms, and what arms are fit for immediate service." The Committee of Supplies was asked "the quantity of powder in their possession and where the same is."

By June 15 a stream of requests was "earnestly recommended to the immediate consideration of the honorable Congress now sitting in Watertown." The army must be further increased. Men destitute of arms must be armed. Militia regiments, the reserve of the army, must be completely officered immediately. Moreover, the Congress was asked that:

"All militia in the colony be ordered to hold themselves in readiness to march on the shortest notice, completely equipped, having 30 rounds of cartridges per man."

Quite clearly, the Committee of Safety knew that Gage's operation was planned for June 18, a Sunday, for the committee begged leave to ask further that the Congress issue "a general recommendation to the people to go to meeting armed, on the Lord's day, in order to prevent being thrown into confusion."

Climax of this activity came June 15 in a unanimous resolution of the Committee of Safety, a resolution regarded as so vital to their cause that they even waited four days before they entered it on their records. Their vote, signed by their chairman Benjamin White of Brookline, urged upon the Council of War that Bunker Hill "be securely kept and defended; and also some one hill or hills of Dorchester Neck be likewise secured."

Bunker Hill was well known to them. The situation on Dorchester Neck (the name then for the entire Dorchester penninsula) was not. So they asked that White and Joseph Palmer, with a committee from the Council of War, go to the Roxbury camp and consult with Gen. Thomas. The Council of War, headed by Gen. Ward, voted "to take immediate possession of Bunker Hill and Dorchester Neck."

This ambitious plan to secure the heights both north and south of Boston was quickly modified by the session that followed in Roxbury with Gen. Thomas. White and Palmer were joined, from the Council of War, by Gen. Putnam and two colonels, Jonathan Ward and Samuel Gerrish. But Thomas and his officers felt the same as during the June 6 survey. With inadequate cannon and powder, Thomas, a courageous man, was convinced that his best service still would be to maintain the Roxbury position he was then holding. He might thus be able to block a British sortie from Boston southward.

For Commander in Chief Ward, the next day, June 16, was crucial. His task was gigantic. Gen. Gage, amply supplied with weaponry and powder, backed by a fleet, in command of a long-established army, would open his attack within 24 hours.

Ward's force was larger, by more than two-to-one. His besieging position though, involved far more miles to cover. The patriots had been openly under arms less than two months. There was at Ward's command no unified military machine, far from a trained and disciplined one, no smooth working staff, hardly an operative chain of command. His ill-supplied, ill-clothed, ill-housed army's great strength was the strength of its cause, an unshakable fervor for liberty. Out of it came the admirable audacity of these uni-

formless provincials to confront in battle the best of George III's regulars.

Toward midday this day, Ward stepped out of his headquarters at Hastings House, mounted a horse and, with some officers, rode to Charlestown.

A lieutenant in Col. Reed's regiment, Thompson Maxwell, saw them. Maxwell, a teamster, had served at Lake George, was a member of the Boston Tea Party, fought in the Lexington-Concord Alarm, and had enlisted as an eight-month volunteer. It was about noon, Maxwell recalled, that the headquarters party appeared and "went onto Bunker Hill." Presently Ward and the officers "returned and went to Cambridge."

Ward was checking the potential battlefield.

While Thomas would try to defend the right wing, Ward would try the same on the center in Cambridge. Gage's plan, as the patriot intelligence knew, included a sweep through the rebel center. Ward could not be certain whether the British would also repeat Lt. Col. Smith's maneuver of April 18 and attempt a landing in the vicinity of Willis Creek on the Cambridge shore.

The patriot move to forestall Gage would be on Ward's left wing, and the man he selected to set it in motion was a man he knew to be aggressive, militarily experienced and wholeheartedly in favor of fortifying the heights of Charlestown: Col. William Prescott. Ward's orders to Prescott would be explicit. Ward must have been thinking of them as he rode back to Cambridge.

Col. Prescott with 300 men of his regiment, along with some companies of the regiments of Col. James Frye of North Andover and Col. Ebenezer Bridge of Billerica and a makeshift company of artillery under Capt. Samuel Gridley, were to assemble on Cambridge Common, grand parade of the colony army, at 6 p.m. on June 16.

Ward's orders to Prescott were that he keep his mission secret until after he should cross Charlestown Neck.

A short while before the assembling hour, Prescott dropped into the headquarters of Gen. Putnam near Harvard Square. Putnam's 16-year-old son Daniel, who had gone along when Putnam made his defiant march through Charlestown, knew a detachment from Putnam's regiment was also under arms for some "secret service." Daniel recalled that "Old Put" had out his pistols, was preparing cartridges and putting in new flints when Prescott entered.

Daniel said that Prescott remarked to Putnam: "I see, General, you are making preparation, and we shall be ready at the time."

The detachment assembled on the side of the Common near Hastings House. It was still broad daylight, the afternoon of a long, pleasant June day, as the men came from their quarters and tents in the scattered Cambridge camp. Each was to have his pack with blanket and provisions for 24 hours. Capt. Gridley's men had two fieldpieces, some cannon of *HMS Diana* taken at Chelsea Creek.

The men, most of them devout churchgoers, gathered in a circle, as Harvard's President Langdon led them in prayer and implored divine blessing on their endeavors.

By 9 p.m., when Prescott gave the order to march, darkness had fallen and two men with hooded lanterns had to march up front to give guiding flickers of light. Prescott, 49, a lean, muscular 6-footer, veteran of the French and Indian Wars, led the way by the old Charlestown-Cambridge road (now Kirkland street). A little more than a mile along the road, the column was joined by 200 Connecticut men under stalwart, tall Capt. Thomas Knowlton Jr. of Ashford, who had come up the road from the Inman farm (near what is now Cambridge City Hall), where Putnam's regiment was stationed.

Prescott's detachment was now complete, "about a thousand men," he estimated, including the drivers of several wagons at the rear who were carting all the entrenchment tools, shovels and spades, that could be found in the Cambridge camp. A short march after Capt. Knowlton joined the column, it passed by Prospect Hill; a little farther it skirted now-vanished Cobble Hill, and, after two and a half miles of quiet-as-possible advance, came to Charlestown Neck.

Prescott called a halt. Ward's orders directed Prescott to build a fortification on Bunker Hill and defend it until he was relieved. It was to be planned by Col. Richard Gridley, chief engineer,

65-year-old veteran of the French and Indian Wars, in command of the patriots' still-incomplete artillery regiment. Gridley had accompanied the column, which included the artillery unit of his son.

Beyond the neck, a road started up Bunker Hill, running off the main road leading into Charlestown. Prescott sent one of his captains, with about 70 men, along the main street into the town as sentinels. And before Prescott started up Bunker Hill, he was joined by Putnam, always eager for activity.

Bunker Hill, 110 feet high, bore an old, familiar name. A low ridge from it connected with what we now call Breed's Hill, 62 feet high. Breed's was a new name and applied then only to one of the hill's many pastures. Both the higher and lower hills were known jointly as Charlestown Hills or Bunker Hill. Somewhere between the two heights (Maj. John Brooks of Bridge's regiment later said at the foot of Breed's Hill), Prescott held a consultation.

Where to place the redoubt? Time was precious. Breed's Hill clearly would be more of a direct threat to the British. But it was commanded by the higher hill, and so the discussion came down to the necessity of having entrenchments on Bunker Hill as a possible rallying place should a redoubt on Breed's Hill be overrun. The decision was to go ahead on Breed's Hill, and Col. Gridley drew the lines, roughly a square, 8 rods or 132 feet to the side, with a small opening on the north. Prescott sent his senior captain, Hugh Maxwell, Lt. Thompson Maxwell's brother, with a patrol to watch any enemy activity on the shore or near the Charlestown ferry, and ordered his men to start digging.

It was now about midnight.

As on their march, the men were cautioned to act as quietly as possible.

Across the mouth of the Charles River was a slumbering Boston, largest community in New England, one of that period's foremost seaports, its silhouette and scattered night lights as exciting to most of the men then as a first view is now of any famous metropolis. Visible, too, were outlines of warships around Boston. The *HMS Lively*, a 20-gun frigate was just below the hill, at the Charlestown-to-Boston ferryway from

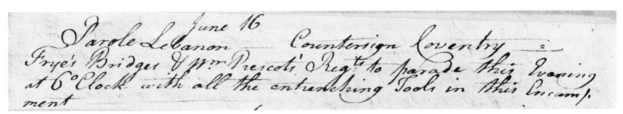

Prescott's orders to fortify Bunker Hill as recorded in Ward's orderly book

Massachusetts Historical Society

which Adm. Graves, worried about shallows, had recently shifted his mammoth 68-gun man-o'-war *HMS Somerset*.

The night sky was starfilled, but its darkness for a few hours shielded from the diggers the extent of their danger. Prescott understood it fully, and twice went down the hillside, past the empty dwellings, to the shore to satisfy his concern. With him went Maj. Brooks. From over the water they could hear the watch on the warships routinely make their cry, "All's well."

Prescott, weeks before he had responded to the Lexington-Concord Alarm, had told his brother-in-law, "I will never be taken alive. The Tories shall never have the satisfaction of seeing me hanged."

Prescott was the bravest of this heroic band. He well knew some might weaken and leave, for he had said "it would be difficult, if not quite impossible, to make raw troops, however full of patriotism, to stand, in an open field, against artillery and well armed and well disciplined soldiers." So he pressed on the digging, the raising of the earthwork to six feet in height.

Maj. Brooks, Prescott's companion to check on the enemy, had led the Reading minutemen to Concord and the fight at Meriam's Corner. Prescott's next in command, Lt. Col. John Robinson, had marched side by side with Maj. John Buttrick and Capt. Isaac Davis to oppose the redcoats at Concord's old North Bridge. Many men digging here would be buried here, pierced by bayonet or musket ball; some would be shattered by cannonball, some would be taken, wounded, as captives to face amputation and die in the brutal prison in Boston.

The coming of dawn underscored the danger

confronting the men in their redoubt — still little more than half-completed — and made still another hazard apparent. Prescott had recalled his two captains and their patrols from the shore. Chief engineer Gridley had become ill from fatigue shortly after midnight and had departed.

(He would return and would be among the wounded.) Capt. Maxwell, on returning, detected the additional hazard:

The redoubt, as it then stood, would have no adjoining breastwork to prevent encirclement.

At this point Lt. Maxwell of Reed's regiment had come uphill to visit the redoubt and overheard his brother, Capt. Maxwell, suggest to "Col. Prescott the propriety of running an entrenchment from the northeast angle of the night's work to a rail fence leading to Mystic River." Prescott approved. Said Lt. Maxwell: "I set up the stakes after my brother." This protective breastwork would not be carried as far as the rail fence, but Prescott did order it extended about 330 feet toward a sharply descending ravine.

Young Cpl. Peter Brown of Prescott's regiment was a soldier, as he put it, "hearty in the cause." On the parade ground at Cambridge Common he had come "readily and cheerfully," though he "knew not where" the march was headed. He now looked about him at what the dawn revealed, and wrote later to his mother:

"Then we saw danger, being against ships of the line, and all Boston fortified against us. The danger we were in made us think there was treachery and that we were brought there to be all slain."

A bit under three-quarters of a mile across

the river mouth rose Copp's Hill, and bristling atop it was a recently built battery with some 24-pounders that would be fired by Gen. Burgoyne. Brown could see that warships besides the *HMS Lively* were riding on station off the Charlestown peninsula: *HMS Falcon,* a 14-gun sloop-o'-war, off Moulton's Point; *HMS Glasgow,* 20-gun frigate, off Boston's West End; and the armed transport *Symmetry,* 18 guns, off School House Hill.

Suddenly, there came a cannon shot at the redoubt and everyone still sleeping within miles was awakened — generals, troops and citizenry. The log of *HMS Lively* tells leanly of this first shot in the battle of Bunker Hill on Saturday, June 17, after recording the weather as moderate and fair:

"At 4 a.m. discovered the rebels throwing up a redoubt on a hill at the back of Charlestown. Began to fire upon them."

Cautious Adm. Graves, who preferred to act under orders, signaled the *Lively* "Cease fire!" Just after the Lexington-Concord Alarm, Gage, on April 21, had warned the Charlestown selectmen that if rebel forces were allowed to occupy the town or erect works on the heights, the warships would be ordered to fire. Gage had repeated the threat. Under it, citizens had fled and the 400 dwellings in Charlestown stood mostly deserted. Graves wanted to be sure that Gage's threat was still in force.

Cpl. Brown, making note of the *Lively's* first fire, said it was soon resumed, lasted about 20 minutes, then again there was silence. "They killed but one of our men," said Brown. Asa Pollard of Billerica was this first casualty of the battle. The cannonball struck him, while outside the entrenchment, and beheaded him. Shocked fellow soldiers came to look. Prescott, so near Pollard he was "besmeared with his blood," was asked what should be done.

"Bury him," replied Prescott, seeking to avoid upsetting any raw troops.

"What! Without prayers?" interposed an officer. A chaplain and some soldiers twice persisted, and there was a brief interment.

Putnam, who had returned to his Cambridge headquarters, was awakened by the cannon shot.

He galloped to Ward's headquarters, conferred with Ward, sped off to Charlestown, saw what had been accomplished on the redoubt and promptly galloped back to Ward to suggest reinforcements. Ward sent a request to Col. Stark in Medford. Stark said:

"I was required by the general to send a party consisting of 200 men with officers to their assistance, which order I readily obeyed." But this detachment, in one of the mix-ups of the day, would arrive at a different place.

Gage, too, had heard the cannon boom on the *Lively.*

A Council of War was summoned, and soon the major generals, other high officers and military aides made their way along Boston's main street to Gage's resplendent Province House with its royal coat of arms.

Uppermost in Gage's mind had to be the question of how this rebel action would affect the long-delayed plans he already had made for seizing Dorchester Heights the next day, Sunday, at daybreak. Such thoughts, to his intense annoyance, may have already been disturbing his sleep, for Gage had been warned about rebel activity in Charlestown hours before the gunners on the *Lively* had fired their cannon.

The warning had come from Maj. Gen. Clinton. This officer, zealous about his forthcoming command in the Dorchester Heights operation, had been reconnoitering during the night and, while traversing the North End, detected the patriot activity on Breed's Hill. It was about midnight.

"I saw them at work, reported it to Generals Gage and Howe and advised a landing in two divisions at daybreak," said Clinton.

Howe, to whom Clinton first rushed with his discovery, approved Clinton's suggestion. But the Commander in Chief was not satisfied as to the meaning of this nighttime enterprise of the rebels. "Gen. Gage," said Clinton, "seemed to doubt their intention." Clinton went back to his quarters and turned in, but not before writing a letter in which he put his conviction that Gage's Sunday operation should now be reversed and be launched at Charlestown instead of Dorchester.

"If we were of active dispositions," wrote Clinton, with manifest tartness, "we should be landed by tomorrow morning at daybreak." Also, at that time, the tides on the Charlestown shore would be favorable.

The British generals were not the only ones in their camp who had wind of Prescott's mission, despite all the colonel's efforts and watchfulness to keep the strenuous digging quiet. Howe, forgetting his own foreknowledge, confirmed that British sentinels had also heard the patriot diggers and done nothing. Howe shortly wrote to England:

"The sentries on the Boston side had heard the rebels at work all night, without making any other report of it, except mentioning it in conversation in the morning."

Contempt for the provincials still persisted in the British camp, from officers' quarters to barracks, contrary to what Lord Percy had learned on April 19. The intervening weeks, the arrival of reinforcements, if anything, had buttressed it. Officers and regulars were supremely confident of their superiority. In the spirit of 18th Century warfare they felt no spur to act with speed.

At 7 a.m., said Lt. Barker, orders were sent to the elite companies, the huge grenadiers and nimble light infantry, "to keep in readiness." Since the Lexington-Concord Alarm these flank companies, removed from their respective regiments, had been combined into two separate corps. These were the striking force of Gage's army, and they had the privilege, recently exercised, of taking men from other regimental companies to keep their own ranks filled.

The Council of War, said Howe, "entirely set aside" the Dorchester Neck "scheme" and "it was therefore instantly determined to change the attack to this (Charlestown) side."

Clinton had another proposal. When Howe should land his force at Moulton's Point, farthest spot on that shore from Charlestown Village, Clinton suggested that he should lead 500 men and land at the old burying ground across from School House Hill and take the redoubt in the rear, or march through the town and cut off the rebels at Charlestown Neck. "My advice was not attended to," wrote twice-squelched Clinton.

The decision of the Council of War was, wrote Clinton, "that the hill was open and of easy ascent and in short it would easily be carried."

Gage and his generals, for Burgoyne said there was ultimate agreement, still clung to the garrison illusion that the rebels, when faced with the scarlet and glitter panoply of the redcoats in formation, would melt like bits of ice in the radiance of a hot sun.

Gage decided to commit about a third of his troops, 2200, to a landing in Charlestown under Howe. Orders now set in preparation would have the rest of the garrison keep "in readiness to march at a moment's notice." The 2200 troops would be ordered to parade at 11:30 "with their arms, ammunition, blankets and the provisions ordered to be cooked this morning."

So time would pass as beef was boiled and bread baked. But Howe was complacent. He noted, writing to England, that "it would be high water at 2 o'clock in the afternoon." (Actually high tide was to be at 2:51.) This would allow the landing boats to come close ashore, and the soldiers, unlike Lt. Col. Smith's on their start to Lexington and Concord, could avoid a soaking.

Clearly, from the three days' provisions to be carried by the regulars, this was not just to be an action to chase the rebels from Breed's Hill. It was to be the start of an expedition, possibly of several days' duration, to press right on, crush the rebel forces in the entire besieging arc, Charlestown, Cambridge, Roxbury and Dorchester Heights.

While the British conferred, Prescott's men kept at their spades and shovels. "Our work went on continually," wrote Thomas Boynton of Andover of Col. Bridge's regiment. Then about 9 o'clock the big cannon on Copp's Hill opened up and, said Boynton, "continued a hot fire." Some of the soldiers, no doubt recollecting Pollard's headless body, made off. Prescott, to keep his men inspired, mounted the earthwork, strode casually up and down it issuing his orders and urging on his soldiers.

Over on Copp's Hill, Gage had arrived to get a firsthand impression. Through his spyglass, Gage studied the tall figure striding on the parapet and asked of those about him who the man might be. Mandamus Councilor Abijiah Willard of Lancaster, stocky, wealthy, former colonel whose first wife had been a sister of Prescott, told Gage his brother-in-law's name. Gage asked:

"Will he fight?"

"Yes, sir," replied Williard, "he's an old soldier, and will fight as long as a drop of blood remains in his veins."

Gage thereupon declared: "The works must be carried."

Prescott's men toiled on, and the June day grew warmer. Prescott's officers requested that he ask Ward for some relief. Actually, Ward, back in Cambridge, had gone to check on relief he had already ordered. Cols. Nixon, Moses Little, John Mansfield and 200 Connecticut troops, with two days' provisions, arms and ammunition, were to parade at 4 p.m. and relieve Prescott and his detachment.

Prescott, indomitable man, was not interested in relief.

Refreshments and reinforcements were other matters, and Prescott favored these and sent Maj. Brooks off to Ward's headquarters to seek them. Brooks arrived there about 10 a.m., but at that hour Ward was not willing to weaken the army center.

Ward suspected that Gage might try just a feint at Charlestown to cover a drive against Cambridge and the army supplies. Ward held to this decision inflexibly, even when a top member of the Committee of Safety, Richard Devens of Charlestown, also appealed for reinforcements.

"About 11 o'clock," said Cpl. Brown, affording an eloquent picture of the effects upon the soldiers of hard labor, little sustenance and encompassing peril, the British batteries and warships "began to fire as brisk as ever, which caused many of our young country people to desert, apprehending the danger in a clearer manner than others who were more diligent in digging and fortifying ourselves. . . .

"We began to be almost beat out, being fatigued by our labor, having no sleep the night before, very little to eat, no drink but rum, but what we hazzarded our lives to get, we grew faint, thirsty, hungry and weary." To get water they had to go, under enemy fire, to wells in the abandoned homesteads of Charlestown Village.

Prescott knew his men well, knew that danger and gnawing need were winnowing them to a noble band that would be as resolute as himself. No, he wanted no relief. To those who insisted he said:

"The men who had raised the works were the best able to defend them. Already they had learned to despise the fire of the enemy. They had the merit of the labor, and they should have the honor of the victory."

About this time, between 11 a.m. and noon, the men suspended their digging. Gen. Heath related how "Gen. Putnam came to the redoubt and told Col. Prescott that the entrenching tools must be sent off, or they would be lost. The colonel replied, that if he sent any of the men away with the tools, not one of them would return. To this the general answered, they shall every man return. A large party was then sent off with the tools, and not one of them returned. In this instance the colonel was the best judge of human nature."

Taking orders, or observing orders from officers of different colonies, was not yet among the military accomplishments of this newly assembled, inexperienced army. Coordination was lacking, promoting confusion. Putnam did not have the staff or officers to get men to return to Breed's Hill. Still, he was able to get started building breastworks on Bunker Hill that could be a vital fall-back position on the line of any retreat.

Putnam had often expressed the view, deep-seated, on his experience in warfare:

"The Americans were not afraid of their heads, though very much afraid of their legs; if you cover these, they will fight forever."

Putnam was simply compressing in a few words the basic difference between the military seasoning of the redcoat and the rebel. The redcoat was taught volley firing. His regulation "Brown Bess" smoothbore had no rear sight. His effectiveness was the blast power of a quick succession of volleys. He also was taught to act in open-field formations.

For the American soldier there had been no training for open-field formations. His experience went straight back to Indian-style warfare, from behind trees or walls or mounds, a warfare natural to his wooded, hilly terrain. His weapons were strictly individual, catch-as-catch-can, of endless variety, many homemade. His training was chiefly self-training in hunting or keeping down wildlife on his farm. This made him usually surer with a target.

The cannon fire of the *Lively* had, as was said on grand occasions of spectacles in the Roman colosseum, produced a vasty multitude of spectators. The clarity and warmth of this June day were conducive to people's crowding to rooftops and hills and surrounding shores. Thousands of eyes followed signs of military action — signal flags on the warships, message boats moving on river and harbor.

Presently the word spread that the redcoats, their drummers beating, were moving toward the wharves. This word was rushed to Ward's headquarters. Ward was left with the question: Where would the British hit? He still felt that their real aim might be the army center in a bid to wipe out both it and the patriot cause. When Putnam's second in command, Lt. Col. Experience Storrs, rushed into headquarters for orders, Ward sent him and his men to strengthen Fort No. 1, a redoubt Putnam had raised slightly downriver from the Great Bridge, a short way from Harvard Square, to prevent any British foray up the Charles River.

Gen. Thomas and patriot regiments in Roxbury, opposite Boston Neck, felt menaced, too, by Gage's moves. Lord Percy, who had commanded the British relief column on April 19, was assigned by Gage to the neck fortifications and batteries to try to keep the rebels in Roxbury pinned down. A patriot soldier there from Sutton, Samuel Bixby, wrote this day how his comrades could clearly see the redcoats marching in Boston and how the patriot right wing reacted at noon:

"We fired an alarm, and rung the bells in Roxbury; and every man was ordered to arms, as an attack was expected."

For Prescott and the tired, hungry men at the redoubt, there was no respite. The British cannon fire, to prepare for a landing, was now intensified.

Patriots strengthen lines for battle

Aboard his flagship *HMS Preston* in Boston harbor, Adm. Graves, at noon, signaled orders for the 28 boats from all ships of the squadron to be "manned and armed." An hour later they all were ordered to repair to the wharves, as the log put it, "to embark the troops and ferry them over . . . to the west side Mystic River."

Graves did not feel, because of the lack of deep water, that he could use his two heavy ships of the line, 68-gun *HMS Somerset* or 50-gun *HMS Preston,* but he did transfer guns and crews from these to the lighter warships he had positioned around Charlestown to keep a "constant fire upon the rebels to prevent their annoying the troops on landing."

HMS Lively lay off the Winnisimmet ferryway, to which it had been shifted after its opening cannon fire. *HMS Falcon* was still off Moulton's Point, and the landing mission now had been joined by *HMS Spitfire,* a sloop-of-war carrying six 3-pounders.

Elevation of cannon, to get distance, was a constant problem for all these vessels that lessened the effectiveness, though not the thunder, of their continual bombardment.

Graves conceded that he had been astounded by the overnight creation of the rebel redoubt, and said:

"As this affair was sudden and unexpected there was no time for constructing floating batteries, or rafts of real service, as any such would have been the work of some days."

Instead, he explained, he put a 12-pounder on each of two scows and ordered them, despite difficulties from the tide, to be placed near the milldam to prevent rebel reinforcements from crossing Charlestown Neck. Every patriot who did try also had to face death from cannon of the frigate *HMS Glasgow* and the armed transport *Symmetry* that now were moved closer to bombard the neck from the west side.

The redcoats embarked at two wharves. The long wharf at the foot of King street jutted deep into the harbor, and it was from here that roughly 1000 stepped into the waiting boats, 10 companies each of grenadiers and light infantry and two regiments of foot, the 5th, Lord Percy's regiment, and the 38th, Brig. Gen. Robert Pigot's regiment. Sailors manning banks of oars rowed them, with military precision, past the North Battery (on what is now Atlantic avenue, North End) toward Moulton's Point.

At the North Battery, roughly 500 more redcoats entered boats, the foot troops of the 43rd and the 52nd Regts. Eight remaining companies of grenadiers and light infantry were to go along, but only two of them went on the first two trips of the boats, for two passages were necessary to get all the first 1500 troops across along with eight fieldpieces and four howitzers with their gun crews.

The brightness of scarlet and gleam of bayonet, making many-colored reflections dance on the water, presented a dazzling sight on this bright June day. Within the next few hours on those rises of land ahead, and along the beach by the Mystic River, roughly half of all these officers and men would be killed, mortally or painfully wounded — a staggering loss that would haunt British generalship all eight years of this Revolutionary War.

Gen. William Howe, in command, 46, tall and dark-complexioned, had fought at the fall of the fortress of Louisburg and on the Plains of Abraham at Quebec, had learned the art of war under heroic Gen. James Wolfe, conquerer of Canada. He was a younger brother of beloved Lord Howe, who had lost his life at Ticonderoga many years ago, and — until recently — was long believed friendly to the American cause. Howe came across to Moulton's Point on the second passage of the boats.

Meantime, none of this spectacle — or its imminent threat to their rustic ranks — was lost upon the men in the redoubt. The North Battery was within their view. They could see the sailors stroke their boats across the mouth of the Charles River and move, on the signal of a red flag, to a landing on the beach.

Prescott took it all in despite the enemy's "incessant fire with their artillery," and acted. "About 2 o'clock," he recounted, "the enemy

Boston Athenaeum, Boston, Mass.

Capt. John Chester

began to land a north-easterly point from the fort, and I ordered the train, with two field-pieces, to go and oppose them, and the Connecticut forces to support them."

Like David facing Goliath, Prescott was a man indifferent to the odds of military might massed against him. The "train" meant the small, untrained group of gunners under Capt. John Callender. Capt. Samuel Gridley, who had come from Cambridge with the detachment and placed his two fieldpieces within the fort, had already taken them out of the redoubt and beyond the breastwork. Cpl. Brown told of this.

Capt. Gridley had fired six or eight shots toward Copp's Hill that hit ineffectually in Boston. Then, said Brown, Capt. Gridley had "swung his hat three times round to the enemy and ceased to fire." Gridley was joined by Capt. Callender and his two fieldpieces. But all four of their cannon afforded but a puny response to the intense bombardment now being aimed at the redoubt.

The Connecticut forces sent out by Prescott

were led by a man who would be one of the great heroes of the day, Capt. Thomas Knowlton Jr., veteran of the French and Indian War, a gallant, handsome man who would give his life in little more than a year in the battle of Harlem Heights. On the Lexington-Concord Alarm he had been the first to lead his Connecticut company into Massachusetts.

Knowlton now led his 200 men to the end of the breastwork. Beyond it was sloughy land, and a ravine, waterfilled in springtime, fell away toward Morton's Hill. To Knowlton's left, 600 feet to the rear, he saw a rail fence at the foot of Bunker Hill that ran almost to the Mystic River. This particular rail fence was made "half of stone with two rails of wood."

Knowlton's selection would become one of the most celebrated barricades in the centuries-long annals of history. He set his men to doubling this rail fence by placing in front of it rails taken from other nearby fences and then stuffing between them "bushes, hay, and grass, which they found on the spot, ready cut." In Knowlton's vicinity the hayfields and pastureland had been recently mowed. This was in contrast to the fence-crossed, uncut pastures that stretched between them and the British regulars.

In front of Howe, as he landed at Moulton's Point, stood Morton's Hill, a 35-foot hillock. Howe ascended it, had his men form in a parade-like three lines and then took an appraising look at the terrain. There had been a significant change.

There no longer was just the redoubt to be taken. There were now rebels behind a breastwork and, farther back, a rail fence stretching toward the shore of the Mystic River. And rebels were active, too, still farther back, atop Bunker Hill.

Howe, unmindful or indifferent to the extra time he was affording the rebels, decided to wait until his reserves, roughly 700 more soldiers, could be ferried to Charlestown. He sent Lt. Col. George Clark, commander of the corps of light infantry, with four companies as an outpost along the Mystic River beach and ordered two battalions, under his second in command, Gen. Pigot, as an outpost toward Charlestown village.

As Howe awaited his reserves, he gave the

word for his redcoats to eat the lunch carried in their haversacks.

News that the redcoats had landed in Charlestown electrified the camp at Cambridge. A soldier in the regiment of Col. John Nixon of Framingham recalled the clanging bell of Christ Church beside the Cambridge Common.

"The bell was ringing," he said. "Our adjutant, Stephen Jenkens, rode up and hallooed, 'Turn out! Turn out! the enemy's all landed at Charlestown!'"

Capt. John Chester of Connecticut had just eaten his midday meal and was walking out when "all at once the drums beat to arms, and bells rang, and a great noise in Cambridge. Daniel Putnam came by on full gallop."

Chester asked: "What is the matter?"

"Have you not heard?" responded young Putnam.

"No," said Chester.

"Why, the regulars are landing at Charlestown; and father says you must all meet, and march immediately to Bunker Hill to oppose the enemy." Chester added: "I waited not, but ran, and got my arms and ammunition, and hasted to my company (who were in the church for barracks) and found them nearly ready to march."

Gen. Ward promptly ordered so many men from the Cambridge camp to Bunker Hill that the main camp soon seemed, to a medical student of Joseph Warren, "quiet as the Sabbath."

Ward retained in Cambridge just some Massachusetts and Connecticut men to guard the camp in general, Prospect Hill, Willis Creek and the Charles River approach and three companies of Col. Bridge's regiment to guard headquarters. The leader of one of these companies, Capt. John Ford of Chelmsford, who had fought at Meriam's Corner on April 19, asked Ward's permission to join the march to Bunker Hill. Ward gave it.

The force Ward ordered to Bunker Hill comprised nine Massachusetts regiments. Men from five of these — the regiments of Col. Jonathan Brewer of Waltham, Col. Little of Newbury, Col. Nixon of Sudbury, Col. Benjamin Woodbridge of South Hadley and Maj. Willard Moore of Paxton, who led the Ephraim Doolittle regiment, would reach the patriot lines before the battle began.

Cols. Brewer and Nixon would be wounded, and heroic Maj. Moore would die of his wounds.

An express was, at the same time, sent off by Ward to Charlestown Common and Medford to order to Bunker Hill the New Hampshire men under Col. James Reed and Col. John Stark.

Col. Stark got Ward's message at 2 o'clock. A man of magnificent independence in thought and action — "Live free or die!" were his words — he had his men ready to move fast. Earlier in the day, when the request came to him for 200 men, he had set his other men to making cartridges. Gunpowder, as in all the patriot camps, was in short supply. Each man had been distributed only "a gill cup full of powder, 15 balls and one flint."

Two regiments were shying away from crossing Charlestown Neck, its 30-yard width further shrunken by the high tide, when Stark and his New Hampshire men reached the hellfire of that isthmus under the deadly whizz and gouging impact of the 9- and 12-pounders of the scows, armed transport and frigate.

Maj. Andrew McClary, Stark's second in command, an athletic giant with a voice stronger than the roar of the cannon, told the hesitant commanders, as Capt. Henry Dearborn recalled, that "if they did not intend to move on he wished them to open and let our regiment pass." This was done immediately, and McClary, who would be killed this day, marched forward.

In front was Col. Stark and beside him, for his company was first, walked Capt. Dearborn.

"I suggested," recalled Dearborn, "the propriety of quickening the march of the regiment that it might sooner be relieved of the galling crossfire of the enemy.

"With a look, peculiar to himself, he fixed his eyes on me and observed, with great composure, 'Dearborn, one fresh man in action is worth ten fatigued ones' and continued to advance in the same cool and collected manner."

Some, as in all battles, were lucky. Still, the peril of instant death was so threatening at the neck that there were some, among them Capt. Dearborn, who thought that floating batteries were firing from both sides of the neck. Cpl. Brown, in the Prescott redoubt, told how the horror at the neck had discouraged some rein-

THE BATTLE OF BUNKER HILL

PATRIOT DEFENDERS
BRITISH SOLDIERS
POSITIONS BEFORE ATTACK
MAJOR THRUSTS
FIRST ATTACK
THIRD ATTACK

CHARLESTOWN NECK

MYSTIC RIVER

BUNKER HILL

LIGHT INFANTRY

MOULTON'S POINT

ARMED SCOWS

rail fence

tongue of land

GRENADIERS

5th

clay pit

brick kiln

outpost

MORTON'S HILL

first landing

CEMETERY HILL

ELM STREET

ravine

BREED'S HILL

breastwork

52nd

38th

SCHOOLHOUSE HILL

HIGH STREET

barn tavern

GREEN'S LA.

redoubt

brow of hill

47th

MARINES

43rd

outpost

flank companies MARINES 63rd

MAIN STREET

SYMMETRY

landing place of reserves

H.M.S. FALCON

CHARLESTOWN VILLAGE

H.M.S. GLASCOW

H.M.S. SPITFIRE

FERRYWAY

H.M.S. LIVELY

COPP'S HILL

Bunker Hill Monument

Maj. Gen. Henry Clinton

Connecticut State Library

Gen. Israel Putnam

Albert Blakeslee Wolfe

Gen. Artemas Ward

National Gallery of Art, Washington, D.C.

"Attack on Bunker Hill with Charlestown Burning" — 18th Century painting

Bennington Museum, Bennington, Vt.

The Catamount Tavern in Bennington

Beverly Historical Society, Beverly, Mass.

Rev. Langdon leads prayer on Cambridge Common with Prescott's detachment

State House, Concord, N.H.

Col. John Stark

U.S. Postal Service

Salem Poor depicted on Bicentennial commemorative stamp

Anne S. K. Brown Military
Collection, Providence, R.I.

Gen. William Howe

State House, Hartford, Conn.

Capt. Thomas Knowlton

Frick Collection, New York

Maj. Gen. John Burgoyne

Beverly Historical Society,
Beverly, Mass.

Facing page: Col. Prescott on parapet of his redoubt on Breed's hill

Fort Ticonderoga, N.Y.

Ethan Allen demands surrender at Ft. Ticonderoga, as shown in diorama

Defenders behind improvised breastwork await second British attack

Spirit of the British launching second attack, by Howard Pyle

Death of Dr. Joseph Warren in John Trumbull's "Battle of Bunker Hill."

forcements and of hearing how "one cannon cut three men in two." Of the reinforcements sent from Cambridge, some did not get past the neck, some got misdirected to other hills, some—after crossing, got no farther than Bunker Hill.

Stark came upon Putnam, who was trying as best one man could to get the fall-back entrenchments dug and urge on reinforcements. Old warrior Stark needed no urging and he was fully able to choose, as most reinforcements did, his spot on the fighting line. Stark saw at once the importance to the redoubt of Knowlton's rail fence and ordered his men to it.

They manned it from Knowlton's position near the gap down to the beach, and then they did something else that would utterly confound Howe's plans for a quick victory over the rebels in the redoubt.

Just where the rail fence ended there was a sharp, almost perpendicular eight- or nine-foot drop to the beach, now narrowed to a small shore by the high tide. An enemy might use this passage to outflank the fence. So Stark ordered his men to take rocks from nearby pasture walls and quickly form a rock extension of the fence across the shore to the water. Like Knowlton, Stark ordered rails and piles of newly cut grass brought to double the rail fence in front of his position. And men on Knowlton's end built some small barriers on his right, in the upper part of the ravine, to strengthen the gap.

Two patriots of the highest military rank now came to the battlefield, but modestly insisted on serving as volunteers.

Maj. Gen. Seth Pomeroy of Northampton, just turned 69, had gone back to his home in Northampton to rest when he learned that the patriots were planning to fortify Bunker Hill. He got on a horse, rode night and day to Cambridge.

At Hastings House he borrowed a fresh horse from Ward and headed for Charlestown. Cannon fire at Charlestown Neck led him to dismount, spare the horse "as too valuable" to risk on the isthmus and stride across and on to the rail fence.

Pomeroy declined proferred command and, amid the cheers of the men, took his post with them — and with the homemade musket (he was

N.H. State House, Concord, N.H.

Capt. Henry Dearborn

a gunsmith) he had carried 30 years earlier in the battle for Louisburg.

There were cheers again as the men at the battle lines recognized the honored countenance of Dr. Joseph Warren. He had been chosen a major general on June 14 during the thwarted drive to complete the regiments, but had not yet received his commission. As patriot governor, his hours had been crammed with duties and anxieties.

Until late Friday night he had worked at Watertown on business of the Provincial Congress, over which he had presided that day. He let some members of the Congress know it was his intention to share the dangers of the battlefield next day. Like Samuel Adams persuading John Hancock not to go to Lexington Green on April 19 because he had greater service to provide his fellowmen, Elbridge Gerry sought to dissuade Warren. Warren's response was to quote the noble Roman maxim:

"Dulce et decorum est pro patria mori — It is sweet and right to die for one's country."

Pressure of his duties had given Warren so intense a headache that after he conferred with the Committee of Safety, on his arrival this morning at Hastings House, he went to an upper room to rest. But when the frantic call came for reinforcements to head for Charlestown, Warren's headache vanished and, dressed in his best clothes, he set out.

Near the rail fence Warren encountered Putnam, who offered, as head of Connecticut's forces, to accept Warren's commands. Warren had come, he told Putnam, just as a volunteer. It was exactly what he had done on April 19 and at Grape Island and at Chelsea Creek. He was not seeking safety. He said to Putnam:

"But tell me where the onset will be the most furious."

Putnam pointed to the redoubt. "That," he said, "is the enemy's object, and if that can be defended the day is ours."

As Warren entered the redoubt there was more cheering. He brought word to these embattled farmers that en route from Cambridge he had passed 2000 reinforcements on their way.

What heartening news for these already wearied and hungry men!

Below them, visible on the slopes, they could see in formation, in uniforms made more showy by the sunshine, regulars of regiments with many inspiring military traditions — the very best troops that King George III could assemble on a battlefield.

Prescott respectfully asked Warren if he had any orders.

Warren, who very shortly would be mortally wounded, replied: "I came as a volunteer, with my musket, to serve under you, and shall be happy to learn from a soldier of your experience."

Defenders turn back redcoats

Howe's request to send over his reserves prompted Adm. Graves to join Howe in Charlestown "for the sake of seeing whether any further aid could be given and of ordering it immediately."

The general had two requests, both of them inspired by changed conditions he had encountered. Rebels had been sniping from abandoned houses in Charlestown Village upon Pigot's advance troops in their outpost, which was beneath the brow of the hill in front of the redoubt, and, being in a depression, was sheltered from any fire from the redoubt.

Graves, whose incendiary instincts had made him suggest unsuccessfully to Gage on April 19 that he set fire to Roxbury and Charlestown, now asked Howe "if he wished to have the place burned" to put an end to any "mischief his left wing sustained." Graves said that Howe answered: "Yes."

This blurted answer doomed all 400 structures, both public and private, in the town, a thriving seaport older than Boston. Graves told how he "immediately sent to the ships to fire red-hot balls (which had been prepared with that in view), and also to Copp's Hill battery to desire they would throw carcasses (fire bombs) into the town; and thereby it was instantly set on fire in many places."

Gen. Burgoyne said that Pigot's force was "exceedingly hurt by musketry from Charlestown." Neither he nor Clinton, who was with him at the Copp's Hill battery, was aware of this until they got instructions to burn the town. "We threw a parcel of shells," said Burgoyne, "and the whole was instantly in flames."

A spectator on Copp's Hill, William Cockran, said that the fire started in "one of the old houses just above the ferry-ways; from that the meetinghouse and several other houses were set on fire by the carcasses." He also saw sailors land from boats and set fires, as did Col. Prescott.

The cannonading from the ships and the 24-pounders on Copp's Hill grew in preparation for the assault and to hold down the rebels until Howe's reserves had been ferried over.

Against this, the return fire of cannon under Capts. Gridley and Callender, in their exposed position in the gap, was dismally inadequate. Capt. Gridley's two 4-pounders were soon disabled, and he started to drag them toward Bunker Hill. Callender, saying he was without ammunition, also drew off his two cannon.

Howe's second request to the admiral sprung from his seeing the rebels forming behind the rail fence. They could be swept in the rear by cannon on the Mystic River, so Howe asked that the scows near the milldam that were firing across Charlestown Neck be moved around the Charlestown peninsula and into the Mystic River. A volunteer artilleryman in command of the scows, Lt. Col. Thomas James, got the order and started them, in the face of contrary tides, on a slow, futile trip around the peninsula.

Now the boats bearing Howe's reserves neared the shore midway between Morton's Hill and Charlestown Village. These carried the men, roughly 700, who had been waiting at the North Battery under orders to "be ready to embark there when ordered" — the men of the 47th Regt. and the 1st Battalion of Marines, about 400 men under Maj. John Pitcairn, the British officer whose troops had fired the first shots of the war two months ago on Lexington Green.

In the boats with them were the light-infantry and grenadier companies of both marine battalions and of the 63rd Regt., which had been left earlier at the North Battery when the boats had made their second trip.

As the British reserves began to land, Prescott, his eyes sharp for any enemy movement, sent his heroic second in command, Lt. Col. John Robinson and Maj. Henry Wood "each with a detachment, to flank the enemy." It was a characteristically brave gesture by Prescott, for with their departure he recalled: "I was now left with perhaps 150 men in the fort."

Prescott could not see where Robinson and Wood went. He was certain, though, that they "behaved with prudence and courage." Their flanking efforts, presumably, were to Prescott's right, in and among the houses nearest the cart-way (now High street) before the conflagration reached these structures. Out of them, still annoying Pigot, the rebels kept up a flanking gun fire.

Ward, when he got word of the landing, immediately ordered forward to Bunker Hill virtually all his remaining troops, including his own regiment under Lt. Col. Jonathan Ward of Southboro. Col. Thomas Gardner of Cambridge, guarding Prospect Hill, headed his men to Bunker Hill on his own. Lt. Col. Ward and three of his companies would fight at the rail fence. Col. Gardner, who had told his friends "I consider the call of my country as the call of God," would be mortally wounded.

It was nearly 3 o'clock.

Howe, his staff of a dozen aides near him to transmit his commands, glanced again along the rebel lines from the village to the Mystic River, the redoubt, the breastwork, the grass-stuffed rail fence, all of such recent and hasty contrivance.

Courage was not wanting on either side as battle approached. But on the rebel side they had the inexhaustible strength of freemen fighting for their rights — for rights guaranteed them by George III's royal ancestors. These were their heritage. None of Gage's spit and polish before their eyes could demoralize them.

Few would fight as units, other than those under Col. Prescott, Capt. Knowlton and Col. Stark. Most of the regiments, after coming through the savagery and torment of enfiladed Charlestown Neck, divided into small groups and chose scattered positions along the lines.

Many Massachusetts men formed at the gap. Capt. John Chester of Connecticut described the situation when his unit reached there:

"Here we lost our regularity as every company had done before us."

There was irrepressible independence and a lot of hit or miss for guides as the patriots got set for the onslaught. They were to have mighty little artillery support. When Capt. Callender with his two cannon withdrew toward Bunker Hill, Gen. Putnam stopped him. Callender said he was out of proper-size ammunition. Putnam opened the side-boxes, saw some there and ordered Callender back to the lines. He went back, but left. Then Capt. John Ford of Chelmsford arrived on the battlefield and, at Putnam's request, had his men drag these fieldpieces back to the gap.

Now the last of Howe's reserves had debarked. Howe was ready. The cannonade ceased and Howe's artillery, the 12-pounders on Morton's Hill and the 6-pounders and howitzers, which had been moved forward with the help of a company of grenadiers, opened fire.

Onlookers in Boston could hear the church bells strike three.

Howe gave the order to attack.

Two lines of men in scarlet, stretching across the peninsula from the village to the river moved forward. Howe personally commanded the right wing, and Pigot the left, both wings of about the same number of troops.

The sight, in the strong sunlight, in the amphitheater setting of surrounding, crowded hills, moved playwright Gen. Burgoyne to eloquence:

"And now ensued one of the greatest scenes of war that can be conceived. If we look to the heights, Howe's corps ascending the hill in the face of entrenchments, and in a very disadvantageous ground, was much engaged; to the left, the enemy pouring in troops by the thousands, over the land; and in the arm of the sea our ships and floating batteries cannonading them; straight before us a large and noble town in one great blaze—the church steeples, being timber, were great pyramids of fire above the rest; behind us, the church steeples and heights of our own camp covered with spectators; the enemy all in anxious suspense; the roar of cannon, mortars and musketry; the crash of churches, ships upon the stocks, and whole streets falling together, to fill the ear; the storm of the redoubts, with the objects described above, to fill the eye; and the reflection that, perhaps, a defeat was a final loss to the British Empire in America, to fill the mind . . . ."

From Copp's Hill the disposition of Howe's troops looked theatrically ideal — "exceeding soldier-like . . . in my opinion, it was perfect," said Burgoyne. But on the Charlestown slopes, things were not so orderly. Burgoyne was to learn that as Howe's troops advanced "they met with a thousand impediments from strong fences, and were much exposed."

In the meadows, pits and pastureland between Morton's Hill and either the redoubt or the rail fence, there were a dozen fences, fences following no formal pattern, fences connecting other fences at right or odd angles. Some were concealed by the high, uncut growth through which the regulars, each carrying pack and equipment Burgoyne estimated at 125 pounds, had to march.

Howe, writing later from camp to another brother, Lord Howe, the admiral, said, "We began the attack by a sharp cannonade ... the lines advancing slowly and frequently halting to give time for the artillery to fire."

Howe did not mention, at this writing, that other hazards on the ground —beyond unexpected holes — interfered with his artillery. Forward of Morton's Hill there were claypits and sloughy land to which springtime runoff flowed down the ravine in the gap. By the claypits stood a brick kiln, and near here Howe's fieldpieces became briefly mired. And there was another problem on the advance:

Suddenly "our artillery stopped firing," wrote a British officer. Howe asked the reason and, when told that a mistake had put 12-pound balls instead of 6-pounders in the side-boxes, ordered them to fire grapeshot, shrapnel-like clusters of small balls. This, nor other mishaps, had the slightest effect on the high-flown spirit of the redcoats. The British officer asserted:

"Our troops advanced with great confidence, expecting an easy victory."

Howe's order to the elite troops in his wing was "Attack with bayonets!" — the sickening lunge of sharpened steel.

The 11 companies of light infantry sent in column along the narrow beach were to try to outflank the rebels at the rail fence and cut off their retreat from the rear as the giant grenadiers were to make a bayonet charge from the front. Howe's 5th and 52nd Regts. were to support these flank troops. Pigot, with his left wing of the 38th and 43rd Regts. and, on his far left,

the 47th Regt. and the marines, were to feint and hold down the rebels at the breastwork and redoubt.

As the redcoats clambered over the last fences the rebels did something, spontaneously, that would forever distinguish this battle for freedom.

They held their fire.

It had the impact of tactical genius.

Almost complete silence from the rebel lines had become eerie, puzzling to the slowly advancing redcoats. Had most of the rebels fled? Were others cowering behind those earthworks? Would they rise suddenly behind those grass-packed rails and lift their arms in surrender?

The patriots, said Joseph Palmer on behalf of the Committee of Safety, on seeing the enemy approach "reserved their fire 'til they came within 10 or 12 rods." The three old French and Indian War warriors, each on his own and in his own way, Prescott, Stark and Putnam, spread this ancient battlefield wisdom. "Don't fire until you see the whites of their eyes" and ordered no firing " 'til the word was given."

Some did fail to obey, or tried impatiently for an early shot, and got an angry response. Col. Prescott's officers kicked up their barrels at the redoubt. Reuben Kemp of Goffstown said, "Gen. Putnam appeared very angry; and passed along the lines quickly, with his sword drawn, and threatened to stab any man that fired without order." Col. Stark took no chances. He strode in front of the rail fence, thrust a stick in the ground and warned that if any fired before the redcoats reached it, "I'll knock him down!"

Presently the redcoats came within effective musket range.

Determined men, many accustomed to drawing a bead on a moving squirrel, pheasant or varmint, had their picked redcoat for a target.

Cries came of "Fire!"

The effect was catastrophic.

The British officer recalled:

"An incessant stream of fire poured from the rebel lines: it seemed a continued sheet of fire ...."

Second redcoat attack fails

"Such a slaughter was, perhaps, never made before upon British troops. . . ."

This was no exaggerated report as made by the Committee of Safety and signed by Joseph Palmer. Most remembered then were the sanguinary struggles that had climaxed the last French and Indian War in the old world at Minden, a few miles from Hanover, and in the new world on the Plains of Abraham outside the walls of Quebec. Many fighting in this battle had fought beside Gen. Wolfe. British losses here today would be far bloodier.

When the signal "Fire!" was shouted, the provincials, said Palmer, "began a furious discharge of small arms. This fire arrested the enemy, which they for some time returned, without advancing a step, and then retreated in disorder. . . ."

The light-infantry companies which advanced, four men abreast, along the beach narrowed by the high tide, save for men of the 35th and 63rd Regts. that had disembarked from Europe earlier this very day, were the same ones that had marched and fought on April 19. The same was true of the grenadier companies which, on the land above the beach, advanced against the rail fence.

In less than two months their leaders had forgotten or, in their overconfidence, had ignored, how effective these Yankees were in Indian-style position behind barriers. Four light-infantry companies had been placed by Howe beyond the claypits as an outpost. One of these, the 23rd, the world-famous Royal Welsh Fusiliers, had been speedier than the others and had taken the lead when the 11 companies formed in column on the beach.

The stone barrier that Col. Stark had improvised on the beach to complete his rail fence was apparently unnoticed or dismissed by Howe.

The British officer who was describing the battle wrote of the fate of both the flank companies — the light infantry and the grenadiers:

"Our light infantry were served up in companies against the grass fence, without being able to penetrate — indeed, how could we penetrate? Most of our grenadiers and light infantry, the moment of presenting themselves lost three-fourths, and many nine-tenths, of their men. Some had only eight or nine men a company left; some only three, four, and five."

The casualty totals, since these companies would be in every action of the battle, do not tell specifically the location or time of each casualty, but they leave no doubt that the heaviest British losses of the day were on Howe's right wing, during the attacks on the rail fence and on the patriot center.

The two flank companies of the Royal Welsh Fusiliers (the remaining eight infantry companies of the regiment were on alert at Fort Hill in Boston) would have roughly nine-tenths of their men killed or wounded. As captains and lieutenants fell, sergeants sought to rally the men. Then against the murderous fire and smoke the next company advanced, the 4th Regt., the King's Own. Its ultimate casualties would be seven in each 10 men.

In the next company, the 10th Regt.'s light infantry — as in its grenadier company — every officer would be wounded and final casualties would be more than eight in 10. Some of the bullet-torn officers of this company had become well known on April 19 — Capt. Lawrence Parsons, who commanded the companies that marched to Col. Barrett's farmhouse in Concord, and Lt. Waldo Kelly, who was wounded at Concord's old North Bridge. Both suffered severe wounds in this battle.

So it was, company after company, until the men recoiled. The just-arrived, light infantry of the 35th Regt., though ninth in the column of companies, would be virtually annihilated. Only three of its men would escape death or wounds by battle's end.

At the redoubt and the breastwork the patriot fire staggered the British front line. "The enemy," recalled Col. Prescott, "advanced and fired very hotly on the fort, and meeting with a warm reception, there was a very smart firing on both sides." Prescott often told his son and namesake:

"There was a simultaneous discharge from the redoubt and the breastwork, and nearly the whole front rank of the enemy fell, and the whole body was brought to a stand for an instant. The fire was continued by the Americans and briskly returned by the British for a few minutes, and then they retreated precipitately to the foot of the hill." Of the British fire on the left wing, Prescott told his son, "they had commenced firing too soon, and generally fired over the heads of his troops."

The patriot fire was "so precise and fatal," said Lt. Thomas Grosvener, one of Capt. Knowlton's officers, that the redcoats in a short time "gave way and retired in disorder out of musket shot, leaving before us many killed and wounded." Lt. James Dana, who was also at the rail fence, told Capt. John Chester: "Many of our men were for pursuing, but by the prudence of the officers they were prevented from leaving so advantageous a post."

Several soldiers, among them Alexander Davidson, of Capt. Ford's company, which had dragged back to the rail fence the cannon abandoned by Capt. Callender, long remembered Gen. Putnam getting these cannon in position and firing them. Davidson could recall "Putnam's expression when the second discharge of one of the guns, loaded with canister, made a lane through the enemy." The canister was bags of musket balls from Putnam's saddlebags.

Col. Stark, too, held back his men from scrambling over the rail fence and chasing the retreating British, but some did get over and replenish their meager powder supply from the military harness of their foe. Stark had magnificent officers to aid him in his second in command, huge Maj. McClary, in Capt. John Moore of Derryfield at the rock barrier on the beach and in Lt. Col. Israel Gilman, who had led Reed's regiment to the rail fence.

In front of the fence, above the beach, the grenadiers suffered casualties of the same appalling severity as the light infantry. Of three officers and 46 rank and file of the grenadiers of the Royal Welsh Fusiliers who went into battle, all but five would be killed or wounded. All grenadiers but eight of the 52nd Regt. would be eventual casualties.

Stark said:

"I never saw sheep laying thicker in a sheep fold than the British regulars in front of my line."

Stark's 16-year-old son Caleb, who fought at the rail fence, said that a man who visited the battlefield late the next day "counted 96 men dead on the beach."

The sight of the redcoats fleeing back toward the shoreline brought exultant cheers all along the patriot lines. In the redoubt young Peter Brown proudly put their mood into words. The redcoats, he said, had advanced to swallow up the provincials "but they found a choky mouthful of us."

Rev. Peter Thatcher, a 24-year-old Malden minister who was among spectators on the north bank of the Mystic River, helped to prepare the account of the Committee of Safety. He watched as Howe rallied his troops for a second assault, saw the British officers run down to the men "using the most passionate gestures, and pushing the men forward with their swords."

Prescott, Putnam, Stark, all praised and encouraged the patriots, urged them again to be sure to hold their fire. The redcoats were not beaten yet, but they were clearly conquerable. And more reinforcements were reaching the patriot lines.

Rough and ready Col. James Frye of North Andover, ardent patriot, a colonel back in the days when he helped to take Louisburg and full of vigor despite his 65 years, galloped from Cambridge when he learned that the battle had begun. His men, the night prior, had been led by his second in command, Lt. Col. James Brickett, and had worked under Prescott digging the redoubt. Brickett, a doctor, had been wounded in the early shooting and had withdrawn to the far side of Bunker Hill to help other doctors there care for the wounded.

Some men, terrified by the cannonading of Charlestown Neck, were still hanging back, and Col. Frye sought to set them an example by dashing across. He told them:

"This day 30 years I was at the taking of Louisburg. This is a fortunate day for America. We shall certainly beat the enemy."

Capt. Samuel Trevett

Crossing the neck was not the only hazard in getting to the battlefield. Cannonballs fell in the valley between the lines and Bunker Hill. Some companies of the regiments of Col. Asa Whitcomb of Lancaster and Col. Samuel Gerrish of Newbury crossed the neck and reached the lines, but Col. Gerrish and some of his men did not get beyond Bunker Hill. Gerrish, a corpulent old warrior of French and Indian War days but a warm patriot who had marched on the Lexington-Concord Alarm, was simply exhausted.

His adjutant, Maj. Christian Febiger of Newbury, a Danish immigrant who would become a brigadier general and be in the struggle all the way to Yorktown, led some of Gerrish's companies to the patriot lines.

Another enthusiastic patriot — with two cannon, both 4-pounders — also came to the lines at the rail fence near the gap. Capt. Samuel Russell Trevett of Marblehead brought his company of matrosses (artillerymen) of Col. Gridley's regiment. Trevett had some weeks ago won a reputation for fearlessness when, right under

the guns of *HMS Lively*, then patrolling Marblehead waters, he had led a group of young men to seize chests of arms from a ship the *HMS Lively* had forced to anchor for inspection.

Near Trevett's cannon were Callender's. Col. Gridley, who had returned to the battlefield before the first attack, would help bring them into action.

Howe had his men back in formation in about 15 minutes. Both wings again would move forward in line formation. Howe's thrust would be all along the lines to try for a breakthrough. However, in this frontal attack, the thinned ranks of the light infantry would move on the land above the beach along with the grenadiers, both against the rail fence.

Howe gave the order to attack.

The scarlet lines, again parade-like, moved forward. Fences still had to be surmounted and the pastureland, now trampled, was bloody. A British observer was surprised how the redcoats stepped over dead bodies "as though they had been logs of wood." Leading the grenadiers was Gage's adjutant and old friend, Lt. Col. James Abercromby, former aide to Lord Jeffery Amherst.

A British officer, advancing, recalled the taunts he heard coming from the rebels:

"Col. Abercromby, are the Yankees cowards?"

Flames and billowing smoke from the conflagration now raging in the town drove back patriot fighters to the stone walls and buildings along steep Green's Lane (now Green street).

The fire could be seen for many miles. From Beacon Hill it looked to a young American Tory "a most awful, grand and melancholy sight." Adj. John Trumbull, the painter, watched from an upstairs window in Gen. Thomas's headquarters in Roxbury and said the fire "extended rapidly, and enveloped the whole (town) in flames," Abigail Adams, holding 7-year-old John Quincy Adams by the hand, watched the flames from a hill back of the Adams homestead in Braintree.

Again the patriots held their musket fire — even longer this time. Prescott halved the distance to five or six rods before he shouted, "Fire!" His son said, "Nearly the whole front rank was swept away by the first fire of the Americans." Stark's men at the rail fence maintained their firing so fast, a New Hampshire officer recalled, that "we did not take the trouble to return ramrods but dropped them by our sides as we reloaded."

In front of the rail fence was a level stretch of pasture called "the tongue of the land." This area was now brought under fire from both the rail fence and the ravine in the gap, ripping the ranks of the grenadiers and the 5th Regt. with fierce impact. Losses in Percy's 5th Regt. would exceed seven out of every 10 men killed or wounded, the highest of any of the regiments engaged. This was one of the deadliest spots on the battlefield.

Of the 5th Regt., Burgoyne would say:

"The 5th has behaved the best and suffered the most."

The gorgets, chest ornaments worn by the officers, made perfect targets. Lt. Col. Abercromby fell, mortally wounded. On the patriot side brave Maj. Willard Moore of Paxton was hit in the thigh, and hit again through the body as he was carried back. He asked for water. There was none, with Charlestown wells enveloped in flame. He told the men to return to the lines, and died.

Howe, with two of his aides killed, was seen standing alone beyond the rail fence. The other 10 of Howe's aides would all be among the wounded. Even Howe's servant Mr. Evans, who persisted in being near the general to serve him, had a bottle of wine in his hand "dashed to bits" and was grazed on his arm by a Yankee musket ball.

The incredibly isolated, intrepid British general watched as the second line of his grenadiers mixed with the first and "by crowding fell into disorder." Then Howe added the desperate reflection: "The light infantry at the same time being repulsed, there was a moment that I never felt before."

Dearborn said the pasture was covered with "dead and wounded."

Rev. Peter Thatcher watched the redcoats take flight again and run "in great confusion towards their boats."

Prescott orders retreat

Col. Prescott, his eyes on the pastureland bloodied with carnage and with the luckier wounded being carried to their boats, assured his men in the redoubt that their enemies "could never be rallied again if they were once more driven back."

Howe's officers took longer this time in their effort to regroup their men. Some officers even protested to Howe against the butchery of again ordering the redcoats to assault the rebel lines.

But Howe was not to be dissuaded. He sent a message to Clinton, still on Copp's Hill, to send across some reinforcements, a task that Gage had assigned earlier in the day to the major general. The remaining foot companies of the 63rd Regt. and the 2nd Battalion of Marines, about 500 men in all, were presently embarked at the Boston wharves. Once again the assault would be all along the line, but Howe's main thrust would be against the gap and the breastwork with Pigot leading a bayonet charge on the rebels in the redoubt. Howe's battered flank companies would feint and hold on the right.

By now Howe had given up his plan of crushing the rebels in a sweep through Cambridge, Brookline and Roxbury. The task before him was prodigious enough for a day, and in deference to the day's warmth, he now ordered his remaining warriors to cast off their ponderous knapsacks. Some even stripped to their shirts.

Putnam, who was mounted and could move fast between the hills, urged reinforcements forward to the lines. Stark and Prescott again urged their men to be prepared to hold their fire. In the redoubt, where powder, unreplenished, was running alarmingly low, Prescott opened a few discarded artillery cartridges and distributed their scanty charge with the caution "not to waste a kernel of it, but to make certain that every shot should tell."

Col. Thomas Gardner, who would be called "heroic" by the Provincial Congress, having left Prospect Hill on his own, now arrived at Bunker Hill where Putnam had some of the men of the Gardner regiment work on shoveling a breastwork. Soon, though, Gardner could hear the British artillery open up. It had been moved forward, in preparation for Howe's assault.

Gardner, a vigorous patriot, could wait no longer on Bunker Hill. When the Tory colonel of his regiment, old William Brattle, had to flee to Boston from patriot wrath, Gardner had been elected colonel. He served on his town's first Committee of Correspondence and in the first Provincial Congress and led his regiment to Battle Road on April 19. Now he headed his men for the patriot lines and sent Capt. Josiah Harris, with his company of Charlestown men, to the rail fence.

Howe had just given the command, and the redcoats had moved forward as the British artillery raked the breastwork.

As Gardner was moving toward the gap he sustained a wound that was plainly mortal. Some of his men fetched rails to carry him to the rear. His 19-year-old son Richard, a lieutenant in Capt. Trevett's artillery company, ran to his father's side. Col. Gardner ordered Richard to go back to his duty and Richard did. The dying colonel was borne to the far side of Bunker Hill.

The raking fire of the British cannon served Howe well and drove patriots from behind the breastwork toward the rail fence and behind obstructions in the gap or into the redoubt. The first fire from the defenders in the redoubt staggered Pigot's division and inflicted heavy losses. At this moment Howe's reinforcements, just landed on the strand where Howe's reserve had earlier come ashore, seemed in such disorder that Clinton, on his own, threw himself into a boat to bring them leadership.

Some of the redcoats of Percy's regiment and the 52nd, Howe's division, sought to mount the breastwork and the redoubt. The 5th's senior captain, George Harris, was trying to ascend the fortifications for a third time when, he recalled:

"A ball grazed the top of my head, and I fell, deprived of sense and motion. My lieutenant, Lord Rawdon, caught me in his arms, and, believing me dead, endeavored to remove me from the spot, to save my body from being trampled on. The motion, while it hurt me, restored my senses, and I articulated, 'For God's sake, let me die in peace.'" Describing the battle scene, Harris continued:

"The hope of preserving my life induced Lord Rawdon to order four soldiers to take me up, and carry me to a place of safety. Three of them were wounded while performing this office (one afterward died of his wounds), but they succeeded in placing me under some trees out of reach of the balls. A retreat having been sounded, poor Holmes (the captain's servant) was running about like a madman in search of me, and luckily came to the place where I lay, just in time to prevent my being left behind, for when they brought me to the water's edge, the last boat was put off, the men calling out they could take no more! On Holmes's hallooing out, 'It is Captain Harris,' they put back and took me in."

Part of the fusillade that hit Harris mortally wounded Maj. Arthur Williams of the 52nd Regt. Lord Rawdon, who, under the heavy patriot fire, got a musket ball through his catskin cap, tried to get young Ens. Martin Hunter of the 52nd to fetch a surgeon for Williams. But Williams was no favorite with Hunter, and Hunter had seen what happened to the grenadiers helping Lord Harris. Also, recounted Hunter, who was temporarily sheltered from the patriot fire above, "I had sense enough to know that I was much safer under the works than I could be a few yards from it."

On the other side of the redoubt Pigot, despite flames fast consuming the Charlestown buildings, was encountering trouble from stiff resistance, and from fences, too.

The men of the 47th Regt. and the 1st Marines suffered many casualties in fighting to clear a barn and tavern behind stone walls on the sharp, short incline of Green's Lane. One of the patriot companies in this area likewise suffered severely. Capt. Nathaniel Warner of Col. Little's regiment went on the hill with 23 men and had all but six of them killed or wounded.

Nearer the redoubt the marines, intending to push a bayonet charge over the entrenchment, were stopped by the first patriot fusillade. Lt. John Waller, adjutant of the 1st Marines, told of the marines and the 47th's men climbing over "rails and hedges." He then went on to describe the fatal wounding of the commander of the 1st Marines, Maj. Pitcairn:

"When we came immediately under the work (the redoubt), we were checked by the severe fire of the enemy, but did not retreat an inch. We were now in confusion, after being broke several times in getting over the rails, & etc. I did all I could to form the two companies on our right, which at last I affected, losing many of them while it was performing.

"Major Pitcairn was killed close by me, with a captain and a subaltern, also a sergeant, and many of the privates; and had we stopped there much longer, the enemy would have picked us all off." Pitcairn's son Thomas, said Burgoyne, carried the dying major "upon his back from the entrenchment . . . to the nearest boat about half a mile" and returned "instantly to his duty."

It was only two months ago that Maj. Pitcairn, on detached duty, rode into history when light infantrymen under him fired at Capt. Parker's minutemen on Lexington Green. Pitcairn had this time been leading his own marines when he was struck in the head by a musket ball fired from the redoubt by Peter Salem, a private from Framingham, who had marched with the Framingham minutemen and fought at Battle Road on April 19.

Peter Salem, a black man, was a member of Capt. Thomas Drury's company of Col. Nixon's regiment. Salem had been given his freedom by Maj. Lawson Buckminster, for only freemen could be enlisted. There were a number of blacks embattled here on the patriot lines just as Prince Estabrook, a black member of Capt. Parker's company, had faced the attack of Pitcairn's force at Lexington Green and had been wounded.

Among them, fighting at the rail fence, was Barzillai Lew, veteran of the French and Indian Wars, who came to the lines with Capt. John Ford's company from Chelmsford. Salem Poor, a black man from Andover, serving in the company of Capt. Benjamin Ames, Col. Frye's regiment, was praised as a "brave and gallant soldier" by several officers, including Col. Prescott, who said Poor "behaved like an experienced officer." There is a legend that Poor's musket brought down Lt. Col. Abercromby.

Poor would serve at Valley Forge and White Plains.

Prince Hall, who would re-enlist later from Medford, was a free black man from the Barbados. A soldier at Bunker Hill, Hall became the Grand Master of the Negro Masons in Boston and was a leader in petitioning for the freedom of slaves, a dedication that helped to make Massachusetts a free state by 1783.

The terror and chaos of battle, while most intense at the lines, stretched all the way back to Charlestown Neck. At the neck, still under punishing cannon fire, there were men yet headed for the lines. Ahead of them the town was in flames, the battlefield erupting smoke and the fury of gunfire; beside them the wounded were being led or carried back in makeshift litters or stretched blankets.

In vivid words, the scene at this moment was pictured by two Connecticut men, relatives, Capt. John Chester and Lt. Samuel B. Webb. Capt. Chester's company of Wethersfield was about the only one in the patriot camp with uniforms, blue trimmed with red, a conspicuousness they covered with their frocks and trousers on going into battle.

"Before we reached the summit of Bunker Hill and while we were going over the neck," said Chester, "we were in imminent danger from the cannon shot which buzzed around us like hail." There, on the neck, said Webb, they passed "through the cannonading of the ships — bombs, chain shot, ring shot, and double headed shot flew as thick as hailstones."

Once atop Bunker Hill, Webb went on:

"For my part I confess, when I was descending into the valley from off Bunker Hill side by side of Capt. Chester at the head of our company, I had no more thought of ever rising the hill again than I had of ascending to heaven as Elijah did, soul and body together. But when we got engaged, to see the dead and wounded around me, I had no other feelings but that of revenge; four men were shot dead within five feet of me." Of the engagement, Webb added:

"Good God, how the balls flew — I freely acknowledge I never had such a tremor come over me before."

Now the battle reached its peak. Col. Prescott recalled:

"Our ammunition being nearly exhausted, could keep up only a scattering fire. The enemy being numerous, surrounded our little fort, began to mount our lines and enter the fort with their bayonets."

Prescott, always indomitable, ordered his men with bayonets to hold the ramparts; others without bayonets were to go to the back of the fort and fire as the redcoats appeared. "The discovery of another cannon cartridge," Prescott told his son, "furnished powder for the last muskets that were fired." Men without powder clubbed their gun barrels, prepared to use their gun butts — brass or wood. Some even picked up rocks, which were plentiful from the digging.

Lt. Waller described the marines and the 47th mounting the ramparts:

"We rushed on, leaped the ditch, and climbed the parapet. One captain and one subaltern fell in getting up, and one captain and one subaltern were wounded of our corps; three captains of the 52nd were killed on the parapet, and others that I know nothing of.

"Nothing could be more shocking than the carnage that followed the storming of this work. We tumbled over the dead to get at the living, who were crowding out of the gorge of the redoubt, in order to form under the defenses which they had prepared to cover their retreat." Within the redoubt there was horror: "'Twas streaming with blood, strewed with dead and dying men, the soldiers stabbing some and dashing out the brains of others."

Friend and foe mingled in the dust-covered melee. As the British poured over the ramparts, others forced their way through the narrow sally port. This gateway, recalled Ebenezer Bancroft of old Dunstable, of Bridge's regiment, "was completely filled with British soldiers.

"I held my gun broadside before my face and rushed upon them, and at first bore some of them down, but I soon lost my gun, a remarkably long item which I had taken from the French at Chamblee, in the old French war." As

Bancroft fled, musket balls struck off his hat, tore his clothes, ripped away his left forefinger.

Cpl. Peter Brown left differently. He wrote his mother:

"I was in the fort when the enemy came in, (I) jumped over the wall and ran half a mile, where balls flew like hail stones and cannon roared like thunder."

A soldier in Col. Prescott's regiment, Amos Farnsworth of Groton, recalled the final moments:

"I did not leave the intrenchment until the enemy got in. I then retreated 10 or 15 rods, then I received a wound in my right arm, the ball going through a little below my elbow, the little shellbone. Another ball struck my back, taking a piece of skin about as big as a penny."

Few words were used by Thomas Boynton of Andover, Col. Frye's regiment, to relate the end:

"We began a hot fire for a short time. The enemy scaling our walls and the number of our men being few, we was ordered to retreat, at which time the enemy were almost round us, and a continual firing at our heels."

Col. Prescott, after giving the order to retreat, was among the last to leave the redoubt. He coolly parried with his sword the bayonet passes made at him by the entering British. He came unharmed through this savage encounter with his clothing, banyan and waistcoat pierced crazily by bayonet thrusts.

The triumphant huzzas of the British within the redoubt could be heard plainly on Beacon Hill in Boston.

The patriots, still to face about the heaviest losses of the day, tried to take their wounded with them. Some seriously wounded, though, had to be left behind. Within the redoubt was Lt. Col. Moses Parker of Chelmsford, Col. Bridge's second in command.

Col. Bridge, slashed on the head and neck, was able to get away. Parker, his knee fractured by a musket ball, would die miserably in the Boston jail after amputation. He had been a hero at the siege of Fort Frontenac in the old wars, a fervent patriot and had fought on the Lexington-Concord Alarm, at Meriam's Corner and along Battle Road.

The regiments that fought mainly in the gap sustained grievous casualties as the withdrawal got under way. Col. Jonathan Brewer was painfully wounded in the arm and his next in command, Lt. Col. William Buckminster of Barre, was crippled for life when a musket ball struck his shoulder and came out in the middle of his back.

Col. Nixon, who had fought at Louisburg and Lake George and had led Sudbury minutemen to Concord on April 19, fought near Col. Brewer and was borne, badly wounded, from the battlefield just moments earlier. Col. Little was luckier. Two men were killed either side of him, and he withdrew unharmed but went back to camp "all bespattered with blood."

Almost unnoticed in the pell-mell rush away from the redoubt, Joseph Warren was struck on the right side of his head by a musket ball and died instantly. His was the loss that would bring most anguish to the patriots. He would be widely mourned and tragically missed.

Howe conceded that the redoubt "was most obstinately defended to the last."

The old warrior, Col. Richard Gridley, was hit by a musket ball just about the time that the redcoats overran the redoubt that he had planned. Gridley managed to get from the field. So did Capt. Trevett, always enterprising, rescuing for another day one of the 4-pounders he had brought to the battle line.

Col. Stark and the men at the rail fence, with their powder almost gone, held their position as the patriots retreated from the center and from the redoubt, thus preventing the patriots from being enveloped and cut off. Capt. Chester helped, too, his men firing for the last few minutes from "a poor stone fence, two or three feet high, and very thin, so that the bullets came through," presumably a pasture wall on Elm street near the Bunker Hill road.

Gallant Col. Stark said, "The regulars almost surrounded me before I retreated." One of the last companies to leave the rail fence comprised the men under Capt. Josiah Harris, all of them enlisted from Charlestown and fighting literally for their own soil.

Burgoyne, in a letter to British authorities, allowed:

"The retreat was no rout; it was even covered with bravery and military skill."

The line of withdrawal, with Main street into Charlestown Village under control of British naval cannon, was along the road over Bunker Hill.

On top of the hill, Gen. Putnam tried in vain to get the patriots to make another stand. But the battle was over. Even Howe, declining Clinton's offer, would not pursue the rebels. Soon Clinton, at the head of Howe's last reinforcements, which had arrived too late for the climax of the battle, had them resume entrenching on Bunker Hill.

There was yet one more tragic loss.

Hearty, fearless Maj. McClary, Stark's ablest lieutenant — "a man full of vigor and blood," as McClary described men he considered the bravest — had recrossed Charlestown Neck to the mainland with all the other patriots and was refreshing himself in the company of Capt. Dearborn when he noticed Clinton's activity on Bunker Hill.

McClary went to reconnoiter, satisfied himself that Clinton was going to attempt no pursuit, and started back across the neck when a random shot from *HMS Glasgow,* said Dearborn, who was only a few yards away, "passed directly through his body, and put to flight one of the most heroic souls that ever animated man. He leaped two or three feet from the ground, pitched forward, and fell dead upon his face."

Losses shock British

After the dangers and exertions Col. Prescott had endured, most men might welcome a respite. But not Prescott.

True to his dauntless spirit, the colonel went straight from the battlefield to Hastings House, headquarters of Gen. Ward, with a proposal. Ward, as Prescott told his son, was worried that the British would now strike at the patriot center "where there was neither artillery, ammunition, nor disciplined troops to oppose them."

What had happened to the redcoats on Bunker Hill, Prescott assured Ward, would not likely encourage them to try any immediate assault on Cambridge, and Prescott made an offer to Ward:

"To retake (Bunker) hill that night, or perish in the attempt, if he would give him 1500 men ... well equipped with ammunition and bayonets."

Bayonets, ammunition, effective cannon, all these were lacking in Cambridge. Even critical James Warren of Plymouth, shortly to succeed Joseph Warren as head of the Provincial Congress, granted that munitions could not get past Charlestown Neck during the battle because "the enemies' constant fire from their ships and floating batteries had prevented any supplies from our main army." Within hours the Provincial Congress would be appealing to Philadelphia for gunpowder because stocks of it in all Massachusetts, public or private, were "very small."

Prescott, of course, was under the stinging impression that the patriots had sustained a defeat. The British were holding the battlefield and this meant, under the 18th Century code of warfare, that they had scored a victory.

How different this was from what the patriots had accomplished on April 19, at Ticonderoga and Chelsea Creek! Many others had Prescott's impression. As a result there would be some harsh courts-martial at Cambridge, as though two months of revolution could make old hands out of beginners in the art of conducting warfare.

Some did sense at once what time would one day clarify. The massive percentage of British casualties, far exceeding those at Blenheim or Minden, suggested the true tale. Of 2200 British soldiers engaged, Gage informed Lord Dartmouth at Whitehall, there had been 1054 officers and men either killed or wounded.

This represented roughly 50 percent casualties, a Pyrrhic victory at best.

The 50 percent was an average. In the flank companies casualties ran into the high 80 percents. For complete regiments the casualties ranged from 35 percent in some to 50 percent in the 5th Regt. Losses among officers overall ran almost 40 percent, high enough to daze Great Britain.

In his general orders of congratulations, Gage duly thanked the officers and men for gaining "a complete victory." Gage knew this was strictly a formality. Gage wrote secretly to his old friend Lord Barrington, secretary of war:

"The loss we have sustained is greater than we can bear. Small armies can't afford such losses, especially when the advantage gained tends to little more than the gaining of a post."

Howe recognized the facts and called Gage's "complete victory" "this unhappy day.

"I freely confess to you," he wrote to England, "when I look to the consequences of it, in the loss of so many brave officers, I do it with horror. The success is too dearly bought."

Clinton knew. "A dear bought victory," he observed, "another such would have ruined us."

From his own losses, Gage told Dartmouth he was sure that the rebels' losses were "considerable." Gage told of finding 100 dead rebels on the battlefield and of 30 wounded prisoners. (Twenty of these would perish in the Boston jail.)

But Gage was mistaken. Lack of records prevent definite knowledge on how many patriots were present. Estimates range from 1500 to 3500, the latter probably a nearer overall figure. But patriot casualties are known and total 441, much less than half the British losses.

Of these, 45 were from Connecticut, 86 from New Hampshire, 310 from Massachusetts. Prescott's regiment sustained the highest losses, 42 killed, 28 wounded. Among them in the redoubt were some of his neighbors from Hollis, N.H., whose captain, Reuben Dow, was wounded and crippled. Eight men from Hollis and eight from Pepperell were killed, a community loss exceeded only by Groton, Prescott's birthplace.

Col. Stark's regiment had losses next to Prescott's, 15 dead, 45 wounded. Next highest were regiments of Cols. Bridge and Frye, both with 15 dead, and Gen. Putnam's with 11 dead, all three with many wounded.

Stark, reporting casualties to New Hampshire, talked of "being well satisfied that where we have lost one the enemy have lost three." Gen. Nathanael Greene, with the Rhode Island soldiers in Jamaica Plain in support of Gen. Thomas holding Roxbury, remarked, "I wish we could sell them another hill at the same price." And Samuel Adams, from Philadelphia, wrote to James Warren, "I dare say you would not grudge them every hill near you upon the same terms."

Burgoyne, like Gage, had noticed how the rebels, on leaving Bunker Hill, "proceeded no farther than the next hill." On the very night of the battle, Gen. Putnam, on reaching nearby Prospect Hill, had set his men to fortifying it while New Hampshire men fortified Winter Hill, both relieved by Massachusetts men.

Gage had more respect now for the Yankees than when he sent his troops into the assault as on a parade. He ruefully informed Dartmouth: "The rebels are not the despicable rabble too many have supposed them to be." An officer of Gage's newly arrived 49th Regt., not in the battle, said he had learned a "melancholy truth" about the rebels. They are, he said, "full as good soldiers as ours." Some regulars who had been in the battle said the rebels "fought more like devils than men."

Indeed, the patriots had won more than they realized at first. They had demonstrated they could confront the regulars. They had won respect for their courage and ability as soldiers.

Their deficiencies as military men, and they had them — in discipline, organization, record keeping, supply and many others — were already on their way to improvement. Unknown to the men who fought at Bunker Hill, John Adams had moved and Samuel Adams had seconded a resolution in the Continental Congress at Philadelphia making George Washington the Commander in Chief of the new Continental Army.

This was two days before the battle of Bunker Hill. Washington soon would be en route to Cambridge.

The fire that consumed Charlestown burned for two days. The ashes of Charlestown, seen or imagined, shocked America. In ashes as well was the great store of goodwill that had so long and happily conjoined England and her colonies, bound so proudly by shared traditions. These feelings were now widely replaced by outrage and deep-seated hostility.

Ahead were eight weary years of warfare.

An olive branch would be proffered — and would be disdained by George III.

Every British general involved in Gage's "complete victory" at Bunker Hill would have his military renown impaired by his activities in the new world.

Gage would be the first to go. George III and Lord North and Lord Dartmouth would not be blind to their true meaning when they eventually weighed all the details of the battle. George III's "mild general" Gage, with his troops still besieged, would be replaced.

The three generals who came on HMS Cerberus so short a while ago would achieve highest commands in America and suffer similar fate. Burgoyne would meet defeat at Saratoga. Who might have imagined this June 17 that the adversaries — Prescott in his cannonless fort and Burgoyne behind his mighty 24-pounders on Copp's Hill — would be present at Saratoga when the British general would turn over his sword at the turning point of the Revolutionary War!

Howe would take Philadelphia, the patriot capital, and be recalled. Clinton, as Cornwallis's chief, would suffer Yorktown. The road to final victory would be long and hard — but Bunker Hill had now placed the patriots on it.

**Washington's
First Victory**

Washington heads north to take over army

George Washington drew quite a throng of admirers as he was about to leave Philadelphia for the camp at Cambridge to take command of the Continental Army.

It was the morning of June 23, 1775 — six days after the battle of Bunker Hill. News of the bloody encounter had yet to reach Congress.

The newly named Commander in Chief was mounted on a horse. A naturally impressive figure, with his unusual height of 6 feet 2 and dignified bearing, Washington was even more admirable on horseback. Thomas Jefferson called him "the best horseman of his age . . . the most graceful figure that could be seen on horseback."

On horseback, too, were two of Washington's top generals, former British officer Maj. Gen. Charles Lee and New York patroon Maj. Gen. Philip Schuyler.

John Adams, the foresighted Yankee principally responsible for picking the Virginian as military leader of the embattled colonies, described the scene in a letter back home to his wife Abigail:

"All the delegates from the Massachusetts, with their servants and carriages attended; many others of the delegates from the Congress; a large troop of light horse in their uniforms; many officers of militia besides, in theirs; music playing, etc. Such is the pride and pomp of war."

The enterprise Washington was commencing would be far more momentous than anyone present imagined. It would be one of the greatest in the annals of mankind — seeing into existence a world power that would eclipse the motherland of Great Britain, then the foremost power in the world.

This lofty assignment had not been sought by Washington. He undertook it strictly as a duty. Months ago, before the outbreak of hostilities, he had informed his brother "Jack" (John Augustine), "It is my full intention to devote my life and fortune in the cause we are engaged in, if need be."

A long, punishing eight years would pass before there would be peace and he would settle back at Mt. Vernon, but at this moment Washington believed firmly that he would be back for good in the fall — and so he had just written to "My dear Patsy," his wife Martha.

Above all, Washington as he set out did not feel that his mission was the independence of the colonies. A declaration of independence was still a year in the future. Most colonists felt certain that the King would rescue them from the dictatorial policies of Lord North's Parliament. Most still drank to the health of the King.

Indeed, this very Continental Congress that had taken over the army and made Washington the Commander in Chief was hopefully at work on another "Olive Branch" petition to King George III, and would dispatch it to London in a few days.

Massachusetts, the current theater of the war, had a decisive role in Washington's selection.

Dr. Joseph Warren, many days before he died heroically at Bunker Hill, had written to Philadelphia in favor of Washington. Elbridge Gerry, disciple of Samuel Adams, favored Washington. John Adams observed to Abigail that Washington was attending sessions of the Continental Congress while attired in his blue and red uniform as colonel of the Virginia Regiment, the uniform he had chosen when his first portrait was painted. This was Washington's way of indicating to all the delegates that Virginia was ready to fight for the common cause.

When Washington learned that he was being proposed as Commander in Chief, he anxiously sought the help of friends to avoid being selected. His modesty persuaded him that he did not have the capabilities that the post would demand.

The leaders of Massachusetts, plunged in battle, had made an attempt back in mid-May to get the Continental Congress to assume control of the makeshift patriot army with which Gen. Artemas Ward was busy besieging Gen. Gage in Boston.

Dr. Joseph Warren, as head of the Massachusetts Provincial Congress, had signed this appeal on May 16 and sent it by the still-undetected

British superspy, Dr. Benjamin Church Jr.

John Adams, discussing this formative period in later years, told how the proposed adoption of the essentially New England Army bestirred various regional fears and jealousies. Some delegates were content merely to await the result of the new "Olive Branch" appeal to the King. Some southern delegates were fearful of being controlled by an army of New Englanders under a New England general. And the many aspirants created division.

When the First Continental Congress had met, Washington had served on no committees. This time he had been serving on several that were concerned with urgent military difficulties — the enormous need for powder and ammunition, the frightening cost of military operations, some organization of the army.

Adams had come to value Washington's military advice and to recognize, as he later wrote to Abigail, that the choice of Washington as Commander in Chief would have "a great effect in cementing and securing the union of these colonies."

Adams's most anxious hours were spent in devising some plan that would push Congress to the verge of action. His anxieties became compounded, as he recalled:

"Apprehending daily that we should hear very distressing news from Boston, I walked with Mr. Samuel Adams in the State House yard, for a little exercise and air, before the hour of Congress, and there represented to him the various dangers that surrounded us. He agreed to them all, but said, 'What shall we do?' "

John Adams conceived an answer. He would prod Congress into action by linking the adoption of the army with the appointment of a Commander in Chief. "I am determined this morning to make a direct motion that Congress should adopt the army before Boston, and appoint Col. Washington commander of it," he told Samuel Adams, and recalled he "seemed to think very seriously of it, but said nothing."

The congressional records do not tell when John Adams made his crucial motion. He did not mention the date when recounting it. It came while Congress was debating the overall total of troops that must be raised, a topic of profound interest to Washington.

"I rose in my place," said John Adams, "and in as short a speech as the subject would admit, represented the state of the colonies, the uncertainty in the minds of the people, their great expectation and anxiety, the distresses of the army, the danger of its dissolution, the difficulty of collecting another, and the probability that the British army would take advantage of our delays, march out of Boston and spread desolation as far as they could go.

"I concluded with a motion, in form, that Congress would adopt the army at Cambridge, and appoint a general; though this was not the proper time to nominate a general, yet, as I had reason to believe this was a point of the greatest difficulty, I had no hesitation to declare that I had but one gentleman in my mind for that important command and that was a gentleman from Virginia whose skill and experience as an officer, whose independent fortune, great talents, and excellent universal character, would command the approbation of all America, and unite the cordial exertions of all the colonies better than any other person in the Union.

"Mr. Washington, who happened to sit near the door, as soon as he heard me allude to him, from his usual modesty, darted into the library room."

John Hancock, presiding, had been one of those hopeful of being named to the post. John Adams vividly recalled the "mortification" that spread on Hancock's face when it became clear that the man about to be mentioned was not himself. John Adams added: "Mr. Samuel Adams seconded the motion, and that did not soften the President's (Hancock's) physiognomy at all."

The formal choice was postponed "to a future day," as Adams recalled, but instantly Adams's shrewd proposal had concentrated debate on the Commander in Chief rather than on the more divisive issue of adopting the army. The ensuing debate and offstage discussions quickly made clear that Washington was the ideal choice. On June 15 the motion was formally presented and Washington, who had absented himself, was unanimously chosen.

Next day Hancock announced the vote from

the chair. Washington rose at his seat, thanked his fellow delegates for this "high honor," pledged himself to "exert every power I possess in . . . support of the glorious cause," disclosed he would serve without accepting the then considerable salary of $500 each month. He spoke as well from a heart reflecting his deep-seated candor:

"I beg it to be remembered by every gentleman in the room that I this day declare with the utmost sincerity, I do not think myself equal to the command I am honored with."

Washington was a man of profound, though invariably well controlled, emotions. When he spoke as he had just done to his fellow delegates he had the anguishing knowledge that he had never commanded any large force of soldiers, was little acquainted with artillery or mounted troops and was totally inexperienced in open-battlefield maneuvers.

Still, to his fellowmen he had the brightest military reputation of any native-born militiaman in America.

Back when Washington was only 21 the governor of Virginia had sent him to the disputed forks of the Ohio River (now Pittsburgh) to warn off the French. Twice he nearly lost his life. His experiences, written in the "Journal of Major George Washington," made him famous when he was only 22. That year, 1754, he was sent again to the Ohio Forks and in a fierce skirmish, a French commander was among those killed. This shooting led directly to renewal of French and English warfare and to the Seven Years War that would see Great Britain conquer Quebec and Canada.

Washington's fame was spread throughout the globe by an eminent British author and Earl, Horace Walpole, who observed:

"The volley fired by a young Virginian in the backwoods of America set the world on fire."

Washington subsequently became a colonel of the Virginia militia and went twice more to the Ohio Forks. Most remembered was his acting as a volunteer aide to the ill-fated Maj. Gen. Braddock and the young Virginian's winning honors by trying to retrieve Braddock's mistakes. As John Adams had noted, no choice for Com-

mander in Chief was more natural or could win wider approval in all the colonies.

The members of Congress pledged "their lives and fortunes" to the cause after naming Washington military chief. There were a few relaxed moments. A patriot leader, Dr. Benjamin Rush, told of a dinner group a few days later at a tavern on the banks of the Schuylkill River with Benjamin Franklin and Thomas Jefferson among those present. Dr. Rush said:

"The first toast that was given after dinner was: 'The Commander in Chief of the American armies.'

"Gen. Washington rose from his seat, and with some confusion thanked the company for the honor they did him. The whole company instantly rose, and drank the toast standing.

"The scene, so unexpected, was a solemn one. A silence followed it, as if every heart was penetrated with the awful, but great events which were to follow the use of the sword of liberty which had just been put into Gen. Washington's hands by the unanimous voice of his country."

The moments of pleasure were not many during the few days Washington remained in Philadelphia. The days were mostly, as John Adams called them, a period of "torment," for several difficult military decisions had to be made by Congress before Washington could depart.

Principal among these was choosing the top command. Four major generals were designated: Maj. Gen. Artemas Ward, now holding the army together around besieged Boston; Maj. Gen. Charles Lee, eccentric, talented, experienced, one of those who had aspired to be Commander in Chief; Maj. Gen. Philip Schuyler and rough-and-ready Maj. Gen. Israel Putnam, just recently distinguished at the battle of Chelsea Creek.

Washington's instructions had to be prepared, finishing touches had to be put on the articles of war and many orders had to be drafted, including those for companies of riflemen to be sent from Maryland, Pennsylvania and Virginia to join the new Continental Army.

Washington, naturally, took a persuasive interest in the selection of his top officers. Two were particularly named because he wanted their experience in his councils of war. These two were former British line officers. In fact, Washington first became acquainted with them when they were serving, as he was, with Gen. Braddock — Charles Lee, then a lieutenant, and Horatio Gates, then a captain. Later they settled in Virginia. Gates was picked as adjutant general.

A curious echo of the Braddock debacle was that another British officer Washington met as an aide to Braddock was then Maj. Thomas Gage — now the British Commander in Chief in Boston, the man Washington would be heading north to defeat.

Only two of all the letters Washington ever wrote to his wife still exist. Both were written during this period of high emotions.

It was not until two days after Washington accepted his new duty that he could bring himself to tell the news to Martha. He felt it would cause her uneasiness and he confided to her his feelings of "inexpressible concern.

"You may believe me, my dear Patsy, when I assure you, in the most solemn manner that, so far from seeking this appointment, I have used every endeavor in my power to avoid it, not only from my unwillingness to part with you and the family, but from a consciousness of its being a trust too great for my capacity. . . .

"It was utterly out of my power to refuse this appointment, without exposing my character to such censures, as would have reflected dishonor upon myself, and have given pain to my friends. This, I am sure, could not, and ought not, to be pleasing to you, and must have lessened me considerably in my own esteem."

He bespoke arrangements for her contentment and tranquility and told her how he had had a will prepared "as life is always uncertain. . . ."

This same day he wrote to his brother Jack:

"I am embarked on a wide ocean, boundless in its prospect, and from whence, perhaps, no safe harbor is to be found."

His other extant letter to Martha was written as he was about to leave Philadelphia on June 23. His thoughts were poignantly of her and Mt. Vernon. He wrote of his trust in Providence, "which has been more bountiful to me than I deserve," and of his trust in seeing her in the fall and of his unalterable affection for her.

Rumors had already been speeding toward Philadelphia that there had been a sanguine clash of arms at Bunker Hill. Washington heard them as he crossed New Jersey in a phaeton drawn by two white horses and as he approached New York City, a community of about 22,000 persons, second only in size to Philadelphia's 34,000.

Schuyler, now near his own colony with its extensive following of loyalists, expressed concern that British war vessels might block Washington's crossing New York harbor. Schuyler soon learned that New York Gov. Tryon, a confirmed loyalist, was scheduled to return from England the very same day.

That Sunday, June 25, Washington crossed the Hudson River just above the city, and came ashore to the cheers of a goodly crowd at the fine mansion of Col. Leonard Lispenard. As happened all along his route, Washington was met by horsemen, a band, volunteers in uniform and a spread of food. Amid the festivities an express bound from the Massachusetts Provincial Congress to Philadelphia arrived at the mansion with a sealed dispatch.

Washington was urged to open it as it might contain accurate information about what had happened at Bunker Hill. He broke the seal and read the contents.

The British troops had made three assaults. British losses had been heavy. Charlestown had gone up in flames.

The peerless patriot Dr. Joseph Warren was among the dead. His successor, James Warren, who signed the message, told of perilous shortages of powder and supplies besetting the army. If Congress had named a Commander in Chief, Warren appealed for his "immediate presence."

Soon came word that Gov. Tryon's barge was coming up New York harbor. It was about 8 p.m. Some welcomers attended both receptions, but numbers and enthusiasm favored Washington's. He, meanwhile, prepared instructions to Schuyler on his taking command in New York and to the north. Washington ordered Schuyler to stop Tryon if he tried anything hostile.

Before leaving for Cambridge on the next day, Washington received an address from the New York Provincial Congress in which the New York body said it was the wish of every American that once accommodation was reached with Great Britain Washington "resume the character of our worthiest citizen."

Washington's reply swelled his popularity:

"When we assumed the soldier, we did not lay aside the citizen."

On entering Massachusetts, Washington was met by a committee at Springfield, and there were welcoming groups and entertainments all the way through Worcester and Marlboro to the meetinghouse of the Provincial Congress in Watertown, where Washington arrived on July 2. He made a cordial response to an address of welcome and pressed on to Cambridge.

It was 2 p.m. when, "with a good deal of fatigue," Washington arrived in the camp at Cambridge Common and went to the quarters prepared for him, Wadsworth House (still standing) in the Harvard University yard. It was the residence of the college president and then had stable and coach house, large gardens and extensive courtyard.

Maj. Gen. Ward gave the new Commander in Chief and his party a dinner at his headquarters, Hastings House, on the opposite side of the college yard.

The British "cannonaded briskly from the lines on Boston Neck" and no relaxation was possible all along the miles of redoubts and entrenchments around Boston. But welcome there was for the new Commander in Chief. Some units had made premature appearances on the parade the past two days and then been dismissed for it had been raining.

July 3 became the day for a camp reception.

Lt. Joseph Hodgkins of Ipswich, a minuteman who answered the Lexington-Concord Alarm and fought at Bunker Hill, wrote home to his wife that Gen. Washington was to "take a view of the army and that will be attended with a great deal of grandeur.

"There is at this time one and 20 drummers and as many fifers beating and playing round the parade."

A joyful moment! But for Washington — as it had been for Artemas Ward — now would begin hours of anxiety, the sleepless passage of nights, the flashing instants of dread that this ill-equipped army of citizen-soldiers might melt away despite its undeniable patriotism and the noble cause that had brought it together.

Howe succeeds Gage in besieged Boston

George III reacted swiftly when he received Gen. Thomas Gage's official June 25 account of the battle of Bunker Hill with its lopsided casualty list that the British leaders, as Lord Dartmouth expressed it, read with "very painful feelings."

At once and, as Dartmouth phrased it, "in the most gracious manner," the King sent His Majesty's thanks to the Boston camp so that Gage could have them read "both to the officers and men for the resolution and gallantry with which they attacked and defeated the rebels." This royal praise, in the 18th Century fashion of communication, took weeks to cross the Atlantic Ocean.

The King held consultations with his Privy Council, and reaffirmed his stern plan to use force against the rebels. "I am certain," he said, "any other conduct but compelling obedience would be ruinous and culpable. . . ."

The King and Privy Council decided a 20,000-man army would be needed to overwhelm the American colonies. This was a prodigious-size army for that age and it would be extra costly and time-consuming to try to raise it in Great Britain. The King turned to Czarina Catherine of Russia with a request for Russian mercenaries.

Gage, along with his official account of the battle, had sent a secret letter to Lord Dartmouth. It proved to be Gage's undoing.

Gage wrote that he thought it his duty to let his lordship "know the true situation of affairs." He emphasized the zeal and enthusiasm of the rebels. He said that they were "not the despicable rabble too many have supposed them to be. . . . They have fortified all the passes and heights round this town from Dorchester to Medford on Mystic, and it's not impossible for them to annoy the town.

"Your lordship will perceive that the conquest of this country is not easy."

Gage, if slow to aggression, had reached a sound conception of the extent of the British military problem in the colonies. His size-up, however, fell on unsympathetic ears in London because Gage, in a moment of euphoria, had long ago misled the King into believing that the troubles in America could be resolved with a handful of troops.

The King concluded that he would recall his "mild general" for consultation. In other words, Gage was to be fired. And steps were taken to issue a royal proclamation from St. James's palace declaring that the deluded subjects in America "have at length proceeded to an open and avowed rebellion." Americans were now rebels all. This proclamation was empire-wide, far beyond Gage's earlier, more limited proclamation of them as rebels.

Prior to the battle of Bunker Hill, Gage's plans had included the seizure of Dorchester Heights to the southeast of Boston. Gage had shifted when the patriots had fortified Bunker Hill. So the taking of Dorchester Heights was still part of Gage's agenda and putting the plan into operation was urged by Gage's subordinate, Maj. Gen. Henry Clinton.

Troops to do this were embarked in boats on June 23. Then, to Clinton's dismay, the operation was canceled. Gage's brother-in-law, Col. Stephen Kemble, Gage's deputy adjutant general, explained:

"The enemy appearing to have taken alarm, and our numbers not very strong, being able to carry only 1200 men into the field and to leave not above 700 in the town of Boston, it was thought proper to lay that project aside, especially as our guns from the blockhouse (on Boston Neck) were thought sufficient to dislodge them should they attempt to annoy us from thence (Dorchester Heights)."

Clinton still felt that seizing Dorchester Heights was more important to the British camp than holding Bunker Hill because Dorchester Heights "lay directly on our water communications and more seriously annoyed the port of Boston." Prophetically, Clinton at that time told Gage:

"If the King's troops should be ever driven from Boston it would be by rebel batteries raised on those heights."

Capt. Charles Stuart, dashing young son of Lord Bute, the former prime minister of George III, and a brother-in-law of Lord Percy, stepped ashore in Boston the day after the battle of Bunker Hill to join his regiment. He wrote home to his father:

"It is impossible to describe the horror that on every side presented itself — wounded and dead officers in every street . . . bells tolling, wounded soldiers lying in tents and crying for assistance to remove some of the men who had just expired. So little precaution did Gen. Gage take to provide for the wounded by making hospitals that they remained in this deplorable situation for three days. . . .

"The hatred the troops have for the rebels lulls the dislike they hold for Gen. Gage, who, by the by, seems the most unhappy man existing. On my first seeing him he asked me if I ever expected to find this continent in such a condition, and upon my replying in the negative he said he feared nor no one at home either could have expected it."

Many others described the Boston scenes produced by the heavy casualties the British took at Bunker Hill.

One of the few clergymen who stayed in Boston, Rev. Andrew Eliot of the New North Church (North End), said:

"It was a new and awful spectacle to us to have men carried through the streets, groaning, bleeding and dying."

Boston merchant Isaac Smith wrote:

"I have seen many from Boston who were eyewitnesses to the most melancholy scene ever beheld in this part of the world. The Saturday night and Sabbath were taken up in carrying over the dead and wounded. All the wood carts in town, it is said, were employed. Chaises and coaches for officers. They have taken the workhouse, almshouse and manufactory house (all in or near present Park street) for the wounded."

Tory Henry Hulton, a customs commissioner, recalled:

"In the evening the streets were filled with the wounded and the dying; the sight of which, with the lamentations of the women and children over their husbands and fathers, pierced one to the soul. We were now every moment hearing of some officer, or other of our friends and acquaintance, who had fallen in our defense, and in supporting the honor of our country."

A British military surgeon, Dr. Mallet, appealed two days after Bunker Hill to Dr. James Lloyd, who wished to remain neutral:

"The general desires me to tell you 'twould be the utmost charity to dress the wounded prisoners in the jail. Our people are fairly worn out and cannot possibly attend this duty. If you can get any of your townsmen to assist in this good office 'twould be an act of the utmost humanity."

Funerals were so frequent that Gage ordered no more tolling of bells. Equally depressing were the encampment auctions of the effects of officers and men who had died. Facilities and doctors were simply inadequate to the catastrophic casualties sustained. Doleful indeed was the departure of vessels bearing widows, their children and amputees.

On one of these vessels, *Charming Nancy*, Gage sent his American-born wife to England to have her out of the area of conflict.

Gage, of course, was blamed for everything. Mistreatment of American prisoners in the jail near the old State House was actually the work of two evil men — both civilians — the odious sheriff Joshua Loring Jr. and the despicable prison provost William Cunningham, a profiteer and bully. Twenty of the 30 American prisoners captured at Bunker Hill, chiefly in and around Prescott's redoubt, perished in this jail in a few weeks.

The shaky, dying signatures of two of the most heroic, Lt. Col. Moses Parker and Capt. Benjamin Walker, are extant on an artfully soothing note claiming they were well and had all they needed except fresh provisions, which, of course, the American siege had about cut off from everybody in Boston.

Spy charges were lodged against the patriot printer John Gill, the Whig teachers John Leach and James Lovell — who had delivered the first anniversary Boston Massacre address in the Old South Meetinghouse — and against the 19-year-old son of another patriot printer, Peter Edes. These four were jammed into the same cell.

Young Peter called the prison "an emblem of hell ... the worst man-of-war is nothing compared with this diabolical place." It took a month for them even to learn the charges against them. They were kept on bread and water, often without light or ventilation despite the stifling summer heat. When a doctor complained to the provost about the prisoners' lack of food, this foul-mouthed monster shouted:

"Let them eat the heads of nails, and gnaw the planks, and be damned."

Washington, on hearing of the abuses in the prison, wrote to Gage, his former comrade in arms. Gage sent back a letter in the pretentious phrasing of his subordinate, Maj. Gen. John Burgoyne, the playwright and member of Parliament, in which he said that he treated the imprisoned soldiers — "destined to the cord" (hanging) — indiscriminately "for I acknowledge no rank that is not derived from the King."

Washington replied that he could not conceive of a more honorable source of rank "than that which flows from the uncorrupted choice of a brave and free people." He warned Gage to remember the occasion if British prisoners "receive a treatment from me different from that I wished to show them." As for further corresponding, Washington said he was closing any "perhaps forever."

Gage's force lacked a multitude of things that make life comfortable.

Food, especially fresh food, practically disappeared in Boston. "Fresh provisions are scarce, and what we have, not of the best quality," said Lt. William Carter. Ens. Jeremy Lister, who fought at Lexington-Concord and Bunker Hill, wrote, "We are now reduced to live upon salt pork and peas as fresh provisions are not to be got for money." In mid-August the "mutton fleet" brought brief respite with some sheep and cattle obtained by ruse from New York loyalists.

The scarcity of food was succinctly put by Henry Pelham, engraver-mapmaker and half-brother of painter John Singleton Copley. He wrote:

"You will form some idea of our present disagreeable situation when I tell you that last Monday I ate at Gen. Howe's table at Charles-town camp the only bit of fresh meat I have tasted for over near four months past."

To relieve his food shortage, Gage in August allowed some Bostonians to depart from Boston by way of the Chelsea ferry route. Their lot, of course, had been worse than that of the troops. Merchant John Andrews observed, "Was it not for a trifle of salt provisions that we have, 'twould be impossible for us to live. Pork and beans one day, and beans and pork another, fish when we can catch it." And Andrews was wealthy.

Wood for cooking was so scarce that houses and wharves were pulled down. Gov. John Winthrop's venerable house at the foot of School street went this way. So did the Liberty Tree. Cut down in bitterness, it provided 14 cords of wood at the cost of the life of one British soldier who tumbled from a top limb.

Hay was short and led to an amazing encounter between two disliked public figures, Adm. Samuel Graves and Commissioner of Customs Benjamin Hallowell. Hallowell owned the hay on Gallup's Island in Boston harbor. The admiral, who wanted the hay for himself, had forbidden Hallowell from doing any haying on the island.

Hot-headed Hallowell encountered the blustering admiral on a waterfront street. In answer to Hallowell's demands, the admiral drew his sword. A struggle followed in which Hallowell broke the admiral's sword and may have given him a black eye. "From what I can gather," remarked Lord Percy, "I believe the admiral has had the worst of it in every respect."

Whichever way Gage glanced landward he could see hills with rebel entrenchments and growing redoubts that would be as costly in casualties to take as was Bunker Hill. He decided that his troops, despite some reinforcements that had arrived, were too few for anything other than defensive action. He set them to strengthening his defensive works, especially on Boston Neck.

There were occasional military actions.

Adm. Graves brought down from Portsmouth harbor a lot of large-size cannon that the Americans had left or overlooked when they raided Fort William and Mary. This would keep these cannon from helping to meet Washington's desperate need for artillery. Early in July, Lord Percy had orders to burn Roxbury but the cannonade, said Col. Kemble, "had not the desired effect."

Clinton, at the end of July, led an advance party into Roxbury but the foray, after setting popular George Tavern in flames, was called off by Gage.

The reasons for what Clinton described as Gage's "strict defensive" were set forth in a letter Gage wrote to Lord Dartmouth. His force, Gage said, was "too small to divide" or try to open up the country for supplies. "Success," he said, "would answer no end by forcing the rebels out of one stronghold into another."

A British officer suggested the British should indeed find some better way than "gaining every little hill at the expense of 1000 Englishmen."

Gage had a proposal. He said that all his generals agreed that New York "appears to be a place preferable to all others" for dealing effectively with the rebellion. He suggested that the campaign for the next year be launched from New York but he would not "presume to put it into execution without first knowing His Majesty's pleasure."

Meantime, so that the rebels could not use Castle William in Boston harbor against him should they seize it, he ordered the sea battery destroyed and the "fort to be mined in order to be blown if the troops should be ordered from Boston.

"No offensive operations," he re-emphasized to Dartmouth, "can be carried on to advantage from Boston."

In this opinion Gage's successor — already chosen in an Aug. 2 dispatch from Dartmouth that was moving slowly across the Atlantic — concurred.

The successor at Boston was to be Maj. Gen. William Howe, the man who had led the British in three charges up Bunker Hill. He was the youngest son of a viscount and his mother had been the natural daughter of King George I. Howe was thus a cousin of George III.

Now 46, three years older than Washington, Howe had been a soldier since he was 18, had led the British up Wolfe's Cove at the taking of Quebec, was brave but noted, too, for his self-indulgence.

Massachusetts colonials intensely admired Howe's oldest brother, the then Lord George Howe, who gave his life in one of the battles at Ticonderoga back in the 1750s. In his honor the Bay colonials had placed a memorial (still to be seen) in Westminster Abbey. John Adams, alluding to this, put in words the general resentment felt against the new British Commander in Chief:

"Such a wretch as Howe, with a statue in honor of his family in Westminster Abbey, erected by the Massachusetts, to come over with a design to cut the throats of the Massachusetts people, is too much.

"I most sincerely and cooly and devoutly wish that a lucky ball or bayonet may make a signal example of him for a warning to such unprincipled, unsentimental miscreants for the future."

In Cambridge camp: 'New lords, new laws'

Roughly three weeks after Washington had taken command of the camp at Cambridge, he wrote to his brother Jack how the army he found on his arrival was "a mixed multitude of people here, under very little discipline, order, or government. . . ."

"Our works, and those of the enemy are so near and the space between is so open, that each sees every thing the other is doing."

Washington thus cited some of the foremost of a multiplicity of problems that, literally under the gunfire of British troops in Boston and Charlestown, would press unremittingly upon him in the ensuing months as he would seek to beset the enemy and simultaneously organize an army.

There would be moments when the soldiers, accustomed to the lax, easygoing practices of the old militia, would crack the composure of the general so that he exploded in writing into bitter feelings about New Englanders. Members of the Provincial Congress, led by their president, James Warren, had sought to warn Washington of the situation in their welcoming address to him at Watertown.

"We wish," they said, "you may have found such regularity and discipline already established in the army, as may be agreeable to your expectations. The hurry with which it was necessarily collected and the many disadvantages . . . have rendered it a work of time; and though, in great measure effected, the completion of so difficult, and at the same time so necessary a task, is reserved to Your Excellency. . . ."

As for individual soldiers:

"The greatest part of them have not before seen service; and although naturally brave, and of good understanding, yet, for want of experience in military life, have but little knowledge of divers things most essential to the preservation of health and even life."

Immediately after arriving at Cambridge, Washington visited and studied the positions of his army, and, when the rains cleared, he employed his spyglass and reconnoitered the lines of the British. He observed that their strongest fortifications were on Bunker Hill, where they had raised a new fort on the very top, and at Boston Neck. In both places, on the two land links to the mainland, he saw Gage had advanced the fortification lines.

Washington had not seen Boston since he visited nearly 20 years earlier when he was a young militia officer. Charlestown, a beautiful companion town to Boston, he now saw in ashes, a forest of blackened chimneys, "a wretched heap of rubbish" that inflamed the indignation of all the colonies.

The British, as Washington perceived, were in the center of a semicircle formed by the American lines, stretching, he figured, eight or nine miles — it was actually more — from Powderhorn Hill in present Chelsea on the north to Savin Hill in Dorchester on the south. The Americans had strongly fortified Winter Hill and Prospect Hill just inland from Bunker Hill. They had done the same on the heights of Roxbury just inland from Boston Neck. There were redoubts and entrenchments scattered along the semicircle inland and at the river approaches in present Somerville, Cambridge, Brookline and Roxbury and at the neck leading to Dorchester Heights.

Washington set his men at "incessant labor, Sundays not excepted" to make fortifications at intermediate points. Even without the aid of his spyglass he could observe that the British had two fundamental advantages that he lacked — a navy and ample artillery. The British completely commanded the water and could make a surprise landing at any place on the American lines that they might select.

The American camp and civilians, as Abigail Adams put it, lived "in continual expectation of alarms." Lt. Samuel Blatchly Webb, Connecticut veteran of the battle of Bunker Hill and a future aide to Washington, said of the British, "We hourly expect them to sally out and attempt to carry our lines. But should they attempt it . . . it will be the most bloody engagement our American world ever knew — our men are resolute and determined."

The day Washington arrived in camp he had handed Maj. Gen. Israel Putnam his new commission in the Continental Army. Washington refrained, though, from handing their new commissions to his eight brigadier generals because he quickly sensed that he had a problem — a problem created unintentionally by the necessity that forced Congress to act fast.

It was a problem Washington could personally appreciate because the trip that he made to Boston nearly two decades back had sprung from his own bitterness at the precedence British army officers claimed over colonial militia officers.

Brig. Gen. Joseph Spencer, who had for some time outranked Putnam in the Connecticut military establishment, was so incensed by Putnam's elevation over him to be major general that he departed the camp without even a courtesy call on Washington. More serious, however, was the disappointment of Brig. Gen. John Thomas of Kingston, Mass., who felt that he could not possibly take orders from men he had just been commanding.

To Washington, Thomas, the skillful commander of the Roxbury fortress that had for nearly three months blocked the British from carrying "fire and sword" out of Boston, "was an able, good officer; and his resignation would be a public loss." Actually, as James Warren observed, there was no likelihood that Thomas would act like Spencer. If Thomas were to leave, said Warren, "he would soon return and serve as a volunteer."

Washington's suggested solution to Congress came as a windfall. An heroic figure at the battle of Bunker Hill, elderly Brig. Gen. Seth Pomeroy, decided not to take up his commission as the first brigadier general. This generalship was accordingly shifted to Thomas, who would become an illustrious figure at the eventual taking of Dorchester Heights. Everything thus came out well, for Spencer finally decided to return and serve in his new rank.

Washington found camp life a catch-as-catch-can affair, as might have been expected in the early stage of a people's revolution.

Rev. William Emerson, who had grabbed his musket and been the first to reach the square in Concord on April 19, had breakfast with Washington and Lee at Wadsworth House and stayed that week in the camp to pray on Cambridge Common with the soldiers "every morning before sunrise and evening at 6 o'clock."

Rev. Emerson wrote his wife: "There is great overturnings in the camp as to order and regularity. New lords, new laws.

"The Generals Washington and Lee are upon

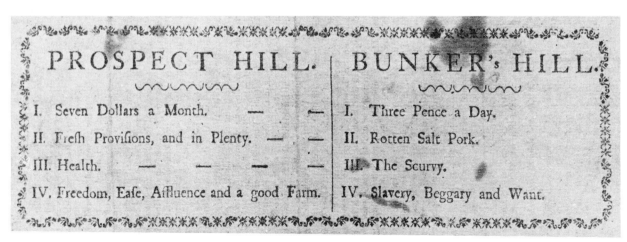

PROSPECT HILL.	BUNKER's HILL.
I. Seven Dollars a Month.	I. Three Pence a Day.
II. Fresh Provisions, and in Plenty.	II. Rotten Salt Pork.
III. Health.	III. The Scurvy.
IV. Freedom, Ease, Affluence and a good Farm.	IV. Slavery, Beggary and Want.

Yankee flier to tempt redcoats

Massachusetts Historical Society

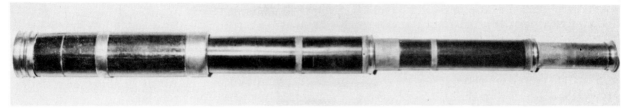

Washington's spyglass

the lines every day, new orders from His Excellency are read to the respective regiments every morning after prayers, the strictest government is taking place: great distinctions made between officers and soldiers, everyone is made to know his place and keep in it, or be immediately triced up and receive (not 1000) but 30 or 40 lashes according to the nature of his crime.

"Who would have thought a 12-month past that all Cambridge and Charlestown (the present Somerville portion) would be covered over with American camps, and cut up into forts and entrenchments, and all their lands, fields and orchards laid common, the horses and other cattle feeding in the choicest mowing land — whole fields of corn eat down to the ground. Large parks of well regulated locusts cut down for firewood and other public uses. This I must say looks a little melancholy."

The same was true along the whole semicircle. In Cambridge itself, abandoned Tory dwellings, from which the loyalist owners had fled to Boston to be behind Gage's guns, Christ Church by the Common, public structures, the Harvard College buildings were all pre-empted for use of the soldiery. Rev. Emerson told his wife it was "diverting to walk among the camps.

"They are as different in their form as the owners are in their dress, and every tent is a portraiture of the temper and taste of the person that encamps in it. Some are made of boards, some of sailcloth, and some partly of one and partly of the other. Others are made of stone and turf, and others again of brick and others brush.

"Some are thrown up in a hurry and look as if they could not help it — mere necessity — others are curiously wrought with doors and windows, done with wreaths and withes in manner of a basket. Some are the proper tents and marquees that look as the regular camp of the enemy."

In one of his first general orders Washington declared:

"It is with inexpressible concern that the general upon his first arrival in the army, should find an officer sentenced by a general court-martial to be cashiered for cowardice — a crime of all others, the most infamous in a soldier, the most injurious to an army, and the last to be forgiven . . . ." Ironically, this cashiered officer, Capt. John Callender, scornfully repudiated the verdict, re-enlisted later as a private and proved so brave in battle that the general cleared his record.

Sensitiveness was rampant in the camp after Bunker Hill in the mistaken belief that the battle had been a complete failure. An intensive hunt got going to ferret out the guilty, and scapegoats, too. Gen. Putnam was so keenly determined that the men responsible for the weak showing of the artillery at Bunker Hill should be punished that a hero of the battle, Capt. Samuel Trevett, was even shoved into the guardhouse "by a mistake."

Rev. Emerson wrote:

"Courts-martial are sitting every day calling colonels, captains, etc., to account for their conduct in the late action. Col. Scammon is to be tried for cowardice this morning and the officers and soldiers are very much divided in their sentiments, some approving and others highly disapproving his conduct; I fear 'tis nothing but envy that has subjected him to trial." Col. James Scammon was found not guilty.

It was this atmosphere that stimulated Washington's anti-New England remarks to his cousin Lund Washington, who was acting as overseer at Mt. Vernon in the general's absence:

"The people of this government have obtained a character which they by no means deserved; their officers generally speaking are the most indifferent kind of people I ever saw. I have already broke one colonel and five captains for cowardice and for drawing more pay and provision than they had men in their command. . . ."

Such reflections expressed more Washington's irritation than his confirmed opinion, for the Virginian, from a region of far less democratic intermingling of officers and men, would come sincerely to admire New Englanders. He would regain his usual self-control and refrain also from anti-New England remarks — as his much-respected secretary Joseph Reed would advise him — because they spread and were damaging to the cause.

Washington had expected to have an army of 18,000 to 20,000. He gave orders on arrival that he be given returns and had expected to send this count off the next day to Congress. He complained of laxity in a letter to his fellow Virginia delegate and friend Richard Henry Lee:

"Could I have conceived that what ought, and in the regular army would, have been done in an hour, would employ eight days!"

The trickling returns showed him he had about 16,000 men with only 14,000 fit for duty. Washington had estimated the British — and his figure was too high — at 11,500, and judged he needed twice as many men as the British in order to defend the infinitely longer American lines. Washington's discovery confronted him, he told Lee, with "an exceedingly dangerous situation."

He **immediately** summoned his first Council of War on July 9. It was an anxious huddle. Washington, Lee and Adj. Horatio Gates were joined by generals longer on the scene, Maj. Gens. Ward and Putnam, and Brig. Gens. John Thomas, William Heath of Roxbury and Nathaniel Greene of Coventry, R.I.

They agreed fully with Washington that the army should have 22,000 men, that officers should be sent from each company to recruit, that the provincial authorities should be asked to furnish temporary reinforcements, militia, who invariably provided a reserve whenever needed.

To spare the communities around Boston from British invasion, the generals agreed on no withdrawal, that "the public service requires the defense of the present posts." But should this prove an impossibility, they agreed to try to make a stand in the rear of the Roxbury lines at Weld's Hill (now in the Arnold Arboretum).

Washington, looking further in the future, had this question for his generals:

"Whether it is expedient to take possession of Dorchester Point, or to oppose the enemy, if they should attempt to possess it?"

The answers: "No."

Washington was now in a position to make his delayed, initial report to Congress. He summarized his situation in a letter July 10 to John Hancock, president of the Congress, a letter emphasizing the camp's "daily expectation of an attack," the camp's desperate, endless shortages, even to a willingness to settle for hunting shirts as any sort of uniform, and especially the want of ammunition, of which, he said, he was "exceedingly destitute." The single abundance, in contrast with the British, was good food.

Patriots seize Ploughed Hill, invite attack

In mid-July, Washington shifted his headquarters to a mansion from which Tory John Vassall had fled, a showplace then and still on old Tory Row, part of the King's Highway from Cambridge to Watertown. Soldiers were encamped on the wide open land on either side of the mansion and here Washington housed his official family, especially his immediate aides, Joseph Reed and Thomas Mifflin of Pennsylvania, both of whom would one day rise to be governors of their own state.

When the artist John Trumbull, remarkable at first to Washington as a mapmaker, became an aide, he observed on joining the staff at Vassall House:

"I suddenly found myself in the family of one of the most distinguished and dignified men of the age; surrounded at his table by the principal officers of the army, and in constant intercourse with them ... it was further my duty to receive company and do the honors of the house to many of the first people of the country of both sexes."

Abigail Adams had written her husband that Washington's appointment gave "universal satisfaction." Though she was mostly a homebody with her children in Braintree, she was among the early visitors Trumbull mentioned, and wrote John Adams how much more impressive Washington was than any advance advice about him:

"I was struck with Gen. Washington. You had prepared me to entertain a favorable opinion of him, but I thought the one half was not told me. Dignity with ease, and complacency, the gentleman and soldier look agreeably blended in him. Modesty marks every line and feature of his face."

Even in these early days Washington was having deep worries, and they would get worse during his residency in Vassall House. There would be many sleepless nights and anguish that would produce "many an unhappy hour when all around me are wrapped in sleep." There would be moments as commander so painful that he wished instead that he had "taken my musket on my shoulder and entered the ranks ... and lived in a wigwam."

To improve the shaky chain of command he split his army into three divisions: Maj. Gen. Ward in command of the right wing in Roxbury, Maj. Gen. Putnam, the center in Cambridge, and Maj. Gen. Lee, the left wing in Medford and present Somerville. Expresses, with horses handy, were stationed to speed any alarm directly to Washington's headquarters.

Creating the three army divisions was part of Washington's efforts "to establish order, regularity and discipline." Next to strengthening his defenses and seeking information on possible enemy movements (one of his earliest expenditures was to hire spies in Boston), Washington regarded discipline as his "great concern." He would enforce it rigorously. Still, the American camp shunned the grim punishments meted out in the British camp — the 1000 lashes mentioned comparatively by Rev. Emerson.

Both sides had desertions. There were hangings of British deserters on Boston Common and at Charlestown Neck. In the American camp the crime brought 39 lashes and being drummed ignominiously out of camp. Washington found this technique of meting out disgrace effective.

He had hardly been in camp a couple of days before he issued a general order in which he expressed the hope that all distinctions of colonies would be laid aside since the soldiers were "now the troops of the United Provinces of North America." Provincial prejudices and ways, though, would die mighty slow deaths.

The first troops enlisted outside New England, and the first enlisted by the Continental Congress, were the companies of riflemen from Pennsylvania, Maryland and Virginia. They were eager recruits. Capt. Daniel Morgan marched his men so fast from Virginia they covered the 600 miles to Cambridge in three weeks.

The reputation of the riflemen was fearsome. A British soldier called "these shirttailed men with their cursed twisted guns, the most fatal widow and orphan makers in the world." Their weapon was virtually unknown in New England. John Adams quaintly described it as "a peculiar kind of musket."

Independence National Historic Park,
Philadelphia, Pa.

Capt. Daniel Morgan

As special troops skilled in picking off British sentries and officers, the riflemen were excused from regular fatigue duty. Being mostly young and mettlesome, many soon became disorderly, provoking camp troubles. Even realistic Gen. Thomas observed, "The army would be as well off without them."

This was embarrassing to Washington for these were troops from his region. He would be chagrined, too, by an eventual near-mutiny. When a rifleman was sent to Cambridge for confinement, after threatening to free a sergeant who had been confined at Prospect Hill, nearly three dozen riflemen grabbed their weapons and headed for Cambridge to free their buddy.

Word was sent on to Washington. He ordered 500 soldiers to reinforce the guard and rode out to meet them. The mutineers, said a soldier, Jesse Lukens, "were not so hardened but upon the general's ordering them to ground their arms they did it immediately." They were put in the guardhouse, convicted of mutiny and fined. The men returned to camp, said Lukens, and

"seem exceedingly sorry for their misbehavior and promise amendment." No longer were they excused from fatigue duty.

Most shocking to Washington was the sudden revelation that powder for the troops was almost nonexistent. This news, a drastic, downward revision of the more than 300 barrels he thought were on hand, came in a note Elbridge Gerry sent from the Chamber of Supplies in Watertown. There remained only 36 barrels — or a mere nine rounds a soldier —of all the powder that had been collected from the towns "this side of Maryland." There are, Gerry added, "also about two tons of lead, and not any flints in store."

This terrible news came on Aug. 1. Brig. Gen. John Sullivan, who was present, described Washington's dismay:

"The general was so struck that he did not utter a word for half an hour."

He summoned a Council of War to discuss means of obtaining powder. Washington said that he "listened to every proposition on the subject which could give the smallest hope." A recent visitor to the camp had disclosed that he thought there was considerable powder in a remote part of Bermuda. Washington thereupon asked Rhode Island Dep. Gov. Nicholas Cooke to send two armed vessels to Bermuda to get this powder and if it was already gone (and it was) to try to purchase some at other islands.

For the moment, Washington issued a general order on Aug. 4 forbidding any firing that would waste ammunition. He warned: "It is with indignation and shame the General observes, that notwithstanding the repeated orders which have been given to prevent the firing of guns in and about the camp, it is daily and hourly practised; that, contrary to all orders, straggling soldiers do still pass the guards and fire at a distance where there is not the least probability of hurting the enemy. . . ."

Some powder eventually arrived from Philadelphia, but serious shortages were recurrent.

This did not dim the spirit of the army. Gen. Lee could say:

"Although we want powder most cruelly we rather approach than retire from the enemy."

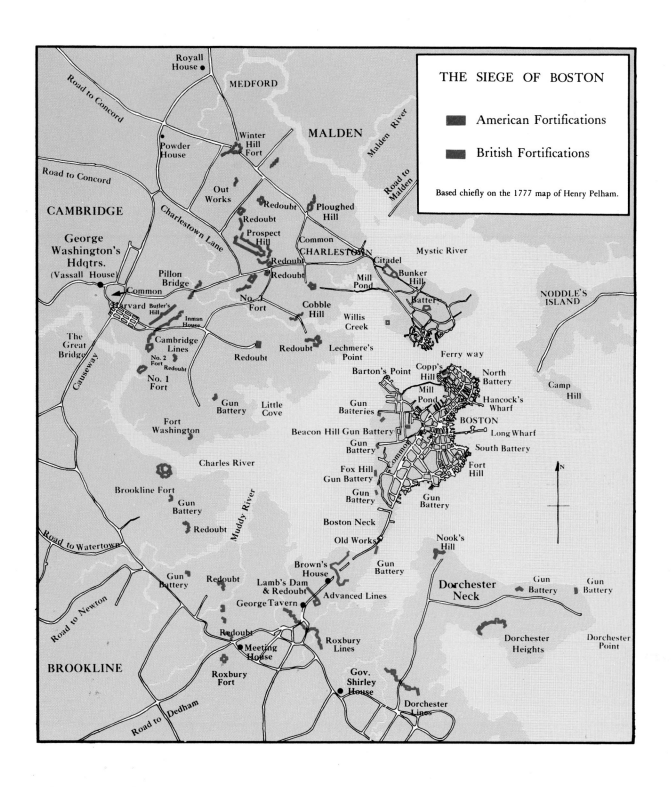

THE SIEGE OF BOSTON

American Fortifications

British Fortifications

Based chiefly on the 1777 map of Henry Pelham.

Martha Washington

John Adams

Abigail Adams

Cambridge Common as Washington takes command in mural by Charles Hoffbauer

Beverly Historical Society, Beverly, Mass.

William Ryerson, Boston Globe

Above, Franklin committee arrives in Cambridge for conference with Washington

Left, Vassall House, Washington's headquarters on Old Tory Row in Cambridge

Independence National Historic Park,
Philadelphia, Pa.

Lt. Col. Rufus Putnam

N.H. State House, Concord, N.H.

Brig. Gen. John Sullivan

Independence National Historic Park,
Philadelphia, Pa.

Joseph Reed

Amanda K. Berls

Wyeth's painting of Arnold's men battling the wilderness

Independence National Historic Park,
Philadelphia, Pa.

Col. Henry Knox

Massachusetts Historical Society
Brig. Gen. John Thomas

Fort Ticonderoga and Joseph Dixon
Crucible Company
*Left, Knox directs cannon over
the snow-covered hills*

The raising of the flag at Prospect Hill on Jan. 1, 1776

School Department, Somerville, Mass.

"Death of Montgomery" painting by John Trumbull

Gallery of Art, Yale University, New Haven, Conn.

Scene on Boston wharf as British head for ships in evacuation of Boston

Right, victory medal that Congress voted to Washington

Below, Washington at the taking of Dorchester Heights in painting by Emanuel Leutze

Boston Public Library, Boston, Mass.

Boston Public Library, Boston, Mass.

During these summer months there were intermittent skirmishes. At 2 a.m. on July 8, Maj. Benjamin Tupper and Maj. John Crane of the artillery crashed through the British advance guard on Boston Neck, seized weapons and burned structures including Brown's house, the outermost British post. This was repeated, and Brown's store burned, on the morning of July 11, and the next forenoon Col. John Greaton with 136 men in whaleboats brought off cattle from Long Island down the harbor and burned buildings. A British sea party cannonaded them and men were killed and wounded on both sides.

Some of the same men raided and drove cattle from Grape Island and Deer Island, all part of the siege plan to tighten the food squeeze on the British camp. On July 21 an American detachment, by way of Nantasket, raided the lighthouse at outer Boston harbor. Gen. Heath said they "took away the lamps, oil, some gunpowder, the boats, etc. and burned the wooden parts of the lighthouse. An armed schooner and several boats with men engaged the detachment; of the Americans, two were wounded."

It was about 1 a.m. on July 31 when Gen. Clinton, retaliating for the attacks on Brown's house, drove in the American sentinels on Boston Neck and burned the George Tavern, the most advanced American post. But at this same time Maj. Tupper and 300 Americans were making a second descent upon the Boston lighthouse, where a marine lieutenant and 32 marines were guarding a crew of 18 carpenters repairing damages from the July 21 raid.

"We killed six persons on the spot, one of which was a lieutenant," Tupper said in his report. Tupper was detained by the tide and attacked by several British boats. Still, he made off with 45 prisoners, several wounded. He said that "Major Crane, with his fieldpiece, which was planted on Nantasket Beach to cover our retreat, sunk one of their boats, and probably killed sundry of their crew, as the enemy approached within 200 yards." Only one American was killed.

Washington, in general orders next day, thanked "Maj. Tupper and the officers and soldiers under his command for their gallant and soldier-like behaviour in possessing themselves of the enemy's post at the lighthouse and for the number of prisoners they took there." These prisoners, including some Tory carpenters from the Massachusetts mainland, were escorted to jail in Worcester.

Gage's adjutant made note of the lighthouse skirmish and observed, "The admiral thought much to blame in this as well as in other things."

Washington's most important move in this summer period came on Saturday night, Aug. 26. A fatigue party of 1000 men with a guard of 2400

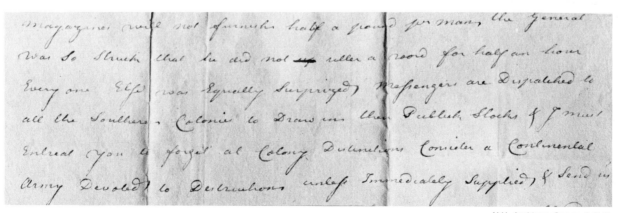

N.H. Archives, Concord, N.H.

Brig. Gen. Sullivan writes from Winter Hill

more under Gen. Sullivan seized and fortified Ploughed Hill (now vanished), an eminence about one-third the way from Prospect Hill to Bunker Hill.

"Sunday morning," Sullivan wrote to the patriot leaders in New Hampshire, "a heavy cannonading ensued which lasted through the whole day ... the floating batteries and an armed vessel attempting to come up and enfilade us as I expected. I opened a battery which I had prepared on purpose, cut away the sloop's foresail, made her shear off, wounded one floating battery and sunk another."

The next day, Sullivan continued, "they sent around a man-of-war to Mystic River, drawed their forces from Boston, formed a long column and prepared to come out, but finding our readiness to receive them declined the combat."

This move, as Washington observed to Congress, "took possession of a hill considerably advanced beyond our former lines." Bombardment went on by the British for days. But what Washington was trying to provoke, a repeat of the British attack on Bunker Hill, did not materialize.

For weeks Washington had been puzzled by the "inactivity of the enemy" despite the arrival of some British reinforcements. Washington's own defenses had by now been so improved he was eager for the British to attack. Washington's secretary, Joseph Reed, declared that the British would be "madmen to think of breaking through the lines we have thrown up." Gen. Lee dubbed the scene an "inactive, staring situation."

Gen. Howe, in later years when asked to defend his performance before Parliament, would concede that Washington "acted judiciously" in avoiding combat. Actually, Washington was hoping that by provoking a British attack he would inflict such losses on the redcoats as to end the war.

Mercy Warren, wife of James Warren, said of all the general inactivity that it was "heartily censured by the more ardent spirits." Washington knew this criticism. Yet, she added, with a "petition still pending to the King, and their allegiance not formally renounced, it was judged by many most prudent for the American Army to remain for the present only on the defensive."

But none of this was Washington's thinking. So, to make aggressive use of his troops, Washington came up with two plans.

Arnold hastens up Kennebec River

On Aug. 20, Washington disclosed one of his plans in a letter to Maj. Gen. Philip Schuyler — a plan that would initiate one of the most grueling marches in all military history. The plan, Washington told Schuyler, "has engaged my thoughts for several days." Washington proposed detaching 1000 to 1200 of his troops:

"To penetrate into Canada by way of the Kennebec River, and so to Quebec...."

Schuyler had been keeping Washington informed by letter of his preparations to cross Lake Champlain from Fort Ticonderoga to take Canadian towns on the Richelieu River and also Montreal on the St. Lawrence River. The British commander in Canada, resourceful Gen. Guy Carleton, with far fewer than 1000 British regulars available throughout his extensive command, was preparing to defend Montreal.

Washington's would be a supporting plan. He emphasized to Schuyler that a surprise march on Quebec would "distract Carleton" and help Schuyler, for Carleton would have to quit Montreal in order to save Quebec, the premier British fortress in Canada, or "suffer that important place to fall into our hands."

Canada and Massachusetts (which then included Maine) had a long, common border. As the revolution had moved toward open warfare there was intense interest at Boston on what course of action this would produce on American neighbors, the Canadians and the Indians. A succession of agents and letters indicated the neighbors would be friendly, or at least neutral. Some St. Francis Indians were visiting Cambridge and were stressing this to Washington as he was writing to Schuyler.

The objective of the Americans in trying to take Canada was not to conquer the Indians and the Canadians, but to expel the British military forces. This would deprive the British of a base from which to launch a drive down the Lake Champlain route and split the American colonies. Washington, who had contemplated raids for British gunpowder at Halifax and Bermuda, knew Quebec was well stocked and might provide him weapons and powder to drive the British out of Boston, as well.

Invasion of Canada had long been debated in the colonies. Samuel Adams was one of its earliest advocates. After the capture of Fort Ticonderoga, Ethan Allen and Benedict Arnold, who had entered that fortress side by side, both advocated a prompt invasion. "'Tis a pity," said Allen, "such a handful of regulars should command Canada!"

The Continental Congress, with Samuel Adams even more urgent, went over the situation and Schuyler was assigned to the mission in July. All this contemplated invasion by the historic Lake Champlain route.

Washington would add something quite different. He would have a twin invasion by an additional route, one far less widely known — up the Kennebec River, up its tributary Dead River to the Canadian border, then down tributaries of Lake Megantic, across this headwater of the Chaudiere River and down the Chaudiere itself to the St. Lawrence River and Quebec. It was a route little known but to Indians, voyageurs and missionaries.

The French, when they had ruled Canada, explored and mapped this route. The British, in their turn, did the same. A highly capable man who would become Britain's chief engineer in America, Lt. John Montresor, explored and mapped it in 1761. For military reasons both the French and British suppressed many of their discoveries.

It was a wilderness trail, replete with natural hazards. It was passable except, Montresor comfortingly reported to the new British masters of Quebec, by a military force armed with cannon, quite an exception.

Washington learned about this almost-forgotten route after he came to New England. Col. Jonathan Brewer of Waltham, who was wounded in the battle of Bunker Hill, had once offered to lead 500 men up the Kennebec River and invest Quebec. He had been there as an old French and Indian warrior. His offer was in the early days — back in mid-May — and was ignored. Col. Brewer and his regiment were now stationed at Prospect Hill. Col. Brewer could have told Washington of the route.

Washington, intent on wasting no time, started assembling information necessary for the mission. He noted that "the season will be considerably advanced" and was aware of some of the dangers that would have to be surmounted in penetrating the wilderness. The very next day after writing Schuyler, Washington had a set of questions prepared for a man who would be a key figure in this expedition, Reuben Colburn of Pittston on the Kennebec River.

Colburn had a shipyard on the east bank of the river six miles below Fort Western (Augusta). High on the bank above his yard he had a fine frame house (still standing) built a decade earlier. He was a prosperous man in this then sparsely settled area, owned large tracts of land, was a captain in the militia.

Colburn, at Washington's request, was to determine how soon he could procure or build "200 light bateaux capable of carrying six or seven men each, with their provisions and baggage (say 100 weight to each man), the boats to be furnished with four oars, two paddles and two setting poles each. . . ."

There were many other questions for Colburn. How much fresh beef could be obtained in his area? How many and the length of the carrying places on the route to Quebec —"whether low, dry land, hills or swamp? Also the depth of water in the river at this season, whether an easy stream or rapid?" Any other necessary intelligence?

Colburn was to inquire, on his way home from Cambridge, if any British warships were off Cape Ann or cruising the Kennebec. He was to send written answers by express to His Excellency as soon as possible. These questions had been put in writing to Colburn by Benedict Arnold.

Clearly, Washington had picked his man to head the expedition. Arnold, 34 years old, had won distinction at the taking of Fort Ticonderoga and in plans for defense of Lake Champlain, though, exasperated by difficulties over his command, he had angrily resigned his commission and was back in Watertown trying to straighten out his accounts with the Massachusetts authorities.

Arnold had continued favoring a Canadian campaign. From his merchant days, when he sailed and traded along the St. Lawrence and in the West Indies, he had acquaintanceship with Quebec. Above all, as Washington could instantly observe, Arnold was a fighter. A 16-year-old Pennsylvania rifleman who would join the expedition described Arnold as:

"Brave, even to temerity . . . a short, handsome man of a florid complexion. . . ."

On getting back to Pittston, Colburn got two men from north of Fort Western, Dennis Getchell and Samuel Berry, to go with three others and an Indian guide to check the route and collect intelligence. They set out on Sept. 1. Colburn also engaged a surveyor from downriver to furnish maps.

This officially "secret" expedition really got moving in the early days of September.

On Sept. 2, Washington sent authorization to Newburyport's Nathaniel Tracy, a wealthy shipowner who would become famous as an immensely successful privateer, to obtain as many vessels as necessary to transport the expedition. Tracy would himself provide four, get seven others from Newbury and Beverly, all of them schooners and sloops — some, in the haste, still smelly from fishing.

Next day came specific orders for Colburn, who was again on a visit to Cambridge.

He was told to go back to his place and start building the 200 bateaux "without delay." He was to arrange 20 artificers, carpenters and guides to aid along the route, "bespeak all the pork and flour you can from the inhabitants upon the River Kennebec" and let them know a commissary would also be seeking sixty 220-pound barrels of salted beef.

In a general order Washington announced that Col. Arnold and officers would be on Cambridge Common on Sept. 6 for an assembling of the detachment and expressed the desire that those volunteering from the various regiments should be "active woodsmen and well-acquainted with bateaux, so it is recommended that none but such will offer themselves for this service."

The chance to see action was so welcome to the rambunctious riflemen that their captains had to draw by lot to decide the three companies to go. The winners: Capt. Daniel Morgan, 39-

Benedict Arnold

Boston Athenaeum, Boston, Mass.

year-old frontiersman of Virginia, and two Pennsylvania captains, one of whom, Capt. William Hendricks, would sacrifice his life.

Washington took those who volunteered off their former roll of duty and they were told to march that evening to Cambridge Common, where "tents and everything necessary are provided for their reception." The three rifle companies from Prospect Hill and Roxbury camp were ordered to join them.

When Washington would hand Arnold his instructions it was little wonder that a fellow colonel and friend from Connecticut, told by Arnold about the expedition, would say of it: "Secret, though known to everybody." Soldiers involved were making preparations at Cambridge for several days and were steadily joined there by volunteers, among them 19-year-old Aaron Burr.

As early as Sept. 11 some of the units headed out of Cambridge for Newburyport, where the

expedition of roughly 1100 men was to embark. The largest number left Cambridge on Wednesday, Sept. 13. Units moved, as the lone, 22-year-old surgeon of the expedition, Dr. Isaac Senter of Rhode Island, explained, "for convenient marching and lodging." Most took two or three nights on the way.

The outlook of the men on the march was hopeful and full of enthusiasm. The soldiers, said 22-year-old musketman Abner Stocking of Connecticut, were "all in high spirits, intending to endure with fortitude all the fatigues and hardships that we might meet with in our march to Quebec."

Mindful of Arnold's troubles over rank during the taking of Fort Ticonderoga, Washington told Arnold that if he joined with Gen. Schuyler, "put yourself under him. In such a cause every post is honorable in which a man can serve his country."

Arnold was, above all, an ambitious man. The most popular military hero of those times was Gen. Wolfe, the man who captured Quebec in the prior war. Here Arnold was being given a chance to repeat Wolfe's triumph. Washington's urging "all possible dispatch" was a delightful injunction to Arnold's ears. If he should get to Quebec all the top honors would be his!

On Sept. 15, the Friday morning after getting his formal instructions, Arnold sped out of Cambridge, dined at Salem where he secured and sent on blankets, and reached Newburyport at 10 p.m. He was entertained at Tracy's big red-brick mansion near the harbor. But his time in Newburyport was crowded with preparations, among them sending three scouting vessels — as Washington had cautioned him — to detect if any British war vessels were skulking anywhere along the 100-mile ocean route to the mouth of the Kennebec River.

It was a prudent move. Word of Arnold's expedition had already reached the British camp. Gen. Clinton proposed "to frustrate it by sweeping the coast from Newburyport to Kennebec River and offered myself for that service if 1000 men could be spared to accompany me." Adm. Graves offered 500 marines. But Gen. Gage decided so many men could not be drawn "from the defenses of Charlestown and Boston."

Had he detected any peril from British warships, Arnold had been ordered to take the more time-consuming land route to the Kennebec River.

By Saturday, all of Arnold's men had arrived. They were housed in town house, church, ropewalks and tents. On Sunday they marched to services, heard the chaplain of the expedition, Rev. Samuel Spring of Northbridge, and held a review for the townsfolk later that day.

On Monday night embarkation was complete and the next morning, Sept. 19, at 10 a.m., when the lead skipper, one of Tracy's men, hoisted his jack on the *Broad Bay*, a vessel carrying Arnold, the transports set sail and cleared the bar. One ship, the *Swallow*, was grounded until high tide in the evening.

People crowded the shores to see them off. Some of the young soldiers particularly remembered the girls. Joseph Ware of Needham said there was a pleasant gale as they weighed anchor, "our colors flying, drums and fifes a-playing, and the hills all around covered with pretty girls weeping for their departed swains."

It became a rough passage. The weather grew thick and foggy. Seasickness, said Dr. Senter, hit "most of the troops" when gale winds swelled the waves in the evening. The ships ran until midnight when a signal was given to heave to, "with head off shore, off Wood Island."

Next day the weather continued "very thick and foggy" but Dr. Senter could spot the mouth of the Kennebec "half an hour after sunrise." By 9 a.m. Arnold and all the fleet, except three transports scattered in the gale winds, had entered the river. A pilot, secured from some armed men at the river mouth, came aboard Arnold's ship.

On the tricky river passage, during which several of the transports temporarily ran aground, the three missing vessels tardily appeared, two of them after coming round about by the Sheepscot River.

It was at this time, back in Cambridge, that Washington wrote a letter to John Hancock to give the Continental Congress its first information that Arnold was off "if possible, to make himself master of Quebec." And, at that moment,

on the other arm of the Canadian invasion, Schuyler had been taken ill and Ethan Allen, in a forlorn, daring attempt to capture Montreal, had been made a prisoner.

On Thursday, Sept. 21, "with wind and tide unfavorable," Arnold left the transports struggling up the river and reached Colburn's shipyard. There, produced amazingly in less than three weeks, were the 200 bateaux. Arnold, though, with a well-trained eye for nautical things, noticed their variations — "many of them smaller than the directions given, and very badly built."

He asked Colburn to make an additional 20, and Colburn put men back at building.

The river was low and the transports could not go the additional six miles to Fort Western, the customary head of ocean navigation on the river. Arnold set the men shifting supplies from the transports, and moving the considerable supplies Colburn had assembled, on to Fort Western by land and bateaux. Capt. Simeon Taylor of Mendon counted 100 men assigned to row the bateaux to the fort.

Arnold's days at Colburn's were crammed with activity.

Colburn's scouts, Getchell and Berry, came to give Arnold a firsthand report. On the Dead River they had met Natanis, chief of the Norridgewock tribe, and they said Natanis, who proved a good guide to them, was in the pay of Carleton. Even more, Natanis said that Carleton had spies at the head of the Chaudiere River and a squad of regulars stationed "some way down the river." Anyway, Getchell and Berry had gone no farther on their mission.

Arnold concluded that Natanis — as he would inform Washington — was "a noted villain" and ordered him shot on sight.

Colburn's mapmaker came to discuss the maps he had prepared. Arnold, of course, already had the maps that had been made by Lt. Montresor back on his 1761 mission along the Kennebec-Chaudiere route.

It was 6 p.m. Saturday evening when Arnold reached Fort Western, which would be his stepping-off place into the wilderness. Actually there were quite a few more miles before Arnold would pass the last American habitation. But he was pretty much in frontier country. There were fewer than 2000 dwellers up and down the Kennebec River countryside.

Fort Western, still standing on the east bank in present Augusta, was built of hand-shaped, foot-thick squared timbers now hidden under shingling. This was back in 1754, and it had been a frontier fort in the last French and Indian War. Later, no longer needed as a fort, it was sold to its first commandant, James Howard, who was running it as a trading post. He built himself a "great house" a mile farther upriver and, as Maj. Return J. Meigs of Middletown, Conn., recalled, "we were exceedingly well entertained." Still, despite the sizable fort and nearby hospitable dwellings, some of the men had to improvise shelters.

Arnold had to see hurriedly to a mass of detail to get his expedition ready to advance. One of his foremost concerns was information about the route beyond the Dead River. Next day, Sunday, he sent off two exploratory parties. He picked Lt. Archibald Steele of Capt. Smith's Pennsylvania riflemen and sent him with six men in birch canoes to Chaudiere Pond (Lake Megantic) to reconnoiter. The other party of 10, including surveyor and pilot, was "to take the exact courses and distances to the Dead River."

Arnold decided to send off his detachment in four divisions, at least a day apart, "for the conveniency of passing the carrying places." Each would carry a hefty 45 days' provisions and there would be a general rendezvous on reaching Lake Megantic.

Arnold had intended to have Lt. Col. Christopher Greene, 38, of Warwick, R.I., in the vanguard with a company of riflemen and two companies of musketmen. But the captains of the riflemen protested that they would be commanded only by big, rugged Capt. Morgan. Morgan indeed thought this was Washington's intention (which Washington would deny) to have the riflemen commanded by a rifle officer. Arnold finally gave in and sent off:

On Monday: Capt. Morgan and the three rifle companies "to clear the roads over the carrying places."

On Tuesday: Lt. Col. Greene and three companies of musketmen.

On Wednesday: Maj. Meigs and four companies of musketmen.

Arnold meantime received by express from Cambridge some manifestos printed in French that he was to distribute to the people of Canada to explain American intentions. He had to send back some sick soldiers and a private court-martialed for killing a young sergeant.

"On Thursday some of the 4th Division, which had with it 20 carpenters engaged by Colburn for the mission, took off. This division was commanded by Lt. Col. Roger Enos of Windsor, Conn., with the duty of moving forward all remaining supplies. It included three companies of musketmen. Enos, with orders to follow as soon as possible, was still busy when Arnold left Fort Western.

It was about noon of Friday, Sept. 29, when Arnold stepped into a swift birchbark canoe to push hurriedly ahead and get in the vanguard of his men.

The contemplated route would be much longer than Arnold figured from his imperfect maps. These men who had been taking off to the northward would never, in their most dreadful dreams, have imagined the hardships they would soon encounter in the wilderness.

Washington creates navy to seize supplies

In his letters, Washington — busy creating his other plan of action — told how he had been analyzing the British position. The two peninsulas of Boston and Charlestown, "surrounded in a manner by ships of war and floating batteries," were so strongly fortified "as to render it almost impossible to force their lines ... without great slaughter on our side or cowardice on theirs."

"We therefore can do no more than keep them besieged, which they are, to all intents and purposes, as closely as any troops on earth can be, who have an opening to the sea."

Also, in entries he was making in his expense account, Washington disclosed how closely he kept an eye on that British "opening to the sea." He wrote of his reconnoitering it from "the seacoast east of Boston harbor" and on "the south and west shore." And later he would look from Mystic (now Medford), from the "shores about Chelsea" and from Roxbury.

In other words, he reconnoitered the opening from every vantage point of his semicircle around the British camp.

This opening was plainly the British lifeline. If Washington could find a way to reduce its ocean-borne flow of supplies and reinforcements, he could strengthen his siege. The situation also presented him an irresistible opportunity to divert to his own camp incoming weapons, ordnance and gunpowder he desperately needed.

Washington was keenly mindful of the daring exploits of men like Col. Greaton and Maj. Tupper in their raids down Boston harbor. Their forays, which he praised, used mere whaleboats. What might such fearless men accomplish in boats of large size?

Washington knew of many brave deeds of coastal patriots from New York to the Carolinas. But the intrepidity of seagoing and ocean-bred New Englanders had sparked events closer at hand and magnified them in his eyes.

Early in May, Capt. Linzee of *HMS Falcon*, 14-gun sloop-of-war, prowled Buzzards Bay and tried to make off with two ships as prizes in a maneuver that outraged the men of the present New Bedford-Dartmouth area. Thirty of them — blind to any danger — went after him in two sloops of their own, boarded, fought and brought back the prizes to port along with 15 prisoners.

Machias and its bay, way Down East in present Maine, was the setting of an exciting sea drama early in June when a Boston loyalist, intent on swapping provisions — which Machias grievously needed — for lumber, arrived from Boston with two sloops laden with provisions, and with an armed schooner, the *Margaretta*, sent by Adm. Graves as convoy. Dickering ensued for so many days that the local Sons of Liberty rightly suspected that the lumber was intended, not for firewood, but for fortifications Gage was planning. They swung into action.

The loyalists tried to flee — at times grounding — as the Sons of Liberty, led by young Capt. Jeremiah O'Brien, made after the *Margaretta* in two loyalist sloops that they had seized. O'Brien lashed one of these sloops beside the *Margaretta* and boarded. In the bloody encounter 10 British were killed or wounded, while there were 14 American casualties — but Capt. O'Brien won the *Margaretta*.

By the time of the battle of Bunker Hill, three of the New England colonies were taking steps to get naval vessels of their own. Indeed, the battle interrupted debate in the Massachusetts Provincial Congress on the "expediency of establishing a number of armed vessels." But in Rhode Island and Connecticut armed vessels were being approved.

Capt. James Wallace of *HMS Rose*, 20-gun frigate, was prowling Narragansett Bay when he learned that Capt. Abraham Whipple, a hardy privateer in French and Indian War days, had been named to command Rhode Island's two newly authorized, armed vessels. Audacious Whipple would capture one of Wallace's small craft. Wallace, enraged, sent word to Whipple in which he revived an old, unsolved crime against the King's navy.

"You, Abraham Whipple, on the 10th of June, 1772, burned His Majesty's vessel, the *Gaspee,* and I will hang you at the yardarm."

To which Whipple nonchalantly responded:

"To Sir James Wallace. Always catch a man before you hang him. Abraham Whipple."

This was the magnificent spirit on which Washington felt he could plan to hound Gage's "opening to the sea." Washington had the experienced men already in his army, the sailors and fishermen of Cape Ann mustered by Col. John Glover — short, stouthearted Marblehead shipowner and veteran Son of Liberty. These were men, as Washington called them, "bred to the sea." Most had been driven from their occupations by Britain's closing the Grand Banks to Yankee fishermen.

Washington decided he would experiment with an armed vessel in the name of the United Colonies.

Col. Glover selected the ship, a fishing schooner from his merchant fleet, the *Hannah* — his wife's name. Outfitting began, early in August, at Glover's wharf in Beverly. Sailors, of course, were picked from Glover's regiment, and so, too, was the skipper, a longtime friend of Glover, Capt. Nicholson Broughton, 50-year-old Marblehead shipmaster, an officer in Glover's regiment.

Sept. 2 was a major day for both of Washington's plans to make aggressive use of his army. This was the day that he wrote to Newburyport to Nathaniel Tracy to arrange ships for Arnold's expedition. It was also the day that Washington drafted Capt. Broughton's orders to unfurl the *Hannah's* sails and take her out from Beverly harbor against the British lifeline.

Broughton, in his orders, was "appointed a captain in the army of the United Colonies of North America."

His mission was explicit — not to take on any and all enemy vessels. His orders read, in part:

"You are particularly charged to avoid any engagement with any armed vessel of the enemy, though you may be equal in strength or may have some small advantage;

"The design of this enterprise being to intercept the supplies of the enemy, which will be defeated by your running into unnecessary engagements."

This beginning of the navy, as an arm of the army, did not lead immediately to glorious events. Three days after getting his orders, Broughton sailed "with a fair wind" from Beverly at 10 a.m. Cruising off Cape Ann at 5 p.m. that day he sighted "two ships of war," which, he wrote Washington, "gave me chase." He wisely veered back toward Cape Ann, where he knew every drift and depth, and there the British ships, as night approached, did not care to follow.

Next morning he set out again and again spotting a formidable British warship, scurried back toward Gloucester harbor. That night after sunset he ventured out again, and next morning sighted and pursued a large ship headed from Portsmouth to Boston. Ship and crew were made captive.

But this first prizetaking turned into a fiasco. On board, when captured, the ship already had a British prize crew. She was a brig, the *Unity,* and belonged to John Langdon, New Hampshire delegate to the Continental Congress. *Unity* had first been captured by *HMS Lively,* one of the warships that had chased the *Hannah.* Washington ordered her returned to her owner, though Broughton — probably with prize money in mind — said he suspected she was intent on trading her lumber to the British in Boston.

An incentive to the American sailors had been a promised one-third share of all prize money over and above their regular pay. Langdon, in gratitude, sent a gift. But some of the *Hannah's* men, angered by the loss of the much greater prize money, mutinied. They were promptly court-martialed. The leading mutineer got 39 lashes and was drummed out. Washington replenished the men with more from Glover's regiment, and this pioneer warship continued her perilous cruise.

It virtually ended Oct. 10 in Beverly harbor.

HMS Nautilus, 16-gun sloop-of-war, late that day chased the *Hannah,* which Broughton, to escape, grounded on a sandbar near the beach. Shots from the *Nautilus* drew nearby townsfolk, who quickly carried ashore the *Hannah's* armament and enthusiastically turned it on the *Nautilus.* The plan of the British captain was to set the *Hannah* on fire. He gave that up as the tide ebbed, even abandoned an anchor, but in withdrawing ran his ship on a mud bank.

More townsfolk — Salem's William Wetmore counted about 200 — flocked to Salem Neck and turned some fieldpieces upon the *Nautilus*. An exchange of fire went on until 8 p.m., when the *Nautilus* was floated by the incoming tide. The British skipper had his rigging and sails slashed, a gun dismounted, 20 shots through the hammacoes (rolled hammocks) and hull. " 'Tis very lucky," he observed, "they fire so high."

The plucky *Hannah,* her structure sprung by the beaching, was soon retired from Washington's service.

Washington, however, had already made up his mind to have a bigger navy. He again visited the shores from which he could see heavily laden British vessels entering Boston harbor. He wrote confidently to his brother Jack, "I have no doubt of making captures of several of their transports."

Col. Glover was sent back to Cape Ann and with him, to speed things up, was sent a Washington aide, Stephen Moylan, mustermaster general of the army. Moylan was a sea merchant from Philadelphia. They were to select and arm two vessels that were "prime sailers" as soon as possible and send notice to Cambridge so a crew of "officers and men may march down."

The next day, Oct. 5, was to be an epochal date in the creation of an American navy. Washington wrote a letter to John Hancock in which he informed the Continental Congress — for the first time — that he had directed that armed vessels be equipped in order to cut off British supplies. From the number of vessels arriving, said Washington, "it may become an object of some importance." He hoped Congress would approve.

This same day Hancock was busy at Philadelphia writing instructions, hurriedly initiated by the Congress, for Washington as fast as possible to procure some armed vessels and send them on a secret mission to the St. Lawrence River. They were to attempt to capture two unconvoyed "north-country-built brigs" which had left England on Aug. 11 and were headed for Quebec loaded with arms and military stores.

What a prize these supplies might make for the munitions-starved Continental Army!

Beverly Historical Society, Beverly, Mass.

Schooner "Hannah"

Congress, and Hancock, had acted completely unaware of Washington's pioneering with armed vessels. Hancock also sent word that he was writing to the authorities of Massachusetts, Rhode Island and Connecticut to ask that they make any of their armed vessels available to Washington. If they had none, Washington was to get some that could "be soonest fitted out." And as an extraordinary incentive, Congress promised the seamen "one half of the value of the prizes by them taken." This went much beyond Washington's bonus offer.

The creation of a navy — which would mean waging war at sea as well as on land — had for months hung upon an irresolute, secret debate among members of Congress. John Adams had been with the foremost in preaching the necessity for an American navy. Other New Englanders aided him, Stephen Hopkins of Rhode Island, Silas Deane of Connecticut, and New Hampshire's John Langdon, lucky owner of the lumber ship that the *Hannah* had recaptured.

Adams had as well the advice and support of South Carolina's Christopher Gadsden, staunch Son of Liberty, though most southerners looked upon creation of a navy as a New England affair. Southern produce had been carried chiefly in British ships. Any American navy would thus seem mostly for the benefit of seafaring New Englanders.

Moreover, creation of a navy seemed to many members as an irrevocable break with Great Britain at a time when an "Olive Branch" petition was being presented to King George III. And when a cold realist considered the mighty reputation of the British fleet, then ruling all the oceans of the earth, opposition, as Adams potently expressed it, made the idea seem "the most wild, visionary, mad project that ever had been imagined. It was an infant taking a mad bull by his horns. . . ."

But Congress would, in succeeding months, step by step, create a continental navy. Some of the ships would be built at Philadelphia on the Delaware River, and from there Commodore Esek Hopkins would sail in his flagship *Alfred*, named, with lingering pride in British traditions, after the legendary founder of the British navy, King Alfred. This would not come to pass until early 1776.

Back on Oct. 5, 1775, Congress was in the drifting, early stage of the naval debate. Rhode Island's assembly had passed a resolution weeks earlier to ask Congress to build a continental navy. The resolve had been formally introduced and argument, which would continue for months, was in progress again when a ship, the *Aurora* from London, arrived at the port of Philadelphia with the sensational tip about the unprotected ammunition brigs bound for Quebec.

The express rushing Hancock's letter from the Congress to Cambridge would not deliver it into Washington's hands until Oct. 11.

Meantime Glover and Moylan, after hiring two Marblehead vessels and starting to outfit them as the armed ships *Hancock* and *Franklin*, were running into all sorts of problems — disputes over extra sails, lack of carpenters, even the price of bread. Washington considered the price asked "monstrous" and flour was provided instead.

Washington's reactions were expressed in a rash of letters from his secretary and confidant, Joseph Reed. The letters grew more demanding after the arrival of Hancock's express and Washington had lifted his sights to outfit four armed vessels at Cape Ann and two more at Plymouth. Expecting the *Hancock* and *Franklin* to be ready, Washington prepared additional orders on Oct. 16 to Capt. Broughton.

His quarry was now to be the two north-country brigs. Broughton in the *Hancock* was "to make all possible dispatch for the River St. Lawrence, and there to take such a station as will best enable you to intercept the above vessels."

Further instructions underscored Washington's soaring hopes for this naval mission and also for Arnold's expedition, which at the moment was approaching the Dead River. Washington told Broughton that, in the event that he missed the ammunition brigs, he was not to return, but to stay on station as long as the season would permit, adding:

"As there is great probability that Quebec will fall into our hands in a very short time, it may be expected that not only the above ordnance vessels, but others from Quebec and Montreal may come down and fall into our hands."

Capt. John Selman, another officer from Glover's regiment, given command of the *Franklin*, was placed under Broughton as commodore.

"The general is much dissatisfied," stormed Reed the next day, when the *Hancock* and *Franklin* failed to sail. He hinted that in Glover there might be hindrance from a mingling of public and private interests. "If they are not soon at sea," declared Reed, "we shall heartily repent it was ever undertaken." Two days later Reed exclaimed to Moylan:

"For God's sake, hurry off the vessels that are to cruise — transports without convoy arrive every day at Boston."

This demand brought word back that Broughton and Selman were at last ready to sail. Reed then proposed: "What do you think of a flag with a white ground, a tree in the middle, the motto 'Appeal to Heaven'? This is the flag of our floating batteries."

Schooners *Hancock* and *Franklin* set sail Oct. 21, but without the proposed flag. Moylan and Glover explained that the vessels "had none but their old colors" — so the signal they would use to each other and friends would be "the ensign up to the main toppinglift."

Moylan had some further words for Reed. He said that the available carpenters were "the idlest scoundrels in nature" with Tory-like dispositions. He defended Glover, said he was mortified by Reed's implications and had done his best for the public service.

"You cannot conceive the difficulty, the trouble and the delay there is in procuring the thousand things necessary for one of these vessels . . . . You must search all over Salem, Marblehead, Danvers and Beverly for every little thing that is wanting."

But problems were overcome both at Cape Ann and Plymouth and by the end of the month Washington had four armed ships of his fleet at sea. Glover and Moylan had another ready to sail at Beverly, and Washington's agent at Plymouth, William Watson, had another ready there.

Broughton and Selman missed their quarry. Instead of following Washington's orders they made unwarranted seizures of small vessels, raided the present capital of Prince Edward Island and made prisoners, all embarrassing to Washington. He abruptly cut off their attempt to report to him on the steps of Vassall House and dismissed them from his fleet.

His fleet, though, would have many successes. One of the greatest of them would be the achievement of Capt. John Manley of Marblehead, formerly of the British navy.

Washington, from his Boston spies, learned that for two weeks Adm. Graves had been trying to find an ordnance transport, the brig *Nancy,* which had been blown by a gale from her convoy and was missing off Cape Cod. Washington ordered his fleet to "keep a good lookout for her." Late on Nov. 27, as dark gathered, Manley sighted the *Nancy* and boarded her after she mistook his ship for a pilot boat.

Nancy's cargo was a virtual arsenal.

Washington was with the other generals at a

Peabody Museum, Salem, Mass.

Capt. John Manley

gathering when an express from Gloucester came at a gallop with the news the *Nancy* was in port. The wife of Dr. John Morgan told of the pleasure that shone on the faces of all, Generals Lee, Putnam and Gates. Gates was in ecstacy, she said.

"As Gen. Washington was reading the invoice there was scarce an article that he did not comment upon and that with so much warmth as diverted everyone present."

At once Washington grew concerned about the safety of this invaluable capture. Indeed, Graves had instructed his captains to set the *Nancy* on fire if found in Gloucester harbor. Washington immediately ordered four companies to protect the stores, teams to start conveying them to Cambridge and Col. Glover to assemble the Cape Ann minutemen "to secure the removal."

There was little gunpowder, but the rest was a needy general's dream: 2000 muskets "with bayonets, scabbards and steel rammers," 100,000 flints, tons of musket shot, round shot, mortar beds, two brass 6-pounders, loads of stores and a stunning, immense 13-inch brass mortar that would be hauled in delight to the Cambridge camp and be dubbed "The Congress" as Gen. Putnam poured a christening bottle of rum.

Manley would soon be made commodore of what Washington called "our little squadron."

There was no joy in Boston. Gen. Howe, who had replaced deposed Gen. Gage when he sailed to London on Oct. 10, in effect complimented Washington's fleet by asking Lord Dartmouth in the future to send out valuable stores in ships of war with "sufficient force to defend themselves against these pirates." The lengthy invoice of stores Washington had read included 34 boxes of 8-inch carcasses and 50 boxes of 13-inch ones. Howe dolefully told Dartmouth that the rebels were "now furnished with all the requisites for setting the town on fire."

Franklin seeks to save the army

Doctor Franklin, the respectful way his colleagues addressed Benjamin Franklin, was about to leave Philadelphia on Oct. 3 on a mission to the camp at Cambridge as Samuel Adams was expressing the feelings of many who placed no faith in the "Olive Branch" petition en route to George III.

"It is folly to supplicate a tyrant.... Under God, our own virtuous efforts must save us.

"I hope that our troops will before long force their way into Boston."

Franklin and two other members of the Continental Congress, Col. Benjamin Harrison of Virginia and Thomas Lynch Sr. of South Carolina, had promptly been made a committee to confer with Washington on receipt of his warnings that problems facing the army had reached a crisis stage. Without an army in the field the revolution could collapse.

Samuel Adams was a member of the group that had drafted instructions to guide the Franklin group. Adams was far from being alone in hoping for an assault on Boston. It was the sense of Congress, the instructions said in part, that if Washington considered it practical, "to make the attack upon the first favorable occasion" and before the expected British reinforcements arrived.

In the Boston camp Gen. Howe wrote Lord Dartmouth that barring some unforeseen accident he felt that his lines "would be in no danger from the enemy during the winter." His expected 2000 reinforcements "would enable us to distress the rebels by incursions along the coast." From the "strength" of the rebel army and his own defensive position, Howe complacently expected "nothing material will probably be attempted."

This right along was far from Washington's intention. The state of inactivity, he had told Congress, "by no means corresponds with my wishes to relieve my country, by some decisive stroke, from the heavy expense its subsistence must create." And Washington had sent on to Congress a report of the Council of War he had called on Sept. 11.

Prior to that council, so that his generals would have three days to think over their advice, Washington had marshaled his reasons for going on the offensive and asked:

"Whether, in your judgments, we cannot make a successful attack upon the troops in Boston by means of boats, cooperated by an attempt upon their lines at Roxbury?"

Winter, he told them, was fast approaching. His army would need barracks, costly wood, unobtainable blankets. "The soldiery grow impatient to get home already," he observed, "and we shall find it a very hard task to detain them, when they feel the severity of the northern winter, without proper covering."

He brought up a problem already haunting his sleeping hours:

"If the present army should not incline to engage for a longer time than the first of January, you must either levy new troops, and have two armies, or partly so, on pay at the same time, or, disbanding one before the other is assembled, expose the country to desolation, and the cause to ruin."

Above all, he noted, "Our powder is daily wasting."

Still his generals were unanimously opposed to the proposed attack. They felt that there might be "some important advices from England" any moment on acceptance by King George of the "Olive Branch" petition. "It was not expedient," they concluded, "to make the attempt at present."

Washington's hopes to get home to Mt. Vernon had recently faded. Reports he got from Boston, from his spies and deserters, showed that the British were getting ready for winter, preparing barracks and trying to bring in coal. His decisive blow that would end the war would have to be delayed. He now put his problems together in a crucial letter sent to Congress Sept. 21. Its dire tone:

"My situation is inexpressibly distressing, to see the winter fast approaching upon a naked army, the time of their service within a few weeks expiring, and no provision yet made for such important events.

"Added to these, the military chest is totally exhausted; the paymaster has not a single dollar in hand; the commissary general assures me he has strained his credit, for the subsistence of the army, to the utmost.

"The quartermaster general is precisely in the same situation; and the greater part of the troops are in a state not far from mutiny, upon the deduction from their stated allowance.

"I know not to whom I am to impute this failure; but I am of opinion, if the evil is not immediately remedied . . . the army must absolutely break up."

His express reached Philadelphia on Sept. 29. Congress heard his stark message, and did not delay. It ordered immediate dispatch of a committee of three to find "the most effectual method of continuing, supporting and regulating a continental army." Next day it named the three men. Col. Harrison was a friend and often a spokesman of Washington in the Congress. Lynch, wealthy planter, was a friend of the eminent Christopher Gadsden and a longtime Son of Liberty.

Franklin's reputation was already worldwide. John Adams said at this time of Franklin: "There's no abler or better American that I know of." Brig. Gen. Nathaniel Greene, who would attain a military reputation second only to Washington's, would tell how on arrival he looked steadily on Franklin "with silent admiration during the whole evening," called him "a very great man."

Franklin's wit and sagacity sparkle in a letter he wrote, on the day he left Philadelphia, to a famous fellow scientist in England, Dr. Joseph Priestley, to tell another friend there who sometimes despaired about America's firmness:

"Britain, at the expense of 3,000,000 pounds, has killed 150 Yankees this campaign, which is 20,000 pounds a head; and at Bunker Hill she gained a mile of ground, half of which she lost again by our taking post on Ploughed Hill.

"During the same time 60,000 children have been born in America. From these data, his mathematical head will easily calculate the time and expense necessary to kill us all and conquer our whole territory."

While Franklin and his associates were en route to the camp, Washington, meeting a request of Congress, again used his prudent technique of giving his generals three days in which to prepare their answers on army organization dealing with size, pay, rations, clothing (very difficult for a nation of strictly home manufacture), enlistments and regimental makeup. The answers were ready at a Council of War on Oct. 8, in effect a preliminary to the forthcoming sessions with the Franklin group.

Both Samuel and John Adams, deeply aware of New England's stake in the mission, wrote to James Warren, then top Massachusetts official as the speaker of the House, to urge that "every kind of civility" be shown the distinguished visitors.

Warren fully complied when the visitors reached Watertown on Sunday, Oct. 15. Col. Harrison pressed on to Cambridge but Franklin and Lynch paused "and drank coffee," and later, in Widow Coolidge's tavern near the Watertown mill bridge, the general officers and the visitors sat down to "the best dinner we could get them, turtle, codfish, etc."

There was a welcoming dinner at Vassall House to which Washington sent his general officers invitations and told them they would be introduced to the delegates. Franklin presented the committee of the Massachusetts assembly 100 pounds sent to him by persons in England for the relief of those wounded on Lexington Green and for the widows and children of the slain.

The opening of the formal conferences was delayed two days because Matthew Thornton, president of the New Hampshire Convention, was detained by family illness. A decision was reached to go ahead on Wednesday morning and have Brig. Gen. John Sullivan fill in for Thornton.

On the eve of the sessions, Tuesday night, there was quite a water scene off Boston Common. Lt. William Carter of His Majesty's 40th Foot related:

"The enemy saluted the camp on Boston Common. They brought three floats (with a piece of cannon in each) out of Cambridge River, and fired a number of shot, some of which went over, several fell short; in fine, we had not even a tent cord broke.

"On the last firing, a very confused noise was heard; and this morning several pieces of oars and planks were picked up by our people on the shore."

Rev. Jeremy Belknap of Dover, N.H., was visiting the camp, and while dining later with the visitors had more exact detail. There were only two floating batteries that came down the Charles River, past Brookline Fort, and "within three-quarters of a mile of the bottom of the Common. They fired about 17 shots into the town, and then a 9-pounder in one of the batteries split; the cartridges took fire, and blew up the covering, or deck, on which several men were standing." One man bled to death, many others were wounded.

The incident emphasized a timely point made by Gen. Greene that the American troops were in general "raw and undisciplined," but they were willing to try.

On Wednesday, the morning sessions began. Washington took time for a Council of War after discovering that the Franklin group's instructions included "an intimation from the Congress that an attack upon Boston, if practicable, was much desired." He therefore again asked their opinions. Their response, in brief:

Gates — "Improper to attempt it."

Greene — "Not practicable under all circumstances; but if 10,000 men could be landed at Boston, thinks it is."

Sullivan — "At this time it is improper."

Heath — "Impracticable at present."

Thomas — "Of the same opinion."

Putnam — "Disapproves of it at present."

Lee — "Too great a risk."

Ward — "Against it."

The underlying reason, of course, was in a letter Washington wrote a few days earlier about the daily cannonade he had to sustain from the British artillery. "These insults," he said, "we are compelled to submit to for want of powder . . . ."

The sessions were lengthy. It took five days to reach answers to the questions raised in the instructions, and then the committee sat two days longer to find answers to a number of problems that had been vexing Washington.

President Thornton arrived early on the second day and took his seat. The leaders from the provinces included Dep. Gov. Matthew Griswold of Connecticut, Dep. Gov. Nicholas Cooke of Rhode Island and James Bowdoin, the chairman of a committee from the Council of Massachusetts Bay (the Senate).

They agreed on the need for an army of 20,372 men with 26 regiments of uniform size rather than the 40 regiments of a variety of sizes; on seeking year-long enlistments in the new army until December of 1776; on continuing the current pay scale; dyed brown uniforms with regimental facings to be bought by the Congress; clearer rules and regulations; and readier availability of money for military needs.

On the last day, Oct. 24, Franklin, Harrison and Lynch sent to Congress a record of the proceedings (made by Washington's secretary, Joseph Reed) and a statement that while every decision reached was subject to congressional approval, they felt that they must anticipate it in a vital respect — enlistments.

Congress, worried about costs, had hoped to reduce the pay of the soldiers. This, said the delegates, was "absolutely impracticable." They declared that "a bare proposal of this nature would cause such discontents, if not mutinies, as would, perhaps, prove the ruin of the army. We are sorry to find this opinion too much confirmed by the difficulty that occurs in prevailing on the troops of Connecticut to enlist for the month of December only."

They felt that Washington "should immediately proceed to a new enlistment of the present army for the next year, without waiting for directions from Congress." They felt every moment's delay was big with danger.

"One more reason for dispatch is, that men may much more probably enlist before, than after, they feel the hardships of a winter campaign."

On enlistments, they continued the practice of not enrolling Negroes, "especially such as are slaves." Washington and time would alter this, for free blacks were already serving in the regiments and had won distinction in the Lexington-Concord action and the battle of Bunker Hill.

A portentous, final question Washington asked them they considered "of too much importance to be determined by them, therefore refer it to the Congress." The question: Whether an attack upon the British troops in Boston "should be avoided when it evidently appears that the town must of consequence be destroyed?"

The Congress would not find itself able to answer that one until late in December.

John Adams was soon writing back from Philadelphia:

"The committee have returned, much pleased with what they have seen and heard .... They say the only disagreeable circumstance was, that their engagements, haste, and constant attention to business, were such as prevented them from forming such acquaintances with the gentlemen of our Province as they wished...."

Lynch wrote Washington on Nov. 13:

"I am happy to inform you that Congress had agreed to every recommendation of the committee....

Washington had received his signal to hold and begin reshaping an army from what amounted to four provincial armies, with their myriad variations in composition and practices, into a continental army. He would find the task, particularly in seeking to overcome old provincial prejudices and ruggedly independent ways, frustrating, often infuriating. As they would soon crowd in upon him he would find these troubles, in his own word, "inconceivable."

Adm. Graves wars on seaports, burns Falmouth

Adm. Graves's Oct. 6 instructions to Lt. Henry Mowat of His Majesty's armed vessel *Canceaux* sounded terrifying:

"My design is to chastize Marblehead, Salem, Newburyport, Cape Ann Harbor (Gloucester), Portsmouth, Ipswich, Saco, Falmouth in Casco Bay (now Portland), and particularly Machias where the *Margaretta* was taken, the officer commanding her killed, and the people made prisoners ... where preparations I am informed are now making to invade the Province of Nova Scotia."

All these seaside communities had angered the admiral in their encounters with His Majesty's navy. All four New England governments, declared Graves, "are in open and avowed rebellion against His Majesty."

Mowat, selected because of his special knowledge gained in a coastal survey, was ordered "to proceed along the coast and lay waste and burn such seaport towns as are accessible to His Majesty's ships...."

The admiral's anger had been approaching the boiling point for some months. Mowat's orders were to take him eastward from Boston to the Canadian border (then) of Massachusetts. The admiral also had standing orders for Capt. James Wallace of *HMS Rose*, 20-gun man-of-war, long remembered for his depredations along the Rhode Island and Connecticut coasts.

He had been instructed in mid-September "to lay waste and destroy every town or place from whence the pirates (rebels) are fitted out, or shall presume to harbor or shelter them, together with all the vessels of what kind soever therein...."

The admiral was keenly in favor of burning. It was he who had suggested to Howe, just before the first assault at Bunker Hill, that Charlestown be set on fire.

Wallace had already provoked an encounter at Stonington, Conn., when he came upon 250 patriots about to head for Block Island and clear it of cattle. Gunfire broke out. The *Rose* fired 120 shots into the town and made off with five schooners and sloops from the wharves as Wal-

lace guessed there were more than 3000 rebels "skulking behind hills and rocks and fences." He had three wounded, the town one. Despite the severe canonading, Gov. Trumbull told Washington the town was "by divine Providence marvelously protected."

Wallace would try to block the removal of cattle, sheep, hogs and turkeys from Newport, R.I., farms, would threaten and fire upon the town after laying it under demand to furnish him fresh meat and beer. The threats, related Rev. Ezra Stiles, then the local minister, created a general panic and scramble with household effects. But it was Bristol that suffered the great wrath of Wallace and of some other British warships with him.

Wallace — "an inhuman wretch," Rev. Stiles called him — drew up his fleet off Bristol and, when his demands for sheep and cattle were not promptly met, ordered a bombardment with cannonball and firebomb that lasted an hour and a half. "The shrieks of women, the cries of children," said an eyewitness, "would have extorted a tear from even the eye of Nero." The local minister, who was ill, expired while fleeing, as did a child. Wallace sailed off with 50 sheep. "Words," said the eyewitness, "can't describe the dreadful scene."

Wallace's activities were impromptu in nature compared with Mowat's punitive expedition. It was in the planning stage for weeks after Graves, early in September, got two transports from Gage to be outfitted. Gage, who supplied far less than Graves hoped, furnished only 100 troops for Mowat's four-vessel flying squadron.

Shortly before its departure, Graves, much relieved to have official sanction, received orders from the Admiralty to pursue — though there would be hedging later in London — the very punishing action he had in mind. Mowat set out just after midnight on Oct. 9, was blown by a gale to Cape Cod and, after several days, arrived off Gloucester.

But the town was spared when Mowat's artillery officer advised him that the "houses stood too scattered to expect success." So Mowat steered a course for Casco Bay and the port of Falmouth. Mowat knew Falmouth well, though not favorably. On duties there just after the Lexington-Concord Alarm started hostilities, Mowat was briefly held as a prisoner and was released only after threats to burn the place.

Now Mowat hauled his squadron into the harbor on Oct. 17 and at 5 p.m. sent ashore his barge and a lieutenant, who proceeded into the town house and delivered Mowat's message to be read to the people, who had assembled pell-mell. It was in stilted phrasing.

Mowat was back, he informed the uneasy assemblage, because of the way in which they had treated "the best of sovereigns" despite "Britain's long forbearance of the rod of correction." He had come "with orders to execute a just punishment on the town." He gave the people two hours in which "to remove without delay the human species out of the said town," and at the end of that period:

"A red pennant will be hoisted at the main-top-gallant masthead with gun" and the punishment would follow.

Telling of the impact, Rev. Jacob Bailey said:

"It is impossible to describe the amazement which prevailed upon reading this alarming declaration: a frightful consternation ran through the assembly, every heart was seized with terror, every contenance changed color, and a profound silence ensued for several moments."

Old Jedediah Preble, who had declined a field command at Cambridge camp because of his years and infirmity, led a committee on board the *Canceaux*. The members read Mowat's orders, recognized the gravity of their situation, got Mowat to postpone execution until the next morning on his agreeing with them, as a pledge, to have the people turn in their arms by 8 p.m. He also wanted five cannon near the town house, but they had been removed from town.

At 8 p.m. the committee came back with only 10 stand of arms. Mowat agreed to hold off until 9 a.m. for further compliance with his concession that he would, if given hostages and all their arms, refer the decreed punishment back to the Commander in Chief of the King's forces in Boston.

One half hour before the deadline the committee came back aboard the warship to tell Mowat that they had not been able to assemble the people. This meant rejection of Mowat's terms.

"Perceiving women and children still in the town," Mowat would report to Graves, "I made it 40 minutes after 9 before the signal was hoisted, which was done with a gun, at the same time the cannonade began from all the vessels . . . ."

The Sons of Liberty had beaten their drums and mustered for some 30 miles. Some had arrived before midnight. But they lacked cannon and powder. The day broke clear and pleasant and, as Rev. Bailey related, "without a breath of wind."

People and carts from the country crowded in to assist in removing goods and furniture. "The streets were replete with people, oxen and horses." Presently they saw "the flag hoisted at the top of the mast and the cannon began to roar with incessant and tremendous fury."

The multitude was struck "into instant alarm and amazement. The oxen, terrified at the smoke and report of the guns, ran with precipitation over the rocks, dashing everything in pieces and scattering large quantities of goods about the streets. In a few minutes the whole town was involved in smoke and combustion."

Mowat, when there was still no wind, could see that "numbers of armed men were employed extinguishing the fire . . . although a regular cannonade was kept up all the time." Mowat felt he had to land some men, and parties were sent ashore "to set fire to the vessels, wharves, storehouses, as well as to many parts of the town that escaped from the shells and carcasses." Eleven vessels were destroyed, four captured.

In the afternoon the wind sprung up and favored Mowat's efforts. The bombardment was continued until 6 p.m. The southern and middle parts of the town were reduced "to a heap of rubbish," said Rev. Bailey. The front of the town house "was torn to pieces by the bursting of a bomb."

"In a word, about three quarters of the town was consumed and between two and three hundred families . . . were now in many instances destitute of a hut for themselves and families;

and a tedious winter was approaching . . . ." Winter prospects so close to the edge of the wilderness were indeed desolate.

The log of the *Canceaux* reported the British were fired upon and the armed vessel had to be withdrawn "out of reach of their musketry."

Days later, as recorded in the log, "the fire still continues in the town."

Rumors of the devastation of Falmouth reached Cambridge while the Franklin committee was still at its labors. It was not until the night of Oct. 23 that an express came into camp with confirmation of what Washington, in a letter prepared immediately for Congress, termed "an outrage exceeding in barbarity and cruelty every hostile act practised among civilized nations."

The Franklin committee also wrote Congress.

"It is easy," the members said, "to conceive what effects this must produce in this camp; every soldier who came from Falmouth insisting on leave to go and take care of his family, and to find a place for them, where they may be covered from the inclemency of the approaching winter. Indeed, it is too reasonable a request to be refused."

"Should the same fate fall to the share of many such towns, it is easy to foretell what must happen to the army, especially should it happen before the new army is enlisted."

For some time coastal communities had pleaded with Washington for detachments of soldiers and powder. He could not, without dissolving his army, respond. As he understood that Portsmouth was next on Mowat's list, Washington did send Brig. Gen. Sullivan to help organize its defenses though he sensed its fortifications would be sufficient to discourage any attackers.

Falmouth was not the first leveling of a coastal community in this war nor would it be the last. The Falmouth casualties were few. The effect did not weaken resistance, but intensified it. America agreed with Washington's appraisal. A wave of outrage swept the colonies. Congress moved closer to building a navy. It was Charlestown all over again . . . and soon it would be Norfolk, Va., sent up in flames.

Mowat in a few days returned to Boston. He had to refit. "The badness of his vessels and stores prevented his doing more than destroying the town of Falmouth," Graves explained to the Admiralty, and added: "You may be assured we shall not allow the rebels to remain quiet."

Secret letter exposes America's first traitor

A traitor!

Americans were shocked when the charges became known. How could this be possible?

Dr. Benjamin Church Jr., 41-year-old surgeon general of the Continental Army, was in the innermost circle of the leaders of the Bay Province, had long been a Son of Liberty and had risked a noose for years.

Doctor Church! His songs and poems had delighted Americans. His ready pen had time and again filled columns in the Whig journals with powerful arguments for the defense of ancient liberties. He was an honored member of Boston's Committee of Correspondence and delivered an eloquent address at the Old South Meetinghouse on the anniversary of the Boston Massacre.

He was a Boston representative in the Provincial Congress. More important, he was a top member of its most important group, the Committee of Safety. He knew all the patriot secrets.

Church was on the committee that had urged the fortifying of Bunker Hill. He signed the commission that sent Benedict Arnold to take Fort Ticonderoga. Only a few weeks ago he was the agent of the Provincial Congress sent to Philadelphia to ask that a general be named to head the army, and he was on the committee that had gone to Springfield to welcome Washingon.

"Good God!" exclaimed John Adams at the sensational news. "What shall we say of human nature?"

"Astonishing and terrifying," said Gen. Lee.

These and similar reactions were heard throughout camp and country when word spread at the end of September that Church had been placed under arrest.

Back in July, Church addressed a folded letter to Maj. Maurice Cane, an aide to Gen. Gage, and handed it to a young woman — who would turn out to be the doctor's mistress — to take with her on a visit to Newport, R.I. She was furnished alternate ways by Church of getting it into the hands of Capt. Wallace of *HMS Rose* for delivery in Boston.

In Newport she went to the home of a baker who had been an acquaintance back in Boston, Godfrey Wainwood, to get his help in speeding the letter on its way. He suspected something irregular and persuaded her to leave the missive with him for delivery. On opening it he found a message addressed to a Mr. Fleming of Boston, but the message was in unintelligible cipher.

Wainwood consulted a local friend, schoolmaster Maxwell. He, too, suspected an illicit correspondence, sought help from Rev. Ezra Stiles, the Newport minister, and talked about going to the army in Cambridge. Meanwhile Wainwood got an illiterate, scrawling note from the young woman asking him to come to Cambridge. She was worried about what had happened to the letter, and told Wainwood, "There is a certain person here wants to see you very much."

Clearly, Wainwood figured, there was a treasonable correspondence — and a second letter must have informed the sender that his original letter had not arrived. He and Maxwell headed north to Providence to lay their facts before the provincial secretary, who gave them instructions to take their evidence on to Brig. Gen. Nathaniel Greene. Greene promptly took it to Vassall House.

The young woman's name (now lost to history) was given by Wainwood. Washington ordered a search. She was located and, tradition in the camp relates, she was fetched at night to headquarters by Gen. Putnam on horseback, riding pillion in back of his saddle.

"For a long time," said Washington, "she was proof against every threat and persuasion to discover the author. However, at length she was brought to a confession."

The questioning had been suspended late that night and it was the next day that she named Dr. Church.

"Upon this," James Warren recounted, "the general sent a note desiring Maj. Joseph Hawley and me to come immediately to Cambridge." Hawley was a leading member of the Massachusetts Legislature. "We all thought," added Warren, "the suspicion quite sufficient to justify an arrest of him (Church) and his papers."

Washington located someone to decipher the letter and meantime sent his secretary across Tory Row to the still-standing mansion of the widow of Henry Vassall, which was Church's residence as surgeon general, to have his papers searched. "It appeared on inquiry," said Washington, "that a confidant had been among the papers before my messenger arrived."

Washington summoned his officers to headquarters on Oct. 3 for a Council of War and presented the evidence. The code had been broken by one of the camp chaplains, Rev. Samuel West. The solution, achieved by a simple process of letter frequencies, was quickly corroborated. Col. Elisha Porter heard of the problem and, assisted by Elbridge Gerry, also provided a decoding. It was identical with Rev. West's.

The generals discussed the evidence and decided to have Church before them the next day.

Church, shown the letter in cipher, agreed that it was his, agreed the deciphering was true but, said Washington, "made solemn asseverations of his innocence."

The Mr. Fleming addressed in the letter was John Fleming, husband of Church's sister, a Boston printer who had been in partnership with a fellow Tory publisher. Church told the generals that his intentions had been to "impress the enemy with a strong idea of our strength . . . to prevent an attack at a time when the Continental Army was in great want of ammunition and in hopes of effecting some speedy accommodation of the present dispute" with Great Britain.

With Church removed from the chamber, Washington asked "Whether it did not appear that Dr. Church had carried on a criminal correspondence with the enemy?" The answer was a unanimous "Yes." The current articles of the army offered, said Washington, "very inadequate punishment" for "the enormity of the crime." So Church was to be closely guarded while punishment was set by the Continental Congress.

The coded letter contained virtually nothing that, on its face, was traitorous. It was its being coded, possibly involving meanings or signals that were hidden, and its being sent in a suspicious way, that looked criminal. Washington remarked that Church could have sent a letter directly into Boston any day, if he had wished.

The disclosure of Church's immorality, in a community of Puritanical beginnings, produced its own shock waves.

John Adams wrote to James Warren that he would never have recommended Church for preferment had he known. "Honor and fidelity violated in such gross instances in private life are slender securities in public." This was Samuel Adam's sentiment, too. If a man would betray his wife it was an easy step for him to betray his country.

Church's young woman, said James Warren, was "an infamous hussy." Young Lt. Ebenezer Huntington wrote home to his brother from the Roxbury camp that the young woman "is now with child by him (Church) and he owns himself the father — for he has dismissed his wife."

Many began thinking back about the famous

Harvard University,
Cambridge, Mass.

Dr. Benjamin Church Jr.

doctor. Among them was Paul Revere and one day he would put it in writing. He recalled three days after the war opened at Lexington Green on April 19 that Dr. Joseph Warren and other patriots were assembled in Hastings House, off Cambridge Common, and Church had astonished them by saying that he was going into Boston. Church insisted, though Dr. Warren warned him that he might be hanged.

On his return, Church, who had indulged in some heroics with Revere on April 19 over bloodstains on his stocking, told of being arrested and questioned by Gage. Revere presently encountered a deacon who saw Gage and Church emerge from Gage's headquarters, Province House, not acting like captor and captive, but "discoursing together like persons who had been long acquainted."

Revere would one day meet a man who had been studying medicine under Church and keeping the doctor's books. Shortly before the Lexington-Concord Alarm the student knew Church "was much drove for money." Then, all at once, Church "had several hundred new British guineas, and that he thought at the time where they came from."

James Warren, Revere and others thought back on how the patriots before Lexington-Concord Alarm had come to believe someone was passing their secrets to Gage. Revere recalled how his group of mechanics, assigned to watch British troop movements, had changed their gathering place in an effort to shake the informer.

James Warren observed, "I have now no difficulty to account for the knowledge Gage had of all our Congress secrets, and how some later plans have been rendered abortive; or for the indulgence shown him (Church) when he went into Boston after the Lexington battle."

Church was no longer an admired doctor. His moments of preoccupation and seeming coldness were now mentioned. Of course Church had been making enemies with his efforts to establish much more efficient army hospitals and do away with the old regimental doctoring. He was in the midst of winning this important battle when he took sick just before the charges against him erupted. Was it illness, or was it agony about the missing letter?

Since Church was a member of the Massachusetts Legislature, Washington sent the evidence to that body in Watertown.

A bar was placed in the center aisle of the old meetinghouse (now vanished) and here, with guards bringing him from Cambridge and guards at the several doors, Church appeared on Oct. 27 before his fellow members. He had been convicted by a Council of War "on a criminal correspondence with the enemy." The House members, "upon proof of the same," were being asked "to manifest their utter abhorrence."

The evidence was presented and Church, with one intermission for refreshments, spoke most of that Friday giving his explanations and answering questions. He employed flowery language, some hairsplitting and a letter from Fleming (which the doctor himself probably concocted) to explain his having used cipher and Newport to transmit his letter. Everything he had done, he protested, was for the public good.

Church later wrote his account of the inquiry and seemed to take satisfaction that he had been conducted the three miles from Cambridge to Watertown by a 20-man guard "with drum and fife," and that the "galleries were thronged with a numerous collection of people of all ranks."

He called his letter "an innocent piece of artifice to serve the common cause." The letter, never delivered, he argued, "never produced any ill consequences but to the guiltless, though unfortunate author." In sum, he asked:

"Why then, may it please your honor, shall unbounded credit be given that letter, which bears such glaring marks of fallacy and design, and couched in terms totally inconsonant with the conduct of my whole life; against the conviction arising from that conduct, against my solemn asseveration, and against sundry concurring circumstances, to prove that it was meant as a piece of political deceit to serve my country...."

Church's protestations did not convince his colleagues. They voted on Nov. 2, after a weekend of consideration, that he "did endeavor to carry on a secret correspondence with the enemy in Boston" in July, a practice "wicked and detestable," and that there were grounds for a "violent presumption that before that time he had secretly communicated intelligence to the said enemy." He was "expelled this House."

James Warren, who presided at the inquiry, emphasized evidence beyond the letters. He called it "collateral evidence ... such as his keeping the correspondence a secret to every one, instead of communicating it to the president or some of the members of the Congress, or to the general, if he intended it for the good of the public, especially," he added, "when the general in great confidence has solicited him to recommend to him some proper person in Boston from whom he might receive intelligence."

The absence of any drastic penalty for treason was discussed during the visit of the Franklin group and a death penalty, approved by Washington, was placed in the rules and regulations of the army.

This, however, was ex post facto law, and the Continental Congress simply ordered that Church be sent to some jail in Connecticut and be closely confined "without the use of pen, ink and paper." He was sent to Norwich.

Washington remarked: "So much for indiscretion, the doctor will say."

This charitable judgment has not been the one rendered by time. Time's judgment has been severe because time has uncovered total, incontrovertible proof that Church was involved in treason and that his glib defense was an interweaving of lies.

Indeed, Church's own handwriting has ultimately confirmed his conviction. An unsigned letter he wrote to Gage rested for more than a century and a half in the Gage papers, and first came to light early in this century when William L. Clements brought it from England to his library in Ann Arbor, Mich. In the letter the writer complains that he has been picked, "to my vexation," to go to Philadelphia on a mission for the Provincial Congress, a mission in part to get a Commander in Chief for the army. Church was the only man sent on that mission.

In the same handwriting is a letter tipping off Gage that the Americans were going to fortify Bunker Hill — this, from the very same man, Church, who signed his name to a report urging that the Americans fortify this very hill.

Church, pleading impaired health, was allowed to write to former friends and to Congress asking to be released. He finally was, on surety. James Warren soon wrote, "I fear the people will kill him if at large. The night before last he went to lodge at Waltham, was saved by the interposition of the selectmen but by jumping out of a chamber window and flying."

Church eventually obtained permission to leave his native land and go to Martinique. He embarked at Boston on a schooner that was overtaken by a gale and lost at sea.

Arnold's crippling battle with the wilderness

Washington, in his instructions to Arnold, emphasized above all:

"The winter season is now advancing and the success of this enterprise (under God) depends wholly upon the spirit with which it is pushed. . . ."

He asked that at every opportunity Arnold should keep him informed of his progress by express. Arnold's enthusiasm on leaving Fort Western must have delighted Washington, to whom Arnold wrote: "We shall be able to perform the march in 20 days; the distance is about 180 miles."

Yet in 20 days, in the struggle now to begin with the wilderness, Arnold would not even reach the disastrous north branch of the Dead River. Nor would this be even the halfway mark, for the distance ahead to Quebec was in actuality much closer to 300 miles. And it would always be much longer for most of the soldiers, for they would have to retrace the portages many times to move ahead all the supplies.

Eighteen miles above Fort Western, in a ruinous condition, was Fort Halifax (in present Winslow), a frontier outpost built at the same time as Fort Western. A neglected military road still ran to it along the east shore of the Kennebec. Part of Arnold's men, as throughout his advance, managed the boats while the rest marched on the shore. Local people, with oxen and horses, helped the soldiers with baggage as long as there were any habitations.

Fort Halifax, located strategically at a river junction, was of especial significance to Arnold's mission. Arnold's chief guide, actually, was the map that Lt. John Montresor, now chief engineer to Gen. Howe in Boston, had made back in 1761.

In scouting the Quebec routes, Montresor had come from Quebec by way of Moosehead Lake, one of the sources of the Kennebec River. He had come only as far as Fort Halifax and then gone back up the Kennebec to explore the other source of the Kennebec, the western branch now named the Dead River. This Dead River route Montresor called the "most eligible" to Quebec.

This was the route that Arnold was now attempting to follow precisely — and his Montresor map would, en route, prove an unintentional trap.

Portages heavily wearing on the soldiers started at once. Less than a mile above Fort Halifax were the ledges of Ticonic Falls. And there another difficulty, one that would be devastating to the expedition, began to show. Dr. Senter observed that several bateaux, having passed shoal water and plenty of rocks, "begun to leak profusely." The bateaux had been made hurriedly and of the only available material, green pine, and were so leak-prone that Senter had bought an old bateau of seasoned wood to convey his precious medical supplies.

The inexperience of the boatmen, jagged rock, riotous ripples and rips in the watercourse and whirlpools combined to take a steady toll of the bateaux — which began an inexorable reduction of the expedition's equipment and food. After passing the fearful, double falls at Skowhegan, many bateaux already needed recaulking, and losses in the rapids forced an overhauling at Norridgewock that cost Arnold a precious week's delay.

"By this time many of our bateaux were nothing but wrecks," Senter noted. Colburn's carpenters recaulked and repaired them as each division's boats put in.

Cargo had shipped water from the river and from the rains. Casks of peas had to be condemned. Salted cod had lost its preserving salt. Soaked bread — most vital — had soured and was tossed into the piles of discard. Pork had to be repacked.

Norridgewock was the actual frontier. Only two or three families lived there. After leaving Norridgewock the soldiers would see no one but members of the expedition until reaching the southernmost Canadian settlement at Sartigan, (now St. George's) 150 miles north of them on the turbulent, rock-strewn Chaudiere River.

Montresor in his journey covered this distance in just one week. That was by canoe in a salubrious mid-summer. For Arnold's men there would be ice and snow, mud and miles of misery. It would take him, perfervid as he was to carry out Washington's plan, three times as long as Montresor to cover the same distance to Sartigan.

Roughly 15 miles above the back-breaking portage of Norridgewock Falls came the 15-foot-high Carritunk Falls. It was here that the soldiers, strung along the river, now started up into more rugged country. "Mountains," said Arnold, "began to appear on each side the river, high, and snow on the tops." The Kennebec became more shallow, swift and hard for the boatmen. The weather grew colder.

About a dozen miles below where the Dead River enters the Kennebec was the Great Carrying Place used by Montresor and Arnold's men. It was roughly a 10-mile route west to an upper part of the Dead River and thus bypassed the virtually impassable lower portion of the Dead River. It had three helpful ponds.

Arnold reached the Great Carrying Place on Wednesday, Oct. 11. The forward divisions had already reached there two days earlier and all the men kept moving steadily across despite swampy ground, snow squalls and high winds that toppled trees and killed a soldier. The route had been blazed by Morgan's men and they were taking time to improve it.

With Morgan's men were the wives of two riflemen. These intrepid, devoted women — Mrs. Joseph Grier, wife of a sergeant, and Jemima Warner, wife of Pvt. James Warner who would die from exhaustion — would share all the hazards and reach Quebec but lose their lives during the siege of that citadel.

Arnold's manifold duties detained him five days in getting across the Great Carrying Place.

Lt. Steele and part of the scouting party Arnold had dispatched from Fort Western met him. Lt. Steele, who had sped back when his men were delayed by accidents to their canoes, reported that the Dead River was deep and good most of the way. Steele was sent forward again with 20 axemen to survey and clear the portages to Lake Megantic, and for Steele to check as far as Sartigan and report again at Lake Megantic.

For emergency use in case of retreat, Arnold ordered a log house built at the first portage and sent word to the commissary to bring up provisions. At the second portage Arnold built a log hospital to care for the victims of fatigue and exposure. "A formidable number," said Senter, were already ill from dysentery, some from rheumatic attack and pneumonia. The hospital, said Senter, was "no sooner finished than filled."

On Oct. 13, a Friday, Arnold sent off, by Eneas and another Indian, two letters that would have a fateful effect upon the expedition. One was to friends of Arnold in Quebec, seeking information, and the other was to be expressed by them to Gen. Schuyler, telling of Arnold's hope to meet in Quebec "in a fortnight." The letters would be intercepted and deprive the expedition of surprising Quebec.

Arnold this same day sent word of his progress to Washington. "We have had a very fatiguing time," Arnold told his anxious Commander in Chief, spoke of the men being "in high spirits" and added a telltale postscript about their struggle with the cumbersome bateaux, each weighing about 400 pounds:

"Your Excellency may possibly think we have been tardy in our march as we have gained so little; but when you consider the badness and weight of the bateaux and the large quantity of provisions, etc., we have been obliged to force up against a very rapid stream, where you would have taken the men for amphibious animals, as they were great part of the time under water; add to this the great fatigue in portage, you will think I have pushed the men as fast as could possibly have been."

Arnold told Washington he was now reduced to 950 effective men and about 25 days' provisions.

Food, of course, was crucial. Lt. Steele reported seeing plenty of game (he brought down some moose), but game would flee on the approach of so many men. Arnold told of men catching "a prodigious number of fine salmon trout" in the ponds. Still, food had already become of concern because Arnold fixed a regular daily ration — a pint of flour, three-quarters of a pound of pork—before leaving the Great Carrying Place.

The very next day lack of food produced a sad tale when the remnant of Lt. Steele's first scouting party — missed by those sent to its rescue — stumbled into the last part of the Great Carrying Place before the Dead River. John Joseph Henry, Pennsylvania rifleman soon to reach his 17th birthday, recounted their agony.

Arnold's adjutant, Maj. Christian Febiger of Newbury, Mass., was busy there with Capt. Dan Morgan's men. Febiger, 29, was one of two heroes of the battle of Bunker Hill with the Arnold expedition. The other was Capt. Henry Dearborn, 24, of Hampton, N.H. Rifleman Henry, his companions with "wan and haggard faces and meager bodies," reached Febiger's campfire and told a story that brought tears "to this brave soldier's eye."

Henry remembered for life how Febiger "handed me his wooden canteen which contained the last spirits in the army" and revived him and his "ghastly" companions with pork and dumplings from his kettle.

There was stern news indeed for Arnold when he soon arrived at the tentground of Lt. Col. Greene. This was past the Dead River hunting lodge of Chief Natanis, who had fled when he saw the first smoke from the soldiers' campfires, and opposite a snow-covered mountain that dominates the entire area, Mt. Bigelow, named later for Greene's Maj. Timothy Bigelow of Worcester, Mass.

Arnold discovered that a great part of Greene's bread had been found damaged and that Greene's division was "very short of provisions." Rations had been suddenly ordered cut in half. Arnold promptly sent Maj. Bigelow and about 100 men back to Col. Enos with orders to give them "as much provisions as you can spare . . . in particular of flour." Four days later Bigelow would return with a mere two barrels of flour!

Maj. Meigs, on Oct. 18, had his men kill for food his last two oxen "which we had drove with great difficulty to this place." This was on the Dead River near Greene's camp. This last fresh meat was shared with all the divisions.

A more immediate crisis was now shaping.

Arnold's journal shows how it came:

Oct. 19—"Small rains the whole of this day. N. B. rained very hard all night."

Oct. 20—"Continues rainy the whole of this day."

Oct. 21—"Prodigious fall of rain for two days past—has raised the river upwards of three feet."

"The wind," said Senter, "increased to an almost hurricane the latter part of this day. The trees tumbling on all quarters that rendered our passage not only exceedingly difficult, but very dangerous." Despite the awesome crash of trees and onrushing debris, Morgan's men and Meigs's men moved onward from the Dead River and up the rockier, narrower, more precipitous north branch.

Arnold, the men in his party "very wet and much fatigued," retook the lead and encamped on a steep bank a mile above Morgan's men — about two miles above present Eustis. They had paddled for hours and the rain had been incessant. It was near 11 o'clock before they could dry their clothes by the campfire and wrap themselves in blankets. Arnold's journal continues:

"Slept very comfortably until 4 o'clock in the morning, when we were awakened by the freshet which came rushing on us like a torrent, having rose eight feet perpendicular in nine hours and, before we could remove, wet all our baggage . . . .Very luckily we had a small hill to retreat to, where we conveyed our baggage and passed the remainder of the night in no very agreeable situation."

Downriver, the riflemen "fled to high ground."

Senter, at the Greene campsite, figured a 10-foot rise in the water there made "marching by land of the utmost difficulty, as the river was no longer confined to her banks, but extended in many low, flat places, a mile or more each way upon the upland."

Pvt. Ephraim Squier, way back with the Enos camp, found "the water next morning four feet deep where we made our fire; the river raised, we judge, 12 feet."

Capt. Simeon Thayer of Mendon, Mass., an old Rogers ranger, and eight of his men from the Greene camp, lost their way in the flood and were "wading through water . . . without victuals or drink until the next morning about 9 o'clock."

To Arnold, the prospect was "very dis-agreeable:

"The country round entirely overflowed, so that the course of the river being crooked, could not be discovered, which with the rapidity of the current renders it almost impossible for the bateaux to ascend the river, or the men to find their way . . . .

"Add to this our provisions almost exhausted, and the incessant rains for three days have prevented our gaining anything considerable, so that we have but a melancholy prospect before us, but in general in high spirits."

Arnold and his men, among them constantly his friend and secretary Capt. Eleazer Oswald, who had been with him at the taking of Fort Ticonderoga, had to spend the day on the bank drying out their baggage. Bateaux had been lost. Barrels of pork, and even powder, had been carried away, but the men still moved ahead, at times grasping bushes on the riverside to advance against the current. Some got lost in tributaries.

Presently, after sending rescue groups the next day, Arnold reached some rapids (Upper Shadagee Falls) where he suffered the "misfortune of oversetting seven bateaux and losing all the provisions."

On a bank nearby Arnold summoned "such officers as were present" — those mainly of the Morgan's and Meigs's divisions — and held a Council of War.

Capt. Oliver Hanchet, 34, of Suffield, Conn., from Meigs's division, was chosen with 50 picked men, each given 10 days' full rations, to push ahead as fast as possible to Sartigan, close to 100 miles away, to send on provisions. Twenty-six sick soldiers were sent back, and instructions were expressed to both Greene and Enos to send back their sick and feeble and hurry on "fast as possible" with the best men they could furnish, with 15 days' provisions.

Arnold's party now strove to reach the van of his men. Next day the rain resumed near nightfall and "continued raining and snowing all night." In the morning the men faced a two-to-six-inch accumulation. Next day "it snowed and blowed very hard." Arnold was crossing a series of lakes, now called the Chain of Ponds, with the storm so bad it obscured the encircling mountains. Beyond the lakes was the "Height of Land," the present U.S.-Canadian border.

That stormy Oct. 25 was an ominous day for the fate of the expedition.

Greene's men had arrived near the snow-covered site of Arnold's Council of War. Food was so scarce, Senter said, that some were "almost destitute of any eatable whatever except a few candles." Greene himself went on in advance that morning in an effort to let Arnold know their plight. But Arnold was too far ahead, and Greene returned and found Enos and his officers had arrived to request a conference.

It was about noon. Enos presided. The question was whether these divisions should go ahead or, because of the scarcity of food, return to Cambridge. Before them were Arnold's messages to send back the sick and feeble and join him with "all possible expedition." Five of Enos's officers voted to return. Greene and his officers, five in all, voted, as Senter put it, "to go through or die."

Enos cast the deciding vote. It was to continue, but immediately Enos's officers held their own huddle and declared that they were going back anyway to Cambridge. Whereupon, Enos said he would go back with them to stay with the three companies of his men.

Greene's officers wrenched an agreement from Enos's officers to share some of their provisions. Capt. Thayer and a volunteer got a boat and went rapidly downriver with the current, but on reaching Enos's men were refused food. "We were utterly deceived," said Thayer. Entreaties finally brought a pittance — two barrels of flour from Capt. Thomas Williams.

Williams, said Thayer, stepped forward, wished him success but looked upon him as doomed. "He never expected to see . . . any of us," said Thayer. Enos pleaded that his men were beyond his control and, said Thayer, Enos "took, as he then supposed and absolutely thought, his last farewell of me."

Major Bigelow wrote to his wife Anna of the plight of his men 100 miles from either American or French habitations, and with food vanishing:

"If the French are our enemies, it will go

hard with us, for we have no retreat left. In that case, there will be no other alternative between the sword and famine."

Greene's men had kept moving faithfully forward during the conferences. They went on though Thayer said there was "only a half-pint of flour per man left," and Senter said "many now were entirely destitute of any sustenance." Forty-eight who were sick, many "excessively exhausted with the diarrhea," were sent back.

"Our men, " said Capt. Dearborn on learning of Enos's departure, "made a general prayer that Col. Enos and all his men might die by the way, or meet with some disaster."

At the time Enos left, Arnold and the remaining soldiers were approaching a still greater crisis of his march — the potential extinction of most of the men — just over the Height of Land.

The Height of Land marks the watershed. All the way from Popham Beach the soldiers had been struggling against the oncoming water flowing from the Height of Land toward the Atlantic. Once they crossed the Height of Land the water all flows downward and eventually reaches the St. Lawrence River.

Beyond the Height of Land was the river Montresor used to reach Lake Megantic. He called it Megantic River, the present Arnold River. Just before the main channel of this river reaches Lake Megantic it takes a sharp turn to the right, and, after a short run, turns sharply to the left into Lake Megantic. Montresor, and Arnold after him, did not follow the main channel when it makes the turns, but went straight ahead into Lake Megantic by a stream called the Black Arnold.

This delta could be a trap. Montresor passed down this river at night and failed to see — or put on his map — the delta outlets, Spider Lake or smaller Rush Lake, both connected by delta rivers, and in turn with Lake Megantic. Swampland, with decaying trees, covered much of the borders of these two lakes and the delta. Anyone marching down Arnold River, and crossing its bend to reach Lake Megantic, would find himself trapped by the swamp.

Arnold and Hanchet's advance party crossed the Height of Land about the same time. Arnold talked with Hanchet about the route and sent word back to Cols. Greene and Enos that carrying places intervening lake to lake were "so many and difficult that I think the whole will get forward much sooner by leaving all the bateaux." Arnold then went downriver to Lake Megantic while Hanchet marched along the river.

Arnold, in a bark wigwam he found on Lake Megantic shore, stopped to await Hanchet. Arnold had with him 15 men and four bateaux ready for his dash to Sartigan. Near sunset he discovered Hanchet's men were in a trap on the low marshy ground and had waded "two miles through water to their waists." He sent his bateaux to rescue them.

To protect the 600 men then moving toward the Arnold River, Arnold sent back a guide and added a postscript on a letter "to all field officers and captains" in which he joyfully told them he had heard from his scouts that the French inhabitants would welcome them and furnish food and that "Quebec may be easily taken." The postscript ominously warned:

"By no means keep the brook (Arnold River), which will carry you into a swamp, out of which it will be impossible for you to get." Instead, he told them to strike off for the highland to the right.

By the same express Arnold made a report to Washington. In it he remarked:

"I have been much deceived in every account of our route, which is longer and has been attended with a thousand difficulties I never apprehended."

All 10 of Arnold's remaining companies had been assembled in what Arnold, copying Montresor, called the "Beautiful Meadow," close to the Arnold River. On Arnold's orders they divided their remaining, pitifully meager provisions. Half of the men, though, resumed advancing and failed to receive Arnold's warning.

Capt. Morgan's men, who had been resentful at Morgan's command that they carry all their seven bateaux over the Height of Land, went off by boat. It was a heartache to see the men carry those boats, said Rifleman Henry, with "the flesh worn from their shoulders, even to the bone." A reward was at hand and they now slipped by the trap, unaware of their fellow soldiers' peril.

The four companies that set out along with them marched into the trap on nearing Lake Megantic. These were Capt. Smith's riflemen and three companies of Maj. Meigs. Capt. Dearborn, who had picked up a canoe, came upon and rescued Capt. Goodrich "almost perished with the cold, having waded several miles backwards, and forwards, sometimes to his armpits in water and ice, endeavoring to find some place to cross this river."

Darkness descended and it was not until next morning that they got to ferrying their men to safety.

James Melvin of Hubbardston, Mass., a man who had responded to the Lexington-Concord Alarm, told of the men wandering that night on "ground giving way under us at every step," how they came upon a little knoll, waded back into the water to chop decayed trees, "made a fire to dry themselves, being almost perished ... laid ourselves down to sleep, 'round the fire, the water surrounding us close to our heads."

The men of these companies did reach firm, though snow-covered, land and continue up the east shore of Lake Megantic. Henry and his group, prior to that, saw the two brave wives as they approached a marsh "covered by a coat of ice half an inch thick." The men broke this with their guns and feet and were "soon waist deep in mud and water."

Mrs. Warner, finding her husband missing, went back to help him. Mrs. Grier's husband, with three other men, was away in the only bateau of Capt. Hendricks, trying to bring to safety the company's stricken lieutenant, an officer so popular with the men that they carried him in a litter over the Height of Land. Despite this devotion, Lt. McCleland would die of pneumonia on reaching Sartigan.

Henry, after sinking at one point to his armpits in frigid water, was humbled and astonished by the exertions of Mrs. Grier, "a large, virtuous woman," just ahead of him. "Her clothes more than waist high," said Henry, "she waded before me to firm ground."

The other five companies followed Arnold's advice and took to high ground after leaving the Beautiful Meadow. Their guide sent by Arnold soon proved to be as lost as any of the soldiers. They would be three days wandering, frozen and starving, in the bogs about Rush Pond, along the river connecting with Spider Lake, skirting the bogs of this irregular lake, fording the four-feet-deep, ice-fringed Spider River, then skirting the northern shore of Spider lake — with despair ever mounting.

Twenty-two-year-old Abner Stocking, marching with Maj. Meigs, soon found himself in an "ocean of swamp ... covered with a soft moss, filled with water and ice. After walking a few hours in the swamp we seemed to have lost all sense of feeling in our feet and ankles."

Rifleman George Morison, of Capt. Hendricks's company, whose comrades had improvidently eaten up their allowance when they heard Arnold's good news back at Beautiful Meadow, lamented: "How happy would we have been to have had no other dangers to face but the enemy" and described some miserable moments at his campsite:

"Never perhaps was there a more forlorn set of human beings collected together in one place ... every one of us shivering from head to foot, as hungry as wolves, and nothing to eat save the little flour we had left...."

Dr. Senter said of the three days:

"We wandered through hideous swamps and mountainous precipices with the conjoint addition of cold, wet and hunger, not to mention our fatigue — with the terrible apprehension of famishing in this desert. The pretended pilot was no less frightened than many of the rest .... We proceeded with as little knowledge of where we were, or where we should get to, as if we had been in the unknown interior of Africa or the deserts of Arabia."

Montresor's map, ironically, also contained a way out of their desperate predicament. Col. Greene and Senter had both map and compass. By persisting in keeping a WNW course, despite their uncertainty all the way, they could come upon Lake Megantic. They did, after first encountering the confirming footprints in the snow of the earlier companies moving north.

"Our arrival here," said Senter, "was succeeded with three huzzas."

Said Rifleman Morison: "In the midst of those hideous and lonesome depths of the world the sight of human footsteps revived our fallen spirits."

By the next day all the soldiers were moving along the shore of Lake Megantic to march to the Chaudiere River. Death by starvation now became a greater menace than the forest. It was Oct. 31. "This day," said Morison, "the whole army as far as I could learn, ran out of provisions entirely." That very morning Arnold, who had reached Sartigan late the night before, had started off cattle, food and rescuers. But Sartigan was some 45 exhausting miles down the Chaudiere.

Arnold told Washington this pathway river to Quebec was "amazingly rapid and rocky." He had entered it Oct. 28 with his birch canoe and four bateaux, the baggage all lashed. The craft were carried headlong by the swift current. Within 15 miles they found themselves in rapids and suddenly, as Arnold recounted:

"We had the misfortune to overset and stave three boats ... lost all the baggage, arms, and provision of four men, and stove two of the boats to pieces against the rocks ... but happily no lives were lost although six men were a long time swimming in the water and were with difficulty saved."

Daredevil, determined Arnold, as soon as the men were dry, ventured out again on the terrifying river. Within minutes men forward yelled, "A fall ahead!" It was unknown to Arnold and his men, who had no guide. "Had we been carried over," noted Arnold, "we must inevitably been dashed to pieces and all lost."

He still did not give up. Soon the canoe was bashed. He simply split the meager food remaining, took again to the river, portaged its frequent rapids, rocks and plunging cataracts, and reached Sartigan.

The end of October and beginning of November brought appalling hours to the soldiers struggling down the Chaudiere. The rapids that first wrecked Arnold's boats smashed all seven of Capt. Morgan's bateaux, drowned one rifleman, claimed all the company baggage and ammunition. Capt. Dearborn passing the rapids counted 10 wrecked bateaux. The rapids ruined Dr. Senter's medicines, save what he had in his knapsack, destroyed Capt. Goodrich's supplies and forced the dying Lt. McCleland to be borne ashore.

The pathetic death of Pvt. Warner came as rescue was on its way. The rifleman, "exhausted with fatigue and hunger fell a victim to the king of terrors. His affectionate wife tarried by him until he died. Having no implements with which she could bury him she covered him with leaves, and then took his gun ... and came up with us," said Abner Stocking.

The men, said Dr. Senter, felt now it was the "zenith of distress. Several had been entirely destitute of either meat or bread for many days."

A dog, said Pvt. Melvin, was killed by the company of 19-year-old Capt. Samuel Ward, son of a former Rhode Island governor. Next day, said Capt. Dearborn: "Capt. Goodrich's company killed my dog and another dog and ate them." They ate "even the feet and skins," said Col. Meigs.

"Nor," said Dr. Senter, "did the shaving soap, pomatum, and even the lip salve, leather of their shoes, cartridge boxes, etc., share any better fate."

Jubilation welled up when the soldiers caught sight of the cattle and other food sent by Arnold.

Joseph Ware of Needham, Mass., exulted:

"It was the joyfullest sight that ever I beheld.... Some could not refrain from crying with joy."

Soldiers would be coming in for a few days. Rescue parties on horseback from Sartigan would help many of the helpless from deep in the forest. Some would become sick and some would die from suddenly gorging themselves. But the ordeal in the wilderness was over.

Arnold knew though, it was not the wilderness he had come to conquer. He concluded Eneas had betrayed him and that the secret of his expedition was known in Quebec. He was keenly aware that his losses in manpower and fire power might make taking Quebec impractical without help from Gen. Schuyler's army. But he wrote Washington he would still try as soon as possible to bring Quebec "to terms."

Washington sends Knox for cannon

"As you have mentioned nothing in your letters of the cannon, etc., to be had from New York, Ticonderoga, etc., I have, in order to reduce the matter to a certainty, employed Mr. Knox to go to those places, complete our wants, and to provide such military stores as St. John's can spare."

Washington wrote this late in November in a letter, a generally gloomy one, to his closest confidant, his former secretary Joseph Reed, who was then back in Philadelphia.

Additional problems had been added to a "burthen," said Washington, which was already "too great for me to stand under with the smallest degree of comfort to my own feelings." The men of his fleet were troubling him — "our rascally privateersmen . . . mutinying if they cannot do as they please." He feared Arnold's expedition was "in a bad way" because of the defection, he sarcastically remarked, of the "noble Col. Enos." And provincial and private jealousies were plaguing his efforts to form a new officer corps.

About the only cheerful portion of the letter was about his wife, Martha, who would soon be passing through Philadelphia en route to Cambridge. She and her son, Jacky Custis, "were perfect strangers to the road, the stages, and the proper place to cross Hudson River." Reed, he hoped, would advise them.

Actually, there was a tinge of cheer in the words about Knox. His mission could help solve a deep-seated problem of the siege. Washington had become convinced that a "scoundrel" had informed Gen. Howe about the weaknesses of the Cambridge camp and that Howe was waiting for a favorable moment "to aim a capital blow."

Early in November, Gen. Clinton had made a raid across the harbor upon Lechmere's Point. Washington came to feel this was a prelude to more action by Howe. Washington personally went along the shore, selected more places to be fortified, planned strong fortifications for Lechmere's Point, and decided to seize and fortify Cobble HIll, which was much closer to Boston than Prospect Hill. All this would require cannon,

and, of course, gunpowder, which, as Washington reminded Reed, "is also so much wanted."

Henry Knox, 25, was a convivial 250-pound, quick-thinking, dedicated man who would become a key general for Washington and one day be his Secretary of War.

At the moment, Knox was a civilian whose engineering abilities had already attracted Washington's attention and made Knox and his wife, Lucy, welcome dining guests at Vassall House. Lucy, big and convivial too, a bride of a year, was the daughter of a leading royal official of the colony, currently among the besieged Tories in Boston.

Military engineers — who, in Revolutionary days, had to have skill both in gunnery and fortification — were woefully scarce in the American camp. Among Washington's innumerable difficulties was finding someone qualified to replace the aging, heroic Col. Gridley as commanding officer of more than 600 men who comprised Washington's artillery regiment, men mostly inexperienced from lack of cannon and gunpowder.

Gridley obtained his own experience in the prior wars. Knox's experience came from books and, curiously, from British officers.

Knox was a poor boy born on Boston's South End waterfront. He was one of 10 sons and when out of grammar school was apprenticed to a bookseller. When he was 21 he got his own shop, first located in old Pi Alley, then opposite it on Boston's old Newspaper Row. This was the London Book Shop.

He was an early Son of Liberty and a military enthusiast. He picked up gunnery and fortification from reading books he had obtained from London for British officers. A gunnery accident down the harbor cost the eager student two fingers of his left hand. British officers advised him in helping to form his Boston Grenadier corps.

Knox's "pleasing manners" and military knowledge impressed a young lawyer, John Adams, whose office was diagonally across the street. A young Rhode Island blacksmith with a limp, Nathaniel Greene, who would become Washington's foremost general, shared Knox's military interest and books. Paul Revere was a close friend.

So, too, were Tories of the colony for whom Knox obtained expensive books from England — Lt. Gov. Andrew Oliver, Councilor Ruggles of Hardwick and Secretary of the Colony Thomas Flucker. Lucy Flucker came to the shop and fell in love. Her father was sternly opposed to any marriage, but the lovers did marry and Lucy at least kept the affection of her brother, who sent his congratulations from Antigua along with "love to Mr. Knox."

On the outbreak of war, Knox abandoned his shop (which was wrecked during the siege, putting him in debt for years) and took his bride to Worcester. She, to hoodwink Gage's soldiers, quilted Henry's sword into her cloak to get it out of Boston. He returned and helped officers of the American army fortify heights around Boston. Most admired — Samuel Adams called it "celebrated" — was the high fort Knox helped to build on Roxbury's old Fort Hill.

A few days after Washington arrived in Cambridge he encountered Knox as he was making his first inspection. Knox was able to write on July 6 to Lucy how the day before Washington had "begged me to return to Roxbury again, which I did." Washington and Gen. Lee viewed the fort, "expressed the greatest pleasure and surprise," and Knox's plan "did not escape their praise."

Washington recommended Knox to Congress to succeed Gridley, as one whose choice would give "general satisfaction." This was Nov. 8. John Adams, to whom Knox wrote because of his desire to be a colonel "to free my country," helped. So did other admirers.

Meantime there was discussion at Cambridge headquarters about Washington's need for cannon. Into the talk came a revival of Arnold's proposal back in April to bring to Cambridge the cannon at Fort Ticonderoga. Washington, thrilled with the idea, would go much farther. The outer forts on the Richelieu River protecting Montreal were at the moment under American attack by Brig. Gen. Richard Montgomery, field commander for Schuyler. Fort Chambly had fallen. St. John's was under siege.

In the orders Washington gave to Knox on Nov. 16, he was instructed to check all artillery needs at the Cambridge camp, go in the "most expeditious manner to New York," and then:

"After you have procured as many of these necessaries as you can there, you must go to Maj. Gen. Schuyler and get the remainder from Ticonderoga, Crown Point, or St. John's; if it should be necessary, from Quebec, if in our hands.

"The want of them is so great, that no trouble or expense must be spared to obtain them." To which Washington hopefully added: "Endeavor to procure what flints you can."

Knox took with him his 19-year-old brother William, for whom he was seeking a commission in the artillery, and a servant and sped off to New York after making his survey in the Cambridge camp. On the way he paused at Worcester to reassure Lucy, now many months pregnant with their first child, that he would be back soon. He reached New York on Nov. 25.

Knox promptly started arranging for available cannon, though of small calibre and not the heavy cannon Washington desired, to be sent to Cambridge. Knox had hardly begun when an officer from Gen. Montgomery passed through New York on his way to the Continental Congress with the glorious news that Montreal had surrendered on Nov. 13 — just 10 days after the capitulation of St. John's. Knox relayed all the detail he could gather to Washington with a report that Arnold was advancing toward Quebec.

"In all probability," Knox added with delight, "our people are now in possession of all Canada." If so, this would leave the British with only a single continental toehold in all the American colonies — the one they were defending in besieged Boston.

Knox, early the next morning, sped off on horseback from New York to meet Schuyler. He moved with utmost expedition, he told Washington, "knowing our whole dependence for heavy cannon" was at Fort Ticonderoga. Schuyler and Knox were soon talking at the general's Albany mansion about transporting the cannon — fully 60 tons of metal alone.

Knox pushed on to Fort George, at the head

of 33-mile-long Lake George, and got there on Dec. 4. Next day his departure was delayed a couple of hours when Schuyler arrived and gave him a list of stores at Fort Ticonderoga.

The prior night Knox had got little sleep. Quarters assigned him on arrival at Fort George had been a one-room log cabin with two beds. The other bed had been assigned to a young British officer of Knox's age who had been captured at St. John's and was now on his way, on parole, to Pennsylvania for a prisoner exchange. The personable young officer was Lt. John Andre.

Five years in the future Knox would sit at Andre's court-martial, for Andre's part in the amazing treason of Arnold, and would have the painful duty of voting to hang Andre.

This night in the log cabin, though, the two young men had things of compelling interest to discuss. Andre, handling dwindling provisions, had been a key soldier in the heroic 55-day ordeal of the British garrison. Its admirable commander, Maj. Charles Preston, refused to surrender to Montgomery despite unbearable crowding, lack of food (they were down to salt pork and roots, and little of those), and ruinous cannon fire.

Finally, when all hope of aid from Carleton, who was about to surrender Montreal, disappeared, Preston sent Andre to negotiate terms with Montgomery. The delay of Montgomery's advance at St. John's would, like the loss of time to Arnold in the wilderness, eventually make it possible for Carleton to hold out at Quebec. But Montgomery had so admired the courage of Preston, Andre and the besieged soldiers that he allowed the British officers to retain their swords.

Fort Ticonderoga stood on Lake Champlain, three miles farther north than the foot of Lake George. Before sailing northward down the lake, Knox wrote to Washington that the weak garrison at Fort Ticonderoga and precarious passage on Lake George made him fear that it would take him 10 days to get everything south as far as Fort George. So it turned out.

Knox also told Washington that, for conveying his cannon southward from Fort George, everything depended on snow and sledding. "With-out good sledding," Knox wrote, "the roads are so much gullied it will be impossible to move a step."

Knox spent four days at Fort Ticonderoga getting his selection — 59 cannon, mortars, cohorns (small mortars) and howitzers, 23 boxes of lead. There were only two barrels of flints and no gunpowder. All was lugged up the difficult bridge of land to Lake George and stowed by the soldiers and teamsters on three shallow-draught, sailing craft — "scow, pettianger and battoe," Knox styled them — to head up the lake to Fort George.

"Exceedingly disagreeable" was the way Knox described the passage back. The weather was freezing. The men would put ashore to make fires and warm themselves. The winds were contrary. They had to row for hours "exceedingly hard," said Knox. The scow grounded on a rock and then actually sank off Sabbath Day Point. Worried Knox, who had pushed ahead to the fort on the bateau, sent an express boat back to check.

"Our scow sunk," William reported, "but luckily so near the shore that when she sank her gunnel was above water, so ... we were able to bail her out and tow her to the leeward shore of the point where we took out three mortars, and by hauling the cannon aft balanced her, and now she stands ready to sail the first fair wind." The pettianger, William added, went "as far as she could get for the ice, for it is frozen a mile which they will have to cut through...."

Knox put in long hours at Fort George on arrangements. Some three days before the cannon arrived he sent an express to Squire Palmer of Stillwater, to whom he had sent prior instructions, asking him to:

"Purchase or get made immediately 40 good strong sleds that will each be able to carry a long cannon clear from dragging on the ground and which will weigh 3400 pounds each, and likewise that you would procure oxen or horses as you shall judge most proper to drag them ...." Knox looked to other details, even to getting "500 fathom three-inch rope to fasten the cannon on the sleds."

At Fort Ticonderoga he had been surprised to find some 13-inch mortars and wrote to New

York asking that shells for them be forwarded to Cambridge. He prepared instructions for putting the cannon on sleds. "Let the touch-holes and vents of all the mortars and cannon be turned downwards." A span of horses was to pull 1000 pounds; "four span for those of 5000 weight"; the sleds to move in groups.

In a progress report to Washington on Dec. 17 on the cannon Knox wrote:

"It is not easy to conceive the difficulties we have had in getting them over the lake owing to the advanced season of the year and contrary winds, but the danger is now past .... Three days ago it was very uncertain whether we could have gotten them until spring but now please God they must go ...."

"The sledding is tolerable to Saratoga about 26 miles; beyond that there is none." Knox hoped there would be a fine fall of snow to "make the carriage easy." If so, "I hope in 16 or 17 days time to be able to present Your Excellency a noble train of artillery." This was optimistic. It would take him twice that long.

In his exuberance, Knox wrote to Lucy — "my dearest companion" — that he hoped to be home in three weeks. He said he and brother William, who "has been of the utmost service to me," were well. He painted a glorious picture for her:

"We shall cut no small figure going through the country with our cannon mortars and drawn by 80 yoke of oxen."

It seemed magnificent. But the very next day Schuyler, top general and aristocrat of upper New York, sent word to Knox to countermand his construction orders to Squire Palmer. The county, said Schuyler, a man as economical as Washington with public funds, had a "sufficiency of carriage suitable" to carry 10 times Knox's load.

Knox soon got the snow he prayed for.

He headed southward for Albany to confer with Schuyler. The snow started Christmas Eve. By nightfall it was so heavy his horses could not pull his borrowed sleigh but a few miles below Saratoga. Next day he started in two feet of snow, had to shift to horseback, borrowed another sleigh at Stillwater but could get only a few miles.

The third day of the storm he set out, but after two miles "our horses tired and refused to go any farther." He had to "march in snow three feet deep through the woods, there being no beaten path." He borrowed another sleigh and got to Albany "almost perished with the cold." He waited on Schuyler and spent the evening with him.

Squire Palmer was sent for next day. Schuyler did not like the prices the squire was asking to provide some more yoke of oxen, and he was dismissed. Knox consoled himself in his diary with the entry: "By reports from all parts the snow is too deep for the cannon to set out, even if the sleds were ready." Schuyler's wagon master was told to put out a call for sleighs with horses.

On the last day of the year the wagon master handed Knox a list of persons who with "near 124 pairs with sleighs" had gone up to the lake with their horses. Knox was afraid some of the sleighs might not be "strong enough for the heavy cannon."

The New Year brought a change in weather.

Knox wrote about it to Washington on Jan. 5. "I was in hopes," he said, "that we should have been able to have had the cannon at Cambridge by this time. The want of snow detained us some days, and now a cruel thaw hinders from crossing Hudson River, which we are obliged to do four times from Lake George to this town."

For the first four days of the new year Knox had been "getting holes cut in the different crossing places in the river in order to strengthen the ice."

The express to Washington also carried a letter to Lucy. "The weather for three or four days has been intolerably warm considering my wishes — the thaw has been so that I've trembled for the consequences .... My brother is now at Lake George busily employed in loading the sleds as they come up."

Knox was "much alarmed ... just as I was going to sit down to dinner" when Schuyler came in and said one of the heaviest cannon had fallen into the river at Half Moon ferry at the northermost mouth of the Mohawk River. Knox headed northward at dusk in a sleigh, sending an express to another wagon master up the Mohawk not to cross until he came.

There had been no lack of precaution, as Knox had feared. Twelve-year-old John Becker had gone up to Fort George with his father, who was handling some of the wagons. The father's safety method was to string a rope between the wagon and the horses, walk with an axe, and, if anything happened to the wagon, cut the rope.

"In the center of the river," said young Becker, "the ice gave way, as had been feared, and a noble 18-pounder sank with a crackling noise, and then a heavy plunge to the bottom of the stream .... Just as the cracking of the ice gave the alarm, the horses were whipped up into a full jump, but to no purpose." But the water was not deep and the cannon was recovered.

When Knox found all was well there, and on the Mohawk, too, he went a bit farther up the Mohawk to gaze at a wonder of the country, 80-foot Cohoes Falls. He returned to Albany "not a little humbled by thoughts of my own insignificance."

The January thaw abruptly ended, but misfortune came again as the last of 11 sleds moved out of Albany across the newly frozen Hudson to the east side. It plunged through "and in its fall broke all the ice for 14 feet around it," said Knox. He tried rescue work that night, gave up until 8 o'clock next morning and succeeded with the help of folks from Albany. In their honor he named the cannon "The Albany."

The cannon column moved on the old New York Post Road through Kinderhook, turned eastward at Claverack and passed through old Nobletown, entering Massachusetts at present Egremont in the Berkshires.

The way over the mountains from Great Barrington to Blandford was called the Green Woods, of fearsome reputation. The original Indian trail had become the only passageway from Boston to Albany when Lord Jeffery Amherst made a military road 16 years earlier.

It was so bad in 1772 that Henry Hulton, a Boston commissioner of customs on a return trip from Quebec, went 40 miles out of his way, by Hartford, to avoid it. It was, he said, "rough, rocky, hilly, every way bad" with so many dangers from dead falling lofty pines that "one rides in terror."

As the teamsters labored toward Township No. 1, South Tyringham, Knox said they "climbed mountains from which we might almost have seen all the kingdoms of the earth."

In Blandford came the highest hills. "It appeared to me almost a miracle," Knox wrote in his diary, "that people with heavy loads should be able to get up and down such hills Here he caught up with his advance division. The men were refusing to continue because five or six miles farther there was no snow and a "tremendous ... mountain to go down." Knox said:

"After about three hours persuasion, I hiring two teams of oxen, they agreed to go."

Fearing the New York teamsters would want to return home on reaching Springfield, Knox decided to obtain teams of horses. Once over the mountains, he said, the horses "will be able to travel much faster than oxen." He would start trying at Westfield, for a long time the westernmost settlement of the province. The Westfield people gave Knox's teamsters so hearty a welcome that Knox, to the town's delight, fired a shot in gratitude from his largest mortar, "The Old Sow."

Knox was so keen for the New York teamsters to carry on to camp he offered them extra pay per day per span of horses. But thaw came again and the New York men left. By the time the roads were ready again Knox moved across the province via Worcester and Marlboro to the Framingham road, where, on Washington's orders, the cannon awaited his disposition.

Knox himself reached Cambridge camp on Jan. 18. He was no longer a civilian. The day after he had departed, Congress, approving Washington's recommendation, had made him a colonel. The desired commission naming Knox the head of the army's artillery awaited his arrival at Washington's office in Vassall House.

Montgomery killed; Arnold's men trapped

Arnold was well aware when he reached Sartigan at the end of October that 60 miles more of marching would bring his men to Point Levis on the St. Lawrence, and his next major difficulty would be to get across the broad, swift river to Quebec.

The intercepted letter of Oct. 13, carried by the Indians from way back on the Great Carrying Place, reached the hands of the Quebec authorities on Nov. 3. Lt. Gov. Hector Cramahe, in command in the absence of Gen. Carleton, who had gone up river to save Montreal, was thus alerted and took hurried defensive actions, among them his order that all "canoes, shallops and craft should be brought off from the opposite shore. . . ."

Arnold learned this when he was about halfway to Point Levis. Twenty canoes were purchased there, at St. Mary's, and Capt. Thayer tells of carrying them "thirty miles on our backs, four men under each canoe." Arnold had already acquired 20 other canoes at Sartigan, where, in one of the big surprises of the expedition, he was joined by Natanis, the Indian chief he had ordered to be shot.

Young John Henry well remembered it, for Natanis appeared on Henry's 17th birthday. Natanis, who had kept up with the expedition, walked out of the woods and shook hands with the scout, with Lt. Steele and with others "in the way of an old acquaintance." Henry said Natanis was asked: "Why did you not speak to your friends?"

"He readily answered and truly, 'You would have killed me.' "

Natanis had been secretly watching since the marchers had passed his hunting lodge on the Dead River. Pvt. Melvin said Natanis and his tribesmen had appeared at Sartigan "all finely ornamented in their way with brooches, bracelets and other trinkets, and their faces painted."

Forty of them, along with Natanis, who would be wounded at Quebec, joined the march. Few Indians, save for scouts and messengers, had entered the army up to this time. Indeed,

marching with Arnold was Capt. Goodrich, who had brought into the Cambridge camp the first Indian recruits, from Stockbridge, Mass.

Arnold, in his first view of the mighty St. Lawrence, could see that the mile across to Quebec, a stretch both tidal and deep though 400 miles from the sea, was patroled by the newly arrived 26-gun frigate *HMS Lizard,* the sloop-of-war *HMS Hunter* and their guard boats. On the cliff opposite stood the Upper Town protected by its virtually impregnable walls, the Lower Town a narrow, shelflike shore at the foot of the cliff with narrow streets, waterfront structures and warehouses.

A third British warship, the schooner *HMS Magdalen* with dispatches from London to Carleton, increased the patrol shortly after Arnold reached Point Levis. The skipper of *HMS Lizard,* zealous Capt. John Hamilton, would get Cramahe to call a Council of War, would himself take command of all the war vessels and shift their men and cannon to the ramparts of Quebec. What Arnold saw, though, did not daunt him.

Washington was keeping prayerful track of the expedition, at times confident Arnold would take both Carleton and Canada, at other times worried that Arnold was "in a bad way" because of Enos's "great defection." When he learned Arnold was at Point Levis he wrote to Schuyler of his "highest satisfaction" that Arnold got there after "almost insuperable difficulties."

To Arnold, Washington wrote:

"It is not in the power of any man to command success, but you have done more, you have deserved it."

Washington called Arnold's work "glorious," thanked him and his "brave followers." Enos, Washington told him, had on his return been arrested and court-martialed. Washington could not wait for Arnold's testimony because Enos's enlistment was expiring. He had been acquitted, said Washington, "on the score of provisions." Soon Enos, denied the regard of his fellow officers, resigned.

Arnold wrote Washington that he was planning to cross the river and expected "to be able to evade" the *Lizard* and *Hunter*. There had been a gale for some days and the wind was too high. Meanwhile, Arnold had his men prepare scaling ladders and spear points.

While Arnold waited, there arrived at Quebec Col. Allan Maclean, a greater enthusiast, if possible, than Capt. Hamilton.

Maclean and the Royal Highland Emigrant battalion of ex-soldiers he had raised had dashed toward Montreal in an effort to help Carleton. When Carleton's effort was collapsing, and Maclean learned by intercepted letter that Arnold was approaching Quebec, Maclean hurried back with his men to protect the town. Cramahe gladly gave Maclean the military command of the citadel.

Arnold's opportunity to cross came on the night, a dark one, of Nov. 13 — the day that far up the river Montreal was capitulating to Montgomery. The wind had moderated. Arnold wrote to Washington that he crossed the river "without

obstruction, except from a barge, into which we fired and killed three men." Arnold had been in the lead canoe passing a man-of-war. The shooting did not come until the warship's barge came by a second time and nosed into the landing place, historic Wolfe's Cove.

The canoes crossed several times. Still, some of the men had to be brought over on the following days.

Once over, Arnold gathered his ragged, haggard, almost powderless and cannonless band on the Plains of Abraham. He had taken as his headquarters the nearby mansion of Lt. Col. Henry Caldwell, head of Quebec's British militia, a mansion well posted. "We carried it sword in hand," said Capt. Morgan. Arnold soon stood about where Wolfe had stood.

"I am ordered by his Excellency George Washington," Arnold informed Cramahe, "to take possession of the town of Quebec. I do therefore, in the name of the United Colonies, demand immediate surrender of the town, fortifications, etc., of Quebec to the forces of the United Colonies under my command."

Arnold was, in effect, demanding about the last British soil in Canada. Capt. Thomas Ainslie of the British militia, collector of customs at Quebec port, said Arnold and his shabby soldiers in their surrender demand:

"Came within 800 yards of the walls of Quebec; they huzza'd thrice — we answered them with three cheers of defiance, and saluted them with a few cannon loaded with grape and cannister shot. They did not wait for a second round."

Col. Maclean was clearly actively in command.

On withdrawing, Arnold took stock. His men had full rations, thanks to the habitants nearby, but as a military force his men grievously showed the ravages of their passage through the wilderness — lack of clothing, hard cash, muskets, gunpowder. He sent an appeal to Montgomery to supply these wants. Writing of this situation to Washington, Arnold said his men were "almost naked" and:

"To my great surprise I found many of our cartridges unfit for use (which to appearance were very good) and that we had no more than

Gen. Guy Carleton

Public Archives of Canada,
Ottawa, Canada

five rounds to each man. It was judged prudent in our situation not to hazard a battle, but retire."

He withdrew about 20 miles upriver to an aspen-covered cape called Point aux Trembles (present Neuville) to await Montgomery. As the men approached this village, young Henry made note of "the rapid passage downstream of two boats." Presently the men could hear the reverberations of Capt. Hamilton's *HMS Lizard* firing a 13-gun salute at Quebec. It could only mean that the royal governor, Carleton, had been on one of those two boats and had arrived at his capital.

Carleton, an astute Commander in Chief, had not awaited the inevitable surrender of Montreal. He had loaded his few remaining men and vital supplies on 11 vessels and headed for Quebec. If he could hold Quebec, despite the fall of all the other places along the Richelieu and St. Lawrence, he might save Canada.

At Sorel, where the Richelieu River joins the St. Lawrence, Montgomery had sent a force to erect batteries and make the St. Lawrence there impassable. Carleton ordered the vital gunpowder dumped from the 11 vessels, which were forced to surrender, and he continued downstream in a whaleboat.

He shifted to a habitant's attire as disguise — and his men, their oarlocks muffled and paddling by hand when necessary, got by the American outposts. Soon Carleton met two boats, British vessels of war, and got to Quebec. Capt. Hamilton's 13-gun salute was answered by the town battery. The British were suffering no shortage of gunpowder in their Quebec fortress.

Arnold had time at Point aux Trembles to reflect on his men and their march. He wrote to Washington.

"Had I been 10 days sooner, Quebec must inevitably have fallen into our hands...." He was talking of the time before Maclean and Carleton reached Quebec. Yet, despite the critical delays, the march began to take on wonder. Leading patriots would liken it to the achievement of Xenophon and Hannibal. Arnold, listing for Schuyler the obstacles overcome, said:

"In about eight weeks we completed a march of near 600 miles, not to be paralleled in history."

Montgomery joined Arnold late on Dec. 2. He had marched downriver and brought supplies, including artillery, in the 11 vessels captured at Sorel. He did bring captured British uniforms sufficient to clothe Arnold's shivering men. But Montgomery had endured disastrous difficulties with his troops overextending enlistments and had been able to bring only 300 soldiers. Montgomery was a beloved and inspiring leader, and the Americans promptly headed for the Plains of Abraham to conquer Quebec.

Carleton could anticipate no outside help. He knew London could send no aid until spring. Howe, deferring to the fears of Adm. Graves that the season was too far advanced, had canceled orders to marines about to embark at Boston. At Montreal, Carleton's defense had suffered fatally from disunity. Now he would avoid that and delivered a master stroke in a proclamation he issued three days after his arrival.

"I do hereby strictly order and enjoin all and every person and persons whatsoever liable to serve in the militia, and residing in Quebec, who have refused to enroll their names in the militia lists and to take up arms ... to quit the town in four days ... under pain of being treated as rebels or spies."

Some left. This, Carleton said, was his aim, to rid Quebec of "all useless, disloyal and treacherous persons." Most of the 5000 still within Quebec gained an increased sense of unity and security.

Montgomery twice demanded that Carleton surrender. Carleton refused to read any surrender demand from a rebel. He would, he said, accept only an "appeal for the King's mercy." To reach the citizenry, Montgomery had Indians with bow and arrow shoot messages over the walls. Carleton conspicuously burned a surrender demand smuggled in by a woman, had her jailed and then drummed out.

Carleton, and Montgomery, too, had been at Quebec when it fell in 1759 to Wolfe. Carleton felt that Gen. Montcalm's mistake that then cost him Quebec was going outside the walls to fight Wolfe on the Plains of Abraham. Carleton was determined to stay within his well-stocked walls. Out of the 5000 population he had 1800 under arms. These defenders comprised mainly militiamen, a handful of regulars, a few merchant seamen and Capt. Hamilton's sailors.

Montgomery on his part had no cannon capable of breaching the walls. The ground was frozen, eliminating any digging or undermining. Montgomery had no choice but to assault Quebec.

Moreover, Montgomery had very little time. Enlistments would be expiring on Jan. 1. On Dec. 27, Montgomery organized an attack for that night but called it off at the last minute. The night had become too light. Confident his luck would hold, Montgomery promised he would soon lead his men "to an easy and glorious victory." He awaited a night that would be dark and stormy.

It came on the night of Dec. 30.

The snow started driving hard by nightfall, shifting to blizzard. Young Henry said, "The storm was outrageous and the cold extremely biting." Ainslie noted, "It snowed all night, it was very dark, the wind was strong at N.E."

That evening Montgomery sent orders to each division to assemble at 2 a.m. and commence the attack at 5 a.m. Rockets would give the signal. There would be a feint by Col. James Livingston and his Canadian volunteers on the Upper Town at St. John's Gate. Livingston had combustibles to set the gate on fire.

The real attack would be on the Lower Town. Montgomery would come with his companies along the river edge from the south and Arnold, also along the river edge, from the north with his three divisions and Capt. John Lamb's artillery company. The two forces would combine in Lower Town at the foot of the road that curves up the cliff to the Upper Town's center, the Place d'Armes.

The soldiers would wear a sprig of hemlock on their hats to distinguish their uniforms from the enemy's. Some would wear bits of paper with the motto: "Liberty or Death."

Carleton, apprised by an escaped prisoner, had been expecting an attack for days. He, his second in command, Col. Maclean, and his off-duty officers had been sleeping in his headquarters in the Recollect Monastery, just off the Place d'Armes.

Montgomery and his staff came as planned from his headquarters, Holland House on the border of the Plains of Abraham, crossed the plain, descended the cliff to the beach and went along the narrow snow-covered path between the cliff and the beach, fringed by the tide with large chunks of ice, toward Cap Diamant. Presently he came to the first of two barriers.

Carpenters, who accompanied him for this purpose, cut away pickets. Montgomery plodded in the snow the short distance to the second barrier, helped the carpenters by pulling away a picket and went through the opening. Fifty yards beyond, barely discernible in the driving snow, was a guardhouse. Montgomery called to his troops, still at a distance, to come on, and led the way.

This approach to the Lower Town was called Pres de Ville. In the guardhouse, a private structure almost blocking the path, were 50 defenders, local militia, seamen, a Royal Artillery sergeant with two 3-pounders managed by a merchantman, Capt. Barnsfare. On lookout was a volunteer, John Coffin, a Loyalist who had fled Boston in June with his wife and 12 children.

Coffin, detecting the oncomers, yelled, "Fire!"

The defenders opened with their muskets and Capt. Barnsfare touched off his cannon.

Montgomery, hit in the head, was killed instantly. So, too, was his aide-de-camp, Capt. John MacPherson. Capt. Jacob Cheeseman, with such a foreboding of death that he had dressed in his best and put gold coins in his pocket for a "decent burial," as he told his comrades, was hit in the body by canister. He still tried to push on, but fell back dead. Ten others were killed.

Montgomery's orderly sergeant, fatally wounded, was carried into the guardhouse but would reveal nothing before he died. Aaron Burr, who had been sent to join Montgomery a month ago, escaped injury. The command fell to Lt. Col. Donald Campbell, an ill-suited commissary officer. Campbell had been entering the second barrier as the fusillade struck. Unnerved, he ordered a retreat.

The death of Montgomery was a tragedy. He seemed invincible — this victor of Chambly, St. John's, Montreal, Sorel, Three Rivers. The colonies would mourn his sacrifice as they did Joseph Warren's and his enemies would bury him with honors. His loss stripped his force of leadership. Now all Carleton's force would be concentrated on Arnold and his men.

To the north of Quebec, in the suburb of St. Roch, Arnold had assembled his force at the agreed time near his headquarters and guardhouse.

All Arnold's men were present save Capt. Dearborn's company. They had recently been housed on the north side of the St. Charles River, which enters the St. Lawrence north of Quebec, in order to clear room they had used at Dr. Senter's hospital. Word of the attack hour had not reached Dearborn because of the high tide. Arnold quickly decided not to wait.

Arnold's party led the way, followed by Capt. Lamb and his 40-man artillery company dragging a 6-pounder on a sled. In line behind were the divisions of Capt. Morgan, Lt. Col. Greene and Maj. Meigs just as they had marched through the wilderness. The men, said Henry, had to travel "covering the locks of our guns with the lappets of our coats and holding down our heads ... against the imperious storm of wind and snow."

As the column struggled past the Palace Gate the defenders on the ramparts caught sight of them and began to fire. This continued intermittently for a quarter of a mile as the column made its way below the ramparts.

"Here," said Henry, "we lost some brave men, when powerless to return the salutes we received, as the enemy was covered by his impregnable defenses. They were even sightless to us....we could see nothing but the blaze from the muzzles of their muskets." It was here, said Capt. Thayer, that Capt. Hubbard was mortally wounded.

The column curved around the ramparts on reaching the beach, and now the path was a narrow way between rampart and beach. It was called Sault-au-Matelot — the sailor's leap. Henry was hit by a hawser that pitched him down a 15-foot snow-laden bank, up which he had to claw his way.

The snow drifts were so deep that Capt. Lamb found that his men could no longer, with their ropes, pull the 6-pounder. He halted to send

a request ahead to Arnold to abandon the cannon. He was already holding up and confusing the column. Arnold approved, but in the meantime Morgan had come with his men and received Lamb's permission to pass ahead.

Arnold and Oswald with him, approached another curve in the ramparts. Up above, roughly 50 feet, was a battery manned by sailors and behind them the old Seminary of Quebec. Ahead of them, blocking the Sault-au-Matelot was a barrier with apertures for two cannon. Arnold had planned to use his 6-pounder on this battery. Now he ordered his men to attack. The sailors from above fired their muskets in this new affray and a musket ball hit Arnold's left leg, penetrating down to his heel.

Some of Arnold's men placed their scaling ladders against the barrier and mounted. Others exchanged fire with the defenders. Capt. Thayer said the two fieldpieces played on the attackers, and added:

"On their drawing them back to recharge, Capt. Morgan and myself quickly advanced through the port, seized them with 60 men rank and file ...." The barrier was taken.

Arnold, suffering profuse loss of blood, had to withdraw to Dr. Senter's care supported by two men, one of them the chaplain, Rev. Spring.

It was a dismaying sight, for again the assault had to sustain a dire loss of inspired leadership. Arnold, moving painfully to the rear, exhorted on the men he passed in the storm. There was no question of the resolution of these volunteers, and Capt. Morgan, to whom Arnold gave the command, was a fearless soldier.

Carleton and his defenders had been taking countermeasures from the moment the rockets went up, sometime, Carleton said, between 4 and 5 a.m.

The defenders' first alert came from the captain of the main guard making his rounds in the Upper Town. He saw the rockets, hastened back to the Place d'Armes. The drummer beat "To arms!" The great bell of the Cathedral clanged. Other bells rang and, said Capt. Ainslie: "In a few minutes the whole garrison was under arms ... even old men of 70 were forward to oppose the attackers."

Sentries on the ramparts had seen the rockets flash in the sky like lightning and started firing. Arnold's battery at St. Roch lobbed cannonballs into the town. Fire flared at St. John's gate.

Col. Maclean sent Lt. Col. Caldwell with a detachment to reinforce the blockhouse at Cap Diamant, where rockets had been seen. An artillery officer sent along soon found, with Montgomery's assault quickly over, that there was "perfect security," sent back to Maclean for further orders and was dispatched to meet Arnold's attack.

Caldwell hurried away to check the St. Louis Gate and next St. John's Gate "where," he said, "I first learned that the enemy had surprised the post at Sault-au-Matelot and had got into the lower town." Caldwell and his militia, picking up reinforcements from the ramparts, rushed to defend a second barrier in the Sault-au-Matelot.

Col. Maclean checked the situation in Sault-au-Matelot and reported to Carleton:

"By heavens 'tis true the enemy has got in at Sault-au-Matelot."

Carleton became satisfied that here was the main attack. He sent reinforcements to the second barrier, and, setting up what he would write to Howe in Boston was "a trap," he sent his chief engineer, Capt. George Laws, and 60 men to make a sortie from the Palace Gate. Col. Maclean quickly doubled their number with a detachment under Capt. Macdougal.

As Laws emerged from the Palace Gate he encountered the middle of Dearborn's company. Dearborn had got his men together, made his way across the St. Charles River, passed Arnold being aided to the hospital. Arnold told him that the barricade had been taken and "we should carry the town." In the storm, without guide, Dearborn's men were bewildered trying to find their way and were quickly made captive by Laws. Some guns — "exceedingly wet," Dearborn said — would not fire. Few managed to escape.

Any retreat of the Americans from Sault-au-Matelot had now been totally cut off.

The second barrier across the Sault-au-Matelot, a barrier about 12 feet high, was about 200 yards from the first. Beyond it, where the road led to the Upper Town, was a platform with a cannon mounted. There was a door in the barrier which was, for a while, unlocked. Capt. Caldwell guessed that an enemy opportunity had been missed in their not rushing this door.

But Morgan had other problems after the first barrier was taken. Rifleman Abner Stocking said Morgan quickly discovered that he was not followed by the main body. Like Dearborn's men behind them, Lt. Col. Greene and Maj. Meigs got lost in the storm in alleys and byways en route. They soon came up, but at the moment Stocking said:

"It was yet extremely dark, and he (Morgan) had not the slightest knowledge of the course to be pursued, or of the defenses to be encountered. Thus circumstanced, it was thought unadvisable to advance further."

Later, when they did advance toward the second barrier with their ladders, Stocking said that they were hailed by a man, Capt. Anderson, a naval officer, who had just come through the barrier gate with a body of troops. "Capt. Morgan ... answered the British captain by a ball through his head, his soldiers drew him within the barricade and closed the gate."

Capt. Laws, in his eagerness, got ahead of his men. Just beyond the first barrier he dashed into the midst of some Meigs's men and coolly announced:

"You are all my prisoners."

Challenged as to the whereabouts of his men, Laws said they would be there, "in a twinkling." Meigs made Laws a prisoner.

The struggle raged in the Sault-au-Matelot for hours. Many were killed and wounded. Capt. Hendricks, taking aim, was hit "by a straggling ball through the heart," staggered back a few feet and died. Capt. Lamb "had nearly one half of his face carried away by a grape or cannister shot." Chief Natanis "received a musketball through his wrist."

There was lingering hope that Montgomery's force would appear. Morgan pressed his attack against the barrier. The scaling ladders were found ineffectual. The riflemen were able to drive the defending gunners from their cannon on the platform, but the defenders went into the upper floors of buildings back of the barrier and fired from the windows.

Henry said that the enemy had such "irresistible power in so narrow a space" that near daylight Morgan ordered his men into the houses. The battle raged from the windows and within the structures. Caldwell made a special, successful bayonet drive to get the attackers out of the corner, riverside house overlooking the barrier. This house also overlooked at its back a battery on its wharf that prevented the barrier from being outflanked.

Caldwell, around 9 o'clock, brought a 9-pounder from this battery to bear upon the attackers in Sault-au-Matelot and said that "their fire ... a good deal slackened."

Near the first barrier Capt. Macdougal had rescued Capt. Laws and was taking many American prisoners. The arms of the Americans were so wet, said Capt. Thayer, "scarcely one in ten would fire.

"There was," added Thayer, "no possibility of retreat ...." Soon, at the second barrier, Caldwell said that the Americans began to surrender "in such numbers that we opened the barrier."

Capt. Morgan, enraged by the turn of events, expressed the bitter disappointment of these men who had overcome so many obstacles and suffered so many hardships in their brave struggle to defend, as they saw it, their ancient hard-won rights and liberties. Morgan scorned his captors, turned to a priest and said:

"I give my sword to you, but not a scoundrel of these cowards shall take it out of my hands."

There were more than 400 prisoners, among them all Arnold's division commanders. Casualties included 42 wounded, 30 dead. Carleton would report just Capt. Anderson and four rank and file killed, 13 wounded, two of whom died in a few days. The American losses were desperately heavy. Pvt. Haskell, returning from the hospital to camp next day, New Year's Day, said:

"Found all my officers and three of my messmates and almost all the company taken or killed, and the rest in great confusion."

Arnold had remained conscious, tried to follow the battle as best he could. When Carleton sent a force to take the battery at St. Roch, Arnold had his sword brought, had himself and the patients armed and sent an officer to drive them off. The officer did — but they got away with the St. Roch cannon.

Conceding at last that he was "not able to act," Arnold resigned the command to Col. Campbell.

This brought such a protest from Arnold's remaining officers that Arnold had to resume the command. He put his mind at once to continuing the wretched siege of Quebec, sent an express to request men and cannon. Indeed, the cannon that Arnold requested were the very ones that Knox at that moment was bringing to Cambridge.

Washington made Arnold a brigadier general. The Commander in Chief clung to his hope of taking Quebec.

An anguished Washington faces many problems

Just a few days after New Year's Day 1776, Washington wrote to Joseph Reed about the agonizing period — the worst that Washington suffered throughout the siege — when he was harassed by unending problems, but especially by the miseries of organizing a new army.

"Search the volumes of history through," he told Reed, "and I much question whether a case similar to ours is to be found; namely, to maintain a post, against the flower of the British troops, for six months together, without powder, and then to have one army disbanded, and another to be raised, within the same distance of a reinforced enemy. It is too much to attempt . . . .

"I wish this month were well over our heads. . . .

"For more than two months past, I have scarcely emerged from one difficulty, before I have been plunged into another. How it will end, God, in His great goodness will direct. I am thankful for His protection to this time. We are told that we shall soon get the army completed, but I have been told so many things, which have never come to pass, that I distrust everything."

Washington's astonishment and shock at the reaction of some of the officers and soldiers to the new army, as well as the perplexities of selecting officers, pushing recruitment of soldiers and expecting at any moment that Howe would pick this time of weakness to launch a capital drive — all took their toll of the Commander in Chief. And often his usually calm temper seemed to vanish.

The goal of a new army of roughly 20,000 men, a truly continental army with old provincial ways discarded, was set in October during the sessions with Benjamin Franklin and the other delegates. Recruiting, Washington well knew, would be far more difficult once the cold of winter struck. As the delegates had given their assent, he started to get this new army under way even before the delegates left for Philadelphia.

In a general order on Oct. 22 he requested that all officers of his current 40 regiments who were intending to retire from the army indicate this in writing. "True patriots" — officers and men willing to serve through 1776 unless sooner discharged by Congress — were also asked to signify their intentions. He gave them three days in which to act.

But old lax ways persisted, and the returns were so meager that Washington gave an additional three days — this time to report "without fail." In his announcement he included an emotional appeal highlighted by the recent British destruction of the town of Falmouth.

"The times," he said, "and the importance of the great cause we are engaged in, allow no room for hesitation and delay — when life, liberty, and property are at stake, when our country is in danger of being a melancholy scene of bloodshed and desolation, when our towns are laid in ashes, and innocent women and children driven from their peaceful habitations, exposed to the rigor of an inclement season, and to the hands of charity perhaps for a support. . . ."

Furloughs for a "reasonable time" were promised to officers and soldiers joining the new army, and Washington promised he would, after present enlistments, see that they would "receive their pay once a month regularly." Soon Washington was promising that new army recruits would have barracks, that clothing obtained by the quartermaster general would be saved for them and not only would a soldier bringing his own blanket get $2 (quite a bounty) but could carry the blanket away at the end of the campaign.

Old ways still intruded. Washington had to stop prospective officers from enlisting men without orders. "Commissions in the new army," he said, "are not intended merely for those who can enlist the most men, but for such gentlemen as are most likely to deserve them."

Washington had been assured the authority to pick the best-qualified officers, a drastic change in an army currently officered by men chosen by the soldiers. Instead of 40 regiments there were to be 28, one of these the artillery. The regiments, unlike the existing ones, were to be of uniform size and have the same number of officers.

To help him select the officers Washington held a Council of War. His generals, he told them, were more intimately informed about the qualities of the various officers. Outside of the artillery command (which would eventually go to Knox) Washington set about picking a colonel, lieutenant colonel and major for each of 27 regiments. It was a fearsome task.

He saved one colonel's rank for Arnold, named three new colonels, retained 23 of his present colonels. This, for some colonels had died or been displaced, meant dropping a dozen colonels. There was a great reduction, too, in lieutenant colonels and majors, and right down the line. Those displaced did not all react like Col. Jonathan Brewer.

Brewer of Waltham, at last recovered from his wounds at Bunker Hill, offered to give up his new regiment to another veteran of the battle, Col. Asa Whitcomb of Lancaster, who had been overlooked in the new assignments. Indeed, Brewer was willing to serve as a private soldier. This news so pleased Washington he made it the subject of a general order and appointed the genial Brewer as barrackmaster.

Officer troubles still appeared despite their being given an increase in pay. Officers sent into the country to enlist recruits were granted an advance of two months. They were to send recruits back as fast as possible in groups of eight or 10. Officers who knowingly enlisted some other officer's recruit were threatened by Washington with being cashiered.

Washington had to squelch a dangerous rumor. He had learned that some lieutenants, feeling they would get company command if a captain failed to obtain sufficient recruits, had become "indifferent and lukewarm in the recruiting business." Washington warned them that, if guilty, they would be dismissed forever "with disgrace."

He had difficulties with some provinces offering higher pay and bounties for their provincial militia. There was difficulty over soldiers being accustomed to being paid in their provinces by the lunar month, which meant an extra month's pay a year. And, Washington knew this

was the season when New England farmers wished to be home "to lay in provisions, stores, etc., for the use of their families." Like Washington, they had not expected warfare to be long lasting.

Provincialism kept showing it was perdurable. Men, and officers, too, of the different colonies did not see why they could not serve with just men from their own colony.

Washington told Congress:

"The trouble in the arrangement of the army is really inconceivable. Many of the officers sent in their names to serve in expectation of promotion, others stood aloof to see what advantage they could make themselves, whilst a number who had declined, have again sent in their names to serve. . . .

"The difficulty with the soldiers is as great, indeed more so if possible, than with the officers. They will not enlist until they know their colonel, lieutenant colonel, major, captain, etc., so that it is necessary to fix the officers the first thing. . . .

"You, sir (the letter was addressed to John Hancock), can easier judge than I can express the anxiety of mind I labor under on this occasion, especially at this time when we may expect the enemy will begin to act, on the arrival of their reinforcement, part of which is already come and the remainder daily dropping in.

"I have other distresses of a very alarming nature. The arms of our soldiers are so exceedingly bad, that I assure you, Sir, I cannot place a proper confidence in them." He went on to mention the constant lack of gunpowder, which had only recently in part delayed repelling Gen. Clinton's raid on Lechmere's Point.

Washington had his generals address the soldiers, urging re-enlistments. Recruitment still lagged. Washington felt certain that Howe was fully aware of his woes. This was quite true. Howe was writing to Lord Dartmouth that rebel enlistments were running out "and there is reason to believe that many of them will decline entering into new engagements."

At about the same time Washington, at the peak of his anguish, was writing to his sorely missed, former secretary, Reed:

"Such a dearth of public spirit, and such want of virtue, such stock-jobbing, and fertility in all the low arts to obtain advantages of one kind or another, in this great change of military arrangements, I never saw before, and pray God I may never be witness to again. What will be the ultimate end of these maneuvers is beyond my scan. I tremble at the prospect."

Just ahead for Washington was another crisis. The enlistments of the Connecticut troops would expire on Dec. 10. Many of them, mistakenly, thought Dec. 1 was the expiration date. "Tarry" was the word in use to mean to remain beyond their agreed seven months. Connecticut officers and some of Washington's generals appealed to the men to stay on, even if only until the end of the year.

The Connecticut colonels, at Washington's request, checked to see if their men would stay. He was told they would, though there were provisos about homesickness, furloughs and winter clothing. As the expiration time drew closer. Col. Ebenezer Huntington of Connecticut observed:

"The universal determination of the soldiers from Connecticut seems to be for home ... although they have been repeatedly solicited in general orders to tarry longer .... The officers and soldiers are possessed to get home."

When Washington learned, to his "surprise and astonishment," that some had left on Dec. 1 "not only without leave, but contrary to express orders," he warned those remaining and said he had "sent an express to the Governor of Connecticut with the names of such men as have left the camp, in order that they may be dealt with in a manner suited to the ignominy of their behavior."

Gov. Jonathan Trumbull of Connecticut, an ardent patriot and staunch supporter of Washington, denounced their conduct as "extraordinary and reprehensible." He promised that "some examples should be made." These men did receive hard treatment on their way — some returned. But there was no such harshness toward the Connecticut men who left on Dec. 10.

Washington had had them on their parade so that their muskets could be examined and those thought worthwhile retained. The men who left on Dec. 1 had taken their arms with them, which

Boston Public Library, Boston, Mass.

Rev. Lemuel Haynes

had been an additional distress to Washington.

During the French and Indians Wars there was a saying: "He's a good soldier who serves his time out." This was still a valid feeling with the soldiers. Loyalty no longer existed toward Great Britain, and this new country was yet to be born. The thinking of the soldiery, despite Washington's endeavors and feelings, was still very much provincial. Rev. William Gordon, at times an army chaplain, said:

" 'Tis the cast of the New Englanders to enlist for a certain time, and when the time is expired to quit the service and return home, let the call for their continuance be ever so urgent."

Connecticut would continue to join with the New England colonies in sending militia to meet Washington's and the continental needs. Washington would appeal to the Massachusetts, New Hampshire and Rhode Island men to "tarry" when their time was to expire on Dec. 31. Many would nevertheless leave, giving up at his request their blankets and muskets. But many of these soldiers would later return.

Some sunshine did break into this bleak period for the distressed and fatigued Commander in Chief. Martha, escorted by her son Jacky Custis, arrived at Cambridge two weeks before Christmas. Jacky brought a sizable donation from Virginians to the poor of Boston.

Washington had maintained a hospitable table at Vassall House for his staff, generals, visiting dignitaries and officers of the day who had a standing invitation to dine at headquarters. Many things were short in the American camp — barracks, gunpowder, arms, firewood, money — but not food, though Washington himself preferred a simple diet.

Martha was a gentle, delightful hostess. The wives of the generals and many officers exchanged visits and dinners. Dr. John Morgan's wife told how it seemed "lively and agreeable all winter." The wife of Speaker James Warren, the celebrated historian and dramatist Mercy Otis Warren, became a close friend of Martha.

"This is a beautiful country," Martha wrote of Cambridge to a friend. Yet there were moments when all was not so beautiful.

"Some days," Martha wrote, "we have a number of cannon and shells from Boston and Bunker Hill, but it does not seem to surprise anyone but me. I confess .I shudder every time I hear the sound of a gun...

"I just took a look at poor Boston and Charlestown .... from Prospect Hill, Charlestown has only a few chimneys standing in it. There seems to be a number of very fine buildings in Boston but God knows how long they will stand; they are pulling apart the wharves for firewood. To me that never see anything of war, the preparations are very terrible indeed, but I endeavor to keep my fears to myself as much as I can."

Though slowly, recruiting did mount. Washington found, as he told Congress, "that free Negroes who have served in this army are very much dissatisfied at being discarded." He had accordingly given instructions to re-enlist them.

Blacks had been serving right along, but, being mostly excluded, not in large numbers in these early months of the war. Among them now was the first black Congregational minister, Rev. Lemuel Haynes of Granville, Mass., and Washington's trusted body servant, Billy Lee, who would serve the general throughout the war.

On New Year's Eve Brig. Gen. Nathaniel Greene observed from Prospect Hill:

"This is the last day of the old enlisted soldiers' service. Nothing but confusion and disorder reign. We are obliged to retain their guns, whether private or public property .... The army cannot be provided in any other way, and those we detain are very indifferent; generally without bayonets, and of different sized bores.

"We have suffered prodigiously for want of wood. Many regiments have been obliged to eat their provisions raw, for want of fuel to cook it; and notwithstanding we have burnt up all the fences, and cut down all the trees for a mile round the camp, our sufferings have been inconceivable. The barracks have been greatly delayed for want of stuff. The fatigues of the campaign, the suffering for want of wood and clothing, have made a multitude of soldiers heartily sick of service.

"We never have been so weak as we shall be tomorrow when we dismiss the old troops."

On New Year's Day, Washington celebrated the birth of his new army with a new flag — the Union flag with 13 stripes — and, with 13 cannon shot, unfurled it atop the fort on Prospect Hill. The flagpole, 76 feet high, was the raised mast of a schooner that had been burned at Chelsea Creek.

A happy scene, but Washington's woes were far from over.

Unaware of the defeat at Quebec, he sent an importunate message to Gen. Montgomery, 12 days after the general's death, to allay the wants of the army at Cambridge. "After powder," he said, "the principal deficiency is that of arms .... Blankets and clothing we are very deficient in. Quebec is, I suppose, the great magazine for them (he listed other needs), and all kind of military stores....

"If they cannot in some part be supplied by you, I do not know where else I can apply."

Returns to show Washington the size of his new army came in so slowly he expressed astonishment and threatened to arrest and try for disobedience officers responsible for the delay.

Then when he got the returns he was amazed that enlistments had been going so slowly "they seem almost at an end."

He called his generals to a Council of War. And it was now he got the news of Montgomery's valiant death — and the desperate appeal from Quebec for men. The decision was to ask the New England colonies to send militia. Washington could spare no soldiers from his incomplete new army. He was already forming plans to attack Boston, and confided to Reed:

"Could I have foreseen the difficulties which have come upon us ... all the generals upon Earth should not have convinced me of the propriety of delaying an attack upon Boston 'till this time."

Washington, a learner in generalship, now knew he must not always defer to his generals' advice but be the master of military decision.

King's stubbornness destroys old loyalties

Toward the close of the year 1775, Thomas Jefferson told how Americans had been changing in their allegiance to their British sovereign:

"It is an immense misfortune to the whole empire, he said, "to have a King of such a disposition at such at time. We are told, and everything proves it true, that he is the bitterest enemy we have . . . .

"To undo his empire, he has but one more truth to learn: that, after colonies have drawn the sword, there is but one step more they can take. That step is now pressed upon us, by the measures adopted, as if they were afraid we would not take it.

"Believe me ... there is not in the British empire a man who more cordially loves a union with Great Britain than I do. But, by the God that made me, I will cease to exist before I yield to a connection on such terms as the British Parliament propose; and in this I think I speak the sentiments of America.

"We want neither inducement nor power, to declare and assert a separation. It is will alone that is wanting, and that is growing apace, under the fostering hand of our King."

For many months Americans had been certain that the enemy of their liberties was the administration of Lord North. They looked upon the British soldiers opposing them as a "Parliamentary army." Most were convinced that the King, when he understood their pleas, would protect them against the tyrannical actions of Parliament.

But in the waning weeks of 1775 the news from London had, to their amazement, shown that His Majesty was solidly on the side of Lord North.

The "Olive Branch" petition of the Continental Congress, a basis for conciliation, had been rushed to London by Gov. Richard Penn of Pennsylvania. An advisory copy was promptly handed to Lord Dartmouth, and arrangements made for the original — signed by John Hancock and the members of the Continental Congress — to be delivered to the King two days later. Penn, revealing what then happened to himself and the American agent Arthur Lee, said:

"We were told, as His Majesty did not receive it (the petition) on the throne, no answer would be given."

Moreover, Dartmouth informed the astonished messengers that the King had refused even to read the petition. The whole thing took on the appearance of a grim farce. The petition was plainly foredoomed for Penn soon learned that this very day had been selected by George III to proclaim formally that the American colonies were in a state of rebellion.

If any question still remained in any American mind as to the true position of the King, it was dismissed forever by the next move of His Majesty — a move of momentous significance for the British empire, for it would open an unbridgeable gap between the motherland and the colonies, and commence an irresistible movement toward American independence.

This move was George III's "Speech from the Throne" at the opening of Parliament for its 1775-1776 session.

The King, reacting to Lexington-Concord and Bunker Hill, had resolved to use force. Besides removing Gage he would replace his naval commander in America, Adm. Graves. He was understandably confident of winning the approval of Parliament for his hard-fisted program because Lord North commanded a majority made pliant by the cynical use of titles, preferments and public funds.

Parliament was summoned earlier than usual. The King, resplendent with crown and royal regalia and surrounded by his chief ministers, delivered his speech in the House of Lords, with the Lords all in their robes, and the speaker and the gentlemen of the House of Commons in attendance.

His Majesty spoke of the "unhappy and deluded multitude" in America and of spurning their protestations of loyalty while a rebellious war was "manifestly carried on for the purpose of establishing an independent empire." He was willing to receive any submissions, of course, and would grant pardons.

But the main thrust of his speech, the part

that literally shocked America, came in these words:

"It is now become the part of wisdom ... to put a speedy end to these disorders by the most decisive exertions. For this purpose I have increased my naval establishment and greatly augmented my land forces .... I have also the satisfaction to inform you that I have received the most friendly offers of foreign assistance...."

There was to be outright war. The Americans could submit or fight.

On the next day, Oct. 27, Lord Dartmouth sent off a copy of the King's speech to Howe. Dartmouth hoped it would "convince the leaders of the rebellion in America of the firm resolution of every branch of the legislature to maintain the dignity and authority of Parliament, and open the eyes of those who have been misled by their wicked artifices."

Dartmouth sent some other interesting news as well. The negotiations with Czarina Catherine of Russia for mercenaries had led only to "embarrassment and disappointment." She, moreover, had shrewdly suggested to King George that he employ instead a peaceful approach to his colonists.

To get the necessary troops in England that the King needed for this war was practically an impossibility. Dartmouth's undersecretary remarked: "Unless it rains men in red coats I know not where we are to get all we shall want." So the King had set about opening negotiations with the rulers of the German principalities.

As the hereditary ruler of Hanover, the King said he would donate Hanoverian troops. These, with the troops of Hesse-Cassel and Brunswick at a price per head, would eventually be delivered to the seaports of Europe for transport. The struggle would thus no longer be a civil war but a war of mercenaries and conquest.

Parliamentary support, while predictably overwhelming, was not so unanimous as Dartmouth had conveyed to Howe. This turning point in the fate of the empire did not come without an intense underdog effort by the opposition to avert disaster, which was ominously predicted, by using the rejected "Olive Branch" petition as the basis for a peaceful solution. The debate went vigorously on after the King departed the House of Lords and lasted until well after midnight.

The foremost and most celebrated advocate of conciliation, William Pitt, Earl of Chatham, was so ill that he could not be present. His role, though, was most ably and, surprisingly, filled by the Duke of Grafton. He was at the time the lord privy seal, a member of the cabinet, a supporter in the past of the North administration. But now Grafton had become convinced that the King had been misled by his ministers.

Lord Grafton was himself in poor health. He said, however, that "the present very critical situation of this country" would have made him, if necessary, "come down to this house in a litter in order to express my full and hearty disapprobation of the measures now pursuing." He denounced the administration efforts of the past year, said that the King and the nation had "been deceived." He had a proposal, simply:

"To bring in a bill for repealing every act (I think there are 13) which has been passed in this country since the year 1763, relative to America."

Grafton and others strenuously attacked the King's proposal to hire foreign troops. The Marquis of Rockingham assailed it as an "alarming and dangerous expedient of calling in foreign forces to the support of His Majesty's authority within his own dominions." And even more dreadful, said Rockingham, was the "calamity of shedding British blood by British hands."

The "madness and absurdity of expecting to reduce them (the Americans) by mere measures of coercion" was attacked by the Earl of Coventry. He told his fellow Lords that they had "no alternative left, but either to relinquish all connection with the colonies or to adopt conciliatory measures; the idea of conquering them was wild and extravagant even in the event of victory...." Above all he cautioned of "the inability of Great Britain to retain, for any considerable time, such a species of dominion."

The arrogant Earl of Sandwich, head of the navy, the man who had called Americans cowards, announced that the navy was to be increased from the 30 armed vessels of 1775 to 70.

Such a force cooperating with the army, said Sandwich, "would render it impossible for the Americans either to resist, keep together, or subsist."

Sandwich said he knew that it was fashionable to cry up the prowess and intrepidity of Americans, but in his opinion "if they had betrayed any proofs of cowardice and want of spirit formerly, nothing had yet happened on their part sufficient to wipe off the aspersion." The provincials had superiority by their entrenchments, as at Bunker Hill, yet, said Sandwich, "the King's troops were victorious."

This was too much for the Duke of Richmond. He said that he "could inform his lordship that the New England people were brave; that they had proved it; that the general who commanded at Bunker Hill had confessed it; that another (Gen. Burgoyne) ... had confirmed it; that an officer, a particular friend ... had united in the same opinion." Richmond added, recalling the American stand in the fort on Bunker Hill, that he "never recollected an instance where lines had been forced and no prisoners taken but such as were wounded."

Lord Dartmouth expressed his astonishment that any — like Grafton — would withdraw support from the administration. It had never been supposed, said Dartmouth, that the reduction of America "would be the work of one summer." The administration measures of 1775, he said, had been directed entirely to the Province of Massachusetts Bay, and he continued:

"As such, they had been wisely planned, and must have been successful, if a variety of events, impossible to be foreseen or provided against, had not united to defeat them; such, in particular ... the unexpected unanimity and unforeseen measures adopted by the Continental Congress." Quite a compliment to the adoption by Congress of the New England Army!

A final appeal was made by the Earl of Shelburne to utilize the "Olive Branch":

"How comes it, that the colonies are charged with planning independency, in the face of their explicit declaration to the contrary, contained in that petition?

"Who is it that presumes to put an assertion, (what shall I call it, my Lords?) contrary to fact, contrary to evidence, notorious to the whole world, in that mouth, from which truth alone, if unprompted, would issue?

"Is it their intention, by thus perpetually sounding independence in the ears of the Americans, to lead them to it, or, by treating them, upon suspicion, with every possible violence, to compel them into that which must be our ruin?"

There could not be, said Shelburne, alluding to the "Olive Branch," "a fairer opportunity offered of extricating this country from the ruinous situation in which the folly of administration has involved us."

The eloquence of opposition was unavailing. Grafton's proposal to wipe the books clean of the successive laws that had produced warfare in America, was heavily beaten down. The Lords then approved the King's address 76 to 33. The dissenters' only recourse was to put a protest on the record, a protest that North and his men had deceived the King and disgraced the nation. The protest touched, in part, on the siege:

"Our arms have been disgraced; upwards of 10,000 of the flower of our army, with an immense artillery, under four generals of reputation, and backed with a great naval force, have been miserably blockaded in one seaport town; and after repeated and obstinate battles, in which such numbers of our bravest men have fallen, the British forces have not been able to penetrate one mile into the country which they were sent to subdue ...."

The debate in the House of Commons, to which the members retired after hearing the King's "Address from the Throne," resulted in the same overwhelming support for the King's course of action, 278 to 108.

Once again there was eloquence. The Lord Mayor of London, John Wilkes, anathema to the King, said:

"The conduct of the present administration had already wrested the sceptre of America out of the hands of our sovereign, and he has now scarcely even a postmaster left in the whole northern continent. More than half the empire is already lost, and almost all the rest in confusion and anarchy ....

"An appeal has been made to the sword; and at the close of the last campaign what have we conquered? Bunker Hill only, and with the loss of 1200 men. Are we to pay as dearly for the rest of America? The idea of the conquest of that immense continent is as romantic as injust."

Col. Isaac Barre, who had fought beside Americans at Wolfe's conquest of Quebec, once again defended their bravery and said Bunker Hill "smacked more of defeat than victory." He urged the House of Commons:

"To embrace the present, the only moment tolerated by Heaven, for an accommodation with the Americans. If they were driven a step further in resistance, the whole American continent was lost forever."

A response for the administration was given by a noted speaker, Solicitor General Alexander Wedderburn, who would be made a lord:

"Relinquish America! What is it but to desire a giant to shrink spontaneously into a dwarf?

"Relinquish America, and you also relinquish the West Indies, and confine yourself to the narrow insular situation, which once made you hardly discernable on the face of the globe.

"My heart swells with indignation at the idea. Relinquish America!"

He urged:

"Establish, first, your superiority, and then talk of negotiation.

"Let us rather second the indignant voice of the nation, which presses in from all quarters upon the sovereign, calling loudly for vigorous measures, and for the suppression of faction. Shall we be deaf to its call?

"Sir, we have been too long deaf; we have too long shown our forbearance and long-suffering; faction must now be curbed, must be subdued and crushed; our thunders must go forth; America must be conquered."

Lord North spoke, too. He declared "that if the scheme of repealing every American act passed since 1763 was adopted, there was certainly an end to the dispute, for from that moment America would be independent of England." He observed:

"The measures the administration meant now to pursue were, to send a powerful sea and land force to America, and at the same time to accompany them with offers of mercy upon a proper submission.

"This will show that we are in earnest, that we are prepared to punish, but are nevertheless ready to forgive; that is, in my opinion, the most likely means of producing an honorable reconciliation."

The King lost no time in having Grafton turn in the privy seals. This vacancy in the cabinet made possible shifts that increased the number of hard-liners at the summit of administration. Lord Dartmouth was shifted to lord privy seal and his crucial post of secretary for the American colonies was given to Lord George Germain.

Germain was a thorough supporter of the war policy. The son of a Duke, Germain, under his earlier name of Sackville, had been court-martialed for his failure to bring the cavalry into action at the great battle of Minden. Most military men, particularly those in America, disliked him. He had difficulty working with colleagues. But he was trusted by George III — a misfortune in store for both King and empire.

Paine's "Common Sense" arouses Americans

"The King's speech was condemned and ordered to be burnt at the center of the camp at Cambridge."

This reaction, recounted Mercy Warren, was the same throughout the American colonies when news of what the King had said to Parliament reached this side of the Atlantic. "The indignation of all ranks," she wrote, "can scarcely be described.

"The wavering were resolved, the timid grew bold, the placid and philosophic lovers of peace left the retired haunts of literary felicity, and beneath the helmet and the buckler, courted the post of danger — vigorous action was now the only line of conduct to be observed. . . ."

Washington's reaction was, in brief:

"We now know the ultimatum of British justice."

The Commander in Chief was highly amused, he told Reed, by a mistake of Howe and his redcoats about the effect of the King's speech on the Cambridge camp. A quantity of reprints of the King's speech was sent out Jan. 1 by "the Boston gentry," said Washington. They came, by way of Roxbury, to Cambridge and gave Washington and his army their first sight of what the King had said.

"Before the proclamation came to hand," Washington explained, "we had hoisted the Union flag in compliment to the United Colonies. But, behold, it was received in Boston as a token of the deep impression the speech had made upon us, and as a signal of submission. So we hear, by a person out of Boston. . . . By this time, I presume, they begin to think it strange that we have not made a formal surrender of our lines."

Howe soon had a more realistic impression. He wrote to Dartmouth:

"From what I can learn of the designs of the leaders of the rebels, they seem determined, since the receipt of the King's speech among them, to make the most diligent preparations for an active war. . . ."

Washington's generals reacted warmly.

Adj. Gen. Gates wrote Maj. Gen. Lee:

"The King's speech has had a noble effect in fixing all the wavering to the cause of freedom and America."

Maj. Gen. Lee's view:

"I formerly and indeed not long ago looked with some degree of horror on the scheme of separation but at present there appears no alternative. . . . We must be independent or slaves."

Brig. Gen. Greene was stoutest of all:

"The tyrant, by his last speech, has convinced us that to be free or not, depends upon ourselves. . . ."

"Permit me . . . to recommend from the sincerity of my heart, ready at all times to bleed in my country's cause, a declaration of independence; and call upon the world, and the great God who governs it, to witness the necessity, propriety, and rectitude thereof."

It was at this time that Americans were widely swayed in favor of considering independence by the writing of an Englishman who had come from his homeland little more than a year ago, 38-year-old Thomas Paine.

The receptiveness of the Americans to Paine's thinking was intensified not only by their sovereign's declaration of a mercenary war but by the New Year's Day deed of the Earl of Dunmore, royal governor of Virginia, who had been trying futilely, from a few warships, to retain control of the Old Dominion.

When the people of Norfolk, Virginia's most active seaport, refused him supplies, Dunmore commenced a cannonade that lasted well into the night, sent marines ashore to set the warehouses in flames, and continued to fire on the community, which burned for nearly three days.

Washington, who had been concerned that Martha's staying at Mt. Vernon might have made her an object of Dunmore's terrorism, expressed the hope that this devastation of Norfolk would indissolubly unite Americans "against a nation which seems to be lost to every sense of

Thomas Paine

American Antiquarian Society

Paine to undertake the task, read each chapter as Paine wrote it and, at Paine's request, suggested the title "Common Sense."

Rush recalled being charmed by a sentence that Paine, by accident or design, omitted:

"Nothing can be conceived of more absurd than 3,000,000 of people flocking to the American shore every time a vessel arrives from England, to know what portion of liberty they shall enjoy."

Paine wished no monetary benefit from his pamphlet. Any proceeds he assigned toward the purchase of mittens for Arnold's army, now suffering through the siege of Quebec. The pamphlet was a runaway top seller and spread rapidly throughout the world. This, though, meant no income because it was pirated. But Paine did reach a mammoth audience in America.

John Adams noted that it contained arguments that had been made for months in debate in the Continental Congress. Such debate was secret. Paine was bringing these arguments for the first time to a widespread audience of Americans and with a skill and flaming spirit that seemed inspired.

The pamphlet was published early in January, 1776, and was published anonymously — an additional interest, a wonder all over the land: "Who wrote it?"

At the outset Paine demolished the divine origin of kings. From his study of the poet Milton he was able to call upon the Holy Bible, especially on the prophet Samuel, to support his argument, a technique immensely effective in a society with deep religious roots.

It was heathens who first introduced government by kings and the Hebrews sinned when they copied them, said Paine. "The idolatrous homage which is paid to the persons of kings ... impiously invades the prerogative of Heaven."

Hereditary kingship in Great Britain, Paine observed, came from William the Conquerer. "A French bastard landing with an armed banditti and establishing himself King of England against the consent of the natives, is in plain terms a very paltry rascally original. It certainly hath no divinity in it."

This was unusual language to give the King's

virtue, and those feelings which distinguish a civilized people from the most barbarous savages."

Paine had met Franklin in London and been favored with a letter intended to help Paine get a job in Philadelphia. On his arrival he encountered the man who had made the first engraving of the battle of Bunker Hill, Robert Aitkin. Aitkin was intent on starting a new magazine, the *Pennsylvania Magazine,* and made Paine his editor.

This quickly brought Paine in contact with some of the leading men of the community, among them Dr. Benjamin Rush. Rush admired Paine's articles, and particularly one assailing slavery and the inconsistency of men seeking freedom for themselves at the same time holding others in bondage.

For some time Rush had been planning an address to Americans urging independence. Now Rush happily discovered that Paine thought independence "necessary to bring the war to a speedy and successful issue." So Rush urged

American subjects. Paine then crushed the lingering notion that having kings was a safeguard against a disturbed society. "The whole history of England disowns the fact. Thirty kings and two minors have reigned in that distracted kingdom since the conquest, in which time there has been (including the revolution) no less than eight civil wars and 19 rebellions."

Reconciliation "like an agreeable dream hath passed away and left us as we were." Since some, said Paine, believed there might be advantages in reconciliation, he thought it proper to examine whether the colonies sustained injuries while connected with Great Britain.

In matters of commerce, he declared, America would have been better off "had no European power taken any notice of her." The commerce of America was in necessaries of life and America "will always have a market while eating is the custom in Europe." As for defense, Britain's interest in that was not from attachment but "for the sake of trade and dominion."

"But Britain," said Paine, "is the parent country, some say. Then the more shame upon her conduct. Even brutes do not devour their young, nor savages make war upon their families .... This new world hath been the asylum for the persecuted lovers of civil and religious liberty.... It is so far true of England, that the same tyranny which drove the first emigrants from home, pursues their descendants still.

"I challenge the warmest advocate for reconciliation to show a single advantage that this continent can reap by being connected with Great Britain ... but the injuries and disadvantages which we sustain by that connection are without number.

"Everything that is right and reasonable pleads for separation. The blood of the slain, the weaping voice of nature cries, 'Tis time to part.

"The authority of Great Britain over this continent, is a form of government, which sooner or later must have an end.... 'Tis repugnant to reason, to the universal order of things, to all examples from former ages, to suppose that this continent can longer remain subject to any external power.

"Every quiet method for peace hath been in-effectual. Our prayers have been rejected with disdain .... Wherefore, since nothing but blows will do, for God's sake let us come to a final separation, and not leave the next generation to be cutting throats under the violated unmeaning names of parent and child.

"There is something absurd, in supposing a continent to be perpetually governed by an island. In no instance hath nature made the satellite larger than its primary planet; and as England and America, with respect to each other, reverse the common order of nature, it is evident that they belong to different systems. England to Europe; America to itself."

Paine gave some suggestions on what sort of government might be established here after remarking:

"If there is any true cause of fear respecting independence it is because no plan is yet laid down." He proposed a constitutional, representative government. It was a beginning. As for having a King, Paine would have only God who "reigns above, and doth not make havoc of mankind like the Royal Brute of Great Britain." He proposed a plan for electing a President.

His eloquence mounted:

"O! ye that love mankind! Ye that dare oppose not only tyranny but the tyrant, stand forth! Every spot of the old world is overrun with oppression. Freedom hath been hunted around the globe.... Europe regards her as a stranger, and England hath given her warning to depart. O! receive the fugitive, and prepare in time an asylum for mankind."

In his peroration he laid down final considerations after declaring that "nothing can settle our affairs so expeditiously as an open and determined declaration of independence."

He asserted that as long as America remained a colony the quarrel could go on forever and no mediator would appear. He affirmed that neither France nor Spain would give any help because these rivals of England would hurt themselves by strengthening America should there be a reconciliation.

While Americans remained as subjects they would always be considered rebels. And lastly, he argued that America should publish a manifesto to all foreign courts of being driven to break off all connection with the British court, assuring all nations of our peaceful intentions and our desire to trade with them.

"Such a memorial," said Paine, "would produce more good effects to this continent than if a ship were freighted with petitions to Britain. Under our present denomination of British subjects, we can neither be received nor heard abroad; the custom of all courts is against us, and will be so, until by an independence we take rank with other nations."

The effect was electrifying.

Speaker James Warren wrote that he and other Massachusetts leaders "should certainly vote for a declaration of independence without delay."

Washington's generals felt the same way.

Maj. Gen. Artemas Ward's secretary wrote to John Adams: "I am persuaded the war would not be long if those sentiments were adopted, and that America would soon be the admiration and glory of the world."

Brig. Gen. John Sullivan, also writing to John Adams, spoke of his admiration of "Common Sense" and noted, "It takes well with the army and the people in general, and I hope so rational a doctrine will be established throughout the continent as the only doctrine that will work out the salvation of America."

Washington's words reflected the steady, flourishing growth in America's response to Paine's summons to action and nationhood.

At first he told Reed:

"A few more of such flaming arguments, as were exhibited at Falmouth and Norfolk, added to the sound doctrine and unanswerable reasoning contained in the pamphlet 'Common Sense,' will not leave numbers at a loss to decide upon the propriety of a separation."

Little more than a week later he told Reed how he would inform the King and his ministers:

"That we have done everything which could be expected from the best of subjects, that the spirit of freedom rises too high in us to submit to slavery, and that, if nothing else would satisfy a tyrant and his diabolical ministry, we are determined to shake off all connections with a state so unjust and unnatural.

"This I would tell them, not under covert, but in words as clear as the sun in its meridian brightness."

Just a few weeks later he told Reed:

"My countrymen I know, from their form of government, and steady attachment heretofore to royalty, will come reluctantly into the idea of independence, but time and persecution bring many wonderful things to pass; and by private letters, which I have lately received from Virginia, I find 'Common Sense' is working a powerful change there in the minds of many men."

Washington sets deadline for attack

Washington's preparation for an assault upon the British forces in Boston monopolized most of his time in the first two months of 1776. He was resolved to act and felt he must do so before anticipated British reinforcements from Europe, despite his own persisting insufficiency of just about everything needed for a campaign.

An attack over the ice was Washington's first choice. As winter increased its grip, Gen. Sullivan had noted, "Old Boreas and Jack Frost are now at work building a bridge over all the rivers and bays, which once completed, we take possession of the town, or perish in the attempt."

The freezing, the January thawing, and the refreezing of the bays (now mostly filled land) between Dorchester and Roxbury and old Boston north of Boston Neck excited Washington's enthusiasm for this pathway of attack — but he did not overlook preparations for his attractive alternative of seizing and fortifying Dorchester Heights.

An attack on Boston had not only become Washington's foremost objective but he had also grown sensitive because of his inability, for strategic reasons, to explain why he had been so many months launching the attack. Franklin and his fellow committeemen, when they left Cambridge, had taken with them a critical question asked by Washington.

Should the attack, as Congress desired, be launched even if it meant that "the town ... must be destroyed?"

When this question was placed before the Congress it kept that body, however sanguine for an attack, in intermittent debate from Nov. 4 to Dec. 22 to decide on the answer, which was: "That if Gen. Washington and his Council of War should be of opinon that a successful attack may be made on the troops in Boston, he do it in any manner he may think expedient, notwithstanding the town and property in it may thereby be destroyed."

John Hancock, who presided at the debate and sent the answer on to Cambridge, gave his blessing to Washington in these words:

"May God crown your attempt with success. I most heartily wish it, though individually I may be the greatest sufferer." Hancock was one of the largest property owners in Boston and on his estate atop Beacon Hill then stood what was probably the finest residence in the community.

To Washington, the greatest of the "stumbling-blocks ... which disturb my present repose" was his lack of gunpowder. This, above everything else, was what basically delayed an assault on Boston. Washington, irked that he could not enlighten his fellow Americans, would be writing to Hancock:

"I have many disagreeable sensations on account of my situation; for, to have the eyes of the whole continent fixed with anxious expectation of hearing of some great event, and to be restrained in every military operation, for want of the necessary means of carrying it on, is not very pleasing, especially as the means used to conceal my weakness from the enemy, conceals it also from our friends, and adds to their wonder."

Washington's seizures of Ploughed Hill and Cobble Hill had, from his point of view, tightened the lines around the Boston citadel. When the British barely responded, he was deeply puzzled unless the British idleness "be to lull us with a fatal security." The British contented themselves with perfunctory cannonading, explained Capt. Charles Stuart in a letter to his father Lord Bute, because they regarded these rebel moves as "merely defensive."

After Gen. Clinton's raid at Lechmere's Point, Washington decided to strengthen that position. His concern that the British might make "a sortie when the bay gets frozen" led him to throw up two half-moon batteries between Lechmere's Point and the mouth of the Charles River on the Cambridge side and he marked three places for entrenchments between Brookline Fort (near Sewall's Point) and Roxbury.

The strengthening of the works at Lechmere's Point, or Phipps's Farm, did surprise the British. Capt. Stuart said, "Frequent consultations were held about it," but added, "our officers still agreed it was defensive." Capt. Archibald Robertson of the Royal Engineers noted that the newer work there and at the causeway leading to Phipps's Farm was but 1500 yards from the new British battery at Barton's Point, present West End. Lord Percy judged the rebels with large cannon there "may trouble us a good deal."

Ground was broken by Gen. Putnam and 400 men. They were laboring two hours on a misty morning until the mist cleared and revealed the parties working at the point and putting a new bridge across the creek that, at high tide, turned Lechmere's Point into an island. Capt. Robertson said that the cannon at Barton's Point commenced firing 10-inch shells.

HMS Scarborough, 20-gun frigate on patrol a half mile off Lechmere's Point, let go a broadside of round and grapeshot. The men, taking their wounded, had to decamp from the point but "Old Put" kept them at work on the bridge.

Over on Cobble Hill some cannon opened fire on *HMS Scarborough.* The gunners, said crusty Lt. John Barker of the King's Own Regiment, "though at a great distance, struck her twice out of six shots." One shot pierced her side. That night the Americans resumed their work at the point and worked all night.

Next morning Gen. Heath relieved Putnam. Fortunately for the men, the gunners on Cobble Hill fired two 18-pounders at the warship, and that vessel, on a signal of two rockets fired at Boston, withdrew out of harm's way to the Charlestown ferryway. The rebels, said Barker, gave "three cheers as she passed. We fired at them from Barton's Point battery ... notwithstanding all our shells and shot they continued working."

Heath told how this was done:

"Two sentinels were posted to watch the British batteries, with orders, on discovering the discharge of cannon, to call out, 'A shot!'

"The men in the works were ordered to be steady; on the signal of a shot, to settle down and remain so, until the shot had struck; or if a shell, until it had burst; then to rise and prosecute the work — no man to step out of his

place." Finally the British commander gave up, figuring the long-distance shelling would only "inure the Americans to danger." But the British did resume. So did the work, and Washington and several general officers came to inspect it.

Washington now tried something different — raiding the British position. In the first attempt Gen. Sullivan led a detachment from Winter Hill that crossed on the ice from Cobble Hill to surprise a British outpost in Charlestown. But a soldier slipped on the ice, his musket went off and alarmed the enemy, so the mission was dropped.

The next attempt was successful.

Maj. Thomas Knowlton Jr., promoted for his gallantry at the battle of Bunker Hill, was to lead a detachment of 200 men to deprive the British of the few remaining houses in Charlestown, those still standing near the milldam, all of them under the guns of the formidable British fortress raised on the summit of Bunker Hill.

The men set out from near Cobble Hill after 8 p.m., Jan. 8, a dark night. Knowlton and his men crossed the milldam, set fire to eight of the 14 dwellings still standing that the British, Washington said, "were daily pulling down for fuel." One British soldier was killed, a sergeant, and four others and the wife of one of them were taken back as prisoners.

Gen. Putnam, watching from Cobble Hill, laughed uproariously when he saw the redcoats, surprised in their big fortress, suddenly erupt into musket fire in every direction. An onlooker with him said:

"Bunker Hill took the alarm; the flashing of musketry, from every quarter of that fort, showed the confusion of its defenders — firing, some in the air, some in the Mystic River; in short, they fired at random, and thought they were attacked at every quarter, which, you may suppose, gave no small pleasure to the general and a number of us who were spectators of the scene from Cobble Hill."

There was a far more amusing scene at the moment in Faneuil Hall. There, a large audience, which included Gen. Howe, had just completed watching the play of the evening and was beginning to enjoy a farce written by some officers of

Dorchester Heights as seen from Beacon Hill

the garrison and called "The Blockade of Boston." A lively account of what followed was written by Dr. James Thacher:

"The figure designed to burlesque Gen. Washington was dressed in an uncouth style, with a large wig and long rusty sword, attended by his orderly sergeant in his country dress, having on his shoulder an old rusty gun seven or eight feet long. At the moment this figure appeared on the stage, one of the regular sergeants came running on stage, threw down his bayonet, and exclaimed,

" 'The Yankees are attacking our works on Bunker Hill!'

"Those of the audience who were unacquainted with the different parts, supposed that this belonged to the farce; but when Gen. Howe called out, 'Officers to your alarm posts!' they were undeceived; all was confusion and dismay; and among the ladies, shrieking and fainting ensued."

In orders of the day Washington gave his thanks to Maj. Knowlton, officers and soldiers. Howe had something different to say. He told his officers of the guard to instruct their sentries "not to fire except in the last extremity upon discovering the enemy," and to the soldiery in general he observed, "It is a great mark of the want of discipline when a soldier fires his piece without cause . . . ."

The glitter that goes with playgoing did not broadly apply to daily life in the British camp. At this time of January thaw, Lt. William Carter of the 40th Foot was saying, "Our little army has suffered severely from the dampness of the season and from living totally on salt provisions, without the smallest portion of vegetables." There was scurvy, of course, and Howe, as winter came, spoke of "smallpox spreading universally about the town."

At first Howe had threatened military execution for any persons leaving Boston without written permission. But the scarcity of food and fuel, and the soaring prices they brought, prompted him to change his orders and allow some civilians to depart by the Winnisimmet (Chelsea) ferryway — which caused Washington, though sympathetic, to take stern measures to prevent the spread of smallpox to his army.

The pathetic 300 men, women and children thus released from Boston gave, said Washington, "shocking accounts of the want of fuel and fresh provisions."

Lord Percy had a guess why the British garrison had so many shortages. He wrote at the time of Knowlton's raid, "We have had the most violent gales of wind for some time past that ever was known, so that we suppose great numbers of the ships destined for this port are gone to the West Indies." Capture of supply transports by Washington's navy also hurt deeply.

An early response of Howe to any of his men trying to forage for wood on their own brought this warning in a general order:

"The frequent depredations committed by the soldiers, in pulling down houses and fences, in defiance of repeated orders, has induced the Commander in Chief to direct the provost to go his rounds attended by the executioner, with orders to hang up upon the spot the first man he shall detect in the fact, without waiting for further proof by trial."

Yet little more than a week later Howe had each corps furnish an officer and 20 men "who understand the use of the ax" to obtain wood and work "till a sufficiency of fuel is provided. The barrack master general or his deputy, will point out such wharves, houses, old ships, and trees as each regiment may use for its share." This order was modified on arrival of some coal.

With all the pulling and axing down of Boston structures, Howe was soon complaining to Lord Dartmouth that "robberies, and housebreaking in particular, had got to such a height in this town, that some examples had become necessary to suppress it." Two soldiers caught robbing a store were ordered "hanged by the neck until they are dead," though Howe commuted hanging for one of them.

Still he inflicted severe punishments. A soldier and his wife were found guilty of receiving stolen goods. The man was ordered to receive "1000 lashes on the bare back with a cat-o-nine-tails" and his wife "100 lashes on the bare back at a cart's tail in different portions in the most conspicuous part of the town and to be imprisoned for three months."

Washington, pushing his preparations for attack, tried to do everything within his power to alleviate the shortages suffered in his camp.

On men, he decided to give little more than a couple of weeks' notice that all officers and soldiers on leave "or pretense whatsoever" be back in camp by Feb. 1 on pain of being cashiered or punished. Colonels were to grant no more leaves of absence or furloughs. He wanted his force in camp, he said, "so our real strength may be fully and clearly ascertained." This applied even to officers out recruiting.

When he discovered recruiting for the new army was still going slowly, he called his generals on Jan. 16 to a Council of War, which was joined by John Adams, shortly to return to Congress, and by James Warren. The council resolved to seek 13 regiments of militia to come to camp on Feb. 1 and serve through March — seven regiments from Massachusetts, four from Connecticut, two from New Hampshire.

During these council sessions came Gen. Schuyler's news of the "melancholy reverse" at Quebec. "The gallant Montgomery is no more; the brave Arnold is wounded." Three of the militia regiments called for Feb. 1 were now to be diverted to Quebec. Besides, Washington, after consulting with Adams, had sent Gen. Lee to strengthen the fortifying of New York, for fear that Gen. Clinton, who had headed southward with a striking force, would hit that seaport.

Arms were so difficult to obtain that Washington permitted each regiment to send one or two officers into the countryside with funds to buy arms where possible and even extended their time for returning to camp to Feb. 4. From all the discharged soldiers Washington had been able to obtain only 1620 arms and all these had to be redelivered to recruits arriving without arms.

When militia started coming to camp without arms, Washington ordered his brigadiers to discharge them at once, for he would have 2000 soldiers without firelocks and with no weapons but spears. Washington called the scarcity of arms "truly alarming" and regarded the endeavor of the officers sent to buy arms as "the last resource left me in this quarter."

Gunpowder continued as Washington's most critical lack. His secretary Reed used to find himself "shuddering at our situation." Washington only recently had written to Reed, "Our want of powder is inconceivable ... a gloomy prospect." To Hancock, Washington had written that once the fortifying at Lechmere's Point was finished the resolve of Congress for an attack would be executed "when we have powder to sport with."

Back in mid-December, two French merchants from Nantes, Penet and Pliarne, had come to the Cambridge camp with offers of trade that induced Washington to send them as swiftly as possible on to the Continental Congress. There they made a contract — portent of military supplies in the future from France. But for the present, gunpowder continued in desperate shortage.

Gunpowder manufacture in the colonies, tried way back in the early colonial days, had never really prospered because of British mercantile policy and the availability of inexpensive gunpowder from overseas. Now that the British supply had been cut off by the King's order in council, manufacture was again attempted, encouraged by the colonies. By early 1776 it was in progress, especially in Pennsylvania, from where Samuel Adams had sent Paul Revere "the plan of a powder mill."

For the present, though, Washington and the patriot cause had to depend chiefly on purchases abroad. American vessels left port with American produce and products to exchange for gunpowder, saltpeter and arms, at times in Europe, more often in non-British ports of the West Indies. This trade had begun to build a good supply. Howe had already complained to Lord Dartmouth about munitions coming in Yankee vessels from Hispanola.

Howe might well do so. Powder in his camp had the advantage of ample supply. Capt. Francis Hutcheson could tell how, just for the fun of it, the British gunners had just packed 27 pounds of powder into a sea mortar to lob a shell into the Cambridge camp between Harvard College and Christ Church on the Cambridge Common. Hutcheson, overjoyed, remarked: "This shows the rebels we can reach them at that distance when we please."

Gen. Heath's reaction mirrored the powder impoverishment of the Americans. The shell landed about as Hutcheson hoped. Heath remarked: "It did not burst. Nearly five pounds of powder was taken out of the shell." Washington could use them.

Washington's preparations moved on many fronts. Col. Jedediah Huntington in the Roxbury camp told early in January that "fascines are now cutting in preparation for possessing an important post to annoy the enemy." Sgt. Silas Goodell, in the Cambridge camp, wrote home late in January:

"Our people have built a new sled for the 'Congress' to carry her to Lechmere's Point and we expect every day she will speak to the Bostonians.

"We have got a large number of cannon within 20 miles of this place and the 'Old Sow' with the rest. I saw the 'Old Sow' on my march down with about 70 other pieces of cannon all bound to this place and we shall have hot work very soon.

"The groups are all in confusion. The militia are going home and the new troops coming in every day, which makes confusion plenty." The militia Goodell meant were those whose time expired between Jan. 15 and Feb. 1.

At this same time Col. Knox, pushing preparations too, was writing to New York for shot and shell promised to Washington and for the loan of two brass 6-pounders at Kingsbridge. "Although I brought 11 very fine fieldpieces from Ticonderoga," Knox wrote, "yet without the additional ones from New York we shall be deficient in field artillery — the shells, etc., are much wanted."

Knox, along with Col. Gridley, the chief engineer, went to study changes on the new bridge at Lechmere's Point "to prevent accidents."

Washington pressed ahead on finishing his fortifications so that he could move heavy cannon into place. He wrote to Reed, "We have had the most laborious piece of work at Lechmere's Point, on account of the frost that ever you saw. We hope to get it finished Sunday." This would be Feb. 11.

That day Washington was busy checking on fortifications. Lt. Col. Rufus Putnam, already noted for his engineering skill, reported that the causeway leading to Dorchester Neck was nearer the British cannon in Boston than was Lechmere's Point, and a covered way was already being built to Lechmere's Point. Putnam figured a covered way of about 3300 feet was thus needed on the approach to Dorchester Neck. Putnam observed:

"Can we, by any means, raise a covered way in this frozen season, it will be of no small consequence in taking posession of this ground in a favorable hour."

The next day some of the generals, accompanied by Knox and chief engineer Gridley, went to plan out works on the frozen ground of Dorchester Neck. At one point they left their horses back of Nook's Hill opposite British works on Boston Neck. Suddenly they had to scamper to safety when they spotted two British officers dash toward their artillery. "Old Put," though, took his time, keeping with lame old Gridley.

Washington was totally resolved on action. He had written to Hancock, on receiving the "Attack Boston" signal from Congress, to assure the Congress it was "not want of inclination" that was delaying him. And again he had written to Hancock: "No man upon Earth wishes more ardently to destroy the nest in Boston, than I do; no person will be willing to go greater lengths than I shall, to accomplish it . . . ."

This he said at the end of the January thaw. In the first two weeks of February the weather had turned frigid. Before his inspection on Feb. 11 Washington had written, "The bay towards Roxbury has been frozen up once or twice pretty hard." The army too began anticipating action. Col. Huntington wrote:

"I hope we shall be ordered to Dorchester before long, for more reasons than one. It is not only an important post to possess, but the militia will soon be uneasy if something considerable is not attempted. They are come with an idea of executing some great business."

The immediate action came, however, from the British. Howe sent word to Lord Dartmouth:

"Having intelligence that the enemy intended to possess themselves of Dorchester Neck, I ordered a detachment from Castle William on the 13th of February, under the command of Lt. Col. Leslie, and one composed of grenadiers and light infantry from Boston, commanded by Maj. Musgrave, to pass over the ice, with directions to destroy the houses, and every kind of cover whatever upon that peninsula."

The spy's information that Howe had received, said Col. Stephen Kemble, Howe's deputy adjutant general, was that the rebels had quantities of fascines (bundles of sticks), gabions (earth- and rock-filled cylindrical baskets) and entrenching tools on the neck to throw up a battery. None of these things was found, for the shrewd reason that anything ready had been secreted out in the countryside.

Robertson sketch of Feb. 14 raid on Dorchester Neck

Boston Athenaeum, Boston, Mass.

The British raid actually started about 4 a.m. on Feb. 14. It was dark and there was some light snow. Capt. Archibald Robertson, who made a picture of the scene, estimated Musgrave had about 400 troops when he reached the shore near Nook's (Foster's) Hill. Col. Leslie, the Alexander Leslie who about a year earlier had nearly touched off the Revolution with his abortive raid on Salem's North Bridge, led another 400 to the shore opposite Castle William.

An American sentry spotted Musgrave's men, fired and ran to the guardhouse to warn his captain. This officer, Capt. Barnes, already alerted by the shot, decided he needed reinforcements and withdrew his guard along the Dorchester road as the redcoats moved about the peninsula setting fire to six dwellings and 10 or 11 barns and shops.

The dozen families who had lived on the peninsula had long since withdrawn into the town of Dorchester. There Deacon James Blake, whose property was at the extreme end of the peninsula opposite Castle William, watched helplessly as his two houses and barn went up in flames. The British withdrew by dawn with six guardsmen they made prisoners.

Rev. William Gordon, Jamaica Plain minister and historian of that day, said Howe was up all night ready to attack the American camp at Roxbury.

Howe, said Gordon, "expected that the burning of the houses would occasion such an alarm, as to put us upon sending from Roxbury lines a large reinforcement, and thereby give him an opportunity of attacking them with advantage; but when day broke he found that our men were as usual at their alarm posts so that he could not prosecute his plan." Howe did extend his thanks to Leslie and Musgrave and their men.

Washington was still thinking of his own attack across the ice and dismissed the burned structures as "of no value to us . . . unless we take post there, they then might have been of some service."

He summoned his generals on Feb. 16 to a Council of War at Vassall House. Congress had stipulated that he should consult them on any assault on Boston. He estimated he had about 10,-000 men, twice the number fit for duty in the British camp. He agreed his stock of "powder was so small" he would have to rely on small arms. But with British reinforcements momentarily expected he told the generals:

"A stroke, well aimed, at this critical juncture, might put a final end to the war, and restore peace and tranquility, so much to be wished for.

"For these reasons, and under these circumstances, and as part of Cambridge and Roxbury bays were so frozen as to admit of an easier entry into the town of Boston than could be obtained, either by water or through lines on the Neck, the general desired to know the sentiments of the general officers respecting a general assault upon the town."

They were still opposed. Rev. Gordon said, "The repulse at Quebec cooled some fiery spirits and prudence prevented such a rash undertaking." The generals, though, gave reasons to Washington.

They figured Howe's force larger than Washington's estimate, noted Howe was "furnished with artillery, assisted by a fleet, and possessed of every advantage the situation of the place affords." They noted 2000 Americans still lacked arms, only half the expected militia had arrived, and they felt an assault should be preceded for some days by a bombardment. A bombardment would be proper only when the Americans should have a supply of powder "and not before."

The generals did, though, assent:

"That, in the meantime, preparations should be made to take possession of Dorchester Hill, with a view to drawing out the enemy, and of Noddle's Island, if the situation of the water, and other circumstances, will admit it."

Washington wrote to Hancock that he felt, despite all handicaps, an assault across the ice might have been "crowned with success." But since he found the Council of War "almost unanimous, I must suppose it to be right." His council had the attendance of two major generals, Artemas Ward and Israel Putnam, and five brigadiers, Thomas, Heath, Spencer, Sullivan and Gates.

Seizing Dorchester Heights now became Washington's paramount objective.

Washington plans to seize Dorchester Heights

The foot and a half of frost that, with the resistance of armor, hardened the ground on Dorchester Heights, made it impossible to shovel up an earth entrenchment overnight as the Americans had done before the battle of Bunker Hill.

The frost seemed impenetrable on the heights because they were bare and, observed Lt. Col. Rufus Putnam, "it was open country."

Washington had this difficulty unhappily emphasized to him by the long hours, day after freezing day, that his troops had been laboring to extend his fortifications at Lechmere's Point. And the British encountered precisely the same hardship a few hundred yards across the water in Boston when they, in reaction to Washington's activity, commenced erecting some new artillery positions.

"Find it difficult to work," noted Gen. Howe's adjutant, "on account of the hardness of the ground, being frozen."

But Washington found a solution, accidentally — even miraculously. Lt. Col. Putnam, who found it, attributed it to "Providence." Putnam, and others concerned with the difficulty, had visited with Washington and after dinner, related Putnam, Washington "desired me to tarry." The Commander in Chief asked Putnam especially to consider what could be done and, "if I think of any way ... to make report to him immediately."

On his route from Vassall House, Putnam called upon Brig. Gen. Heath. "I had no thoughts of calling until I came against his door," said Putnam. Once inside Putnam spotted a book on field engineering. Heath, it developed, had a policy of never lending books. Putnam had to beg several times, and did not succeed until he reminded Heath that it was Heath himself who had forced him, in the early, emergency days of the war, to act, though untrained, as an engineer.

While reading the book next day in his quarters Putnam came upon a tool of warfare entirely novel to him: "chandeliers." In military terms a chandelier is a wooden framework for stacking fascines. Putnam went on:

"No sooner did I turn to the page where it was described with its use but I was ready to report a plan for making a lodgment on Dorchester Neck. (Infidels may laugh if they please.)"

Soon Putnam was conferring, as Washington had directed, with Cols. Knox and Gridley. "They fell in with my plan. Our report was approved by the General and preparations immediately set on foot to carry it into effect...."

Other preparations went ahead steadily. They appeared in daily general orders from Vassall House. "The entrenching tools of every kind are to be carefully looked up, and put in good order... No time is to be lost in the doing of it." At the same time — coinciding with the Feb. 16 Council of War — came the command: "Col. Knox is to report the exact number of cannon cartridges, which are filled and ready for use, specifying the sorts and sizes."

Washington even brought up scarce regimental insignia "as the season is fast approaching for taking the field."

The bloody scenes at Bunker Hill were not forgotten. Dr. James Thacher, little more than a week before orders would be given to take Dorchester Heights, told of his regiment being moved from Prospect Hill to old Gov. Shirley's house on the Roxbury-Dorchester road, and how "orders have been received for surgeons and mates to prepare lint and bandages, to the amount of 2000, for fractured limbs, and other gunshot wounds."

Washington went further in his concern. He declared in general orders:

"It being a matter of too much importance to entrust the wounds and lives of officers and soldiers to unskilled surgeons, the general requests the director general and surgeons of the hospital ... will sit and examine the surgeons and mates of the whole army."

Washington's preparatory bombardment for taking Dorchester Heights would open on the night of March 2, a Saturday. It was only on the previous Monday, Feb. 26, that Washington completed his works at Lechmere's Point, and wrote to Reed that he had "two platforms fixed for mortars, and everything but THE thing (powder) ready for an offensive operation."

He wrote to Gen. Lee that he also had finished another platform at Lamb's Dam, an outermost work on Boston Neck. And he now had strong guards mounted at Lechmere's Point and Cobble Hill. It would be these three fortifications, Lechmere's Point, Cobble Hill and Lamb's Dam, from which he would bombard Boston.

As these became ready, Washington ordered Col. Knox's regiment to move heavy cannon and mortars into position. Knox had his second in command, Lt. Col. William Burbeck, play a big role because Mrs. Knox was "exceedingly ill." She was about to have her first baby.

Burbeck saw to the moving of 18-pounders and 24-pounders from Prospect Hill to Lechmere's Point. Over in Roxbury, Knox's Maj. John Crane, a hero of the Boston Tea Party, moved cannon into position, among them some 24-pounders from the high Roxbury Fort down to Lamb's Dam.

Washington spoke of "an amazing quantity of chandeliers and fascines" being prepared. New carriages had to be built for "almost all our heavy cannon," said Col. Jedediah Huntington. Great quantities of hay were screwed into bundles at Chelsea to be used as a blind along the neck to Dorchester Heights. Master carpenter Jacob Rhoades was busy up the Charles River preparing flat-bottomed boats, whaleboats, oars and paddles for a projected amphibious landing in Boston from across the Back Bay.

Howe's Feb. 14 raid and burning on Dorchester Neck seemed to leave him content that he was secure from attack from that quarter.

The British, though, made several responses to Washington's move. Col. Kemble told of a new battery for three 32-pounders opened on Beacon Hill opposite Lechmere's Point and below that, near the water, a battery for a 13-inch mortar. A new battery was started near the magazine on Boston Common. The battlements in the redoubt at Barton's Point were heightened.

From time to time, during this preliminary activity, Washington obtained reports out of Boston that indicated the British might be intending to sail away. Useful vessels were being pressed into service of the crown. British ships were taking on water. Some heavy ordnance — mortars from Bunker Hill — were being stowed on shipboard. Large quantities of biscuit were being baked.

Washington was left to guess the meaning. He did send warnings off to Gen. Lee in New York. But he declared: "Whether they really intend to embark or whether the whole is a feint is impossible for me to tell."

Washington had a sudden new worry on Wednesday, Feb. 28, and rushed off orders to Gen. Artemas Ward about a deserter to Boston:

"A rascally rifleman went in last night and will no doubt give all the intelligence he can." Ward was asked to assign special patrols this night at either end of Dorchester Neck, the point opposite Fort William and Castle Island and at Nook's Hill opposite Boston's South End. Washington asked Ward to order:

"Particular regiments to be ready to march at a moment's warning to the Heights of Dorchester; for should the enemy get possession of those hills before us they would render it a difficult task to dispossess them; better it is therefore to prevent than to remedy an evil."

Washington's preparations were about complete. He had sent Gen. Thomas to consult with the Massachusetts authorities to arrange signals for the militia of the neighboring towns to be ready to march as an extra reserve. Six regiments would arrive on March 4 under the command of Brig. Gen. Benjamin Lincoln. And Washington would even order that "all the spears ... be examined, cleaned and collected in their proper places."

He addressed an inspirational message to the soldiers "as the season is now fast approaching when every man must expect to be drawn into the field of action ....

"It is a noble cause we are engaged in. It is the cause of virtue, and mankind, every temporal advantage and comfort to us, and our posterity, depends upon the vigor of our exertions; in short, freedom or slavery must be the result of our conduct, there can therefore be no greater inducement to men to behave well.

"But it may not be amiss for the troops to know, that if any man in action shall presume to skulk, hide himself, or retreat from the enemy, without the orders of his commanding officer; he will be instantly shot down, as an example of cowardice; cowards having too frequently disconcerted the best formed troops, by their dastardly behavior."

Washington was now about as set for action as was possible, in view of the paucity of gunpowder. His aim was clear. He wrote to congress:

"If anything will induce them (the British) to hazard an engagement, it will be our attempting to fortify these heights, as on that event's taking place, we shall be able to command a great part of the town and almost the whole harbor, and to make them rather disagreeable than otherwise. . . ."

To a Virginian friend, Landon Carter, Washington put the situation thusly:

"To . . . force the enemy to an engagement or make the town too hot for them."

To Reed he expressed his most ardent hope: "I am preparing to take post on Dorchester Heights, to try if the enemy will be so kind as to come out to us."

That Wednesday, Feb. 28, and on Leap Year's Day the following day, Washington relaxed, wrote some personal letters. One was to the celebrated black poetess, Phillis Wheatley, who had been educated and made free by her Boston owners, the John Wheatleys. Miss Wheatley had written a poem on Washington and his letter invited her to visit him at Vassall House. Another letter was to his brother-in-law, Burwell Bassett, to thank him for his care of Washington's Ohio River lands. With the hoped-for battle at hand he said of the lands:

"In the worst event, they will serve for an asylum."

In the first half of March, Washington would be getting letters from Hancock and Reed that five tons and then 10 tons of gunpowder were on their way from Philadelphia. But at the moment that Washington was planning to act, America was just on the eve of its own manufacture flourishing and of receiving a dependable supply from foreign ports.

The trickle into the Cambridge camp did swell a bit so that diarists recorded arrival of two loads from Providence, 30 barrels from Connecticut and some "small parcels" — Washington called them "a seasonable supply" — also from Connecticut. Still, Washington, at the moment of action, summed up his powder situation for his brother Jack as mighty lean:

"Having received a small supply of powder, very inadequate to our wants, I resolved to take possession of Dorchester Point . . . ."

Washington summoned his generals to a Council of War to fix the time. Col. Thomas Mifflin, the Quartermaster General, was invited to attend and had a suggestion. The anniversary of the Boston Massacre would fall on March 5 and Mifflin thought "it would have a wonderful effect upon the spirits of the New Englanders" to go on Dorchester Heights on the night of March 4 for battle the next day.

On March 2, Washington's orders were sent to Maj. Gen. Ward, who, supported by Brig. Gens. John Thomas and Joseph Spencer, was in command of the army's right wing. The orders were brief:

"Sir:

"After weighing all circumstances of tide, etc., and considering the hazard of having the posts on Dorchester Neck taken by the enemy, and the evil consequences which would result from it, the gentlemen here are of the opinion that we should go on there Monday night. I give you this early notice of it, that you may delay no time in preparing for it, as everything here will be got in readiness to cooperate. In haste I am, sir, etc."

On the outside of the orders was written:

"Saturday evening. Remember — barrels."

Barrels? Dorchester Heights was steep and free of any trees or brush. Barrels, said Brig. Gen. Heath, comprised "a very curious and novel mode of defense" suggested by a Boston merchant. Heath, delighted with the idea, said he had rushed it to Washington. The barrels would be filled with stone or sand, be placed outside the parapet and, when the British should attack, chocks on the barrels could be removed and the barrels plummet downhill into the enemy.

That Saturday night Abigail Adams, in her home in Braintree, having put her children to bed, was writing a letter to her husband in praise of Paine's "Common Sense" and wondering why Congress should hesitate a moment in accepting these arguments for independence, when abruptly she interjected:

"But hark! The house this instant shakes with the roar of cannon . . . .

"I have been to the door and find 'tis a cannonade from our army. Orders I find are come for all the remaining militia to repair to the lines a Monday night by 12 o'clock. No sleep for me tonight . . . ."

The cannonade under Col. Knox began about 11 p.m., belching from the big cannon and mortars mainly of the advanced posts Washington had built on Cobble Hill and Lechmere's Point, and from Lamb's Dam. The cannonade, which would thunder for three nights, was intended by Washington "to divert the enemy's attention from our real design." In this he had complete success.

"The violent crash of heavy artillery," said Lt. William Carter of the King's 40th Foot, was answered by the British batteries, mainly from the new ones on Barton's Point and westside Beacon Hill.

The rebel shells, observed Capt. Charles Stuart, "were thrown in an excellent direction, they took effect near the center of the town, and tore several houses to pieces." Rising to eloquence, Stuart added:

"A nobler scene it was impossible to behold: sheets of fire seemed to come from our batteries; some of the shells crossed one another in the air, and then bursting looked beautiful. The inhabitants were in a horrid situation, particularly the women, who were several times drove from their houses by shot, and crying for protection."

The bombardment went on until daylight. Adj. Kemble saw several shells that "came into the town and through some houses" and exploded in yards of fellow officers. Testy Lt. John Barker thought the rebels had the advantage. "Our shells very bad," he noted; "most of 'em bursting in the air or not at all."

On the American side there was an unlucky loss.

The commissary general, Joseph Trumbull, was at Lechmere's Point watching the cannon fire. "The 13-inch mortar," he said, "was directed at the Province House (Howe's headquarters), and the shells went very near it, I believe." But, alas! The beloved 13-inch mortar, "The Congress," after two or three discharges, burst. So did two 10-inch mortars.

"To what cause to attribute this misfortune, I know not," Washington wrote Hancock; "whether to any defect in them, or to the inexperience of the bombardiers." Gen. Heath felt that the cannon "were not properly bedded, as the ground was hard frozen." Whatever the cause, there were more similar losses when the bombardment resumed.

Washington had another exhortation for his army on Sunday:

"As it is not unlikely but a contest may soon be brought on, between the ministerial troops and this army; the general flatters himself, that every officer, and soldier, will endeavor to give such distinguished proofs of his conduct, and good behavior, as becomes men, fighting for everything that is dear and valuable to free men . . . ."

The soldiers were cautioned not to fire at too great a distance "as one fire well aimed does more execution than a dozen at long-shot." And every man in the army was firmly ordered by the general that "No officer, or soldier, under any pretense, is to be absent from his post, without leave in writing from his brigadier general . . . ."

Washington had a special message for Gen. Ward, not so much outright orders, as, he said, "my ideas generally."

Washington said he would send over Cols. Gridley and Knox on Monday to lay out the lines of fortification. He discussed what relief — "I should think from two to three thousand as circumstances may require" — should be sent on "the morning after the post is taken." Two regiments of riflemen from Cambridge would be sent to join this relief force.

For holding the post, Washington observed, Ward would have five companies of riflemen in all who could "gall the enemy sorely in their march from their boats and in landing."

Washington thought "a blind along the causeway should be thrown up . . . nearest the enemy's guns and most exposed." He estimated 250 axe-men would be sufficient to fell trees (these would be in the orchards on Dorchester Neck) to make abattis, obstructions of sharpened tree limbs placed on the approach to ramparts. Covering parties should be placed at either end of the Neck, at Nook's Hill and opposite Fort William, and sentries between them, even on the Squantum side, the back shore.

And barrels again! Washington told Ward, "I have a very high opinion of the defense which may be made with barrels from either of the hills . . . . Perhaps single barrels would be better than linking them together, being less liable to accidents; the hoops should be well nailed or else they will soon fly, and the casks fall to pieces."

The American cannon reverberated again on Sunday night. Col. Knox kept count, undoubtedly with vast delight, for the shells were all the King's, either from the King's stores in New York or from Capt. Manley's sensational capture last November of the British ordnance brig *Nancy*.

"I went to bed after 12 but go no rest," noted Abigail Adams; "the cannon continued firing and my heart beat pace with them all night."

Howe, on Sunday, had instructed his soldiers that "in case of shells falling at or near their posts, so as to endanger the houses catching fire, they will immediately apprise the neighborhood of it, that it may be extinguished as soon as possible." Lt. Barker had a bit better report on British gunfire on the second night:

"Our artillery a little mended, a few of our shells answering." Fire on both sides, he thought, was warmer than on Saturday night.

Howe was getting concerned by Monday and ordered that his troops, if they did not already. have them, obtain sufficient supplies so that each man would have 60 rounds of cartridges. He also ordered that the troops "have one day's provision, ready dressed, to carry with them, in case of their being ordered out at short notice."

Washington, with combat at hand, was issuing last-minute orders. The signal for a general alarm was to be the hoisting of a flag on Prospect Hill and the laboratory building at the rear of Cambridge Common. No flags were to be

hoisted in either place except on a general alarm — and this was made a "standing order until the Commander in Chief shall please to direct otherwise."

Washington's mind, as always, was on his men. He gave instructions that all the surgeons from the army's left wing and center were to meet at 5 p.m. with the director general of the hospital on dispositions for their sick, that the barracks at Prospect Hill were to be got in immediate readiness to receive some of the wounded. Sufficient men were to be selected to carry wounded and hand-barrows were to be provided.

At 7 p.m. Col. Knox began the third night of cannonading and the British cannoneers replied with a "very hot" fire of shot and shell.

Tonight, though, something else was afoot, at 7 o'clock, something slightly to the southeastward of Boston — barely outside the range of this booming artillery duel — something that would go generally unnoticed in the British camp.

"About 7 o'clock," Brig. Gen. Thomas wrote in a quick summation to his wife, "I marched with about 3000 picked men, besides 360 ox teams and some pieces of artillery. Two companies of the train of teams were laden with materials for our works.

"About 8 o'clock we ascended the high hills, and by daylight got two hills defensible . . . ."

The cannonade concealing this tremendous activity exceeded the intensity of the first two nights. A Maryland rifleman, Pvt. Daniel Mc-Curtin, was among those from Roxbury and Cambridge sent to "lay in ambush close by the water side expecting every moment that the butchers belonging to the tyrant of Great Britain would be out among us."

McCurtin, who could watch artillery exchange, noted:

"Those other two nights . . . I thought was bad enough. But O my God the wonders of last night.

"I can't, it's impossible I could describe the situation of this town and all about it. This night you could see shells, sometimes seven at a time in the air and as to cannon the continual shaking of the earth by cannonading dried up our wells."

During the battle of Bunker Hill Abigail Adams, holding by the hand her son, future President John Quincy Adams, had watched from Penn's Hill near her Braintree farmhouse. This night she witnessed the "amazing roar of cannon" from the same spot. "I could see every shell which was thrown," she said.

There were casualties on both sides. Gen. Heath told of British shot from Boston Neck hitting troops on the Roxbury parade ground and mortally wounding a lieutenant, a ball carrying away a thigh. Lt. Carter told of an 18-pound shot from Roxbury going through a regimental guardhouse and wounding six men, one of them mortally, "having his legs and thighs broke in shocking manner."

Heaviest of the American cannonfire was from the Lamb's Dam 24-pounders and 18-pounders. Lt. Col. David Mason, of Knox's artillery, was in charge there with Maj. Crane. Mason, at the time of Col. Leslie's raid at Salem, was the patriot who had taunted Leslie from atop the raised old North Bridge. Mason was now wounded when a 10-inch mortar burst.

There was a gigantic task of moving materials and cannon. A veteran and vigorous Son of Liberty, John Goddard of Brookline, was wagon master general and often used his farm for hiding patriot powder and supplies. Working with him was James Boies of Milton, a member of the Provincial Congress. A lot of the fascines were cut on his farm.

Boies's 13-year-old son Jeremiah rode pillion behind his father "to take care of the horse when father might have occasion to dismount and issue orders." Jeremiah related that many of the supplies, to cover where they were going to be used, had been "carted to Brookline, lying in a different direction, as a plan of disguise.

"Numerous teams were ordered to the place of deposit, and at the close of day, to load and cart the same through Roxbury and over Dorchester neck of land to the heights.

"In passing through Dorchester great caution was taken that no teamster should speak loud to his cattle. The fascines were unloaded on the summit of the hill without being discovered

in Boston, although the writer could plainly see several of the inhabitants open and shut their outer doors...."

Roxbury was the bustling center for the expedition and a local clergyman, Rev. Gordon, spoke with many of the participants. Gordon described Thomas's march:

"The covering party of 800 men lead the way; then come the carts with the entrenching tools; after them the main working body of about 1200 under Gen. Thomas: a train of more than 300 carts, loaded with fascines, hay in bundles of 7 and 800 weight, etc., close the martial procession.

"The bundles of hay are designed for Dorchester Neck, which is very low, and exposed to be raked by the enemy; and are to be laid on the side next to them, to cover the Americans in passing and repassing.

"Every man knows his place and business.

"The covering party, when upon the grounds, divides; half goes to the point nearest to Boston, the other to that next to the castle.

"All possible silence is observed. But there is no occasion to order the whips to be taken from the waggoners, lest their impatience, and the difficulty of the roads should induce them to make use of them, and occasion an alarm.

"The whips used by the drivers of these ox-carts, are not formed for making much noise, and can give no alarm at a distance. The men in driving their oxen commonly make most noise with their voices; and now a regard to their own safety dictates to them, to speak to their cattle, as they move on, in a whispering note.

"There are no bad roads to require an exertion; for the frost having been of long continuance, they are so hard frozen, as to be quite good. The wind lies so as to carry what noise cannot be avoided by driving the stakes and picking against the ground ... into the harbor between the town and the castle, so that it cannot be heard and regarded by any who have no suspicion of what is carrying on, especially as there is a continued cannonade on both sides.

"Many of the carts make three trips, some four; for a vast quantity of materials have been collected, especially chandeliers and fascines...."

"Gen. Thomas told me that he pulled out his watch and found that by 10 o'clock at night, they had got two forts, one upon each hill, sufficient to defend them from small arms and grape shot. The men continued working with the utmost spirit....The night was remarkably mild, a finer for working could not have been taken out of the whole 365.

"It was hazy below so that our people could not be seen, though it was a bright moonlight night above on the hills."

As Gen. Thomas was pulling out his watch, someone in Boston noticed the rebel activity. Royal engineer Capt. Robertson said: "About 10 o'clock at night Lt. Col. Campbell reported to Brig. Smith that the rebels were at work on Dorchester Heights."

Lt. Col. John Campbell of the 22nd Regt. was the one whose guardhouse was hit and six wounded, and Brig. Gen. Francis Smith was the officer who had led the redcoats to Lexington and Concord the day the war began. The warning, however, as the one to Gage before the battle of Bunker Hill, brought no action in the British camp.

Cannon resounded ceaselessly through the night. "I went to bed about 12 and rose again a little after one," recounted Abigail. "I could no more sleep than if I had been in the engagement. The rattling of the windows, the jar of the house and the continual roar of the 24-pounders, the bursting of shells give us such ideas, and realize a scene to us of which we could scarcely form any conception."

Some relief troops started marching about 3 a.m. Dr. Thacher was with his regiment, which was ordered to march at 4 a.m. from the Gov. Shirley mansion.

"On passing Dorchester Neck," he related, "I observed a vast number of large bundles of screwed hay, arranged in a line next the enemy, to protect our troops....The carts are still in motion with materials....

"On the heights we found two forts in considerable forwardness....The amount of labor performed during the night, considering the earth is frozen 18 inches deep, is almost incredible." Gen. Heath's comment was: "Perhaps there never was so much work done in so short a space of time."

Thomas thought the British surprise was total.

"About sunrise," he said, "the enemy and others in Boston, appeared numerous on the tops of houses and on the wharves viewing us with astonishment, for our appearance was unexpected to them.

"The cannonading which had been kept up all night from our lines at Lamb's Dam, and from the enemy's lines, likewise at Lechmere's Point, now ceased from these quarters, and the enemy turned their fire towards us on the hills, but they soon found it was to little effect."

Capt. Charles Stuart felt that what the rebels had created: "Appeared more like magic than the work of human beings."

If not magical, it was awesome. With an engineer's eyes, Capt. Robertson studied the two forts, the parapet connecting them across the intervening tableland and a kind of redoubt on a small hill below. "The materials for the whole works must have been carried ... a most astonishing night's work must have employed from 15,000 to 20,000 men."

Vice Adm. Molyneux Shuldham, too, studied this sudden peril to his main anchorage and the entire harbor. The rebels had improvised a reversal which Shuldham found "so alarming and ... unexpected" from what, he believed, had been all along "an advantageous situation." He told Howe his ships "could not possibly remain in the harbor under the fire of the batteries from Dorchester Neck."

Howe readily understood the menace — indeed, potential disaster — now confronting him.

Rev. Gordon said Howe was seen to scratch his head and say to those about him, "The rebels have done more in one night than my whole army would have done in months." Howe also figured it was the work of 12,000 or even 14,000 rebels and informed Lord Dartmouth:

"In a situation so critical, I determined upon an immediate attack with all the force I could transport."

Howe called an immediate Council of War at Province House. All the field officers were ordered to attend. On his way, Lt. Carter was thinking how the rebels now "command old Boston entirely: the enemy must inevitably be driven from thence, or we must abandon the town."

Howe ordered five regiments to embark immediately on five transports at Long Wharf (at the end of present State street). These, under command of Brig. Gen. Valentine Jones, were to proceed to Castle William to prepare to attack the rebels from the Castle side of Dorchester Neck.

Presently, four corps of shock troops — two of light infantry and two of grenadiers — along with two foot regiments were ordered to parade at 7 p.m. and be ready to embark at Long Wharf. This force would be under command of Howe, Lord Percy and Gen. James Robertson. It would attack from the side opposite Boston, the point at Nook's Hill.

The attack would be with bayonet. The forces would start moving in boats to the shore at 9 p.m.

Meantime the British cannon had been aimed at Dorchester Heights. The distance and the elevation caused problems. The British, Brig. Gen. Sullivan reported, "endeavored to elevate their cannon, so as to reach our works, by sinking the hinder wheels of the cannon into the earth, but after an unsuccessful fire of about two hours, they grew weary of it and desisted."

The surprise seizure of Dorchester Heights was only one of the surprises Washington had prepared for his foe. Should Howe make "any formidable attack upon Dorchester," Washington had prepared a force of 4000 soldiers who had been on the alert since daybreak for an amphibious assault on Boston. The signal was to come from atop old Roxbury Meetinghouse in present Eliot square, a hilltop structure easily visible then in Cambridge.

Maj. Gen. Putnam would be in command.

Three floating batteries, the flat-bottomed boats and the whaleboats were in readiness at the mouth of the Charles River and the soldiers were paraded nearby at Fort No. 2 in the lines of the Cambridge camp. Brig. Gen. Greene was to land in the West End at Barton's Point and Brig. Gen. Sullivan at Boston Common to take Beacon Hill. They were to join, force the British works at Boston Neck and let in the Roxbury troops.

Dr. Thacher said that during the British bombardment directed at Dorchester Heights there was also some firing from ships in the harbor. "Cannon shot are continually rolling and re-bounding over the hill; and it is astonishing to observe how little our soldiers are terrified by them.

"During the forenoon we were in momentary expectation of witnessing an awful scene; nothing less than the carnage of Breed's Hill battle was expected."

"We were in high spirits," said Maj. John Trumbull, the artist who was on the heights, "well prepared to receive the threatened attack. We had at least 20 pieces of artillery mounted on them, amply supplied with ammunition.... We waited with impatience for the attack, when we meant to emulate, and hoped to eclipse, the glories of Bunker Hill."

Thomas was joined by his 10-year-old son John Jr., who had run away from school in the morning and, as Thomas would write to his wife, "got by the sentries and came to me on Dorchester Hills." Studying the scene, Thomas said:

"About 10 o'clock we discovered large bodies of troops embarking in boats with their artillery, which made a formidable appearance. After some time they were put on board transports, and several of the ships came down near the castle, as we supposed, with a design to land on our shore. Our people appeared in spirits to receive them."

Rev. Gordon, who was among the spectators, pictured the setting:

"The surrounding hills and elevations about Boston ... are alive with the numerous spectators that throng them. A more interesting and bloody scene is apprehended to be just upon commencing, than what presented at Charlestown." When the spectators saw the redcoats, said Rev. Gordon:

"The Americans expect they are intended for an immediate attack, clap their hands for joy, and wish them to come on.

"Gen. Washington happens at that instant to be on one of the heights; thinks with his men; and says to those at hand: 'Remember it is the Fifth of March, and avenge the death of your brethren.'

"It is instantly asked by such as are not near enough to hear: 'What says the general?' His words are given in answer. They fly from man to man through all the troops upon the spot, and add fuel to the martial fire already kindled, and burning with uncommon intenseness."

The tide turned and late in the afternoon, when it was far ebbed, the soldiers and the waiting throng became convinced that the British attack would come later. The wind shifted and was now blowing "pretty fresh and almost full against" the British. Some of the redcoats landed at the Castle before dark. Their transports were fired upon from a fieldpiece the Americans moved down to the shore facing the Castle.

The winds grew stronger, preventing some transports from getting down to the Castle and blowing ships ashore on a harbor island. *HMS Centurion* lost a gunboat swamped with its 12-pounder. The raging surf made it impossible to have the flat-bottomed boats proceed. "The attempt," Howe decided, "became impractical."

By late afternoon, even before the storm struck, Capt. Robertson had become alarmed for the fate of the British force. As embarkation was still afoot he decided "I think the most serious step ever an army of this strength in such a situation took considering the state the rebels' works are in and the number of men they appear to have under arms. The fate of this whole army and the town is at stake not to say the fate of America."

He went to Province House but could not get admittance. Then he started expressing his views to several officers, two lieutenant colonels, two majors, three captains. At 7 p.m. he hurried again to headquarters to press his suggestion that the British "ought immediately to embark" — get out. After waiting an hour, Robertson said:

"Capt. Montresor (his immediate superior, and one of the captains he had spoken with) came down from the general, told me he had been in council and had advised the going off altogether, that Lord Percy and some others seconded him and that the general said it was his own sentiments from the first, but thought the honor of the troops concerned. . . . "

Montresor, best remembered for his mapmaking, was right. Howe put it this way to Lord Dartmouth:

"The weather continuing boisterous the next day and night gave the enemy time to improve their works, to bring up their cannon, and to put themselves into such a state of defense, that I could promise myself little success by attacking them under all the disadvantages I had to encounter; wherefore I judged it most advisable to prepare for the evacuation of the town, upon the assurance of one month's provision from Adm. Shuldham. . . . "

Washington's fleet and the unusual winter gales that had driven Howe's provision ships to the West Indies, and held them there, had made his food supply precarious, close to desperate. Shuldham had already been transfering naval provisions to the army and was convinced "except a supply arrives very speedily for both services, the consequences must be fatal."

In the forenoon, at 11 o'clock, Howe called his commanding officers of corps together at Province House. Boston, said Adj. Kemble, was considered "untenable" as the rebels might take Nook's Hill. So, said Kemble, "the general thought proper to embark all the stores and sail away as fast as possible." Halifax, which Shuldham called "the nearest and most likely place of refuge," was now Howe's destination.

To his troops Howe declared:

"The general desires the troops may know that the intended expedition was unavoidably put off by the badness of the weather."

This day, March 6, Washington found British troops sailing back from the Castle to Boston "whether," he observed, "from an apprehension that our works are now too formidable to make any impression on, or from what other causes I know not. . . . If we had powder (and our mortars replaced, which I am about to do by new cast ones as soon as possible) I would, so soon as we were sufficiently strengthened on the heights to take possession of the point just opposite Boston Neck (Nook's Hill), give them a dose they would not well like. . . .

"I will not lament or repine at any act of Providence," Washington told Reed, "because I am in a great measure, a convert to Mr. (Alexander) Pope's opinion, that whatever is, is right, but I think everything had the appearance of a successful issue, if we had come to an engagement. . . . "

Howe flees Boston

Howe was more candid than Adm. Shuldham on why he chose to retreat to Halifax. His explanation, given to Lord Dartmouth, underscored the low estate to which the flight from Boston would bring British dominion in North America.

Halifax, said Howe, was: "The only place where the army can remain until supplies arrive from Europe."

For Howe there now arose, as he bemoaned, "a thousand difficulties." The prior fall, he had received the King's permission to begin the 1776 campaign in New York, but he had remained in Boston because he said he did not have sufficient vessels. Now Howe had even less serviceable shipping.

Washington's surprise offensive caught Howe without the reinforcements he needed to initiate any attack on New York, and the men Howe had were far from prepared for a descent upon that community. Under hostile guns, Howe now had to move out his troops, artillery and military supplies and transport more than 1000 Tories who had sought shelter behind his lines.

A supreme worry for Howe was what might be Washington's next move. And further moves were already part of Washington's plan. "Our taking possession of Dorchester Heights," Washington told Congress, "is only preparatory to taking post on Nook's Hill, and the points opposite to the south end of Boston." To do this, said Washington, it was "absolutely necessary" that Dorchester Heights be fortified.

Nook's Hill (now vanished) was so close to the center of Boston it was even behind the British blockhouse battery and both the old and advance batteries on Boston Neck. Mingling with worry over Nook's Hill was fear that the Americans might also fortify Noddle's Island (East Boston), and thus control the main harbor channel from either side.

Adj. Kemble, directly following Howe's orders for the camp to prepare as soon as possible for embarkation, kept nervous, daily accounts on what was happening at both these points. Capt. Robertson was assigned to reconnoiter them each day.

A new consideration, essentially diplomatic, entered the tense situation on March 8. Boston's selectmen were, Washington later wrote to Reed, "under dreadful apprehension for the town" and, through Maj. Gen. James Robertson, sought to learn if Howe was planning to incinerate it. Robertson spoke to Howe, and told them that Howe would "not molest the town unless His Majesty's troops should be molested during the embarkation, or at their departure."

Soon a flag of truce appeared outside the British works on Boston Neck and Maj. Richard Bassett of the 10th Foot handed a message to Col. Ebenezer Learned, whose regiment had long been posted at the advance American lines on Boston Neck, for delivery to Gen. Washington "as soon as possible."

The paper had been prepared by prominent Bostonians, Thomas and Jonathan Amory and Peter Johonnot, who had spoken to Gen. Robertson. It told of having Howe's assurances within Boston that it would not be consumed like Charlestown and sought assurance that "so dreadful a calamity may not be brought on by any measures without." To attest Howe's assurance, Chairman John Scollay and three other selectmen signed their names.

Washington consulted with general officers handy to Vassall House. They agreed that no official recognition should be accorded the appeal but Col. Learned was to say he had handed it to the general and to state his position. Learned did this in a brief note next morning, March 9. Washington had told him "that, as it was an unauthenticated paper, without an address, and not obligatory upon Gen. Howe, he would take no notice of it."

Any understanding between the camps was strictly tacit. Washington was nevertheless resolved to proceed with his plans as they were before he heard from the Boston selectmen and decided to "have a battery thrown up on Nook's Hill" that night "with a design of acting as circumstances may require."

Capt. Robertson had been keeping faithful watch. At 5 a.m. that morning he even went in a six-oared boat of a man-of-war to reconnoiter

Noddle's Island and reported, "Saw nothing." But that night he did see something: "Rebels . . . bringing materials" to Nook's Hill. "At dusk orders were given to cannonade them."

Gen. Heath said British attention was attracted to Nook's Hill when "the men imprudently kindled a fire behind the hill previous to the hour for breaking ground." But Robertson had not missed a rebel move. That night, said Heath, there was a "continual roar of cannon and mortars." Four Americans were killed, some wounded. Robertson said "peppery fire" continued on successive nights on materials behind Nook's Hill.

Sharp-tongued Lt. Barker's description of Boston, after Howe came to his decision to get out, was identical to that of most observers:

"Nothing but hurry and confusion."

Loyalists, who had comforted themselves with the belief that Great Britain was invincible, were overwhelmed by Howe's impending flight. Rev. Gordon said: "The Tories were thunderstruck, and terribly dejected."

John Rowe, Boston merchant and shipowner (one of his vessels was in the Boston Tea Party), had remained in Boston throughout the occupation and kept a diary. He had shrewdly guessed on March 6 that Howe would be quitting Boston. Soon as Howe's intentions spread through the town, Rowe recorded next day that the troops and inhabitants were frantically busy getting goods and effects on board the vessels in the harbor.

" 'Tis impossible to describe the distress of this unfortunate town," commented Rowe.

And two days later:

"Nothing but hurry and confusion, every person striving to get out of the place."

Howe's original intention was to depart by March 11. All women, children, sick and convalescents were embarked. As that day approached he gave strict orders on fires. "Any person detected setting fire to the town without authority will suffer immediate death." All troops and Tories were warned to have all baggage on shipboard by 5 p.m. on March 11: "If any is found on the wharfs after 6, it will be thrown into the sea."

But Howe could not keep that deadline, though all the precious brass artillery was on board and a large part of the troops' baggage and such of the King's stores as were designated to be saved. One of the reasons Howe could not get away came from a notice he issued March 10 authorizing one Crean Brush, an unsavory New Yorker, to remove all linen and woolen goods, "articles much wanted by the rebels."

The idea had originated with Capt. Robertson, he said, and had been passed to Howe by Montresor. Brush, a man "with sharp nose," an arrogant, officious individual, far exceeded his orders. He and his crew crashed into the stores and warehouses of numerous merchants, among them Rowe's, grabbed what they wanted helter-skelter, jammed it unmarked on board the brig *Elizabeth*.

"There never was such destruction and outrage committed any day before this," said Rowe. Selectman Samuel Austin, who was among those trying to save the town, said he was stripped of "everything worth carrying away and that others are sharing the same fate."

Plundering, incipient in the withdrawal of hostile troops, was stimulated by Brush's example. This led to intoxication in the garrison — as did prosperous civilians paying exorbitant prices to offduty troops to help them escape with their valuables.

Some regulars and sailors were officially busy destroying things, useful to the rebels, that could not be shipped. Iron cannon were spiked or their trunnions knocked off. Vessels Howe could not utilize, with and without cargo, were scuttled at their wharves. Three ships of 300 or more tons being built were wrecked, two of them Hancock's and one of them at his own wharf.

Howe strove to keep order. He had officers remain with their men to keep them as much as possible in quarters before departure. Efforts were made to suppress drunkenness. On plundering, Howe would have to threaten "that the first soldier who is caught plundering will be hanged on the spot." Even the portraits of the King and Queen hanging in the town house (old State House) were cut and defaced and public papers destroyed.

British troops departing from Boston

Howe set a new date for departure — March 13 — and finding shipboard space woefully inadequate, he ordered "all household furniture and other useless luggage to be thrown overboard." Soon the debris, along with gun carriages and ammunition wagons systematically wrecked by the regulars, would be drifting in around all the shores of Boston harbor.

Washington, who "fully expected, before this, that the town would have been entirely evacuated," held a Council of War at Gen. Ward's headquarters in Roxbury on present Mission Hill. He was concerned about the safety of New York, for he was convinced New York would be Howe's objective because its possession could split the northern and southern colonies and control the Hudson River approach to Canada.

The Council agreed that a battalion of riflemen could be sent off to New York, to be followed by five regiments and some artillery units. The Council further felt that if Howe was still in Boston the next day, Washington the following night should fortify Nook's Hill "at all events."

The fate of Boston was still far from settled. "Whether the town will be destroyed," said Washington, "is a matter of much uncertainty." He did feel, though, that the piecemeal destruction might mean that it would not "be involved in one general ruin."

On the 13th, Howe had all the rowers freed from other duties and paraded at noontime. Brig. Gens. Robertson and Sir James Grant were to supervise the embarkation at Long Wharf, and Brig. Gens. Valentine Jones and Francis Smith at Hancock's Wharf. "But the wind came against us," said Lt. Barker.

Next day Howe, determined to depart, ordered "all officers and soldiers on board ship not to come on shore on any account without the general's express permission." Those on shore were ordered to be careful about making fires on hearths from which stoves had been removed.

But the winds proved foul. And the next day, the troops were ordered under arms to embark at noon — suddenly Boston's famous east wind started to blow, and that evening the winds continued contrary with "rainy bad weather." The weather did not deter Washington's riflemen from setting out that night on their march to New York.

Now Howe, on Saturday morning, wished to wait no longer. He gave orders that on Sunday morning, March 17, at 3 a.m., the rowers were to report for duty in King street, and the whole garrison be ready under arms at 4 a.m. to embark. Protective barricades had been built at the head of each of the two wharves and a similar one near the old Liberty Tree on the way to Boston Neck. A rear guard of shock troops was set.

The night of the 16th, Washington's troops took and fortified Nook's Hill, precipitating a cannonade.

All did go next morning as Howe had hoped. "Fine weather and fair wind," recorded Adj. Kemble.

Capt. Robertson had special duty. Boston might still go up in flames. Robertson stood on Long Wharf. He saw that, by 6:15 a.m., all the regiments but the rear guard of grenadiers and light infantrymen were embarked. "The wind though fair was very faint," he said. The rear guard received orders to embark at 8 a.m. An hour later all the guard, as well as those from Charlestown, were on board.

Robertson said at this time that he and Capt. Montresor, aided by three corpsmen, shut the barricade opening on Long Wharf. They were prepared "to fire some houses if there had appeared any enemy in our rear, but none appeared and we went off. ..." With the fleet at anchor in King Road, Robertson and Montresor boarded their transport.

To Robertson it was: "The finest day in the world, and fair breeze."

Kemble had already landed at the Castle, and said, on his passage down, that he could see rebels "upwards of 1000 drawn up before their redoubts as we passed." Robertson had seen them and said that they made a great parade on the heights of Dorchester."

There was naval etiquette on the warships.

As Howe and his officers moved down the harbor's main channel, King Road, there were salutes from the ships. On the log of Adm. Shuldham's flagship, the 50-gun *HMS Chatham*, moored in King Road, was this entry on Sunday, March 17:

"Came on board Maj. Gen. Howe, Earl Percy, Gen. Pigot and several other officers .... .

Saluted them with 15 guns. At 12, *HMS Fowey* (which, with its heavy cannon, had covered the embarkation) saluted with 13 guns. Returned 11 guns."

Howe's fleet did not put out to sea at once. Rather, it lingered for many days in the main roads of the harbor, to the steadily mounting puzzlement and suspicion of Washington.

Howe would contend, when his performance in America would come under attack in England, that his manner of leaving Boston had not brought "any disgrace .... upon His Majesty's arms." This, though, was far from the reaction at this moment of many Americans, men and women.

Mercy Warren called it a "disgraceful flight."

Elbridge Gerry exclaimed:

"What an occurrence is this to be known in Europe! I am at a loss to know how Great Britain will reconcile all this to her military glory."

Abigail Adams could not resist being impressed as she looked from Penn's Hill, Braintree, toward Boston harbor and "the largest fleet ever seen in America. You may count upwards of 170 sail. They look like a forest. It was lucky for us that we got possession of Nook's Hill .... Our general may say with Caesar, 'Veni, vidi, vici.' " Then she added:

"To what a contemptible situation are the troops of Britain reduced!"

Washington described Howe's 22 regiments as "the flower of the British army" beaten "into a shameful and precipitate retreat out of a place the strongest by nature on this continent, and strengthened and fortified at an enormous expense."

They embarked, he said, "in as much hurry, precipitation, and confusion, as ever troops did, not taking time to fit their transports, but leaving the King's property" to such an amount — including all the destroyed baggage wagons and artillery carts, things thrown into the docks, and set adrift — that it reminded him of Gen. Braddock's defeat.

The American troops entered the town by both land and sea.

Maj. General Ward, Col. Learned with a detachment and Ens. Samuel Richards with a Union flag, like the one that had been unfurled on New Year's Day at Prospect Hill, picked their way to the gate through crows' feet — pointed metal devices — strewn on Boston Neck.

Col. Learned, who unbarred the deserted gate, was the first to enter. Many more crows' feet had been scattered on the roadway ahead to slow troops.

Col. Jedediah Huntington's sentries in Roxbury were soon told by several lads that the British were gone and "the selectmen were coming out to see us." The selectmen went on to Cambridge to meet Washington and "give him the best intelligence they could concerning the state of the town and the intentions of the enemy."

"Never," said Huntington, "was joy painted in higher colors than in the faces of the selectmen of Boston and other of the inhabitants of that distressed town when we first had an interview with them this forenoon." Huntington had gone right into Boston.

To the north of Boston, Brig. Gen. Sullivan had been on Ploughed Hill watching the British departure with his spyglass.

Satisfied that they were not aiming at Dorchester but boarding their ships, Sullivan rode toward Charlestown Neck. Soon, through his glass, he detected that the usual sentries on Bunker Hill were not moving. They were dummies — "only effigies set there by the flying enemy." Sullivan was ordered by Washington to take possession of Charlestown.

Maj. Gen. Putnam, with 1000 men, went by boat from the Charles River to the foot of Boston Common. Washington had been concerned for days about smallpox in Boston and had included in this detachment only men who had had the disease. Putnam was commanded to take possession of the town and its heights. Washington wanted to have them fortified against a possible return of the enemy.

Putnam's chaplain, Rev. Abiel Leonard, held a Sunday thanksgiving service for the troops in the old meetinghouse in Harvard Square. Washington and camp leaders attended and heard Rev. Leonard preach from Exodus: "Let us flee from the face of Israel, for the Lord fighteth for

them against the Egyptians."

Washington entered Boston the next day. He particularly visited the mansion of John Hancock, the president of the Continental Congress, a man Adm. Shuldham called a "notorious rebel" when he sent sailors to destroy two of Hancock's big ships nearing completion. Washington wrote to Hancock:

"I have a particular pleasure in being able to inform you, sir, that your house has received no damage worth mentioning. Your furniture is in tolerable order and the family pictures are all left entire and untouched." Some owners would find that conscientious departing British occupants had left rent money and no damage, but these instances were few.

Washington decided to have strong works raised on Fort Hill commanding the harbor front, and this would be done in about a week. Gridley was to demolish at once the fortifications that blocked the natural gateway to the town.

While what he saw was not in so bad a state as he had expected, he found that "the inhabitants have suffered a good deal, in being plundered by the soldiery at their departure." He found the enemy works in Boston and on Bunker Hill "formidable." He wrote of this to Reed:

"Their works all standing ... especially that at Bunker Hill, we find amazingly strong: 20,000 men could not have carried it against 1000, had that work been well defended. The town of Boston was almost impregnable ... every avenue fortified."

Washington was astonished by the amount of provisions and stores Howe left behind. He estimated not "less than 30,000 pounds worth of his Majesty's property." He ordered that it be inventoried, and the resulting estimate would be nearly double his original one.

Brig. Gen. Heath, at the head of five regiments and two companies of artillery, was dispatched to New York to push the fortifications there that had been planned by Maj. Gen. Lee. Bad road conditions had held them up for four days — and Washington also had a concern that the British military might be tempted to pay another visit to Boston. For that reason he would order no more troops to New York until the British should depart the lower harbor.

Soldiers and all officers were "positively forbid going into Boston without a pass or being sent expressly on duty" until the selectmen reported the town cleansed from smallpox infection. Arrangements were made at the Charlestown ferry and at Boston Neck to issue permits so that inhabitants might be able to return to their dwellings if still standing.

On his return to Cambridge, Washington would express strong views to his brother Jack on loyalists and government men "who have acted an unfriendly part in the great contest.... One or two have done, what a great number ought to have done long ago, committed suicide. By all accounts there never existed a more miserable set of beings than those wretched creatures now...."

"When the order issued ... for embarking the troops in Boston, no electric shock, no sudden explosion of thunder, in a word, not the last trump could have struck them with greater consternation. They were at their wits' end, and, conscious of their black ingratitude, they chose to commit themselves ... to the waves at a tempestuous season, rather than meet their offended countrymen."

The troops in general were allowed to enter Boston on March 20. Dr. Thacher, marching in with his regiment, said, "the inhabitants appeared at their doors and windows; though they manifested lively joy on being liberated from a long imprisonment, they were not altogether free from a melancholy gloom which 10 tedious months' siege has spread over their countenances.

"The streets and buildings present a scene, which reflects disgrace on their late occupants, exhibiting a deplorable desolation and wretchedness."

Life aboard the British vessels had its desolation, too. Capt. Charles Stuart found the men "crowded with two regiments in each ship, and nothing could be more horrid." Another passenger had some bitter reflections from the flagship to a gentleman in London: "The people in the town who were friends to government, took care of nothing but their merchandise, and found means to employ the men belonging to the transports in embarking their goods; by which means several of the vessels are entirely filled with private property instead of the King's stores.

"By some unavoidable accident, the medicines, surgeons' chests, instruments, and necessaries, were left in the hospital."

The exodus, said the writer, was not like breaking camp. "It was like departing your country, with your wives, your servants, your household furniture, and all your encumbrances. The officers, who felt the disgrace of their retreat, did their utmost to keep up appearances.

"In bad plight we go to Halifax. What supply we are to expect there I do not know; our expectations are not very sanguine. The neglect shown us bears hard on us all; the soldiers think themselves betrayed, the officers blame the Admiralty, and your friend, Lord Sandwich, is universally execrated."

Capt. Robertson's duties included going to Castle William and checking the mines. He was there on March 18 and reported them ready for loading. He went back the next day and found all but a dozen loaded, and then unloaded them all because Howe wanted it that way for "some days." But Howe found that Americans in whaleboats with small cannon had been landing on harbor islands and firing on British working parties getting water for their ships.

Orders to reload the mines were conveyed from Howe to Castle Island on the afternoon of March 20 by Col. Leslie. This was just after seven regulars were wounded by the bursting of a cannon being fired from the Castle at the new 3-gun battery the Americans had raised near Dorchester Point. The reloading of the mines went on as the 64th Regt., assigned to the Castle since its abortive foray on Salem's old North Bridge, embarked. The night was squally.

Robertson said that at 8 p.m. "the boats lay off until the mines — more than five dozen of them — were fired, which was done a half-hour afterwards and they had a very good effect. The barracks and other houses were then set on fire and at 9 the rear guard ... embarked and we got all safe on board the transports."

The burning of the Castle, the shocks and explosions made a sensation wherever visible.

Gen. Heath, who had reached Mendon with his troops en route to New York, could see from there the conflagration lighting up the sky. Next day Adm. Shuldham made the signal for weighing anchor and the fleet dropped farther down the harbor to Nantasket Road.

Bay colonists in general were permitted to enter Boston by March 22, when Dr. Thacher observed:

"A concourse of people from the country are crowding into town, full of friendly solicitude .... It is truly interesting to witness the tender interviews and fond embraces of those who have been long separated under circumstances so peculiarly distressing."

Thacher, like others, looked around. The church of the Mathers in old North Square had been demolished for firewood. Dozens of other structures and wharves had filled the same insatiable need. One of the town's most sacred buildings, the Old South Meetinghouse, had been turned into a riding school for Burgoyne's dragoons and a carved pew was removed to make a pigsty.

Sightseeing became in vogue. Rev. Gordon could see American soldiers eager to get into Boston. "Many of them came from inland places and were never in a seaport; their curiosity was much excited on a variety of accounts."

Nor was Charlestown forgotten. Mercy Warren said that early one morning Martha Washington sent her chariot for her, and they went "to see the deserted lines of the enemy and the ruins of Charlestown, a melancholy sight, the last which evinces the barbarity of the foe and leaves a deep impression of the sufferings of that unhappy town."

A harsh gale, with rain and snow, struck in the next days, driving a couple of the British ships ashore. When the gale was spent, Adm. Shuldham gave the signal at his main top masthead and the first division of ships came to sail and departed early on the afternoon of March 25

... brigs, schooners, frigates and transport ships, "about 49 vessels," said Robertson, under convoy of *HMS Fowey*, a 20-gun frigate. The division was led by Brig. Gens. Grant and Robertson.

Despite the bad weather and the partial departure of the British ships, Washington was confounded by the large number of ships still in the lower harbor. He could figure no satisfactory reason, he informed Congress, telling of the destruction of the Castle and how the British left a great number of cannon there.

"They ... have rendered all of them, except a very few, entirely useless by breaking off the trunnions, and those they spiked up; but may be made serviceable again; some are already done."

Those ships still in Nantasket Road!

"The enemy," he wrote to Reed, "have the best knack of puzzling people I ever met with in my life." He grew interested in a scheme of Maj. Benjamin Tupper to load two lighters with combustibles and set them loose as fire rafts some windy night to burn the remaining fleet.

It departed, though, before Tupper could strike.

Adm. Shuldham on March 27 at 8 a.m. ran up the signal to unmoor and prepare for sailing. In his convoy he had 66 sail of transports and other vessels to which, at 3 p.m., he gave the signal to weigh anchor and in an hour *HMS Chatham* was a mile northwest of the Boston lighthouse, the fleet under her stern, with fair wind but soon a high, uneasy sea.

Shuldham left behind the 50-gun *HMS Renown*, Capt. Francis Banks, and three transports to lie in Nantasket Road to receive any incoming British vessels. Any supply ships approaching were to be sent right off to Halifax. The fleet and army, Shuldham told Banks, "are in extreme want of them." As for other ships, Shuldham's orders to Banks read:

"You are to take, sink, burn, or destroy, all rebel vessels you may meet with, and to continue upon this service 'till further notice."

Congress votes first gold medal

"An inglorious retreat," was Washington's comment.

King George III, through his new secretary for the colonies, Lord Germain, would very much approve what Howe had done under the circumstances. The King would remark, however, that he had hoped that Howe would have received enough supplies to maintain himself "at Boston until a force was collected adequate to some decisive blow."

A chilling debate was provoked in Parliament when the North administration sought to dismiss the news with a brief, government-inspired paragraph in the *London Gazette* to make it all seem like a routine shifting of regiments.

North did not quiet the opposition when he claimed:

"The troops were not compelled to abandon Boston."

Edmund Burke told the House of Commons that "the troops could not have remained in that town 10 days longer, if the heavens had not rained down manna and quails." Sir George Yonge declared that "the ruin and disgrace of the nation, and the loss of America, were inevitable." David Hartley observed:

"Gen. Howe was driven from Boston, and . . . nothing but the dread of having his whole army cut to pieces, or made prisoners, induced him to make so precipitate and unexpected a retreat."

This, too, was the tenor of argument in the House of Lords, where the administration, nevertheless, was able to muster a 4-to-1 majority. The Duke of Manchester appealed in vain for the North administration to revise its judgments, "to retrace the steps we may too hastily have trod."

He pictured that "a chosen army, with chosen officers, backed by the power of a mighty fleet, sent to correct revolted subjects; sent to chastise a resisting city; sent to assert Britain's authority, has, for many tedious months, been imprisoned within that town by the provincial army . . . ."

Manchester said he had intelligence, despite the government's short, uncircumstantial account, "that Gen. Howe quitted not Boston of his own free will; but that a superior enemy, by repeated efforts, by extraordinary works, by fire of their batteries, rendered the place untenable.

"My lords, circumstances obliged him to quit that post he could not possibly maintain. The mode of the retreat may do the general infinite honor; but it does dishonor to the British nation."

As the British fleet had sailed off, Abigail Adams was joined on Penn's Hill by James and Mercy Warren. Emotion swelled in Abigail as she wrote her husband:

"I think the sun looks brighter, the birds sing more melodiously, and nature puts on a more cheerful countenance."

Washington went to a thanksgiving service in Boston the day after the fleet departed and he had arranged to send more of his regiments to New York. The service, given by Rev. Andrew Eliot of the new North Church, was held in the Old Brick Meetinghouse diagonally across the street from the town house.

After the service Washington, some of his officers and gentlemen of the town joined at the town house and went down King street to a celebrated tavern, "Bunch of Grapes," at the corner of present Kilby street, for a banquet. It was along this street that the British troops, from their first arrival in Boston, and in all their chief movements — to Bunker Hill, Dorchester Heights and in departure — had come and gone to their ships.

There were honors for Washington. The selectmen thanked him. The Massachusetts Legislature, led by Speaker James Warren, made him a grateful address. He replied delightedly, for it was "pleasing testimony" as he told his brother Jack, "that my reputation stands fair."

Congress, on motion of John Adams, warmly expressed its thanks to Washington and the officers and soldiers under his command "for their wise and spirited conduct in the siege and acquisition of Boston."

A gold medal, first to be authorized by Congress, was ordered as a present to Washington. It would be months, many months, before it would be minted.

His attention always on his work, Washington went right after the banquet to inspect nearby Fort Hill. He now set about breaking camp, arranging Boston's defenses, and on the afternoon of April 6 he set out for New York, via Norwich, with the rest of his army, leaving Gen. Ward with a force to protect Boston and Col. Knox to find hundreds of teams to bring on the cannon.

There was a poignant day in Boston when the body of the venerated Dr. Joseph Warren, sought since the British left Bunker Hill, was located and brought back to the town he loved. The service was held two days after Washington's departure, in present King's Chapel, which to avoid royalty, had for the time being been rechristened the "Stone Chapel."

There was a highly gratifying day in Boston. Capt. Manley, dogging the departing British fleet on Washington's orders, captured the brig *Elizabeth*. It had to be "the richest vessel in the fleet," said Boston merchant John Andrews. Its cargo approximated in value everything military that Howe had left behind. "That cursed villian Crean Brush," as Andrew called him, was lodged in Boston jail to face his irate victims.

There was worry in Boston, too, as the few British warships lingered week after week.

And there were clashes.

Capt. James Mugford of Marblehead, master of Washington's schooner *Franklin*, made a sensational capture of a richly laden British munitions transport, *Hope*, as it approached Boston harbor. She ran aground at ebbtide as he was bringing her through Shirley gut, once a harbor entrance on the north side of Deer Island. From there her precious supplies, especially 1500 whole barrels of gunpowder, were taken in boats to Boston and much of it forwarded to the army in New York.

Capture of the *Hope* had been under the noses of the British patrol and vengeance was in the air. Two nights later, on May 19, the lookouts on two 50-gun warships, HMS *Renown* and HMS *Experiment*, spotted a schooner aground in Shirley gut. It was Capt. Mugford's vessel which had been headed outward on another cruise.

Thirteen boats of the two warships, manned and armed with seamen and marines, went after the stranded schooner. As they approached, the *Franklin* was joined by a half-dozen men in a small privateer. In the uneven struggle that followed Capt. Mugford, after discharging his cannon and driving off the attackers, was run through by a lance and slain.

Logs of the British warships recount the loss of the *Renown's* first lieutenant, six other sailors and marines killed or drowned, a barge overset and lost and many wounded. Intrepid Capt. Mugford was the only American casualty.

Efforts were continually made to harass and drive away the British patrol at the entry of the harbor. A surprise attack finally succeeded.

Gen. Ward, on June 13, sent Col. Asa Whitcomb and 500 men, with a 13-inch mortar and two cannon, to land on Long Island that night and entrench. Next morning their fire from the 13-inch mortar so amazed the British that they slipped cable and headed out of the harbor. En route they were fired upon by militia, under Brig. Gen. Benjamin Lincoln, and from the field-piece on a headland.

But as they departed, as a final salute, they blew up the Boston lighthouse.

Their departure was two years from the month Gen. Gage had begun the punishment of Boston and the Bostonians for the Boston Tea Party by closing the port. Now, for any oncoming British troops, Boston harbor was actually a trap — and into it sailed, unaware of Howe's departure, two vessels carrying reinforcements for Howe.

The British, taken by surprise from every quarter, put up a gallant struggle but gave up, with a major and 10 soldiers killed and many wounded. Their commanding officer, a member of Parliament, Col. Sir Archibald Campbell, was made prisoner and eventually exchanged for an early hero of the war, Ethan Allen.

"These events are extremely pleasing," Washington, on being informed of the departed patrol and the captures, wrote to Ward.

Bostonians all had reason to be pleased.

For the first time since troops came to Boston harbor in 1768, Boston was free from hostile troops, fleet or customsmen backing the King's assault on ancient liberties. Boston harbor now belonged to Bostonians.

America proclaims Declaration of Independence

Tall, lean Richard Henry Lee, an early Virginia Son of Liberty and one of the great orators of this era, rose in the Continental Congress on June 7, 1776, and urged a resolution that would presently give birth to the United States of America:

"Resolved:

"That these United colonies are, and of right ought to be, free and independent states, that they are absolved from all allegiance to the British crown, and that all political connection between them and the state of Great Britain is, and ought to be, totally dissolved.

"That it is expedient forthwith to take the most effectual measures for forming foreign alliances.

"That a plan of confederation be prepared and transmitted to the respective colonies for their consideration and approbation."

Lee, in offering the motion, was putting into effect the votes of the Virginia Convention, and of county after county in Virginia, in favor of independence. Washington expressed great gladness when he heard of the Virginia Convention action and called it "so noble a vote."

The move toward independence, already gathering strength during May, became virtually irresistible with this support of Virginia, the largest of the colonies. John Adams, noting that identical instructions to their delegates had just come in from Georgia, South Carolina and North Carolina, exulted:

"Every post and every day rolls in upon us, Independence like a torrent."

This rush for independence was not something that suddenly, excitingly — like the burst of a fireworks — appeared on the American scene. It was a development of long, slow growth, nurtured not so much by any eagerness of the colonials as by the obstinacy of George III and the insensitiveness and ineptness of Lord North's administration.

Richard Henry Lee, who was a cheerful, companionable man as well as being perspicacious, used to visit John and Samuel Adams in their quarters across from the City Tavern back when they first came to Philadelphia. Their views, in which Lee heartily concurred, led him to dub their quarters "Liberty Hall."

Dr. Benjamin Rush, often host to the Adamses, credited John Adams with first putting the idea of independence in the public mind when a letter Adams wrote in 1775 was intercepted by the British and published by Gen. Gage in Boston. But Massachusetts' old royal governor Hutchinson long before that attributed a connivance for independence to Samuel Adams, "Father of the Revolution."

When Samuel Adams learned of Washington's having driven Howe out of Boston he thought independence should be proclaimed immediately. "The salvation of this country depends on its being done speedily. Every day's delay tries my patience . . . . the only alternative is independence or slavery."

Certainly proclaiming independence had been discussed for months among the soldiers in the camp at Cambridge, long before they liberated Boston. Visitors heard soldiers discuss it in the fall of 1775. And, officers, too. Brig. Gens. Nathaniel Greene and John Sullivan were asking, "Why, in God's name, is it not done?"

King George's refusing even to read colonial grievances in the "Olive Branch" petition, his proclaiming all Americans as rebels and instituting mercenary warfare gave boundless allure to the arguments advanced by Paine's "Common Sense." And Paine's "Common Sense" gave initial momentum to the united colonial move for independence.

John Adams constantly sought to have the Congress support measures that implied independence. One of them, his proposal to open all American ports to foreign commerce, he regarded as a "bold step to independence. Indeed, I urged it expressly with that view . . . ." This was early in 1776 and its passage in Congress was impeded by the bloc of moderate and proprietary delegates from the middle colonies and the South, led by John Dickinson of Pennsylvania.

Lord North, ironically, came to Adams's rescue when word spread through the colonies in

March of 1776 about what was to be North's last enactment concerning the American colonies: the Prohibitory Act.

"Restraining Act, or Prohibitory Act, or Piratical Act, or Plundering Act, or Act of Independency — for by all these titles it is called," declared John Adams.

"I think the most apposite is the Act of Independency; for King, Lords, and Commons, have united in sundering this country from that, I think, forever. It is a complete dismemberment of the British Empire. It throws 13 colonies out of the royal protection, levels all distinctions, and makes us independent in spite of our supplications and entreaties.

"It may be fortunate that the Act of Independency should come from the British Parliament rather than the American Congress; but it is very odd that Americans should hesitate at accepting such a gift from them."

Curiously, the Prohibitory Act repealed the old "Intolerable Acts" that had originally closed the port of Boston and brought Gen. Gage's army. Enacted instead were provisions that would stop all American trade with British ports, order the seizure of all American trading vessels and, on June 1, 1776, start the seizure of any foreign vessels trading with America.

"Was there ever anything more absurd," inquired Washington of Reed, "than to repeal the very acts, which have introduced all this confusion and bloodshed, and at the same time enact a law to restrain intercourse with the colonies for opposing them?"

Lord North's Prohibitory Act did contain a provision for peace commissioners to come to America, but merely to receive submission and grant pardons. The Duke of Grafton, opposing the entire act in Parliament, had warned that this new idea of unconditional surrender for talking peace would make the Americans desperate.

It did appeal to Dickinson and his supporters seeking a middle ground. To John Adams it was another "ministerial bubble." Washington considered the terms of pardon "insulting" and "only designed . . . to set us up . . . in Great Britain as a people that will not hearken to any propositions of peace." Reed, speaking of the re-

action in Philadelphia said, "No man of understanding expects any good from the commissioners."

Why was Congress still hesitant on independence? Benjamin Franklin, en route in April, despite his age and illness, to report on the deteriorating American military situation in Canada, explained to a Bay Colony friend:

"The novelty of the thing deters some, the doubts of success, others, the vain hope of reconciliation, many. But our enemies take continually every proper measure to remove these obstacles, and their endeavors are attended with success, since every day furnishes us with new causes of increasing enmity, and new reasons for wishing an eternal separation . . . ."

Events in May met even restless John Adams's high expectations. The Massachusetts House of Representatives on May 10 asked each town, in full town meeting, to declare, if the delegates to Congress should vote for independence, would the inhabitants "solemnly engage, with their lives and fortunes, to support them in the measure?" Pledges started flooding in from the towns. And this was repeated in colony after colony.

On May 15, John Adams brought forward another proposal that implied independence. It was a resolution that, in light of George III's hostile actions, "it is necessary that the exercise of every kind of authority under the said crown should be totally suppressed" and each colony that had not already done so, set up its own government "under the authority of the people."

There was intense debate. John Adams called it "the most important resolution that ever was taken in America" and, when it was adopted, he observed:

"Great Britain has at last driven America to the last step, a complete separation from her; a total absolute independence, not only of her Parliament, but of her crown, for such is the amount of the resolve of the 15th. I have reasons to believe that no colony, which shall assume a government under the people, will give it up."

It was on this same May 15 that the Virginia Convention had voted for independence. And now Washington was able to forward to Philadelphia the texts, brought by packet from England of the treaties for mercenaries that George III had made with the rulers of Hesse Cassel, Brunswick, Waldeck and Hanau. This brought thunder from Richard Henry Lee on both the treaties and on Parliament's rejection of the Duke of Grafton's call for a suspension of warfare:

"The infamous treaties with Hesse, Brunswick, etc., of which we have authentic copies and the ministerial reply to Grafton's motion leave no doubt that our enemies are determined upon the absolute conquest and subduction of North America.

"It is not choice then but necessity that calls for independence, as the only means by which foreign alliances can be obtained . . . .

"Contrary to our earnest, early and repeated petitions for peace, liberty, and safety, our enemies press us with war, threaten us with danger and slavery. And this, not with her single force, but with the aid of foreigners."

Lee no sooner finished proposing his resolution for independence on June 7 than John Adams was on his feet, and seconded it. Consideration was postponed until 10 a.m. next day.

Debate, on Saturday June 8, lasted into the evening. Dickinson — tall, slender, pale — a London-trained lawyer, repeated the arguments against departing from the British empire, particularly when peace commissioners were on their way. Adams put again into action arguments he had often expressed to Congress. Others spoke.

When Congress met again Monday morning it was decided to postpone action on the Lee resolution for three weeks, until July 1. The purpose of the supporters of independence was to give doubtful middle colonies — New York, New Jersey, Pennsylvania, Delaware, Maryland — "an opportunity . . . to let their delegates unite in the measure."

Congress, however, did take three fateful steps. It named committees to make a plan of treaties with foreign powers, to prepare the form of a confederation of the colonies, and to have ready, should it be the final decision of the Congress, a declaration of independence. To the last committee were named Thomas Jefferson, John

Adams, Benjamin Franklin, Roger Sherman of Connecticut and Robert R. Livingston of New York.

To John Adams, America was now really in a revolution dealing with measures of "stupendous magnitude . . . in which the lives and liberties of millions yet unborn are intimately interested."

Jefferson, a tall sandy-haired man, one of the youngest members of the Congress, was picked for the drafting committee because, as a member of the House of Burgesses and for a year in the Congress, he had won a reputation as a felicitous writer. On his feet he was almost inarticulate. A "silent member," Adams called him, but "a masterly pen."

After discussing contents at several meetings, the committee handed the actual drafting to Jefferson and Adams. Jefferson suggested that Adams do it. Adams replied, "I will not." "Why?" "Reasons enough," replied Adams. Jefferson, he said, was Virginian, a Virginian should do it, and "you can write 10 times better than I can."

Jefferson took off for the second-floor parlor in his boarding house a few blocks from the Congress and began writing.

The substance of his composition had often been expressed in debate in the Congress, and, before that, by James Otis and Samuel Adams in Boston. Essentially, as written by Jefferson, it drew upon Virginians — George Mason's "Bill of Rights," Jefferson's own recently written preamble to the Virginia constitution and Richard Henry Lee's resolution for independence.

Jefferson's draft delighted John Adams — ". . . its high tone . . . the flights of oratory with which it abounded, especially that concerning Negro slavery, which I knew his southern brethren would never suffer to pass in Congress." Adams suggested no changes. Nor did the other members of the committee when it was read to them. "We were all in haste . . . Congress was impatient." said Adams.

The military situation was a troubled one. The British foray against Charleston, S.C., was beaten off, and Gen. Clinton would be heading back to join Gen. Howe in an attack against New York. Washington, still suffering from shortages of every sort, was trying to strengthen the defenses of that seaport. The campaign to win Canada had collapsed. Gen. Guy Carleton had triumphantly re-entered Montreal.

Adams attributed the loss in Canada to lack of unity, to the obstructionist maneuvers of Dickinson and his team of proprietary powers and southern barons, as well as their delusive faith both in the "Olive Branch" petition, which Dickinson had written, and now in the approach of Lord North's "peace commissioners."

Still, Adams would, philosophically, see a silver lining, a great advantage. "The hopes of reconciliation, which were fondly entertained by multitudes of honest and well-meaning, though weak and mistaken people, have been gradually and at last totally extinguished.

"Time has been given for the whole people maturely to consider the great question of independence and to ripen their judgment . . . by discussing it in newspapers and pamphlets, by debating it . . . so that the whole people in every colony of the 13 have now adopted it as their own act. This will cement the union . . . ."

Jefferson's draft was reported to the Congress on June 28. That very day Maryland's convention voted for independence. New Jersey was sending new delegates to vote for independence. Pennsylvania was organizing a people's government and discarding the proprietary one, as envisaged in Adams's resolution of May 15. The independence party was busy in a similar way in New York, but would a change there come in time?

July 1 was set for what Adams called "the greatest debate of all."

Dickinson spoke at great length — "with great ingenuity and eloquence." Adams hoped someone "less obnoxious" than himself — "believed to be the author of all the mischief" — would rise to answer. No member did, so Adams rose. As he finished, the New Jersey delegates arrived and said they would like to hear the arguments. "All eyes were turned upon me," said the reluctant Adams, so he obliged. Then followed the vote.

All but four colonies voted affirmatively.

Pennsylvania and South Carolina voted "No." New York abstained. Delaware was divided, 1 to 1. Since Congress was acting as a committee of the whole, it was decided to sit again on the matter the next day.

A Delaware delegate, Thomas McKean, suggested to Adams that he would see if they could get Dickinson to stay away next day; he would also send an express back the 80 miles to the Delaware capital, Dover, to call back Delaware's third delegate, Caesar Rodney, who had left to help the patriot cause there. And so events proved the next day.

The vote was 12 to 0, with New York abstaining. Caesar Rodney, booted, spurred and mud-covered, arrived in the nick of time to swing Delaware in favor. The vote was for passage of the Lee resolution for independence. The declaration itself was adopted on July 4 but all the signatures, including those of new delegates from Pennsylvania and New York, would not be affixed until New Hampshire's Matthew Thornton signed on Nov. 4.

Dickinson, true to his belief that America would be more secure within the British empire, was the only delegate who would not sign. He did believe in the patriot cause, entered the army, became a brigadier general of militia and later a governor of Pennsylvania.

Jefferson, who had been seated in front next to Franklin, writhed as changes were moved and made in his declaration. Soothing, wry tales Franklin whispered did not comfort him. He regarded changes as "depredations." Jefferson and Adams regretfully saw some of the "best of it" go — "the vehement philippic against Negro slavery," deleted to keep Georgia and South Carolina and unity.

Still adoption of the declaration, said Adams, would be "the most memorable epocha in the history of America.

"It ought to be commemorated, as the day of deliverance by solemn acts of devotion to God Almighty. It ought to be solemnized with pomp and parade, with shows, games, sports, guns, bells, bonfires and illuminations from one end of this continent to the other from this time forward forever more."

The Tea Party participants

The list of those in the Tea Party?

Peter Edes said that his father, the patriot publisher, had a list in his desk, but an old Whig gentleman came along and it disappeared. Maybe this was only the list of those who volunteered to guard the tea ships. We will never know.

Benjamin Thatcher, in preparing his story about Hewes, who was then thought to be the oldest survivor, in 1835 presented a list of 58 names furnished to him by "an aged Bostonian well acquainted with the history of our subject."

"Of course it is not complete," noted Thatcher, hoping for additions and corrections from the nine survivors then alive. Thatcher also frankly conceded that the list had contained names of those "more or less actively engaged in or present at the destruction of the tea." In other words, no separation of performers and spectators.

Most thorough presentation of all — and the definitive one — was made by Francis S. Drake in his Tea Leaves in 1884. Drake gave an additional 55 names "derived principally from family tradition." There is a list on the Slater grave in Worcester but it contains some evident errors.

The following list of 119 combines these sources with the additions of others in Drake's text and in genealogical records.

NATHANIEL BARBER, 45, merchant, member of Whig Club, member of first Committee of Correspondence 1772, Committee of Safety, Mason, became a major; muster master for Suffolk County, naval officer in Boston 1784, died 1787.

SAMUEL BARNARD, 36, led Watertown minutemen to Lexington April 19, 1775, at capture of Dorchester Heights, major in Revolutionary Army, died 1782.

HENRY BASS, 34, merchant, member of Loyal Nine, member of first volunteer guard on Dartmouth, son-in-law of moderator Samuel Phillips Savage, cousin of Samuel Adams, died 1813.

EDWARD BATES

THOMAS BOLTER, 38, housewright, died 1811.

DAVID BRADLEE, 31, captain in Col. Crafts's regiment, died 1811.

JOSIAH BRADLEE, 19, died 1798.

NATHANIEL BRADLEE, 27, died 1813.

THOMAS BRADLEE, 29, died 1805.

JAMES BREWER, pump and blockmaker, member of volunteer guard on Dartmouth, wife and daughter helped some Tea Party members blacken their faces with burnt cork at his house on Summer street, prisoner-of-war from privateer in 1781, Mason, Mass. Charitable Mechanic Assn., died 1805.

SETH INGERSOLL BROWN, 23, carpenter, later a tavernkeeper, cached ammunition in his Charlestown shop for use at Bunker Hill, wounded in leg at Bunker Hill, in army to end of Revolutionary War, died 1809.

STEPHEN BRUCE, merchant, member of first volunteer guard on Dartmouth, first state inspector of beef and pork, Mason, died 1801.

BENJAMIN BURTON, 24, carpenter, of Thomaston, Maine, became a colonel in Revolutionary Army, at surrender of Burgoyne, captured in 1781, imprisoned with Gen. Peleg Wadsworth (grandfather of poet Henry Wadsworth Longfellow), engineered escape for self and Wadsworth, magistrate, member of Legislature, died 1835.

NICHOLAS CAMPBELL, 41, sailor, died 1829.

GEORGE CARLETON

THOMAS CHASE, distiller, part-owner of Chase & Speakman distillery where Sons of Liberty met, member of Loyal Nine, member of first volunteer guard on Dartmouth, Mason.

BENJAMIN CLARKE, cooper, Mass. Charitable Mechanic Assn., Ancient & Honorable Artillery, died 1840. Three of Clarke's sons may have been in Tea Party, too.

JOHN COCHRAN, 24, farmer, one of first settlers of Belfast, Maine., last survivor of the original proprietors of Belfast, died 1839.

GILBERT COLESWORTHY, 29, member of family that moved to Nantucket and were ship carpenters and whaling masters, died 1818.

GERSHOM COLLIER, from Chesterfield, Mass., died about 1825.

ADAM COLLSON, 35, leather dresser, member of volunteer guard on Dartmouth, member Long Club, Mason, died 1798.

JAMES FOSTER CONDY, member of first volunteer guard on the Dartmouth, bookseller, died 1809.

S. COOLIDGE

SAMUEL COOPER 18, officer in Crane's artillery regiment, became regimental quartermaster 1778-83, died 1840.

THOMAS CRAFTS JR., 33, painter, japaner and carpenter, member of Loyal Nine, colonel of Boston militia that drove British ships out of Boston harbor in 1776, under him served Lt. Col. Paul Revere and Major Thomas Melvill, selectman, county official; Boston heard Declaration of Independence for first time when Crafts read it from the balcony of the old State House, Ancient & Honorable Artillery, married to sister of Samuel and Gov. Gore, died 1799.

JOHN CRANE, 29, carpenter, served in French and Indian War when only 15 years old, member of first volunteer guard on Dartmouth, brought Rhode Island company to serve in Continental Army forming in Cambridge, commissioned a major under General Knox bringing cannon from Ticonderoga to Dorchester Heights, wounded in New York campaign, raised Massachusetts artillery regiment which served at Saratoga, settled in Maine after war, became a judge, Mason, married to Josiah Wheeler's sister, died 1805.

THOMAS DANA JR., of Roxbury, brother-in-law of Thomas Williams.

ROBERT DAVIS, 26, importer, major in Crafts's regiment, Ancient & Honorable Artillery, Mason, died 1798.

EDWARD DOLBEAR, apprentice cooper, in cooper business later with Henry Purkitt, died 1796.

JOSEPH EATON, hatter, member of Ancient & Honorable Artillery, styled himself a general in later life, eccentric, claimed to have loaded cannon to block British regulars landing on King street in 1774.

JOSEPH EAYRES, housewright, member of volunteer guard on Dartmouth.

ECKLEY, barber, only one imprisoned for the Tea Party, Sons of Liberty provided for his family, secured his release from prison.

Brewster Doggett — *Nathaniel Bradlee*   Mrs. Lammot Copeland Jr. — *Joseph Lovering*   Detroit Institute of Art — *Lendall Pitts*

BENJAMIN EDES, 41, printer, part owner of patriot mouthpiece, the *Boston Gazette,* which he edited for 43 years, member of Loyal Nine, member of first volunteer guard on the *Dartmouth,* Ancient & Honorable Artillery, died 1803.

WILLIAM ETHERIDGE, masonry business.

SAMUEL FENNO, 28, housewright, died 1806.

SAMUEL FOSTER, sergeant of Roxbury's minutemen at Lexington April 19, 1775, served in Revolutionary War, died 1778.

NATHANIEL FROTHINGHAM, 27, coachmaker, died 1825.

JOHN FULTON, 40, of Medford, his wife Sarah helped disguise his four Bradlee brothers-in-law. Fulton was a cousin of steamship inventor Robert Fulton.

JOHN GAMMELL, 24, carpenter, in Stamp Act rioting, served in construction department of the Revolutionary Army, died 1827.

THOMAS GERRISH

SAMUEL GORE, 22, painter, elder brother of future Gov. Christopher Gore of Massachusetts, Ancient & Honorable Artillery, first treasurer of Mass. Charitable Mechanic Assn. Mason, died 1831. His father was a wealthy Tory and left with the British in 1776 but returned.

MOSES GRANT, 30, upholsterer, member of first volunteer guard on the *Dartmouth,* member of Committees of Correspondence and Safety, deacon of the Brattle Street Church, died 1817.

NATHANIEL GREENE, register of deeds, ardent Son of Liberty.

SAMUEL HAMMOND, 24, farmer, settled on New York frontier but hostility of Indians drove him to farming in Vermont, died 1842.

WILLIAM HENDLEY, 25, Mason, of Roxbury, died 1830.

GEORGE ROBERT TWELVES HEWES, 31, farmer, fisherman, shoemaker, at scene of massacre, testified at trial he could not see Capt. Preston's lips give order to shoot, helped injured boy when attacked by customs informer John Malcolm, who was tarred and feathered in 1774, died in 1840.

JOHN HICKS, 48, served with Cambridge minutemen and was killed in Arlington during the intense shooting as the British retreated from Lexington-Concord April 19, 1775.

SAMUEL HOBBS, 23, tanner and currier, of Roxbury, later a farmer, tanner and town official in Sturbridge, died 1823.

JOHN HOOTON, apprentice oarmaker and later a wood-wharfinger in the North End.

SAMUEL HOWARD, 21, shipwright, nephew of Theophilus Lillie, Tory violator of non-importation which infuriated the patriots in 1770 and led to the killing of 12-year-old Christopher Seider. Another uncle, Major John Lillie, was an aide to General Knox and military commander at West Point, died 1797.

EDWARD C. HOWE, 31, ropemaker near Gray's ropewalk in Hutchinson (Pearl) street, died 1821.

JONATHAN HUNNEWELL, 14, Mason, later a Boston selectman, member of the Legislature, president of the Mass. Charitable Mechanic Assn., died 1842.

RICHARD HUNNEWELL, Mason, member of volunteer guard on the *Dartmouth,* had two sons, Jonathan and Richard Jr., in the Tea Party, Mass. Charitable Mechanic Assn., died 1805.

RICHARD HUNNEWELL JR., 16.

THOMAS HUNSTABLE, 20, member of the Masons.

ABRAHAM HUNT, 25, wine merchant, colonel in the Revolutionary Army, served at Ticonderoga, in siege of Boston, at Valley Forge in 1777, Ancient & Honorable Artillery, Mason, died 1793.

DANIEL INGERSOLL, 23, housewright, Mason, died 1829.

DANIEL INGOLDSON

DAVID KINNISON, 37, farmer at Lebanon, Maine, served throughout Revolutionary War from the Lexington-Concord call, Bunker Hill, until captured at Saratoga Springs by Indians, served in the War of 1812, badly wounded by a cannon at Sackett's Harbor, was the last survivor of the Tea Party, died at Chicago in 1852 at the age of 115. He came to Boston with a group of comrades from Lebanon who were determined to help destroy the tea.

JOSEPH LEE, 28, merchant, Mason, died 1831.

AMOS LINCOLN, 20, housewright apprentice, served at Bunker Hill with Gen. John Stark, became Lt. Colonel in Crafts's regiment, served against Shays' insurrection, was in charge of woodwork in construction of the State House, married successively two daughters of Paul Revere, Mason, died 1829. His elder brother Levi was acting governor of Massachusetts and in Jefferson's cabinet, his nephews were simultaneously governors of Maine and Massachusetts.

MATTHEW LORING, 23, cordwainer, died 1829.

JOSEPH LOVERING, 15, apprentice tallow chandler, Ancient & Honorable Artillery, died 1848.

THOMAS MACHIN, 29, engineer, wounded at Bunker Hill, officer in Knox's artillery regiment, laid out fortifications for Boston harbor, Hudson River, wounded in 1777, laid out works while Revolutionary Army besieging Yorktown in 1781, Mason, died 1816.

EBENEZER MACKINTOSH, 36, shoemaker, served in French & Indian War at Ticonderoga, leader of the South End gang in Pope's Day clashes, became "First Captain-general of Liberty Tree" when South and North End gangs united, leader in the Stamp Act riots, Oliver's resignation at Liberty Tree, destruction of Gov. Hutchinson's house, left Boston after Tea Party and settled in New Hampshire, joined patriots there when Gen. Burgoyne was raiding Connecticut River communities in 1777 and again in 1780 at the sacking of Royalton, Vt., died 1816.

ARCHIBALD MacNEIL, 23, died 1840.

MARTIN

THOMPSON MAXWELL, 31, teamster, in French & Indian War under Capt. Lovewell of the Rangers, went with Bedford minutemen to Concord April 19, 1775, fought at Bunker Hill, served throughout the war, was member of the convention drafting, the Massachusetts constitution, captain in forces against Shays' Rebellion, moved to Ohio, served in War of 1812 when 70, made prisoner, died in 1835.

JOHN MAY, 25, colonel of the Boston regiment, one of agents and movers in formation of the Ohio Company after the Revolutionary War, Maysville in Ohio named after him, selectman in Boston 1804-12, Ancient & Honorable Artillery, died 1812.

MEAD

THOMAS MELVILL, 22, merchant, graduate of Princeton University, 1769, member Long Room Club, Harvard University honorary M.A. 1773, aide to Joseph Warren at Bunker Hill, major in Crafts's regiment, first to discharge his cannon against British ships still in harbor 1776, served in Rhode Island campaign, naval officer for Boston after Revolutionary War, member of Legislature, president Mass. Charitable Society, Mason, died 1832. He married John Scollay's daugher and was grandfather of Herman Melville, the author.

WILLIAM MOLINEUX, 57, merchant, member Long Club, Sons of Liberty from start in 1765, on first Boston Committee of Correspondence 1772, worked with Adams to get troops out of Boston in 1770, leader against tea consignees. Thomas Newell in his dairy said "Molineux died a martyr to the interest of America." His last words

were for his country. "Oh, save my country, Heaven," he pleaded, died in 1774.

THOMAS MOORE, 20, wharfinger, died 1813. His father was arrested in 1765 along with Mackintosh at time of Stamp Act riots.

ANTHONY MORSE, lieutenant during the Revolutionary War.

JOSEPH MOUNTFORD, 23, cooper, was with his cousin Samuel Maverick when Maverick was killed during massacre, died 1838.

ELIPHALET NEWELL, 38, artillery officer in 1775, of Charlestown, Mason.

JOSEPH PEARSE PALMER, merchant, brigade major and quartermaster general during Revolutionary War, served in Boston and Rhode Island, Mason.

JOHNATHAN PARKER, farmer, of Roxbury, wagon master among Revolutionary Army artificers stationed at Boston.

JOSEPH PAYSON, 30, housewright.

SAMUEL PECK, cooper, member North End Caucus, one of volunteer guard on the *Dartmouth,* Mason.

JOHN PETERS, 41, served at Lexington, April 19, 1775, wounded at Bunker Hill, in campaigns at Trenton, Princeton and Monmouth, at capture of Burgoyne and Cornwallis and was wounded again, died 1832.

WILLIAM PIERCE, 29, barber in North End, told of shaving Benjamin Franklin who lived nearby, died 1840.

LENDALL PITTS, 26, merchant, officer in Hancock's cadets. His family mansion off Scollay Square was favorite meeting place for Sons of Liberty. Pitt's mother was a sister of James Bowdoin, died 1787.

SAMUEL PITTS, 28, merchant, brother of Lendall Pitts, officer in cadet company.

THOMAS PORTER, merchant, died 1800.

HENRY PRENTISS, 24, merchant, saw massacre, served as captain in Revolutionary War at Cambridge, Long Island and Trenton, Ancient & Honorable Artillery, Mason, died 1821.

JOHN PRINCE, 22, pewterer apprentice, Harvard University 1776, minister First Church in Salem 1779 to death in 1836, Mason.

EDWARD PROCTOR, 40, importer, captain of first volunteer guard on the *Dartmouth*, member of Committees of Correspondence and Safety, colonel in Boston regiment, Ancient & Honorable Artillery, Mason, died 1811.

HENRY PURKITT, 18, cooper's apprentice, in Revolutionary Army at Trenton and Brandywine, sergeant in Pulaski's cavalry, became colonel of cavalry after the Revolutionary War, Mass. Charitable Mechanic Assn., died 1846.

JOHN RANDALL, 23, marched with Watertown minutemen to Lexington April 19, 1775.

PAUL REVERE, 38, engraver, goldsmith, lieutenant of artillery in French and Indian War, member of first volunteer guard on the *Dartmouth*, rose to lieutenant colonel in Crafts's regiment, in Penobscott expedition 1779, established gunpowder mill for Congress, express rider for patriots, first president Mass. Charitable Mechanic Assn., Mason, died 1818.

BENJAMIN RICE

JOSEPH ROBY, was living in Hanover, N.H., **in 1817.**

JOHN RUSSELL, Mason, died 1778.

American Antiquarian Society
Col. John May

Stuart Goldman
Thompson Maxwell

Gallery of Art, Yale University
Gen. Ebenezer Stevens

WILLIAM RUSSELL, 25, teacher, sergeant-major, adjutant in Crafts's regiment, in Rhode Island campaign, sailed on privateer, captured, imprisoned two and a half years in England, then on notorious prison-ship *Jersey*, Mason, died 1784. Wife's father was killed at Lexington April 19, 1775.

ROBERT SESSIONS, 21, laborer, rose to lieutenant in Revolutionary Army, after war settled in present Hampden, Mass., local official, justice of peace, in Legislature, died 1836.

JOSEPH SHED, 41, carpenter, later grocer, worked on enlarging Faneuil Hall, died 1812.

BENJAMIN SIMPSON, 19, bricklayer's apprentice, served in Revolutionary Army, moved to Saco, Maine, died 1849.

PETER SLATER, 14, served in Revolutionary Army, in Crane's regiment, moved to Worcester, died 1831.

SAMUEL SLOPER

THOMAS SPEAR, living in Boston in 1789.

SAMUEL SPRAGUE, 19, Mason, father of poet Charles Sprague, died 1844.

JOHN SPURR, 25, of Dorchester, joined Revolutionary Army in Providence, served throughout the war, rose to major, settled in Charlton, Mass., served in Legislature, died 1822.

JAMES STARR, 32, cooper, served in French and Indian War, at capture of Montreal, in Revolutionary Army, taken prisoner to Halifax; on transport en route to prison-ship *Jersey*, prisoners rise and capture

transport and bring it into Marblehead, died 1831.

PHINEAS STEARNS, 37, farmer, blacksmith, of Watertown, served in French and Indian Wars, marched with Watertown minutemen to Lexington April 19, 1775, commanded company at Dorchester Heights when British evacuated Boston, rose to colonel in Revolutionary Army, died 1798.

EBENEZER STEVENS, 22, carpenter, lieutenant in Crane's Rhode Island company, served at siege of Boston, captain in Knox's artillery regiment, on expedition to Canada, at surrender of Burgoyne, lieutenant colonel in John Lamb's artillery regiment, served with Lafayette in Virginia and at Yorktown, after war member of New York Legislature, major general of militia in War of 1812, founder of Tammany Society, member of Society of Cincinnati, died 1823.

ELISHA STORY, 30, doctor, member of first volunteer guard on the *Dartmouth*, volunteer at Lexington and Bunker Hill, with Washington at Long Island, White Plains and Trenton, settled in Marblehead, died 1805.

JAMES SWANN, 19, clerk in countinghouse, wounded at Bunker Hill, major in Crafts's regiment, secretary of Mass. Board of War, in Legislature from Roxbury, adjutant general of state, major in cavalry corps, made huge fortune in France, served 22 years in debtors' prison in Paris, Mason, died 1831.

ABRAHAM TOWER

JOHN TRUMAN

THOMAS URANN, ship-joiner, one of volunteer guard on the *Dartmouth*, with Revolutionary Army artificers stationed at Boston, Mason, died 1791.

JOSIAH WHEELER, 30, housewright, member of first volunteer guard on the *Dartmouth*, foreman of Revolutionary Army artificers at Boston, superintended erection of Fort Dorchester Heights, died 1817.

DAVID WILLIAMS

ISAAC WILLIAMS

JEREMIAH WILLIAMS, blacksmith of Roxbury, father of Maj. Edward Payson Williams of Revolutionary Army who died in service.

THOMAS WILLIAMS, 19, marched with Roxbury minutemen to Lexington April 19, 1775, died 1817.

NATHANIEL WILLIS, 18, printer, migrated to Ohio, published one of first newspapers in Ohio territory, Sciotto *Gazette*, Mason, died 1831.

JOSHUA WYETH, 16, journeyman blacksmith of Cambridge, served in Revolutionary Army, migrated to Ohio, living in Cincinnati in 1827.

THOMAS YOUNG, 41, doctor, active patriot against Stamp Act in Albany, N.Y., first president of North End Caucus, delivered first massacre memorial address, member of first Committee of Correspondence 1772, patriotic writer, first to suggest throwing tea in the harbor, moved to Philadelphia, friend of Ethan Allen and tried to help Vermont's independence, senior surgeon in Revolutionary Army hospital, caught fever, died 1777.

Index

Acknowledgments

Full acknowledgment would stretch back from present times to a poet and childhood. It was then that fascination began with the exciting tale of the revolutionary birth of our nation — back in committing to memory Longfellow's "Listen, my children, and you shall hear/Of the midnight ride of Paul Revere...."

Deeper appreciation began with the discovery that poetic license had the poet wander from the true story in many more ways than having Revere gallop as far as Concord's old North Bridge.

Understanding increased over the years in repeated visits to historic scenes, in absorbing all available biographies and the works of historians Richard Frothingham, Samuel Adams Drake, Benson J. Lossing, Francis S. Drake, Justin Winsor, Allen French and many others obtainable in bookstore, library or house of a friend.

Peter Force's great, though tragically incomplete, "American Archives" brought revelation that no presentation, however skillfully put together, was so powerful and moving as the unadorned story to be found in original sources. Thus began the search that took the writer to source materials — and to their honored repositories — to diaries, letters, documents, journals, orderly books, memoirs, contemporary likenesses, sketches and maps, and so on.

Many courtesies have been given. In particular they have come from Stephen T. Riley, Winifred Collins, John D. Cushing and Malcolm Freiberg of the Massachusetts Historical Society; Rodney Armstrong, Jack Jackson and Anne Wardsworth of the Boston Athenaeum; Harriet Ropes Cabot and Thomas W. Parker of the Bostonian Society; Sinclair Hitchings, John Alden and Yen-Tsai Feng of the Boston Public Library; Elliott B. Knowlton of the American Antiquarian Society; Leo D. Flaherty, Richard Hale and Alan Fox of the Massachusetts Archives and State Library; Clementine Brown of the Museum of Fine Arts in Boston; Howard H. Peckham and Arlene Kleeb of the William L. Clements Library, Ann Arbor, Mich.

Others include William P. Campbell, National Gallery of Art; John Milley, Independence National Historic Park, Philadelphia, Pa.; William H. Bond and Harley Holden, Harvard University; Gallery of Art, Yale University; Jane Lape, Fort Ticonderoga, N.Y.; Edouard Stackpole, Nantucket Whaling Museum; John Wright and Dorothy M. Potter, Essex Institute, Salem; Philip C.F. Smith, Peabody Institute, Salem, Mass.; Lewis W. Whittemore, Ancient & Honorable Artillery Company, Boston; Philip H. Dunbar, Connecticut Historical Society; Richard B. Harrington, Anne S.K. Brown Military Collection, Providence, R.I.; Margaret DeGrace, Detroit Institute of Art.

Still others include officers and members of many local historical societies, especially White Nichols of Wiscasset, Maine; Rev. Honorious Provost of Quebec; Forrest D. Bradshaw of Sudbury; Ruth Henderson Hill, Beverly Historical Society; Mrs. Thomas Doig, Concord Antiquarian Society; Richard B. Trask, Danvers Archival Center; Beatrice A. Turner, Framingham Library; Roland B. Greeley and S. Lawrence Whipple, Lexington Historical Society; Charles R. Morris, Milton Historical Society; Dorothy Vaughan, Portsmouth, N.H., Library; Margaret E. Durkin, Somerville Library; Mary McNally, Watertown Library, and Allister F. MacDougall of Westford.